Lecture Notes in Computer Science 6193

Commenced Publication in 1973
Founding and Former Series Editors:
Gerhard Goos, Juris Hartmanis, and Jan van Leeuwen

W0246093

Masatoshi Yoshikawa Xiaofeng Meng
Takayuki Yumoto Qiang Ma Lifeng Sun
Chiemi Watanabe (Eds.)

Database Systems for Advanced Applications

15th International Conference, DASFAA 2010
International Workshops:
GDM, BenchmarX, MCIS, SNSMW, DIEW, UDM
Tsukuba, Japan, April 1-4, 2010
Revised Selected Papers

Springer

Volume Editors

Masatoshi Yoshikawa
Graduate School of Informatics, Kyoto University, Yoshida-Honmachi
Sakyo-ku, Kyoto 606-8501, Japan
E-mail: yoshikawa@i.kyoto-u.ac.jp

Xiaofeng Meng
Information School, Renmin University of China
Beijing 100872, China
E-mail: xfmeng@ruc.edu.cn

Takayuki Yumoto
Graduate School of Engineering, University of Hyogo
2167 Shosha, Himeji, Hyogo 671-2280, Japan
E-mail: yumoto@eng.u-hyogo.ac.jp

Qiang Ma
Graduate School of Informatics, Kyoto University
Yoshida-Honmachi, Sakyo-ku, Kyoto 606-8501, Japan
E-mail: qiang@i.kyoto-u.ac.jp

Lifeng Sun
Institute of HCI and Media Integration, Tsinghua University
Beijing 100084, China
E-mail: sunlf@tsinghua.edu.cn

Chiemi Watanabe
Department of Information Science, Ochanomizu University
2-1-1, Otsuka, Bunkyo-ku, Tokyo 112-8610, Japan
E-mail: chiemi@is.ocha.ac.jp

Library of Congress Control Number: 2010930790

CR Subject Classification (1998): H.3, H.4, I.2, C.2, H.2, H.5

LNCS Sublibrary: SL 3 – Information Systems and Application, incl. Internet/Web and HCI

ISSN 0302-9743
ISBN-10 3-642-14588-4 Springer Berlin Heidelberg New York
ISBN-13 978-3-642-14588-9 Springer Berlin Heidelberg New York

springer.com

Printed in Germany

Typesetting: Camera-ready by author, data conversion by Scientific Publishing Services, Chennai, India
Printed on acid-free paper 06/3180

Preface

Database Systems for Advanced Applications (DASFAA) is an international forum for academic exchanges and technical discussions among researchers, developers, and users of databases from academia, business, and industry. DASFAA has been a leading conference in the areas of databases, large-scale data management, data mining, and the Web. Workshops of the 15th DASFAA were held in Tsukuba, Japan on April 4, 2010. These proceedings contain papers of DASFAA2010 workshops. Among the proposals submitted in response to the call-for-workshops, we decided to hold the following six workshops:

- First International Workshop on Graph Data Management: Techniques and Applications (GDM 2010)
- Second International Workshop on Benchmarking of Database Management Systems and Data-Oriented Web Technologies (BenchmarX 2010)
- Third International Workshop on Managing Data Quality in Collaborative Information Systems (MCIS 2010)
- Workshop on Social Networks and Social Media Mining on the Web (SNSMW 2010)
- Data-Intensive eScience Workshop (DIEW 2010)
- Second International Workshop on Ubiquitous Data Management (UDM 2010)

The research area of DASFAA is growing rapidly. The topics of each workshop cover specific area of DASFAA and complement topics of the main conference.

We are grateful to the workshop organizers for their effort in soliciting papers, selecting papers by peer review, and preparing attractive programs. We would like to express our appreciation to Qiang Ma, Lifeng Sun and Takayuki Yumoto for their dedicated work. Our thanks also goes to Chiemi Watanabe for her hard work in preparing this proceedings volume.

April 2010

Xiaofeng Meng
Masatoshi Yoshikawa

DASFAA 2010 Workshop Organization

Workshop Committee Co-chairs

Masatoshi Yoshikawa	Kyoto University, Japan
Xiaofeng Meng	Renmin University, China

Workshop Committee

Qiang Ma	Kyoto University, Japan
Lifeng Sun	Tsinghua University, China
Takayuki Yumoto	University of Hyogo, Japan

Publication Chair

Chiemi Watanabe	Ochanomizu University, Japan

First International Workshop on Graph Data Management: Techniques and Applications (GDM 2010)

Workshop Co-chairs

Sherif Sakr	University of New South Wales, USA
Wei Wang	University of New South Wales, USA

Program Committee

Ghazi Al-Naymat	University of New South Wales, Australia
Toshiyuki Amagasa	University of Tsukuba, Japan
Ahmed Awad	University of Potsdam, Germany
Sourav S. Bhowmick	Nanyang Technological University, Singapore
Stephane Bressan	National University of Singapore, Singapore
Lei Chen	Hong Kong University of Science and Technology, China
Hong Cheng	Chinese University of Hong Kong, China
James Cheng	Nanyang Technological University, Singapore
Claudio Gutierrez	Universidad de Chile, Chile
Herman Haverkort	Technische Universiteit Eindhoven, The Netherlands
Huahai He	Google, USA
Jun Huan	University of Kansas, USA

Yiping Ke	Chinese University of Hong Kong, China
Mohamed F. Mokbel	University of Minnesota, USA
Yuanyuan Tian	IBM Almaden Research Center, USA
Alexander Wolff	University of Würzburg, Germany
Raymond Wong	National ICT Australia, Australia
Lei Zou	Peking University, China
Rui Zhang	University of Melbourne, Australia

Second International Workshop on Benchmarking of Database Management Systems and Data-Oriented Web Technologies (BenchmarX 2010)

Workshop Organizers

Irena Mlýnková	Charles University in Prague, Czech Republic
Martin Nečaský	Charles University in Prague, Czech Republic
Jiří Dokulil	Charles University in Prague, Czech Republic

Program Committee Chairs

Martin Nečaský	Charles University in Prague, Czech Republic
Eric Pardede	La Trobe University, Bundoora, Australia

Program Committee

Radim Bača	Technical University of Ostrava, Czech Republic
Geert Jan Bex	Hasselt University, Belgium
Martine Collard	INRIA Sophia Antipolis, France
Sven Hartmann	Clausthal University of Technology, Germany
Kazuhiro Inaba	National Institute of Informatics, Japan
Agnes Koschmider	Institute AIFB, Universität Karlsruhe, Germany
Michal Krátký	Technical University of Ostrava, Czech Republic
Sebastian Link	Victoria University of Wellington, New Zealand
Sebastian Maneth	University of New South Wales, Australia
Alexander Paar	Universität Karlsruhe, Germany
Incheon Paik	The University of Aizu, Japan
Sherif Sakr	University of New South Wales, Australia
Dmitry Shaporenkov	University of Saint Petersburg, Russia
Jakub Yaghob	Charles University in Prague, Czech Republic

Third International Workshop on Managing Data Quality in Collaborative Information Systems (MCIS 2010)

Workshop Organizers

Shazia Sadiq	The University of Queensland, Australia
Xiaochun Yang	Northeastern University, China
Xiaofang Zhou	The University of Queensland, Australia
Ke Deng	The University of Queensland, Australia

Program Committee

Lei Chen	Hong Kong University of Science and Technology, Hong Kong
Jun Gao	Peking University, China
Marta Indulska	University of Queensland, Australia
Adam Jatowt	Kyoto University, Japan
Cheqing Jin	East China Normal University, China
Marek Kowalkiewicz	SAP Australia
Jiuyong Li	University of South Australia, Australia
Qing Liu	CSIRO, Australia
Mohamed Medhat Gaber	Monash University, Australia
Wanita Sherchan	CSIRO Australia
Yanfeng Shu	CSIRO Australia
Bin Wang	Northeastern University, China

Workshop on Social Networks and Social Media Mining on the Web (SNSMW 2010)

Workshop Co-chairs

Yoshinori Hijikata	Osaka University, Japan
Guandong Xu	Victoria University, Australia

Program Co-chairs

Lin Li	Wuhan University of Technology, China
Munehiko Sasajima	Osaka University, Japan

Program Committee

James Bailey	University of Melbourne, Australia
Yixin Chen	Washington University in St. Louis, USA
Irene Ggarrigos	University of Alicante, Spain
Kenji Hatano	Doshisha University, Japan
Yoshinori Hijikata	Osaka University, Japan

Makoto Iguchi	Synclore Corporation, Japan
Fumihiro Kato	Keio University, Japan
Yukiko Kawai	Kyoto Sangyo University, Japan
Hideyuki Kawashima	Tsukuba University, Japan
Sang-Wook Kim	Hanyang University, Korea
Ichiro Kobayashi	Ochanomizu University, Japan
Tadahiko Kumamoto	Chiba Institute of Technology, Japan
Yuefeng Li	Queensland University of Technology, Australia
Wenxin Liang	Dalian University of Technology, China
Mitsunori Matsushita	Kansai University, Japan
Harumi Murakami	Osaka City University, Japan
Hidetsugu Nanba	Hiroshima City University, Japan
Ikki Omukai	National Institute of Informatics, Japan
Shingo Otsuka	National Institute for Materials Science, Japan
Hitomi Saito	Aichi University of Education, Japan
Hiroshi Sakamoto	Kyushu Institute of Technology, Japan
Shigeaki Sakurai	Toshiba Corporation, Japan
Munehiko Sasajima	Osaka University, Japan
Hiroko Shoji	Chuo University, Japan
Taro Sugihara	Japan Advanced Institute of Science and Technology, Japan
Yasufumi Takama	Tokyo Metropolitan University, Japan
Xiaohui Tao	Queensland University of Technology, Australia
Kenji Tateishi	NEC Corporation, Japan
Masashi Toyoda	University of Tokyo, Japan
Botao Wang	Northeastern University, China
Guoren Wang	Northeastern University, China
Kazuaki Yamada	Toyo University, Japan
Zhenglu Yang	University of Tokyo, Japan
Koji Zettsu	National Institute of Information and Communications Technology, Japan
Jianwei Zhang	Kyoto Sangyo University, Japan
Yanchun Zhang	Victoria University, Australia

Data-Intensive eScience Workshop (DIEW 2010)

Workshop Organizers

Kento Aida	National Institute of Informatics (NII), Japan
Geoffrey Fox	Indiana University, USA
Neil Chue Hong	Open Middleware Infrastructure Institute (OMII), UK
Isao Kojima	National Institute of Advanced Industrial Science and Technology (AIST), Japan
Masatoshi Ohishi	National Astronomical Observatory of Japan (NAOJ), Japan

Program Committee

Takeshi Horinouchi	Hokkaido University, Japan
Toshiaki Katayama	University of Tokyo, Japan
Akira Kinjo	Osaka University, Japan
Akiyoshi Matono	National Institute of Advanced Industrial Science and Technology (AIST), Japan
Yuji Shirasaki	National Astronomical Observatory of Japan (NAOJ), Japan
Yukio Yamamoto	Japan Aerospace Exploration Agency (JAXA), Japan
Shohei Yokoyama	Shizuoka University, Japan

External Reviewers

Yoshiharu Ishikawa	Nagoya University, Japan
Hiroko Kinutani	University of Tokyo, Japan
Steven Lynden	AIST, Japan
Toshiyuki Shimizu	Kyoto University, Japan

Supported by

KAKEN-fuzoroi (20240010)
RENKEI project

The Second International Workshop on Ubiquitous Data Management (UDM 2010)

Honorable Workshop Chair

Katsumi Tanaka	Kyoto University, Japan

Organization Co-chairs

Yutaka Kidawara	NICT, Japan
Ki-Joune Li	Pusan National University, Korea

Program Co-chairs

Koji Zettsu	NICT, Japan
Hannu Jaakkolam	Tampere University of Technology, Finland

Publication Co-chairs

Kyoungsook Kim	NICT, Japan
Sungwoo Tak	Pusan National University, Korea

Local Arrangements Co-chairs

Takafumi Nakanishi	NICT, Japan
Hisashi Miyamori	Kyoto Sangyo University, Japan
Yuhei Akahoshi	NICT, Japan

Publicity Chair

Mitsuru Minakuchi	Kyoto Sangyo University, Japan

Program Committee Members

Paolo Atzeni	University of Rome 3, Italy
Bostjan Brumen	University of Maribor, Slovenia
Takahiro Hara	Osaka University, Japan
Hannu Jaakkola	Tampere University of Technology, Finland
Christian S. Jensen	Aalborg University, Denmark
Sang-Wook Kim	Hanyang University, Korea
Yong-Jin Kwon	Korea Aerospace University, Korea
Ray R. Larson	University of California, Berkeley, USA
Robert Laurini	INSA de Lyon, France
Mario A. Lopez	Denver University, USA
Cyrus Shahabi	University of Southern California, USA
Shashi Shekhar	University of Minnesota, USA
Kazutoshi Sumiya	University of Hyogo, Japan
Guangzhong Sun	University of Science and Technology of China, China
Bernhard Thalheim	Christian Albrechts University at Kiel, Germany
Peter Vojtas	Charles University, Czech Republic
Ouri Wolfson	University of Illinois at Chicago, USA
Xing Xie	Microsoft Research Asia, China
Koji Zettsu	NICT, Japan
Aoying Zhou	East China Normal University, China

Organizers

University of Tsukuba   The Database Society of Japan (DBSJ)

In Cooperation with:

KIISE Database Society of Korea
The China Computer Federation Database Technical Committee
ARC Research Network in Enterprise Information Infrastructure
Asian Institute of Technology (AIT)
"New IT Infrastructure for the Information-explosion Era", MEXT (Ministry of Education, Culture, Sports, Science and Technology) Grant-in-Aid for Scientific Research on Priority Areas, Japan
Information Processing Society of Japan (IPSJ)
The Institute of Electronics, Information, and Communication Engineers (IEICE)
Japan PostgreSQL Users Group
MySQL Nippon Association
The Japanese Firebird Users Group

Sponsoring Institutions

Platinum Sponsors

BeaconIT, Japan

MITSUBISHI ELECTRIC CORPORATION, Japan

Gold Sponsors

National Institute for Materials Science (NIMS), Japan

KDDI R&D Laboratories Inc., Japan

National Institute of Advanced Industrial Science and Technology (AIST), Japan

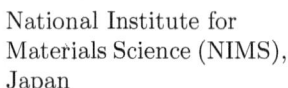

FUJITSU LIMITED

TOSHIBA CORPORATION

Silver Sponsors

Ricoh Co., Ltd., Japan

NTT DATA CORPORATION, Japan

Hitachi, Ltd., Japan

Bronze Sponsors

Ricoh IT Solutions Co., Ltd., Japan

SRA OSS, Inc., Japan

Table of Contents

1st International Workshop on Graph Data Management: Techniques and Applications (GDM 2010)

Data Intensive e-Science Workshop (DIEW2010)

3rd International Workshop on Managing Data Quality in Collaborative Information Systems (MCIS2010)

2nd International Workshop on Benchmarking of Database Management Systems and Data-Oriented Web Technologies (BenchmarX'10)

Workshop on Social Networks and Social Media Mining on the Web (SNSMW2010)

The 2nd International Workshop on Ubiquitous Data Management(UDM2010)

GDM2010
Workshop Organizers' Message

Sherif Sakr and Wei Wang

University of New South Wales, Sydney, Australia

The graph is a powerful tool for representing and understanding objects and their relationships in various application domains. Recently, graphs have been widely used to model many complex structured and schemaless data such as semantic web, social networks, biological networks, chemical compounds, multimedia databases and business process models. The growing popularity of graph databases has generated interesting and fundamental data management problems which attracted a lot of attention from the database community such as: subgraph search queries, supergraph search queries, frequent subgraph mining and approximate subgraph matching. In principle, efficient management of large graph databases is a key performance issue in any graph-based application.

The 1st International Workshop on the techniques and applications of graph data management (GDM'10) was held on April 4, 2010 at the University of Tsukuba, Japan in conjunction with the 15th International Conference on Database Systems for Advanced Applications (DASFAA'10). The overall goal of the workshop was to bring people from different fields together, exchange research ideas and results, encourage discussion about how to provide efficient graph data management techniques in different application domains and to understand the research challenges of such area.

The workshop attracted eight submissions in addition to an invited paper. The submissions are highly diversified, coming from Australia, Germany, Sweden, China, Chile and Japan. The program committee consisted of 19 members from 8 different countries. All submissions were peer reviewed by three program committee members for its technical merit, originality, significance, and relevance to the workshop. The program committee selected three papers for inclusion in the workshop proceedings (Acceptance Rate 38%). The accepted papers covered important research topics and novel applications on business process model, mining timely graph patterns, and spread activation queries.

In fact, this workshop would not be successful without the help of many people. We would like to thank the program committee members for evaluating the assigned papers in a timely and professional manner. The great efforts of the members in the organization committee of DASFAA 2010 in accommodating and supporting the workshops are highly appreciated. Certainly, running this workshop would not have been possible without the support from the authors for their submissions.

After this successful first edition of the workshop which provided many insights for interesting ideas and research problems, we believe that the GDM workshop will become a traditional annual meeting for the community of researchers in the different topics of the graph data management field.

M. Yoshikawa et al. (Eds.): DASFAA 2010, LNCS 6193, p. 1, 2010.

On-Line Preferential Nearest Neighbor Browsing in Large Attributed Graphs

Jiefeng Cheng[1,*], Jeffrey Xu Yu[2], and Reynold C.K. Cheng[1]

[1] University of Hong Kong, China
{jfcheng,ckcheng}@cs.hku.hk
[2] The Chinese University of Hong Kong, China
yu@se.cuhk.edu.hk

Abstract. Given a large weighted directed graph where nodes are associated with attributes and edges are weighted, we study a new problem, called preferential nearest neighbors (NN) browsing, in this paper. In such browsing, a user may provide one or more source nodes and some keywords to retrieve the nearest neighbors of those source nodes that contain the given keywords. For example, when a tourist has a plan to visit several places (source nodes), he/she would like to search hotels with some preferred features (e.g., Internet and swimming pools). It is highly desirable to recommend a list of near hotels with those preferred features, in order of the road network distance to the places (source nodes) the tourist wants to visit. The existing approach by graph traversal at querying time requires long query processing time, and the approach by maintenance of the pre-computed all-pairs shortest distances requires huge storage space on disk. In this paper, we propose new approaches to support on-line preferential NN browsing. The data graphs we are dealing with are weighted directed graphs where nodes are associated with attributes, and the distances between nodes to be found are the exact distances in the graph. We focus ourselves on two-step approaches. In the first step, we identify a number of reference nodes (also called centers) which exist alone on some shortest paths between a source node and a preferential NN node that contains the user-given keywords. In the second step, we find the preferential NN nodes within a certain distance to the source nodes via the relevant reference nodes, using an index that supports both textural (attributes) and and the distance. Our approach tightly integrates NN search with the preference search, which is confirmed to be efficient and effective to find any preferential NN nodes.

1 Introduction

Recently, with the rapid growth of Internet and the World-Wide-Web, the fast-paced data archiving and analyzing techniques sparkle increasing interest in efficient search of nearest neighbors (NN) that meet a user's preferences. In this paper, we study a new nearest neighbors search problem by taking keyword search into consideration. Several examples are given below to motivate our study. As an example, in a large road network [19], a tourist, who plans to visit a few places, would like to find near hotels

* This work was mainly done while Jiefeng Cheng was working in The Chinese Univ. of Hong Kong.

M. Yoshikawa et al. (Eds.): DASFAA 2010, LNCS 6193, pp. 2–19, 2010.

with some preferred features (e.g., Internet and swimming pools), and wants to know the exact distances between the hotels and the places he/she wants to visit in order by the distance. As another example, a user may give hotel names and search restaurants with some features that are near to the given hotels. It is desirable to see the hotel which is closest to a restaurant with the requested features to be visited is returned first. Examples can be also found in a collaborative network. Suppose that a researcher is interested in a new topic and is looking for people who have done the relevant work to collaborate. On the collaborative network, she/he can search authors who study that topic and are close to her/his friends in the collaborative network. The possible collaborators can be ranked by the distances to her/his friends.

Motivated by these requirements and the applications, in this paper, we study a new nearest neighbors search problem, which we call the preferential NN browsing. In detail, we use the common graph distance: Let $G = (V, E)$ be an edge-weighted directed graph, where V is a set of nodes, and E is a set of edges, and every edge weight is a non-negative number. The *shortest distance* from a node u to a node v, denoted $\delta(u, v)$, is the minimum total weight along a path from u and v. And a *shortest path* from u to v is a path from u to v with the minimum total weight $\delta(u, v)$. A node is associated with attributes to describe its features. A number of literals, $\{t\}$, are used to represent the node attributes or a user's preferences (keywords).[1] For preferential NN browsing, a user provides one or more source nodes $\{q\}$ and a number of keywords $\{t\}$. A list of node pairs is returned where one node is one taken from $\{q\}$ and the other is a node, v, that contains all the required $\{t\}$. The list is ranked by the distance between q and v.

This kind of queries can also be applied as building blocks for emerging graph-distance-based applications: graph-structured XML data, bio graphs, and keyword search. The twig query against graph-structured XML data [12] intensively processes the required node pairs of the ancestor/descendant relationship with the corresponding distance information, where one node in a pair is derived from an intermediate result while the other node corresponds to a certain label (literal) and connects to the first node with a specified distance. Those node pairs are enumerated in the increasing order to their distances for top-k queries. The approach of [13] finds star-like tree answers for a set of user-given keywords in large graphs. For each tree answer, all leaf nodes contain all keywords. [13] enumerates node pairs (r, v_t) in the increasing order of their distances in a large graph where r in the pair is the root node of a possible answer which can be any node in the large graph while v_t in the pair is required to contain the keyword t.

Efficient algorithms to explore shortest paths and corresponding distances on demand in main memory [8] or with graphs organized on the secondary storage [16] have been studied. To perform the preferential NN browsing, a naive graph traversal approach is to use the shortest path algorithm multiple times on all specified source nodes ($\{q\}$). While visiting nodes in the increasing order of distance from a source node, a node is returned as a result if it contains all user-given keywords. However, the average number of nodes within a certain distance from a specific node increases dramatically as the distance increases [21], which results in a high processing cost. Moreover, while only a few nodes may contain the user-given keywords, the shortest path algorithm can

[1] In this paper, we use literals and keywords interchangeably about attributes or preferences.

visit a huge number of nodes, in order to find them. On the other hand, an alternative and simple solution is to use pre-computed edge transitive closure with distance information, which has been adopted by [13] to support keyword search and by [12] to support twig queries, in graphs. Let D_G be the *all-pairs distances* for G, namely, D_G consists of all pairs $\langle(u, v)\colon \delta(u, v)\rangle$, which records the distance $(\delta(u, v))$ from node u to node v, for all $u, v \in V$, if there is a directed path from u to v in G. This solution materializes D_G and is effective in finding the distance between two arbitrary nodes, because no shortest path computation is needed at querying time. However, the solution by pre-computing edge transitive closure with distance suffers from the large storage overhead as $O(|V|^2)$. Moreover, if we want to be able to directly retrieve any node pairs containing a user-given keyword in order, using the edge transitive closure, we need to maintain many edge transitive closures for different keywords. The overall storage cost can be $O(N_t \cdot |V|^2)$, where N_t is the total number of different keywords.

In this paper, we propose a compact index approach to support on-line preferential NN browsing. In contrast to the hop-by-hop graph traversal approach, we efficiently find any specified number of preferential NN nodes of different distances to source nodes based on a two-step search method. In the first step, we identify a number of reference nodes (also called centers) which exist alone on some shortest paths between a source node and a preferential NN node that contains the user-given keywords. In the second step, we find the preferential NN nodes within a certain distance to the source nodes via the relevant reference nodes, using an index that supports both textural (attributes) and and the distance. Furthermore, we associate each attribute with a list of centers, which can be used to find all relevant index keys. And those index keys suggest that only relevant nodes with a given attribute will be searched in the two-step search. The index size is manageable. Our approach tightly integrates NN search with the preference search, which is fast and effective to find any preferential NN nodes. Our approach is motivated by the fact that there are too many pairs in D_G (in $O(|V|^2)$) while the total number of centers must be less than $|V|$. Therefore, our approach only includes all keyword to center lists, which require $O(N_t \cdot |V|)$ space, and a search structure for all centers to buckets of encoded nodes. In our approach, all buckets consume $O(|V| \cdot \sqrt{|E|})$ space. We can obtain all node pairs corresponding to a keyword efficiently.

Contributions. (1) We characterize and address an important problem, the preferential NN browsing; (2) we investigate the solution to use all-pairs shortest distances, D_G, for this problem. (3) we design a compact index which does not need to store D_G directly but can be used to find any pairs in D_G, which supports searching with the textural information and and the distance. of ranking queries and a tightly integration of NN search with the preference search, for this problem; (5) we conducted extensive experimental evaluation with real data to verify the superiority of our approach over the existing approach.

Paper organization. We briefly state our problem in Section 2. Then we investigate a straightforward solution which uses pre-computed edge transitive closure with distance information in Section 3. We introduce a center-based processing framework in Section 4, including a detailed implementation to cope with the ranking query and preference search in NN browsing. The experimental results are discussed in Section 5. Related work is given in Section 6. Section 7 concludes this paper.

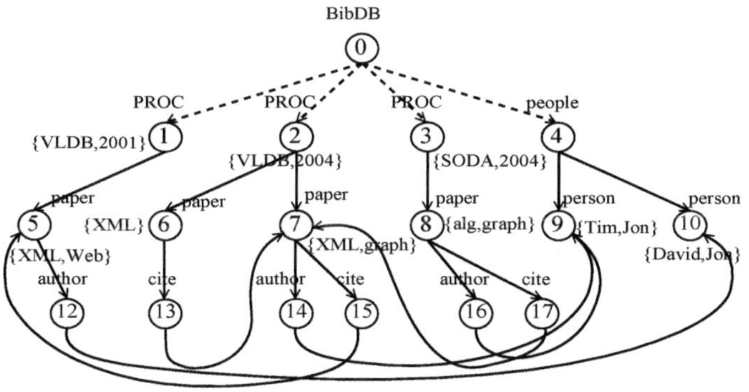

Fig. 1. An Example

2 Problem Statement

Our preferential NN browsing problem is considered on a large attributed graph $G(V, E)$, where each node has one or more keywords to represent its attributes. Similarly, a user also provides one or more keywords to represent her/his preference that should be matched by a neighbor's attributes. Suppose that $I(t)$ consists of all nodes containing keyword t in G. We use several kinds of queries that characterize our NN browsing problem. Given a keyword t and a node set Q of interest, the main form of our query is $Q \overset{d}{\hookrightarrow} t$ (or $Q \overset{d}{\hookleftarrow} t$), asking for a specified number of $\langle (u, v)\colon \delta(u, v)\rangle \in D_G$ ordered by $\delta(u, v)$, for all $u \in Q$ and $v \in I(t)$ (or $u \in I(t)$ and $v \in Q$), where $\delta(u, v) \neq \infty$. This is a ranking query, where the actual number of all node pairs returned is decided by the user or application. Note that the two directions for the above query indicate the outgoing/incoming path between any node in Q and its neighbors. A typical case exists in terms of Q: there is $Q = I(t')$ and t' corresponds to another keyword. Next, we introduce a number of generalizations from this query. However, for the interest of space in this paper, we focus on the processing for this kind of queries in this paper, and discuss how our approach can be extended to support other variants of this query.

Example 1. A sample graph is shown in Fig. 1, which shows a bibliography database. Each node has a label which is common in XML and other semi-structure data. Each edge in this graph has a unit weight, that is, all edge weight is 1 and we thus do not list them in Fig. 1. In this example, there are labels PROC, paper and so on. Each node in the graph is also described by some texture information. For example, node 1 contains `VLDB` and `2001`. A keyword t is either the name of a label or from the containing text. Suppose Q is $I(\texttt{PROC})$ and t is `Jon`. Then, $I(\texttt{PROC}) = \{1, 2, 3\}$ and $I(\texttt{Jon}) = \{9, 10\}$. Then, a ranked list consisting of all the query results for $Q \overset{d}{\hookrightarrow}$ `Jon` is $\langle (1, 10)\colon 3\rangle$, $\langle (2, 9)\colon 3\rangle$, $\langle (3, 9)\colon 3\rangle$, $\langle (2, 10)\colon 5\rangle$ and $\langle (3, 10)\colon 7\rangle$.

To perform the preferential NN browsing, a naive method is to use multiple instances of the shortest path algorithm on all specified source nodes. Upon each visited node in the increasing order of distance, if it contains all user-given keywords then we return it as one result. However, the average number of nodes within a certain distance from a specific node increases dramatically as the distance increases [21], which results in necessitating processing cost. Moreover, while only a few nodes may contain those keywords, the shortest path algorithms can visited a huge number of nodes in order to find them. Therefore, we first study a quick solution that pre-computes and stores edge transitive closure with distance information, which has been adopted by [12,13].

3 Pairwise Processing

Our first target is a thorough investigation for methods using pre-computed and materialized D_G, which is effective in finding the distance between two arbitrary nodes, because there is no shortest path computation needed at querying time. Because it relies on D_G directly, it is called *pairwise processing* in this paper. It is straightforward to solve preferential NN browsing based on D_G, where $Q \overset{d}{\hookrightarrow} t$ (or $Q \overset{d}{\hookleftarrow} t$) can be viewed as $|Q| \times |I(t)|$ several individual queries $Q_d(q, v)$ for all $q \in Q$ and $v \in I(t)$. And each individual query $Q_d(q, v)$ asks for the distance from q to v in G. A straightforward method is to index all $\delta(u, v)$ in D_G by (u, v) with a B^+-tree or a hash table. Then it is sufficient to find out $\delta(u, v)$ via a single index look-up. Thus, $Q \hookrightarrow t$ can be evaluated by first using $|Q| \times |I(t)|$ look-ups for all $\delta(u, v)$ and then sorting all obtained $\langle (u, v)\colon \delta(u, v)\rangle$. However, we thus need to find all query results and sort all obtained $\langle (q, v)\colon \delta(q, v)\rangle$ even if the user only request several top-ranked results. This can be costly and unwise especially when $|Q| \times |I(t)|$ is large and only few results is requested from the user.

We consider a better choice as to index D_G by u (or v) for all $\langle (u, v)\colon \delta(u, v)\rangle$ and to search for results in D_G progressively, that is, we find a few top-ranked results first instead of all results, for $Q \overset{d}{\hookrightarrow} t$. Now the key issue is how to organize and store D_G on disk for efficient processing of $Q \overset{d}{\hookrightarrow} t$ (or $Q \overset{d}{\hookleftarrow} t$). In particularly, we store all different $\langle (u, v)\colon \delta(u, v)\rangle$ into a cluster in terms of some specific u (or v). For the two cases for u or v, we first discuss the design of indexing D_G by the source node u to process $Q \overset{d}{\hookrightarrow} t$.

For a single node u, it is possible to materialize all results of $\{u\} \overset{d}{\hookrightarrow} t$ in the cluster of u. To fast process $Q \overset{d}{\hookrightarrow} t$, it is possible to materialize all $\langle (u, v)\colon \delta(u, v)\rangle \in D_G$ for each t such that $v \in I(t)$ or $u \in I(t)$. However, the number of different t, denoted by N_t, can be large. The total storage can be $O(N_t \cdot |V|^2))$, which is prohibitive for a large data graph. Therefore, a more practical storage is to organize D_G and not to duplicate portions of D_G with different t. Under such a guideline, we group all $\langle (u, v)\colon \delta(u, v)\rangle \in D_G$ in terms of some specific u. And the main idea to process $Q \overset{d}{\hookrightarrow} t$ is to scan all cluster of $u \in Q$ and in the same time to check whether $v \in I(t)$ is true for each encountered $\langle (u, v)\colon \delta(u, v)\rangle$. And all $\langle (u, v)\colon \delta(u, v)\rangle$ in the cluster of u are sorted in the ascending order of $\delta(u, v)$.

Algorithm 1 scans $|Q|$ clusters of $u \in Q$ sequentially in a round-robin fashion. That is, in one round, it accesses all clusters for one δ value, where it examines all pairs $\langle (u, v)\colon d\rangle$ in those clusters for requested results. Then, in the next round, it increases δ by one to repeat the scan on all clusters for all requested results. All sequential scans are

Algorithm 1. *PairwiseProcessing*

Input: $Q \overset{d}{\hookrightarrow} t$.
Output: $\langle (u,v){:}\delta(u,v)\rangle \in D_G$ sorted by $\delta(u,v)$, where $u \in Q$ or $v \in I(t)$.

1: $\delta \longleftarrow 1$;
2: **while** TRUE **do**
3:     **for all** $\langle (u,v){:}\delta\rangle$ in u's clusters based on D_G, where $u \in Q$ **do**
4:         **if** $v \in I(t)$ **then**
5:             output $\langle (u,v){:}\delta\rangle$ for $Q \overset{d}{\hookrightarrow} t$;
6:         **end if**
7:     **end for**
8:     $\delta \longleftarrow \delta + 1$;
9: **end while**

u	v	δ
1	5	1
1	12	2
1	10	3

(a) Node 1

u	v	δ
2	6	1
2	7	1
2	13	2
2	14	2
2	15	2
2	5	3
2	9	3
2	12	4
2	10	5

(b) Node 2

u	v	δ
3	8	1
3	16	2
3	17	2
3	7	3
3	9	3
3	14	4
3	15	4
3	5	5
3	12	6
3	10	7

(c) Node 3

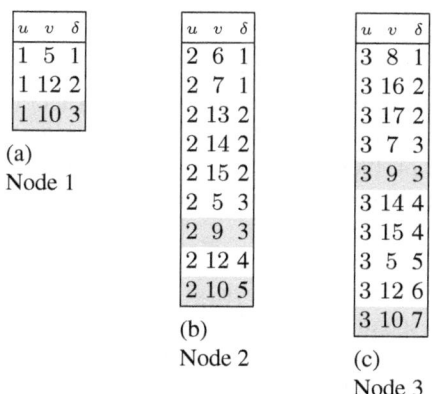

Fig. 2. The Clusters Based on Transitive Closure

started from the records with the smallest δ, suggested by Line 1 of Algorithm 1. Line 2 assumes the results of $Q \overset{d}{\hookrightarrow} t$ are requested on demand and the loop can be stopped at the user's will if the user does not request more results or all pairs in clusters of $u \in Q$ are consumed. For each $\langle (u,v){:}d\rangle$ encountered, we check if v is in $I(t)$. If it is, $\langle (u,v){:} d\rangle$ can be output as a result of $Q \overset{d}{\hookrightarrow} t$. Note that Algorithm 1 has to rely on sequential scan to find all proper $\langle (u,v){:}\ \delta(u,v)\rangle$. Therefore, even if $I(t)$ is a very small set, the sequential scan can access all pairs in those clusters, which include at most $|Q| \cdot |V|$ pairs. Moreover, processing $Q \overset{d}{\hookrightarrow} t$ and $Q \overset{d}{\hookleftarrow} t$ requires storing two copies of D_G, one copy is indexed by u and the other by v, for all $\langle (u,v){:}\delta(u,v)\rangle \in D_G$. It is worth noting that only a kind of indexing scheme on D_G, which organizes $\langle (u,v){:}\ \delta(u,v)\rangle \in D_G$ independent of the first node u or the second node v, can support both $Q \overset{d}{\hookrightarrow} t$ and $Q \overset{d}{\hookleftarrow} t$ by storing D_G once.

Example 2. In order to process $Q \overset{d}{\hookrightarrow}$ Jon for our running example, where $Q = \{1, 2, 3\}$, pairwise processing accesses the clusters of node 1, 2 and 3, as the three tables shown in Fig. 2. According to each δ value, the three tables are scanned for all records with the same δ. So, starting with $\delta = 1$, $\langle(1, 5){:}\,1\rangle$, $\langle(2, 6){:}\,1\rangle$, $\langle(2, 7){:}\,1\rangle$ and $\langle(3, 8){:}\,1\rangle$ are obtained and examined for query results. When $\delta = 3$, the first result $\langle(1, 10){:}\,3\rangle$ is spotted. It is also required to scan all 22 records in those tables to find all results of $Q \overset{d}{\hookrightarrow}$ Jon, shown as the shadowed rows in Fig. 2.

4 Center-Based Processing

In this section, we introduce a center-based processing framework to support preferential NN browsing. In this framework, the NN search is based on a number of important *reference nodes*, where the reference nodes are used to suggest all target nodes $v \in I(t)$ connected by all source node $q \in Q$, for evaluating $Q \overset{d}{\hookrightarrow} t$ or $Q \overset{d}{\hookleftarrow} t$. This is possible because those reference nodes carry distance information for other nodes. Recently, the idea of selecting a number of reference nodes in graphs to support processing distance or shortest path queries are widely used, including *landmarks* [11,18] and *centers* [6]. However, the landmark approach does not support finding exact distances directly and can only derive an approximate distance value with the upper and lower bounds [11]. However, as required by our problem, we prefer that the distance between v and q can be obtained with the reference nodes. Hence we will not use the landmark-like reference nodes in this paper.

A essential property for the reference nodes we need is that we can use each reference node to represent a number of distances in the graph. In detail, each reference node resides on a number of shortest paths in G, and those shortest paths are preferred to be as many as possible. Then, we can use the reference node to represent the set of distances corresponding to those shortest paths. In detail, there can be a number of shortest paths in G, say from a to d, all go through w. Thus, we can have w as a reference node for all those (a, d) pairs. Therefore, we can group all pairs $\langle(a, d){:}\,\delta(a, d)\rangle$ in D_G according to different w, where a cluster of w is said to include all such $\langle(a, d){:}\,\delta(a, d)\rangle$. In literature, this kind of reference nodes are studied in [6]. It first proposes finding a set W of such reference nodes, called *centers*, to insure that any $\langle(a, d){:}\,\delta(a, d)\rangle$ in D_G is included in some cluster of $w \in W$. [6] focuses on the cluster construction in order to minimize the overall storage cost for all clusters, which we will review more shortly.

Example 3. For our running example, we have 6 centers in total on all shortest paths in the graph, as shown in Fig. 3. Specifically, Fig. 3(a) shows the center 7, with a circle on it, and a cluster of 7 containing a number of shortest paths from different a to d going through 7. The set of all a, A_7, and the set of all d, D_7, are marked by two shadowed areas with two background colors. Similarly, Fig. 3(b) and Fig. 3(c) show the other centers and clusters. Then we obtained all centers assigned to all associated nodes as illustrated by Fig. 5 (a), where for a node v in A_w, we assign v with the center w and the distance d from v to w, such as $\langle w, d\rangle$. And similar operations are performed for each d in D_w.

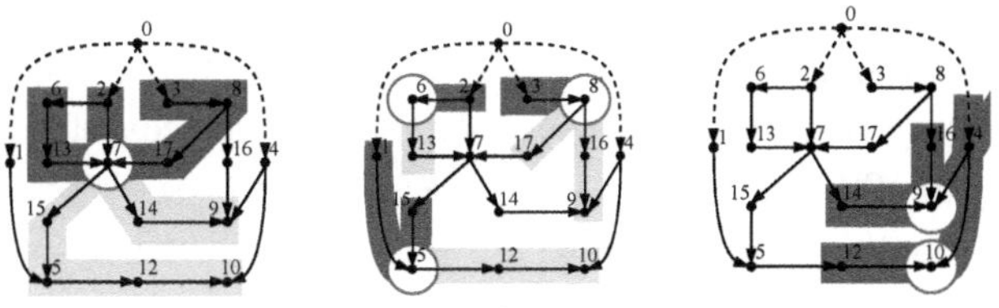

(a) (b) (c)

Fig. 3. The Clusters of All Centers

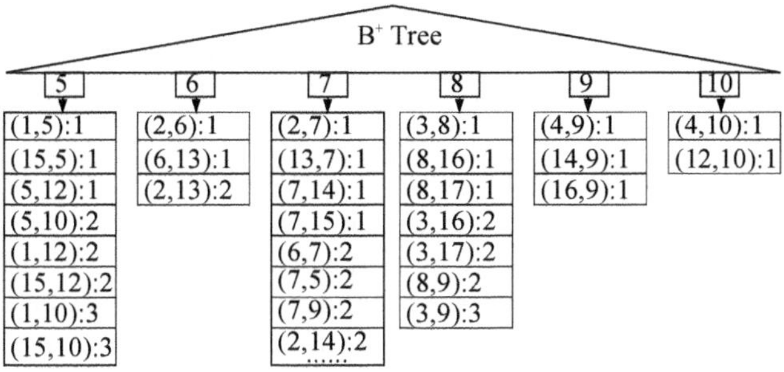

Fig. 4. Indexing All-Pairs Distances Clustered by Centers

v	centers (L_{out})
1	$\langle 5:1 \rangle$
2	$\langle 6:1 \rangle \langle 7:1 \rangle$
3	$\langle 7:3 \rangle \langle 8:1 \rangle$
	...

(a) Centers for q

t	centers (L_{in})
Jon	$\langle 5:2 \rangle \langle 7:2 \rangle \langle 8:2 \rangle \langle 9:0 \rangle \langle 10:0 \rangle$
Tim	$\langle 7:2 \rangle \langle 8:2 \rangle \langle 9:0 \rangle$
David	$\langle 5:2 \rangle \langle 7:4 \rangle \langle 10:0 \rangle$
	...

(b) Centers for t

Fig. 5. Obtaining Relevant Centers

4.1 Indexing All-Pairs Distances by Centers

Recall that in pair-wise processing, we have to store two copies of the transitive closure of G: one copy is clustered by a and the other by d, for all $\langle (a,d)\colon \delta(a,d) \rangle \in D_G$, in order to support both $Q \overset{d}{\hookrightarrow} t$ and $Q \overset{d}{\hookleftarrow} t$. Such a limitation is essentially caused by the way that we search clusters and distances based on the two end nodes a and d of $\langle (a,d)\colon \delta(a,d) \rangle$. It is possible to avoid such an awkward treatment: in our first solution as the center-based processing, we propose an all-pairs distance index based on centers where only one copy of the transitive closure of G is sufficient to support both $Q \overset{d}{\hookrightarrow} t$ and $Q \overset{d}{\hookleftarrow} t$. In detail, consider all $\langle (a,d)\colon \delta(a,d) \rangle \in D_G$ included in a cluster of w, we store them in a list sorted by $\delta(a,d)$ in the increasing order of it. We use a search structure such as a B^+-tree to support finding the sorted list (the cluster of w) with a specified w. For our running example, the all-pairs distance index is given in Fig. 4. It shows that 6 sorted lists are formed based on the 6 clusters in Fig. 3, which are indexed by corresponding centers.

A framework. With this all-pairs distance index, we can explain our two-step search framework for the preferential NN browsing. In particular, here are the two steps: (i) Compute all relevant centers; (ii) use those centers to compute requested $\langle (q,v){:}\,\delta(q,v)\rangle$ (or $\langle (v,q){:}\ \delta(v,q)\rangle$) sorted by $\delta(q,v)$ (or $\delta(v,q)$ progressively. These are the overall steps that can be used to process both of $Q \overset{d}{\hookrightarrow} t$ and $Q \overset{d}{\hookleftarrow} t$ with only slightly difference. Therefore, we use $Q \overset{d}{\hookrightarrow} t$ to describe the processing in this section. We next explain the processing in the first step, followed by an explanation for the second step using this all-pair distance index first.

The first step. For a query $Q \overset{d}{\hookrightarrow} t$, a relevant center w (or the cluster) indicates one or more query results is included in the cluster of w. This is to say, there must exist one or more (q,v), $q \in Q$ and $v \in I(t)$, such that a shortest path from q to v goes through w. Therefore, we should consider those centers connected to any $q \in Q$ as well as any $v \in I(t)$. Recall that all centers are already assigned with each individual node (Fig. 5 (a)), it allows us easily obtain those centers for each $q \in Q$. For $Q \overset{d}{\hookrightarrow} t$ where there is $Q = \{1, 2, 3\}$, we can find all centers connected with Q center are node 5, 6, 7, and 8 based on Fig. 5 (a). On the other hand, in order to obtain centers connected to any $v \in I(t)$, we maintain a keyword to center list for each t, called the *c-list* of t, based on those centers connected to any $v \in I(t)$. Specifically, if v contains a keyword t and some $\langle (a,v){:}\ \delta(a,v)\rangle$ or $\langle (v,d){:}\ \delta(v,d)\rangle$ is included the cluster of w, then a record of w is added to the c-list of t. The record of w in a c-list also includes a min distance d between w and any $v \in I(t)$ such as $\langle w : d\rangle$. In Fig. 5 (b), we illustrate such c-lists for some keywords. For example, consider Jon and $I(\texttt{Jon}) = \{9, 10\}$. Excluding the cluster of 6, all other 5 clusters include some distance involving 9 and 10, then the c-list of Jon consists the records of 5, 7, 8, 9 and 10, as illustrated in the first row of Fig. 5 (b). Considering the records of 7 in the c-list of Jon, it is $\langle 7 : 2\rangle$ because the distance between 7 and 9 is 2, which is smaller than the other distance between 7 and 10 by 1. Now, we can find the relevant centers to be those one appear as the centers for each $q \in Q$ and in the c-list of t. For example, to process the sample query for $Q = \{1, 2, 3\}$ and $t =$ Jon, we obtain relevant centers as 5, 7 and 8 based on all center records of Fig. 5 (a) and the first row of Fig. 5 (b).

For different t, it is practical and beneficial to materialize all centers w. Thus, we can immediately obtain the relevant centers of $Q \hookrightarrow t$ (or $Q \hookleftarrow t$) for different t, while the total storage cost is $O(N_t \cdot |V|))$, in contrast to the $O(N_t \cdot |V|^2))$ storage of pairwise processing to materialize pairs of D_G for different t. For example, all centers for Jon, Tim, David and so on, can thus be stored as disk index (Fig. 5 (b)).

The second step. With all relevant centers w and the B$^+$-tree, we can find all all relevant clusters. Then, we use similar processing as the pair-wise processing to find all requested results (Section 3).

Example 4. On all relevant clusters for the centers 5, 7 and 8 for our sample query, we perform sequential scan in a round-robin fashion. All scanned pairs $\langle (a,d){:}\,\delta(a,d)\rangle$ are not requested results for δ is set to 1 and 2, because no pair satisfies $a \in Q$ and $d \in I(t)$. Then, when δ is set to 3, we obtain the first results $\langle (1,10){:}\,3\rangle$ in the cluster of 5.

On the other hand, in order to illustrate processing of $Q \overset{d}{\hookleftarrow} t$ using the same index, consider $Q = \{9, 10\}$ and $t = \texttt{PROC}$. There is $I(\texttt{PROC}) = \{1, 2, 3\}$ and the c-list of PROC can be obtained based on Fig. 5 (a), which consists of 5, 6, 7 and 8. Note that the center connected to any node in $Q = \{9, 10\}$ is 5, 7, 8, 9 and 10, which is the same to the c-list of Jon. Therefore, the relevant center is again 5, 7 and 8. Therefore, on the clusters of 5, 7 and 8, we use the similar processing in the previous previous example to find the requested results.

A main setback of the all-pairs distance index is its huge storage cost to store all-pairs distances in $O(|V|^2)$ space, therefore the I/O cost to access the clusters is high.

4.2 The Implementation for a Compact Index

In this section, we discuss a new index structure for the all-pairs distances. We first review the 2-hop labeling to support on-line processing of exact distance queries, which is extensively studied in the literature recently [6,24,3]. in [6], which aims at a compressed form of the whole edge transitive closure of a given graph.

The 2-hop labeling is based on the centers discussed in Section 4, which assigns the center w to all a and d where the shortest path from a to d is contained in the cluster of w. Let the set of all a be A_w and that of all d be D_w, for w. Thus, with $|A_w| + |D_w|$ space, total $|A_w| \cdot |D_w|$ several distances between nodes in A_w and D_w can be remembered this way. Therefore, the 2-hop labeling is conjectured to encode all all-pairs distances in $O(V \cdot \sqrt{E})$ space [6]. Particularly, it assigns every node $v \in V$ a label $L(v) = (L_{in}(v), L_{out}(v))$ for G, where $L_{in}(v)$ and $L_{out}(v)$ are subsets of D_G whose entries are in the form of $\langle (w, v)\colon \delta\rangle$ and $\langle (v, w)\colon \delta\rangle$, or simply $\langle w : \delta\rangle$. Then, a query, $Q_d(u, v)$, querying the shortest distance from u to v, can be answer by

$$\min\{\delta_1 + \delta_2 | \langle (u, w)\colon \delta_1\rangle \in L_{out}(u) \wedge \langle (w, v)\colon \delta_2\rangle \in L_{in}(v)\} \tag{1}$$

It means to find a center, w, in both $L_{out}(u)$ and $L_{in}(v)$ with the minimum $\delta_1 + \delta_2$. $Q_d(u, v)$ is infinite if there is no such w found using Eq. (1). A 2-hop distance labeling of G can be obtained with the computation of a *distance-aware 2-hop cover* of G. A distance-aware 2-hop cover of G, denoted by L, is defined to be a set of clusters of all centers in G, denoted by S_w, then we have $L = \{S_{w_1}, S_{w_2}, \cdots, S_{w_m}\}$. Each S_w is exactly a cluster based on the center w, which we briefly mentioned in the previous section. Here we give a formal description for it. A 2-hop clusters S_w, where $S_w = S(A_w, w, D_w)$, compactly represents a subset of D_G. Formally, let $ancs(w)$ and $desc(w)$ be the sets consisting of all entries in the form of $\langle (a, w)\colon \delta\rangle$ and $\langle (w, d)\colon \delta\rangle$ in D_G, respectively. Let $A_w \subseteq ancs(w)$ and $D_w \subseteq desc(w)$. A 2-hop cluster $S(A_w, w, D_w)$ covers the shortest paths from $a \in A_w$ to $d \in D_w$ via w as many as possible, where we abuse $a \in A_w$ (or $d \in D_w$) by signifying $\langle (a, w)\colon \delta\rangle \in A_w$ (or $\langle (w, d)\colon \delta\rangle \in D_w$). If the following equation (Eq. (2)) holds:

$$\delta(a, w) + \delta(w, d) = \delta(a, d) \tag{2}$$

for some $a \in A_w$ and $d \in D_w$, then it is said the $\langle (a, d)\colon \delta(a, d)\rangle \in D_G$ is "covered". This suggests that the shortest path from a to d is the concatenation of the shortest path from a to w and the shortest path from w to d. Note that it is possible that for some

center:	5		
	from	to	
distance:	1	1	2
keyword:	Paper, cite, XML, Web	author,	person, David, Jon
node:	1,15	12	10

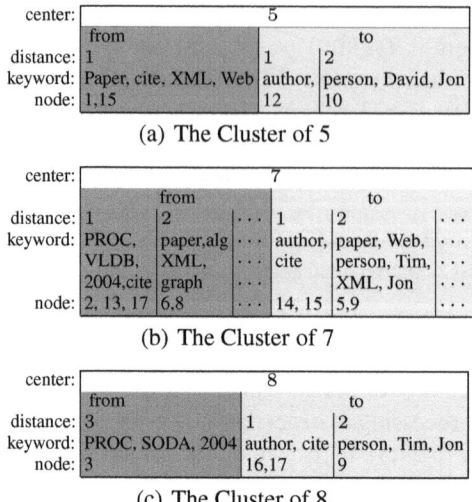

(a) The Cluster of 5

center:	7					
	from			to		
distance:	1	2	···	1	2	···
keyword:	PROC, VLDB, 2004,cite	paper,alg XML, graph	···	author, cite	paper, Web, person, Tim, XML, Jon	···
node:	2, 13, 17	6,8	···	14, 15	5,9	···

(b) The Cluster of 7

center:	8		
	from	to	
distance:	3	1	2
keyword:	PROC, SODA, 2004	author, cite	person, Tim, Jon
node:	3	16,17	9

(c) The Cluster of 8

Fig. 6. Organizing Clusters

v	L_{in}	L_{out}
1	∅	⟨5:1⟩
2	∅	⟨6:1⟩⟨7:1⟩
3	∅	⟨7:3⟩⟨8:1⟩
4	∅	⟨9:1⟩⟨10:1⟩
5	⟨5:0⟩⟨7:2⟩	⟨5:0⟩
6	⟨6:0⟩	⟨6:0⟩⟨7:2⟩
7	⟨7:0⟩	⟨7:0⟩
8	⟨8:0⟩	⟨7:2⟩⟨8:0⟩
9	⟨7:2⟩⟨8:2⟩⟨9:0⟩	∅
10	⟨5:2⟩⟨7:4⟩⟨10:0⟩	∅
12	⟨5:1⟩⟨7:3⟩	⟨10:1⟩
13	⟨6:1⟩	⟨7:1⟩
14	⟨7:1⟩	⟨9:1⟩
15	⟨7:1⟩	⟨5:1⟩
16	⟨8:1⟩	⟨9:1⟩
17	⟨7:1⟩	⟨8:1⟩

Fig. 7. An example for the distance-aware 2-hop cover

$a \in A_w$ and $d \in D_w$, the corresponding $\langle (a,d)\colon \delta(a,d)\rangle \in D_G$ is not covered by $S(A_w, w, D_w)$, due to the constraint given in Eq. (2).

The distance-aware 2-hop cover L of G compactly encodes all entries in D_G by computing 2-hop clusters. Given L, the 2-hop distance labeling for G is determined by adding $\langle w : \delta(a,w)\rangle$ into each $L_{out}(a)$ for $\langle (a,w)\colon \delta(a,w)\rangle \in A_w$ and adding $\langle w : \delta(w,d)\rangle$ into each $L_{in}(d)$ for $\langle (w,d)\colon \delta(w,d)\rangle \in D_w$, for every $S(A_w, w, D_w)$ in L. Similarly, we also abuse $w \in L_{out}(a)$ (or $w \in L_{in}(d)$) by signifying $\langle (a,w)\colon \delta\rangle \in L_{out}(a)$ (or $\langle (w,d)\colon \delta\rangle \in L_{in}(d)$). Let P_L be the set of all entries $\langle (a,d)\colon \delta_1 + \delta_2\rangle$ for any $\langle (a,w)\colon \delta_1\rangle$ and $\langle (w,d)\colon \delta_2\rangle$ in L, a 2-hop cover of G guarantees $P_L \supseteq D_G$ as shown in [6], which guarantees that any distance query can be answered using the 2-hop distance labeling with Eq. (1). Recent work [3,24] on 2-hop labelings focuses on improvement for better construction efficiency. Fig. 7 shows the 2-hop distance labels, $L_{in}(v)$ and $L_{in}(v)$, of all nodes in our sample graph (Fig. 1). With the 2-hop distance labels of the sample graph, we already obtained the clusters of all centers (Fig. 3) as well as all c-lists (Fig. 5).

Now we discuss a better all-pairs distance index. Specifically, we organize the sorted list for $S_w = S(A_w, w, D_w)$ associated with a center w (Fig. 4) according to A_w and D_w. Then, we further group nodes in the two parts by their distances to/from w into a number of a *F-buckets*/*T-buckets*. Those *F-buckets*/*T-buckets* are arranged in the increasing order of the node distance. We collect all keywords for all nodes in a bucket. For example, the cluster of 7 as illustrated in Fig. 6(b), where A_7 and D_7 is shown in different background and each *F-buckets*/*T-buckets* is shown as a column in Fig. 6(b). For the *F-bucket* with distance 1, we have three nodes 2, 13 and 17, which have total 4 keywords, `PROC`, `VLDB` and `2004` from node 1, and `cite` from node 13 and 17. We can sequentially scan the two ordered lists of *F-buckets*/*T-buckets* in order to obtain

Query	t_1	t_2	$\lvert I(t_1)\rvert$	$\lvert I(t_2)\rvert$
Q_1	`conference`	`database`	9792	1156
Q_2	`SIGMOD`	`VLDB`	1309	1061
Q_3	`VLDB`	`SIGMOD`	1061	1309
Q_4	`VLDB`	`cacm`	1061	688
Q_5	`system`	`VLDB`	672	1061
Q_6	`cacm`	`book`	688	540
Q_7	`query`	`rule`	469	129
Q_8	`query`	`efficient`	469	121
Q_9	`tkde`	`performance`	329	135

Fig. 8. Queries

the sorted lists as shown in Fig. 4 progressively. Due to the space constraint, we do not discuss it in detail. Interested readers can refer to [12]. Then, we again relies on similar processing described in Section 4.1 for $Q \overset{d}{\hookrightarrow} t$ and $Q \overset{d}{\hookleftarrow} t$. Therefore, both the storage cost and access overhead can be largely relieved.

5 Performance Evaluation

In this section, we evaluate the performance of our approach experimentally. All those algorithms are implemented using `C++`. We experimented on the real dataset, DBLP[2].

For the DBLP dataset, we get all paper nodes and author nodes from elements in the XML data, and edges are obtained as bibliographic links and co-authorship relationships. And a node is removed from the graph to make it more dense, if the corresponding paper has no citation to other papers, or is not cited by other papers. We also add some other nodes to make it more like a graph. That is, we create nodes to indicate the conference name or journal name for the paper, such as SIGMOD, VLDB and so on, of each individual years. Those paper nodes are added with edges to those corresponding conference nodes or journal nodes being created. The DBLP graph contains $30K$ nodes and $122K$ edges.

We test nine queries as shown in Fig. 8. We construct each query $Q \overset{d}{\hookrightarrow} t$ using t_1 and t_2 which are two keywords based on those extracted from the DBLP graph. And for $Q \overset{d}{\hookrightarrow} t$, the node set Q is $I(t_1)$ and t is t_2. For those queries, Q_1 to Q_9, the number of nodes in Q or $I(t)$ is gradually decreasing roughly in three categories: (a) Both $|Q|$ and $|I(t)|$ are larger than 1 thousand (large sets); (b) both $|Q|$ and $|I(t)|$ are larger than 5 hundreds but smaller than about 1 thousand (middle sets) and (c) both $|Q|$ and $|I(t)|$ are smaller than 5 hundreds (small sets). The $|Q|$ and $|I(t)|$ are used to differentiate those queries because they relate to the maximum possible number of results, which is $|Q| \cdot |I(t)|$, and indirectly reflex the cost of accessing 2-hop labels and c-lists. We experimented with the pairwise processing, represented as Pairwise in all figures, and three algorithms of center-based processing, where each algorithm

[2] http://dblp.uni-trier.de/xml/

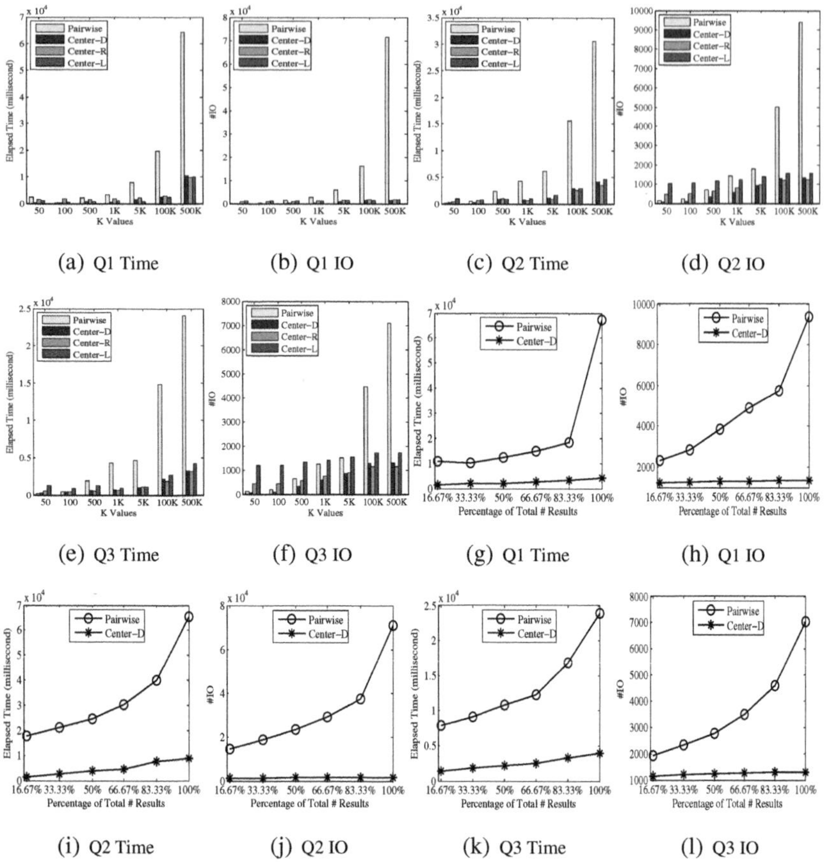

Fig. 9. Performance on Large Sets

corresponds to a different way of obtaining relevant centers. Specifically, we use (i) the algorithm to use the two stored c-lists for both t_1 and t_2, represented as Center-D in all figures; (ii) the algorithm to use the stored c-list for t_1 and access all 2-hop labels for t_2, represented as Center-R in all figures; and (iii) the algorithm to use the stored c-list for t_2 and access all 2-hop labels for t_1, represented as Center-L in all figures. We compare the processing performance of the pairwise and the center-based with two important measurements, the elapsed time and number of IO, for all nine queries against the DBLP graph. For each query, we first test all algorithms by giving a number of fixed K values: 50, 100, 500, 5,000, 10,000, 100,000 and 500,000, which ask the top-K results for those queries. Then, we further examine the performance when K is increasing, we specify different K values which are 16.67%, 16.67%, 33.33%, 50%, 66.67%, 83.33% and 100% of the total result number for each individual query. We conducted all the experiments on a PC with a 3.4GHz processor, 180G hard disk and 2GB main memory running Windows XP.

5.1 The Large Sets

Fig. 9 shows the performance of different algorithms for Q_1, Q_2 and Q_3, which belong to the large sets. Specifically, the figures from Fig. 9(a) to Fig. 9(f) show the performance of Pairwise, Center-D, Center-R and Center-L in terms of a number of fixed K values. In general, the superiority of all center-based processing algorithms over Pairwise is quite obvious. Center-D, Center-R and Center-L are very close to each other while they all spend less processing time and IO numbers than those required by Pairwise up to an order of magnitude. For example, when $K = 500,000$, Pairwise requires 24,013.76 milliseconds while Center-D, Center-R and Center-L spend 3,257.48, 3,199.33 and 4,199.69 milliseconds, respectively, for Q3. As for the IO number for Q3, Pairwise consumes 7,092 while Center-D, Center-R and Center-L spend 1,290, 1,141 and 1,714, respectively.

On the other hand, the figures from Fig. 9(g) to Fig. 9(l) show the performance of Pairwise and Center-D when the K value is increasing. Because all algorithms of center-based processing have close performance, in which all three corresponding curves become too close for this experiment, therefore, those figures only show the performance for Center-D. Based on those figures, we can perceive that the superiority of the center-based processing is even stronger when K value is increased to a large value, for both elapsed time and IO number. For example, in Fig. 9(g), the elapsed time for Center-D is from 1,392.42 to 3,974.71. However, that for Pairwise is from 7,882.60 to 23,924.01. Furthermore, those figures indicate that the IO numbers of Center-D for those queries are not sensitive to the increasing K. For example, the IO numbers for Center-D is from 1,139 to 1,290. However, that for Pairwise is from 1,928 to 7,051.

5.2 The Middle Sets and the Small Sets

Fig. 10 shows the performance of different algorithms for Q_4, Q_5 and Q_6, which belong to the middle sets. And the figures from Fig. 10(a) to Fig. 10(f) illustrate the performance of Pairwise, Center-D, Center-R and Center-L in terms of fixed K values. In these figures, there is still a clear difference in terms of the elapsed time of all center-based processing algorithms v.s. that of Pairwise. However, similar of even more IO numbers are consumed by those center-based processing algorithms. This can be explained by the fact that the Pairwise uses much less IO numbers that those for the large sets. Because the numbers of Q nodes are descreased noticiablely for Q_4, Q_5 and Q_6, compared to Q_1, Q_2 and Q_3. Pairwise needs to access much less clusters to answer all queries. When K is large, Pairwise still has to consume more IO numbers, as suggested by Fig. 10(d) and Fig. 10(f). For example, when $K = 5,000$, Pairwise requires 6,093.36 milliseconds while Center-D, Center-R and Center-L spend 1,247.18, 752.97 and 1,169.249 milliseconds, respectively, for Q5. As for the IO number for Q3, Pairwise consumes 991 while Center-D, Center-R and Center-L spend 973, 807 and 1428, respectively.

The figures from Fig. 10(g) to Fig. 10(l) show the performance of Pairwise and Center-D when the K value is increasing. We can also observe that Pairwise still has to consume more IO numbers when K is large, as suggested by Fig. 10(j) and Fig. 10(l). For example, in in Fig. 10(l), the IO numbers for Center-D is 730, 1,030, 1,156 and

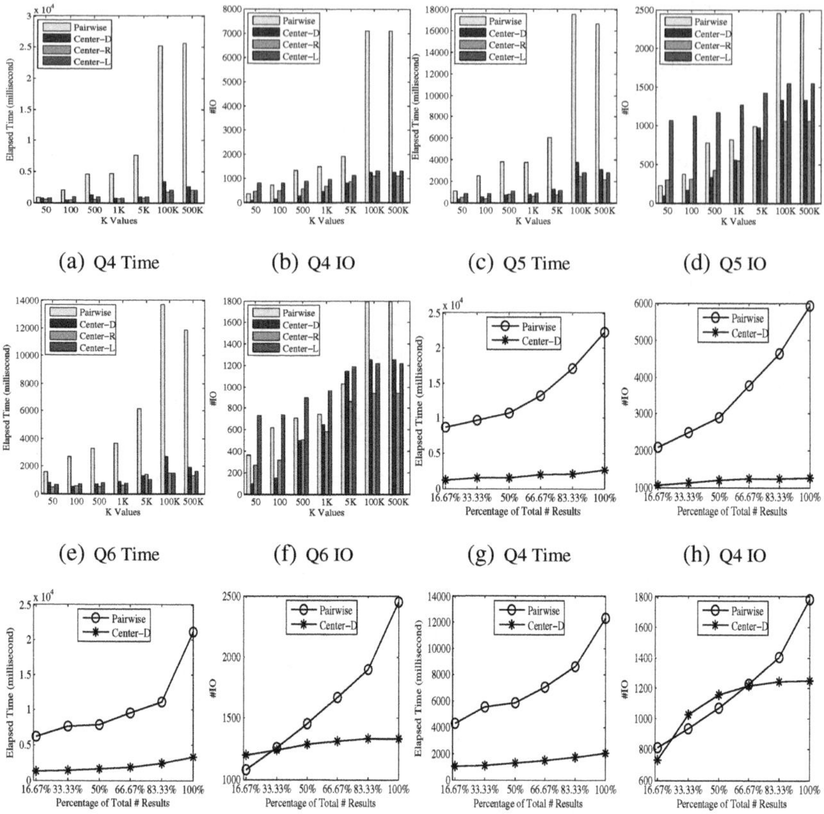

(a) Q4 Time (b) Q4 IO (c) Q5 Time (d) Q5 IO

(e) Q6 Time (f) Q6 IO (g) Q4 Time (h) Q4 IO

(i) Q5 Time (j) Q5 IO (k) Q6 Time (l) Q6 IO

Fig. 10. Performance on Middle Sets

so on. However, that for Pairwise is 813, 939, 1,070 and so on; on the other hand, in Fig. 10(k), the elapsed time for Center-D is from 1,252.35 to 3,337.12. However, that for Pairwise is from 6,188.12 to 21,109.82. The main reason for the more IO numbers consumed by the center-based processing is that it has to access many small *F-buckets*/*T-buckets*, while Pairwise only need to access much less clusters. Even though, the center-based processing can still be faster than Pairwise, because it process much less $\langle (a, d) \colon \delta(a, d) \rangle$ for required number of query results.

Fig. 11 shows the performance of different algorithms for Q_7, Q_8 and Q_9, which belong to the small sets. For all the three queries, the center-based processing outperforms Pairwise in terms of both the elapsed time and the IO number. In terms of IO number, the margin of the center-based processing over Pairwise is not so large as that for the large se, because Pairwise operates on large storage requirement. On the other hand, Pairwise can not use less IO number than the center-based processing, like the middle set, because there are only a few nodes $|Q|$ and $I(t)$ and less results for the center-based processing. In all, the center-based processing is always faster than Pairwise.

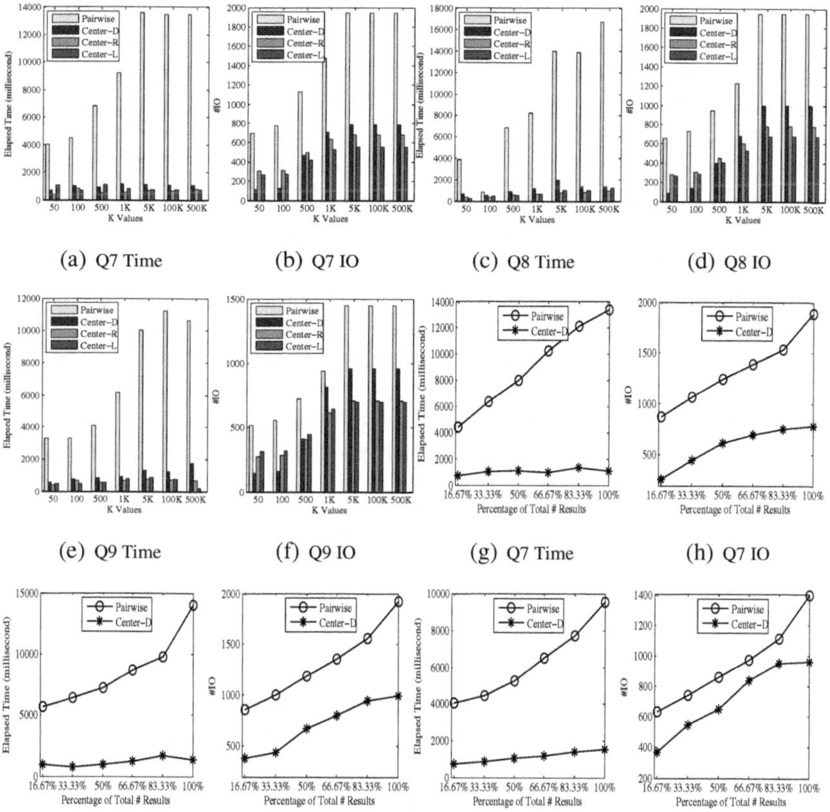

(a) Q7 Time (b) Q7 IO (c) Q8 Time (d) Q8 IO

(e) Q9 Time (f) Q9 IO (g) Q7 Time (h) Q7 IO

(i) Q8 Time (j) Q8 IO (k) Q9 Time (l) Q9 IO

Fig. 11. Performance on Small Sets

6 Related Work

In this paper, we focus on using the disk index to support the preferential nearest neighbors (NN) browsing in graphs. Recently, preprocessing the data graph to support efficient path finding in the graph receives intensive study. Many work are on reachability query processing in graphs. For example, [1,26] all considered assigning intervals to each node to encode the set of reachable nodes from that node in the underlying graph. However, this type of work can hardly be extended to support shortest-path queries, because these intervals are usually based on a spanning tree (called tree-cover in [1,2,17]) of the underlying graph, where the distance information is incomplete for the whole graph. The similar setback also exists in the work [15,17] which decomposes the graph into a number of simple structures, such as chains or trees, to compress the transitive closure.

Fast distance query processing was considered by [20,25,9]. But they are for undirected graphs and can not be applied to directed graphs. Recently, on supporting the processing of k nearest neighbor queries in road networks, [14] discusses distance signatures for distance computation over long distances from single source node. But for our ranked distance queries, multiple source nodes and arbitrary distances will be searched. [22,23] have proposed a compact distance oracle where any distance and shortest path can be found in $O(\delta \cdot |V|)$ time. However, its index construction relies on the spatial coherence of the data, and it is not easy to obtain such structures in arbitrary general directed graphs. Some recent work [10,11,18,7] pre-computes distance information for a number of selected nodes, which are called *landmarks*, and considers approximating the distance of any given two nodes based on pre-computed distance information. These approaches can avoid pre-computing all-pairs shortest paths. But they are thus unaware of the number of shortest paths and exact distance information that can be recorded by those landmarks, and can not support the exact distance and shortest path answering required by our problem. [27] preprocesses a graph in $\tilde{O}(|E| \cdot |V|^{\omega})$ time, where $\omega < 2.376$ is the exponent of matrix multiplication. And any single distance query can be processed in $O(|V|)$ time, which can still be expensive if the total number of distances queried is very large. To handle the intensive processing of shortest path queries to support top-k keyword queries [13] and twig matching [12] in graphs, even the whole edge transitive closure with distance information of the underlying graph is employed. However, even with the all-pairs shortest distances, a close examination in this paper indicates the processing cost to use it can still be high.

The index used in this paper has similar spirit to the join index in [4,28], but the join index of [5,28] can not be used to progressively process ranking queries, which is required in our problem. To search for all node pairs which has a distance smaller than a given threshold, [28] develops an indexing scheme based on landmarks. This indexing scheme can help filter out the node pairs with a larger distance than the threshold, but can not support finding the exact distance. Therefore, it can not be directly used for our problem either.

7 Conclusion

In this paper, we propose a two-step search framework to support a new problem called preferential NN browsing. In such browsing, a user may provide one or more source nodes and some keywords to retrieve the nearest neighbors of those source nodes that contain the given keywords. The first step identifies a number of reference nodes (also called centers) which exist alone on some shortest paths between a source node and a preferential NN node that contain the user-given keywords. In the second step, we find the preferential NN nodes within a certain distance to the source nodes via the relevant reference nodes, using an index that supports both textural (attributes) and and the distance. Our approach has innovations to progressively process ranking queries as well as to tightly integrates NN search with the preference search, which is confirmed to be efficient and effective to find any preferential NN nodes.

Acknowledgment. The work described in this paper was supported by grants of the Research Grants Council of the Hong Kong SAR, China No. 419008 and 419109.

References

1. Agrawal, R., Borgida, A., Jagadish, H.V.: Efficient management of transitive relationships in large data and knowledge bases. In: Proc. of SIGMOD 1989 (1989)
2. Chen, L., Gupta, A., Kurul, M.E.: Stack-based algorithms for pattern matching on dags. In: Proc. of VLDB 2005 (2005)
3. Cheng, J., Yu, J.X.: On-line exact shortest distance query processing. In: EDBT (2009)
4. Cheng, J., Yu, J.X., Ding, B., Yu, P.S., Wang, H.: Fast graph pattern matching. In: Proc. of ICDE 2008 (2008)
5. Cheng, J., Yu, J.X., Lin, X., Wang, H., Yu, P.S.: Fast computing reachability labelings for large graphs with high compression rate. In: Proc. of EDBT 2008 (2008)
6. Cohen, E., Halperin, E., Kaplan, H., Zwick, U.: Reachability and distance queries via 2-hop labels. In: Proc. of SODA 2002 (2002)
7. Dabek, F., Cox, R., Kaashoek, F., Morris, R.: Predicting internet network distance with coordinates-based approaches. In: SIGCOMM (2004)
8. Dijkstra, E.W.: A note on two problems in connection with graphs. Numerische Math. 1, 269–271 (1959)
9. Gavoille, C., Peleg, D., Pérennes, S., Raz, R.: Distance labeling in graphs. J. Algorithms 53(1), 85–112 (2004)
10. Goldberg, A.V., Werneck, R.F.: Computing point-to-point shortest paths from external memory. In: ALENEX (2005)
11. Goldberg, A.V., Werneck, R.F.: Reach for a*: Efficient point-to-point shortest path algorithms. In: ALENEX (2006)
12. Gou, G., Chirkova, R.: Efficient algorithms for exact ranked twig-pattern matching over graphs. In: Proc. of SIGMOD 2008 (2008)
13. He, H., Wang, H., Yang, J., Yu, P.S.: Blinks: ranked keyword searches on graphs. In: Proc. of SIGMOD 2007 (2007)
14. Hu, H., Lee, D.L., Lee, V.C.S.: Distance indexing on road networks. In: VLDB (2006)
15. Jagadish, H.V.: A compression technique to materialize transitive closure. ACM Trans. Database Syst. 15(4), 558–598 (1990)
16. Jiang, B.: I/o-efficiency of shortest path algorithms: An analysis. In: ICDE (1992)
17. Jin, R., Xiang, Y., Ruan, N., Wang, H.: Efficiently answering reachability queries on very large directed graphs. In: Proc. of SIGMOD 2008 (2008)
18. Ng, T.S.E., Zhang, H.: Predicting internet network distance with coordiantes-based approaches. In: INFOCOM (2001)
19. Papadias, D., Zhang, J., Mamoulis, N., Tao, Y.: Query processing in spatial network databases. In: VLDB (2003)
20. Peleg, D.: Proximity-preserving labeling schemes. J. Graph Theory 33, 167–176 (2000)
21. Rattigan, M.J., Maier, M., Jensen, D.: Using structure indices for efficient approximation of network properties. In: KDD (2006)
22. Samet, H., Sankaranarayanan, J., Alborzi, H.: Scalable network distance browsing in spatial databases. In: SIGMOD (2008)
23. Sankaranarayanan, J., Samet, H.: Distance oracles for spatial networks. In: ICDE (2009)
24. Schenkel, R., Theobald, A., Weikum, G.: Efficient creation and incremental maintenance of the HOPI index for complex XML document collections. In: Proc. of ICDE 2005 (2005)
25. Thorup, M., Zwick, U.: Approximate distance oracles. In: Proc. of STOC 2001 (2001)
26. Trißl, S., Leser, U.: Fast and practical indexing and querying of very large graphs. In: Proc. of SIGMOD 2007 (2007)
27. Yuster, R., Zwick, U.: Answering distance queries in directed graphs using fast matrix multiplication. In: Proc. of FOCS 2005 (2005)
28. Zou, L., Chen, L., Özsu, M.T.: Distancejoin: Pattern match query in a large graph database. In: VLDB (2009)

Mining Useful Time Graph Patterns on Extensively Discussed Topics on the Web (Position Paper)

Taihei Oshino, Yasuhito Asano, and Masatoshi Yoshikawa

Department of Social Informatics, Graduate School of Informatics, Kyoto University
Yoshida Honmachi, Sakyo-ku, Kyoto, 606–8591 Japan
oshino@db.soc.i.kyoto-u.ac.jp, {asano,yoshikawa}@i.kyoto-u.ac.jp

Abstract. Temporal characteristics of the web have been analyzed widely in recent years, but graph patterns have served important roles for analyzing the web's structural characteristics. Although temporal characteristics of the web have not been estimated in previous patterns, we specifically examine a novel kind of pattern, *time graph patterns*, estimating time-series data including the creation times of pages and links. We find useful time graph patterns representing the process by which a topic is discussed extensively during a short period without manual investigations of web graphs. We have also analyzed the patterns and the web pages corresponding to the patterns. Three characteristic pages are contained in the patterns. Additionally, we have succeeded in finding a subgraph matching a mined pattern. We observed that the subgraph corresponds to an extensively discussed topic.

1 Introduction

The world-wide web has been changing since its inception. In recent years, many researchers have devoted attention to temporal characteristics of the web. For example, studies have been undertaken to analyze blogs [1] and social bookmark services [2] using time-series data such as time stamps of blog entries or user access logs and tags annotated to bookmarks. Several models, such as the "forest fire model" proposed by Leskovec et al. [3], have been proposed for simulating the growth of a social network, a community of sites, and the whole web. Kumar et al.[4] introduced a "web time graph" to depict the bursty growth of communities. These studies confirmed that analyses of the temporal characteristics of the web are useful for information retrieval.

A web is a graph structure whose nodes are pages and edges are links. "Graph patterns" on a web graph have played important roles in analyzing structural characteristics of the web. A *graph pattern* is a property that should be satisfied by specified subgraphs. It is used as the object of matching or enumeration for a graph. Trawling, proposed by Kumar et al. [5], enumerates complete bipartite subgraphs on a web graph to identify communities. In addition, the HITS algorithm, proposed by Kleinberg [6], computes the importance of web pages using

M. Yoshikawa et al. (Eds.): DASFAA 2010, LNCS 6193, pp. 20–32, 2010.

graph patterns representing hubs and authorities. Several studies are useful to analyze the patterns of growth processes of graphs. Leskovec et al.[7] introduced a technique to analyze the blogosphere using "cascade" graph patterns whose nodes are blog pages and whose edges are links as propagations of information. They enumerate all cascades in a huge blog networks and count frequency, and analyze characteristics of the blogs and cluster them. Innumerable possible graph patterns exist, although few have proved to be useful for information retrieval on the web. Therefore, finding a new and useful graph pattern, even a single pattern, is expected to constitute a valuable research endeavor.

The graph patterns described above are based on the structural topology of a web graph: they estimate only a link structure, not temporal characteristics including the creation and deletion time of pages. Most previous studies dealing with graph patterns on a web graph predict useful patterns, such as a complete bipartite subgraph for trawling, by investigating the graph manually; then those studies find subgraphs matching the pattern. Such graph patterns based on structural topology have been sought extensively during the last decade. It is considered difficult to find a new and useful graph pattern today. However, finding unprecedented graph patterns that are useful for information retrieval on the web can be expected if we introduce time-series data to a web graph. For example, even if two communities of web pages have similar graph structures, one might have grown rapidly, whereas the other might have grown slowly. We might distinguish them and enumerate only those rapidly grown communities if we were able to construct a graph pattern estimating the creation time of links. Furthermore, existing studies of information propagation do not distinguish whether the information spreads rapidly or slowly. Therefore, we seek such a useful graph pattern estimating time-series data on the web, named a *time graph pattern*, without manual investigation. However, the prediction seems difficult for time graph patterns whose nodes and edges have a limited lifetime because time graphs are much more complicated.

"Dynamic graph" mining has been studied for dealing with temporal changing of graphs [8]. However, dynamic graphs can not represent the increase of nodes; it is assumed that edge creations and deletions are frequent. Therefore, dynamic graphs are not considered to be useful for analysis of the web. Few reports describe analysis of the web using dynamic graphs.

The purpose of our research is to find useful time graph patterns without manual investigation of huge web graphs, and to analyze the web using time graph patterns. As described in this paper, we found a new and useful time graph pattern representing the process by which a topic was discussed in blogs and news sites extensively during a short period. In our method, we first construct several web graphs; then labels the nodes and edges are assigned in the graphs by analyzing their creation times. We then mine time graph patterns that appear commonly on most graphs using an existing method for graph mining. Graph mining methods are unable to return results in a practical time for a large graph, including typical web graphs, without a certain number of labels. We propose a method to mine time graph patterns representing the process described above in practical time: we assign labels that are appropriate for the process to the nodes of web graphs by analyzing the creation times of the pages. Results revealed patterns of several characteristics from extensively discussed topics on the web. We also discover several subgraphs matching these patterns from the web. Each subgraph also corresponds to pages discussing a topic that has spread quickly. Therefore, finding time graph patterns using our method is useful for information retrieval on the web. An additional direction is web page clustering. Existing clustering methods specifically examine only link structures. However, it is expected that clustering can be done in greater detail using time graph patterns.

The remainder of the paper is organized as follows, Section 2 surveys the related work. Section 3 describes our method for finding useful time graph patterns. Section 4 explains how we find a time graph pattern representing the process by which a topic was discussed extensively, and evaluate the obtained pattern using case studies. Finally, we conclude with a discussion of the results in Section 5.

2 Related Work

In this section, we introduce the studies using time-series data of the web. Then, we introduce studies related to graph patterns. Subsequently, we state general graph mining applications in the real world. Finally, we explain an existing graph mining algorithm "gSpan" proposed by Yan and Han. We use this algorithm to enumerate frequent time graph patterns in our technique.

2.1 Analysis of the Web Using Time-Series Data

In recent years, several studies have been made of temporal properties of the web. For example, some studies identify influential bloggers by analyzing the time stamps of blog entries [1]. They specifically examine the degree to which the pages or entries in a blog community increase during a particular period, and also analyze the degree of the rapid spread of topics. Other studies predict attractive pages among newly posted pages on a social bookmark service using time-series data, such as user access logs and tags annotated to bookmarks [2]. Several models have been proposed [3,9,10] for simulating the growth of a social network, a community of sites, and the whole web. For example, the "forest fire model" proposed by Leskovec et al.[3] can simulate properties of the web such that their degree distribution follows a power law [11]; their diameter shrinks over time [3]. Kumar et al.[4] introduced a "web time graph" to discover the bursty growth of communities. A *web time graph* is an extension of a web graph showing nodes as pages and edges as links: in a web time graph, each node is given the creation and deletion time of the corresponding page; each link between two pages is regarded as valid for the duration that both pages exist. Their studies analyze time variation of the number of pages or bookmarks in the community statistically, but our research analyzes the time variation of graph structures.

"Dynamic graph" mining has been studied for dealing with temporal changes of graphs [8]. A *dynamic graph* represents a graph that is transformed n-times such as $G_1, G_2, \cdots, G_n$ during a period. In a dynamic graph, the number of edges might change, but the number of nodes does not change. Each edge is labeled with an n bit sequence $\{0|1\}^n$. The i-th bit of the sequence is 1 if the edge exists in G_i, and 0 if the edge does not exist in G_i. These algorithms can enumerate frequently occurring dynamic patterns from a dynamic graph. However, dynamic graphs can not represent increases of nodes. It is assumed that edge creations and deletions are frequent. On the web, the increase of pages is frequent. The links are created once; they usually remain unchanged. Therefore, a dynamic graph is not considered to be useful to analyze web contents. Few studies analyzing the web use dynamic graphs.

2.2 Graph Patterns

Several studies have examined information retrieval using graph patterns. Existing methods that use patterns to discover web communities are given below.

The HITS algorithm proposed by Kleinberg [6] uses the two concepts of "hub" and "authority" in the web graph. Hub pages and authoritative pages have a mutually reinforcing relation. In fact, HITS finds better pages on a specific topic using the pattern by which a good hub page links many good authoritative pages and by which a good authoritative page is linked by many good hub pages. Trawling, as proposed by Kumar [5] discovers communities by finding subgraphs matching patterns called complete bipartite graphs. Other studies use a maximal clique enumeration method to identify web communities from an inter-site graph whose nodes are web sites and whose edges are links between sites [12]. A subgraph is called a clique if there is an edge between every pair of nodes. Maximal cliques and isolated pseudo-cliques of sites are also used as graph patterns to find communities or *link farms*: sets of spam links [12,13,14,15].

In addition, studies exist that find spam pages. The HITS algorithm described above has properties by which pages of densely linked structures are assigned high scores. Consequently, the method of extracting cliques is used to detect *link farms* [13]: groups of spam pages linked densely together so that their pages are assigned high scores. Additionally, some studies have examined the distribution and evolution of link farms using time-series dates of web graphs [14]. Studies exist to enumerate maximal cliques efficiently [15]. In addition, Uno proposed a method for detecting pseudo-cliques, which are subgraphs obtained by removing a few edges from cliques [16].

2.3 Applications of Graph Mining

Graph mining has been applied in many fields. For example in the field of chemical informatics, common protein structure patterns are enumerated from a set of graphs of chemical compounds. In the field of sociology, many graph mining methods are used to analyze social networks to obtain various social characteristics [17]. Another application in the real world is improving hospital processes

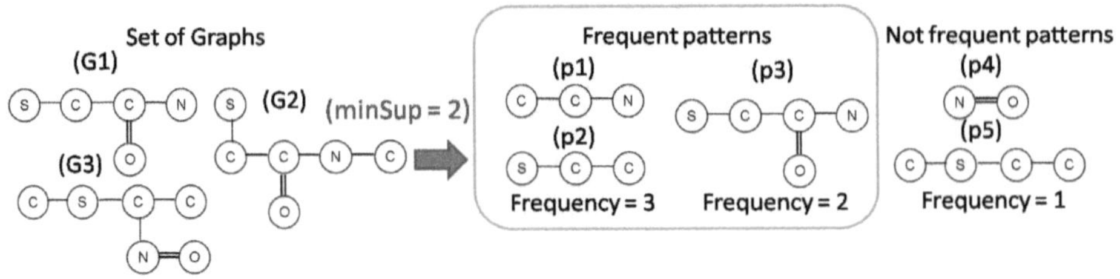

Fig. 1. Mining frequent patterns

by mining frequent combination operations from time-series data and graphs representing clinical pathways [18]. Several researchers have examined frequent graph pattern enumeration. Frequent graph pattern mining delivers useful information. An outline of the frequent graph pattern enumeration algorithms is shown in Figure. 1. We explain how to mine frequently occurring patterns from a set of graphs in Section 2.4.

2.4 Frequent Graph Pattern Mining Algorithm

We explain the gSpan algorithm proposed by Yan and Han [19], which enumerates frequent graph patterns from a set of graphs. Target graphs are simple graphs. Their nodes and edges are labeled. Regarding a molecular structure, for example, each node is labeled with its atomic symbol; each edge is labeled with a symbol representing a single bond or covalent bond. Looking at the set of graph $\{G_1, G_2, G_3\}$ shown in Figure. 1, various patterns are apparent in them. Patterns p_1 and p_2 appear on all three graphs. Pattern p_3 appears on two graphs: G_1 and G_2. Patterns p_4 and p_5 appear on a single graph G_3.

The inputs of gSpan are a set of graphs as D and minimum support as *minSup*. In fact, gSpan outputs all patterns appearing in more than *minSup* graphs, where *minSup* is a parameter meaning the minimum support, in a set D of graphs. Consequently, in the case of Figure. 1, it is assumed that we input as $D = \{G_1, G_2, G_3\}$ and $minSup = 2$. The results are all patterns appearing in more than two graphs such as p_1, p_2, and p_3. As described in this paper, we use a library of gSpan[1].

3 Our Method to Mine Time Graph Patterns

In this section, we propose a method to identify useful time graph patterns by estimating temporal characteristics of the web without manual investigation of huge graphs. The proposed method comprises the following five steps (1)–(5). (1) Prepare several desired topics (e.g., topics discussed extensively in a short time) about which a user wants to extract patterns. (2) For each topic, collect pages using a search engine. Then construct a set of graphs. Furthermore, obtain the creation time of each page. (3) Label every node by analyzing the creation

[1] Parsemis: http://www2.informatik.uni-erlangen.de/research/ParSeMiS/index.html

time of the page. Then construct a set of time graphs. (4) Enumerate frequent time graph patterns using gSpan. (5) Detect characteristic time graph patterns from enumerated patterns.

We can identify other topics whose link structure similar to the intended topics by discovering several subgraphs matching these patterns from the web if useful time graph patterns are mined in this way.

3.1 Construct Web Graph Sets

First, we construct a set of graphs for the input of gSpan. To do so, we prepared some topics that have been discussed extensively on the web in advance. For each topic, we construct a set of graphs whose nodes are the pages containing the topic. We use the Google search engine[2] to collect web pages related to the topics. We query the characteristic keywords representing a topic and an approximate time period. In this way, we can restrict results pages for our target of interests. Consequently, we can obtain the top k, say 300, web pages and their indexed time by Google, and construct a web graph consisting of the pages and links between them. We can regard the indexed time as the creation time of the page because it almost always corresponds with its posted time in the text of the blog entry or the new page.

We use a search engine to construct a set of graphs because it is sufficient for this case to collect pages referring to particular topics in certain periods. However, in considering other applications, we might use another method to construct graphs. For example, we might use a crawler instead of a search engine to collect web pages and extract date information of the page by HTML parsing.

3.2 Analyzing Time-Series Data for the Labeling Method

For each graph, we collect a set of web pages whose topic is discussed extensively in a specified period. On such topics, few pages discuss the topic at first. After that, the topic spreads gradually, i.e., few pages related to the topic are created. An explosive spread then occurs: many pages are created in a few days. Subsequently, new pages referring to the topic do not increase so much. The spread enters a stable period. Thereafter, if some progress or change is made on this topic, then a second or third explosion occurs.

To use characteristics of the spread, we assign the nodes labels reflecting the growth period of a graph. We were able to consider the following simple method for labeling: dividing the whole period into n sub-periods, the nodes created during the i-th sub-period are labeled N_i. Using this method, the meaning of the fixed i-th sub-period might differ from topic to topic. For example, the second sub-period for a topic might correspond to a period when the topic spreads gradually; the same sub-period might correspond to an explosive spread for another topic. We desire to use the same label for the periods with the same temporal characteristics, such as how the topic spreads, as possible. Therefore, we

[2] http://www.google.co.jp/

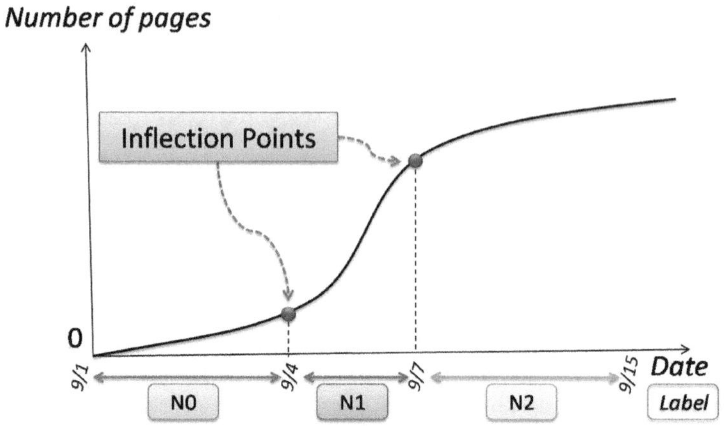

Fig. 2. Example of the growth of a graph

find the time points at which the graph growth changes drastically. Subsequently, we label the nodes of graph in the order of periods whose boundaries are these time points.

Let us consider an example of a web graph whose pages increase during September 1–15, 2009, as depicted in Figure. 2. In this example, the first page appeared on September 1; then pages increased slowly. On September 4, the graph suddenly expanded; after September 7, the graph showed a stable period. Consequently, two inflection points of the pages were identified: September 4 and September 7. Therefore, the nodes made during September 1–3 are labeled as N_0, representing the early period of the graph; the nodes made during September 4–6 are labeled as N_1, representing the growth period, and the nodes made during September 7–15 are labeled as N_2, representing the stable period.

A specific method for calculation of inflection points is that we divide the period of the topic into n sub-periods and let the first date of each sub-period be $t_1, t_2, \cdots, t_n$. (In our experiment explained in Section 4, n is set to 10.) At that time, the i-th period d_i is defined as $t_i \leq d_i < t_{i+1}$ $(i = 1, 2, \cdots, n-1)$. Therein, v_i is the number of pages created in each period d_i. This is the velocity of the increase of pages. Additionally, $a_i = v_i - v_{i-1}$ $(i = 1, 2, \cdots, n)$ can be regarded as acceleration of the increase at t_i. The growth of a graph changes considerably if the absolute value of this acceleration is greater than a certain value θ. As described in this paper, letting the number of all nodes of the graph be N, we define θ as $\theta = \frac{N}{n}$. Then, t_i that meets $|a_i| > \theta$ is regarded as an inflection point, and as the boundary point of labeling. We assume that two inflection points a_p and a_q $(1 < p < q < n)$ are obtained. The nodes made during $d_1 \cup \cdots \cup d_{p-1}$ are labeled N_0. The nodes made during $d_p \cup \cdots \cup d_{q-1}$ are labeled N_1. The nodes made during $d_q \cup \cdots \cup d_n$ are labeled N_2. Using such a method, we can enumerate the time graph patterns successfully in this time.

Labels are necessary for existing graph pattern mining algorithms such as gSpan. It is difficult to obtain results in practical time without appropriate labeling because frequent pattern mining problems are NP-hard. We use the labeling method described above in this case. However, another method would be more effective for another case. Generally, if many labels exist, then the computational cost is not so high because few frequent patterns exist. If few labels exist, then the computational cost is high because many frequent patterns exist. Therefore, an effective labeling method for each case would be obtained by considering periodical characteristics for the case (e.g. specifying a period during which the number of nodes increase rappidly in a short time.)

3.3 Mining Time Graph Patterns

We enumerate frequent graph patterns from the set of graphs labeled as explained in 3.2. The number of enumerated patterns depends on *minSup*. If *minSup* is not so large, then many patterns are enumerated. They contain both useful patterns and uninteresting ones. Therefore, we must identify them from the enumerated patterns to characteristic patterns and detect useful structures. Enumerated patterns have several clusters consisting of patterns whose structures are mutually similar. The similar patterns are inferred to represent the same characteristics of the topic. Therefore, we regard the patterns involving the maximum cluster as characteristic patterns. As described in this paper, we detect such characteristic patterns manually.

Enumerating subgraphs containing detected patterns from the web is another difficult problem, but we are not concerned with that problem here.

4 Experiments and Analysis

In this section, we mine time graph patterns around the extensively discussed topics in out method as an experiment. we explain our analysis and considerations to evaluate our method. In addition, we verify that we can mine useful time graph patterns feasibly using our method. We construct a set of web graphs from the actual topics discussed extensively, and enumerate frequent graph patterns. Consequently, our target web pages are blogs and news sites. All experiments were done using a PC (Core i7; Intel Corp.) with 4 GB memory and a 64-bit operating system (Windows Vista; Microsoft Corp.).

4.1 Choosing Topics

We mine time graph patterns around the extensively discussed topics in our method. Particularly, we specifically examine discussions found on blogs and news sites. In such discussions, once an entry about a topic is posted on a blog or news site, then bloggers discuss the topic by creating links to the entry and posting their personal comments. We choose and investigate seven topics that have been discussed in the past, and determine the input for each topic, i.e. the search query and the time period, to a search engine, as listed below. We also explain the outline of each topic.

(1) Discussion of the average cost for producing a web site. It is also discussed whether the quality of a site corresponds to the cost.
(2) Discussion about the relation between school records and a person's intelligence.
(3) Discussion about *hakenmura*—makeshift shacks for temporary workers whose contracts have been terminated—in a Japanese park.
(4) Discussion about a problem by which some persons post illustrations tracing other illustrations in *pixiv*; *pixiv* is a Japanese SNS specializing in posting illustrations.
(5) Discussion about *yominige*, where a person reads another person's diary in *mixi* without commenting on the diary; *mixi* is a popular SNS in Japan.
(6) Rumors about the release date of a software game "Final Fantasy 13" presented by Square Enix Holdings, a Japanese company.
(7) Discussion related to the coding style of HTML on a blog community.

For each topic (1)–(7), we construct a web graph as explained in the previous section. The graph structures and the labels of nodes are depicted in Figure. 3. The graphs for topics (2)–(6) are shrunk because of space limitations.

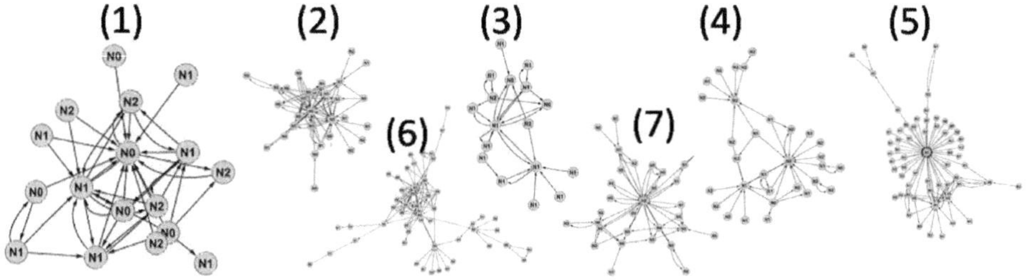

Fig. 3. Input graphs of the topics

4.2 Discovering Patterns

We apply the gSpan algorithm to the constructed seven graphs (Figure. 3) by setting *minSup* to 4. If *minSup* is too large, then the number of nodes in each maximal pattern becomes extremely small. Small patterns are usually found on almost all web graphs other than the constructed graphs. Therefore, the patterns are not useful for finding interesting topics. In contrast, if *minSup* is too small, then the structures of enumerated patterns would depend on the constructed graphs considerably: consequently, the patterns would not be sufficiently versatile to find new useful information for many topics. In addition, the number of patterns would be too large to compute them in practice. We actually investigated various values for *minSup*. It is difficult to discover versatile patterns when *minSup* is 5 or greater, although we cannot obtain results in a particular time when *minSup* is 3 or less. Therefore, we regard frequent patterns as all maximal patterns appearing in more than four graphs in seven input graphs. When

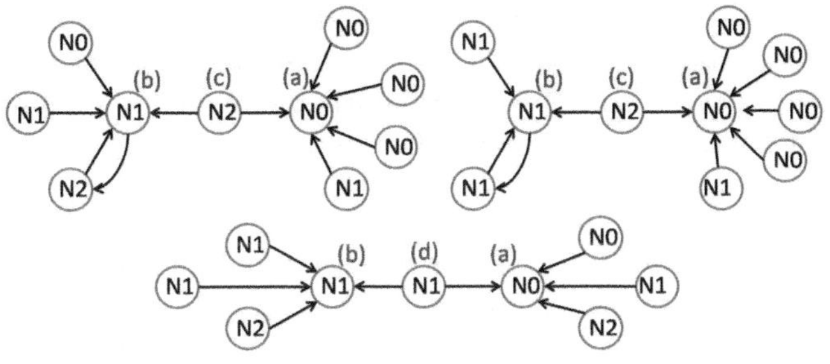

Fig. 4. Characteristic patterns

minSup = 4, we can obtain results in a few minutes. The mined characteristic patterns are presented in Figure. 4.

Analyzing the mined patterns, we found that the following nodes of four types (a)–(d) appear commonly in all those patterns.

(a) A page created during the early period, corresponding to label N_0, and linked to many pages created during various periods.
(b) A page created during the growth period, corresponding to label N_1, and linked by many pages created during the growth period and the stable period, corresponding to label N_2.
(c) A page created during the stable period, and linking to many pages including pages of types (a) and (b).
(d) A page created during the growth period, linking to many pages including pages of types (a) and (b).

Figure. 4 depicts which nodes correspond to types (a)–(d) in each pattern. We also verified what roles pages of the three types play for spreading a topic by investigating the pages carefully. It is particularly interesting that the following facts are observed in all patterns. Page (a) is either a page reporting the topic first on a news site, or the first blog entry discussing the topic. Therefore, we can say that page (a) is a *primary source* for the topic. Page (b) often links to page (a). It usually contains an attracted opinion or good information about the topic. Page (b) is often written by a famous blogger. Many bloggers are interested in the topic by reading such a page. Consequently, many pages linking to page (b) appear. Page (b) is regarded as a *trigger* for the growth period for the discussion. Actually, the pages discussing the topic were increased gradually before page (b) was made, although they were increased drastically after page (b) was made. Page (c) and page (d) are hub pages linking to authoritative pages, i.e., pages linked from many pages created during the growth period. Pages (c) and (d) often summarizes the past discussion, defines a conflict in the discussion, and concludes. Therefore, we call them *summarizers*.

4.3 Information Retrieval Using Mined Patterns

We could retrieve extensively discussed topics, other than the used topics, from the web by enumerating subgraphs matching to the patterns mined as explained above. The ideal way is expected to be development of a method for enumerating such subgraphs automatically. For example, trawling is a method for enumerating complete bipartite subgraphs automatically to find communities. Kumar et al. [5] investigated samples among the enumerated subgraphs manually and confirmed that most samples actually correspond to communities. They concluded that their pattern is effective for information retrieval. We unfortunately have not established an automatic method for enumeration yet. We verify whether our patterns are useful by finding a subgraph matching to one of the patterns from the web and analyzing the subgraph manually. If the identified subgraph represents the spread of a topic similarly to the mined patterns, then the patterns would be useful for information retrieval.

We collect web pages using a crawler with hub pages for many topics as sources, and construct a web graph consisting of the pages. To find a subgraph matching a mined pattern, we first find page p with large out-degree. Let $t(p)$ be the creation time of page p. We then find pages q and r linked from many pages including p such that $t(r) < t(q) < t(p)$. We expect here that r might be a primary source, q might be a trigger, and p might be a summarizer. We finally check whether a subgraph containing p, q, and r matches a mined pattern by assigning label N_0 to the pages created before $t_0 = (t(r) + t(q))/2$, and label N_1 to the pages created after t_0 and before $(t(q) + t(r))/2$, and label N_2 to the remaining pages. In this way, we actually found a subgraph matching a mined pattern. We observed that the subgraph corresponds to an extensively discussed topic. As we expected, pages r, q, and p are, respectively, a primary source, a trigger and a summarizer. We explain this topic as well as the topics used in the previous subsection.

Outlines: Topic related to NHK's interview of a comic artist. A comic artist posted an entry on his blog to complain about NHK's interview of him. NHK is the Japanese national public broadcasting organization.
Primary source: http://blog.livedoor.jp/dqnplus/archives/1301496.html
A famous blogger refers to the blog above in his own blog.
Trigger: http://blog.nawosan.com/archives/51567295.html
After this topic was discussed extensively, the comic artist posted a new entry to give comments on his blog.
Summarizer: http://homepage3.nifty.com/DOCUMENT/pakuri301.html
This page links to many pages related to this topic.

This observation implies that the mined patterns are useful for information retrieval. Therefore, we confirm that mining time graph patterns found according to our method is meaningful for analyzing temporal characteristics of the web. We expect that other useful time graph patterns can be mined using our method in the future.

5 Conclusion

We have proposed a method for mining time graph patterns representing temporal characteristics of the topics discussed extensively on web graphs. We have analyzed the patterns and web pages corresponding to the patterns. Results show that three characteristic pages are contained in the patterns. Additionally, we have succeeded in finding a subgraph matching a mined pattern. We observed that the subgraph corresponds to an extensively discussed topic. Consequently, we have claimed that time graph patterns are useful for information retrieval and web analysis.

Our future work includes the following two subjects: (1) developing a general method for mining time graph patterns; and (2) analyzing web using time graph patterns. The proposed method uses labels specialized to extensively discussed topics, and chooses characteristic patterns manually. We should try to develop a generalized labeling, and a method for choosing characteristic patterns automatically. Leskovec used the cascade for analyzing web; they classified blogs into conservative and humorous ones by investigating the number of cascades in blogs. We could analyze web using time graph patterns in a similar way if we propose a method for enumerating subgraphs matching to a specified time graph pattern.

Acknowledgment

This work was supported in part by the National Institute of Information and Communications Technology.

References

1. Nakajima, S., Tatemura, J., Hara, Y., Tanaka, K., Uemura, S.: A method of blog thread analysis to discover important bloggers. Journal of Japan Society for Fuzzy Theory and Intelligent Informatics (2007)
2. Menjo, T., Yoshikawa, M.: Trend prediction in social bookmark service using time series of bookmarks. In: Proceedings of DEWS, vol. (2), pp. 156–166 (2008)
3. Leskovec, J., Kleinberg, J., Faloutsos, C.: Graphs over time: densification laws, shrinking diameters and possible explanations. In: Proceedings of the eleventh ACM SIGKDD International Conference on Knowledge Discovery in Data Mining, pp. 177–187 (2005)
4. Kumar, R., Novak, J., Raghavan, P., Tomkins, A.: On the bursty evolution of blogspace. In: Proceedings of the 12th International World Wide Web Conference, pp. 159–178 (2005)
5. Kumar, R., Raghavan, P., Rajagopalan, S., Tomkins, A.: Trawling the web for emerging cyber-communities. Computer Networks 31, 1481–1493 (1999)
6. Kleinberg, J.M.: Authoritative sources in a hyperlinked environment. Journal of the ACM 46(5), 604–632 (1999)
7. McGlohon, M., Leskovec, J., Faloutsos, C., Hurst, M., Glance, N.: Finding patterns in blog shapes and blog evolution. In: Proceedings of ICWSM (2007)
8. Borgwardt, K.M., Kriegel, H.P., Wackersreuther, P.: Pattern mining in frequent dynamic subgraphs. In: Proceedings of ICDM, pp. 818–822 (2006)
9. Tawde, V.B., Oates, T., Glover, E.: Generating web graphs with embedded communities. In: Leonardi, S. (ed.) WAW 2004. LNCS, vol. 3243, pp. 80–91. Springer, Heidelberg (2004)

10. Pennock, D.M., Flake, G.W., Lawrence, S., Glover, E.J., Giles, C.L.: Winners don't take all: Characterizing the competition for links on the web. Proceedings of the National Academy of Sciences of the United States of America, National Acad Sciences, 5207 (2002)
11. Huberman, B., Adamic, L.: Growth dynamics of the world-wide web. Nature 401, 131 (1999)
12. Asano, Y., Imai, H., Toyoda, M., Kitsuregawa, M.: Finding neighbor communities in the web using inter-site graph. IEICE transactions on information and systems 87(9), 2163–2170 (2004)
13. Wu, B., Davison, B.D.: Identifying link farm spam pages. In: Proceedings of the 14th International World Wide Web Conference (2005)
14. Joo Chung, Y., Toyoda, M., Kitsuregawa, M.: A study of link farm distribution and evolution using a time series of web snapshots. In: Proceedings of AIRWeb, pp. 9–16 (2009)
15. Makino, K., Uno, T.: New algorithms for enumerating all maximal cliques. LNCS, pp. 260–272. Springer, Heidelberg (2004)
16. Uno, T.: An efficient algorithm for solving pseudo clique enumerating problem. Algorithmica 56(1), 3–16 (2008)
17. Coffman, T., Marcus, S.: Pattern classification in social network analysis: a case study. In: Proceedings of IEEE Aerospace Conference, vol. 5, pp. 3162–3175 (2004)
18. Lin, F., Chou, S., Pan, S., Chen, Y.: Mining time dependency patterns in clinical pathways. International Journal of Medical Informatics 62(1), 11–25 (2001)
19. Yan, X., Han, J.: gSpan: Graph-based substructure pattern mining. In: Proceedings of the 2002 IEEE International Conference on Data Mining, pp. 721–724 (2002)
20. Cook, D.J., Holder, L.B. (eds.): Mining Graph Data. Wiley-Interscience, Hoboken (2005)

Querying Graph-Based Repositories of Business Process Models

Ahmed Awad[1] and Sherif Sakr[2]

[1] HPI, University of Potsdam, Germany
ahmed.awad@hpi.uni-potsdam.de
[2] CSE, University of New South Wales, Australia
ssakr@cse.unsw.edu.au

Abstract. With the rapid and incremental increase in the number of process models developed by different process designers, it becomes crucial for business process designers to be able to look up the repository for models that could handle a similar situation before developing new ones. In this paper, we present an approach for querying repositories of graph-based business process models. Our approach is based on a visual query language for business processes called BPMN-Q. BPMN-Q is used to query business process models by matching the structure of a graph query to that of a process model. The query engine of our system is built on top of traditional RDBMS. We make use of the robust relational indexing infrastructure in order to achieve an efficient and scalable query evaluation performance.

1 Introduction

Business process modeling is an essential first phase in the business process engineering chain. Business process models are created by business analysts with an objective to capture business requirements, enable a better understanding of business processes, facilitate communication between business analysts and IT experts, identify process improvement options and serve as a basis for the derivation of executable business processes. Designing a new process model is a highly complex, time consuming and error prone task. As the number of business process models increases, providing business process designers with a query engine for reusing previously designed business process models (by themselves or others) is of a great practical value. Reusing implies the need an intuitive, easy-to-use and expressive query languages of business process models.

In this paper, we present a query engine for repositories of graph-based business process models. The query engine relies on a novel Business Process Models Query language called BPMN-Q [2]. BPMN-Q allows expressing structural queries and specifies proceedings of determining whether a given process model (graph) is structurally similar to a query graph. A primary challenge in computing the answers of graph queries is that pairwise comparisons of graphs are usually hard problems. For example, subgraph isomorphism is known to be NP-complete [8]. A naive approach to compute the answer set of a BPMN-Q graph query (q) is to perform a sequential scan on the stored graph models and check

M. Yoshikawa et al. (Eds.): DASFAA 2010, LNCS 6193, pp. 33–44, 2010.

whether each model satisfies the conditions of (q). However, the business process repository can be very large which makes a sequential scan over the repository impracticable. Moreover, the query processing of BPMN-Q queries is more challenging than the traditional graph queries in the sense that the edges between the nodes of the BPMN-Q queries are not always *simple* or *direct* connections that can be evaluated using intuitive retrieval mechanisms. However, BPMN-Q query edges can represent more complex and recursive types of connections between the nodes of the business process graph models. Therefore, it is apparent that the efficiency of BPMN-Q query processor is directly dependent on its back-end graph indexing and query processing mechanisms.

Relational database management systems (RDBMSs) have repeatedly proven to be highly efficient, scalable and successful in hosting different types of data such complex objects [7] and XML data [9,6]. In addition, RDBMSs have shown to be able to handle vast amounts of data efficiently using their powerful indexing mechanisms. Thus, we decided to build the storage and query engines of our business process query engine on top of traditional RDBMS. We use a fixed-mapping storage scheme to store the graph-based models of the business process repository. We make use of the robust relational indexing infrastructure in order to achieve an efficient and scalable query evaluation performance.

The remainder of this paper is organized as follows. Section 2 describes BPMN-Q as a language for querying repositories of business process models. The design and implementation of the back-end relational query processor is presented in Section 3. In Section 4 we experimentally demonstrate the efficiency of our query engine. Related work is discussed in Section 5 before we conclude the paper in Section 6.

2 BPMN-Q

BPMN has been recently considered as the *defacto* standard for business process modeling [12]. Figure 1 shows the core process modeling concepts in BPMN notation. In principle, a process model based on BPMN can be viewed as a directed typed attributed labeled graph. The process model shown in Figure 2 is a simplified loan handling process using BPMN notations. We will use this process model to describe queries and their matching to the process. When a customer applies for a real-estate credit, the customer's credit rating, the real estate construction documents and the land register record are checked. As a result of those assessments, the application will be either rejected or the contract is to be prepared. After the contract has been prepared, the process can either end or the bank might offer additional products: a loan protection insurance and a residence insurance. Conceptually, process models are considered as graphs with nodes and edges which are formalized as follows:

Definition 1. *[Process Model] is a tuple $P = (A, E, D, G, S, CF, DF)$ where:*
- *A is the set of activities in a process model.*
- *E is the set of events where E_s, E_e represent the start and end events.*
- *D is the set of data objects/elements that are needed for the activities*
- *G is the set of control flow routing gateways.*

Control Objects		
Event	A trigger or a result that "happens" during the course of a business process and which affect the flow of the Process.	
Activity	The work that is performed within a business process An Activity can be atomic or compound.	
Gateway	are decisions_points that are used to control how sequence flows interact as they converge and diverge within a process. Internal Markers indicates the type of behavior control.	
Data Objects		
Data Object	A mechanism to show how data is required or produced by activities.	
Flow Objects		
Control (Sequence Flow)	it shows the sequence in which the activities will be performed in a Process.	
Data Flow (Association)	It is used to associate data, text, and other Artifacts with flow objects.	

Fig. 1. Representation of Core Concepts in BPMN Notation

- *S is the set of states(values) a data object can assume.*
- *$CF \subseteq A \cup G \cup (E \setminus E_e) \times A \cup G \cup (E \setminus E_s)$ is the control flow relations*
- *$DF \subseteq (D \times (A \cup E \cup G) \times S) \cup ((A \cup E) \times D \times S)$ is the data flow relation between control objects and data objects.*

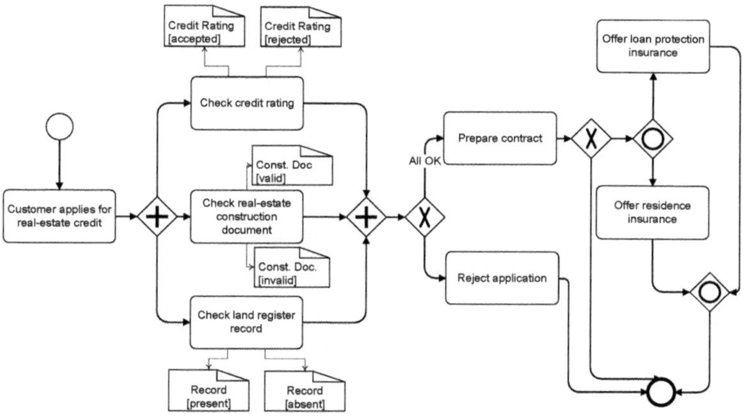

Fig. 2. A Banking Business Process (in BPMN Notation)

The BPMN-Q query language is designed to help the business process designers on querying repositories of graph-based business process models. The language relies on the notation of BPMN as its concrete sytax and supports querying on all its core concepts. Figure 3 summarizes the symbols used to represent the query concepts of BPMN-Q. We describe in detail the meaning of the querying constructs of BPMN-Q as follows:

- **Path edges:** a path edge connecting two nodes in a query represents an abstraction over whatever nodes could be in between in the matching process model. Moreover, path edges have an *exclude* property. When the *exclude*

Variable Node	It is used to indicate unknown activities in a query. It resembles an activity but is distinguished by the @ sign in the beginning of the label.	@Variable
Generic Node	It indicates an unknown node in a process. It could evaluate to any node type.	*
Generic Split	It refers to any type of split gateways.	S
Generic Join	It refers to any type of join gateways.	J
Negative Sequence Flow	It states that two nodes A and B are not directly related by sequence flow.	—X→
Path	It states that there must be a path from A to B. A query usually returns all paths.	—//→
Negative Path	It states that there is not any path between two nodes A and B.	—X //→

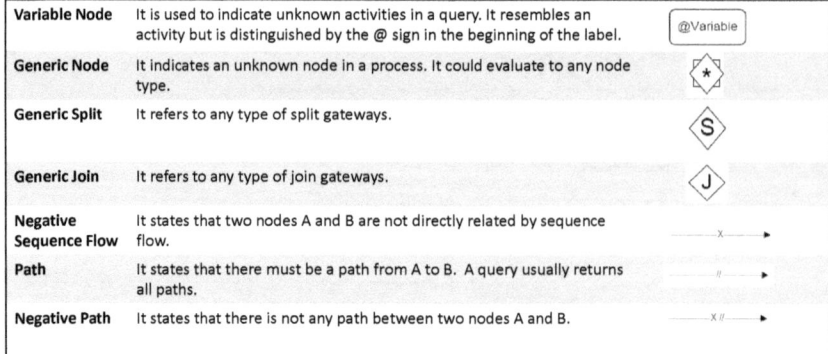

Fig. 3. BPMN-Q Query Constructs

(a) A Query with Path edge

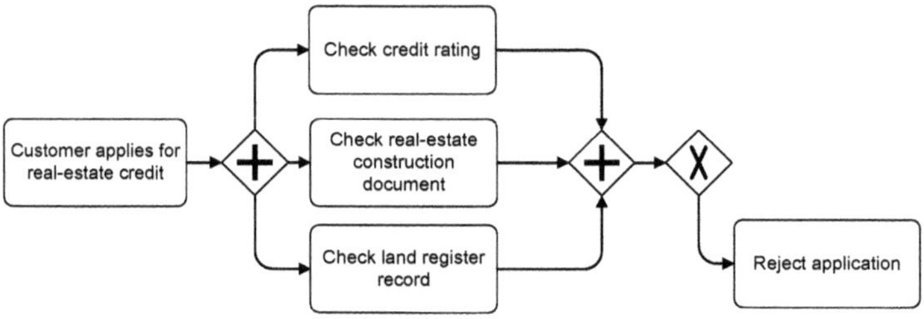

(b) Match of the Query to Process in Figure 2

Fig. 4. A Path Query and its Match

property is set to some node. The evaluation of the path edge succeeds only if there are sequences of nodes between the source and destination nodes to whom *excluded node* does not belong.

- **Undirected Data Flow edges:** this type of edges is used to connect a data object to a path edge in a query. This is also an abstraction mechanism to find paths on which there are nodes that access the specified data object.
- **Anonymous activities and data objects:** They are used users who may need to issue a query on the form, what activities read/update the insurance claim data object. Since, the user does not know that activity, he/she can start its label with the '@' symbol to declare it as an anonymous activity the query processor has to find. Similarly, data objects can be anonymous.
- **Negative control flow and path edges:** They are used to express that nodes A and B must have no control flow edge from A to B (negative control flow), or there must be no path at all from A to B (negative path).
- **Concrete ControlObject and GateWay:** These classes are no longer *abstract*. i.e., in a query, the user is able to put a generic node, generic split,

generic join in order to abstract from the details and let the query processor figure out the match to that node in the inspected process model.

Nodes and path edges can be assigned with variable names which start with the symbol '?'. These names can be used in the *exclude* property of paths to help describe non-trivial queries. For example, matching a path from activity "customer applies for real-estate credit" to activity "Reject application", see Figure 4(a), succeeds in the process model in Figure 2 because there is at least one sequence of nodes and control flow edges that connects "Identify Respondent Bank" to activity "Add Respondent Bank to Black List", see Figure 4(b). Setting the *exclude* property of the path in Figure 4(a) to "Check land register record" would yield no matches. we can define a BPMN-Q query graphs as follows:

Definition 2. *[Query] a BPMN-Q query is a tuple* $Q = (QO, QA, QE, QD, QG, QS, QCF, QP, QDF, QUF, isAnonymous, isNegative, exclude)$ *where:*

- QO *is the set of generic objects in a query.*
- QA *is the set of activities in a query.*
- QE *is the set of events where* QE_s, QE_e *represent the start and end events respectively.*
- QD *is the set of data objects/elements that are needed for the activities*
- QG *is the set of control flow routing gateways.*
- QS *is the set of states(values) a data object can assume.*
- $QCF \subseteq QO \cup QA \cup QG \cup (QE \setminus QE_e) \times QO \cup QA \cup QG \cup (QE \setminus QE_s)$ *is the control flow relation between control nodes*
- $QP \subseteq QO \cup QA \cup QG \cup (QE \setminus QE_e) \times QO \cup QA \cup QG \cup (QE \setminus QE_s)$ *is the* path *relation between control nodes*
- $QDF \subseteq (QD \times (QO \cup QA \cup QE \cup QG) \times QS) \cup ((QO \cup QA \cup QE) \times QD \times QS)$ *is the data flow relation between control objects and data objects.*
- $QUF \subseteq QD \dot{\times} path$ *is the set of undirected associations between data objects and paths.*
- $isAnonymous : QA \cup QD \rightarrow \{true, false\}$ *is a functions that determines whether activities and data objects in a query are anonymous.*
- $isNegative : QCF \cup QP \rightarrow \{true, false\}$ *is a function that determines whether the control flow or path edges are negative.*
- $exclude : \{p \in QP : isNegative(p) = false\} \rightarrow 2^{QO \cup QA \cup QE \cup QG}$

Since BPMN-Q is designed to match queries to process definitions in a repository, it is necessary to identify a candidate set of process models that might have the chance to provide a match to the query, rather than scanning the whole repository. A process model is said to match a BPMN-Q query if it satisfies all sequence flow and path edges as in Definition 3 which is formalized as follows:

Definition 3. *A process model* $P = (A, E, D, G, S, CF, DF)$ *matches a query* $Q = (QO, QA, QE, QD, QG, QS, QCF, QP, QDF, QUF, isAnonymous, isNegative, exclude)$ *iff:*

- $QE \subseteq E$.
- $QG \subseteq G$

- $\forall o \in QO \cup \{a \in QA : isAnonymous(a) = true\} \exists a \in A \cup E \cup G : (o, \_) \in QCF \wedge isNegative((o, \_)) = false \rightarrow (a, \_) \in CF \wedge (\_, o) \in QCF \wedge isNegative((\_, o)) = false \rightarrow (\_, a) \in CF$. *All non negative control flow edges must be satisfied for anonymous activities and generic objects.*
- $\forall d \in QD \exists d' \in D : (d, \_) \in QDF \rightarrow (d', \_) \in DF \wedge (\_, d) \in QDF \rightarrow (\_, d') \in DF$. *All data flow edges must be satisfied for data objects.*
- $(x, y) \in QCF \wedge isNegative((x, y)) = true \rightarrow (x, y) \notin CF$. *a process must not have control flow edges specified as negative control flows in the query.*

3 Relational Processing of BPMN-Q Queries

3.1 Relational Encoding of Process Models

The starting point of our SQL-based processor for BPMN-Q graph-based queries is to design an efficient and suitable mapping scheme for each business process graph model BPM_i of the business process repository (BPR) [11]. In our implementation, we use a *fixed-mapping* storage scheme to store the models of the BPR. In this mapping scheme, each business process model is assigned a unique identity, *ModelID*. Each element of the business process model is assigned a unique identity, *elementID*. Each element is represented by one tuple in a single table (*Elements table*) which stores all elements of the business process repository. Additionally, each element has additional attributes to store the element name and type (*activity, event* or *gateway*). Similarly, each edge in the business process models is assigned a unique identity *EdgeID* and all edges of the graph database are stored in a single table (*BPEdges table*) where each edge is represented by a single tuple in this table. Each edge tuple describes the business process model to which the sequence flow belongs, the unique identity of the *source* element of the edge, the unique identity of the *destination* element of the sequence flow and the edge type (*Sequence flow* or *association*). The overhead of checking the existence of *indirect* sequence between the elements of the business process models can be *optionally* reduced by encoding paths with all lengths that are extracted from process models in an *incremental* fashion according to the user query workloads. The relational storage scheme of business process repository is therefore described as follow:

- BPModel(ModelID, ModelName, ModelDescription).
- BPElements(ModelID, ElementID, ElementName, ElementType).
- BPEdges(ModelID, EdgeID, SElementID, DElementID, EdgeType).
- BPPaths(ModelID, PathID, SElementID, DElementID, ElementList).

Figure 5 illustrates an example of storing business process models which are defined using BPMN notations into our defined relational mapping scheme. In this example, BPMN elements with the kind *start event, end event* or *gateway* do not have labels. Therefore *null* values are stored in the *ElementName* attribute for their encoding tuples. Integer codes are used to represent the different types of BPMN elements (for example 1 represents start events, 2 represents activities and 3 represents gatways). With the aim of reducing the cost of the verification phase of the query evaluation process, table *BPPaths* represents a materialization for *some* paths of the stored business process graph models. The records of this table is added *incrementally* based on the query workload. In this table the symbol G is used to represent gateway elements in the *ElementList* attribute.

3.2 BPMN-Q Query Evaluation

The query processing of BPMN-Q queries goes beyond the traditional sub-graph query processing in two main aspects: 1) BPMN-Q subgraph queries do not treat all nodes of the graph repository or graph query in the same way. Each node has its own *type* and *characteristics*. The nodes of BPMN-Q queries can be also *generic* nodes which means they can be matched to nodes with different types on the source repository models. 2) The edges between the nodes of the subgraph query is not always *simple* or *direct* connections that can be evaluated using the intuitive retrieval mechanisms. However, these query edges can represent more complex and recursive types of connections (*paths, negative paths* and *negative connections*). Therefore, in order to achieve an efficient execution for BPMN-Q queries and avoid the high cost of evaluating the recursive constructs, we have divided this task into two phases: *filtering* and *verification*. The first phase retrieves from the repository all candidate business models to match the structure of the input query. The second phase verifies each candidate model to ignore the ones which does not satisfy the recursive constructs of the input queries. More specifically, using our defined relational storages scheme, we employ the following SQL-based *filtering-and-verification* mechanism to speed up the search efficiency of BPMN-Q queries.

- **Filtering phase:** In this phase we use an effective and efficient pruning strategy to filter out as many as possible of the non-required business process models early. Specifically, in this phase we specify the set of graph database members which contain the set of nodes and edges that are described by the BPMN-Q query. Therefore, the filtering process of a BPMN-Q query q consists of a set of nodes QE with a size that is equal to m and a set of edges QS equal to n is achieved using the SQL translation template which is represented in Figure 6. In this template, each referenced table E_i (Line number 2) represents an instance from the table *BPElements* and maps the information of one element of the set of query nodes QE. Similarly, each referenced table S_j represents an instance from the table *BPEdges* and maps the information of one edge of the set of query edges QS. f is the mapping function between each element of QE and its associated *BPElements* table instance E_i. Lines number 4 and 5 of the SQL translation template represents a set of conjunctive conditions to ensure that all queried elements and egdes belong to the same process model graph. Line number 6 represents the set of conjunctive predicates of the element labels with exclusion of *variable* and *generic* nodes. Line number 7 represents the set of conjunctive predicates of the element types with exclusion of *generic* nodes and *generalization* for the *generic split* and *generic join* constructs. Line number 8 represents the set of

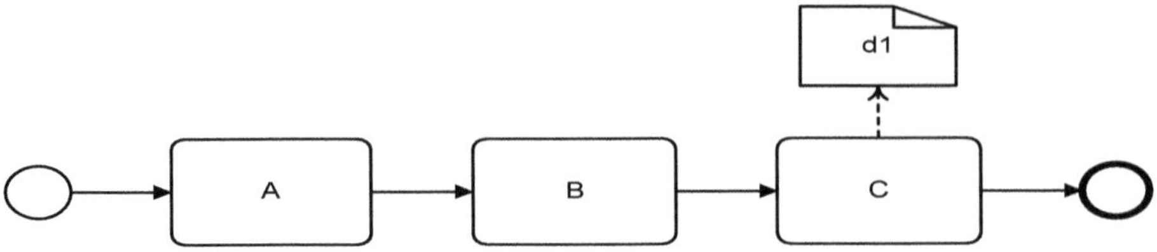

(a) Sample business process model (BPMN1)

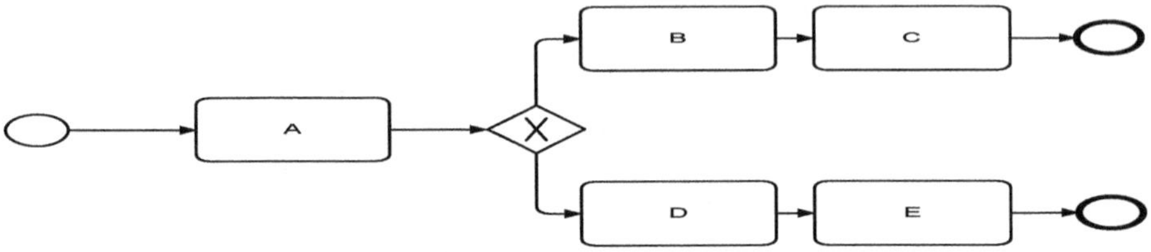

(b) Sample business process model (BPMN2)

modelID	elementID	Element Name	Element Type
1	1		1 (start)
1	2	A	2(Activity)
1	3	B	2(Activity)
1	4	C	2(Activity)
1	5	d1	5(Data Obj.)
1	6		4(End)
2	1		1 (start)
2	2	A	2(Activity)
2	3		3(Gateway)
2	4	B	2(Activity)
2	5	C	2(Activity)
2	6		4(End)
2	7	D	2(Activity)
2	8	E	2(Activity)
2	9		4(End)

BPElements

modelID	sElement	dElement	edgeType
1	1	2	1 (sequence)
1	2	3	1 (sequence)
1	3	4	1 (sequence)
1	4	5	2 (association)
1	4	6	1 (sequence)
2	1	2	1 (sequence)
2	2	3	1 (sequence)
2	3	4	1 (sequence)
2	4	5	1 (sequence)
2	5	6	1 (sequence)
2	3	7	1 (sequence)
2	7	8	1 (sequence)
2	8	9	1 (sequence)

BPEdges

modelID	pathID	sElement	dElement	elementList
1	1	A	C	B
2	1	A	C	*GB*
2	2	A	E	*GD*

BPPaths

(c) Relational encoding of process graphs

Fig. 5. An example of relational encoding of business process graphs

1 SELECT DISTINCT $E_1.modelID, E_i.ElementID$
2 FROM BPElements as E_1,..., BPElements as E_m, BPEdges as S_1,..., BPEdges as S_n
3 WHERE
4 $\forall_{i=2}^{m}(E_1.modelID = E_i.modelID)$
5 AND $\forall_{j=1}^{n}(E_1.modelID = S_j.modelID)$
6 AND $\forall_{i=1}^{m}(E_i.ElementName = QE_i.ElementName)$
7 AND $\forall_{i=1}^{m}(E_i.ElementType = QE_i.ElementType)$
8 AND $\forall_{j=1}^{n}(S_i.EdgeType = S_J.EdgeType)$
9 AND $\forall_{j=1}^{n}(S_j.SElementID = E_{f(S_j.SElementID)}.ElementID$
10 AND $S_j.DElementID = E_{f(S_j.DElementID)}.ElementID)$;

Fig. 6. SQL treanslation template of the filtering phase of BPMN-Q queries

conjunctive predicates of the edge types (*sequence flow* or *association*). Due to their very expensive evaluation cost, these conditions are not represented for *recursive* or *negative* edges and delayed to the verification phase after uploading the *candidate* process models into the main memory. Lines number 9 and 10 represent the conditions of the edge connection information between the mapped elements.

- **Verification phase:** This phase is an *optional* phase. We apply the verification process only if the BPMN-Q query contains any of the *Path*, *Negative Path* or *Negative Sequence Flow* constructs. Although the fact that the conditions of evaluating these constructs could be injected into the SQL translation template of the filtering phase as *nested* or *recursive* queries, we found that it is more efficient to avoid the cost of performing these conditions over each stored business process and delay their processing, *if required*, in a separate phase after pruning the candidate list. In this phase we load the candidate process models (which are passed from the filtering phase) into the main memory and verify the conditions of the recursive and negative edge constructs. We use the aid of the information of *BPPaths* table to accelerate the evaluation process of this phase.

4 Experiments

To demonstrate the efficiency of our query engine in processing BPMN-Q graph-based queries [1], we conducted our experiments using the IBM DB2 DBMS running on a PC with 2.8 GHZ Intel Xeon processors, 4 GB of main memory storage and 200 GB of SCSI secondary storage. In our experiments we use a real dataset which is collected from the online business process modeling repository, ORYX[1]. This real dataset consists of 250 business process models. The average number of nodes in each business process model graph is 12 nodes and the average number of edges between these nodes are 17. We mapped the available RDF presentation of these models into our relational storage scheme. A query set which consists of 10 manually designed BPMN-Q queries has been used

[1] http://oryx-editor.org/backend/poem/repository

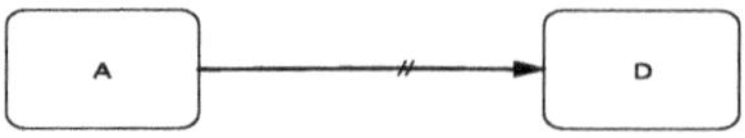

(a) (Q1): Path query between two activity objects

(b) (Q2): Path query between a starting event and an activity object

(c) (Q3): Association query between a data object and an activity

(d) (Q4): Association query between a data object and a variable activity

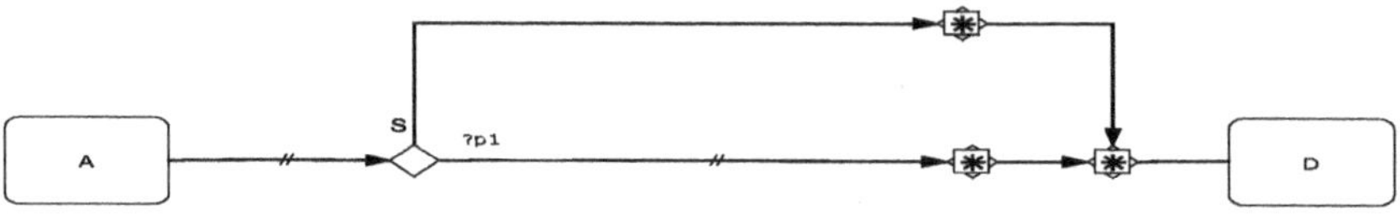

(e) (Q5): Multipath query with generic nodes and generic gateway

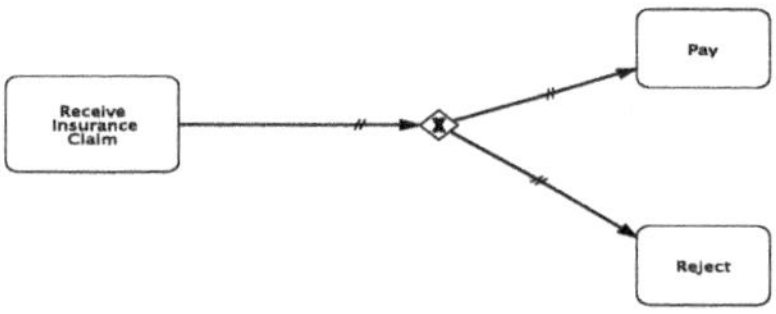

(f) (Q6): Multipath query with an XOR splitting gateway

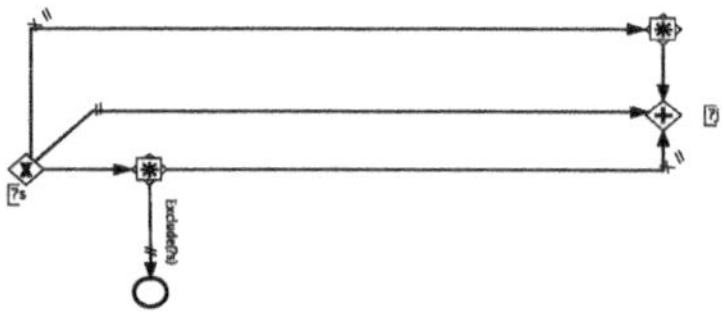

(g) (Q7): And join query with multiple sources

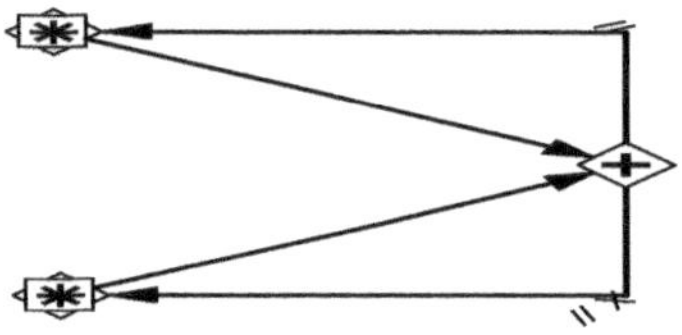

(h) (Q8): A query for detecting deadlock situations

(i) (Q9): An association query between an activity and a variable data object

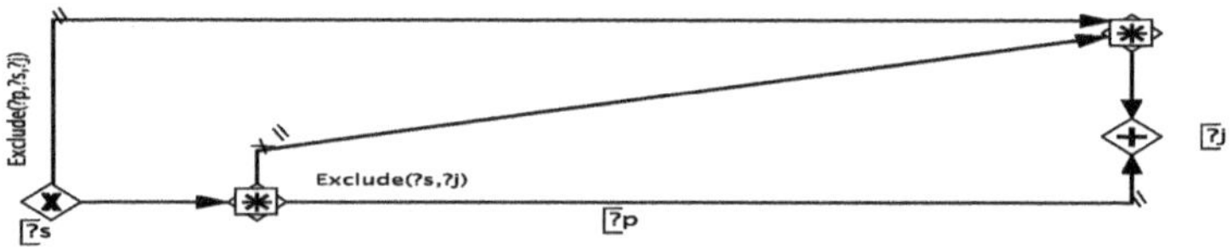

(j) (Q10): A query with an XOR split that matches an AND join

Fig. 7. Queries of the Performance Experiments

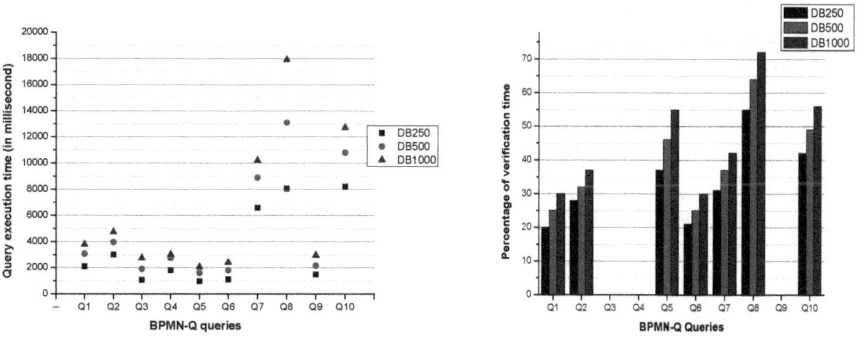

(a) Scalability of BPMN-Q query processor (b) Verification time of BPMN-Q queries

Fig. 8. Performance Evaluation of BPMN-Q Query Processor

(Figure 7). These queries have be designed with ranging number of elements and covering the most important constructs of the BPMN-Q query languages. To demonstrate the scalability of our approach, we run our experiments using larger database sizes of business process models. We duplicated the instances of the available two process models two times to generate another two datasets with sizes of 500 and 1000 process models respectively.

Figure 8(a) illustrates the average execution times for the relational processor of BPMN-Q queries. In this figure, the X-axis represents BPMN-Q queries while the execution time of each query is presented in the Y-axis . The execution times of these experiments include both the filtering and verification phases. The results show that the execution times of our system performs and scales in a decreasing linear fashion with respect to the increasing size of the process model repository. The main reason behind this is the scalability of the relational-based filtering phase to avoid a high percentage of the false positive process models and to reduce the size of the candidate process models. Figure 8(b) illustrates the percentage of the verification phase with respect to the total execution time of BPMN-Q queries. The reported percentages are computed using the formula: $(1 - \frac{V}{T})$ where V represents the execution time of the verification phase while C represents the total execution time of the BPMN-Q query. Queries $Q3, Q4$ and $Q9$ does not require any verification phase because they do not include any recursive or negative edge connections. In principle, the more recursive or negative edges the query has, the longer the time for the verification phase is required. Thus, queries $Q5, Q8$ and $Q10$ have the highest percentage of their execution times reserved to verify their multiple generic nodes and recursive connections. The experiment results confirm the importance of applying efficient filtering mechanisms to avoid the high cost of the verification phase. Although it is expected that the number of candidate process models is increasing linearly with respect to the size of the process model repository, the efficiency of the filtering phase is shown by the decreasing linear increase of the verification time in comparison to the increase of the repository size.

5 Related Work

Several authors have developed process query languages to query about the allowed executions of a BPM [3,10]. The main difference between those graphical languages and BPMN-Q is that BPMN-Q is used to formulate queries about the business process model itself (i.e. its structure), not about the state space of its executions. This makes it possible to use BPMN-Q for searching for modeling problems without having to compute the state space of all possible executions. Beeri et al. [4,5] have presented a query language for querying business processes called BP-QL. The query language is designed based on the BPEL standard and thus focuses on querying executable processes. Our work focuses on the reuse of higher level business knowledge. In addition, our query specification language is more expressive in that apart from constraints on data and control flow, the user can specify additional properties of the structure of the models.

6 Conclusion

In this paper we described the design and implementation of a query engine which provides the business process designers with effective querying mechanisms. The query engine relies on a visual, easy-to-use and expressive query language to specify their queries against the repository of business process models. Using the robust relational infrastructure, our experiments demonstrate the efficiency and scalability of the implementation of our query engine to deal with large business repository. As a future work, we are planning to consider the social aspect in the context of collaborative building and reusing of process models.

References

1. QBP: A Flexible Framework for Querying and Reusing Business Process Models, `http://bpmnq.sourceforge.net/`
2. Awad, A.: BPMN-Q: A Language to Query Business Processes. In: EMISA (2007)
3. Eshuis, R., Grefen, P.: Structural Matching of BPEL Processes. In: ECOWS (2007)
4. Beeri, C., et al.: Querying Business Processes with BP-QL. In: VLDB (2005)
5. Beeri, C., et al.: Querying Business Processes. In: VLDB (2006)
6. Yoshikawa, M., et al.: XRel: a path-based approach to storage and retrieval of XML documents using relational databases. TOIT 1(1) (2001)
7. Cohen, S., et al.: Scientific formats for object-relational database systems: a study of suitability and performance. SIGMOD Record 35(2) (2006)
8. Garey, M.R., Johnson, D.S.: Computers and Intractability: A Guide to the Theory of NP-Completeness. W. H. Freeman, New York (1979)
9. Grust, T., Sakr, S., Teubner, J.: XQuery on SQL Hosts. In: VLDB (2004)
10. Momotko, M., Subieta, K.: Process Query Language: A Way to Make Workflow Processes More Flexible. In: Benczúr, A.A., Demetrovics, J., Gottlob, G. (eds.) ADBIS 2004. LNCS, vol. 3255, pp. 306–321. Springer, Heidelberg (2004)
11. Sakr, S.: Storing and Querying Graph Data Using Efficient Relational Processing Techniques. In: UNISCON (2009)
12. Wohed, P., Aalst, W., Dumas, M., Hofstede, A., Russell, N.: On the Suitability of BPMN for Business Process Modelling. In: Dustdar, S., Fiadeiro, J.L., Sheth, A.P. (eds.) BPM 2006. LNCS, vol. 4102, pp. 161–176. Springer, Heidelberg (2006)

SGDB – Simple Graph Database Optimized for Activation Spreading Computation

Marek Ciglan and Kjetil Nørvåg

Dep. of Computer and Information Science, NTNU, Trondheim, Norway
marek.ciglan@idi.ntnu.no

Abstract. In this paper, we present SGDB, a graph database with a storage model optimized for computation of Spreading Activation (SA) queries. The primary goal of the system is to minimize the execution time of spreading activation algorithm over large graph structures stored on a persistent media; without pre-loading the whole graph into the memory. We propose a storage model aiming to minimize number of accesses to the storage media during execution of SA and we propose a graph query type for the activation spreading operation. Finally, we present the implementation and its performance characteristics in scope of our pilot application that uses the activation spreading over the Wikipedia link graph.

1 Introduction

The graph data structure is one of the most important data structures in computer science and it is also an useful structure for data modeling. Many real-world objects can be naturally described by graphs. The most straightforward examples are those of various types of networks; e.g., transportation networks, delivery networks, hypertext networks, citation networks, social networks or communication networks.

Although the relational data model is dominant in nowadays information systems, modeling data in the graph structure is gaining noticeable interest. Graph databases are information systems providing graph abstraction for modeling, storing and accessing the data. In the graph data model, relations between modeled objects are as important as the data describing the objects. This is the most distinctive feature from other database models - graph databases aim to provide efficient execution of queries taking into account the topology of the graph and the connectivity between stored objects.

Graph traversal and graph analysis operations are traditionally implemented by pre-loading whole graph in the memory and process it in memory, due to performance reasons. This approach naturally suffers from memory size limits. Graph databases aim to provide efficient persistent storage for graph data that also allow for fast graph traversal processing.

In this paper we present the storage model for the graph structure together with the architecture and the implementation of a graph database, named Simple Graph Database[1] (SGDB). The storage model of SGDB is optimized for execution of Spreading Activation (SA) algorithm over stored graphs. Spreading Activation algorithm was designed for searching semantic and association networks. Its basic form, as well as the most

[1] https://sourceforge.net/projects/simplegdb/

M. Yoshikawa et al. (Eds.): DASFAA 2010, LNCS 6193, pp. 45–56, 2010.

common variations, are extensively described in [6]. The nodes in graph structure represents objects and links denotes relations between objects. The algorithm starts by setting activation of the input nodes and the processing consists of iterations, in which the activation is propagated from activated nodes to their neighbor nodes. Mechanism of SA utilize breadth first expansion from activated nodes to identify other nodes in the network that are strongly associated with initial nodes (have high activation value). The breadth first traversal, utilized in SA, can be characterized by random accesses to the underlying graph structure, to retrieve edges of activated nodes.

To motivate the use of Spreading Activation algorithm over graph databases, we provide several use-cases. In the domain of *Semantic Web* , SA technique was successfully used for mining socio-semantic networks [18]. In the enterprise environment, SA can be used for *product recommendation systems* to identify the products that the customer have not purchased yet, but are highly associated with the products he already bought. *Social networks* can be naturally represented by graphs. Also in this application domain, we can find uses for SA technique. E.g., recommendation of people that the user might know.

Motivated by presented use-cases, we propose a graph database optimized for execution of SA algorithm. The main contributions of the paper are the following:

- proposal of the storage model for graph data, aiming at supporting the random access pattern for retrieval of the connectedness information of nodes activated during SA process.
- proposal of the query type for the Spreading Activation operation for graph databases, to facilitate the usage of the SA over stored graph data.

The paper is organized as follows. In Section 2, we discuss related work, we then describe the SA procedure in Section 3 to define the context of the work. The storage model for SGDB is proposed in Section 4 and we propose the graph query type for the SA operation over graph database in Section 5. The architecture of proposed system is described in 6, providing also few important implementation details (6.1). We conclude the paper by describing performance characteristics of the system, evaluated using a pilot application for finding connections in Wikipedia link graph (Section 7).

2 Related Work

The concept of a graph database was popular in academic studies in nineties. An extensive survey of the graph database models proposed in this period is presented in [2]. Proposed models ranged in the complexity, from simple directed graphs with labeled nodes and edges [8, 9] to complex representations of nested objects [13, 12]. Also variety of graph query languages were proposed and ranged from SQL-like languages [1] to graphical queries [16].

For a period of time, the interest in graph databases disappeared. The emergence of *Semantic Web* shifted attention to RDF[2] stores. RDF can be also viewed as a graph data structure. Early RDF stores were design to operate in-memory or used relational

[2] http://www.w3.org/RDF/

database back-ends for the data persistence [17]. Later, specialize persistent stores optimized for semantic data were developed [11] [7]; those are designed as triple stores to support RDF model.

The focus on graph databases recently re-emerged. Several companies in the industry have developed graph databases systems (e.g. Freebase [4], DirectedEdge[3], Neo4j[4]). There is also an effort for providing systems for large-scale graph processing in distributed environment (e.g. Google Pregel [14], graph package in Hama[5], or [10]). The data in [10] as well as Hama is stored in a distributed key value store, used in conjunction with Map-Reduce systems and the graph structure is modeled as the adjacency matrix.

3 Preliminaries

In this section, we first describe the structure that is being modeled, we then describe the Spreading Activation algorithm to define the context for the proposed approach. We discuss the modified SA technique that allows to observe the value of activation received from distinct initial nodes. We highlight important points that influence the design of presented system.

3.1 Modeled Data Structure

The aim of this work is to support the SA technique over a graph with weighted and typed edges, stored on a persistent medium. We can define the modeled structure using equation

$$G = (V, E, f, w, T, t)$$

where G is the graph label, V is a set of nodes, E is a set of edges, f is a function $f : V \times V \rightarrow E$ defining mapping between nodes and edges, w is a function defining edge weights $w : E \rightarrow \langle 0, 1\rangle$, T is a set of edge type labels and t is a function defining edges types $t : E \rightarrow T$.

The operations considered for this data structure are insertion,deletion of nodes and edges, retrieval of outgoing and incoming edges for a given node and iteration over node and edges sets. Due to the space limitation, we define only insertion operations. Similarly, operations for nodes and edge deletion, edge weight, type modification and others can be defined. Operation of node insertion can be defined as

$insert(G = (V, E, f, w, T, t), v) = (V' = \{V \cup v\}, E, f' : V' \times V' \rightarrow E, w, T, t)$;
edge insertion operation is

$insert(G = (V, E, f, w, T, t), (e_{new}, i, j, w_{val}, t_{val})) =$
$(V, E' = \{E \cup e_{new}\}, f', w', T, t') \mid i, j \in V; f(i, j) = \perp; w_{val} \in \langle 0, 1\rangle; t_{val} \in T$
where $f' : V \times V \rightarrow E'$, $w' : E' \rightarrow \langle 0, 1\rangle$, $t' : E' \rightarrow T$ and

$$f'(k,l) = \begin{cases} f(k,l) \ ; k \neq i \wedge l \neq j \\ e_{new} \ \ ; k = i \wedge l = j \end{cases} ; \ w'(e) = \begin{cases} w(e) \ ; e \in E \\ w_{val} \ ; e = e_{new} \end{cases}$$

[3] http://www.directededge.com (visited: 10.12.2009)
[4] http://neo4j.org/ (visited: 10.12.2009)
[5] http://wiki.apache.org/hama (visited: 10.12.2009)

$$t'(e) = \begin{cases} t(e) \ ; e \in E \\ t_{val} \ ; e = e_{new} \end{cases}$$

Edge retrieval operations can be defined as follows:
$outgoing(G, n) = \{e \mid n, i \in V; e : f(n, i) \neq \perp\}$ and
$incoming(G, n) = \{e \mid n, i \in V; e : f(i, n) \neq \perp\}$

In addition to the graph topology, we want to store user defined attributes that can be associated with nodes and edges. In our approach, the user defined data (node and edges attributes) are stored in a separate structure, linked with graph by node identifiers. The storage of the user defined data is out of the scope of this paper, as it does not influence the graph traversal operations.

3.2 Spreading Activation Algorithm

The Spreading Activation algorithm is based on the breadth first expansion from activated nodes in the graph data structure. Edges can be weighted or typed (or both) and can be directed or undirected. The input of the SA algorithm is a set of initially activated nodes and a set of parameters influencing the activation process, the output is a set of nodes activated by the SA process. The SA process consists of iterations in which the activation is spread in breadth first manner. Each iteration is composed of a spreading phase and a pre-adjustment or post-adjustment phases. In pre/post-adjustment phases the activation decay can be applied on activated nodes. In the spreading phase, activated nodes send impulses to their neighbors. The value of the impulse propagated from an activated node is a function of the node's input value. In the basic SA variant, the input value of a node n is equal to the sum of weighted output values of nodes connected with n by outgoing edges. The output values are weighted by the edge weights. Let T be a set of edge types of the graph and $Q \subseteq T$ be the types allowed in the SA computation. Function a is

$$a(t, Q) = \begin{cases} 1 \ ; t \in Q \\ 0 \ ; t \notin Q \end{cases}$$

The output value is described by following formula: $I_n = \sum_i O_i w(e_{i,n}) a(t(e_{i,n}), Q)$; where I_n is the input value of the node n; O_i is the output value of the node i connected to n by an outgoing edge and $w(e_{i,n})$ is the weight of the edge connecting i and n; $w \in \langle 0, 1 \rangle$; $t(e_{i,n})$ is the type of the edge $e_{i,n}$. The most commonly used output function is the threshold function, where the output is zero when the node input value is below the user defined threshold th. In case that $I_n > th$ the output is equal to one.

The activation thus spreads from initial nodes over the network. The algorithm finishes when the there are no nodes with $O_n > 0$ in an iteration. The convergence and the fix point of the SA process has been studied in [3]. In practice, some additional termination conditions are used (e.g., distance constraint).

3.3 Activation Vector Spreading

In the standard SA algorithm, we can not distinguish whether a node received an activation from one or multiple initial nodes. To obtain richer information about activation spread, we have introduced a modification of the standard SA technique in [5], called Activation Vector Spreading (AVS).

We store the node activation as a vector, its length is equal to the number of input nodes and the n-th element of the vector represents the amount of the activation originating from the n-th input node. The activation vector n-th input node is initiated as follows: all the values in the vector are equal to zero, expect n-th element, which is initially set to one. The activation spread is computed individually for each element of the activation vector. Informally, the activation spread is computed individually for each input node. In addition to that, in each iteration, if the individual elements of node's input vector are lower than the defined threshold th but the sum of all the elements is greater than t, we spread an output activation vector with a non-zero element, which is the element with highest value in the input activation vector. The AVS method is described in detail in [5].

This modification allows us to observe which sources the node received the activation from (non-zero values in the activation vector) and the amount of activation from each source. Important aspect of the SA algorithm for the graph storage design is the use of breadth first expansion from activated nodes. The activation value of a node n dependents on activation values of the connected nodes and weights and/or types of connecting edges. Those are the only values necessary to compute the activation value of a node.

4 Storage Model

The aim of this work is to design a persistent graph database system allowing for fast execution of the spreading activation algorithm, without pre-loading the whole graph to the memory prior to the execution. As the access to the persistent medium is the most time costly operation, we aim at minimizing the number of accesses to the storage medium. The SA procedure utilize the breadth first expansion, characterized by a number of random accesses to the graph data. The addressed problem can be formulated as follows: Propose a persistent storage system for representation of a directed, weighted graph with typed edges that allows for an implementation of the spreading activation algorithm with the minimum number of accesses to the persistent storage media.

We can not avoid the random access pattern in general; however we organize the data in a way to reduce the number of disk access operations for retrieving the information needed to compute the activation spreading.

This section describes the storage model proposed for SGDB system, aiming at reducing storage lookups for the SA technique. Adjacency list is an ideal representation of a graph structure for breath first traversals, a graph representation, where each node n has an associated list of nodes that are connects to n by an edge. The adjacency list can be viewed a set of tuples, where first element of each tuple is a node n and the second element is the list of nodes adjacent to n.

A practical data structure for adjacency list is $key - value$ map, where key is the identifier of the node and $value$ is the list of identifiers of the adjacent nodes. As the $key - value$ map is a practical data structure, there has been already a considerable

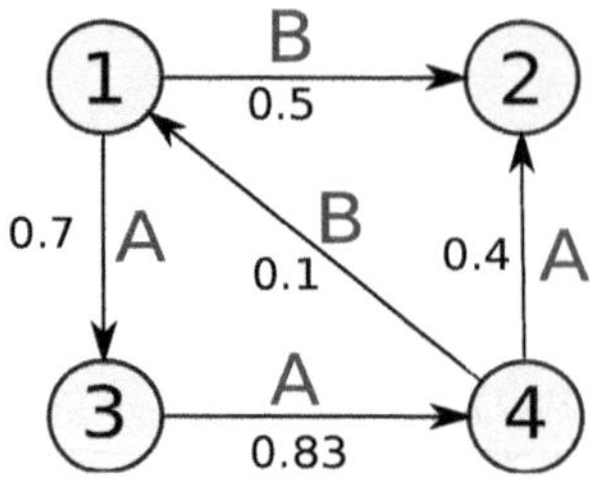

Key	Value			
1	2	(3;0.7;A)	(2;0.5;B)	(4;0.1;B)
2	0	(1;0.5;B)	(4;0.4;A)	
3	1	(4;0.83;A)	(1;0.7;A)	
4	2	(1;0.1;B)	(2;0.4;A)	(3;0.83;A)

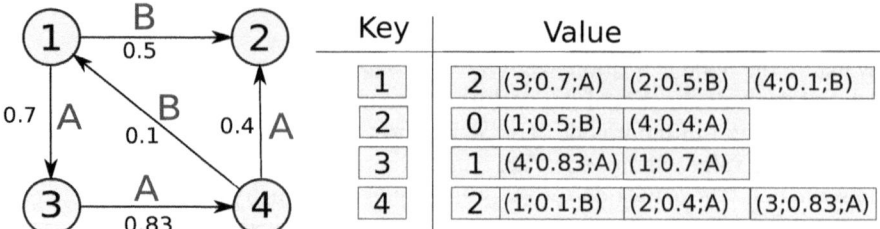

Fig. 1. Example of graph representation in proposed storage model

amount of work done and there are numerous persistent $key - value$ stores available (e.g. Berekeley DB, JDBM[6], BabuDB[7]), able to store large amount of data.

Using this representation, given a starting node n, we need $1 + d$ lookups (where d is the number of nodes adjacent to n) in a $key - value$ store to obtain a set of identifiers of nodes distant two hops from n. Spreading Activation method requires more than structural information. As stated in 3.2, to compute activation values in the SA algorithm we need additional data - weights and/or edge types. To keep the number of lookups low and to avoid additional retrieval from the data storage, we propose to keep the edges weights and types directly in the adjacency list as they are required by the SA algorithm. This simple, even trivial, change brings important time savings for SA processing, oppose to the approach where the edge weights and types are modeled as edge attributes and are stored in a separate structure.

In our storage model, the graph is stored as a set of $key - value$ pairs (i, N_i), where i is the identifier of the node and N_i is the representation of edges adjacent to node i. Each edge e is represented by a triple $e = (j, w_{(i,j)}, t_{(i,j)})$ where j is the identifier of adjacent node, $w_{(i,j)}$ is the weight of the edge connecting i and j and $t_{(i,j)}$ is the type of the edge. We model the weight by a float value and the type by an integer value. As we need to model directed graphs, we must distinguish the direction of edges. We model adjacent edges N_i as a tuple $N_i = (k, \{e_1, e_2, \ldots, e_m\})$, were k denotes the number of outgoing edges; $\{e_1, e_2, \ldots, e_m\}$ is a list of edges and all $e_l : l < k$ represent outgoing edges and all $e_l : l > k$ represent incoming edges. An example of a graph represented using proposed storage model is depicted in Fig. 1. Let us examine the record encoding node 1; the first element of the $Value$ part of the record indicates that there are two outgoing edges from node 1 (those are the first two in the list - $(3, 0.7, A)$ and $(2, 0.5, A)$) and the rest of the list represents incoming edges (in this case only the edge $(4, 0.1, B)$).

This representation allows us to retrieve outgoing and incoming edges of a node n together with edge weights and types in one lookup. The disadvantage of this approach is that information on edges are redundant; i.e., edge $e_{(i,j)}$ is stored as an outgoing edge in the record of node i and as an incoming edge in the node j record. This necessitates to modify both records, in case of edge manipulation (e.g., update of the weight, type values or deletion).

[6] http://jdbm.sourceforge.net/ (visited: 10.12.2009)

[7] http://code.google.com/p/babudb/ (visited: 10.12.2009)

5 Spreading Activation Queries

As mentioned in 3.2, the input of the SA algorithm is a set of initially activated nodes and set of parameters influencing the activation spread. In this section, we propose a query syntax for executing the SA operation over the stored graph with the aim to allow the definition of SA process using simple plain text string. The purpose of the SA query is to facilitate the usage of the system, the execution of SA operation over stored graph.

The set of parameters considered for the SA algorithm is the following: activation threshold (Th), activation decay ($Decay$) , allowed edge types ($Types$) , use of incoming edges for spreading ($Incoming$) and maximal number of SA iterations ($MaxIteration$). The specification of activated nodes is done in terms of node properties that identify nodes. Proposed syntax for the SA query is the following:

([node([prop=val;]);]*) ; SAProperties: Th:threshold_val; Decay: decay_value; Types=([[edge_type]* / all]); Incoming=[true/false]; MaxIteration=max_iterationt*

We explain the SA query on the following example. In our pilot application, we use the graph constructed from Wikipedia articles (modeled as nodes) and links (modeled as edges). Following example query executes the SA algorithm from nodes representing articles 'Spreading Activation' and 'Wikipedia', with activation threshold 0.4 and decay 0.8, using all edge types and both directions of edges, constrained to three SA iterations:

(node(name='Spreading Activation'); node(name='Wikipedia')) ; SAProperties: Th:0.4; Decay: 0.8; Types=all; Incoming=true; MaxIteration=3

Query execution is done in two phases. In the first phase, the input for SA operation is constructed. This involves identification of the initial activation nodes, using attributes specified in the node definition part of the query. Nodes with given attributes and attribute values are selected and the initial nodes vector is constructed. From the node definition part of the query, we construct a vector of initial nodes. E.g., initial nodes vector constructed from the example query would be ['Spreading Activation', 'Wikipedia'] (for simplicity, article names represent nodes of the graph).

Initial nodes vector, together with other parameters, is then used as inputs for SA operation. In the second step the AVS algorithm is executed, taking advantage of the underlying storage model for fast retrieval of information required to compute the activation spread. The results of the SA query is a set of tuples; each tuple contains following elements: (Activated node, activation, partial activations vector, number of impulses vector, distance vector). *Activated node* is the node activated in the process of activation spreading, *activation* is the node's total activation, *partial activations vector* contains partial activations received from distinct initial nodes (n-th element of the vector corresponds to the activation received from the n-th element of initial nodes vector). *Number of impulses vector* contains information on the number of impulses received by the node from distinct initiators and the distance vector contains information on the distance of the node from distinct initiators.

E.g., part of the result set for the example query is:

(Semantic Web; 12.42; [2.4182642, 10.0,]; [3, 10,]; [2,2,])
(Web search engine; 12.12; [0.7190919, 11.407564,]; [1, 21,]; [1,3,])
(Knowledge management; 10.80; [4.8060675, 6.0,]; [5, 6,]; [2,2,])

Proposed SA query can be formulated in the plain text and its result set can be also communicated in the plain text. Another advantage of proposed SA query is that the upper bound of query selectivity can be estimated based on query specification (use of outgoing and incoming links) and the information about initial nodes in/out-degrees.

6 SGDB Architecture

This section presents the overall high-level architecture of SGDB system and its implementation. The architecture of the SGDB is depicted in Figure 2. The system is decomposed into modules with distinct functionality; modules are organized in layers, where each layer provide a simplified abstraction for the upper layer, making the complexity of underlying layers transparent.

The base stone of SGDB is the **key-value store** that maintains the adjacency lists of the graph structure in form of the key-value tuples. The main responsibility of this module is to provide fast lookups for adjacency lists based on the given key (node identifier).

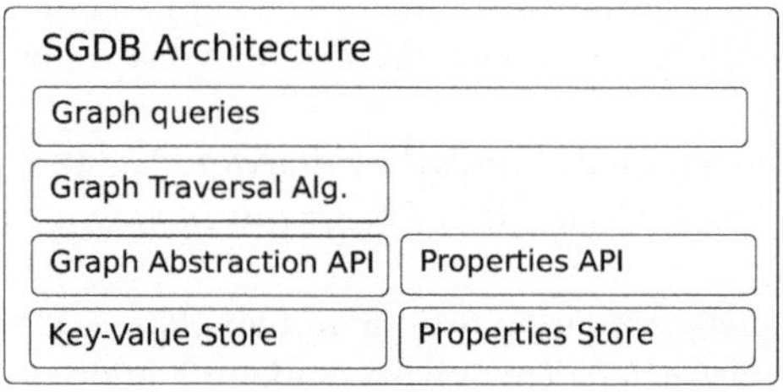

Fig. 2. Architecture of SGDB

Properties store component is responsible for storing data (properties) related to the objects modeled by nodes and relationships modeled by edges. E.g. let us suppose that node n in the graph represents a person; properties associated with n could be name of the person, address of the person. The property store is independent of the graph structure store and allows for retrieval of the graph nodes based on their attributes. **Graph Abstraction API** (GAAPI) provide graph abstraction layer, so that users can access and manipulate the graph data using graph theory concepts - nodes and edges, instead of node identifiers and adjacency lists. GAAPI provide functions for iterating over collection of graph nodes, retrieval of graph nodes based on node identifiers or user defined properties, retrieval of outgoing and incoming edges. In addition GAAPI provide functionality to modify the graph structure - insertion and removal of nodes and edges. **Properties API** provides access to properties store. **Graph traversal layer** contains implementations of graph traversal operations, such as the Spreading Activation algorithm or path finding algorithms. It exploits (GAAPI) to access the graph structure. Finally, **graph queries layer** is a presentation layer, providing access to the database functionality using graph queries (current implementation provides SA queries (described in Section 5)).

6.1 Implementation

SGDB[8] is implemented in JAVA programming language. Current implementation does not support transactions and can be used as an application embedded database (it can not be run in a standalone mode). SGDB is available as an open source software. It exploits Oracle Berkeley DB Java Edition[9] as a key-value store.

The storage model used in SGDB allows to retrieve outgoing and incoming edges together with edge weight and type data in one lookup. This is convenient for breath first traversals, especially the SA. The drawback of this approach, from the implementation point of view, is that for update operations on the graph (insertion, deletion of nodes and edges) the edge list must be retrieved from the storage, modified and then stored back, rewriting the whole original record. In addition, the data describing edge $e_{i,j}$ are stored twice in the storage - it is stored as an outgoing edge in the record of node i and as an incoming edge in the record of node j. This is the trade-off of proposed storage model, more demanding update operations are compensated by efficient retrieval operations.

7 Evaluation

In this section we first compare performance of the proposed approach with a general purpose graph database for retrieval of weighted and typed links using the random access pattern. Secondly, we provide performance characteristics of SGDB in the scope of our pilot application. We describe the application and properties of used graph data, describe the evaluation setting and present achieved performance characteristics.

Experiments were conducted over data set of Wikipedia link graph. The graph structure was generated by a custom parser from Wikipedia XML dump (dump from 03.11.2009 was used). The resulting graph contained 3.3 millions nodes and over 91 millions edges. As shown by previous research [15], Wikipedia link graph exhibits small-world properties. Small-world networks are characterized by small average path length between nodes and high values of the clustering coefficient.

In the first part of the evaluation, we have studied the performance of a general purpose graph database for SA technique, in which the link weights and types are modeled as edge attributes. We have compared the time required to retrieve edges for a randomly chosen node without and with weight and type data. We have used Neo4j[10]), an open source graph database as a general purpose graph database for the tests. The default settings of Neo4j database were used in the tests. The experiment was conducted in a black-box testing fashion.

Wikipedia link graph data set was used in the experiment. All the experiments were conducted on a PC with 2GHz Intel Core 2 Duo-processor and 7200 RPM hard drive.

First, we have generated lists of identifiers of randomly chosen nodes from the graph. We have created lists containing 10, 100, 1 000 and 10 000 node identifiers; we used 10 identifiers sets for each. This setup was used to test the random access pattern that is typical in SA computation. Pregenerated lists of identifiers were used to ensure the

[8] https://sourceforge.net/projects/simplegdb/

[9] http://www.oracle.com/technology/products/berkeley-db/je/index.html (visited: 10.12.2009)

[10] http://neo4j.org/ (visited: 10.12.2009)

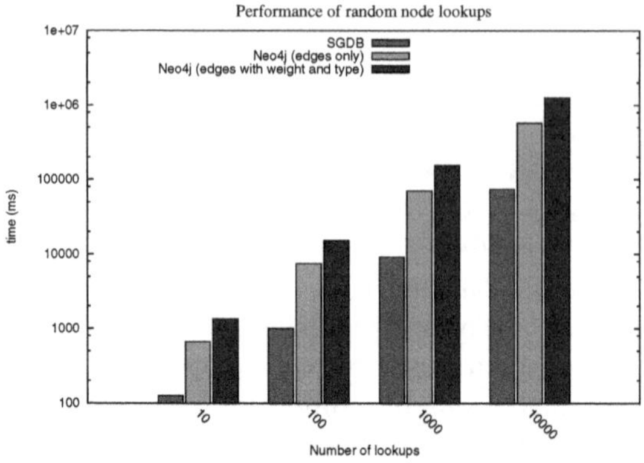

Fig. 3. Time required to perform sets of random lookups; X-axis depicts the number of lookups per set; Y-axis represents the time required to perform lookups. Log scale is used for both axes.

same conditions for distinct tests. We have then measured the time required to retrieve both outgoing and incoming edges for the nodes in the lists. We used generic graph database to retrieve edges without retrieving weight and type attributes. Next, we have measured the time required to retrieve the edges for the same nodes, but with weight and type data. In average, the time required to retrieve weighted and typed edges was 2.1 times higher than the retrieval of edges without weight and type attributes.

We have performed the same experiments using SGDB, where the weight and type data are stored together with link targets. The edges retrieval (with weight and type data) was 16.9 times faster compared to the retrieval of typed and weighted edges from general purpose graph database. The reason is that in SGDB the weight and type data are coupled together with edges definitions, so only one disk access can be used to read all the data for the SA expansion from a given node; in addition, SGDB random access operation for retrieval of node's edges was slightly faster. Figure 3 shows histogram of the time required to retrieve the edges using SGDB, and general purpose graph database (with and without retrieving weight and type attributes).

In the second series of tests, we have run our pilot application. The pilot application aims at finding connections between two or more given input nodes in Wikipedia link graph. Nodes in the Wikipedia link graph model articles and edges represent links between articles. The pilot application uses the activation spreading over the Wikipedia link graph to find highly activated nodes (named connecting nodes), and identifies the paths with the highest sum of activation on the nodes between initial nodes to connecting node. In each test, we have measured the time required for finding connections between two randomly chosen nodes, constrained to two iterations of activation spread. Under the two iterations constraint, we can identify the connections of the maximal length of 4 between two initial nodes. Because of the small average distance between nodes in the test set (one of the properties of the small-world graphs), we found connections for randomly chosen nodes in 86.4% of cases. We have performed 1000 queries, both incoming and outgoing links were used, decay parameter was set to 1 (meaning

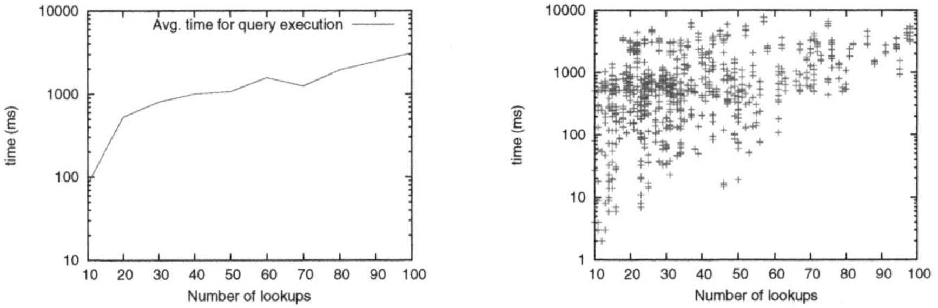

Fig. 4. X-axis represents number of node lookups in queries. Y-axis (log scale) represents time in ms the queries took to execute. Plot on the left represent averaged values and figure on the right depicts points representing values for individual queries.

no decay in iterations) and activation threshold was set to minimal values. The effect of this setting was the full breath first expansion from the initial nodes in two iterations.

Figure 4 depicts the time required to execute queries with an increasing numer of node lookups for a query. The average execution time was 1136.4 ms, the activation values for 181820.1 nodes in average was computed for a single query. The average number of edge retrieval operations from the SGDB storage was 49.7.

8 Conclusion

In this paper, we have proposed a storage model for a graph database, designed to provide fast data store for execution of the Spreading Activation (SA) technique. We have described the motivation for the SA usage over graph databases. In addition, we have presented the architecture and implementation of SGDB, the graph database that utilize proposed storage model.

We have compared performance of our approach with the performance of a general purpose graph database, for the activation spreading over the stored graph. The evaluation showed important time savings using proposed approach. As our approach was designed for a specific problem, it is not surprising that it performs better (for that problem) than a generic one. However, we believe that the SA technique has a wide number of possible uses in context of graph databases and it is worth to exploit the optimization for the SA even at the graph structure storage level.

We have also proposed a query type for the Spreading Activation operation over the graph database. The SA query has an easily interpretable definition and results and the upper bound of query selectivity can be easily estimated. We have described the performance characteristics of SGDB, using proposed SA operation in the scope of our pilot application that exploits the Wikipedia link graph.

References

1. Amann, M., Scholl, B.: Gram: A graph data model and query language. In: Proceedings of the European Conference on Hypertext Technology (ECHT), pp. 201–211. ACM, New York (1992)

2. Angles, R., Gutierrez, C.: Survey of graph database models. ACM Comput. Surv. 40(1), 1–39 (2008)
3. Berthold, M.R., Brandes, U., Kötter, T., Mader, M., Nagel, U., Thiel, K.: Pure spreading activation is pointless. In: CIKM 2009: Proceeding of the 18th ACM conference on Information and knowledge management, pp. 1915–1918. ACM, New York (2009)
4. Bollacker, K., Evans, C., Paritosh, P., Sturge, T., Taylor, J.: Freebase: a collaboratively created graph database for structuring human knowledge. In: SIGMOD 2008: Proceedings of the 2008 ACM SIGMOD international conference on Management of data, pp. 1247–1250. ACM, New York (2008)
5. Ciglan, M., Rivière, E., Nørvåg, K.: Learning to find interesting connections in wikipedia. In: Proceeding of APWeb 2010 (2010)
6. Crestani, F.: Application of spreading activation techniques in information retrieval. Artif. Intell. Rev. 11(6), 453–482 (1997)
7. Erling, O., Mikhailov, I.: RDF support in the virtuoso DBMS. In: Conference on Social Semantic Web. LNI, vol. 113, pp. 59–68. GI (2007)
8. Gyssens, M., Paredaens, J., Gucht, D.V.: A graph-oriented object model for database end-user. In: Proceedings of the 1990 ACM SIGMOD International Conference on Management of Data, pp. 24–33. ACM Press, New York (1990)
9. Hidders, J.: A graph-based update language for object-oriented data models. Ph.D. dissertation. Technische Universiteit Eindhoven (2001)
10. Kang, U., Tsourakakis, C.E., Faloutsos, C.: PEGASUS: A peta-scale graph mining system implementation and observations. In: Ninth IEEE International Conference on Data Mining, ICDM 2009, December 2009, pp. 229–238 (2009)
11. Kiryakov, A., Ognyanov, D., Manov, D.: OWLIM - a pragmatic semantic repository for OWL. In: Proc. Workshop Scalable Semantic Web Knowledge Base Systems
12. Levene, M., Poulovassilis, A.: The hypernode model and its associated query language. In: Proceedings of the 5th Jerusalem Conference on Information technology, pp. 520–530. IEEE Computer Society Press, Los Alamitos (1990)
13. Mainguenaud, M.: Simatic XT: A data model to deal with multi-scaled networks. Comput. Environ. Urban Syst. 16, 281–288 (1992)
14. Malewicz, G., Austern, M.H., Bik, A.J., Dehnert, J.C., Horn, I., Leiser, N., Czajkowski, G.: Pregel: a system for large-scale graph processing. In: PODC 2009: Proceedings of the 28th ACM symposium on Principles of distributed computing, p. 6. ACM, New York (2009)
15. Mehler, A.: Text linkage in the wiki medium: A comparative study. In: Proceedings of the EACL 2006 Workshop on New Text: Wikis and Blogs and Other Dynamic Text Sources, pp. 1–8 (2006)
16. Paredaens, J., Peelman, P., Tanca, L.: G-Log: A graph-based query language. IEEE Trans. Knowl. Data Eng. 7, 436–453 (1995)
17. Rohloff, K., Dean, M., Emmons, I., Ryder, D., Sumner, J.: An evaluation of triple-store technologies for large data stores. In: Meersman, R., Tari, Z., Herrero, P. (eds.) OTM-WS 2007, Part II. LNCS, vol. 4806, pp. 1105–1114. Springer, Heidelberg (2007)
18. Troussov, A., Sogrin, M., Judge, J., Botvich, D.: Mining socio-semantic networks using spreading activation technique. In: International Workshop on Knowledge Acquisition from the Social Web, KASW 2008 (2008)

Introduction to the Data Intensive e-Science Workshop (DIEW) 2010

Isao Kojima, Kento Aida, Geoffrey Fox, Neil Chue Hong, and Masatoshi Ohishi

National Institute of Advanced Industrial Science and Technology, Japan
National Institute of Informatics, Japan
Indiana University, USA
Open Middleware Infrastructure Institute, United Kingdom
National Astronomical Observatory of Japan

As the amount and the complexity of scientific data is rapidly increasing, data has become a key aspect in scientific research. Creating the computer infrastructure which enables scientists to extract scientific knowledge by linking, processing and analyzing these distributed and diverse data would be a crucial issue towards a fourth paradigm ? Data Intentive Scientific Discovery proposed by late Jim Gray. This e-Science infrastructure is also a basis for constructing digital repositories which can archive and share valuable knowledge among science communities.

As the climate change problem shows, scientific research needs to be conducted collaboratively on a global scale, and the distributed data infrastructure which can support various science communities would be indispensable. Based on this motivation, this workshop aims to bring scientists from diverse fields together, and to serve them an opportunity to share their research experiences on how data intensive computing has been facilitating scientific discoveries.

In the rigorous review process, each submitted paper was reviewed by three experts and we selected five papers to be included in the workshop proceedings. The paper by J.Terazono et al. presented a Web-GIS based collaboration environment for lunar and planetary science. The work by I.Elsayed and P.Brezany proposed a large-scale scientific data management based on their concept of dataspaces for e-science applications. T.Takagi et al. proposed an event detection method by using satellite images and web contents. A web-based knowledge server for Geophysical fluid science is presented by T.Horinouchi et al., and its REST-based programming interface is presented by S.Nishizawa et al. An excellent invited talk was given by Prof. Malcolm Atkinson, who is UK e-Science envoy.

We are very grateful to the efforts of all authors while writing and revising their papers. Finally, we appreciate the indispensable support of the members of the Programming Committee and External Reviewers, who provided excellent feedback and valuable directions for the authors to improve their work.

M. Yoshikawa et al. (Eds.): DASFAA 2010, LNCS 6193, p. 57, 2010.

WISE-CAPS: Web-Based Interactive Secure Environment for Collaborative Analysis of Planetary Science

Junya Terazono[1], Ryosuke Nakamura[2], Shinsuke Kodama[2], Naotaka Yamamoto[2], Hirohide Demura[1], Naru Hirata[1], Yoshiko Ogawa[1], Jun'ichi Haruyama[3], Makiko Ohtake[3], and Tsuneo Matsunaga[4]

[1] The University of Aizu, Tsuruga, Ikki-Machi, Aizu-Wakamatsu, Fukushima 965-8580, Japan
{terazono,demura,naru,yoshiko}@u-aizu.ac.jp
[2] National Institute of Advanced Industrial Science and Technology (AIST), Higashi, Tsukuba, Ibaraki 305-8651, Japan
{r.nakamura,s.kodama}@aist.go.jp, naotaka@ni.aist.go.jp
[3] The Institute of Space and Astronautical Science, Japan Aerospace Exploration Agency 3-1-1, Yoshinodai, Sagamihara, Kanagawa 229-8510, Japan
{haruyama.junichi,ohtake.makiko}@jaxa.jp
[4] National Institute for Environmental Studies (NIES) 16-2, Onogawa, Tsukuba, Ibaraki 305-8506, Japan
matsunag@nies.go.jp

Abstract. We are now developing Web-GIS based collaboration environment for lunar and planetary science. This system, called WISE-CAPS aims for promotion of researchers' collaboration and data sharing through the network. In WISE-CAPS, all data are stored in server and data access to server is controlled with security modules of the server and control files. This system combines easy-to-use user environment and flexible and robust security.

Keywords: Web-GIS, planetary science, security, data exchange, web server, access control.

1 Introduction

Location-based information is essential for lunar and planetary exploration to combine. Here "location-based" means mainly the map. By comparing data obtained by different instruments in one map overlapping, researchers can find new knowledge on the planetary bodies inspired by difference of data in the same location.

Currently, Geographical Information System (GIS) is widely used in terrestrial expression of location. In conventional GIS, users can display any data provided by variety of organizations and companies as layers over the base map. Particularly, Web-GIS, the system that displays maps and layers in the web browsers, are becoming common. The merit of using Web-GIS is that users only need to prepare browsers to obtain data. Users do not need to care their operating platform or access environment, and to prepare special and proprietary GIS software.

M. Yoshikawa et al. (Eds.): DASFAA 2010, LNCS 6193, pp. 58–68, 2010.

The Web-GIS infrastructure is becoming common in lunar and planetary exploration field. Several platforms are provided for displaying and distributing data of exploration. These sites include Map-a-Planet [1], operated by USGS (US Geological Survey), and Marsoweb [2]. These sites offers map-based interface to browse a map and ancillary scientific data in the browser.

However, these sites are now offering data browsing and downloading function. Therefore, more capabilities are required for such site to become data sharing platform based on Web-GIS. One of the key functions are security assurance.

The term security is widely used not only in computer technology but in daily computer operation. In our context, security means the following part:

- Security from vulnerabilities: These reside in the platform software and can be fixed by frequent application to patches provided by software creators. This is a operational problem and not an essential one in technology.
- Security from network attacks: The security attack frequently happens in the network environment. The purpose of cracker is to steal information from servers or personal computers. Though our system will not have financially important information or personal data, the scientific results and their derivatives are still very important for us. Therefore the data should be protected from these attacks.
- Security from internal users: Many security incidents are induced by the employees or members who belong to same group or share same security clearance. These internal security threat is the most difficult problem as these are sometimes provoked by poor security settings (such as insufficient user access mode settings, neglect of system management) or mistake operation (human errors).

The third problem is the most crucial threat for data sharing platform, as system users usually do not care about this. In scientific data sharing platform, it can be happen that some data should not be opened to other individuals or group members. Also, even the data should be opened to all members in shared platform, some data should not be opened until some days, such as release data of the journal. The security system used in scientific research platform should have capability to handle these requirements specific in scientific purposes. Also, the system should be capable to protect from other security issues.

Here we propose our prototype data sharing and research platform, WISE-CAPS (Web-based Integrated Secure Environment for Collaborative Analysis for Planetary Science). Our system has flexible and robust security enhancements so that researchers can put their analyzed data without worrying seeing (and copying, altering) from unauthorized or unpermitted members or groups in the same system.

In the meantime, users can share any data with users who she or he admitted. This scheme promotes online data sharing and discussion based on the data, and ideal for group works for writing research papers and building theories. Using our system, users can use this system as "virtual laboratory" in the network. Users do not need to gather in one place frequently to discuss, bringing with large amount of data with risk of divulgation.

2 System Design

Here we show the basic system design and requirement of WISE-CAPS.

2.1 Open-Source Based System

All platform software, including operating system and key software, are open-source based. This enables us to use cutting-edge technology provided by developing communities. Also, as the all sources and derived system application software is also open-source based, the developers can link and combine any function in their system using mash-up scheme or API-based coalition [3].

2.2 Limitation of Access Method to Servers

Multiple data path to servers (download and upload) makes system more vulnerable as system administrator must prepare corresponding server software. For example, upload method by FTP, while still widely used worldwide, is less secure in the viewpoint of security as the protocol communicates with server software with unencrypted password in the packets. Even using Secure Shell (ssh), system administrators should prepare the sudden security updates of ancillary software upon discoveries of vulnerabilities. These labors make system administrators' load more.

By confining users' access method to HTTP protocol only, we can assure more protected system security and simplification of access method. Even data upload can be made from dedicated web pages and users do not need to prepare special software to upload. Also users only need to prepare web browsers to see and download data.

2.3 Security Awareness

As noted in the Introduction section, the security enhancement is the key element of the WISE-CAPS.

2.4 Capability of Large Data Handling

Current lunar and planetary exploration are producing large amount of data. For example, Japanese lunar explorer "Kaguya" produced approximately 20 terabytes as a published data. America's Mars Reconnaissance Orbiter communicates with the Earth with 3 to 4 Mbps and approximately seventy terabytes of data will be obtained [4]. It is virtually impossible for researchers to keep all these data in their desktop or local storage, as the data will increase during their analysis phase. And these data should not kept only in the researchers' individual storage but shared in the same server storage to discuss about their ongoing analysis.

This means the system should be capable of handling large amount of data. High-speed network systems and powerful processors are mandatory. The system also should keep quick turn-around time for every data processing even for the large amount of data. Users will not want to use the system if the system response is too slow. For example, Map-a-Planet system has a map zooming capabilities, however, the page reloading is required in every time we change the map focus and zoom changes. This makes less usability for the system.

The WISE-CAPS system has broad network connection and powerful processors with large amount of storage. Furthermore, the system uses most current web technology to increase usability and system response.

3 The System

3.1 Hardware

The WISE-CAPS system consists of two servers, one for web servers and one for database servers. These two servers have same configuration and specification. These servers (Fujitsu Primagy RX2000) have Intel Xeon 5130 single CPU, 8GB in memory and 73 GB RAID-1 type disk array [5].

These two servers are connected to an external storage (Fujitsu ETERNUS 2000) , approximately 12 TB in total capacity. This storage has 48 disks with single 750 GB SATA connection inside and they are configured as RAID-5 system. Due to the file system capacity limitation of ext3, the disk is divided into approximately 6TB and 6TB to be attached in each server. The individual partition is connected using 4Gbps optical fibrechannel to each server.

Fig. 1. The WISE-CAPS servers (two servers in the center of the rack) and an attached storage (the bottom of the rack)

These servers are directly connected with Japan Gigabit Network (JGNIIPlus), gigabit connection network of Japan, via a router. Currently, the maximum speed to the external connection is confined to 100Mbps because of the router specification.

The WISE-CAPS servers and an attached storage are installed with a half-height 19-inch system rack at the Information Center at The University of Aizu, Fig. 1 shows the server installation.

3.2 Software

As noted in the section 2, all software used in servers are open-source based. Base system is Red Hat Enterprise Linux (RHEL) version 4, with unnecessary software uninstalled. The RHEL 4 is widely used system platform and it ensures stable system operation and immediate security response.

In the web server, Apache 2.0, the most prevailed web server in the world, is used. The most current version of 2.0 branch is used due to affinity of the security module, which will describe later.

To enable map drawing in Web-GIS system, the MapServer [6], open-source based map drawing application, are installed. The MapServer act as a CGI (Common Gateway Interface) program on the web server to draw the map according to the parameter assigned from the map configuration file, or "Mapfile". This scheme enables us to make flexible mapping and easy settings of map drawing.

MapServer supports wide variety of image formats such as TIFF (GeoTIFF), PNG, JPEG as well as proprietary GIS software image formats. This feature is useful for web mapping ofdata produced by proprietary image processing software.

MapServer has built-in support of WMS (Web Mapping Server) function which complies with the OGC (Open Geospatial Consortium) standard data transfer protocol [7]. Therefore, coalition with other OGC-compliant servers can be enabled by operating MapServer with WMS mode.

OpenLayers [8], an open-source implementation of JavaScript files, are used upon map drawing. It has built-in Ajax support so that web page creators can write Ajax-capable pages with few lines of JavaScript. The Ajax technology enables quick display redrawing in the browsers without re-loading pages upon re-zooming and moving of map focus.

Also, as OpenLayers' programming scheme is generally object-oriented, the adding and removing of objects can be realized easily. For example, adding a layer object variables of JavaScript means adding a layer in the map. Once users create objects, their behaviors can be changed by modifying parameters in objects.

Upon using OpenLayers, users only need several lines of JavaScript codes to write. By setting several parameters and writing JavaScript codes of objects (layers) creation, users can realize multi-layer mapping in the web browser.

4 Mapping Data

We are currently using lunar data obtained by Clementine as a base layer for mapping. And adding layers on Kaguya data are in progress. Clementine was a lunar explorer of America launched in 1994 [9], and obtained global digital lunar images for the first time in the world.

Our data is based on UVVIS (UV and Visible ray camera) data of 750 nm wavelength, processed and distributed by USGS (US Geological Survey) [9]. The data is freely downloadable and arranged for immediate use as a GIS layer.

Upon the Clementine base layer, we mapped some images obtaind by Kaguya mission. Currently, two crater regions, Jackson and Yamamoto, are mapped in our system. Figure 2 shows the mapping of Jackson crater using Kaguya TC (Terrain Camera) images, DTM (Digital Terrain Model) derived from TC data and a ratio image created by data obtained by MI (Multi-band Imager).

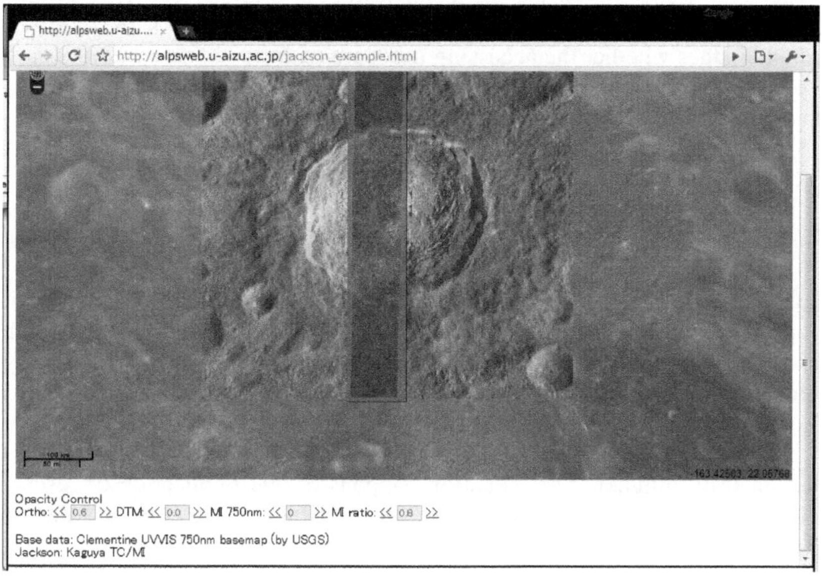

Fig. 2. Webpage snapshot of WISE-CAPS system displaying multiple images near Jackson crater on the moon. The base image is Clementine UVVIS image data, and the sharper image is Kaguya TC image. The red and blue strip is the ratio image created from Kaguya MI data. As the opacity of individual images can be changed in the control window below the map, users can display multi-layered images in WISE-CAPS.

However, MapServer currently do not support any lunar and planetary coordinate. Moreover, we have no lunar standard coordinate system for the projection of maps currently. Therefore, we used mapping by using terrestrial coordinate system instead of lunar coordinate.

5 Security Integration

5.1 Policy of Security Control

As noted in Introduction section, the concept of security has variety of meanings in current networked environment. In WISE-CAPS system, we focused security control for the following three parts:

- Security at the local computer system.
- Security at the data transmission through the network (the Internet).
- Security for the server protection.

The secure HTTP protocol (HTTPS) are widely used to maintain data transmission security through the Internet. However, HTTPS protocol only protects the content of transmission by encrypting, and it does not guarantee the identification of origination and destination. We cannot evaluate whether correct user is coming to our system by their originating addresses and names as they are sometimes falsified.

The general measure to ensure the identification of origination is to use digital certificate storing in users' computer. The server program checks the certificate as needed and judges whether the accessing users are real.

Also, these digital certificates need to be revoked regularly to maintain latest security information, however, the frequent change and re-installation of certificates makes both users and administrators involved in laboring works. The identification mechanism which can use easily for even non-expert people such as scientists is necessary.

Additionally, the digital certificate system is not common particularly in Japan. This fact means that users (researchers) must create their digital certificates from scratch, and few user-friendly tools are prepared.

One more requirement for identification system in WISE-CAPS is the flexible grouping. It happens often that researchers share their data and documents with their collaborators upon writing papers and discussing their result in the laboratory. The same function should be implemented in our virtual laboratory. In this mechanism, one user which another user allowed to access his/her resources can share, see or, in some cases, modify them. In other cases, users can publish the data after a date which is determined by him/her. This situation happens on the publication of research papers. The security mechanism that allows the flexible change of users' demand are also required.

5.2 GridSite Security Module

To solve these problems and satisfy with the above security requirements, we adopted the security module for Apache, called "GridSite" [10] for security enhancement of the WISE-CAPS.

GridSite is a security module developed for Apache web server, developing mainly or security improvement in computer grid environment. However, its security capability can be used also for our environment.

GridSite module uses its own access control file, GACL (Grid Access Control List), variant of XML. It controls access to resource (mainly users' file) upon the description in GACL. Users can put GACL files on the directory, like .htaccess file used for access control used in Apache, to manage access to the files in the directory. The grammar of GACL is so simple with inheritance of XML format that users can write the file easily.

Upon security checking, users' certificate files are sent to the server enhanced with a GridSite module to check validity to access to each resource. The certificates are transmitted via HTTPS protocol.

By setting specific data sharing group, Virtual Organization (VO), the users belonging to same VO can share the same information such as files and directories. This function enables users to share with other users who want to work with the same subject. This scheme is similar to SIG (Specially Interest Group) in the Internet, but different in the point that users' verification is made automatically using their certificates.

However, it is not so common for users, particularly Japanese users, to have their own certificate in their computer. Therefore, our system uses proxy server, OGC Proxy, to issue the certificate based on the ID and password which are registered in the proxy server in advance.

Users who want to access to the server protected by GridSite access first to the OGC Proxy server using their ID and password. Once authentication is successful, the proxy server issues the certificate and sends it to the destination server. Once the authentication is successful, user can access to the destination server, with continuing logging in to the proxy server. The destination server inspects the certificate created by OGC Proxy and determines whether the user can access to the specific resource. Through these processes, no transaction of ID and password between the destination server and users are necessary. The schematic procedure are shown in Figure 3.

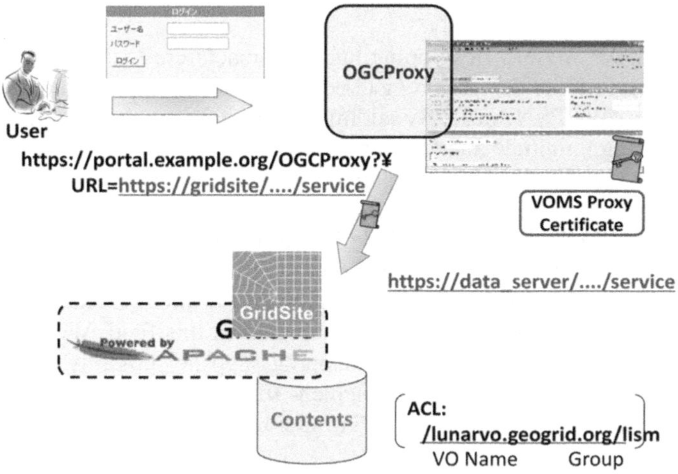

Fig. 3. Schematic concept of GridSite authentication and OGC Proxy

6 Current Implementation Issues

The Virtual Organization should be defined in its own server, however, the server is currently outside the WISE-CAPS system. As current group is only one, this is not becoming a major problem. However, it will need our own VO server as the number of group and users increase.

The WISE-CAPS system carefully implements security features, however, current GACL scheme is not effective for local access. This problem is currently safe for our system as the system confines direct access to the server except HTTP/HTTPS access. However, we cannot assure that the administrator(s) make a malicious access to the server using other protocol such as SSH. Also, if the server is attacked and hijacked using SSH or other controllable protocol, the server is under the external threat of leaking information and security violation. To protect from such threat, the establishment of conventional security measures such as port closing and IP-address based access control are necessary.

As a general and fundamental concept, the authentication by ID and password is weaker in security viewpoint than ones used with the individually issued digital certificate. Our system can use directory their own certificate, without using OGC Proxy server, however, the configuration of our system is result of trade-off between usability and security. The combination of ID-and-password based security and certificates is the current best solution to realize the flexible and robust security system according our operation experience. However, other authentication methods should be incorporated into our system in future advancement of security enhancement requirements.

7 Future Prospective

As our system is open-source based and has flexible implementation, the linkage with other system can be realized easily.

For example, we are now developing lunar nomenclature search system [11] which can query from all lunar features registered in IAU Planetary System Nomenclature Working Group (WGPSN) [12]. By adding an interface to show the portion of web page display using longitude and latitude of target object, users can see the map of the feature with the search result. This implementation is currently in progress.

There are many possibilities to link the WISE-CAPS with the external system. One possibility is the usage of KML (Keyhole Markup Language) as a glue language. The KML is XML-based language which is commonly used to describe geospatial information. As the popular application such as Google Earth can handle KML to control its behavior, the KML is now the de facto standard in this field. We are now investigating how to output KML in specific mapping snapshot possibly by using internal function in OpenLayers. If we can implement this function, our map can be linked with other applications such as Google Earth and NASA WorldWind which can handle KML.

As this system aims for scientists' collaboration platform, the validation of usability is also required. Currently, the targeted scientific subject are:

- Geoscience: Any data which can be described as maps are able to put into our platform. The most typical type of science is geosciences, which is closely related with the distribution of minerals and elements. For example, the webpage snapshot shown in Figure 2 includes the ratio image, the composite image between bands to enhance the difference of spectroscopic absorption of characteristic minerals. By substituting band ratio to three primary colors (RGB), we can enhance the difference of spectroscopy. In most cases, the occurrence of material is closely related with the topographic features, the comparison with material distribution and topography will combine the origin of the material and topography, hence the history of geology in the target area.
- Topography: GIS can express the topography viscerally, in any form like image-based maps and contour drawings. These data can be shown in conjunction with

geosciences data which has been described above. Topography data can be used for large variety of scientific research such as clarification of geologic history and terrain formation. These scientific elements will lead to larger questions such as origin of the region, and consequently origin of the moon.

On the other hand, WISE-CAPS has no function to display subsurface and aerial location data now. This fact does not mean the system cannot map these data, but the ability of expression is severely restricted as all data should be express as one plain layer or several units of layers. This is also a limit of current GIS that cannot handle continuously variable quantities in the vertical direction. The development of system that enables the expression of three dimensional distributions of quantities as a form of GIS will be a future topic, and we think our most current task is to enhance currently available functions of WISE-CAPS.

8 Conclusion

We have developed Web-GIS based lunar and planetary collaboration environment which can share the data among the users under the control using Apache module. The system has flexible and robust security features and it is ideal for research purpose for planetary science. System is open-source based and open standard compliant, and thus the any system which supports such standards can be collaborated with our system.

The security implementation is ACL (Access Control List) basis, and this enables flexible control of security. Also, the proxy server which can interpret ID and password into digital certificate can reduce users' labor to prepare it.

The system is under intensive development and new features are adding. We will continue to improve this system into the network-based collaboration platform to add more functions and linkage with external system.

References

1. USGS Map-A-Planet, `http://www.map-a-planet.org/`
2. Marsoweb website, `http://marsoweb.nas.nasa.gov/`
3. Terazono, J., Asada, N., Demura, H., Hirata, N., Saiki, K., Iwasaki, A., Oka, R., Hayashi, T., Suzuki, T., Miyamoto, H.: Web-GIS based Collaboration Environment Using Scientific Data of the Moon. In: Proceedings of the XXI Congress of the International Society for Photogrammetry and Remote Sensing (2008)
4. Chin, G., Brylow, S., Foote, M., Garvin, J., Kasper, J., Keller, J., Litvak, M., Mitrofanov, I., Paige, D., Raney, K., Robinson, M., Sanin, A., Smith, D., Spence, H., Spudis, P., Stern, S.A., Zuber, M.: Lunar Reconnaissance Orbiter Overview: The Instrument Suite and Mission. Space Science Reviews 129(4), 391–419 (2007)
5. Terazono, J., Sobue, S., Okumura, S., Asada, N., Demura, H., Hirata, N., Fujita, T., Yamamoto, A.: Web-GIS based collaboration environment and remote GIS application experiment using lunar exploration data. In: Proceedings of the International Symposium on GeoInformatics for Spatial-Infrastructure Development in Earth and Allied Science, pp. 239–244 (2008)
6. MapServer website, `http://www.mapserver.org/`

7. Open Geospatial Consortium, http://www.opengeospatial.org/
8. OpenLayers website, http://www.openlayers.org/
9. Nozette, S., Rustan, P., Pleasance, L.P., Kordas, J.F., Lewis, I.T., Park, H.S., Priest, R.E., Horan, D.M., Regeon, P., Lichtenberg, C.L., Shoemaker, E.M., Eliason, E.M., McEwen, A.S., Robinson, M.S., Spudis, P.D., Acton, C.H., Buratti, B.J., Duxbury, T.C., Baker, D.N., Jakosky, B.M., Blamont, J.E., Corson, M.P., Resnick, J.H., Rollins, C.J., Davies, M.E., Lucey, P.G., Malaret, E., Massie, M.A., Pieters, C.M., Reissse, R.A., Simpson, R.A., Smith, D.E., Sorenson, T.C., Vorder Breugge, R.W., Zuber, M.T.: The Clementine Mission to the Moon: Scientific Overview. Science 266(5192), 1835–1839 (1994)
10. Clementine Basemap Mosaic Version 2, http://webgis.wr.usgs.gov/pigwad/down/moon_warp_clementine_750nm_basemap.htm
11. Gridsite website, http://www.gridsite.org/
12. Terazono, J., Bhalla, S., Izumta, T., Asada, N., Demura, H., Hirata, N.: Construction of Lunar Nomenclature Search System. In: The 26th International Symposium on Space Technology and Science (2008)
13. Gazetter of Planetary Nomenclature, http://planetarynames.wr.usgs.gov/

Towards Large-Scale Scientific Dataspaces for e-Science Applications

Ibrahim Elsayed and Peter Brezany

University of Vienna, Department of Scientific Computing
Nordbergstrasse 15/C/3, A-1090 Vienna, Austria
{elsayed,brezany}@par.univie.ac.at
http://www.par.univie.ac.at/

Abstract. This work intends to provide a large-scale scientific data management solution based on the concepts of dataspaces for e-Science applications. Our approach is to semantically enrich the existing relationship among primary and derived data items, and to preserve both relationships and data together within a dataspace to be reused by owners and others. To enable reuse, data must be well preserved. Preservation of scientific data can best be established if the full life cycle of data is addressed. This is challenged by the e-Science life cycle ontology, whose major goal is to trace semantics about procedures in scientific experiments. jSpace, a first prototype of a scientific dataspace support platform is implemented and deployed to an early core of adopters in the breath gas research domain from which specific use cases are derived. In this paper we describe the architecture, discuss a specific prototype implementation and outline the design concepts of a second prototype.

Keywords: Scientific Dataspace, Scientific Data Management, e-Science.

1 Introduction

Dataspaces are not a data integration approach, rather they are a data coexistence approach [1]. The goal is to rise the abstraction level at which data is managed. Dataspaces consist of participants and relationships. Participants can be any data element and relationships should be able to model any interconnection among these participants. Dataspace support platforms (DSSPs) represent the collection of software pieces and services that control the organization, storage and retrieval of data in a dataspace. The challenges of dataspaces discussed in [2] have influenced many research groups of the data management community. However, most effort was put on the mainstream related dataspace research [3,4,5] or on development of personal dataspace systems [6,7].

A major challenge faced by the scientific data management community is to efficiently organize data products used in and generated by scientific experiments of diverse e-Science applications. The challenge to derivate history of a data product is known as data provenance [8]. In contrast to the mainstream related dataspace research scientific dataspaces can be seen as an umbrella to those

M. Yoshikawa et al. (Eds.): DASFAA 2010, LNCS 6193, pp. 69–80, 2010.

research challenges with the goal to establish a distributed large-scale scientific repository where the full life cycle of scientific data is well preserved. In our previous work we have addressed a scientific dataspace paradigm [9] aiming at semi-autonomous creation of semantically rich relationships among data sets used in scientific studies and further, at preserving both, relationships and their corresponding data sets within a distributed space of data.

Breath gas analysis in medicine [10], an emerging new scientific field with a growing international scientific community, represents our driving life science application from which we derive specific dataspace use cases [11]. Breath gas researcher are addressing many different breath gas studies in terms of investigating and screening for hundreds of compounds in exhaled breath gas. Such studies include several experiments. There is a need to provide structured representations of scientific experiments for the breath gas analysis domain. It is hardly possible for a breath gas researcher to re-run an experiment that was conducted at a different research lab from his own, far less to understand its semantics. Both formal research works in publications and also scientific data used in or produced by corresponding experiments should be interlinked with semantics. The e-Science life cycle ontology [12] addresses the precise description of scientific experiments by taking advantage of well-defined semantics of the Resource Description Framework (RDF) [13] and the expressive formal logic-based OWL language [14]. Experiments described by the ontology are referred to as *Life Cycle Resources* (LCRs). A LCR in fact represents the semantic relationship among dataspace participants. We differentiate three kinds of participants (a) data sources being accessed for investigation (primary data), (b) its corresponding findings (derived data), and (c) the set of activities defining concrete preprocessing and analysis methods (background data). Instances of those kinds of data sets are interconnected by LCRs within the scientific dataspace.

In this paper we discuss the implementation of *jSpace*, which is our first experimental prototype of a scientific dataspace system based on semantic web technologies. It represents a further development of the dataspace paradigm introduced in [1], in particular it implements the scientific dataspace framework proposed in [9]. jSpace is an important key-point for collaboration of members of the breath gas analysis research community. After a brief review of related work in dataspace research in the next section we describe the architecture of the scientific dataspace support platform by breaking the system into its major tools in Section 3. That followed, we present the implementation status of jSpace version 1.0 in Section 4 and discuss it in Section 5. Finally, we conclude the paper and outline our next steps, which are towards developing the *semantic grid-enabled* version of jSpace in Section 6.

2 Related Systems

The concept of dataspaces introduced by Franklin et al. [1] gave rise to new data management challenges. Much dataspace research is applied in terms of personal information management. For example Yukun et al. describe in [7] a personal dataspace management system, named OrientSpace, which implements data integration and data query functions. They introduce the CoreSpace framework, which represents a subspace of the personal dataspace containing only objects that are frequently accessed by the owner. The data model used is based on the vertical data model, which takes a vector to describe attributes of an object.

iMeMex [6] provides data management functionalities, such as querying, updating, performing backup and recovery operations. All data is presented using a single graph data model and queried using an own query language, called the iMeMex Query Language (iQL) [15]. Special converters convert the contents of data sources into the internal graph structure. Core idea of iMeMex is a logical layer called Resource View Layer that abstracts from underlying subsystems and data sources. A Data Source Proxy connects to the data sources and provides plugins for file systems, IMAP email servers and RSS feeds, which shows that iMeMex is designed for personal information management, however not limited to it. Another personal dataspace management approach is proposed by Lei et al. in [16]. It introduces the Galaxy data model, which is an extension of the iMeMex data model in order to better consider security issues, primarily access policies.

Also the initiators of dataspaces proposed solutions to major dataspace research challenges like indexing dataspaces [3] and pay-as-you-go data integration approaches for dataspace systems [4,5]. This relates to the mainstream dataspace research. However, so far to our best knowledge no effort was put on applying dataspace concepts to e-Science applications in order to establish a large-scale scientific repository, that preserves scientific studies in conjunction with all its interconnected scientific data sets.

3 jSpace Architecture

In this Section we provide a summary of the architecture of jSpace. Main entities of the architecture (Figure 1) are the *Life Cycle Composer* - for creation of LCRs, the *RDF Store* - for storing those resources, the scientific dataspace itself - for storing participating data sets, the *Dataspace Indexer* - for their subscription, the *Search&Query Processor* allowing scientists to find those LCRs, and the *Dataspace Browser* for exploration of the dataspace. These, with each other cooperating software programs represent the environment in which the scientific dataspace is able to grow and evolve into a remarkable space of well preserved scientific data. They also provide the organization and retrieval of scientific data including their well defined semantics within the dataspace.

3.1 e-Science Life Cycle Composer

The aim of the e-Science life cycle composer is to provide a simple interface to the acting scientists to describe their experiments according to predefined attributes given by a scientific community. It can be seen as the feeding interface to the scientific dataspace. It is an easy but efficient way to capture semantically rich information about dataspace participants and relationships. It guides the

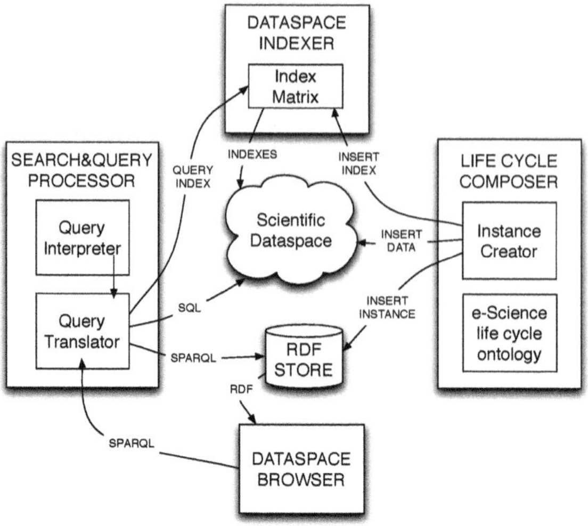

Fig. 1. Overview of the system architecture

user through the five e-Science life cycle activities, creates new individuals, and attaches them to a new LCR. It communicates with the *Dataspace Indexer*, which indexes new individuals. The indexing mechanism and its purpose are described in Section 3.4. Based on guidelines defined by responsible persons of the e-Science application domain to whom the dataspace is deployed, the scientist fills out a number of mandatory fields during experiment execution. Also references to data sets being used in the experiment are recorded. The information entered is used to create individuals of classes defined by the e-Science life cycle ontology. These individuals, consolidated within a LCR describe on a semantically high level a scientific experiment. The resulting RDF graph represents a LCR. It is saved within the RDF store.

3.2 RDF Store

The RDF store manages LCRs persistently. The SPARQL query language [17], which has been accepted as a W3C recommendation for querying RDF resources is used to query LCRs. There might be many dataspace instances set up at multiple research centers, which work together in terms of collaborative science. In such a very common scenario each center will host their own RDF store for storing their LCRs, which results in a distributed RDF data environment. There are two main approaches to handle the problem with multiple RDF stores.

Approach 1 - Global centralized RDF Store. This data warehouse alike approach provides a global centralized RDF store that organizes LCRs on a multi-institutional level. Local stores should guarantee high performance for the people working on the local site. Scientific experiments being conducted at any research lab that participates in a dataspace environment are stored in local stores as long as access should be limited to researchers of the local organization. Once researchers want to share their experiments with other external collaborators or make them public to the scientific community, its corresponding LCRs will be stored in a central global store, which is shared with other dataspace instances.

Approach 2 - Distributed RDF Storage. This solution requires a middleware that supports federated SPARQL query processing. Currently, concepts from traditional approaches of federated query processing systems are adapted to provide integrated access to RDF data sources. Basic idea is to query a mediator, which distributes subqueries to local RDF stores and integrates the results. The DARQ engine [18] is an extension of the Jena-embedded query engine ARQ to support federated SPARQL queries. Very similar to the DARQ approach the SemWIQ [19] system contains contains a mediator service that distributes the execution of SPARQL queries. DAI-RDF [20] is a service-based RDF database middleware suite which extends the OGSA-DAI middleware to support RDF data processing activities including SPARQL query language, ontological primitives, and reasoning functions. Since DAI-RDF is based on service-based grid architecture, it is most promising to realize large-scale distributed scientific dataspaces.

Both approaches are feasible with the architecture. There might be use case scenarios and application domains where one approach fits better due to scale of the dataspace infrastructure or legal issues of participating institutions, etc. Also, a hybrid approach is plausible, for instance, when multiple already deployed dataspaces of homogenous application domains will be merged into a large scale dataspace infrastructure. We discuss such a scenario in Section 5.

3.3 Scientific Dataspace

While dataspace relationships are stored in the RDF store, the dataspace participants are organized in multiple heterogeneous databases that might be geographically distributed. In jSpace a participant represents a data set that either is the input data to a scientific experiment, or the analytical method being used within an experiment, or it is a dataset that has emerged during execution of an experiment. We therefore classify three types of participants: (a) primary data participants - the input data set, (b) background data participants i.e. an analytical method (web service, MATLAB script, etc.), and (c) derived data participants - emerged data sets i.e. histograms. The decision what DBMS to select for storing those different types of dataspace participants depends on the schemas of the corresponding data sets, to be used by the scientific community, to whom the dataspace is deployed. The OGSA-DAI [21] middleware is being used as common interface for all dataspace participants. Thus relational, XML, and file based resources can be organized as dataspace participants.

Dataspace participants are interconnected by relationships, which provide semantic information about the participant and the LCR they are connected to. Meta data of participants is organized by the OWL class *metaData* of the e-Science life cycle ontology. It allows the scientist to describe data sets according to user-defined attributes. An instance of the class *metaData* has the form of

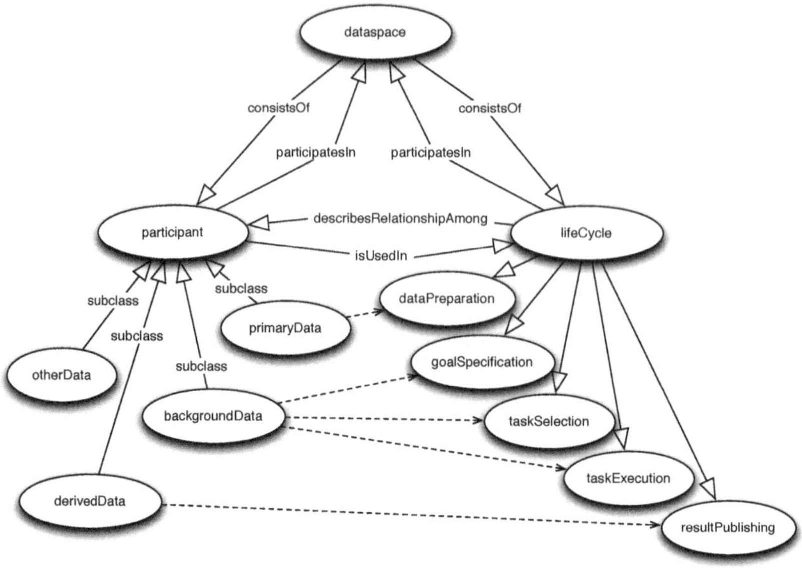

Fig. 2. Scientific dataspace modeled in the e-Science Life Cycle ontology

a triple `<instanceID, attribute, value>`. In Figure 2 we illustrate the main OWL classes and properties defined in the e-Science life cycle ontology showing how the scientific dataspace is modeled. It shows that the class *dataspace* consists of a class *participant* and a class named *lifeCycle*, which in fact represents relationships among participants. Instances of the lifeCycle class model how data sets (primary, background, or derived participants) were used in a specific experiment.

3.4 Dataspace Indexer

The purpose of the Dataspace Indexer is to organize LCRs, including their subscription. It implements a storage and indexing mechanism that allows to quickly evaluate the state of the dataspace in terms of calculating specific measures such as (total number of unique LCRs, number of reran LCRs, etc). Also questions like - *What activity was re-used most?* - can simply be answered without the need to access any RDF store. The examination of dataspace measures allows to monitor system usage and thus helps improving the system. The LCR indexes are organized in a flat table. Each row in the table represents a LCR key, which identifies the index of the resource itself and the indexes of all its participating individuals of the e-Science life cycle activities.

3.5 Search and Query Processor

Searching and querying a dataspace in general is not like querying a database. In a dataspace we need to drift away from the one-shot query to query-by-navigation.

Users will have to pose several queries, which results in an *Information Gathering Task* (IGT). IGT was introduced by Halevy et al. in [2] as one of the major principles of a dataspace system. In jSpace this task is implemented as a multi-level process where different types of queries can be submitted. In level 1 the RDF-Store, which organizes individuals of the e-Science life cycle ontology, is queried using SPARQL queries. The information a scientist is gathering in this first level represent semantics about applied scientific experiments, like what were the research goals, what data set was used, what analytical methods, etc. It will lead the scientist to those LCRs he might be interested in and to those that are interconnected to them. In the second level data items that are used within previously identified LCRs can be retrieved, by submitting queries to data sources that are participating the dataspace. Such data sets are for example the input data set used, or the data set derived from selected scientific experiments. In order to apply such kind of deeper searching and querying more sophisticated queries are submitted to the scientific dataspace, in particular to the corresponding DBMS that participates in the dataspace. Such level-2 queries can be in any other query language that is supported by the underlying data source.

Dataspace relationships and participants are precisely described by individuals of the e-Science life cycle ontology, therefore organized as RDF resources. The *Search&Query Processor* consists of a *Query Interpreter* and a *Query Translator*. The query interpreter receives a request, which can be expressed either as a SPARQL-Query or as keyword based search string or in any query language format that is supported by the underlying participants of the dataspace. For level-1 queries, the request is forwarded to the *Query Translator*, who generates a SPARQL query (if not yet already expressed in SPARQL) search string. This SPARQL query is then submitted to the RDF store. Level-2 queries are directly submitted to the OGSA-DAI client of the dataspace participant.

3.6 Dataspace Browser

The dataspace browser is a tool that allows the user to navigate trough the LCRs available in the dataspace in a visual way. It sends requests to the *Query Processor* in terms of SPARQL queries to be submitted to the RDF store. The response represents RDF data and is used as input for the dataspace browser.

There are a number of tools available that visualize RDF data. Some example projects include Welkin [22], multiple plugin tools for the Protege environment [23], and Semantic Analytics Visualization (SAV) [24]. These tools need to be elaborated and probably an appropriate tool might be adapted or some bits of the tools might be reused. However the jSpace architecture allows to easily attach own tools for browsing the dataspace. The decision what tools to use might depend on the community the dataspace system is deployed for.

4 Implementation Status

A first prototype of jSpace has beed applied to a small research group of a leading breath gas research institute [25], which is acting as an early core of adopters.

Guidelines defining mandatory descriptions for breath gas experiments were elaborated. This first prototype is based on the Jena framework with MySQL databases to provide persistent RDF data storage. We used the persistent ontology model provided in the Jena framework in order to create and store LCRs according to the concepts defined in the e-Science Life Cycle ontology. A dataspace client has a local copy of the ontology, which is used by the *RDF Store Connection Manager* to create a local ontology model. This model is then used to create new individuals and properties according to the ontology. Three MySQL databases for storing primary, background, and derived datasets were set up as OGSA-DAI resources, to be accessible on a service-based grid architecture.

The e-Science life cycle composer, a tool implemented in Java provides an easy graphical user interface to the breath gas researcher allowing to describe and publish breath gas experiments. It organizes text fields for pre-defined descriptions of breath gas experiments in five tabs according to their activity. For instance the *TaskSelection* activity, shown in the e-Science Life Cycle Composer GUI in Figure 3, requires to fill in a brief textual description and some corresponding keywords and to upload an archive file of the analytical methods being used in the experiment. The acting breath gas research group mainly uses MATLAB for their calculations. A typical background data set therefore is the collection of MATLAB functions used in an experiment compressed as zip archive. Once an experiment has beed finished, it can be published into the scientific dataspace by a single click on the OK button of the GUI. The information entered is used to create a new LCR, which then is saved in the corresponding RDF store. Connection details about local and global RDF Store as well as about corresponding OGSA-DAI resources are stored in a configuration file. A web service that communicates with an OGSA-DAI client stores the uploaded datasets into their corresponding databases.

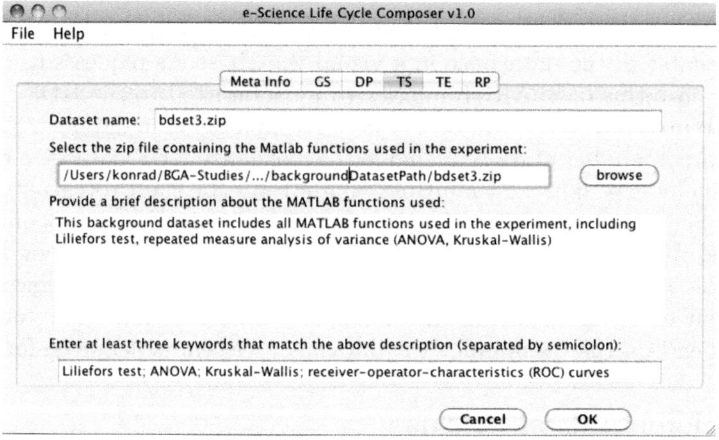

Fig. 3. The e-Science life cycle composer GUI

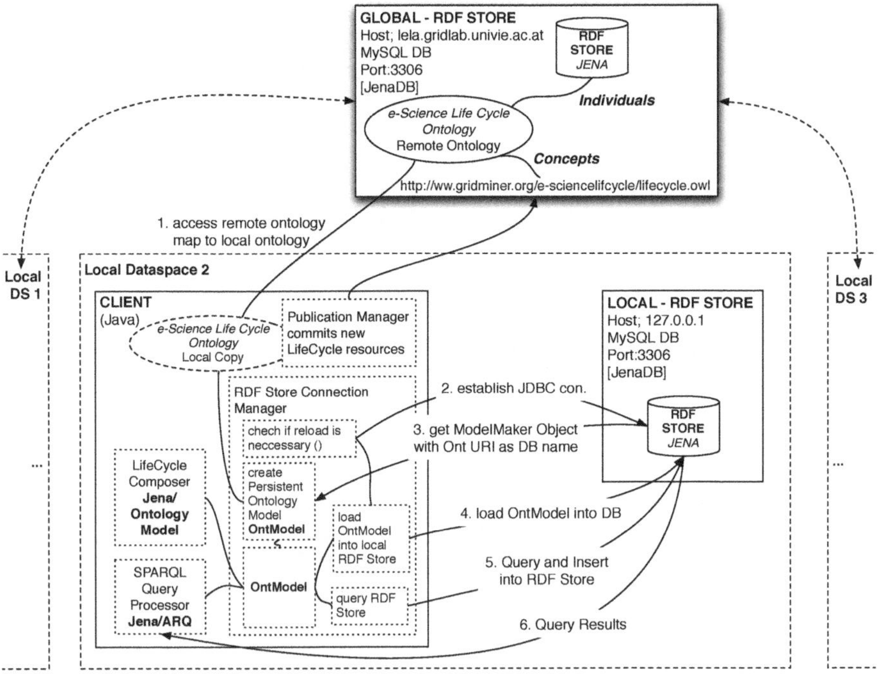

Fig. 4. Local and global RDF Store in a Scientific Dataspace Environment

In the first jSpace version we have chosen the data warehouse alike approach in order to provide efficient access to scientific experiments that were conducted at different research centers. However at the moment we only simulate a second dataspace instance. The *Connection Manager* handles a connection to a global and one to a local RDF store. Figure 4 illustrates one global RDF store, where meta data of breath gas experiments (LCR) that are public to the community is stored. There are three scientific dataspace instances illustrated, each deployed for a specific research group, which might be geographically distributed. Every dataspace instance has their own local RDF store to organize meta data of experiments that should be available only for the local organization. A *Publication/Update Manager* commits new LCRs to the global store. On the dataspace participants layer each dataspace instance deploys at least three databases as OGSA-DAI resources, where data sets used in an experiment are stored. Due to limit of space, this is not illustrated in the figure.

The e-Science life cycle model [9] has been applied as relationship model for the scientific dataspace. Jena SDB Version 1.3.1 with MySQL Version 5.0.67 as underlying RDBMS is used to implement multiple local and one global RDF stores. For the search and query interface we provided Joseki Version 3.4 as HTTP interface. A number of most important queries, such as {*Get me all experiments with VOC 'keyword'*}, and {*Get me all experiments from researcher 'name' where specified goal includes 'keyword'*}, or {*Get me all experiments with*

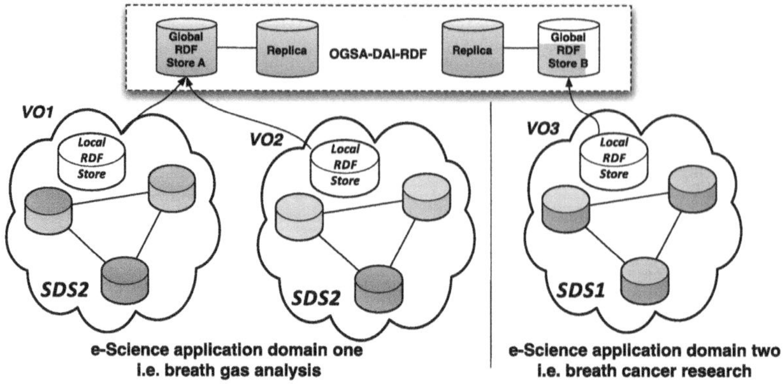

Fig. 5. Large-scale scientific dataspace infrastructure

ANY keyword equals 'keyword' and input dataset 'datasetName' is used} were predefined in SPARQL to enable the breath gas researcher to easy interact with the SPARQL query interface. However, the scientific dataspace is still in an early stage of evolution. It will need some time in order to get a large amount of LCRs including its corresponding dataspace participants into the dataspace.

5 Discussion

Currently, three breath gas research teams from our driving e-Science application produce at an average 48 breath gas experiment in three different studies in a single week. The total size of a LCR of a typical breath gas experiment including its primary, derived, and background data sets amounts to approximately 7 MB. The average number of triples that correspond to a single LCR is 170 with an average size of 150 KB stored in Jena's SDB triple layout. From this we can estimate the total size of the scientific dataspace after six month with a single research lab involved to roughly 8.7 GB with about 8160 triples in the local RDF store (approx. 50K triples in three years). In regard to the Berlin SPARQL benchmark [26], which states that the overall runtime for executing 50 query mixes on a 250K triples Jena SDB test data set is short above one minute, we can be confident that the presented solution provides reasonable performance. Based on this high-level estimation jSpace might need to scale up not before three years of deployment. However having multiple organizations or even various related e-Science application domains involved, it might be much earlier.

Vertical scalability can be achieved by interconnecting multiple dataspace instances, which leads to a large-scale scientific data space infrastructure. Such a scenario is illustrated in Figure 5. In this scenario we assume that each dataspace was already deployed for a specific virtual organization where acting scientist are feeding the dataspace continuously with their regularly running experiments. The global centralized RDF store approach was chosen to support exchange with a second virtual organization of the same domain. Now, as both research domains are related scientific fields, it might be the case that scientists would like to share their knowledge among each other. In order to utilize this arising large-scale dataspace it will be necessary to provide a distributed RDF storage solution on top of global RDF stores. Most promising candidate to realize this is DAI-RDF, since it is based on OGSA-DAI, which we already use for organizing dataspace participants.

We are aware that we rely on active participation of members from the scientific community in order to establish a large scale scientific dataspace for breath gas analysis. Therefore we provide a simple interface that can easily be used by scientists from diverse research domains, especially for non-computer scientists, which was a major requirement from our driving application. However, we suspect that young-researchers (Master and PhD students) will be the major user group of the e-Science life cycle composer, while senior researcher will most likely interact with the system in terms of submitting requests. Once a first release is ready we expect that it enforces building of collaborations among breath gas research institutions as it supports the community in exchanging data and knowledge. This will build the basis for automation-based breath gas analysis.

6 Conclusions and Future Work

This paper presented the architecture of a scientific dataspace paradigm build on top of the e-Science life cycle ontology. A first prototype was developed on top of existing semantic web technology and deployed to a small core of early adopters in a highly relevant life science domain from which specific use cases are derived. It is the bases for development of an intelligent and more powerful second prototype, which will be based on semantic grid technology. One of the most promising technology for distributed SPARQL query processing in a large-scale context, which is a key concern for a wider acceptance of the presented dataspace paradigm seems to be the RDF(S) Realization [27], of the Data Access and Integration Working Group of the Open Grid Forum. However, as our prototype has shown that in order to get semantically rich scientific data from e-Science applications that can be further used we need first to ensure that the experiments being conducted are well preserved. Preservation of scientific data can best be established if the full life cycle of data is addressed [28]. This goal was successfully implemented by the first prototype of jSpace. We see in our future work both, to improve and automatize the preservation process and the upgrade from semantic web to semantic grid technology, which provides more powerful middleware for distributed management of storage systems that expose SPARQL endpoints.

References

1. Franklin, M., Halevy, A., Maier, D.: From databases to dataspaces: A new abstraction for information management. In: SIGMOD (2005)
2. Halevy, A., et al.: Principles of dataspace systems. In: PODS (2006)
3. Dong, X., Halevy, A.: Indexing dataspaces. In: SIGMOD, pp. 43–54 (2007)

4. Jeffery, S.R., Franklin, M.J., Halevy, A.Y.: Pay-as-you-go user feedback for dataspace systems. In: SIGMOD, pp. 847–860 (2008)
5. Das Sarma, A., Dong, X., Halevy, A.: Bootstrapping pay-as-you-go data integration systems. In: SIGMOD, pp. 861–874 (2008)
6. Dittrich, J.P., et al.: Imemex: escapes from the personal information jungle. In: VLDB. VLDB Endowment, pp. 1306–1309 (2005)
7. Li, Y., et al.: Research on personal dataspace management. In: IDAR, pp. 7–12 (2008)
8. Simmhan, Y.L., Plale, B., Gannon, D.: A survey of data provenance in e-science. SIGMOD Rec. 34(3), 31–36 (2005)
9. Elsayed, I., et al.: Intelligent Dataspaces for e-Science. In: CIMMACS, WSEAS, pp. 94–100 (2008)
10. Amann, A., et al.: Applications of breath gas analysis in medicine. International Journal of Mass Spectrometry 239, 227–233 (12 2004/12/15/print)
11. Elsayed, I., et al.: Towards realization of scientific dataspaces for the breath gas analysis research community. In: IWPLS, CEUR, UK (2009)
12. Elsayed, I., et al.: The e-science life cycle ontology (owl documentation) (2008), `http://www.gridminer.org/e-sciencelifecycle/owldoc/`
13. W3C: Resource description framework, RDF (2003), `http://www.w3.org/RDF/`
14. W3C: Web ontology language, OWL (2004), `http://www.w3.org/2004/OWL/`
15. Dittrich, J.P., Salles, M.A.V.: IDM: a unified and versatile data model for personal dataspace management. In: VLDB. VLDB Endowment, pp. 367–378 (2006)
16. Jin, L., Zhang, Y., Ye, X.: An extensible data model with security support for dataspace management. In: HPCC, pp. 556–563 (2008)
17. Prud'hommeaux, E., Seaborne, A.: SPARQL query language for RDF (2008), `http://www.w3.org/TR/rdf-sparql-query/`
18. Quilitz, B., Leser, U.: Querying distributed RDF data sources with SPARQL. In: Bechhofer, S., Hauswirth, M., Hoffmann, J., Koubarakis, M. (eds.) ESWC 2008. LNCS, vol. 5021, pp. 524–538. Springer, Heidelberg (2008)
19. Langegger, A., et al.: A semantic web middleware for virtual data integration on the web. In: Bechhofer, S., Hauswirth, M., Hoffmann, J., Koubarakis, M. (eds.) ESWC 2008. LNCS, vol. 5021, pp. 493–507. Springer, Heidelberg (2008)
20. Kojima, I., et al.: Implementation of a service-based grid middleware for accessing RDF databases. In: Meersman, R., Herrero, P., Dillon, T. (eds.) OTM 2009 Workshops. LNCS, vol. 5872, pp. 866–876. Springer, Heidelberg (2009)
21. Antonioletti, M., et al.: OGSA-DAI 3.0 - the whats and the whys. In: Proceedings of the UK e-Science All Hands Meeting 2007 (September 2007)
22. Mazzocchi, S., et al.: Welkin - a graph-based RDF visualizer (2004), `http://simile.mit.edu/welkin/`
23. Protege: a free, open source ontology editor and knowledge-base framework (2010), `http://protege.stanford.edu/`
24. Deligiannidis, L., et al.: Semantic analytics visualization. In: Mehrotra, S., Zeng, D.D., Chen, H., Thuraisingham, B., Wang, F.-Y. (eds.) ISI 2006. LNCS, vol. 3975, pp. 48–59. Springer, Heidelberg (2006)
25. Amann, A., et al.: Volatile organic compounds research group (2009), `http://www.voc-research.at/`
26. Bizer, C., et al.: The berlin sparql benchmark. Int. J. Semantic Web Inf. Syst. 5(2), 1–24 (2009)
27. Gutiérrez, E., et al.: Accessing RDF(S) data resources in service-based grid infrastructures. Concurr. Comput.: Pract. Exper. 21(8), 1029–1051 (2009)
28. Lynch, C.: Big data: How do your data grow? Nature 455(7209), 28–29 (2008)

Providing Constructed Buildings Information by ASTER Satellite DEM Images and Web Contents

Takashi Takagi[1], Hideyuki Kawashima[2], Toshiyuki Amagasa[2], and Hiroyuki Kitagawa[2]

[1] Graduate School of Systems and Information Engineering, University of Tsukuba, Tennodai 1-1-1, Tsukuba, Ibaraki, 308-8573, Japan
t_takagi@kde.cs.tsukuba.ac.jp

[2] Graduate School of Systems and Information Engineering, University of Tsukuba, and Center for Computational Sciences, Tennodai 1-1-1, Tsukuba, Ibaraki, 308-8573, Japan
{kawasima,amagasa,kitagawa}@cs.tsukuba.ac.jp

Abstract. It has become easy to accumulate and to deliver scientific data by the evolution of computer technologies. The GEO Grid project has collected global satellite images from 2000 to present, and the amount of the collection is about 150 TB. It is required to generate new values by integrating satellite images with heterogeneous information such as Web contents or geographical data. Using GEO Grid satellite images, some researches detect feature changes such as earthquakes, fires and newly constructed building. In this paper, detections of feature changes from time series satellite image are referred to as events, and we focus on events about newly constructed buildings. Usually, there are articles about such newly constructed buildings on the Web. For example, a newly started shopping center is usually introduced in a news report, and a newly constructed apartment is often on the lips of neighboring residents. So, we propose an event detection system that extracts candidate events from satellite images, collects information about them from the Web, and integrates them. This system consists of an event detection module and a Web contents collection module. The event detection module detects geographical regions that have differences with elevation values between two satellite images which are temporally different. The expressions of regions are translated from latitudes/longitudes to building names by using an inverse geocoder. Then, the contents collection module collects Web pages by querying names of buildings to a search engine. The collected pages are re-ranked based on temporal information which is close to event occurrence time. We developed a prototype system. The result of evaluation showed that the system detected some information of building construction events with appropriate web contents in Tsukuba, Japan.

1 Introduction

It has become easy to accumulate and to deliver scientific data by the evolution of computer technologies. The GEO Grid project has collected global satellite

M. Yoshikawa et al. (Eds.): DASFAA 2010, LNCS 6193, pp. 81–92, 2010.

images from 2000 to present, and the amount of the collection is about 150 TB. The original utilization purpose of satellite images is just simply observing the earth. However, satellite images have rich information compared with sensor devices facilitated on the ground. Therefore satellite images can be utilized in a variety of ways over the original purpose. For example, GEO Grid satellite images, some researches detected feature changes including earthquakes, fires and newly constructed buildings [7][10].

This paper focuses on the detection of newly constructed buildings by using satellite images obtained by the ASTER sensing device. It is because earthquakes and fires occur rarely, while building constructions occur frequently. Urban development projects are always running all over the world. Also at Tsukuba city which we live in, large scale shopping centers and apartment buildings have been constructed in these years.

The detection of building constructions can be achieved by using web. When a building is constructed, usually the information is posted to web as a content by press persons or people living around it. Many people can post contents because of user friendly systems are available now such as the twitter, blogs, social networks, wikipedia, etc.

As written above, there are two methods to detect building constructions. Both methods have advantages and disadvantages. The advantage of satellite images is regional completeness. All the constructed buildings can be completely detected by using a satellite image. On the other hand, the disadvantage of satellite images is the lack of content information. Images inform the existence of building constructions, however it does not inform the name of companies, restraints, shops, etc in the buildings. This disadvantage can be overcome by using web contents which include utilization details of the buildings. Therefore, if we can smoothly integrate satellite images and appropriate web contents, then we can provide rich information with newly constructed buildings. This paper presents such a system. To the best of our knowledge, this is the first paper which detect newly constructed buildings by integrating satellite images and web contents.

The system consists of an event detection module and a web contents selection module. The event detection module detects constructed buildings by using satellite images which are temporally different, but regionally the same. For each image, a digital elevation model (DEM) image is generated and then elevation values for each pixel for two images are compared. If the difference of a region is more than the threshold, the system output the region as a constructed building. The web contents selection module receives the region from the event detection module. The region is identified by latitudes/longitudes which is has not contents information. Therefore our system translates latitudes/longitudes to building names by using an inverse geocoder. Then, the names of buildings are queried to a search engine using API. Then, returned contents are re-ranked based on temporal information which is close to event occurrence time.

The rest of this paper is organized as follows. We describe GEO Grid and data used in this research in Section 2. In Section 3, we describe the proposed system. It includes calibration method and efficient event detection algorithm. In Section 4, we describe experimental results. In Section 5, we describe related works. Finally, we conclude this paper and indicate future directions in Section 6.

2 GEO Grid

In this section, we describe GEO Grid and ASTER sensor data archived in GEO Grid. Our research group participates in GEO Grid project. GEO Grid (Global Earth Observation Grid) is a system for archiving and high-speed processing satellite large quantities of satellite observation data by using grid technique. GEO Grid introduce the design concept called VO (Virtual Organization), where necessary data or service is provided depending on a demand from a research community (e.g., disaster prevention, environmental conservation, geological research). Our research group belongs to "BigVO", in which we can get data sensed by MODIS and ASTER.

2.1 MODIS Optical Sensor

MODIS is name of an optical sensor on NASA's earth observation satellite "TERRA/AQUA". MODIS sensor is mounted on both TERRA satellite and AQUA satellite, and the observation cycle is once a day. A spatial resolution of MODIS is $250m$ (band 1-2), $500m$ (band 3-7), $1000m$ (band 8-36) and can observe waveband of 0.4-14μm with 36 channels. From satellite images from MODIS, cloud, radiated energy, aerosol, ground coverage, land use change, vegetation, earth surface temperature, ocean color, snow cover, temperature, humidity, sea ice, etc., can be observed with the use of 36 channels.

2.2 ASTER Optical Sensor

ASTER is one of optical sensors on TERRA satellite, and can sense waveband from visible to thermal infrared. The observation cycle of ASTER is 16 days. ASTER consist of three independent sensors (VNIR, SWIR, TIR).

ASTER Sub-system. VNIR is an optical sensor which can sense reflected light of geosphere from visible to near infrared, and intended to do resource survey, national land survey, vegetation, and environment conservation. SWIR is a multi bands optical sensor which can sense short wavelength infrared region from 1.6μ to 2.43μ, and intended to do resource survey, environment conservation such as vegetation, volcanic action with a rock or mineral distinction. TIR is multi bands optical sensor which can sense thermal infrared radiation on earth surface, and intended to do distinct mineral resource or to observe air, geosphere, or sea surface.

Digital Elevation Model (DEM). ASTER has another near infrared sensor (stereoscopic band) at the 27.6-degree back added, and is able to stereoscope with the just downward sensor which sense same band (band 3). The elevation value can be generated by stereo matching these two images (stereoscopic band

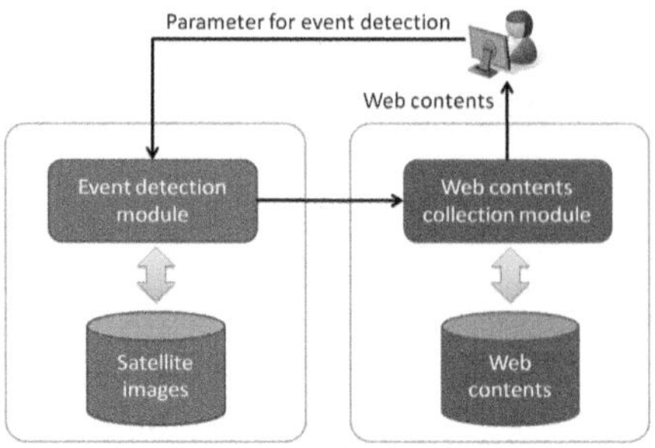

Fig. 1. System overview

and band 3). It is called Digital Elevation Model (DEM) image. A DEM image is used for making three dimensional graphic, geomorphological analysis, and so on. The detection of constructed buildings is performed by using DEM images for the same region.

3 Proposed System

In this section, we propose a constructed buildings information service system. Fig. 1 shows the overview of the proposed system. The proposed system consists of two modules. They are an event detection module and a web contents selection module. In the event detection module, the input is assumed as the amount of change with cubic volume, and the output is assumed as spatial regions. In the web contents selection module, the input is assumed as a spatio-temporal region, and the output is assumed as web contents related to buildings at the region. The rest of this section describes the event detection module and the web contents selection module in detail.

4 Event Detection Module

In this section, we describe the event detection module. This module detects newly constructed buildings from two DEM images, and a building construction is denoted as an event.

Event Model. An events is expressed by a spatio-temporal region and the amount of change with cubic volume. Here we define the word "event" by introducing notations. *time_stamp* denotes event occurrence time. S denotes the region where a building construction is detected. V denotes a grand total of an elevation value change on time section *time_stamp* at S. v_{ij}^{t} denotes a pixel value of position (i, j) on a DEM image at the time. $|v_{ij}^{t_1} - v_{ij}^{t_2}|$ denotes the difference of cubic volume on spatially (i, j) and on temporally (t_1, t_2). An event is defined by a rectangular solid decided uniquely on domain S, volume V and a temporal interval (t_1, t_2).

$$\begin{aligned} event &= (time\_stamp, S, V) \\ time\_stamp &= (t_1, t_2) \\ S &= (x_1, x_2, y_1, y_2) \\ V &= \sum_{i=x_1}^{x_2} \sum_{j=y_1}^{y_2} |v_{ij}^{t_1} - v_{ij}^{t_2}| \end{aligned}$$

Query by User. The input of module is a condition about the amount of change with cubic volume, and a temporal interval (t_1, t_2). The condition is issued by a user. The output of module is a set of spatio-temporal regions $(x_1, x_2, y_1, y_2, t_1, t_2)$ where a condition holds. However, for all regions, (t_1, t_2) are the same since it is specified by a user.

Satellite Images Pair Generation. After receiving a query, the module selects images that satisfy the query condition from all images in the database[1] The selection procedure first filters images by *time_stamp* condition. Therefore images sensed between t_1 and t_2 are obtained. From the obtained images, the module enumerate all the pairs. Therefore if the number of images is n, $nC2$ pairs are generated.

4.1 Calibration of ASTER DEM

For each image of pairs, a DEM image is generated. Unfortunately, a DEM image has vertical/horizontal errors. ASTER DEM has relatively 7.8 meters offset in a vertical direction, 1.18 *px* offsets in a horizontal X direction and 0.67 *px* offset in a horizontal Y direction[5]. Therefore before conducting event detection procedure, the error should be corrected. Here we describe our approach.

Removing Offsets in a Horizontal Direction. At first, we calculate offset in a horizontal direction by a method similar to [5]. For each image for a region, we sum up the differences of the image and base image with elevation values of all the pixels. The base image is common through this calibration procedure, and it was one observed on March 29, 2000. Then, we continually perform the same summing up procedure by moving 1 *px* in horizontal XY direction (latitude longitude direction). Matching cost R_{SAD} is the average of the difference value in a domain overlapping between images, which is expressed in formula. For each image, we choose i and j which minimizes the following R_{SAD}.

$$R_{SAD} = \frac{\sum_{i=0}^{M-1} \sum_{j=0}^{N-1} |PixelDiff(i + offset_i, j + offset_j)|}{s} \tag{1}$$

Where $M \times N$ is the number of pixels in an image. Please note that all the images have the same size. *PixelDiff* is the difference of elevation value with pixels with an image and base one.

1 Although GEO-Grid has images all over the world, our database includes a part of it. The region is limited to only Tsukuba area, Japan. The database is just a collection of image files, and it is not managed by any DBMSs.

Removing Offsets in a Vertical Direction. Vertical offsets is calculated by comparing ASTER DEM with a ground truth dataset. 10 m mesh (altitude) of base map information is published by geographical survey institute, Japan[6]. We used is as a ground truth dataset. In the dataset of ASTER DEM and the ground truth dataset, the average of altitudes with some geographical points are calculated. The selected points are widely known to be flat from 2000 to now in Tsukuba city. For each image, we modified elevation values of all the pixels. For example, assume the average of selected points in the base image $avgH_{base}$ is 100, and one in an image X, $avgH_X$ is 10. Then, for each pixel in X, its elevation value is added 90 so that it fits into the model of base image.

The Result of Removing Offsets. We conducted a calibration experiment. All the data are provided from portal site of GEO Grid with the cooperation of Advanced Industrial Science and Technology. The target region is Tsukuba city, Ibaraki, Japan. In each image, offsets are removed by methods in Section 4.1 and 4.1. In each image after the removing offset, Table 1 shows result that calculated each standard deviation for ten observation points. In Table 1, σ denotes standard deviation in case without offset removal, σ_{XY} denotes the one in case with only horizontal offset removal, σ_Z denotes the one in case with vertical offset removal, and σ_{XYZ} denotes the one in case with both a horizontal and vertical offset removal. Table 1 shows that σ_{XYZ} is better than σ at nine of ten observation points after calibration. Even in the only exception (Football ground in Univ. of Tsukuba), the difference is just only 0.09. Therefore it is considered that our approach succeeded calibration.

Event Detection. The proposed system performs event detection by division algorithm to detect an event efficiently. At first, a difference image is generated from two DEM images each other different time. For detecting events, the whole image is divided into four parts in the top, bottom, right and left. Next, among the domains that are divided, domains where quantity of volume change exceeds threshold are divided into four parts again. The event detection is stopped on

Table 1. Removing Offsets of ASTER DEM

Observation point name	$\sigma(m)$	$\sigma_{XY}(m)$	$\sigma_Z(m)$	$\sigma_{XYZ}(m)$
Baseball ground in Univ. of Tsukuba	3.78	3.76	2.80	2.51
Football ground in Univ. of Tsukuba	3.96	4.33	3.76	4.05
Athletics track field in Univ. of Tsukuba	4.37	4.18	2.76	2.66
Play ground in Univ. of Tsukuba	3.89	4.09	3.37	3.30
Play ground in Doho park	3.95	3.73	2.63	2.34
Baseball ground in Doho park	4.17	4.16	1.99	2.17
Meteorological Research Institute	4.40	4.56	2.73	2.70
Play ground in Azuma junior high school	5.22	4.63	4.05	3.75
Play ground at campus of Kasuga in Univ. of Tsukuba	3.83	3.59	2.78	2.72
Play ground in Azuma junior school	4.07	4.52	3.08	3.18
Average	4.16	4.16	3.00	2.94

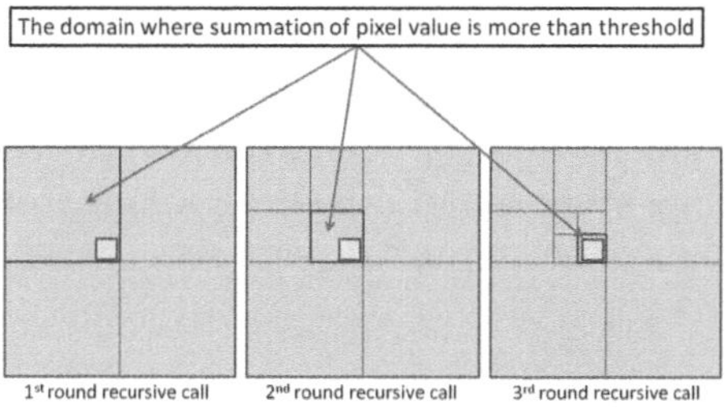

Fig. 2. Method for Detecting an Event

domains where quantity of volume change does not exceed threshold because it is thought that these domains do not include events moreover. Furthermore, domains divided into four parts are performed a threshold processing, and domains where quantity of volume change exceeds threshold are divided again and again. A threshold processing and division processing are repeated recursively in this way, and domains where an area becomes a minimum as an event occurred domain are output. Fig. 2 shows an overview of proposed method for detecting events in this paper.

5 Web Contents Selection Module

Fig. 3 shows the web contents selection module. Events are output by the event detection module, and they are input into a this module. First, the position coordinate of an event is input into an inverse geocoder, and then the name of the geographical object which intersects the position coordinate is output. Second, the name is queried by using the Yahoo! search engine API, and 1000 pages are returned. It should be noted that when only a position name is queried, pages whose position name is same but whose location is different are often returned. To avoid it, each query is expanded so that it is unique by adding the municipality name. The result pages of expanded query is routed to re-ranking module. In this module, representations with time are extracted from pages by

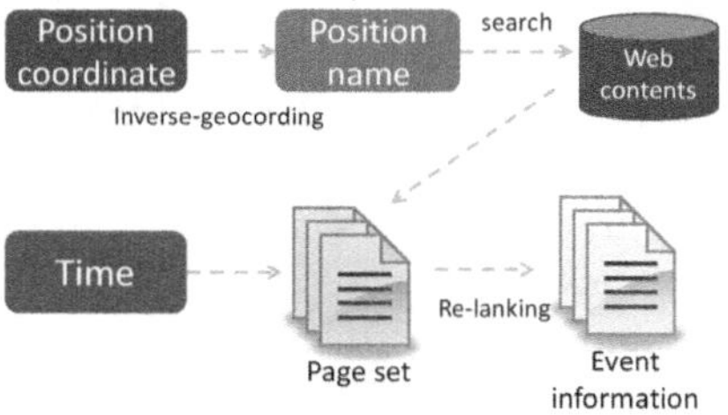

Fig. 3. Web contents collection module

using regular expression. Next, an event occurrence time and a extracted time representation are converted into UNIX TIME, and time lag of the two times is calculated. A ranking score is assumed the minimum value of time lags with event occurrence time among time representations on the page. Calculated for all input pages, this ranking score is performed re-ranking from one having a small score sequentially. Among the re-ranked page sets, pages having high score is output for the system.

6 Evaluation

In this section, we develop the proposal system described in Section 3 and show the evaluated result. Satellite images to use is acquired from portal site of GEO Grid and is images observed by optics sensor ASTER carried in TERRA satellite. The image format is GeoTiff format, and the coordinate system is world coordinate system. The data form of DEM to use in this system is two-dimensional raster type 2 bytes signed integer, and the space resolution is 15m. The programming language for development is C++, and the development environment is as follows.

IDE: Visual Studio2005 CPU: Intel Core2 Quad Q6700 2.66GHz RAM: 3.25GB

6.1 Evaluation of Event Detection Module

Events detected from a the proposal system are mapped onto on Google Maps to evaluate the event detection module and evaluate whether these events accord with events occurred in real world. Fig. 4 shows the result that performed the event detection using images observed at January, 2008 and February, 2009, and the input for the system is volume change $450000m^3$. In fig. 4, the domain surrounded in a red circle is the shopping center started a business in October, 2008. Because this shopping center started a business between the time of difference image generation, it is thought that the construction of the building in the real world is able to be detected. Fig. 5 shows the result that performed the event detection using images observed at November, 2006 and January, 2009, and the input for the system is volume change $225000m^3$. In fig. 5, the three rectangles shown centrally are detected events. In the detected domain, there is a completion planned apartment in the end of January, 2009, and it is thought that the event that occurred in real world is able to be detected because the images used for a calculation for a difference is 2006 and 2009. Fig. 6 shows the result that performed the event detection using images observed at January, 2004 and November, 2006, and the input for the system is volume change $225000m^3$. In fig. 6, the three rectangles shown centrally are detected events, and the shopping center which started a business in March, 2005 was detected. Because this shopping center starts a business between the time of difference image generation, it is thought that the construction of the building in the real world is able to be detected. Fig. 7 shows the result that performed the event detection using images observed at June, 2002 and December, 2004, and the input for the system is volume change $225000m^3$. In fig. 7, though an event does not occur clearly in the time interval on the domain surrounded in a circle, it is detected as an event. We was able to detect some real events, but have detected the domain where an event did not occur clearly as an event according to fig. 7 when the proposal method for a real satellite image is applied. It is thought that a reason is a noise included in a DEM image.

6.2 Evaluation of Web Contents Collection Module

We developed the Web contents collection module, performing an experiment to collect contents about an event detected by satellite images on the WEB. A house map database of Tsukuba-city by ZENRIN Co., Ltd. is used for performing inverse geocoding in this experiment. Input is event object in a domain surrounded in a red circle in fig. 4 in subsection 6.1.

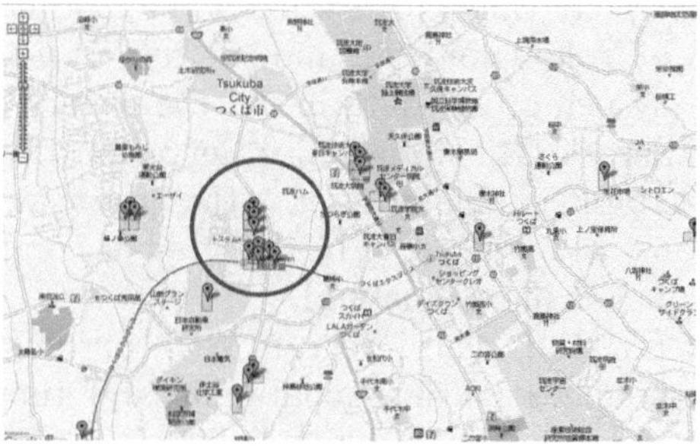

Fig. 4. Event detection result for real data 1

Fig. 5. Event Detection Result for Real Data 2

Evaluation result. Inverse geocoding is performed for an input event object, and so name of shopping center "iias Tsukuba" at Tsukuba-city is output. As a result for collecting contents based on this name and time information on the Web, documents "iias Tsukuba was built newly" are described in top four contents. In addition, precision is 0.4 when the re-ranking is performed though precision is 0.2 when the re-ranking is not performed in Web contents collection module, and so a page about an event was able to be post in the high rank by performing re-ranking.

7 Related Work

As a study of event detection from satellite image, in [3], the method for detecting newly constructed building is proposed, comparing latest GIS data to a high resolving power satellite image for event detection. In this method, the detection of the buildings not included in GIS data is performed based on an edge and vegetation index of the pixel value. [3] evaluates the method for detecting buildings for the city area of Yokohama-city, and the rate of detection is from about 75 to 80%. Detected by using GIS data in [3], the events can be detected only between generation time of GIS data and observation time of satellite image. Generally, GIS data is built manually, so it is thought that generating GIS data takes long time. In contrast, events can be detected at comparatively short time to compare satellite images in our method.

Additionally, there is a study that integrate Web contents with satellite images [8]. [8] proposes a system extracting geographic and time information about the events from free encyclopedia "Wikipedia" on the Web and mapping into satellite images. From an aspect of the information integration, [8] integrates

Fig. 6. Event Detection Result for Real Data 3

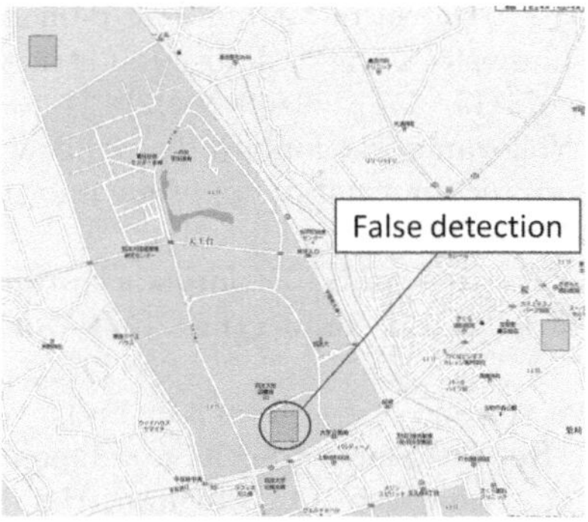

Fig. 7. Event Detection Result for Real Data 4

the satellite image with the event extracted from the Web resource, and it is a inverse approach from our study that integrate Web contents based on the event extracted from a satellite image. Moreover, [8] uses limited information resource on "Wikipedia", but the events, which [8] cannot detect, can be integrate in our study because our study intend for the whole Web content.

8 Conclusions and Future Work

This paper proposed methods and the architecture of a system that collect information about newly constructed buildings by using satellite images and web contents. The system integrates web contents with satellite images, therefore it was mentioned that web contents related to an event is able to be collected.

In future work, we improve event detection algorithm and make the detection precision of the event detection 100%. In addition, we focus on structure of the HTML in re-ranking for contents and are going to perform evaluation of relevance between the event and the article unit of the page.

References

1. Aster Science Project, `http://www.science.aster.ersdac.or.jp/t/`
2. GEO Grid, `http://www.geogrid.org/`
3. Miura, H., Midorikawa, S.: Automated building detection from high-resolution satellite image for updating gis building inventory data. Journal of social safety science (5), 37–44 (November 2003)
4. Honda, S., Ohishi, M., Shirasaki, Y., Tanaka, M., Kawanomoto, S., Mizumoto, Y.: A mechanism in federating internationally distributed databases and computing resources to realize virtual observatories. DBSJ Letters 4(1)
5. Kodama, S., Arioka, M., Mio, A., Nakamura, R., Iwao, K.: Geometric accuracy of aster dem. RSSJ (5), 55 (December 2007)
6. Base Map Information, Geographical Survey Institute, `http://www.gsi.go.jp/kiban/index.html`

7. Matsuoka, M., Yamazaki, F.: Detection of building damage areas due to earthquakes using satellite sar intensity images. Journal of structural and construction engineering. Transactions of AIJ (551), 53–60 (2002)
8. Okamoto, A., Kuroi, S., Yokoyama, S., Fukuta, N., Ishikawa, H.: Proposal of extraction technique of geographic information and time information form wikipedia. In: DEIM Forum 2009 (March 2009)
9. Tamamoto, N., Tatebe, O., Sekiguchi, S.: Performance evaluation of astronomical data analysis tools on grid datafarm architecture. In: SWoPP 2003, August 2003, pp. 185–190 (2003)
10. Urai, M., Fukui, K.: Global volcano observation plan and a volcano image database with aster. Journal of the Remote Sensing Society of Japan 32, 75–76 (2009)
11. Takagi, T., Kawashima, H., Amagasa, T., Kitagawa, H.: Integration of Satellite Images and Web Contents based on Event Detection. In: DEIM Forum 2009 (March 2009)

Gfdnavi, Web-Based Data and Knowledge Server Software for Geophysical Fluid Sciences, Part I: Rationales, Stand-Alone Features, and Supporting Knowledge Documentation Linked to Data

Takeshi Horinouchi[1], Seiya Nishizawa[2], Chiemi Watanabe[3], Akinori Tomobayashi[4], Shigenori Otsuka[5], Tsuyoshi Koshiro[6], Yoshi-Yuki Hayashi[2], and GFD Dennou Club

[1] Faculty of Environmental Earth Science, Hokkaido University, N10W5 Sapporo, Hokkaido 060-0810, Japan
[2] Department of Earth and Planetary Sciences, Kobe University
[3] Department of Information Sciences, Ochanomizu University
[4] Shouganji
[5] Department of Geophysics, Kyoto University
[6] Climate Research Department, Meteorological Research Institute
`www.gfd-dennou.org`

Abstract. In recent years, many data centers and research groups provide data on geophysical fluids such as the atmosphere and oceans through the Internet along with on-line visualization. However, their services are not available once data files are downloaded. This paper presents open-source software named Gfdnavi developed to reduce the limitation and to support data handling beyond initial "quick-looks". Gfdnavi extracts metadata from scientific data and stores them in a database. They can be accessed with web browsers for search, analysis, and visualization. It supports a wide range of usage such as public data services, group data management, and desktop use. As its unique feature, Gfdnavi supports writing and archiving documents based on knowledge obtained through data analysis. The documents are linked with the original data and analysis/visualization procedures. It has a wide variety of applications such as interdisciplinary- and collaborative-study support, a realization of falsifiability, and educational use.

Keywords: Data server, Geophysical fluid sciences, Visualization, Web application, Knowledge archive.

1 Introduction

Contemporary scientists of "geophysical fluids", such as the atmosphere and the ocean, are facing a rapid increase of data. Observational data from satellites, ground-based remote-sensing instruments, and *in situ* measurements have been

M. Yoshikawa et al. (Eds.): DASFAA 2010, LNCS 6193, pp. 93–104, 2010.

increasing year by year in both amount and kinds. Also, numerical simulations, such as climate prediction, produce vast amount of data. Therefore, to enhance information technology (IT) infrastructure for data access and handling would be helpful for the sciences.

There is also increasing demand for interdisciplinary studies to solve environmental problems. In such studies scientists have often to use data from fields of studies that are not familiar to them. Thus, IT infrastructure would also be needed to assist them.

Recently, many research organizations provide geophysical fluid data through the Internet. Some provides server-side visualization as well. Although many data servers are still custom made, it is becoming common to use data-server construction tools such as Live Access Server (LAS)[1]. LAS is the most advanced tool used for geophysical fluid sciences. A LAS server enables its users to visualize data using web browsers. It is highly configurable so that its administrator can design a façade suitable to its contents.

There are, however, still problems with currently used data servers for geophysical fluid sciences as follows:

1. Visualization capability is generally limited, so only "quick-looks" on the initial stage of researches are possible.
2. The features of the servers are not available once data files are downloaded. Therefore, the data need to be analyzed and visualized independently. In such a case, even to opening the files could be time-consuming, since a number of binary data formats are used in these sciences.
3. Most of the browser-based advanced data servers support only georeferencing data, despite the fact that non-georeferencing data are also important and frequently required for conducting researches.
4. The search capability of these servers is often limited. Furthermore, it is difficult to search for data across network, except for their documents that are available via Internet search engines.
5. Interdisciplinary and/or collaborative studies would require communication among scientists for the purpose of exchanging know-hows, results, and so on. However, to the best of authors' knowledge, none of the existing data servers for geophysical fluid sciences support such communication.

To solve all these problems, we have developed software named *Gfdnavi* [2], which stands for Geophysical fluid data navigator. Our approach is to create software that seamlessly support a variety of use cases from the management and analysis of local (desktop) data by individual scientists to public data services, where one can not only download but also interactively analyze and visualize data.

An alternative approach to help remote data access is to provide a good library to support client-side data analysis and visualization. In geophysical fluid sciences, it is OPeNDAP [3] that is widely used for such purposes. OPeNDAP provides remote access to numerical data situated in directory trees. The OPeNDAP server is a CGI program and is frequently installed on web servers of public data centers to allow data access through application programming interfaces (APIs). OPeNDAP has an abstract data model to hide file formats and supports subsetting. The two approaches, client-side analyses with OPeNDAP and server-side analyses with LAS or Gfdnavi, can complement each other.

This paper describes the design and features of Gfdnavi as a stand-alone web application. The companion paper [4] describes its web services and synergetic use across multiple Gfdnavi servers. The rest of the paper is organized as follows. Design principles and decisions made are explained in Section 2. Section 3 introduces Gfdnavi as a stand-alone data server. In Section 4, we argue the usefulness to support collection of knowledge that users obtained through data analysis, and we introduce its implementation. Conclusions are drawn in Section 5.

2 Design Rationales

Gfdnavi is designed and implemented to solve the problems stated in the previous section. In this section we introduce the principles and decisions made when designing it.

Since it is impossible to predefine all possible scientific data-analysis and visualization functionalities, in order to solve the problem 1 it is necessary to provide some kind of programmability for clients. We chose to provide programmability in multiple ways as follows:

1. To support web services.
2. To allow its user to download a subset of data and a script to reproduce what is conducted on the server. Then, one can further refine the analysis and/or visualization.
3. To allow its registered users to upload scripts to conduct data analysis and visualization on the server.

Here, we chose the Ruby programming language as the primary language to provide programmability, so the second and the third of the programmability are implemented for this language. Also, we provide a Ruby library to access the web service as introduced by [4].

The language choice is justified as follows. We earlier developed a Ruby class library GPhys [5], which represents multi-dimensional numerical data and is used by a growing number of scientists to conduct geophysical fluid data analysis and visualization. It supports a variety of data formats and solves the problem 3, so it is quite suitable for our purposes. By extensively supporting programmability, we can bridge the gap between public data services and desktop data handling (the problem 2) in terms of programming.

Our design principle in providing programmability is to unify application programming interfaces (APIs) irrespective of data location (whether they are on run-time memory or in locally accessible external files or over network) and access method (whether through Gfdnavi or other network data services such as OPeNDAP or local IO calls). Ruby is an object-oriented language suitable for such unification.

The problem 2 still remains in terms of browser access. That is, one can access public data servers with a web browser, but he/she cannot use the same browser interface to access local data. The problem can be solved if he/she installs the same data server software locally. To make it practical, the server software should be easy to install, manage, and run for scientists, who are often unfamiliar with web server installation and database management systems. Gfdnavi is designed as such.

The problem 4 should also be treated. Search among a single Gfdnavi server is introduced in what follows, and search across multiple Gfdnavi servers is introduced by the companion paper [4].

Last but not least, to tackle the problem 5 is important. Other data servers only provide access to data and do not have features to collect knowledge obtained through data analysis. We propose to support document creation on data servers, in which data analysis processes are automatically recorded and saved with the documents created. As shown in Section 4, a variety of applications can be made possible by inter-linking scientific data, analysis and visualization procedures, and the documents. This is a unique feature of Gfdnavi.

3 Overview of Gfdnavi as a Data Server

Gfdnavi is a set of software to build and run a data server. Figure 1 shows an overview of the system components of Gfdnavi. A user of a Gfdnavi server accesses it with a web browser or through web service APIs. The server serves data in local file systems or on remote servers for analysis and visualization. It also serves metadata, stored in a relational database (RDB), for browsing and search.

Gfdnavi was developed with the Ruby on Rails application development framework [6][7], which helps develop web applications that utilize RDBs.

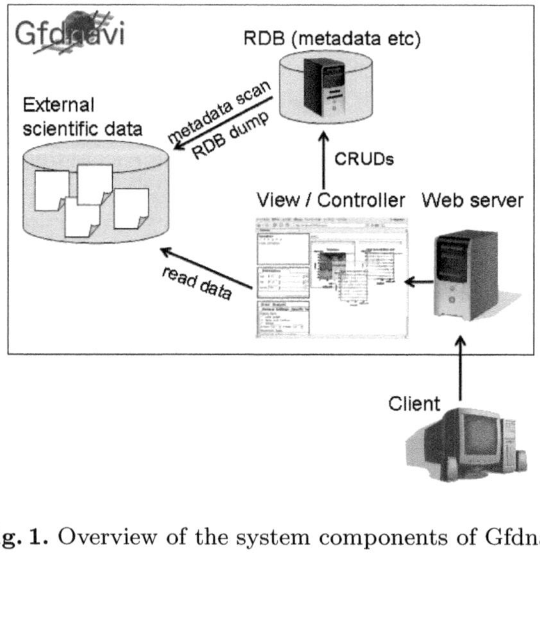

Fig. 1. Overview of the system components of Gfdnavi

It supports most of major RDB managements systems (RDBMSs). Owing to the use of the framework, Gfdnavi is equipped with a custom web server program, which runs on arbitrary communication port with a single command. Therefore, one can run a Gfdnavi server easily on a PC whenever needed, which makes it easier to use Gfdnavi personally on a PC than other data-server tools such as LAS. Gfdnavi can also be operated with commonly used web servers such as Apache, which is suitable to long-term public data services. Since most scientists are not familiar with RDBMSs, the installer of Gfdnavi suggests to use SQLite, a non-daemon type RDBMS, if a desktop configuration is selected, which makes it easy to use Gfdnavi furthermore.

Basic features of Gfdnavi are available for anonymous users. However, it has a "login" system in order to allow access limitation and to support features that are not necessarily safe, such as uploading source codes, or computationally demanding. The basic account system is local to each Gfdnavi server, supposing that the administrators give accounts only to reliable persons. In addition, Gfdnavi supports OpenID[1] for authentication that is available across servers. For security, OpenID accounts are restricted, so, for example, uploading source codes is prohibited.

3.1 Scientific Data and Metadata Database

To start up or maintain a data server, Gfdnavi collects metadata from data files under specified directories in local file systems or on remote OPeNDAP servers (Fig. 2). Most scientific data formats used in geophysical fluid sciences such as NetCDF [8] have metadata embedded. In addition, Gfdnavi supports texts files to supplement metadata. The metadata collected are stored in a RDB along with the structure of directory trees.

The metadata of numerical data consists of keyword attributes and space-and-time attributes. A keyword attribute is a combination of a name and a value

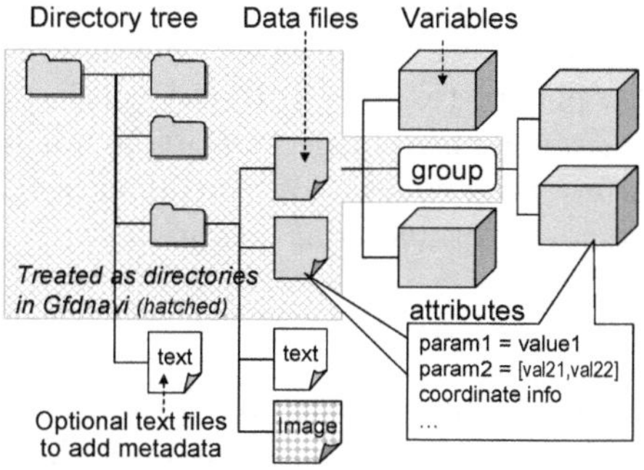

Fig. 2. A schematic illustration of the directory tree (on local storage or remote OPeNDAP servers) to be served by Gfdnavi

[1] http://openid.net/

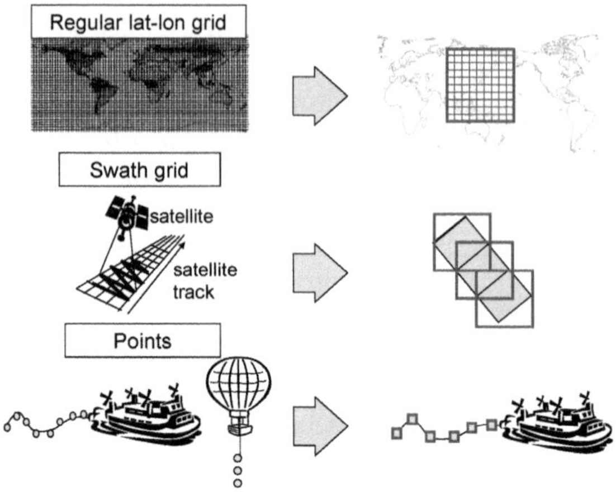

Fig. 3. Treatment of a variety of spatial sampling by bounding boxes. Irregular sampling in terms of longitude and latitude are bounded by multiple boxes, as shown by thick gray lines in the rhs panels.

(or values). A space-and-time attribute is a three-dimensional bounding box in terms of longitude, latitude, and time. As shown in Fig. 3, this simple strategy covers a variety of sampling by allowing to have multiple bounding boxes.

Note that Gfdnavi can handle data without georeferencing and/or time dimensions. Such data are simply excluded from searches based on space and/or time, but they can be found by keyword search or in the directory tree. As for numerical analysis and visualization, any kinds of coordinates are accepted. For example, spectral data that are functions of frequencies are accepted.

Scientists normally organize data directories hierarchically, so metadata of a directory are likely to be applicable to its children. Therefore, in order to make automatically generated metadata practical, we treat metadata to be inherited downward the tree. This treatment is useful to supplement data files with poor metadata. Because of this downward inheritance, metadata in Gfdnavi can be supplemented efficiently by placing text files at right levels in the directory hierarchy.

The downward inheritance may not necessarily be adequate. However, a good ranking and user interface (UI) could allow screening of false match. It is, therefore, rather important not to exclude data wanted.

3.2 Browser User Interface

Finding data on a Gfdnavi server using web browser is based on two UIs: a directory tree viewer and a search window. Figure 4 shows a screen-shot of the directory tree viewer. With this page, one can browse and select data to analyze and/or visualize. The tree viewer uses asynchronous communication and caching, so a huge data tree with numerous files is handled lightly.

Figure 5 shows a screen-shot of the search window. It provides a variety of searches: free text search, faceted navigation of keyword attribute search, search

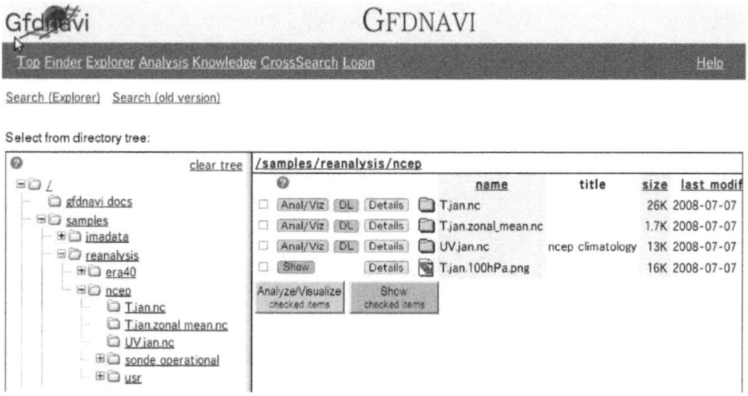

Fig. 4. A screen-shot of the directory-tree viewer. By clicking the the "Anal/Viz" buttons, variables under the files are put in a "cart", and the browser is directed to the visualization/analysis page.

by location and time. Here, multiple queries can be combined. Also, data types such as numerical data and knowledge documents can be specified.

Numerical data selected in either of the interfaces mentioned above can be analyzed and visualized in a single UI. Figure 6 shows a screen-shot of the UI.

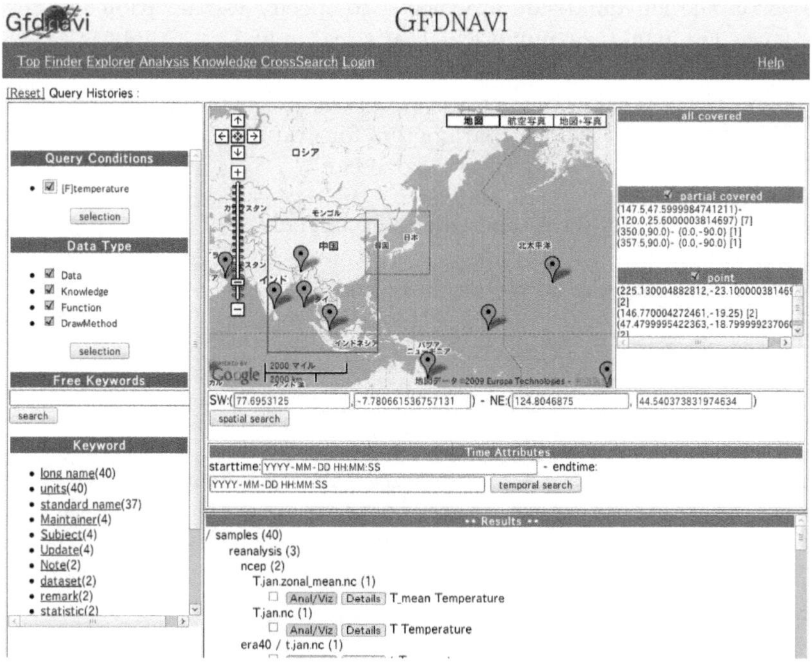

Fig. 5. A screen-shot of the search window

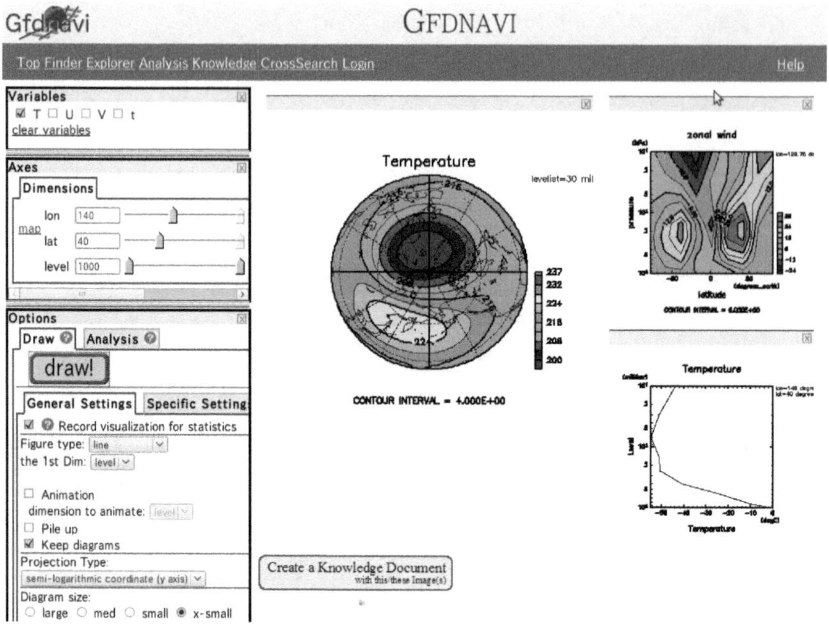

Fig. 6. A screen-shot of the visualization/analysis UI

Windows on the left-hand-side are the UI to specify visualization ("Draw" tab in the lower left panel) or numerical/statistical analysis ("Analysis" tab). The upper-left window is a "cart" of selected numerical variables. The middle-left panel shows dimensions in the variable and is used for subsetting. The lower-left panel is used to specify various parameters for graphics, including animation.

After visualization, as shown Fig. 7, one can

– download the Ruby script and the minimum subset of data to reproduce the visualization,
– save the image on the server (login required),

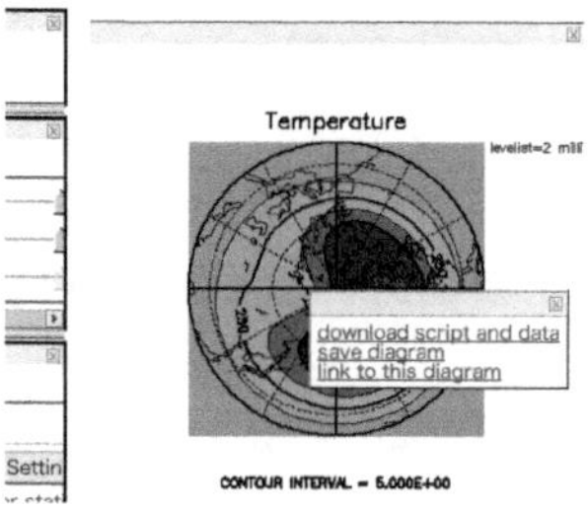

Fig. 7. A pop-up window to navigate user for further operations after visualization

- get the URL, with which a window to redo the visualization can be obtained, and
- create a document with figures that consist of visualization results (see Section 4).

4 Supporting a Knowledge Archiving System in a Data Server

The cycle of a scientific data analysis of geophysical fluids would typically start with visualizing and analyzing numerical data, saving graphics obtained, which is often along with memos, to end by writing a report or paper to publish. It is meaningful to support the entire cycle with one database application, since cross referencing would be available for all the entities involved in the cycle.

Our scope is to support personal research memos, technical documentation, exchange of knowledge and know-hows for interdisciplinary and collaborative studies, outreach or public relations of data centers (such as to create "What's new" pages), and educational materials. We do not aim to support peer-reviewed electronic journal publication systems within Gfdnavi, but in future supplementary materials of research papers could include URLs on Gfdnavi.

A knowledge document in Gfdnavi consists of a title, a summary, a text body, and figures, along with attributes such as category. A figure has not only a caption and an image file but also the script used to create the image. Therefore, if one finds a knowledge document on a Gfdnavi server. He or she can follow links in its figures to reproduce them and further to visualize data with different conditions or even to make additional analysis. This feature is useful to support *falsifiability*, which is important for sciences.

This feature is also useful for collaborative and/or interdisciplinary studies. For example, one can document an example of data analysis, with which actual operations may be reproduced. Then its readers can directly follow or extend it.

In order to further support interactions, knowledge documents can take "comments", which are also knowledge documents. With this feature, collaborators can make threads of interactions, where each of the comments can have dynamic links to data.

The knowledge documentation system of Gfdnavi brings a new depth to outreach and education. Many data centers have "what's new" pages or educational materials, in which scientific outcomes are documented for broad readers. By using the knowledge documentation system of Gfdnavi, such a documents can have figures that are linked to the data used and are dynamically reproducible. The readers can follow links from the figures to further explore scientific data by themselves.

The knowledge documents annotate numerical data. If scientists work with Gfdnavi and stores what they find as knowledge documents, the numerical data used are annotated with text and visual information. Therefore, it can be regarded as a system to collect high-level metadata from scientists. For example, one may leave a document on a specific typhoon found in year 2009 using an

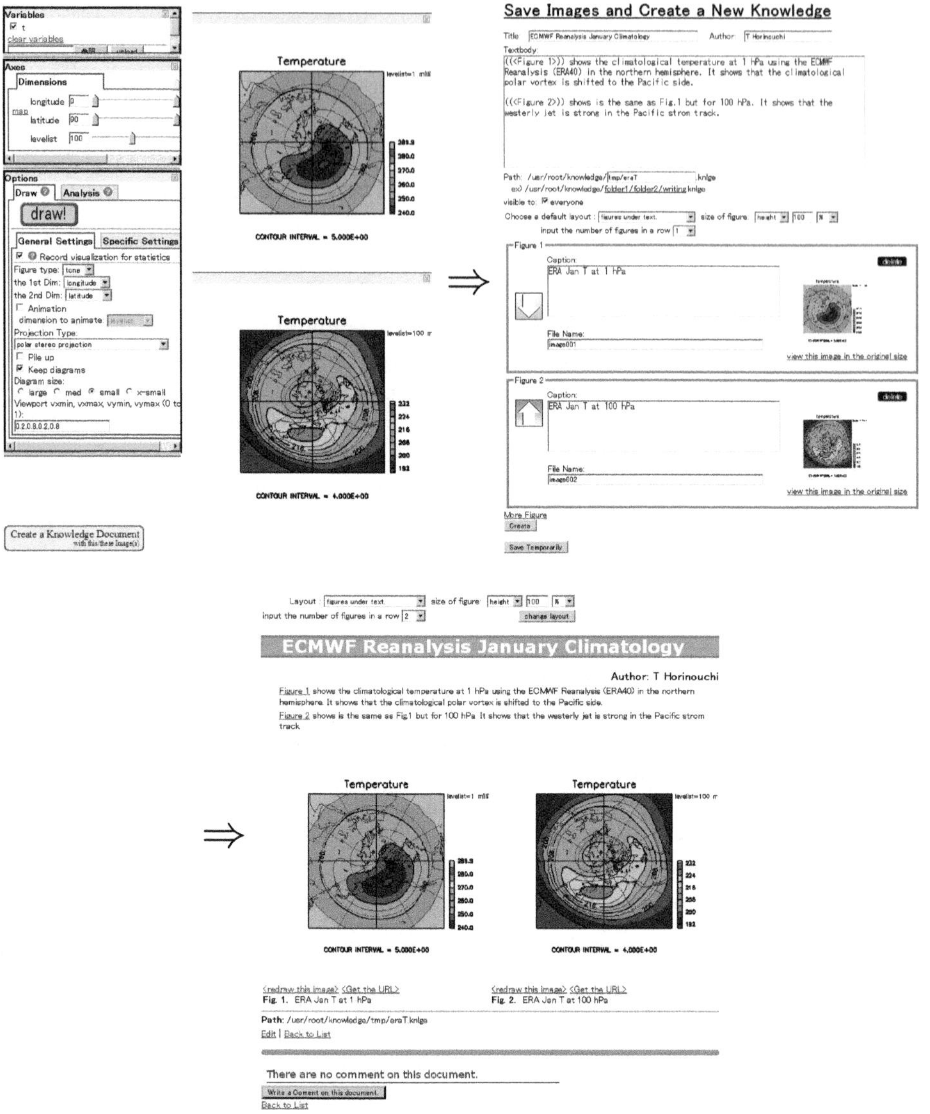

Fig. 8. Demonstration of knowledge document creation from visualization results. By clicking the rounded rectangle below at the bottom of the visualization window (upper-left panel), the user is lead to a document input form (lower-left panel), in which the images on the visualization window are set to figures by default. The lower panel shows the document created.

image made from a global rainfall dataset based on satellite-borne microwave radiometers. Since the image is saved with visualization parameters, it automatically has space-time information on the typhoon. In other words, saving the document annotates the rainfall data with text, image, and space-time information on the typhoon. The annotation enriches the metadata of the dataset significantly, since the original metadata of microwave rainfall data may not even have the word "typhoon". In terms of data search, one may find the microwave radiometer data useful to visualize typhoons because of this document. This is useful especially for those whose specialty is not the atmospheric sciences.

Figure 8 demonstrates how a knowledge document can be created from visualization results. By clicking a button on the visualization window (upper-left panel), the user is lead to a document input form including the visualization results as default figures (lower-left panel). By using the form, visualization procedures are recorded automatically. The procedures to reproduce the visualization from the original data are recorded automatically, and the document created have links to them (bottom panel).

The documents made with Gfdnavi can be browsed and searched in many ways. They are covered by the search UI introduced in Section 3. In addition, Gfdnavi has a window specialized for document browsing and search.

5 Conclusions

In this paper, we presented the problems that the web-browser-based data servers for geophysical fluid sciences have, and we introduced our software Gfdnavi to solve them. The gap between network data services and desktop data handling can be solved by extensively supporting programmability and by making the server software easy to install, manage, and run. A unique feature of Gfdnavi is to support writing and archival of documents based on knowledge that its users obtained through data analysis. It has a wide variety of applications such as accumulation of knowledge, interdisciplinary- and collaborative-study support, a realization of falsifiability, and creation of dynamic documents for outreach and education.

Acknowledgments. This study was supported by the MEXT grant-in-aid "Cyber infrastructure for the information-explosion era" A01-14 (19024039, 21013002). We thank Masato Shiotani, Masaki Ishiwatari, Masatsugu Odaka, and Tomohiro Taniguchi for supporting and promoting this work. We thank Takuji Kubota, Kazuki Joe, Yumi Yanagitaira, Asami Sato, Mai Saito, Eriko Touma, Toshitaka Tsuda, Yasuhiro Morikawa, Youhei Sasaki, Eriko Nishimoto, and Mariko Horikawa for their contributions and comments.

References

1. Hankin, S., Callahan, J., Sirott, J.: The Live Access Server and DODS: Web visualization and data fusion for distributed holdings (2001), `http://ferret.wrc.noaa.gov/Ferret/LAS/LASoverview.html`
2. Horinouchi, T., Nishizawa, S., Watanabe, C., collaborators.: Gfdnavi homepage, `http://www.gfd-dennou.org/arch/davis/gfdnavi/`

3. Cornillon, P., Gallagher, J., Sgouros, T.: OPeNDAP: Accessing data in a distributed, heterogeneous environment. Data Science Journal 2, 164–174 (2003)
4. Nishizawa, S., Horinouchi, T., Watanabe, C., Isamoto, Y., Tomobayashi, A., Otsuka, S., GFD Dennou Club: Gfdnavi, Web-based Data and Knowledge Server Software for Geophysical Fluid Sciences, Part II: Web services. In: Yoshikawa, M., et al. (eds.) DASFAA 2010. LNCS, vol. 6193, pp. 105–116. Springer, Heidelberg (2010)
5. Horinouchi, T., Mizuta, R., Nishizawa, S., Tsukahara, D., Takehiro, S.: GPhys – a multi-purpose class to handle gridded physical quantities (2003), `http://ruby.gfd-dennou.org/products/gphys/`
6. Hansson, D.H., et al.: Ruby on Rails, `http://www.rubyonrails.org/`
7. Thomas, D., Hansson, D.H.: Agile Web Development with Rails, The Pragmatic Programmers LLC, USA (2005)
8. Rew, R., Davis, G.: NetCDF – An interface for scientific-data access. IEEE Computer Graphics and Applications 10(4), 76–82 (1990)

Gfdnavi, Web-Based Data and Knowledge Server Software for Geophysical Fluid Sciences, Part II: RESTful Web Services and Object-Oriented Programming Interface

Seiya Nishizawa[1], Takeshi Horinouchi[2], Chiemi Watanabe[3], Yuka Isamoto[3], Akinori Tomobayashi[4], Shigenori Otsuka[5], and GFD Dennou Club

[1] Department of Earth and Planetary Sciences, Kobe University, 1-1 Rokohdai-cho Nada-ku Kobe, Hyogo 657-8501, Japan
[2] Faculty of Environmental Earth Science, Hokkaido University
[3] Department of Information Sciences, Ochanomizu University
[4] Shoganji
[5] Department of Geophysics, Kyoto University

Abstract. In recent years, increasing amounts of scientific data on geophysical and environmental fluids, e.g., in the atmosphere and oceans, are being available. Further, there is increasing demand for web-based data services. Several browser-based data servers, on which geophysical-fluid data can be analyzed and visualized, have been developed. However, they are suitable only for initial "quick-looks" and not for subsequent research processes. As a solution, we developed data server software named Gfdnavi. One of its important features is that it provides extensive support for programming (scripting). With Gfdnavi, users can easily switch between operations using a web browser and operations using scripts or command lines. This paper describes its network features: web services, which is an important part of Gfdnavi's programmability, and the functionality to search across multiple Gfdnavi servers. To develop the web services, we adopted the REST architecture. We also developed a client library to ensure access to web services in the programming language Ruby. Using this library, data can be analyzed and visualized on either the server side or client side. It also enables data handling on multiple servers. Search across multiple web servers is made possible by a simple peer-to-peer network with a central server, with the peer-to-peer communication based on web services.

1 Introduction

In recent years increasing amounts of scientific data on geophysical and environmental fluids, e.g., in the atmosphere and oceans, are being available. Many data centers and research organizations or groups are now providing data through the Internet, and some are also providing on-line visualization capabilities.

M. Yoshikawa et al. (Eds.): DASFAA 2010, LNCS 6193, pp. 105–116, 2010.

As stated in the companion paper [1] (hereafter referred to as "Part I"), the following problems are encountered by existing web-based data servers during browser-based access employed in geophysical fluid sciences:

1. The visualization capability of existing web-based data servers is limited, because of which only initial "quick-looks" are possible; the resultant diagrams would not be of sufficiently high quality suitable for publication.
2. The features of the servers are not available once the data files are downloaded. Therefore, the data need to be analyzed and visualized independently. In such a case, even the opening of files could be difficult, because a number of binary data formats are used in these sciences.
3. Most of the browser-based advanced data servers support only georeferencing data, despite the fact that non-georeferencing data are also important and frequently required for conducting researches.
4. The search capability of these servers is often limited. Furthermore, it is difficult to search for data across networks, except for documents that are available via Internet search engines.
5. Interdisciplinary and/or collaborative studies would require communication among researchers for the purpose of exchanging know-hows, results, and so on; however, to the best of the authors' knowledge, none of the existing data servers for geophysical fluid sciences support such communication.

To solve all these problems, we have developed web-based data and knowledge server software for application in geophysical fluid sciences, termed Gfdnavi [2]. The basic features of Gfdnavi are described in Part I. Part II of this paper deals mainly with the solution to problems 1 and 4 by the use of the developed Gfdnavi. It is, however, also useful for solving problem 2.

In order to ensure the usefulness of data servers in all stages of scientific studies, it is necessary to provide programmability to clients. A browser-based graphical user interface (GUI) would be useful in initial trial-and-error stages; however, it would not necessarily be productive in the later stages, in which repetition is frequently required; instead, programming would be effective for such repetition. Therefore, the support of a smooth transition between GUI operations and programming by a data server would be a useful feature.

In order to improve the practical applicability of Gfdnavi, we have included in it multiple ways of programmability; as a result, it can be used to

1. support web services
2. allow the user to download a subset of data and a script for reproducing the action that he or she performed on the server with the GUI
3. allow a registered user to upload scripts to carry out his/her original data analysis and visualization on the server

The web services (item 1 in the above list) are described in the present paper, whereas the other two items have been described in Part I.

We have not only included support for web services in Gfdnavi but also provided a client library for accessing the web services in the object-oriented programming (hereafter referred to as "OOP") language Ruby [3]. As will be shown subsequently, because of the library, the programmability associated with Gfdnavi is unified irrespective of the data location (e.g., on the run-time memory, in locally accessible external files, or over the Internet) and access method (e.g., through Gfdnavi, other network data services, or local input-output calls). This unification is the basis for achieving a smooth transition between GUI operations and programming.

Researchers in the field of geophysical fluid sciences frequently combine data from multiple sources for conducting research. It is, therefore, important to support the combining by realizing search and analysis across multiple data servers. However, existing browser-based data servers have limited capability in this respect. In particular, searching across networks (hereafter referred to as "cross search") is rather important, since researchers must first know what kinds of data are available for the task at hand and also the location of the data.

It would be ideal to conduct a search over a variety of heterogeneous data servers. Our scope, however, is limited to a search among Gfdnavi servers. Such a limited search would still be useful if Gfdnavi is used extensively. A typical use case that we aim to cover is as follows: Suppose that a researcher conducts a study using data obtained by his/her own observations or numerical simulations or those of his/her research group. In many cases, the researcher would additionally use external data such as satellite observations, which may be stored locally or available only on servers of data centers. In such a case, a search should be conducted across data on both local and remote servers.

In this paper, we present the design and implementation of two network features of Gfdnavi: web services and cross search. The rest of this paper is organized as follows. In Sect. 2, we present the design of Gfdnavi web services. Then, we describe the implementations of the web services in Sect. 3, a client library in Sect. 4, and functionality of use of multiple servers in Sect. 5. Finally, we present the conclusions and discussions in Sect. 6.

2 Design of Gfdnavi Web Services

2.1 Motivating Scenario

We show an example use case of Gfdnavi web services in research in the field of geophysical fluid sciences. Suppose that a researcher in the field having performed several numerical simulations of the future climate with different scenarios for future emission of carbon dioxide wants to compare these results. At first, he or she analyze and visualize result data of one simulation run out of the simulations with the GUI of Gfdnavi web applications, in order to figure out characteristics of spatial pattern of temperature. After that, he or she would want to apply the same analysis and visualization to result data of the other runs. Carrying out them with programming would be more efficient than that with GUI. A Ruby script reproducing the action performed with the GUI can be downloaded; e.g., Fig. 1. Methods in the script send an HTTP request to Uniform Resource Locator (hereafter referred to as "URL") of Gfdnavi web services, which is as shown in

```
1: require "numru/gfdnavi_data"
2: include NumRu
3: t = GfdnaviData.parse("http://example.com/data/T.exp01.nc/T")
4: t_mean = t.analysis("mean","longitude")
5: tone = t_mean.plot("tone")
6: png = tone.to_png
```

Fig. 1. Example of Ruby script reproducing the action with the GUI on Gfdnavi web applications

```
line 3: /data/T.exp01.nc/T.yml
line 4: /data/T.exp01.nc/T/analysis(mean;longitude).yml
line 5: /data/T.exp01.nc/T/analysis(mean;longitude)/plot(tone).yml
line 6: /data/T.exp01.nc/T/analysis(mean;longitude)/plot(tone).png
```

Fig. 2. URL paths of HTTP requests yielded by methods in the Ruby script in Fig. 1. The number at left side of each line represents line number in the script.

Fig. 2. He or she modifies the script to perform the analysis and visualization with data of all the runs; e.g., Fig. 3.

Further, he or she would want to compare the results with those of simulations performed by other researchers. Using the cross search feature of Gfdnavi, he or she could find other simulation data than his/hers. Then the same analysis and visualization can be applied to these data, and comparison of those results can be performed.

2.2 Web Services and Client Library

We developed web services of Gfdnavi for ensuring programmability and a client library for programming irrespective of the data location and access method. We designed the web services such that they can be used from programs, particularly from the client library, and designed the client library such that it behaves in a manner similar to a library for data analysis and visualization at the local level.

RESTful Web Services. Several technologies for developing web services are available, two of the popular ones being REST [4] and SOAP [5]. REST is based on resource-oriented architecture. It uses a uniform interface, i.e., an HTTP method. RESTful web services are stateless because of the use of HTTP methods. SOAP is a protocol for remote procedure call (RPC). Web services based on SOAP could be either stateful or stateless.

We decided to develop Gfdnavi web services with REST, the most important reason for this being that REST is based on resource-oriented architecture, which has similarities with OOP, and as a result, it would be easy to develop the Ruby client library having access to RESTful web services.

```
require "numru/gfdnavi_data"
include NumRu
NRUNS = 10  # number of runs
pngs = Array.new
for n in 0...NRUNS # loop for all the runs
  crun = sprintf("%02d", n+1) #=> "01", "02", ...
  t = GfdnaviData.parse("http://example.com/data/T.exp"+crun+".nc/T")
  t_mean = t.analysis("mean","longitude")
  tone = t_mean.plot("tone")
  pngs[n] = tone.to_png
end
```

Fig. 3. Example of Ruby script modified for repetition from the script in Fig. 1

Statelessness is an important feature of RESTful web servers. A stateless system is advantageous over a stateful system in some ways. For example, scaling out a stateless system is easy. Scalability of Gfdnavi is important, because its operations such as analysis and visualization could require large computing resources such as CPU usage time and memory space. Further, testing of a stateless system is easier than that of a stateful system.

However, making Gfdnavi web services RESTful is somewhat difficult because of certain problems. One problem is how to define URL of dynamic resources, which are generated dynamically as result of operations such as analysis and visualization. In this study, we defined URLs such that they have correspondence with OOP. In OOP, dynamic objects generated from a static object are represented in the form `a_static_object.method1[.method2[....]]` with a method chain. In a similar manner, the URL path of the dynamic resources is defined as follows: `/a_static_resource/method1[/method2[/...]]` The path of dynamic resources generated from multiple static resources is also defined on the basis of the correspondence of the URLs with OOP.

Another problem is dealing with temporary data in sequential programming. A program is usually a set of sequential operations. Results of operations are set to temporal variables and used later. In stateless web services, temporary resources are usually not used, though they are used to represent transactions in some systems. For simplicity, we decided not to use temporary resources in Gfdnavi. This could result in unnecessary duplicate executions. For example, an operation applied to a result of other operations could result in repeated executions of all those other operations. To prevent such duplication, we introduce delayed execution and cache mechanisms.

Ruby Client Library. Many researchers in the field of geophysical fluid sciences use Ruby and a Ruby class library GPhys [6], which represents multi-dimensional numerical data and supports a variety of data formats, for data analysis and visualization at the local level. We developed a client library of Gfdnavi web services using Ruby in order to enable users to analyze and visualize data on Gfdnavi servers in a manner similar to programming with GPhys.

Using the library, users can carry out data analysis and visualization on either the server side or the client side and select either side for execution, on the basis of efficiency or other factors.

2.3 Use of Multiple Servers

For researchers in the abovementioned field, who often work with several kinds of data, network capability is an important requirement, as explained in Sect. 1. Gfdnavi provides the features of cross search and analysis/visualization with multiple data provided by different Gfdnavi servers. The web services is used in Gfdnavi web applications, in order to access remote resources of other Gfdnavi servers.

Cross Search. In the case of use of multiple servers for data analysis and visualization, the location of resources is specified by users. For cross search, however, users would want to search data on not only known servers but also unknown servers.

The following are some of the candidates for implementing cross search. One is a client-server model, which is a central server having all the information of all the data on servers forming a network for cross search; all the search requests are sent to the central server. Another is a pure peer-to-peer (P2P) network model, which contains all the information shared in the network. Yet another candidate is a hybrid P2P model, which is a server list managed by a central server; in this model, search requests are sent to each peer.

Generally, the pure P2P model has the advantage of scalability over the client-server model and does not require a high-performance central server. However, the development of the pure P2P model tends to be difficult. We decided that at least for the time being, the hybrid P2P model is suitable for Gfdnavi.

3 Implementation of Gfdnavi Web Services

In this section, we present the implementation of Gfdnavi web services.

There are two types of resources in Gfdnavi web services: static and dynamic. A static resource represents column data in database tables, such as data in files and knowledge data. These data are organized as a directory tree structure, and each data set is called a node. A dynamic resource represents results of operations such as search, analysis, or visualization.

3.1 URL Syntax

Each resource of Gfdnavi web services has at least one URL, which consists of prefix for Gfdnavi web service, resource path, extension, and parameters: `http://{host}:{port}/.../{resource_path}.{extension}?{params}`, where "`var`" is a variable name and is substituted to the value of the variable. "`Extension`" specifies the media type for representing the response for a requested resource (Table 1).

Table 1. Extensions for URL of Gfdnavi web service

extension	media type
html	text/html (HTML)
xml	text/xml (XML)
yml	text/x-yaml (YAML [7])
nc	application/x-netcdf (NetCDF [8])
png	image/png (PNG)
knlge	text/x-yaml (YAML for Gfdnavi knowledge data)
gphys	application/octet stream (GPhys marshaled binary)

"`Params`" are parameters for representation, and they can be omitted along with the leading question mark. "`Resource_path`" is an appropriately encoded resource path, which is the identifier of a resource in the Gfdnavi web services; here, the encoding is done by percent-encoding [9].

3.2 Resource Path

The path of a static resource is simply its node path in the directory tree. The path of a dynamic resource is `/{orig_resource}/{operation}`, where "`orig_resource`" is the resource path of original data and "`operation`" is the operation to be performed.

Currently, three types of operations are performed: search, analysis, and visualization. The search `operation` is `find({all_or_first};{queries};{params})`. If `all_or_first` is "`all`", all the search results are returned, whereas if it is "`first`", only the first result is returned. "`Queries`" are search queries joined with an ampersand. Available queries are shown in Table 2. "`Params`" represents search parameters other than the queries joined with a comma. The currently available parameters are `offset={offset}` and `limit={limit}` to specify offset and number of search results to be returned, respectively. Results for searching are sorted by descending order, a parameter to specify the order will be available.

The currently available parameters for analysis and visualization are `analysis({method};{arguments})` and `plot({method};{arguments})`, respectively. Here, "`method`" is the node path of analysis functions or visualization methods, such as `/usr/{user_name}/functions/{method_name}` for analysis functions and `/usr/{user_name}/draw_methods/{method_name}` for visualization methods. The methods can be written as `{method_name},{user_name}`. `User_name` and the leading comma can be omitted when `user_name` is `root`. Methods whose `user_name` is `root` are provided by a server administrator and available to all the users in the server, while other methods are added by users.

The original resource could be either a dynamic resource or a static data resource. The resource path for the result of multiple operations is written as a method chain in OOP, such as `object.method1.method2.....` The resource path is written as `/{orig_resource}/{operation1}/{operation2}/....`

Table 2. Query types for search

search type	query syntax
keyword search	`kw.{attribution_name}={attribution_value}`
free keyword search	`fw={keyword}`
data type search	`datatype={datatype}`
node path search	`path={path}`
spatial search	`sp.overlap=[{slon},{slat},{elon},{elat}]`
time search	`tm=[{start},{end}]`

An array of resources is also a resource, and its path is `[{resource1},{resource2},...]`. Though every operation can take only one original data resource, the array resource can be used for operations that require multiple data, e.g., `[{resource1},{resource2}]/{operation}`. Further, every operation returns an array resource, and `[{indexes}]` is available to specific required elements of the array. "`Indexes`" denotes an index number of arrays, beginning from 0 or a list of the index joined with a comma; e.g., `/{resource}/{operation}[0,2]` represents an array resource that consists of the first and third elements of an array result.

4 GfdnaviData

We have developed a Ruby class library, named GfdnaviData, as a web service client. GfdnaviData class is a class whose instance object corresponds to a resource of Gfdnavi web services.

Figure 1 shows an example of Ruby script for server-side analysis with GfdnaviData; it yields four HTTP requests shown in Fig. 2. Methods `#find`, `#analysis`, and `#plot` correspond to `/find()`, `/analysis()`, and `/plot()` in the resource path, respectively, where the leading "`#`" in the method name indicates that the method is an instance method. These methods send an HTTP request to an appropriate URL whose extension is "yml", which requires a result in the YAML format. The reason why the result is in the YAML format and not the XML format is that the YAML format is simpler and easier to handle in Ruby. The instance method `#to_{type}` acquire a resource in the specified format corresponding to "`type`" by setting the extension of the URL; `#to_html` (html), `#to_xml` (xml), `#to_nc` (nc), `#to_knlge` (knlge), `#to_gphys` (gphys), and `#to_png` (png).

Some methods having similarity to GPhys are provided in GfdnaviData. Naive execution of four arithmetic operations with GfdnaviData is slightly complex. For example, to add objects `dataA` and `dataB`, we must write

```
GfdnaviData[dataA,dataB].analysis("addition"),
```

where the `GfdnaviData[]` class method creates an object corresponding to an array resource. Methods `#+`, `#-`, `#*`, and `#/` are added for convenience and for ensuring similarity with GPhys, and then, we can write "`dataA + dataB`" for the above example.

Basic authorization is used for access control in the Web services. Adding your user name and password to `GfdnaviData.parse` as its arguments, or using `#user` and `#password` methods, you can specify your user name and password, respectively. You might not want to embedding password into a script for security reason. GfdnaviData ask your password to you interactively, if you has not specified your password.

4.1 Delayed Execution and Caching

The generation of dynamic resources in Gfdnavi web services, such as analyzed and visualized resources, could cause serious performance problems. The method chain of OOP requires a return object for every method call, which could result in repetition.

Then, in the example shown in Fig. 1, averaging could be executed three times at the last three method calls. In order to prevent such repetition, we introduced delayed execution and caching in Gfdnavi. Operations such as search, analysis, and visualization are not executed, and only resource information is returned for HTTP requests, except for those requests that really require result data. Such a request requiring result data has the following extensions: `html` and `xml` for search, `nc` and `gphys` for analysis, and `png` for visualization. The `#find`, `#analysis`, and `#plot` methods acquire information about only resources in the YAML format. Consequently, in the case of the above example, averaging is executed only once at the last HTTP request, which requires PNG image data, and results in the execution of both averaging and plotting.

As mentioned above, we also included a caching system in Gfdnavi. Analyzed binary data and drawn image data are cached in the memory or storage and used for later requests for the same data. Their lifetime depends on the frequency of use and time required for generating the data.

5 Use of Multiple Servers

We have provided the network capability of use of multiple servers in Gfdnavi. Gfdnavi web services are used internally in Gfdnavi web applications, and GfdnaviData is used in Gfdnavi web services for obtaining remote resources from other Gfdnavi servers.

A request for a resource with a URL of the Gfdnavi web services is converted into a GfdnaviData class instance. This instance would send requests to other Gfdnavi servers for remote resources, which implies that Gfdnavi servers could serve as a web service client during cross-server use (Fig. 4). The flowchart of this process is as follows:

1. The GfdnaviData class instance in a client constructs a URL and sends an HTTP request to the server identified by the URL.

2. In the server, the web service controller creates a GfdnaviData class instance corresponding to the requested resource.
3. If required, the instance repeats the process in step 1 as a web service client.
4. The instance executes necessary operations using local data and the results obtained in step 3.
5. The instance returns an object of the requested resource to the controller.
6. On the basis of the returned object, the controller returns a representation of the requested resource to the requesting instance.
7. This instance in the client creates another GfdnaviData class instance or data object such as a binary or image data object, depending on the response.

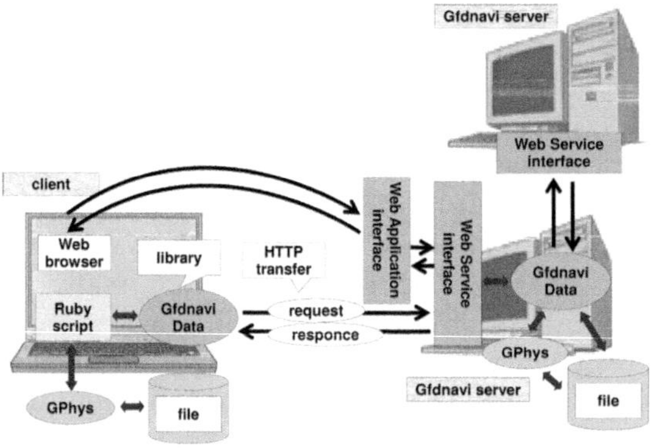

Fig. 4. Structure of web applications and web services provided by Gfdnavi

5.1 Cross Search

Cross search enables users to search for data on all Gfdnavi servers forming a network for cross search, even if the users know only one server out of them. Cross search has been developed in the Gfdnavi web application using the Gfdnavi web services.

To enable cross search, we have to activate a central server that contains a list of Gfdnavi servers forming a network for cross search. Each Gfdnavi server makes a request to the central server and receives the server list.

Figure 5 shows a screen shot of the cross search page in the Gfdnavi web application. For performing cross search, users select target servers on which search is to be performed.

The flowchart of the cross search is as follows:

1. A user accesses the search page of a Gfdnavi server, specifies search conditions, and selects those servers from the list that he or she wants to include as search targets.
2. The user can also add other servers that are not in the list to the targets.
3. The search request is sent to the Gfdnavi server.
4. The server executes search for its own data.

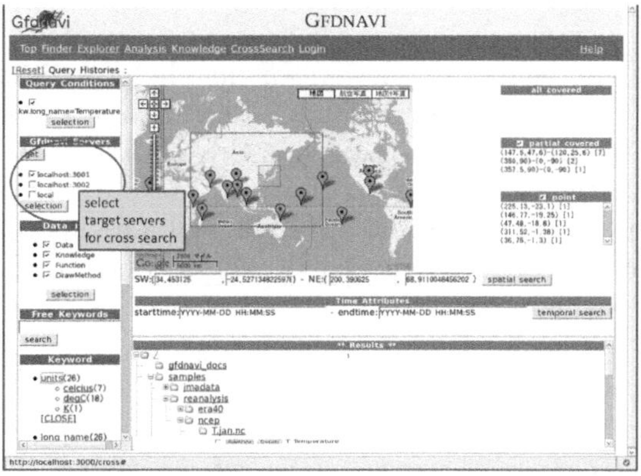

Fig. 5. Screen shot of cross search page in Gfdnavi web application

5. The server sends the request to the servers specified as search targets via the web services.
6. Then, it collects results from all the specified servers.
7. Finally, it returns the result to the user.

6 Concluding Remarks

In this paper, we have presented the development of the network capability of Gfdnavi. The Gfdnavi web services are developed on the REST architecture. A Ruby client library, termed GfdnaviData, is also developed in order to enable researchers in the field of geophysical fluid sciences to carry out data analysis and visualization on either the server side or the client side and to handle data on multiple servers. A cross search feature across multiple Gfdnavi servers is realized by using a simple peer-to-peer network with a central server, where the peer-to-peer communication is based on the Gfdnavi web services.

It should be noted that we could not control the reliability and quality of remote data in the cross search. However, it is obvious that in a scientific research, the reliability and quality of data used in analysis are vital. In a conventional way of research, researchers in the field of geophysical fluid sciences directly download data from a known generator or distributor. They usually know the nature and quality of the data that they are working with. In contrast, by using the cross search feature, researchers can acquire unknown data. The data may be of varied quality levels or could be incomplete. In the future, we need to find a way to determine the quality and reliability of data and convey the same to users. At the very least, traceability information of data, such as their generator and distributor, should be made available to users.

Acknowledgments

We appreciate three anonymous reviewers for their helpful comments. This study was supported by Grant-in-Aid for Scientific Research on Priority Areas "Cyber Infrastructure for the Information-Explosion Era" A01-14 (19024039, 21013002) by the MEXT. We thank Yoshi-Yuki Hayashi, Masato Shiotani, Masaki Ishiwatari, Masatsugu Odaka, and Tomohiro Taniguchi for supporting and promoting this work. We also thank Tsuyoshi Koshiro, Yasuhiro Morikawa, Youhei Sasaki, and Eriko Nishimoto for their valuable contributions and comments.

References

1. Horinouchi, T., Nishizawa, S., Watanabe, C., Tomobayashi, A., Osuka, S., Koshiro, T., GFD Dennou Club: Gfdnavi, Web-based Data and Knowledge Server Software for Geophysical Fluid Sciences, Part I: Rationales, Stand-alone Features, and Supporting Knowledge Documentation Linked to Data. In: Yoshikawa, M., et al. (eds.) DASFAA 2010. LNCS, vol. 6193, pp. 93–104. Springer, Heidelberg (2010)
2. Gfdnavi, `http://www.gfd-dennou.org/arch/davis/gfdnavi/`
3. Ruby, `http://www.ruby-lang.org/`
4. Fielding, R.T.: Architectural Styles and the Design of Network-based Software Architectures. Doctoral dissertation, University of California, Irvine (2000)
5. SOAP, `http://www.w3.org/TR/soap/`
6. Horinouchi, T., Mizuta, R., Nishizawa, S., Tsukahara, D., Takehiro, S.: GPhys - A Multi-purpose Class to Handle Gridded Physical Quantities (2003), `http://ruby.gfd-dennou.org/products/gphys/`
7. YAML, `http://www.yaml.org`
8. Rew, R., Davis, G.: NetCDF – An interface for Scientific-data Access. IEEE Computer Graphics and Applications 10(4), 76–82 (1990)
9. RFC3986, `http://tools.ietf.org/html/rfc3986`

MCIS2010 Workshop Organizers' Message

Shazia Sadiq[1], Xiaochun Yang[2], Xiaofang Zhou[1], and Ke Deng[1]

[1] The University of Queensland, Australia
[2] Northeastern University, China

In today's global information sharing environments, poor data quality is known to compromise the credibility and efficiency of commercial as well as public endeavours. Several developments from industry as well as academia have contributed significantly towards addressing the problem. These typically include analysts and practitioners who have contributed to the design of strategies and methodologies for data governance; solution architects including software vendors who have contributed towards appropriate system architectures that promote data integration; and data experts who have contributed to data quality problems such as duplicate detection, identification of outliers, consistency checking and many more through the use of computational techniques. The attainment of true data quality lies at the convergence of the three aspects, namely organizational, architectural and computational. At the same time, importance of managing data quality has increased manifold, as the diversity of sources, formats and volume of data grows.

The MCIS workshop provided a forum to bring together diverse researchers and make a consolidated contribution to new and extended methods to address the challenges of data quality in a collaborative settings. Topics covered by the workshop include data integration, linkage; consistency checking, data profiling and measurement; methods for data transformation, reconciliation, consolidation; etc. Following the success of MCIS2008 in New Delhi, India and MCIS2009 in Brisbane, Australia, the 3rd MCIS was held on April 4, 2010 at the University of Tsukuba, Japan in conjunction with the 15th International Conference on Database Systems for Advanced Applications (DASFAAf10). In this year, MCIS workshop attracted eight submissions from Australia, China, Greece, and Italy. All submissions were peer reviewed by at least three program committee members to ensure that high quality papers are selected. On the basis of technical merit, originality, significance, and relevance to the workshop, the program committee decided on four papers to be included in the workshop proceedings (acceptance rate 50%).

The workshop program committee consisted of 12 experienced researchers and experts in the area of data analysis and management. We would like to acknowledge the valuable contribution of all the PC members during the peer review process. Also, we would like to show our gratitude to the DASFAA 2010 workshop chairs for their great support in ensuring the success of MCIS2010.

M. Yoshikawa et al. (Eds.): DASFAA 2010, LNCS 6193, p. 117, 2010.

Checking Structural Integrity for Metadata Repository Systems by Means of Description Logics

Xiaofei Zhao[1] and Zhiqiu Huang[2]

[1] Department of Computer Science and Technology
Nanjing University of Information Science and Technology
210044 Nanjing, China
zxf-first@nuaa.edu.cn
[2] Department of Computer Science and Engineering
Nanjing University of Aeronautics and Astronautics
210016 Nanjing, China
zqhuang@nuaa.edu.cn

Abstract. The organization of the metadata in repository systems exhibits a complex structure which is layered, multi-level and dynamically adaptable; it is insufficiently specified in existing repository system standard how to ensure structural integrity, the above two reasons lead to the violation of structural integrity frequently during the creation of the metadata structure based on Meta Object Facility(MOF), thus affect the stability of repository systems. However, structural integrity checking for repository systems based on MOF is difficult because MOF is rendered to users by graphs, which lack precise semantics. In this paper, we try to solve this problem by means of Description Logics (DLs). The approach is based on a particular formal logic of the family of Description Logics. We make a study of how to formalize the different levels of MOF architecture into the DL knowledge base and how to check inconsistencies automatically using query and reasoning mechanism provided by the Description Logic. We perform performance evaluation for structural integrity checking prototypical system implemented in terms of the approach, the results are encouraging.

1 Introduction

The organization of the metadata in repository systems[1](metadata structure) exhibits a complex structure which is layered, multi-level and dynamically adaptable, so preserving the consistency of the systems is a major challenge. Consistency in repository systems has several aspects: (1) operational consistency: deals with the interaction between repository applications and is closely related to the notion of repository transactions. There are two sub-aspects: concurrent multi-client access; and cooperative atomicity; (2) metadata integrity: comprises the notions of well-formedness and structural integrity. Well-formedness ensures the syntactical correctness of the model definitions within a meta-layer. Structural integrity guarantees the conformance of objects on one level to type definitions on the adjacent higher meta-level[1].

Structural integrity is the most important aspect of repository systems consistency. Without structural integrity, repository applications might create or modify metadata

M. Yoshikawa et al. (Eds.): DASFAA 2010, LNCS 6193, pp. 118–129, 2010.

elements on M_{n-1} inconsistent with respect to their meta-classes on M_n. For example, an application may read the value of an attribute of an object whose meta-object does not exist and is therefore invalid. A database system contains layers M_0 through M_2, where M_2 is immutable. To provide a custom-defined and extensible system catalogue repository systems utilize an additional layer. Therefore the layer M_3 is introduced allowing for custom-defined M_2, repository systems allow for dynamic modification of M_2, M_1 and M_0 at run time. This however entails the specific problem of consistency between adjacent layers, i.e. the problem of structural integrity. Other systems do not face this kind of issues because they assume that the catalogue is static at run time.

As a well-accepted and widely applied repository system standard from Object Management Group(OMG), *Meta Object Facility*(MOF)[2] provides several mechanisms for controlling metadata integrity. Firstly, MOF defines a set of MOF Model constraints. Secondly, MOF defines a set of closure rules and computational semantics for the abstract mapping, and JMI defines computational semantics for the Java mapping. Thirdly, MOF provides the MOF constraint model element for expressing domain rules. Last but not least, MOF (and JMI) defines a set of repository interfaces. However all of the above contribute to well-formedness, but not structural integrity, i.e. propagation of changes to underlying layers when instances exist. This also leads to the violation of structural integrity frequently during the creation of the metadata structure, thus affect the stability of repository systems.

Aiming at this situation, in this paper, we study how to check structural integrity for repository systems based on MOF. Because MOF is rendered to users by graphs, which lack formal semantics, we believe that structural integrity checking has to based on a powerful underlying formalism. We try to check structural integrity by means of logic. Description Logics(DLs)[3], which are subsets of First-Order Logic, provide powerful description ability and equipped with reasoning engines such as LOOM[4], RACER[5], Fact[6], etc. which can perform various reasoning tasks, become our first choice.

First, in order to fully represent MOF architecture, according to the specialities of MOF architecture, we propose a DL which supports identification constraints on concepts, then we make a study of how to formalize the different levels of MOF architecture by means of the DL, next, we study how to check structural integrity using query and reasoning mechanism provided by the DL, finally, we discuss performance evaluation for the prototypical structural integrity checking system implemented by our approach and conclude the paper.

2 Related Work

The idea of supporting consistency across different meta-levels is not repository system specific - it emanates from the field of computational reflection[7] and Meta Object Protocols[8]. Metadata integrity is a key characteristic of reflective systems[12] supporting different Meta Object Protocols: OpenC++[9], MPC++[10], SOM[11]. A number of languages contain built-in reflective facilities supporting MOP with high levels of intercession: SmallTalk [14], CLOS, Schema etc. All of the above MOPs support intercession, which is the kind of reflection most relevant in the context of metadata integrity. However, in the field of repository systems, how to ensure structural integrity is still not well solved due to the particularity of the systems, also the concept of structural integrity is insufficiently specified in current MOF specification. Bernstein et al.[1] and Ilia et al.[13] elaborate conditions ensuring structural integrity for repository systems, they classify the structural integrity inconsistencies and present strategies to resolve them. Logic and theorem proving have been proposed by several authors for expressing software models and the derivation of inconsistencies from these models resp., e.g., [15][16][17], the logics they use are all not Description Logics. Compared with their approaches, the advantages of our approach is that reasoning problems in Description Logics are decidable, and a lot of work has investigated DLs wrt their expressive power and computational complexity. Diego et al. [19] introduce DLR, an expressive Description Logic with n-ary relations, for specifying and reasoning on a great variety of data models, including the relational, the entity-relational, and the object-oriented model. In [20], they further analyse the internal mechanism of DLR and discuss the decidability problems and computational complexity of reasoning in DLR. In addition, Simmonds [18] proposes the approach to deal with inconsistencies between UML class, statechart and sequence diagrams by means of Description Logics. Franz et al. [21] survey the related researches on the relationship between expressive power and computational complexity of reasoning of Description Logics.

3 The Description Logic DL_{id}

The basic elements of Description Logics are *concepts* and *relations*, which describe the types of objects and the relations between them in a domain, respectively. Complex concepts and complex relations can be formed from atomic concepts and atomic relations by constructors. The set of allowed constructors characterizes the expressive power of a Description Logic. Various Description Logics have been considered by the DL community. According to the specialities of MOF architecture, in this paper we propose a DL which supports identification constraints on concepts, here called DL_{id}. The DL_{id} offers highly expressive power for structuring mechanisms of MOF architecture and is equipped with decidable reasoning procedures, thus provides the description and reasoning of MOF architecture a rigorous formal and reasoning framework. The DL_{id} can be seen as a fragment of the Description Logic DLR presented in [20] by Diego et al.. The basic elements of DL_{id} are *concepts*(unary relations) and *roles*(binary relations). Atomic concepts and atomic roles are denoted by A and P, respectively. Arbitrary concepts, denoted by C, and arbitrary roles, denoted by R, are built according to the following syntax:

$$R ::= \top_2 \mid P \mid (i/2{:}C) \mid \neg R \mid R_1 \sqcap R_2$$

$$C ::= \top_1 \mid A \mid \neg C \mid C_1 \sqcap C_2 \mid (\leq k[i]R)$$

where i denotes the i-th component of role R, it can be 1 or 2; k denotes a non-negative integer; (i/2:C) denotes that the i-th concept associated with role R is concept C, sometimes we abbreviate (i/2:C) with (i:C); $\leq k[i]R$ is the multiplicity constraint on the participation to role R of the i-th component of R. We consider only concepts and roles that are *well-typed*, which means that $i \leq 2$ whenever i denotes a component of a role R.

A DL_{id} *knowledge base* (KB) is constituted by the *Tbox* and the *Abox*. The Tbox is the set of *axioms* describing domain structure and contains *inclusion assertions* of type $R_1 \sqsubseteq R_2$, $C_1 \sqsubseteq C_2$. Besides inclusion assertions, DL_{id} KBs allow for assertions expressing identification constraints.

An *identification assertion* on a concept has the form:

$$(\text{id}\ \ C\ \ [i_1]R_1, \ldots, [i_h]R_h)$$

where C is a concept, each R_j is a role, and each i_j denotes one component of R_j. Intuitively, such an assertion states that if two instances of concept C both participate to R_j as the i_j-th component, then they coincide.

The Abox in DL_{id} is the set of axioms describing instances, it is constituted by *concept assertions* stating whether an object belongs to a certain concept and *role assertions* stating whether two objects satisfy a certain relation.

The semantics of DL_{id} is specified through the notion of interpretation. An *interpretation* $\mathcal{I} = (\Delta^{\mathcal{I}}, \cdot^{\mathcal{I}})$ of a DL_{id} KB $\mathcal{K}$ is constituted by an *interpretation domain* $\Delta^{\mathcal{I}}$ and an *interpretation function* $\cdot^{\mathcal{I}}$ that assigns to each concept C a subset $C^{\mathcal{I}}$ of $\Delta^{\mathcal{I}}$ and to each role R a subset $R^{\mathcal{I}}$ of $(\Delta^{\mathcal{I}})^2$. More semantics are shown in table 1:

Table 1. Semantic rules for DL_{id}

$\top_2^{\mathcal{I}} \subseteq (\Delta^{\mathcal{I}})^2$	$\top_1^{\mathcal{I}} = \Delta^{\mathcal{I}}$
$P^{\mathcal{I}} \subseteq \top_2^{\mathcal{I}}$	$A^{\mathcal{I}} \subseteq \Delta^{\mathcal{I}}$
$(i/2{:}C)^{\mathcal{I}} = \{t \in \top_2^{\mathcal{I}} \mid t[i] \in C^{\mathcal{I}}\}$	$(\neg C)^{\mathcal{I}} = \Delta^{\mathcal{I}} \setminus C^{\mathcal{I}}$
$(\neg R)^{\mathcal{I}} = \top_2^{\mathcal{I}} \setminus R^{\mathcal{I}}$	$(C_1 \sqcap C_2)^{\mathcal{I}} = C_1^{\mathcal{I}} \cap C_2^{\mathcal{I}}$
$(R_1 \sqcap R_2)^{\mathcal{I}} = R_1^{\mathcal{I}} \cap R_2^{\mathcal{I}}$	$(\leq k[i]R)^{\mathcal{I}} = \{a \in \Delta^{\mathcal{I}} \mid \#\{t \in R_1^{\mathcal{I}} \mid t[i]=a\} \leq k\}$

To specify the semantics of a KB we have the following definitions:

(i) An interpretation $\mathcal{I}$ *satisfies* an inclusion assertion $R_1 \sqsubseteq R_2$ (resp. $C_1 \sqsubseteq C_2$) if $R_1^{\mathcal{I}} \subseteq R_2^{\mathcal{I}}$ (resp. $C_1^{\mathcal{I}} \subseteq C_2^{\mathcal{I}}$).

(ii) An interpretation $\mathcal{I}$ *satisfies* the assertion $(\text{id}\ \ C\ \ [i_1]R_1, \ldots, [i_h]R_h)$ if for all a, $b \in C^{\mathcal{I}}$ and for all $t_1, s_1 \in R_1^{\mathcal{I}}, \ldots, t_h, s_h \in R_h^{\mathcal{I}}$ we have that:

$$\begin{array}{l} a=t_1[i_1]=\ldots=t_h[i_h], \\ b=s_1[i_1]=\ldots=s_h[i_h], \qquad \text{implies } a=b \\ t_j[i]=s_j[i], j\in\{1,\ldots,h\}, i\neq i_j \end{array}$$

An interpretation that satisfies all assertions in a KB $\mathcal{K}$ is called a *model* of $\mathcal{K}$.

Several reasoning services are applicable to DL_{id} KBs. The most important ones are KB satisfiability and logical implication. A KB $\mathcal{K}$ is *satisfiable* if there exists a model of $\mathcal{K}$. A concept C is *satisfiable* in a KB $\mathcal{K}$ if there is a model $\mathcal{I}$ of $\mathcal{K}$ such that $C^{\mathcal{I}}$ is nonempty. A concept C_1 is *subsumed by* a concept C_2 in a KB $\mathcal{K}$ if $C_1^{\mathcal{I}} \subseteq C_2^{\mathcal{I}}$ for every model $\mathcal{I}$ of $\mathcal{K}$. An assertion α is *logically implied* by $\mathcal{K}$ if all models of $\mathcal{K}$ satisfy α.

Reasoning in the basic DL ALC[3] is EXPTIME-complete, on the other hand, DL_{id} can be mapped to a fragment of the Description Logic DLR[20] in which reasoning is also EXPTIME-complete, hence reasoning in DL_{id} is decidable, and is EXPTIME-complete.

4 Formalization of Different Levels in Repository System

In MOF architecture, the relationship between elements on two adjacent levels is the type-instance relationship, so we translate the elements on meta-levels M_{n+1}(n=0 or 1) into the Tbox and the elements on levels M_n which are the instances into the Abox. In detail, in the case of n=1, we formalize level M_2 and M_1 into the Tbox and the Abox, respectively, and the consistency checked is the consistency between level M_2 and M_1; in the case of n=0, we formalize level M_1 and M_0 into the Tbox and the Abox, respectively, and the consistency checked is the consistency between level M_1 and M_0. To be precise and brief, the following formalization is described in DL_{id} expressions.

4.1 Formalization of Meta-levels M_{n+1}

(1) Metaclasses

In the meta-level, a metaclass is also a class, so in the following we don't distinguish metaclass and class. A metaclass is graphically rendered as a rectangle divided into two parts, as shown for example in Figure 1. The first part contains the name of the metaclass; the second part contains the attributes of the metaclass, each denoted by a name and with an associated class, which indicates the domain of the attribute values. For example, the attribute namespace: Namespace of metaclass ModelElement means that each namespace is an instance of Namespace. Each "/" indicates that the type of the attribute is the metaclass already included in the meta-level, i.e., the metaclass that the attribute belongs to is associated with the metaclass that is the type of the attribute.

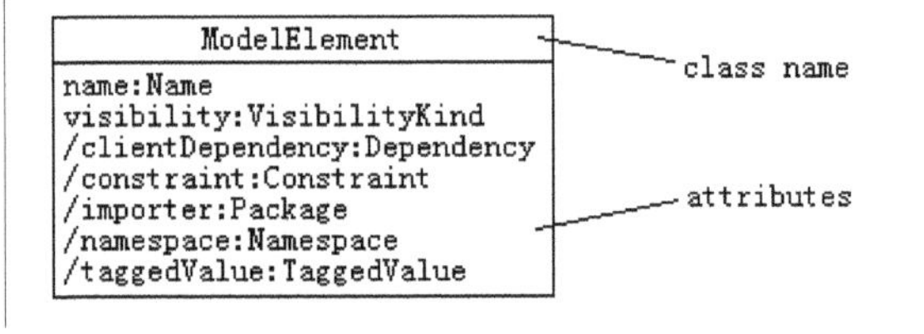

Fig. 1. Representation of a metaclass in level M_{n+1}

A metaclass is represented by a DL_{id} concept. This follows naturally from the fact that both metaclasses and DL_{id} concepts denote sets of objects.

An attribute a of type C' for a class C associates to each instance of C, zero, one, or more instances of a class C', so we think of an attribute a of type C' for a class C as a binary relation between instances of C and instances of C'. We capture such a binary relation by means of a role a of DL_{id}. To specify the type of the attribute we use the assertion:

$$C \sqsubseteq \forall[1]\,(a \Rightarrow (2 : C'\,))$$

Such an assertion specifies precisely that, for each instance c of the concept C, all objects related to c by a, are instances of C'. It also indicates that an attribute name is not necessarily unique in the whole meta-level, and hence two different metaclasses could have the same attribute, possibly of different types. Note that although the attributes after "/" denote associations between C and C', the formalization of such attributes is necessary, because one attribute of C may has several corresponding associations between C and C', if we only formalize the corresponding associations, the name of the attribute may be lost.

(2) Aggregation Associations
An *aggregation association* in the meta-level, graphically rendered as in Figure 2 (attributes are ignored), is a binary relation between the instances of two metaclasses, denoting a part-whole relationship. For example, the aggregation association between metaclass *Classifier* and *Feature* specifies that each instance of *Classifier* is made up of a set of instances of *Feature*. Observe that in MOF architecture, names of aggregation associations (as names of metaclasses) are *unique*. In other words, there can't be two aggregation associations with the same name.

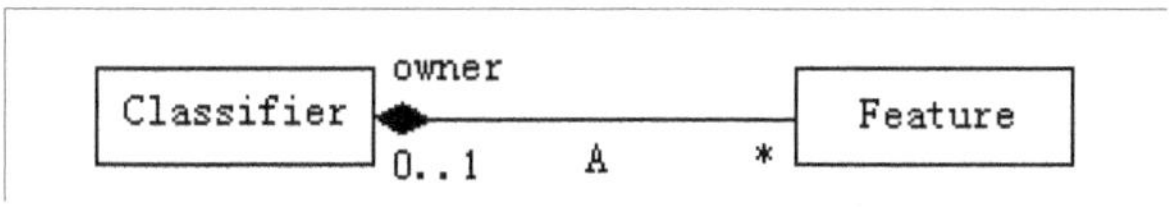

Fig. 2. Aggregation association in level M_{n+1}

The general form of the formalization of aggregation association is that if instances of the metaclass C_1 have components that are instances of metaclass C_2 by aggregation association A, the multiplicity on C_1 is $m_1..m_2$, the multiplicity on C_2 is $n_1..n_2$, then A is formalized in DL_{id} by means of a role A, and the following assertions are added to the Tbox:

$$A \sqsubseteq (1 : C_1) \sqcap (2 : C_2)$$
$$C_1 \sqsubseteq (\geq n_1[1]A) \sqcap (\leq n_2[1]A)$$
$$C_2 \sqsubseteq (\geq m_1[2]A) \sqcap (\leq m_2[2]A)$$

The second assertion specifies that for each instance of C_1, there can be at least n_1 and at most n_2 instances of C_2 related to it by role A. Note that the distinction between the contained metaclass and the containing metaclass isn't lost. Indeed, we simply use the following convention: the first argument of the role is the containing class. So the aggregation association shown in Figure 2 is formalized by means of the assertions (the multiplicities 0..* on *Feature* and 0 on *Classifier* are omitted):

$$A \sqsubseteq (1 : \text{Classifier}) \sqcap (2 : \text{Feature})$$
$$\text{Feature} \sqsubseteq (\leq 1[2]A)$$

Role names are not formalized, such as the role name *owner* of *Classifier*, because if we want to keep track of them in the formalization, it suffices to consider them as convenient abbreviations for the components of the DL_{id} role modeling the aggregation.

(3) Ordinary Associations

In MOF architecture, each *ordinary association* has a corresponding association class. To capture the information of an ordinary association, we formalize each ordinary association into a DL_{id} concept and two roles.

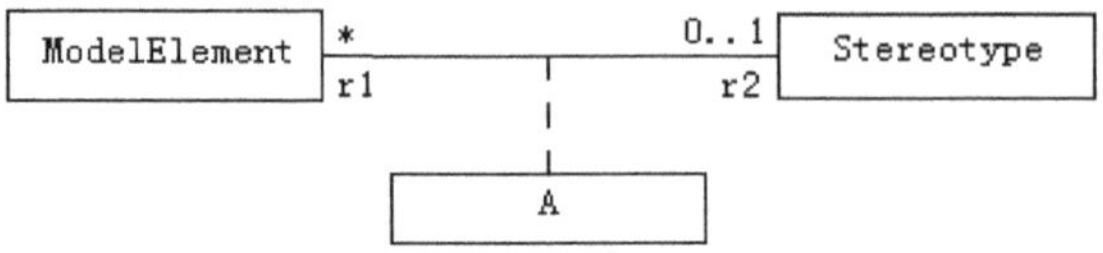

Fig. 3. Ordinary association in level M_{n+1}

For example, we represent an ordinary association shown in Figure 3 by introducing a concept A and two roles r_1, r_2, one for each component of the ordinary association A. Each role has A as its first component and concept *ModelElement* or *Stereotype* as its second component. Then we enforce the following assertion:

$$A \sqsubseteq \exists[1]\, r_1 \sqcap \forall[1]\, (r_1 \Rightarrow (2 : \text{ModelElement})) \sqcap$$

$$\exists[1]\, r_2 \sqcap (\leq 1[1]\, r_2) \sqcap \forall[1]\, (r_2 \Rightarrow (2 : \text{Stereotype}))$$

Note that the presentation of r_1 and r_2 is different from that in aggregation association because the names of DL_{id} roles (which correspond to the components of an ordinary association) are unique wrt the ordinary association only, not the entire meta-level. $\exists[1]\, r_i (i \in \{1,2\})$specifies that the concept A must have all components r_1, r_2 of the ordinary association A; $\leq 1[1]\, r_2$ specifies that the corresponding component is single-valued; $\forall[1]\, (r_1 \Rightarrow (2 : \text{ModelElement}))$specifies that the second component of r_1 has to belong to *ModelElement*. Finally we use the assertion:

$$(\text{id } A\ [1]r_1,\ [1]r_2)$$

to specify that each instance of the concept A indeed represents a distinct tuple of the corresponding association. By imposing suitable number restrictions on r_1 and r_2, we can easily represent a multiplicity on an ordinary association. Differently from aggregation association, the names of DL_{id} roles (which correspond to the components of an ordinary association) may be not unique wrt the entire meta-level, so the assertions which represent the multiplicities of an ordinary association are slightly different from those of an aggregation association. The multiplicities shown in Figure 3 are captured as follows:

$$\text{ModelElement} \sqsubseteq (\geq 0\ [2]\, (r_1 \sqcap (1 : A))) \sqcap (\leq 1\ [2]\, (r_1 \sqcap (1 : A)))$$

(4) Generalization and Inheritance
In MOF architecture, one can use *generalization* between a parent class and a child class to specify that each instance of the child class is also an instance of the parent class. Hence the instances of the child class inherit the prosperities of the parent class, but typically they satisfy additional properties that do not hold for the parent class.

Generalization is naturally supported in DL_{id}. In MOF architecture, the metaclass *Element* generalizes *ModelElement*, we can express this by the DL_{id} assertion: ModelElement $\sqsubseteq$ Element.

Inheritance between DL_{id} concepts works exactly as inheritance between metaclasses. This is an obvious consequence of the semantics of "$\sqsubseteq$" which is based on subsetting. Indeed, in DL_{id}, given an assertion $C_1 \sqsubseteq C_2$, every tuple in a role having C_2 as i-th argument type may have as i-th component an instance of C_1, which is in fact also an instance of C_2. As a consequence, in the formalization, each attribute of C_2, and each aggregation association and each ordinary association involving C_2 are correctly inherited by C_1. Observe that the formalization in DL_{id} also captures directly multiple inheritance between metaclasses.

(5) Constraints
In MOF architecture, there are constraints expressed in the Object Constraint Language(OCL). These OCL constraints are used to express in an informal way information which can not be expressed by other constructs of model. Some constraints can be captured in DL_{id}, and reasoning about them is decidable. For example, the OCL constraint in level M_2: An Interface can only contain Operations, can be captured by:

$$\text{Interface} \sqsubseteq \forall \text{Classifier-Feature} . \text{Operation}$$

The other OCL constraints are essentially full first order logic formulas, hence they would make reasoning undecidable, so we don't consider these OCL constraints.

4.2 Formalization of Levels M_n

Each element in level M_n is an instance of the corresponding metaclass in level M_{n+1}, each relation between elements is the instance of the corresponding association between metaclasses, so the elements in level M_n should be formalized into the Abox in DL_{id} knowledge base. General forms are as follows:

(1) if element c in level M_n is the instance of metaclass C in meta-level, then we have:

$$c : C \text{ or } C(c)$$

(2) if element c_1 in level M_n aggregates c_2, the corresponding metaclsss C_1 (its ancestor) aggregates C_2 (its ancestor) by aggregation association A, aggregation association A is translated as role A in the Tbox, then we have:

$$< c_1 , c_2 > : A$$

(3) if element c_1 in level M_n is related to c_2 by non-aggregation, the corresponding metaclass C_1 (its ancestor) is related to C_2 (its ancestor) by an ordinary association

which is translated as concept A and roles r_1, r_2, then the relation between c_1 and c_2 can be captured by three assertions:

$$a : A \qquad < a , c_1> : r_1 \qquad < a , c_2> : r_2$$

5 Structural Integrity Checking

After the construction of DL_{id} knowledge base, the query and reasoning mechanism of the reasoning tool will allow the query and reasoning on the levels in repository system so that various inconsistencies can be detected. After a study of each reasoning tool, we choose LOOM which has a very expressive concept definition language and a powerful query and retrieval mechanism. The query facility and production rules of LOOM can be used to detect inconsistencies. Although the classification algorithm of LOOM is incomplete[4], it is complete on the knowledge base we introduce. The following is an illustration in which LOOM is used to detect the violation of structural integrity.

Structural integrity constraint specifies that when the type of an attribute in the meta-level is changed, if the primitive type is the metaclass which is already included in the meta-level and the new attribute type is not a super-class of the old one, then the change should be propagated to underlying layers, otherwise inconsistency will arise[1]. The inconsistency can be detected by the following function(assume that the type of the attribute *referencedTableType* which belongs to the metaclass *Column* is changed from *SQLStructuredType*(which is shown in Figure 4) to *SQLSimpleType*, but not the super-class of *SQLStructuredType*, e.g. *SQLDataType*):

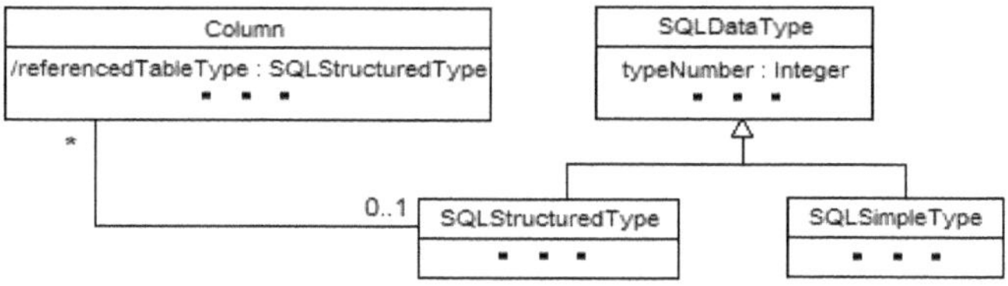

Fig. 4. An example for structural integrity inconsistency

```
(defun  AttributeTypeCheck (referencedTableType)
... //the part omitted queries the Tbox, detects
metaclass Column which is the owner of
referencedTableType and metaclass SQLSimpleType which
is the type of referencedTableType and the
instances ?column of Column.
(let* ((?count1 (length (retrieve (?sqldatatype)
(:and
(referencedTableType  ?column  ?sqldatatype)))))
(?count2 (length (retrieve (?sqldatatype)
(:and
(referencedTableType  ?column  ?sqldatatype)
(SQLSimpleType ?sqldatatype))))))
(if (>  ?count1  ?count2)
(format t "Attribute type conflict: some fillers don't
belong to the type ~S."  referencedTableType))))
```

Given the metaattribute, the function queries the Tbox to obtain the metaclass which is the type of the attribute, and then queries the Abox, if there are fillers which are not of the type of the attribute, structural integrity is violated and the user is notified.

The next example is about the change of the multiplicity. Structural integrity constraint specifies that the change of the multiplicity of an attribute or an association end in the meta-level should be propagated to underlying layers, otherwise the number of corresponding instances in underlying layers may be inconsistent with the modified multiplicity. Assume that the multiplicity on metaclass *AssociationEnd* which is related with metaclass *Association* by a association is changed from 1 to 2, while the instances in underlying layers are not changed, we can apply the following function to detect the inconsistency:

```
(defun  MultiplicityCheck (?association)
...  //the part omitted queries the knowledge base,
detects Association which is the corresponding
metaclass of ?association and Association aggregates
AssociationEnd by aggregation association Association-
AssociationEnd.
(let* ((?count1 (length (retrieve (?associationEnd)
(:and
(Association-AssociationEnd
?association  ?associationEnd)))))
(?count2 (get-role-min-cardinality (get-concept
'Association)(get-relation 'Association-AssociationEnd
))))
(if (<  ?count1  ?count2)
(format t "Multiplicity conflict: ~S is associated with
~S elements, at least ~S is needed."  ?association
?count1  ?count2))))
```

Given the metadata element, the function queries the Tbox to obtain the bottom limit of the multiplicity range of the association related to the element imposed by the meta-level, and then compares it with the result that is obtained by querying the Abox, if the constraint is violated, the information about the inconsistency will be printed.

6 Performance Evaluation

In this section we briefly discuss the performance of structural integrity checking prototypical system implemented in terms of the above approach. We performed extensive tests to prove experimentally the validity of the proposed approach. The tests covered fully every case in structural integrity constraints: inconsistencies about changes of the generalization hierarchies; inconsistencies about the creation, deletion and modification of classes; inconsistencies about changes of the multiplicities of attributes and association ends; inconsistencies about the creation and deletion of packages; inconsistencies about changes of references, etc. The experimental results showed that the proposed approach can detect these inconsistencies accurately.

The performance tests were performed on a Pentium 4, 1.7GHz computer with 512 MB RAM. All measured times are in milliseconds.

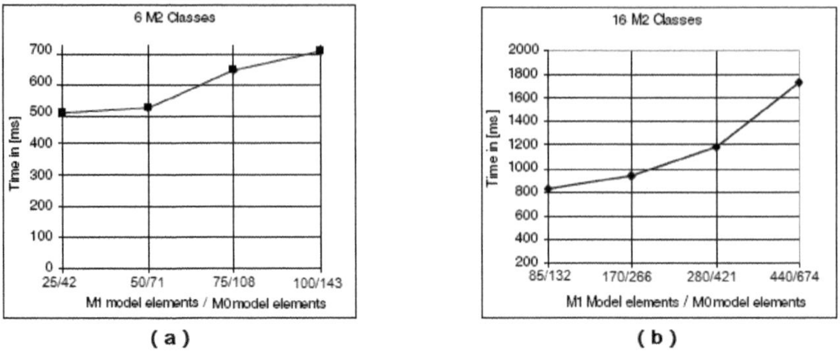

Fig. 5. Evaluation for time performance

Figure 5 shows the time performance of structural integrity checking system when the size of M_2, M_1 and M_0 models are changed. Figure 5(a) depicts the time performance in the case of a small M_2 model with 6 classes (total of 9 elements), while varying the number of corresponding M_1 and M_0 models instances and checking for consistency. Figure 5(b) depicts the time performance in the case of larger M_2 model and larger corresponding M_1 and M_0 models. An approximately linear dependency between the time performance of the prototypical system and the size of checked models can be seen, as it may be expected. The test results also show that the prototypical system exhibits acceptable time performance, on the average, on the small set of data.

7 Conclusion

In this paper, we propose an approach to check structural integrity for MOF-based repository systems. Using a particular formal logic of the family of Description Logics, this approach can provide support for the development of repository systems, so as to improve the reliability and the stability of repository systems. We have implemented a prototypical system in terms of the approach, the elementary performance evaluation results are encouraging.

References

1. Bernstein, P., Dayal, U.: An overview of repository technology. In: 24th International Conference on Very Large Databases, pp. 705–713. Morgan Kaufmann, San Francisco (1998)
2. Object Management Group: Meta Object Facility Specification Version 2.0 (2006)
3. Franz, B., Diego, C., Deborah, M., Daniele, N., Peter, F.P.: The description logic handbook: Theory, implementation, and applications, 2nd edn. Cambridge University Press, Cambridge (2007)
4. University of Southern California. Loom Knowledge Representation System 4.0 (2004)
5. Haarslev, V., Moller, R., Wessel, M.: RacerPro User's Guide Version 2.0 (2009)
6. Horrocks, I.: FaCT and iFaCT. In: International Workshop on Description Logics (DL 1999), pp. 133–135 (1999)

7. Albertini, B., Rigo, S., Araujo, G., Araujo, C., Barros, E., Azevedo, W.: A computational reflection mechanism to support platform debugging in SystemC. In: 5th IEEE/ACM international conference on Hardware/software codesign and system synthesis (CODES+ISSS 2007), pp. 81–86. ACM Press, New York (2007)
8. Eisenberg, A.D., Kiczales, G.: A simple edit-time metaobject protocol: controlling the display of metadata in programs. In: 21st ACM SIGPLAN symposium on Object-oriented programming systems, languages, and applications (OOPSLA 2006), pp. 696–697. ACM Press, New York (2006)
9. Pirkelbauer, P., Solodkyy, Y., Stroustrup, B.: Open Multi-methods for C++. In: 6th International Conference on Generative Programming and Component Engineering, pp. 123–134. ACM Press, New York (2007)
10. Ishikawa, Y., Hori, A., Sato, M., Matsuda, M., Nolte, J., Tezuka, H., Konaka, H., Maeda, M., Kubota, K.: Design and Implementation of Metalevel Architecture in C++, MPC++ Approach. In: 1996 International Conference on Reflection, pp. 141–154 (1996)
11. Bingham, E., Kuusisto, J., Lagus, K.: ICA and SOM in text document analysis. In: 25th annual international ACM SIGIR conference on Research and development in information retrieval (SIGIR 2002), pp. 361–362. ACM Press, New York (2002)
12. Coulson, G., Blair, G., Grace, P.: On the performance of reflective systems software. In: 2004 IEEE International Conference on Performance, Computing, and Communications, pp. 763–769. IEEE Press, New York (2004)
13. Petrov, I., Jablonski, S., Holze, M., Nemes, G., Schneider, M.: iRM: An OMG MOF Based Repository System with Querying Capabilities. In: Atzeni, P., Chu, W., Lu, H., Zhou, S., Ling, T.-W. (eds.) ER 2004. LNCS, vol. 3288, pp. 850–851. Springer, Heidelberg (2004)
14. Black, A.P., Schärli, N., Ducasse, S.: Applying traits to the smalltalk collection classes. In: 18th annual ACM SIGPLAN conference on Object-oriented programing, systems, languages, and applications (OOPSLA 2003), pp. 47–64. ACM Press, New York (2003)
15. Liau, C.-J.: A modal logic framework for multi-agent belief fusion. J. ACM Transactions on Computational Logic (TOCL) 6(1), 124–174 (2005)
16. Halpern, J.Y., Weissman, V.: Using First-Order Logic to Reason about Policies. J. ACM Transactions on Information and System Security (TISSEC) 11(4) (2008)
17. Emmerich, W., Finkelstein, A., Antonelli, S., Armitage, S., Stevens, R.: Managing standards compliance. J. IEEE Transactions on Software Engineering 25(6), 836–851 (1999)
18. Simmonds, J.: Consistency maintenance of uml models with description logic. Master's thesis, Vrije Universiteit Brussel, Brussel (2003)
19. Calvanese, D., De Giacomo, G., Lenzerini, M.: Identification constraints and functional dependencies in description logics. In: 17th International Joint Conference on Artificial Intelligence (IJCAI 2001) (2001)
20. Calvanese, D., De Giacomo, G.: Expressive description logics. In: The Description Logic Handbook: Theory, Implementation and Applications, pp. 178–218. Cambridge University Press, Cambridge (2003)
21. Baader, F., Lutz, C.: Description Logic. In: The Handbook of Modal Logic, pp. 757–820. Elsevier, Amsterdam (2006)

On Memory and I/O Efficient Duplication Detection for Multiple Self-clean Data Sources

Ji Zhang[1], Yanfeng Shu[2], and Hua Wang[1]

[1] Department of Mathematics and Computing,
The University of Southern Queensland, Australia
{Ji.Zhang,Hua.Wang}@usq.edu.au
[2] CSIRO ICT Centre, Hobart, Australia
Yanfeng.Shu@csiro.au

Abstract. In this paper, we propose efficient algorithms for duplicate detection from multiple data sources that are themselves duplicate-free. When developing these algorithms, we take the full consideration of various possible cases given the workload of data sources to be cleaned and the available memory. These algorithms are memory and I/O efficient, being able to reduce the number of pair-wise record comparison and minimize the total page access cost involved in the cleaning process. Experimental evaluation demonstrates that the algorithms we propose are efficient and are able to achieve better performance than SNM and random access methods.

1 Introduction

Data cleaning is of crucial importance for many industries over a wide variety of applications [5]. Aiming to detect the duplicate or approximately duplicate records that refer to the same real-life entity, duplicate record elimination is a very important data cleaning task attempting to make the database more concrete and achieve higher data quality. There are two major branches of research efforts in duplicate detection, with one mainly focusing on the efficiency issue of duplicate detection through developing high-level duplication detection frameworks, and the other on its effectiveness through studying more accurate record similarity measurements.

In terms of high-level duplication detection frameworks, the Sorted Neighborhood Method (SNM) [7] is among the first proposed to speed up the duplicate detection process by only examining neighboring records for a specific record. It involves three major steps: create key, sort data, and merge records. First, a key is computed for each record in the database by extracting relevant fields or portions of fields for discriminating records. Then all the records are sorted by the chosen key, and finally in the step of record merging, a window of fixed size is moved through the sequential order of records, limiting the record comparison to be carried out only within the window. SNM only compares a newly entered record with all the records in the window. The first record in the window will slide out upon the entry of a new record into the window. SNM serves as the basis of many existing duplicate detection methods. Among the variants of SNM are Duplicate Elimination SNM (DE-SNM) [6], Multi-pass-SNM [6], Clustering-SNM [7], SNM-IN/OUT [12] and RAR [14]. In DE-SNM, the records

M. Yoshikawa et al. (Eds.): DASFAA 2010, LNCS 6193, pp. 130–142, 2010.

are first divided into a duplicate list and non-duplicate list. The SNM algorithm is then performed on the duplicated list to produce the lists of matched and unmatched records. The list of unmatched records is merged with the original non-duplicate list using SNM again. Multi-pass-SNM uses several different keys to sort the records and perform SNM algorithm several times, rather than only one pass of SNM based on a single key. Generally, combination of the results of several passes over the database with small window sizes will be better than the result of the single pass over the database. Clustering-based SNM clusters records into a few clusters and the record comparison/merging process is performed independently for every cluster using SNM. SNM-IN/OUT and RAR use several properties based on the lower and upper bounds of the Longest Common Subsequence (LCS) Similarity and TI-Similarity, to save record comparisons without impairing accuracy under the framework of SNM.

Instead of using a fixed window in scanning the sorted databases, the Priority Queue method [10] clusters the records and uses the structure of priority queue to store records belonging to the last few clusters already detected. The database is sequentially scanned and each record is tested as whether it belongs to one of the clusters residing in the priority queue. The information-theoretic metric and clustering technique have also been used to identify groups of similar tuples, which will be considered duplicates [2].

In addition to the above window-based and clustering-based methods, an on-the-fly detection scheme for detecting duplicates when joining multiple tables [8]. This method, however, is not directly applicable for detecting duplicates in a single table where no join operations will be involved. A fuzzy task-driven duplicate match method is proposed to detect duplicates for online data [1][4]. Technique for detecting duplicate objects in XML documents is also proposed [16]. Zhang et al. proposed a partition-based duplicate detection method without using the sliding window or clusters [17].

The effectiveness of duplicate detection is typically addressed by using various metrics to measure the similarity of records. So far, there have been two broad classes of similarity metrics applied in measuring similarity of records: *domain-dependent* and *domain-independent metrics*. As for the domain-dependent metrics, an approach that uses an equational theory consisting of a set of rules to decide whether two records are duplicates is adopted [9]. This set of rules typically involves human knowledge and therefore are highly application-dependent. The major disadvantages of domain-dependent metrics are: (i) the rules can only decide whether two records are duplicate or not, and cannot reflect the degree to which the two records are similar to each other; (ii) the creation of such rules is time-consuming and must be updated to allow for the data updates; and (iii) the rule-based comparison is normally slow and cannot well scale up for large databases. The domain-independent measures, such as Edit Distance, LCS-Similarity and TI-Similarity, are used to measure the similarity of two fields of records by considering each field of the records as an alphanumeric string [10], [11], [13]. N-Gram is used to measure record similarity in [15]. These metrics are domain-independent since they can be applied in a wide range of applications without any major modifications. The adaptive combination of different domain-independent metrics is also studied using machine learning technique in order to achieve a higher level of accuracy than using each of them alone [3].

This paper falls into the first research direction, *i.e.*, investigating ways to improve the efficiency of duplicate detection. However, unlike existing methods that primarily focus on detecting duplicates from a single data source that can be fully loaded into memory, we study the case where data comes from multiple sources and duplicate detection needs to take into account memory constraints.

In this research, we assume that all the workloads are collected and processed in a single physical location. The transferring of data in this collection process is out of the scope of this paper. In addition, each data source are assumed to be self clean, meaning that each of them does not contain any records that are duplicated from others in the same source. This assumption is reasonable as it is pretty easy to apply whatever duplication methods that are appropriate to conduct cleaning for each data source before they are transfered to the same physical site for further cleaning. Each data sources is called a *cleaning workload* in the reminder of this paper.

As the technical contributions of this paper, we propose a number of duplicate detection algorithms for multiple self-clean data sources under memory constraint. These algorithms are memory and I/O efficient. They are able to reduce the number of pair-wise record comparison and minimize the total page access cost involved in the cleaning process. Experimental evaluation demonstrates that the algorithms we propose are efficient and are able to achieve better performance than SNM and random access methods.

Roadmap. The reminder of this paper is organized as follows. In section 2, we will present our duplicate detection algorithms for multiple self-clean data sources. We report the experimental results in Section 3. Section 4 concludes the whole paper.

2 Our Duplication Detection Algorithms

In this section, we will discuss in details the duplicate detection algorithms we propose for multiple self-clean data sources under memory constraint. Specifically, three possible cases will be explored and the corresponding memory or I/O efficient algorithms will be developed.

1. **Case 1**: All the workloads can be accommodated in the memory, that is, $\sum_{i=1}^{n} |CW_i| \leq M$. This also implicitly indicates that $\forall i, |CW_i| \leq M$;
2. **Case 2:** Not a single pair of workloads can be entirely accommodated in the memory, that is, $\forall i, j$, $1 \leq i \leq n$, $1 \leq j \leq n$, $i \neq j$, we have $|CW_i| + |CW_j| \geq M$;
3. **Case 3:** The cases other than case 1 and 2, that is, $\exists i, j, |CW_i| + |CW_j| < M$ and $\exists k, \sum_{i=1}^{k} |CW_i| > M$.

Note that there is another possible case that not a single workload can be accommodated in the memory. However, from the prospective of duplication detection where we need to have pair-wise evaluation between workloads, there is no difference between this case and Case 2. In other words, this case has been inexplicitly encompassed in Case 2.

The algorithm we propose for Case 1 is an in-memory algorithm as all the data sources can be fully loaded into the memory. However, the algorithms for Case 2 and Case 3 have to be external memory ones as the memory is not sufficiently large to hold all the data sources simultaneously.

2.1 In-Memory Duplication Detection Algorithm

We first discuss the in-memory duplication detection algorithm for Case 1. Since pairwise evaluation needs to be conducted for all the memory-resident workloads, thus it suffice to only discuss the duplication of two memory-resident cleaning workloads for Case 1. Let denote by m and n the number of records of two cleaning workloads CW_1 and CW_2 that will be performed and we have $|CW_1| = m$ and $|CW_2| = n$, where $|CW_i|$ denotes the number of records in cleaning workload CW_i. Intra-workload cleaning work is unnecessary since each cleaning workload itself is clean (We have assumed that each cleaning workload has undergone cleaning locally and the records in each of the workloads are already sorted). Hence, the duplication detection only involves inter-workload cleaning that aims to detect duplicate records across different cleaning workloads. Two straightforward methods can be applied to detect duplicates from these two workloads:

A. Pairwise Comparison
In the pairwise comparison method, each record in CW_1 will be compared with each record in CW_2. Obviously, the complexity of the pairwise comparison method is $O(m * n)$.

B. Sorted Neighborhood Method (SNM) Variant
We can also adopt the standard SNM method with some modifications for cleaning the two workloads. The two general steps of this SNM variant are as follows:

1. Sort the merged workload $CW = CW_1 \cup CW_2$;
2. Apply SNM on CW.

At the first glance, this variant of SNM is identical to the standard SNM method, however, there are a few important differences between them, as elaborated below.

- First, in the sorting step, the SNM variant does not have to re-sort the whole workload CW from scratch. Instead, it can take advantage of the fact that CW_1 and CW_2 are pre-sorted and thus it is able to sort CW more quickly. This is because (i) for two records r_1 and r_2 in CW_1, if r_2 comes after r_1 based on the sorting order in CW_1, then it is definitely that r_2 comes after r_1 based on the sorting order in CW; (ii) find the appropriate position in CW_2 for a certain record in CW_1 is efficient since CW_2 has been sorted, and vice versa;
- Second, when the window used in SNM slides through CW in the second step, comparison is only performed among the records that are both in the current active window and come from different workloads.

In light of the above discussions, we can see that this SNM variant is more efficient than the standard SNM method. But the question still remains that whether this SNM variant is more efficient than the pairwise comparison method which is more easily implementable. To answer this question, we will discuss in details their respective computational complexity to get insight on how to select the more efficient record comparison method between them.

Now, let us analyze the complexity of each step in the SNM variant as follows:

1. In the sorting step, we can either insert the m records in CW_1 into the n records in CW_2 or insert the n records in CW_2 into the m records in CW_1 in order to sort the merged workload CW. Since the records in both workloads are sorted, the worst-case complexities of the first and second strategies are $O(m * logn)$ and $O(n * logm)$, respectively. Hence, the complexity of this step is $O(m * logn)$ if $m < n$ or $O(n * logm)$ otherwise;
2. In the comparison step, we identify two extreme cases to study the complexity: (i) the records of the two workloads involved are *uniformly distributed* in the merged workload CW, and (ii) the records of the two workloads involved are *highly skewed* in the merged workload CW, *i.e.*, the records of one workload are all located at the beginning of CW while the records of another workload are all located at the end of CW. Given the window size ω is normally small in practice, thus it is safe to assume that $m >> \omega$ and $n >> \omega$ in our analysis.

In the first case discussed above, the number of records with which each of m records in CW_1 have to compare is in the order of $O(\omega * \frac{n}{m+n})$, where ω denotes the size of the sliding window used in SNM, and $\frac{n}{m+n}$ denotes the probability that the records in the current window are from CW_2. Likewise, the number of records with which each of n records in CW_2 have to compare is in the order of $O(\omega * \frac{m}{m+n})$. Therefore, the total computation of this step in this case will be

$$O(m * \omega * \frac{n}{m+n} + n * \omega * \frac{m}{m+n}) = O(\frac{mn\omega}{m+n})$$

In the second case discussed above, records comparison will be performed only when the sliding window moves to the position that overlaps the records of the two workloads. Thus, the number of records comparison need to be performed is equal to $(\omega - 1) + (\omega - 2) + \ldots + 3 + 2 + 1 = O(\omega^2)$. Therefore, the total computation of this step in this case will be $O(\omega^2)$.

Without losing generality, we assume that $m > n$, then we have

$$\frac{mn\omega}{m+n} > \frac{mn\omega}{2m} = \frac{n\omega}{2} >> \omega^2$$

since $n >> \omega$. This also holds when $m < n$. This analysis indicates that a higher complexity occurs for record comparison when the records of two workloads are uniformly or near uniformly distributed in the merged workload because, for each record, there will be a higher number of records need to be compared in the current window. We will thus use the complexity of this case as the complexity of the second step of the SNM variant in the sequel.

Combining the complexities of the above two steps, we can obtain the total complexity of this SNM variant as

$$O(min(m * logn, n * logm) + \frac{mn\omega}{m+n})$$

Again, we assume that $m > n$, the complexity of the SNM variant will become

$$O(n * logm + \frac{mn\omega}{m+n})$$

Since we have:

$$n * logm + \frac{mn\omega}{m+n} < m * logm + \frac{1}{2} * \omega(m+n) < m * logm + \omega m = m(logm + \omega)$$

The complexity of this SNM variant is thus bounded by

$$O(m(logm + \omega))$$

This analysis is consistent with our preceding claim that our SNM variant is more efficient than the standard SNM method which has a complexity of $O((m+n)log(m+n)+\omega(m+n))$, where $O((m+n)log(m+n))$ is the complexity for sorting the records in the two workloads and $\omega(m+n)$ corresponds to the complexity of scanning all the records in the two workloads using the sliding window.

Therefore, if $n >> logm+\omega$, then $O(mn) >> O(m(logm+\omega))$, in which case we should choose the SNM variant method since it features a lower complexity. Otherwise, we choose the pairwise comparison method.

Since ω is normally small, a more general and approximated selection strategy can thus be given as: if $min(m,n) >> log\, max(m,n)$, then we choose the SNM variant method with a complexity of

$$O(max(m,n) * (log\, max(m,n) + \omega))$$

the pairwise comparison method with a complexity of $O(m * n)$ will be picked otherwise.

2.2 External Memory Duplication Detection Algorithms

In this subsection, we will investigate Case 2 and 3 where not all the cleaning workloads are able to be loaded simultaneously into the memory. External memory algorithms are developed for addressing these two cases.

• **Algorithm for Case 2**

In this case, not a single pair of workloads can be fully loaded into the memory for processing. Thus, we have to perform *workload partitioning* in order to re-size the workloads for memory loading. Here, we classify the workload partitions as the *resident workload partition* and the *streaming workload partition*. The resident workload partitions are the partitions that reside in the memory as long as possible and the streaming workload partitions are those that are discard from memory when they have been compared with the current resident workload partition in memory.

Corresponding to the above categorization of workload partitions, we split the memory available into two parts accordingly: the memory allocated for the resident workload partitions and the memory allocated for the streaming workload partitions. We denote by M_r as the size of the memory allocated for resident workload partition, thus the memory for streaming workload partition is $M - M_r$, where M is the total memory available.

Now, let us give a description of the algorithm. In each step, we pick up a cleaning workload as the resident workload (all its partitions obtained are the resident workload

Algorithm Clean_Workloads_In_Case_2

Input: All the n workloads to be cleaned;

Output: The cleaned workloads;

$WorkloadSet = \emptyset$;

FOR i=1 to n DO

  $WorkloadSet = \cup\{i\}$;

WHILE $WorkloadSet \neq \emptyset$ DO {

  Pick workload r as resident workload from *Workloadset* based on Equation (3);

  $WorkloadSet- = \{r\}$;

  WHILE r has not been fully loaded into memory DO {

    Load r with a size of M_r into memory;

  WHILE the streaming workloads have not been fully loaded

   into memory DO {

      Load the streaming workloads with a size of $M - M_r$ into memory;

      Compare the currently loaded resident and streaming workloads;

      Label duplicates in the current resident and streaming workloads;

      Discard the loaded streaming workload;

      }

    }

}

Remove duplicates from all the workloads;

Fig. 1. Algorithm to compare two workloads in Case 2

partitions), and all the remaining workloads are the streaming workloads (all its partitions obtained are the streaming workload partitions). When each resident workload partition is loaded into the memory, all the streaming workload partitions will sequentially stream into the memory and compared with the current resident workload partition. The streaming workload partitions are then removed from the memory afterwards. After each step, the resident workload will be deleted from the set of workloads, and a new resident workload will be selected for the next round of comparison. The whole comparison process is terminated when there are no any workloads that can be potentially picked up as the resident workloads. The detailed algorithm is presented in Figure 1.

If we model each workload partition as a *page*, we will be able to analyze the number of page access in each step of the algorithm. Suppose CW_j is the resident workload selected in a step when there are $k-1$ workloads left, with a total workload of W (i.e., $W = |CW_1| + |CW_2| + \cdots + |CW_k|$). The number of page access of CW_j will be $\frac{|CW_j|}{M_r}$, and the number of page access of the streaming workload CW_i ($1 \le i \le k$ and $i \neq j$) is $\frac{|CW_i|}{M-M_r}$. Therefore, the total number of page access when CW_j is chosen as the resident workload is

$$f(CW_j) = \frac{|CW_j|}{M_r} * (\frac{|CW_1|}{M-M_r} + \frac{|CW_2|}{M-M_r} + \frac{|CW_{j-1}|}{M-M_r} + \frac{|CW_{j+1}|}{M-M_r} + \ldots + \frac{|CW_k|}{M-M_r})$$

$$= \frac{|CW_j| * (W - |CW_j|)}{M_r * (M - M_r)} \quad (1)$$

Taking the first derivative of $f(CW_j)$ w.r.t M_r, we have

$$\frac{\partial f(CW_j)}{\partial M_r} = \frac{-|CW_j|(W - |CW_j|)(M - 2M_r)}{M_r^2(M - M_r)^2}$$

Let $\frac{\partial f(CW_j)}{\partial M_r} = 0$, we can get the optimal M_r, denoted as M_r^*, as

$$M_r^* = \frac{M}{2} \tag{2}$$

Obviously, $M_r^* \neq 0$ and $M_r^* \neq M$, so it is always guaranteed that $\frac{\partial f}{\partial M_r}$ is meaningful. By specifying M_r as in Equation (2), we can minimize the function $f(CW_j)$. Note that the optimal size of memory allocated to resident workload partitions (and also to streaming workload partitions) is independent of CW_j, the actual workload we choose in each step as the resident workload.

Now, the unsolved question is that which workload should be chosen as the resident workload in each step. In other words, how CW_j can be decided in each step. Based on Equation (1), let us take the first derivative of $f(CW_j)$ w.r.t CW_j as

$$\frac{\partial f(CW_j)}{\partial CW_j} = \frac{W - 2|CW_j|}{M_r(M - M_r)}$$

Let$\frac{\partial f(CW_j)}{\partial CW_j} = 0$, we can get

$$|CW_j| = \frac{W}{2}$$

Note that when $|CW_j| = \frac{W}{2}$, the objective function $f(CW_j)$ will reach its maximum. Therefore, to minimize $f(CW_j)$ we need to choose workloads whose sizes are as far from $\frac{W}{2}$ as possible. In other words, the optimal value for $|CW_j|$, denoted as $|CW_j^*|$, is specified as

$$CW_j^* = argmax(||CW_j| - \frac{W}{2}|) \tag{3}$$

• Algorithm for Case 3

In the third case where there exists some workload pairs that can be loaded into the memory but not all the workloads can be loaded into the memory, we will perform the cleaning in the following five steps:

1. All the workloads are sorted in a descending order by their sizes, that is, in the sorted order, if CW_i come before CW_j then $|CW_i| \leq |CW_j|$;
2. Starting from the first workload in the sorting order, we pick as many workloads as possible whose total size will not exceed the memory limit and load them into the memory simultaneously. To be more specific, we pick the first l workloads in the ordered list to load into the memory if $\sum_{i=1}^{l} |CW_i| \leq M$ and $\sum_{i=1}^{l+1} |CW_i| > M$. Remove these l workloads from the sorting list;
3. Like Case 1, the in-memory duplication detection algorithm can be employed to clean all these k workloads. After this is done, all these k workloads are merged to form a new workload as $CW' = CW_1 \cup CW_2 \cup, \ldots, \cup CW_l$;

4. Repeat Step 2 and 3 until there not long exists a pair of workloads that can be loaded into the memory simultaneously for cleaning;
5. The algorithm of Case 2 is then used to clean the new set of merged workloads that are obtained after Step 4.

We present the following lemma to ensure that the condition of case 2 is alway satisfied after Step 4 of the above algorithm.

Lemma 1. For any pair of merged workloads CW_1 and CW_2 after Step 4 of the above algorithm, we have $|CW_1| + |CW_2| > M$.

Proof. By contradiction. We assume that there exist two workloads CW_1 and CW_2 such that $|CW_1|+|CW_2| \leq M$. $|CW_1|$ and $|CW_2|$ are two maximal memory-loadable workloads and are obtained by merging m and n workloads in the sorting list, respectively, i.e.

$$CW_1 = CW_{11} \cup CW_{12} \cup, \ldots, \cup CW_{1m}$$

$$CW_2 = CW_{21} \cup CW_{22} \cup, \ldots, \cup CW_{2n}$$

Without losing generality, we assume that CW_1 come before CW_2 in the sorting list. Let $CW_{1\,m+1}, CW_{1\,m+2}, \ldots, CW_{1\,m+n}$ be the n consecutive workloads after CW_1 in the sorting list. Thus, $\forall i, 1 \leq i \leq n, |CW_{1\,m+i}| \leq |CW_{2i}|$. Therefore, $\sum_{i=1}^{n} |CW_{1\,m+i}| \leq \sum_{i=1}^{n} |CW_{2i}|$, that is, $\sum_{i=1}^{n} |CW_{1\,m+i}| \leq |CW_2|$. Because $|CW_1| + |CW_2| \leq M$ (by assumption), thus $|CW_1| + \sum_{i=1}^{n} |CW_{1\,m+i}| \leq M$, which is contradicted with the fact that CW_1 itself is a maximal memory-loadable workload.

This lemma ensures that the algorithm of Case 2 can be safely employed on the merged workloads in the Step 5 of the algorithm of Case 3.

2.3 Duplication Labeling

Before finishing this section, we would like to give some remarks on *duplication labeling*, which are applicable to algorithms of all the three cases. When two records are identified as duplicates, then we need to mark these two records as duplicates to each other. Suppose that two records $r_1 \in CW_1$ and $r_2 \in CW_2$ are detected as duplicates, then we have the following labeling for these two records:

For Record r_1 in CW_1, we label "duplicated with r_2 in CW_2"

For Record r_2 in CW_2, we label "duplicated with r_1 in CW_1"

The duplicate records are not removed from workloads until the whole detection process is finished. This is to ensure that more duplicate records can be detected. Following the above example, Record r_1 and r_2 are detected as duplicates. If r_2 is deleted immediately but it is duplicated with another record r_3, then r_3 cannot be detected due to the deletion of r_2. The duplication labeling is particularly important for the algorithm of Case 2 (and Case 3 as well which is based on the algorithm of Case 2) because not all the workloads can be simultaneously loaded into memory and duplication labeling helps maintain all the duplication information amongst records across different cleaning workloads.

3 Experimental Results

In this section, we will report the experimental results on the algorithms we proposed. The experimental evaluation is divided into major parts. The first part mainly evaluates the efficiency of the dual-workload in-memory duplication detection algorithm we proposed, while the second part is on the efficiency of our I/O-efficient external memory algorithm.

3.1 Efficiency of In-Memory Duplication Detection Algorithm

In the first part of our experimental evaluation, we compare our in-memory duplication detection method with the traditional Sorted Neighborhood Method (SNM). It suffices to only investigate the dual-workload case in this experiment. Both our method and the traditional SNM method first merge the two different cleaning workloads and use a sliding window to scan the merged cleaning workloads. They differ in that our method will not compare two records in the sliding window if they come from the same cleaning workload. The number of pair-wise record comparison is counted for both methods under varying degree of record skewness in the two cleaning workloads. The skewness of the records is measured by the metric of *overlapping ratio*. Let us suppose that the records are sorted by the same single key for two cleaning workloads CW_1 and CW_2 and we have $max(KeyValue(CW_1)) < max(KeyValue(CW_2))$. Also, the records within each cleaning workload are uniformly distributed. The overlapping ratio is defined as the ratio between the number of record pair $\{r_1, r_2\}$ where $r_1 \in CW_1$ and $r_2 \in CW_2$ that satisfy $KeyValue(r_1) > KeyValue(r_2)$ against the total number of records in the merged cleaning workload. Intuitively, the higher the value of overlapping ratio, the lower degree of record skewness will be for the merged workloads from CW_1 and CW_2. We evaluate in this experiment the number of pair-wise record comparison under varying overlapping ratio ranging from 10% to 90%. The size of the two cleaning workloads are both set to be 100 and window size $\omega = 10$. The number of pair-wise

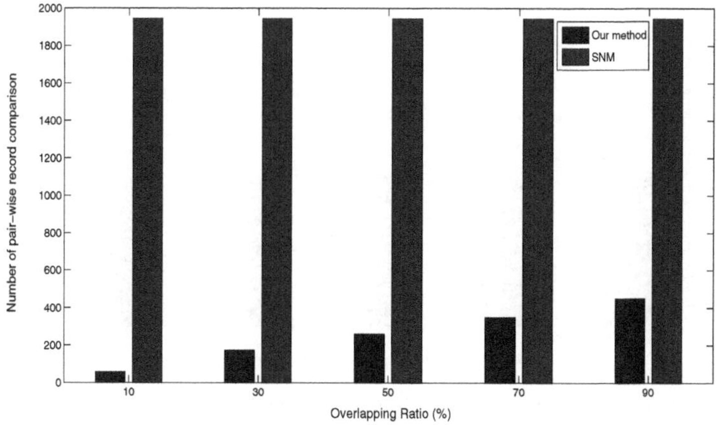

Fig. 2. The number of pair-wise record comparison of our method and SNM method

record comparison for the two methods are averaged over 10 runs for each overlapping ratio under study. The result is presented in Figure 2. As the figure shows, our proposed dual-workload in-memory cleaning method features a much smaller number of pair-wise record comparisons than the traditional SNM method, indicating a better efficiency of other method, espcially when a higher degree of skewness (*i.e.*, a lower overlapping ratio) exists between the two cleaning workloads.

3.2 Efficiency of External-Memory Duplication Detection Algorithm

For the external memory duplication detection algorithm, we investigate the total number of pages that need to loaded into memory during the duplication detection process. We only study the second case, as discussed in Subsection 2.2, where not a single pair of cleaning workloads can be fully loaded into memory for processing. Experiments are not conducted for the third case as it has been proven that the third cases can be reduced to the second case. We compare our method with the *random access method* in this experiment. The random access method randomly chooses the size of the memory allocated to the resident workload partitions (i.e., M_r) and the order in which the streaming cleaning workloads are loaded into memory. Without losing generality, we simply limit the memory M being only able to accommodate 100 records and a total of 5 cleaning workloads are created with varying sizes ranging from 200 to 1000, with 200 increment, in our experiment. This ensures that the condition of the second case is satisfied. Due to the nature of randomness for the random access method, we present the results of 5 different runs of the random access method in the figure and compare it with our method. The results are presented in Figure 3. The results show that in all of the 5 runs, our method outperforms the random access method, achieving a considerably lower number of pages that need to be loaded by delicately optimizing the size of resident workload partition and the loading order of streaming cleaning workloads.

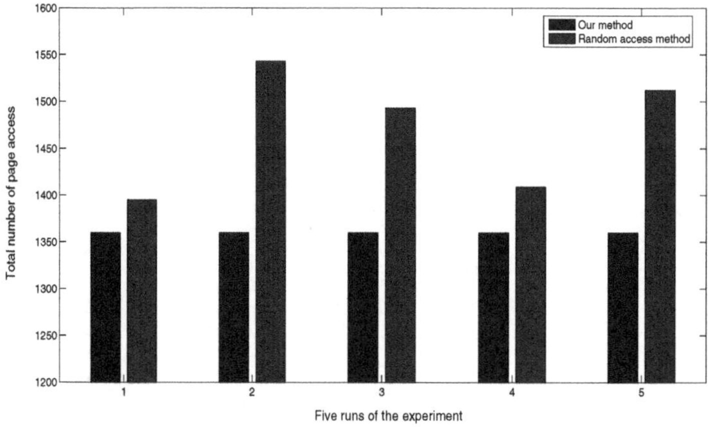

Fig. 3. The number of page access of our method and the random access method

4 Conclusions and Future Work

We investigate in this paper the problem of duplicate detection from the prospective of developing more memory and I/O-efficient algorithms for multiple self-clean data sources. Three possible cases are considered given the size of the data sources to be cleaned and the available memory. An in-memory efficient algorithm is proposed for dealing with the case that all the data sources can be fully loaded into the memory. This algorithm makes a good use of the characteristics of self duplicate-free for the data sources that need to be cleaned. It is faster than the traditional SNM method by reducing unwanted record comparison in the detection process. We also propose I/O-efficient duplicate detection algorithms for another two possible cases where the memory is not big enough to accommodate all the data sources simultaneously. These algorithms can minimize the page access overhead. Experimental results illustrate the better performance of our proposed algorithms.

Our methods require that all the data sources be obtained in one physical site to conduct duplicate detection. However, this may be quite expensive in practice if the data sources are geographically distributed due to the huge transfer overhead involved. We are interested in investigating in our future work the problem of how to deal with distributed self-clean data sources in order to achieve a small transfer overhead.

References

1. Ananthakrishna, R., Chaudhuri, S., Ganti, V.: Eliminating Fuzzy Duplicates in Data Warehouses. In: Proceedings of the 28th International Conference on Very Large Databases (VLDB 2002), Hong Kong, China, pp. 586–597 (2002)
2. Andritsos, P., Miller, R.J., Tsaparas, P.: Information-Theoretic Tools for Mining Database Structure from Large Data Sets. In: Proceedings of ACM SIGMOD 2004, Paris, France, pp. 731–742 (2004)
3. Bilenko, M., Mooney, R.J.: On Evaluation and Training-Set Construction for Duplicate Detection. In: Proceedings of the KDD 2003 Workshop on Data Cleaning, Record Linkage, and Object Consolidation, Washington, DC, August 2003, pp. 7–12 (2003)
4. Chaudhuri, S., Ganjam, K., Ganti, V., Motwani, R.: Robust and Efficient Fuzzy Match for Online Data Cleaning. In: Proceedings of ACM SIGMOD 2003, San Diego, USA, pp. 313–324 (2003)
5. English, L.P.: Improving Data Warehouse and Business Information Quality. J. Wiley and Sons, New York (1999)
6. Hernandez, M.: A Generation of Band Joins and the Merge/Purge Problem. Technical Report CUCS-005-1995, Columbia University (February 1995)
7. Hernandez, M.A., Stolfo, S.J.: The Merge/Purge Problem for Large Databases. In: Proceedings of the 1995 ACM-SIGMOD International Conference on Management of Data, pp. 127–138 (1995)
8. Gravano, L., Ipeirotis, P.G., Koudas, N., Srivastava, D.: Text Joins for Data Cleansing and Integration in an RDBMS. In: Proceedings of ICDE 2003, Bangalore, India, pp. 729–731 (2003)
9. Low, W.L., Lee, M.L., Ling, T.W.: A Knowledge-Based Framework for Duplicates Elimination. Information Systems: Special Issue on Data Extraction, Cleaning and Reconciliation 26(8) (2001)

10. Monge, A.E., Elkan, C.P.: An Efficient Domain-independent Algorithm for detecting Approximately Duplicate Database Records. In: Proceedings of SIDGMOD Workshop on Research issues and Data Mining and Knowledge Discovery (1997)
11. Monge, A.E., Elkan, C.P.: The Field Matching Problem: Algorithms and Application. In: Proceedings of International Conference on Knowledge Discovery and Data Mining (SIGKDD 1996), pp. 267–270 (1996)
12. Li, Z., Sung, S.Y., Sun, P., Ling, T.W.: A New Efficient Data Cleansing Method. In: Hameurlain, A., Cicchetti, R., Traunmüller, R. (eds.) DEXA 2002. LNCS, vol. 2453, p. 484. Springer, Heidelberg (2002)
13. Smith, T.F., Waterman, M.S.: Identification of Common Molecular Subsequences. Journal of Molecular Biology 147, 195–197 (1981)
14. Sung, S.Y., Li, Z., Peng, S.: A Fast Filtering Scheme for Large Database Cleansing. In: Proceedings of Conference on Information and Knowledge Management (CIKM 2002), pp. 76–83 (2002)
15. Tian, Z., Lu, H., Ji, W., Zhou, A., Tian, Z.: An N-gram-based Approach for Detecting Approximately Duplicate Database Records. International Journal of Digital Library 3, 325–331 (2002)
16. Weis, M., Naumann, F.: Detecting Duplicate Objects in XML Documents. In: Proceedings of IQIS 2004, Paris, France, pp. 10–19 (2004)
17. Zhang, J., Ling, T.W., Bruckner, R.M., Liu, H.: PC-Filter: A Robust Filtering Technique for Duplicate Record Detection in Large Databases. In: Galindo, F., Takizawa, M., Traunmüller, R. (eds.) DEXA 2004. LNCS, vol. 3180, pp. 486–496. Springer, Heidelberg (2004)

Top-K Generation of Mediated Schemas over Multiple Data Sources

Guohui Ding, Guoren Wang, and Bin Wang

College of Information Science & Engineering, Northeastern University, China
dgh_acheng@sina.com, {wanggr,binwang}@mail.neu.edu.cn

Abstract. Schema integration has been widely used in many database applications, such as Data Warehousing, Life Science and Ontology Merging. Though schema integration has been intensively studied in recent yeas, it is still a challenging issue, because it is almost impossible to find the perfect target schema. An automatic method to schema integration, which explores multiple possible integrated schemas over a set of source schemas from the same domain, is proposed in this paper. Firstly, the concept graph is introduced to represent the source schemas at a higher-level of abstraction. Secondly, we divide the similarity between concepts into intervals to generate three merging strategies for schemas. Finally, we design a novel top-k ranking algorithm for the automatic generation of the best candidate mediated schemas. The key component of our algorithm is the pruning technique which uses the ordered buffer and the threshold to filter out the candidates. The extensive experimental studies show that our algorithm is effective and runs in polynomial time.

1 Introduction

Schema integration has been a long-standing research problem and continues to be a challenge in practice [1, 11, 2]. Most of previous approaches that we know focus on outputting only one mediated schema which is just adapted to a given scenario. However, if this scenario changed, additional effort is needed to reintegrate the original data sources for a new mediated schema. So, it makes sense to create multiple mediated schemas. The work of [11] designs a tool that enumerates all possible mediated schemas and exploits user constraints to restrict their enumeration. However, their method is not an automatic process and relies heavily on user interaction; so, it is time consuming and labor intensive. An automatic approach for generation of multiple mediated schemas is proposed in [14], but they restrict the size of the input source schemas to only two; thus, their approach is helpless in the face of multiple data sources.

Based on the analysis above, in this paper, we propose an automatic approach to schema integration, which explores multiple possible mediated schemas over a set of source schemas. As opposed to the work of [14], our approach has no constraints on these source schemas, except they come from the same domain. The input to our method is multiple source schemas and correspondences between attributes, which are user-specified or discovered through the automatic schema

M. Yoshikawa et al. (Eds.): DASFAA 2010, LNCS 6193, pp. 143–155, 2010.

matching tools [5], while the output is multiple interesting mediated schemas. Firstly, the concept graph is introduced to abstract away the physical details of schemas with different models(relational or XML models). Then, the similarity between concepts is divided into intervals to generate three kinds of merging edges: positive edges, possible edges and negative edges, which are used to decide whether to merge two concepts. Finally, we design a novel top-k ranking algorithm for the automatic generation of the best candidate mediated schemas. The key component of the algorithm is the process of enumerating candidate schemas and the pruning technique. We test the time complexity of the algorithm, and the experimental results show that our algorithm is effective and runs in polynomial time. The contributions of this paper are summarized as follows:

1. For the first time, we propose an automatic approach to explore multiple mediated schemas over a set of source schemas.
2. We divide the similarity between concepts into intervals to form the merging edges which can be used to decide whether to merge the concepts.
3. A top-k ranking algorithm attached the pruning technique is designed to derive the best candidate mediated schemas.
4. The extensive experimental studies show that the proposed algorithm runs in polynomial time and has good performance.

The rest of this paper is organized as follows. Section 2 describes the concept graphs. The assignments and the top-k ranking algorithm are discussed in Section 3. The extensive experimental results are given in Section 4. A brief related work is reviewed in Section 5. Finally, we conclude in Section 6.

2 Preliminaries

In this section, we first describe the correspondences between attributes. Then, the concept graphs are presented, followed by some instances of the input source schemas and the concept graphs.

2.1 Attribute Correspondences

The traditional correspondence is a binary relationship between two elements both of which refer to the same object. However, our approach needs to tackle a set of source schemas, so the binary correspondence is invalid. As a result, we need to extend it to multivariate correspondence. The definition of multivariate attribute correspondence in our approach is given in the following.

Definition 1. *Let S be a universe of the input source schemas. Let U be a universe of attributes of S. Let $A = \{a_1, a_2, ..., a_i, ..., a_n\}$ be an attribute set and $A \subset U$. If the attribute set A satisfies the following constraints:*

- *all attributes in set A have the same semantics,*
- *for any attribute $x \in U$ and $x \notin A$, the semantics of attribute x is different from the semantics of the attribute set A,*

then we call the set A multivariate attribute correspondence, MAC for short.

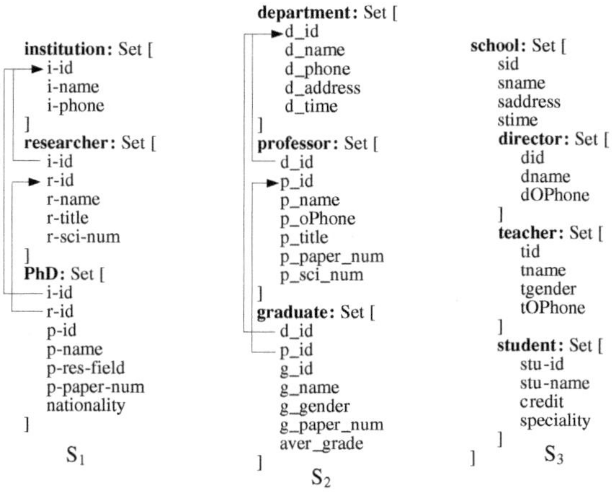

Fig. 1. The Input Source Schemas

According to Definition 1, we can see that the correspondence in our approach is an attribute set where the binary correspondence exists between any pair of attributes; thus, MAC satisfies a $(m : n)$ mapping cardinality constraint. As an example, the set mac ={"i-name", "d_name", "sname"} is a MAC, where the attributes are shown in Figure 1 (be introduced in detailed later). They have the same semantics, which represents the name of a group or a department.

2.2 The Graphs of Concepts

The source schemas may exist within different data models. For example, the three source schemas which are the input to our approach, are depicted in Figure 1. S_1 and S_2 are the relational schemas, while S_3 is the XML schema. The arrows represent the reference relationship. As in [11], we make use of the concept graphs with the edges depicting the *has-a* relationships to represent, at a higher-level of abstraction, the input source schemas.

The concept graph is a pair (V, has) where V is a set of concept nodes and has is a set of directed edges between concepts. Each concept node has an associated set of attributes and represents one category of data (an entity type) that can exist according to its schema, such as a relation name or a specific class in ontology. An edge of the graph depicts a directional reference relation between concepts. Please see [11] for more details.

The concept graphs corresponding to the input schemas S_1, S_2 and S_3, are shown in Figure 2 (overlooking the edges across the schemas for now). For simplicity, we omit the *has* edges of S_2 from the figure. As it can be seen, each relation name in the source schemas corresponds to exactly one concept node in Figure 2, for example, the relation table "PhD" corresponding to the concept node labeled "PhD". The method that transforms the source schemas into the concept graphs can be found in [14]. We shall use this example of the concept graphs in Figure 2 throughout this paper.

3 Top-K Generation of Mediated Schemas

In this section, we first describe how to merge the concept graphs, then introduce the assignment and the scoring function. Finally, we present the top-k ranking algorithm for the generation of the best candidate mediated schemas.

3.1 Merging the Concept Graphs

In general, there may exists much overlapping information and similar semantics between schemas from the same domain. For example, the relation "department" of S_2 is quite similar to the XML segment "school" of S_3, so they need to be combined to one. That's the reason for why we merge the concepts of the graphs.

Definition 2. *Let* $cs = \{c_1, c_2, ..., c_i, ..., c_n\}$ *be a concept set where* $n \geq 2$. *Let* $mac = \{a_1, a_2, ..., a_i, ..., a_n\}$ *be a MAC. If* a_i *is an attribute of* c_i *for* $1 \leq i \leq n$, *we say that cs is matched.*

The meaning behind the matched concepts is that these concepts have overlapping semantics. If two concepts are matched, an edge labeled with weight is created between them, and we call it merging edge. In Figure 2, the lines connecting nodes across schemas are the merging edges, and the weight is the similarity showing how well the two concepts overlap. To keep the fluency, we compute the weight later. According to Definition 2, we can also conclude easily that any subset of a matched concept set is matched too. So, if a concept set $cs = \{c_1, c_2, ..., c_i, ..., c_n\}$ is matched, there exist $n - 1$ merging edges which are outgoing from c_i. However, only the edges with the highest value of weight are reserved, because we would like to merge the most similar concepts.

In Figure 2, the similarity between "school" and "department" is very high (0.9), and all attributes of "school" have the same semantics with the corresponding attributes of "department". Obviously, they need to be merged into one single concept. On the contrary, only one attribute of "PhD" has the same semantics with the attribute "p-paper-num" of "professor", so they are different and we can not merge them. However, for "graduate" and "student", we can't make a decision about whether they should be combined or not, because of their vague similarity value (different users have different decisions). For the three cases above, we divide the similarity (weight) into three intervals from high to low: positive interval, possible interval, negative interval; then, obtain three kinds of merging edges with associated intervals. We list them in the following:

- **positive edges:** the weight of these edges locates at the positive interval and is very high. The two concepts connected by them have the same semantics over most of their attributes, so, we merge them to a single one;
- **possible edges:** these edges are associated with the middle weight which locates at the possible interval, so the combining relationship between the two concepts connected by them is vague. Thus, we take two merging strategies: combining them to a single concept or leaving them alone respectively.

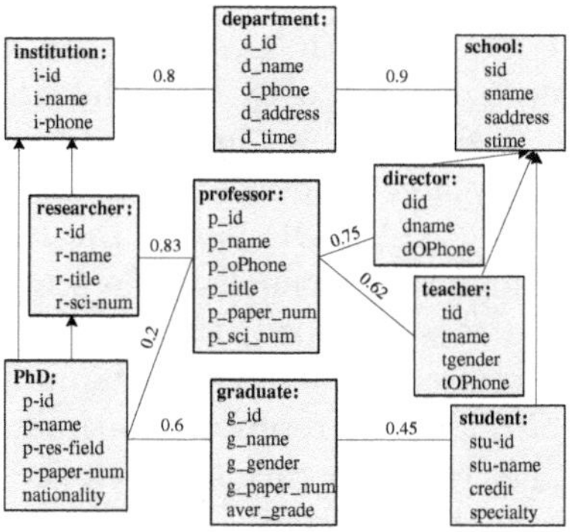

Fig. 2. Concept Graphs

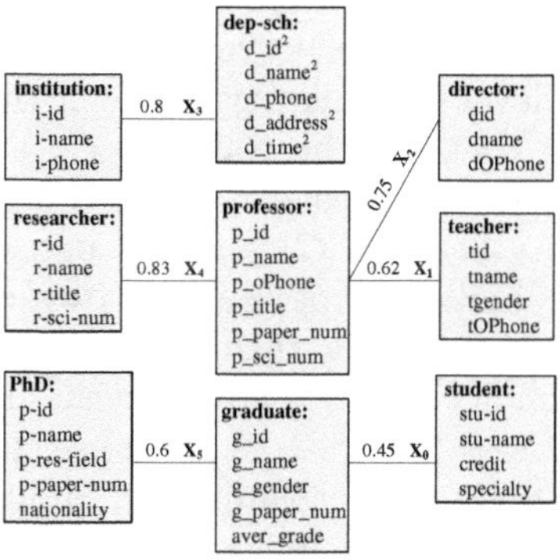

Fig. 3. Merging Graph

- **negative edges:** the weight of these edges locates at the negative interval and is very low, so, we break the edges and leave the concepts alone.

We use the binary vector, denoted as $\delta = (v_1, v_2)$, to represent the intervals, where v_1 indicates the right end point of the positive interval, while v_2 indicates the left end point of the negative interval. For example, $\delta = (0.9, 0.3)$ represents the following intervals: $[1, 0.9]$, $(0.9, 0.3)$ and $[0.3, 0]$. With these intervals, we can merge the "department" and " school" into the new concept "dep-sch", and break the edge between "PhD" and "professor"; then, the new graph, called merging graph, is obtained in Figure 3, with a set of possible edges X_0 to X_5 (not showing the *has* edges). For a possible edge, there exist two merging strategies; thus, we can get 2^6 mediated schemas based on X_0 to X_5. Obviously, the space of the candidate mediated schemas exhibits exponential growth in the size of possible edges. In what follows, we focus on how to retrieve the top-k candidate mediated schemas in this space.

3.2 Assignment and Scoring Function

Following the approach in [11], we use bit assignments to capture all the alternatives for using or not using the possible edges. We assume the edge x has a value of 0 or 1, where $x = 0$ represents one state (merging concepts or not), while $x = 1$ signifies the other state. Thus, all the possible edges make up of a bit *assignment* $\boldsymbol{X}$ which is a fixed-sized, ordered vector of bits. For now, we don't restrict that the value 0 or 1 denotes a specific state ($X_0 = 0$ be "merging", while $X_1 = 0$ may be "not merging"). As an example, all the possible edges in Figure 3 constitute an *assignment* $\boldsymbol{X} = [X_5\ X_4\ X_3\ X_2\ X_1\ X_0]$, and each specific assignment yields a possible mediated schema.

We design a scoring function for the *assignment* X, further, to find the top-k assignments which give rise to the most likely mediated schemas. The scoring function attaches a score to each possible assignment by aggregating the scores associated with the individual bits within the assignments. So, we need to compute first the score of the individual decision about whether to use or not use an edge. Here, we leverage the thought in [14]; that is, the score of the possible edge x, must reflect how much the decision to use or not the edge x agrees with the level of similarity between the two concepts connected by x. If the edge x that connects the concepts C_a and C_b is not used, then we impose a penalty which is referred to as the score for this strategy and is equivalent to the similarity between C_a and C_b, namely $score_x = S(C_a, C_b)$. Obviously, the higher the similarity between the two concepts, the higher the penalty (the score) is for not merging them. Conversely, if the edge x is included, then we impose a penalty which is equal to the dissimilarity between the two concepts, namely $score_x = 1 - S(C_a, C_b)$. We use the notation $D(C_a, C_b)$ to represent the quantity $1 - S(C_a, C_b)$ for simplicity. Similarly, the higher the difference between the two concepts is, the higher the penalty is for merging the concepts.

Now, we present the definition of the scoring function for the *assignment*. Let $\boldsymbol{X} = [X_n...X_i...X_0]$ be an *assignment*, and X_i is any individual bit within $\boldsymbol{X}$. Let C_i and C_i' be two concepts which are connected by the possible edge X_i. We define the scoring function to be:

$$score(\boldsymbol{X}) = \frac{1}{n}\sum_{i=1}^{n} f(X_i)$$

$$f(X_i) = \begin{cases} \min(S(C_i, C_i'), D(C_i, C_i')), & X_i = 0 \\ \max(S(C_i, C_i'), D(C_i, C_i')), & X_i = 1 \end{cases} \tag{1}$$

According to this definition, if we set the value of one bit to 0 within the assignment, the bit signifies the state which makes less contribution to the overall penalty of the assignment. In Figure 3, if X_1 is set to 0, then it suggests that the concepts "professor" and "teacher" should be combined (using the edge X_1), while if X_0 is set to 0, then it suggests that we can not merge the concepts "graduate" and "student" (ignoring the edge X_0). Now, we show an example for the computation of the score of the specific assignment $\boldsymbol{X} = [001001]$. Applying the equation 1, we obtain $score(\boldsymbol{X}) = \frac{1}{6}(0.4+0.17+0.8+0.25+0.38+0.55) = 0.425$.

3.3 Top-K Ranking Algorithm

We can discuss the problem of finding the top-k assignments which yield the most likely mediated schemas. The likelihood of the assignment being in the top-k results is inversely proportional to its score, so, our aim is to find the assignments with the lowest scores. In general, there exist 2^n possible assignments for a merging graph including n possible edges. Thus, the naive approach is infeasible.

Here, we develop a novel algorithm for the top-k assignment problem. Our algorithm enumerates the possible assignments and attaches the pruning technique to the enumeration. We use an example for the top-3 assignments, in Figure 4, intuitively to demonstrate the process of the algorithm. The *assignment* $\boldsymbol{X}$ corresponds to the possible edges in Figure 3. Our first step is to find the optimal assignment, namely the top-one. The state 0 of each individual bit represents the merging strategy making less contribution to the overall penalty. So, we set each bit to 0, within a given *assignment*, to derive the first optimal assignment.

X	X_5	X_4	X_3	X_2	X_1	X_0	score(X)	Top-3 Buffer
A_0	0	0	0	0	0	0	0 .308	A_0
A_1	0	0	0	0	0	1	0 .325	A_0, A_1
A_2	0	0	0	0	1	0	0 .348	A_0, A_1, A_2
A_3	0	0	0	0	1	1	0 .365	A_0, A_1, A_2
A_4	0	0	0	1	0	0	0 .392	A_0, A_1, A_2
A_5 - A_7	*						*	A_0, A_1, A_2
A_8	0	0	1	0	0	0	0 .408	A_0, A_1, A_2
A_9 - A_{15}	*						*	A_0, A_1, A_2
A_{16}	0	1	0	0	0	0	0 .418	A_0, A_1, A_2
A_{17} - A_{31}	*						*	A_0, A_1, A_2
A_{32}	1	0	0	0	0	0	0 .342	A_0, A_1, $\mathbf{A_{32}}$

Fig. 4. Example of The Top-k Ranking Algorithm

With our example, A_0 is the top-one assignment, and is inserted into the buffer. Based on the first assignment A_0, the rest of $\boldsymbol{X}$ is enumerated from the low bit to the high bit. If the binary assignment is represented as a decimal number, actually, we may perform an enumeration from 0 to 2^n (i.e. the subscript of the assignment notation A). So, A_1 (the decimal 1) and A_2 are the next two assignments, and we insert them directly into the buffer, because the size of the buffer is less than 3. We refer to the maximum of the scores of the assignments in the buffer as the threshold for the unknown assignments, denoted as λ. Because of $score(A_3) > \lambda$, A_3 is not the result. Next, according to the Theorem 1 and the fact, $score(A_4) > \lambda$, we can infer that the scores of the following three assignments, A_5, A_6, A_7, are all exactly greater than λ; thus, they are pruned from the following exploration. This is our pruning technique. The situation for the following A_8 and A_{16} is the same as A_4. The assignments pruned are denoted in red color to be distinguished from the assignments enumerated. Subsequently, the next assignment A_{32}, as the new result, replaces A_2 in the buffer, because of $score(A_{32}) < score(A_2)$, and becomes the new threshold. The subsequent enumeration of the unknown assignments is similar to the above process for exploring from A_0 to A_{32}, and we omit it due to space limitation.

Theorem 1. *Let* $\boldsymbol{X} = [X_n...X_i...X_0]$ *be an assignment, and* X_i *is any bit of* $\boldsymbol{X}$ *for* $n \geq i > 0$. *Let* $dec(\boldsymbol{X})$ *denotes the decimal number that* $\boldsymbol{X}$ *corresponds to. If* $X_i = 1$, $X_j = 0$ *for* $i-1 \geq j \geq 0$, *and* $score(\boldsymbol{X}) > \lambda$, *then we can infer that all the scores of the next sequential* $2^i - 1$ *assignments of* $\boldsymbol{X}$ *are greater than* λ, *formally described as* $score(\boldsymbol{A}) > \lambda$, *where* $\boldsymbol{A}$ *is any assignment of* $\boldsymbol{X}$ *and satisfies the constraint:* $dec(\boldsymbol{X}) + (2^i - 1) \geq dec(\boldsymbol{A}) > dec(\boldsymbol{X})$.

Proof. Here, we also refer to the assignment as a binary number. We rewrite the $\boldsymbol{X}$ to $[B_x B_0]$, where B_x denote the high bits $[X_n...X_i]$, while B_0 represents the low bits [0...0] which consists of all 0. The upper bound $dec(\boldsymbol{X}) + (2^i - 1)$ can also be rewritten to binary form $[B_x B_1]$, where B_x is the same as the above, and B_1 denotes the low bits [1...1]. Now, we can rewrite $\boldsymbol{A}$ to $[B_x\ X'_{i-1}...X'_j...X'_0]$, and get $[B_x\ X'_{i-1}...X'_j...X'_0] > [B_x B_0]$, according to the

Algorithm 1. Top-k Ranking Algorithm

$X[n]$: the *assignment* corresponding to n possible edges;
$Buffer$: the ordered buffer for the top-k results;
Initialize $X[n]$, λ, $i = n - 1$;

1: *topk*(i) **begin**
2: **for** (**int** $v = 0$; $v \leq 1$; v++) **do**
3: $X[i] = v$;
4: **if** $X[i] == 1$ **and** $i \neq 0$ **and** $buffer.size == k$ **then**
5: **set** $X[i - 1$ *to* $0] = 0$;
6: **if** $score(X[]) > \lambda$ **then**
7: **break**;
8: **end if**
9: **end if**
10: i−−;
11: **if** i $\geq$ 0 **then**
12: *topk*(i);
13: **else**
14: **if** $score(X[]) < \lambda$ **then**
15: $buffer.push(X[])$; **update** $buffer$, λ;
16: **end if**
17: **end if**
18: i++;
19: **end for**
20: **end**

constraint above. Further, we can obtain $[X'_{i-1}...X'_j...X'_0] > [0...0]$. Thus, there exist one bit at least in $[X'_{i-1}...X'_j...X'_0]$, whose value must be 1. Consequently, we can get $score([X'_{i-1}...X'_j...X'_0]) > score([0...0])$, because the value 1 signifies more penalty than the value 0, further, obtain $score(\boldsymbol{A}) > score(\boldsymbol{X}) > \lambda$. Because $\boldsymbol{A}$ is any assignment between $dec(\boldsymbol{X})$ and $dec(\boldsymbol{X}) + (2^i - 1)$, we conclude that all the scores of the next sequential $2^i - 1$ assignments of $\boldsymbol{X}$ are greater than λ, and the above theorem is true.

As the above example shows, we use the threshold and the Theorem 1 to prune the sequential assignments during each enumeration. The buffer preserves the temporary top-k assignments that have been enumerated. We may get the true top-k results cached in the buffer, in the end, when the algorithm terminates. The details are described in Algorithm 1. The algorithm is a recursive procedure. The data structure "$Buffer$" is the buffer of the top-k results generated so far. The lines $4 - 9$ are the filtering condition for pruning the following assignments (line 12). In lines 14 to 16, the threshold and the top-k buffer is updated, if the score of the new assignment is less than the threshold.

Now, we will make a little change to Algorithm 1 in order to improve its efficiency, just like in [14]. The notation $\Delta\alpha = score_{x=1} - score_{x=0}$ is referred to as the increased score flipping the bit x from 0 to 1. If the assignment A corresponding to n edges includes m bits whose values are 1, the total increment in score is $\frac{1}{n}\sum_{i=1}^{m}\Delta\alpha_i$ with respect to the score of the optimal assignment (the top-one). It can be seen that if A includes less bits whose values are 1, and each bit owns smaller $\Delta\alpha$, then A becomes the true results with high possibility. As a result, we rank the bits of the assignment $\boldsymbol{X}$ in a descending order of their $\Delta\alpha$ from the higher bits to the lower bits. This ensures that the assignments with smaller $\Delta\alpha$ are enumerated early and, further, enables most of the true top-k results to distribute in the early enumeration. Thus, the λ can quickly converge to the true threshold, and filter much of the following assignments.

3.4 Concept Similarity

Here, we regard the concept as a set which owns a number of attribute elements. Then, the improved Hausdorff distance [3] can be used to compute the distance between concepts and, further, we can calculate the concept similarity.

Definition 3. *Let C_a and C_b be two concepts, $C_a = \{a_1, a_2, ..., a_i, ..., a_n\}$ and $C_b = \{b_1, b_2, ..., b_j, ..., b_m\}$. We define the similarity between C_a and C_b to be:*

$$S(C_a, C_b) = 1 - \frac{1}{2}\left(\frac{1}{n}\sum_{i=1}^{n} d(a_i, C_b) + \frac{1}{m}\sum_{j=1}^{m} d(b_j, C_a)\right) \tag{2}$$

In the above equation, the portion computing the average of the summation is the improved Hausdorff distance, which is asymmetric. The first represents the distance from C_a to C_b, while the second signifies the reverse distance. So, we use the average for our concept similarity. The notation $d(a_i, C_b)$ denotes the distance from the element a_i to the set C_b. If no attributes in C_b with a_i are in the same MAC (no correspondences between a_i and any attribute in C_b), then the value of $d(a_i, C_b)$ is 1, else is 0.

4 Performance Evaluation

In this section, we first present the synthetic integration scenarios, then, show the simulation results evaluating the performance of our top-k ranking algorithm along three dimensions: the number of the input schemas, the number k of results retrieved, and the parameter δ which is used to divide the similarity. Furthermore, we compare the top-k algorithm with its improved version in which the bits of the assignments are ranked, and we call them "original" and "improved" algorithm respectively in our experiment. Our algorithm is implemented using C++ language and the experiments were carried on a PC compatible machine, with Intel Core Duo processor (1.73GHz).

We describe how to generate the synthetic schemas. For one input schema, we randomly generate a number of concepts between 2 and 7, then, we randomly assign 3 to 8 attributes to a given concept. In what follows we focus on simulating the correspondences between attributes, namely MAC. The perfect integration scenario is that all input schemas are the same as each other, namely any schema can be referred to as the duplicate of one of them. The number of MACs for this scenario is the number of attributes of a schema, denoted as m, and each

MAC contains all the duplicates of an attribute. Because of the real-world input schemas to our approach coming from the same domain, we assume that 80% of the attributes are similar; this means that 8 of 10 attributes from different schemas have the same semantics. So, we get the computation for the number of MAC in our synthetic scenario, denoted as $\frac{aver}{0.8}$, where $aver$ represents the average of the attribute number in each schema. Based on the MAC generated, we randomly distribute the attributes to any MAC. For each time of running the algorithm, we randomly generate a set of synthetic schemas according to the requirement of the algorithm. Aa a result, all the simulation results are the average performance of running the algorithm for some times.

Figure 5 shows the change in the running times as the effect of varying the number of the input schemas. As it can be seen, the time increase with the variation in the number of the input schema from 10 to 100. Both of the two algorithms perform well, even the original one itself have good performance, less than one second for retrieving 20 results from the 100 input schemas. We also observe that the improved one take less time than the original algorithm, and varies slowly with the increase of input schemas. And this is consistent with the analysis for using the ordered *assignment* in the end of subsection 3.3.

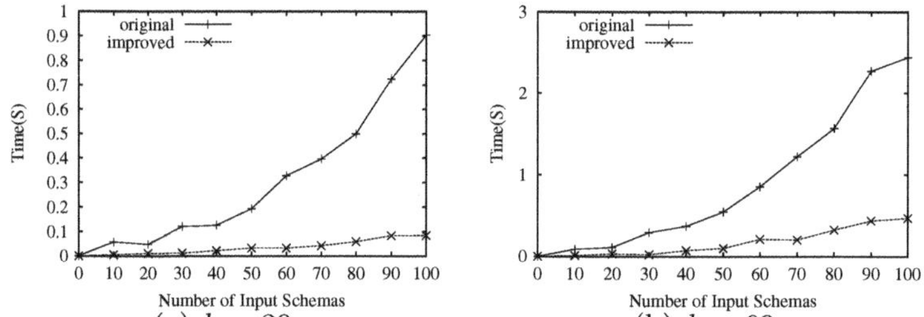

(a) $k = 20$ (b) $k = 60$

Fig. 5. Time Cost Vs. Input Schemas With $\delta = (0.9, 0.3)$

The study in the Figure 6 is similar to the above experiment. But we decrease the δ to $(0.7, 0.4)$, and this significantly affect the variation of the running time, especially the case for $k = 60$. The curve first reach up to the maximum, then decrease with the increase of the input schemas. The reason is that the similarity between concepts augments with the increase of the input schemas because of the stable number of MAC; thus, much of the edges whose weights exceed 0.7 is filter out by the config $\delta = (0.7, 0.4)$, when the number of the input schemas increases beyond some value, for example 60 in Figure (b).

We study the effect of the number k on the performance in Figure 7. We observe that the time of the original algorithm increases as the k increase. This answers to the fact that the more the results are found, the more computation cost is. But the curve for the improved one changes slowly and is less sensitive to the variation of the k. The reason is the same as the above experiment.

Finally, we test the possible edges with varying the input schemas from 10 to 100. To consist with the above writing format, we show the experimental results

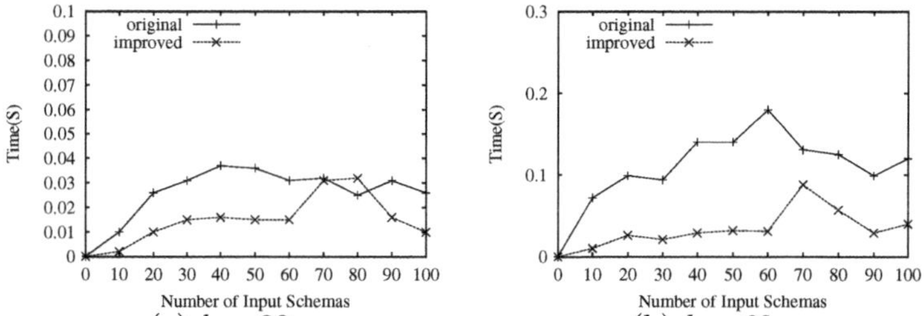

(a) $k = 20$ (b) $k = 60$

Fig. 6. Time Cost Vs. Input Schemas With $\delta = (0.7, 0.4)$

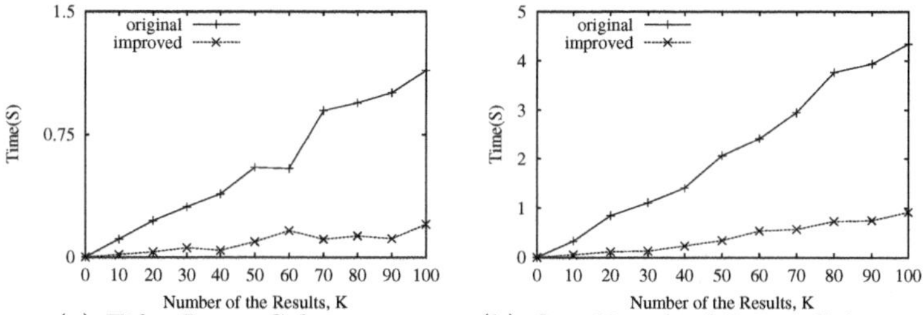

(a) Fifty Input Schemas (b) One Hundred Input Schemas

Fig. 7. Time Cost Vs. Results Retrieved

with config $\delta = (0.9, 0.3)$ in Figure 8(a), and $\delta = (0.7, 0.4)$ in Figure 8(b). In Figure (a), the number of possible edges reaches up to around 300 while the input schemas increase to 100. The reason is that the later concepts caused by the increase of the schemas result in many edges, while much of them is survived from $\delta = (0.9, 0.3)$ which leaves a larger space of weight for the possible edges. By contrast, the possible edges decrease with the input schemas beyond 50. As the analysis above, the similarity of the edges augments as the increase of the schemas; thus much of the edges are filtered out for the smaller space generated by the config $\delta = (0.7, 0.4)$.

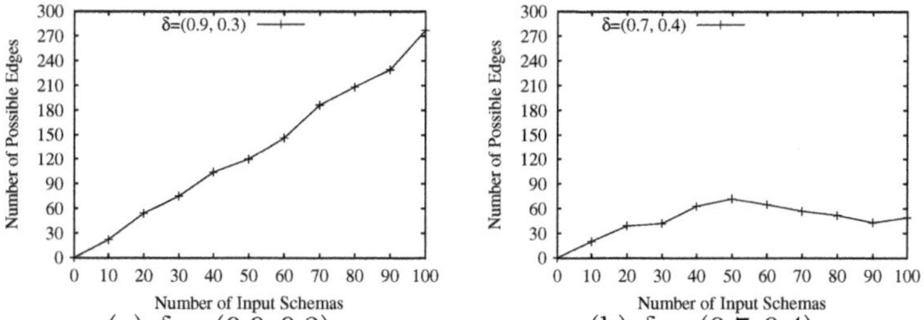

(a) $\delta = (0.9, 0.3)$ (b) $\delta = (0.7, 0.4)$

Fig. 8. Possible Edges Vs. Input Schemas

5 Related Work

A basic problem in the data integration is the schema integration [11,6,4,12,14,8]. A pay-as-you-go integration system is proposed in [12], which uses the possible mapping to create the target schemas. The recent work of [11] developed a tool that systematically enumerates multiple mediated schemas. But their approach relies heavily on the user's interaction. Another recent work [14] proposed an automatic approach to schema integration. Their main disadvantage is that they can not achieve the schema integration over multiple source schemas.

The work of [7] provide a generic framework that can be used to merge models in all these contexts. One of the their main features is the use of a mapping, which can be seen as a "template" for the integrated model. A formalism-independent algorithm for ontology merging and alignment, named PROMPT, is developed in [4], which automates the merging process as much as possible. An ontology merging system FCA-MERGE [6] is developed, following bottom-up techniques which offers a structural description of the merging process.

The correspondences used in our approach are the results of schema matching, which is another long-standing research problem [5, 9, 10, 12, 13]. The automatic approach to schema matching is summarized in [5]. A multi-column substring matching [9] is presented to discovery complex schema translations involving substrings from multiple database columns. Recently, different from the tradition, the possible mapping is introduced to the schema matching [10, 12], which presents another research mode for schema matching.

6 Conclusions

In this paper, we propose an automatic approach to schema integration. Our approach explores multiple possible mediated schemas over a set of source schemas from the same domain. To tackle multiple source schemas, we define the multivariate correspondence MAC to represent the attribute set where all the attribute elements have the same semantics. We introduce the parameter δ to divide the similarity between concepts into intervals, and this generates three kinds of edges, namely positive edges, possible edges and negative edges. We merge the concepts connected by the positive edges, and break the negative edges leaving the concepts alone. The concepts connected by the possible edges can either be merged or not merged (different users have different opinions). As a result, we introduce the *assignment* to represent the two state (merging or not) of the possible edges. Then, we design the top-k ranking algorithm to find the assignments resulting in the best mediated schemas. The algorithm is an enumeration of all the possible assignments. We make use of the top-k buffer and the threshold to prune much of the assignments. The experiment shows that our algorithm has good performance and runs in polynomial time.

References

1. Buneman, P., Davidson, S.B., Kosky, A.: Theoretical Aspects of Schema Merging. In: Pirotte, A., Delobel, C., Gottlob, G. (eds.) EDBT 1992. LNCS, vol. 580, pp. 152–167. Springer, Heidelberg (1992)
2. Miller, R.J., Ioannidis, Y.E.: The Use of Information Capacity in Schema Integration and Translation. In: Proc. of VLDB, pp. 12–133 (1993)
3. Dubuisson, M.-P., Jain, A.K.: A Modified Hausdorff Distance for Object Matching. In: Proc. of Int. Conf. on Pattern Recognition, pp. 566–568 (1994)
4. Noy, N.F., Musen, M.A.: PROMPT: Algorithm and Tool for Automated Ontology Merging and Alignment. In: Proc. of AAAI/IAAI, pp. 450–455 (2000)
5. Rahm, E., Bernstein, P.A.: A survey of approaches to automatic schema matching. VLDB Journal 10(4), 334–350 (2001)
6. Stumme, G., Maedche, A.: FCA-MERGE: Bottom-up merging of ontologies. In: Proc. of IJCAI, pp. 225–234 (2001)
7. Pottinger, R., Bernstein, P.A.: Merging Models Based on Given Correspondences. In: Proc. of VLDB, pp. 826–873 (2003)
8. Dong, X., Halevy, A.: A Platform for Personal Information Management and Integration. In: Proc. of CIDR (2005)
9. Warren, R.H., Tompa, F.: Multicolumn Substring Matching for Database Schema Translation. In: Proc. of VLDB, pp. 331–342 (2006)
10. Dong, X., Halevy, A.Y., Yu, C.: Data integration with uncertainty. In: Proc. of VLDB, pp. 687–698 (2007)
11. Chiticariu, L., Kolaitis, P.G., Popa, L.: Interactive Generation of Integrated Schemas. In: Proc. of SIGMOD, pp. 833–846 (2008)
12. Sarma, A.D., Dong, X., Halevy, A.: Bootstrapping Pay-As-You-Go Data Integration Systems. In: Proc. of SIGMOD, pp. 861–874 (2008)
13. Chan, C., Elmeleegy, H.V.J.H., Ouzzani, M., Elmagarmid, A.: Usage-Based Schema Matching. In: Proc. of ICDE, pp. 20–29 (2008)
14. Radwan, A., Popa, L., Stanoi, I.R., Younis, A.: Top-K Generation of Integrated Schemas Based on Directed and Weighted Correspondences. In: Proc. of SIGMOD, pp. 641–654 (2009)

A Graphical Method for Reference Reconciliation

Zheng Yongqing, Kong Qing, and Dong Guoqing

Department of Computer Science, Shandong University
zyq@sdu.edu.cn, xiaoqinger4848@126.com, dgq@sdu.edu.cn

Abstract. In many applications several references may refer to one real entity, the task of reference reconciliation is to group those references into several clusters so that each cluster associates with only one real entity. In this paper we propose a new method for reference reconciliation, that is, in addition to the traditional attribute values similarity, we employ the record-level relationships to compute the association similarity values of references in graphs, then we combine this kind of similarity with the traditional attribute values similarity and use the clustering algorithm to group the closest references.

Keywords: reference reconciliation, record-level relationships, association similarity, attribute values similarity.

1 Introduction

Nowadays much work needs to integrate information from heterogeneous data sources into one database. This can lead to the occurrence of similar references, some of which may exist originally in one of the data sources; others can be generated from the integration of several data sources. Similar references which potentially refer to one real entity must be reconciled before this database can be efficiently used for further process. The problem of similar references referring to one real entity appears because one real entity may have many descriptions. Many reference reconciliation methods have been proposed to solve this problem.

Reference reconciliation focuses on reconciling and grouping similar references which potentially refer to the same real entities into clusters so that each cluster corresponds to one real entity. Reference reconciliation has something to do with the problem of entity resolution [13], record linkage [1], and duplicate detection [2], object consolidation [5] and so on. Record linkage [1] is dedicated to merging similar records which are judged to refer to the same entity in the real world. It is a little different from reference reconciliation: record linkage deals with records in the database, whereas reference reconciliation deals with references— a concept of a finer grain. Another related problem is reference disambiguation [9], the goal of which is to match object representations (references) with the list of possible objects which are known in advance. Object Distinction [4, 11] considers a problem which is different from the above. It mainly focuses on distinguishing different objects with identical names.

Traditional methods usually utilize textual similarity [2] or attribute values similarity like the context attributes similarity [6] or the feature-based similarity (FBS).

M. Yoshikawa et al. (Eds.): DASFAA 2010, LNCS 6193, pp. 156–167, 2010.

There are also some other methods which use the relational information between the references [5, 8, 9, 10, 15].

But most of the previous works which employ relational information only consider relationships between attributes within records and they compute the similarity values between similar references based on these relationships. In this paper, we proposed an algorithm which employs record-level relationships, that is, we use records as the carriers of references and take the relationships between records as the association similarity values of similar references within these records.

Our algorithms have many advantages: first of all, the record-level relationships taken as the association similarity values of similar references within these records combine multiple attribute-level relationships which are always employed by traditional works. Second, the record-level relationships could also improve the performance of reference reconciliation in single relation since traditional works on single relations only considers textual similarity or context attributes similarity. Although there are also some works focusing on employing relational information in single relation, like works by X. Dong et al [8] and Parag and Pedro Domingos [19], they only consider attribute-level relationships, too.

Single relation means that only one relation exists in the problem and no E-R model can be constructed. In this problem there is only single relation and the records inside represent a certain kind of real entities like books, movies, papers or orders. And in these records, some attributes can refer to other kind of real entities, such as publisher in book relation, director in movie relation, author in paper relation or commodity in order relation (these attributes are called references). All of the above kind of references may have the problem of similar references referring to the same real entity and our algorithm in this paper is able to reconcile these references.

We build similarity matrix for all the records in the single relation at first, and based on this, we build the similarity association graphs (SAG) for all the references we want to reconcile, then we combine the association similarity we acquire from the SAGs with the traditional attribute values similarity to get the overall similarity values between similar references. Finally we use clustering algorithm to group the references into clusters so that each cluster corresponds to one real world entity.

Our contributions in this paper can be summarized as follows:

- A novel algorithm which employ record-level relationships to build the similarity association graphs to compute the association similarity values between references in single relation.
- A method to combine the association similarity with the attribute values similarity to compute the overall similarity values between references.
- An empirical result evaluation and analysis of our algorithm. Our experiments test our algorithm's performance on large real datasets and manual datasets.

The rest of this paper is organized as follows. Section 2 describes the problem of reference reconciliation through an example. Section 3 formalizes the problem. Our algorithm is introduced in detail in Section 4 and Section 5. Experimental results are presented in Section 6. Section 7 is the related work. Section 8 is the conclusion.

2 Problem Description

In the real world, many datasets only contain single relation, like DBLP, Cora in the author matching problem. A segment of the relation contains the following data:

1. <P_1, 'Ekkart Rudolph', 'Title1...', 'venue1'>
2. <P_2, 'Wilhelm K. Hackmann', 'E. Rudolph', 'Hans Seidl', 'Title2...', 'venue2'>
3. <P_3, 'P. Graubmann', 'E. R', 'Hans Seidl', 'Title3...' 'venue3'>
4. <P_4, 'P. Graubmann', 'Toshio Uchiyama', 'Title4...','venue1'>

The schema for this relation is <id, author_name, author_name... title, venue>. Notice that in this data segment there are several similar author_names which potentially refer to one real entity, they are 'Ekkart Rudolph' in P_1, 'E. Rudolph' in P_2, 'E. R' in P_3....The goal of our reference reconciliation algorithm is to group all these references into clusters so that each cluster corresponds to only one real entity.

We build similarity matrix for all the paper records as follows (sim(P_1,P_2) represents the similarity between paper P_1 and P_2, the computing method will be illustrated later):

$$\begin{bmatrix} \cdots & sim(p1,p2) & sim(p1,p3) & sim(p1,p4) \\ \cdots & \cdots & sim(p2,p3) & sim(p2,p4) \\ \cdots & \cdots & \cdots & sim(p3,p4) \\ \cdots & \cdots & \cdots & \cdots \end{bmatrix}$$

Fig. 1. The similarity matrix

Then, based on this matrix, we are able to build many similarity association graphs (SAG) for all the author_name references in these records and compute the association similarity values between the references. The similarity association graph (SAG) for this exemplary data segment is shown in Figure 2. Notice that in this SAG, nodes represent records, some of which contain references needing reconciliation, some do not. Edges (solid lines) represent the associations between two records, and the dotted lines represent how the two records are connected. For example, in Figure 2 P_2 and P_3 are connected because they share the same co-author ‘Hans Seidl’. In this algorithm the similarity values of the two records are employed to represent the association similarity values of the two similar references included in the two records. We combine this kind of similarity (called association similarity) with the traditional attribute values similarity to get a whole similarity value for further process.

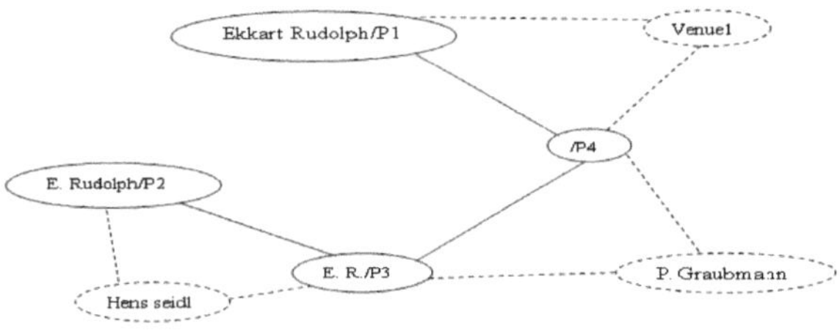

Fig. 2. The similarity association graph for the data segment

3 Notation

Suppose that there is only single relation in our dataset, and the records included in the relation are in set P= $\{P_1, P_2...., P_m\}$ (in the example above are papers). The schema for this relation is <...$Ref_{1,1}$, $Ref_{1,2}$, $Ref_{1,3}$..., $Ref_{2,1}$, $Ref_{2,2}$... $Ref_{i,j}$...>. In $Ref_{i,j}$ ' i ' represents the ith kind of references in each record in P and ' j ' represents the jth reference in all the ith kind of references.

For example, in the relation shown in Section II, author_name represents the first kind of references and venue represents the second kind of references in the records, and the author_name is the exact kind of references needing reconciliation.

Suppose that in the dataset being processed, all real entities underlying the references needing reconciliation are in set A= $\{A_1, A_2, A_3... A_n...\}$. In the set P, the ith kind of references is the exact kind needing reconciliation. All the ith kind of references will be put into a set R=$\{P_1.Ref_{i,1}, P_1.Ref_{i,2},..., P_2.Ref_{i,1}, P_2.Ref_{i,2}, P_2.Ref_{i,3},..., P_m.Ref_{i,1}....\}$. Our goal is to group all the references in R into clusters set C= $\{C_1, C_2...C_n...\}$, each cluster in C contains references referring to the same real entity in A.

4 Computing Similarity Values between References

4.1 Similarity Matrix

A similarity matrix will be built for all the records in P as $sim(P_i,P_j)$ ($P_i,P_j \in P, 1<=i, j<=|P|$). The process is as follows: Suppose that a reference from P_1 and a reference from P_2 (denoted as $P_1.Ref_{m,i}$ and $P_2.Ref_{m,j}$) are from the same field (they are both the mth kind of references) and share the same value ($P_1.Ref_{m,i} = P_2.Ref_{m,j}$), we think that P_1 and P_2 are connected by these two references $P_1.Ref_{m,i}$ and $P_2.Ref_{m,j}$. Then we compute their strength of connecting the two records P_1 and P_2 and add them to the prior similarity value of P_1 and P_2 which is denoted as $sim(P_1, P_2)$ in the similarity matrix, the initial value of which is zero. The computation of the connection strength is as follows:

$$P_1.Ref_{m,i} = P_2.Ref_{m,j} \tag{1}$$

$$sim(P_1, P_2) = sim(P_1, P_2)+1/frequency(P_1.Ref_{m,i}) \tag{2}$$

$$frequency(P_1.Ref_{m,i})=frequency(P_2.Ref_{m,j}) \tag{3}$$

The $frequency(P_1.Ref_{m,i})$ in formula(2) represents the number of times $P_1.Ref_{m,i}$ has appeared in the overall single relation, in other words, it represents how many references are from the same field and share identical values as $P_1.Ref_{m,i}$ in this single relation. We compute the connection strength of this reference as the reciprocal of frequency because we assume that the more frequently the reference appears in the relation the less important it will be. For example, in the problem of author matching, if the reference which connect two records refer to the venue of VLDB, then it will be less important than the reference referring to one of the same co-authors of the papers, i.e. if the two papers are connected by same venues like VLDB, then the connection strength will be smaller than those two papers which are connected by the same co-authors. In the example above, after we find that $P_1.Ref_{m,i} = P_2.Ref_{m,j}$, then frequency($P_1.Ref_{m,i}$) will increase by 1, so does frequency($P_2.Ref_{m,j}$), the process is shown in Figure 3.

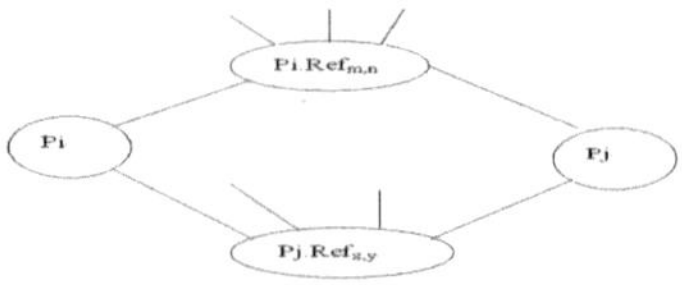

Fig. 3. Computing the Strength of connecting. In this example, the number of branches represents the frequency of the reference. Then sim(Pi,Pj)=1/5+1/4.

4.2 Similarity Association Graph

In Section 3 we assume that all the ith kind of references are put into a set $R=\{P_1.Ref_{i,1}, P_1.Ref_{i,2},..., P_2.Ref_{i,1}, P_2.Ref_{i,2}, P_2.Ref_{i,3},..., P_m.Ref_{i,1}....\}$. Since set R contains references which may refer to many different real entities, we can not process them all at a time, we must divide them into groups roughly based on the attribute values similarity. Here the attributes contain the ones that characterize the underlying entities. For example, in the author matching problem, the author's name is that kind of attribute when we want to reconcile author references. In this state, similar references which potentially refer to one real world entity will be put into approximate groups.

There are many techniques to achieve this. One of them is that we can find some attributes as the blocking attributes to decrease the number of pairs needing comparison by blocking [12]. Another method is that we can use clustering algorithm to merge the most similar clusters of references based on the attribute values similarity.

After we get the approximate groups, each of which contains references possibly referring to one real entity, we can build many similarity association graphs (SAG) based on these approximate groups. In the SAGs, initially, references from the same approximate group form all the nodes in one SAG. In Figure 2, initially 'Ekkart Rudolph' in paper P_1, 'E. Rudolph' in paper P_2 and 'E. R.' in paper P_3 formed a SAG, and only 'E. Rudolph' and 'E. R.' have path (solid line) between them because initially only P_2 and P_3 have connections by the same co-author 'Hans Seidl'. As shown in Figure 4.

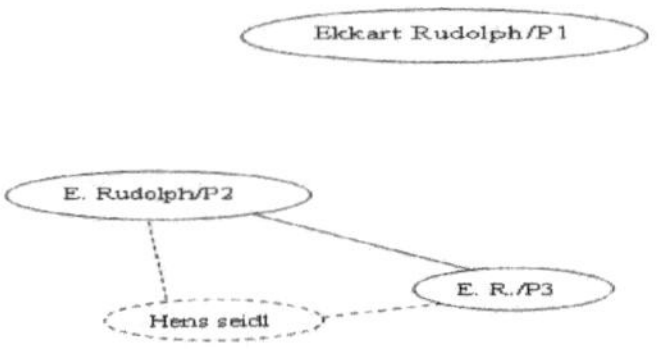

Fig. 4. The initial SAG of the data segment

4.3 Expansion of the Similarity Association Graphs

In the state above, the SAGs only contain direct connecting paths between two references (nodes) since the two records (P_i and P_j) which the two references belong to have direct connection thus sim(P_i,P_j) is not zero. From Figure 4 we can see these paths are all with length 1. In this state we will expand the SAGs to develop paths that are longer than 1 and are not directly connecting two nodes of references in the SAG.

As shown in Figure 2, 'Ekkart Rudolph' in P_1 doesn't have any direct connection with 'E. R.' in P_3, but they can still be connected indirectly through their common neighbour node P_4, so in this state we will expand the existing SAGs to add indirect paths into them. The goal can be easily achieved through the search of the similarity matrix. Since in the similarity matrix, if there is association between two records in P, the similarity value between the two records is positive, otherwise it will be zero. So we can use some algorithms on Graph Theory like FindPath [16] to find paths of given length, in these SAGs we will find paths longer than 1 to connect references.

After this state, many final SAGs like the one in Figure 2 are built. Then we will compute the connection strength of the newly added paths and add them to the existing similarity values of two references.

Suppose that reference No.1 belongs to record Pa, reference No.2 belongs to Pb, they are connected by record Pd, some other records and Pc.

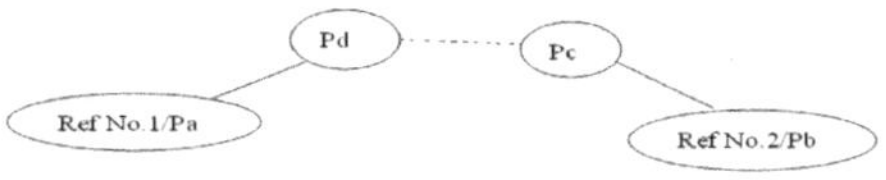

Fig. 5. Computing the connection strength of the newly added paths

Then the connection strength of the newly added path (Pa->Pd...->Pc->Pb) is computed as follows (this connection strength is denoted as cs(Pa,Pb)):

$$cs(Pa,Pb)=sim(Pa,Pd)*...*sim(Pc,Pb) \quad (4)$$

$$sim(Pa,Pb)=sim(Pa,Pb)+cs(Pa,Pb) \quad (5)$$

$$asso\_sim(Ref\ No.1,Ref\ No.2)=sim(Pa,Pb) \quad (6)$$

In formula (4) we compute the connection strength of the newly added paths. We can treat the cs(Pa,Pb) as the probability of reaching Pb from Pa. Based on the random walk probability [4], we multiply the similarity values of all the associations in the paths to get the overall connection strength of the newly added paths.

The initial similarity value sim(Pa,Pb) which only contain connection strength of direct paths is also updated in formula (5). Then the association similarity value between two references could be computed as the similarity value between the two records they belong to in formula (6).

4.4 Combination of Associate Similarity and the Attribute Values Similarity

The final similarity value between two references can be computed as follows:

$$\text{sim(Ref No.1,Ref No.2)}=\alpha*\text{asso\_sim(Ref No.1,Ref No.2)}+(1-\alpha)*\text{attributes\_sim (Ref No.1,Ref No.2)} \quad (7)$$

In this formula asso_sim(Ref No.1,Ref No.2) is the association similarity of the two references and α represents the weight of the association similarity in the final similarity value. attributes_sim ($P_i.Ref_{m,x}$, $P_j.Ref_{m,y}$) represents the similarity value of the attributes which characterize the entities underlying the references. For example, book name, isbn are attributes which characterize the property of a book. Another example, for a person, his/her name, email, address can be attributes characterizing the person. Here the attribute is different from the concept of references: references are the kind of attributes which refer to real entity, but attributes only characterize entity but do not refer to any other real entities. Attributes_sim can be computed using some methods such as string-based distance and vector-based cosine similarity.

5 Clustering Algorithm

Since in many applications we don't know how many clusters we should get in advance, we can use the Hierarchical cluster algorithm to group the closest clusters of references in a SAG repeatedly until the algorithm meets the termination conditions.

There are many methods to evaluate the performance of the clustering algorithm and its result, some are unsupervised [17], such as the cluster cohesion, cluster separation, and others are supervised like the entropy [5]. In this method, as we don't know how many clusters to get in advance, we choose the unsupervised methods.

As it is supposed in preceding paragraphs, the set of clusters our method outputs is C= {C_1, C_2,...C_n,...}, the evaluation of the cluster validity [17] are as follows:

$$\text{overallvalidity}=\sum_{i=1}^{|C|} wi * validity(C_i)$$

$$\text{cohesion}(C_i)=\sum_{\substack{x\in ci \\ y\in ci}} finalsim(x,y)$$

$$\text{separation}(C_i,C_j)=\sum_{\substack{x\in ci \\ y\in cj}} finalsim(x,y) \quad (i!=j)$$

In the formulas above, overallvalidity represents the overall validity of all the clusters. The validity of a cluster C_i can be computed in many ways. Some are based on the cohesion, which means the extent of agglomeration, some are based on the separation, and others use both of them. *wi* represents the weight of the validity of cluster C_i. As we always want the cohesion to be large or the separation to be small, so when we use cohesion as the validity of the cluster, when the overallvalidity gets the maximum we believe the result is the best and vise versa.

6 Experimental Results

We test our method on 2 real world datasets; one is DBLP-SUB series which contains 3 datasets, dblp-sub-01(475KB), dblp-sub-02(1278KB), dblp-sub-03(6316KB). Another is a smaller dataset s-dblp which we completely arrange it manually.

We will measure the quality of our result by precision, recall and f-measure. They are defined as follows: as it is supposed before, the clusters our method outputs are in set $C=\{C_1,C_2,...C_n,...\}$, and the ground truth is in $A=\{A_1, A_2, A_3... A_n...\}$. In each cluster C_i in C, we check all the reference pairs, if references in the pairs also belong to the same element in A, we add 1 to the tp(true positive), else we add 1 to fp(false positive). In each cluster A_i in A, we check all the reference pairs, if references in the pairs don't belong to the same cluster in C, we add 1 to the fn(false negative).

$$\text{Precision}=\frac{tp}{tp+fp},\quad \text{Recall}=\frac{tp}{tp+fn},\quad \text{F-measure}=\frac{2*precision*recall}{precision+recall}$$

As we always want the fp and fn to be close to zero so that the closer the precision and the recall are to 1, the better the performance our algorithm will be, so does the F-measure which is a combined criterion of the both the precision and the recall.

6.1 DBLP-SUB

There are 3 datasets in this series, we will introduce the experiment on dblp-sub-01, and the other 2 datasets are the same as the first one.

In dblp-sub-01 there are 1509 papers and 4961 authors, we first traverse all the elements in the xml document, like the author, venue etc and record their frequency, but we remove all the elements named "year" because we think that kind of elements are useless in our experiments. Then we build the similarity matrix for all the paper records in set P and compute the similarity value $sim(P_i, P_j)$ for all of them. We assume that $sim(P_i,P_j)=sim(P_j,P_i)$ and $sim(P_i,P_i)$ is meaningless so we can decrease the number of times of computation greatly. Since the similarity matrix is very large, we keep the result in a document so that we don't have to compute it every time. The text document we get is 17815KB.

Then we use a hierarchical cluster method to get initial SAGs in which we merge the most similar clusters of references repeatedly until there are no two clusters having the similarity value greater than a threshold, we set the threshold value to be 0.63 to get all the SAGs in this experiment.

After the initial SAGs are built we execute the search algorithm to add paths longer than 1 but shorter than 3 to the SAGs and compute connection strength for all the paths to get the association similarity of every pairs of references. In the state of expansion of the SAGs, we set the length of the paths to be no longer than 3 since our experiments show that much longer paths will be helpless.

We compute the attribute values similarity for all the author_name pairs using the TFIDF method.

After that we use the same cluster method as the one used for building the SAGs, which is merging the most similar clusters of references repeatedly until no two clusters having similarity value greater than a threshold t. The figures below illustrate the impact of different parameters to the result.

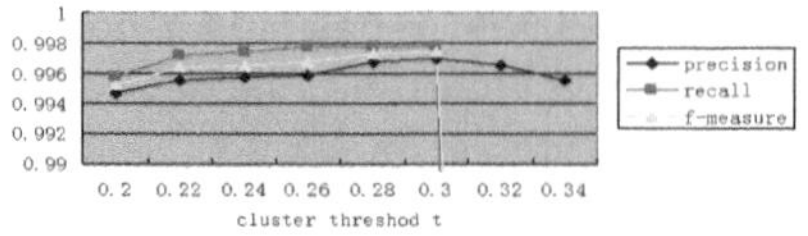

(a) Hierarchical cluster threshold t and the result quality (α=0.7)

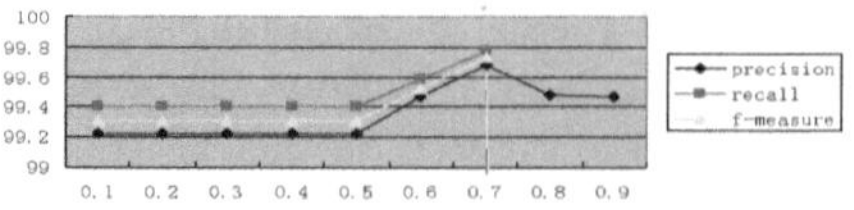

(b) á and the result quality

Fig. 6. Different methods of computing the similarity of clusters

In Figure 6(a), the broken line shows that when cluster threshold t is 0.3, the experiment gets the best result, precision is 0.997, recall is 0.9978, f-measure is 0.9974. In Figure 6(b), the result is best when **α** is 0.7, precision is 0.9968, recall is 0.9978, f-measure is 0.9973. This indicates that the association similarity value accounts for major proportion in the final similarity value. In this experiment, our precision is always very high, but the recall has bigger up and downs because, in the Figure 6(a), when the threshold t is greater than 0.31, the algorithm will divide some clusters into many smaller clusters which are false and impact the recall greatly. In Figure 6(b), α (from formula (7)) can not be too closer to 1. It means that association similarity and the attribute values similarity should be combined to get the best result.

The results of the experiments are also impacted by the different clustering methods as shown in the following figure:

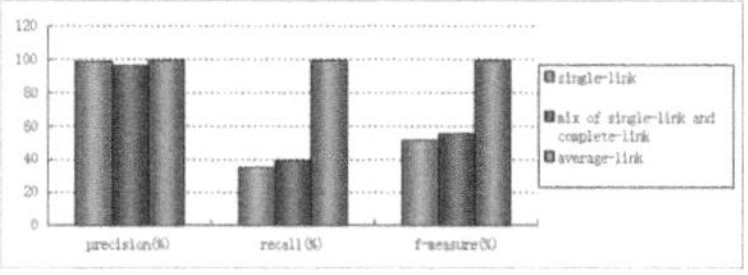

Fig. 7. Different methods of clusters

The figure above shows that average-link method can achieve the best result. For single-link and mix of single-link and complete link, they get lower recall values because they can not get accurate SAGs which impact the final result greatly.

6.2 Artificial Dataset s-dblp

In the above Section we have shown our experiments on some real world datasets, but those datasets have some deficiency to test the performance of our algorithm. First, in most of the SAGs there are no more than 10 references and most of them share the same name and refer to the same author, so the performance has a lot to do with the formation of the SAGs. In this experiment we want to find a dataset in which a SAG has many references (more than 20) which refer to many different real world entities (more than 3), so we construct a dataset manually from the DBLP website about several names, they are shown in the following table:

Table 1. Names corresponding to multiple authors

Name	Authors	References	Name	Authors	References
Ajay Gupta	4	28	Micheal Wagner	3	18
Hui Fang	3	20	Rakesh Kumar	2	8
Jim Smith	3	16	overall	15	90

We apply our algorithm to this dataset with some changes: First of all, we don't need to build the SAGs because naturally references with identical names fall into the same SAGs. This can reflect the performance of our algorithm in a better way because it will not be impacted by the quality of the formation of the SAGs. Second, we use the clustering criterion functions described in Section 5 combined with the following formula:

$$wi=1/|C_i| \tag{8}$$

$$\text{validity}(C_i)=\text{cohesion}(C_i) \tag{9}$$

As illustrated in former experimental section, association similarity and the attribute values similarity separately should be combined to get the best result. In this experiment, the attributes_similarity is always 1 because all the references in the same SAG share identical name, so we can just add a small real number p to all the association similarity values to get better performance. The impact of p to the quality of the result is shown in the following figure:

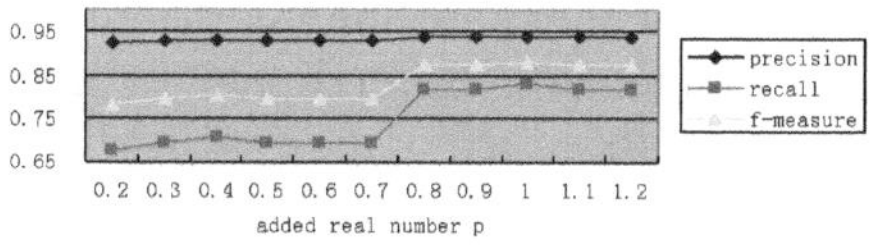

Fig. 8. The impact of p to the quality of the result

From the figure above we can see that when p is set to 1.0 the experiment can achieve the best result.

The following figure shows that the impact of different lengths of paths.

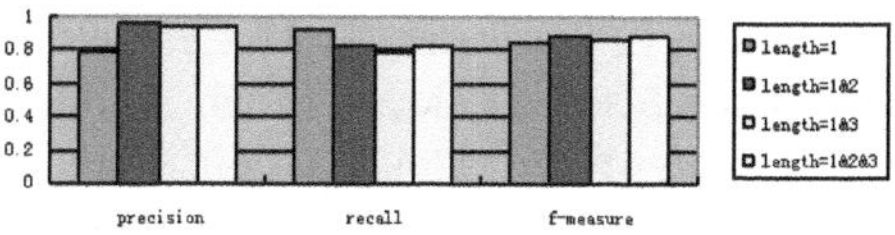

Fig. 9. The impact of different lengths of paths

This figure shows that when the paths with the length 1 and 2 are combined, the experiment can achieve the best F-measure of 0.8853. When we add the paths with length of 3, the result is good too but worse than the situation above, because when we add paths of length 3, the recall will be lower. This result indicates that much longer paths are helpless, sometimes even harmful to the result.

We compare the performance of our method with our preceding method based on decision tree but without employing relationships between multi-type entities [11] and the work DISTINCT by Jiawei Han et al [4] which employing relationships between multi-type entities. The comparison results are shown in the following figure.

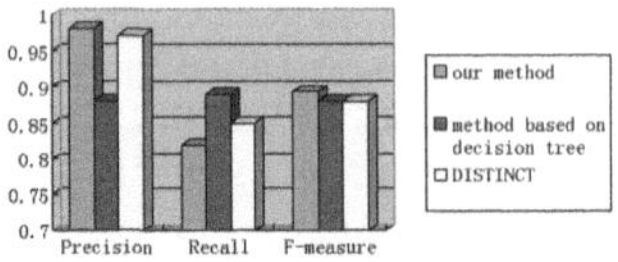

Fig. 10. Performance comparison

From the figure we can conclude that this method acquire higher precision and F-measure on real datasets.

7 Related Work

Traditional work on record linkage can be summarized into two parts: First, how to acquire the object pairs which need to be distinguished. In this field, what we need to do is to increase the efficiency, which is trying to reduce the number of candidate pairs, so we can compare for less times. M. A. Hernandez and S. J. Stolfo [18] developed the sorted neighbourhood method for limiting the number of potential duplicate pairs that require distance computation. Second, how to increase the accuracy of the record linkage, that is, to use higher performance method to distinguish records with identical names or merge similar records. Traditional methods usually based on textual similarity [2] or attribute values similarity like the context attributes similarity [6] or the feature-based similarity (FBS). Some of these methods focus on developing different algorithm to compute the similarity values of attributes. Typically, some string similarity metrics like edit distance [14] or TFIDF [11] or learnable string similarity measure [2] are used to get the similarity values. Other methods always use some machine learning methods such as decision tree[11], SVM [4], perceptron learning [7] to combine these similarity values based on different weights which have been learned to get a whole similarity value to determine whether the two references associate with one real world entity. In the paper [6] M. Lee et al also developed a method to discover these context attributes and calculate their similarity, which is using association rules to determine the set of attributes that constitute each object's context.

There are also some other methods which use the relational information between the references or the references and their attributes. In the paper [8] X. Dong et al describe an algorithm based on a general framework for propagating information from one reconciliation decision to another using dependency graph. In several papers of D. V. Kalashnikov et al [5, 9, 10], the methods which analyses not only object features, but also additional semantic information: inter-objects relationships for the purpose of object consolidation have been developed. In paper [15], some iterative methods are developed to group similar references in an iterative way, as the common authors are identified the additional potential co-references are also identified.

8 Conclusion

In this paper we study the problem of reference reconciliation in single relation. We develop a new method to solve this problem using record-level relationships to get the association similarity values combined with the traditional attribute values similarity to get the overall similarity value. Then we use the hierarchical cluster method to group references into different clusters so that each cluster corresponds with one real world entity. Experiments show that our algorithm can achieve high accuracy.

References

1. Winkler, W.E.: The state of record linkage and current research problems. Technical report, Statistical Research Division, U.S. Bureau of the Census (1999)
2. Bilenko, M., Mooney, R.: Adaptive duplicate detection using learnable string similarity measures. In: SIGKDD (2003)
3. Chaudhuri, S., Ganjam, K., Ganti, V., Motwani, R.: Robust and efficient fuzzy match for online data cleaning. In: Proc. of ACM SIGMOD Conf. (2003)
4. Yin, X., Han, J., Yu, P.S.: Object Distinction: Distinguishing Objects with Identical Names. In: ICDE 2007 (2007)
5. Chen, Z., Kalashnikov, D.V., Mehrotra, S.: Exploiting relationships for object consolidation. In: ACM IQIS (2005)
6. Lee, M., Hsu, W., Kothari, V.: Cleaning the spurious links in data. IEEE Intelligent Systems (2004)
7. Ananthakrishna, R., Chaudhuri, S., Ganti, V.: Eliminating Fuzzy Duplicates in Data Warehouses. In: Proceedings of 28th VLDB conference (2002)
8. Dong, X., Halevy, A., Madhavan, J.: Reference reconciliation in complex information spaces. In: SIGMOD (2005)
9. Kalashnikov, D.V., Mehrotra, S., Chen, Z.: Exploiting relationships for domain-independent data cleaning. In: SIAM SDM (2005)
10. Kalashnikov, D.V., Mehrotra, S., Chen, Z., Nuray-Turan, R., Ashish, N.: Disambiguation algorithm for people search on the web. In: ICDE 2007 (2007)
11. Kong, Q., Li, Q.: Object distinction based on decision tree. In: ITCS 2009 (2009)
12. Baxter, R., Christen, P., Churches, T.: A comparison of fast blocking methods for record linkage. In: ACM KDD 2003 workshop on Data Cleaning, Record Linkage and Object Consolidation, Washington DC, pp. 25–27 (2003)
13. Bhattacharya, I., Getoor, L.: Relational clustering for multi-type entity resolution. In: MRDM Workshop (2005)
14. Gusfield, D.: Algorithms on Strings, Trees and Sequences. Cambridge University Press, New York (1997)
15. Bhattacharya, I., Getoor, L.: Iterative record linkage for cleaning and integration. In: DMKD Workshop (2004)
16. Sahni, S.: Data Structures, Algorithms, and Application in C++. Silicon Press
17. Tan, P.-N., Steinbach, M.: Introduction to Data Mining. Addison Wesley Press, Reading
18. Hernandez, M.A., Stolfo, S.J.: The merge/purge problem for large databases. In: Proceedings of the 1995 ACM SIGMOD International Conference on Management of Data (SIGMOD 1995), San Jose, CA, May 1995, pp. 127–138 (1995)
19. Singla, P., Domingos, P.: Multi-relational record linkage. In: MRDM Workshop (2004)

BenchmarX'10 Workshop Organizers' Message

Irena Mlýnková, Martin Nečaský, and Jiří Dokulil

Department of Software Engineering, Charles University in Prague, Czech Republic

The 2nd International Workshop on Benchmarking of Database Management Systems and Data-Oriented Web Technologies (BenchmarX'10) was held on April 4, 2010 at the University of Tsukuba, Japan in conjunction with the 15th International Conference on Database Systems for Advanced Applications (DASFAA'10). It was organized by Irena Mlynkova, Martin Necasky and Jiri Dokulil from the Department of Software Engineering of the Charles University in Prague, Czech Republic.

BenchmarX'10 was aimed at benchmarking (and related issues) of all stages of data processing in the context of up-to-date database management systems and data-oriented web technologies in general. Typical (but not the only) representatives of such applications and technologies can be web services and semantic web services, Web 2.0 applications, social networks etc. Similarly, new data types, such as data streams, sensor data or imprecise/uncertain data, triggered proposal and implementation of new strategies for their storage, processing and management that need to benchmarked, tested and compared specifically.

Even though data management and data-oriented applications are involved in topics of many conferences around the world, the community dealing with benchmarking of such applications and related issues is still scattered. The aim of BenchmarX is to bring it together and provide a platform for common discussion of all the related topics.

The program committee of the workshop consisted of 14 researchers and specialists representing 11 universities and institutions from 8 different countries. To ensure high objectiveness of the paper selection process 2 PC chairs from different institutions were selected, in particular Martin Necasky from the Charles University in Prague, Czech Republic and Eric Pardede from La Trobe University, Bundoora, Australia. Each of the papers submitted for BenchmarX'10 was reviewed by 3 PC members for its technical merit, originality, significance, and relevance to the workshop. Finally, the PC chairs decided to accept 42% of the submitted papers.

The final program of the workshop consisted of an invited talk on "Benchmarking Holistic Approaches to XML Tree Pattern Query Processing" and 2 sessions involving the accepted papers. The invitation was kindly accepted by Jiaheng Lu from the University of China.

M. Yoshikawa et al. (Eds.): DASFAA 2010, LNCS 6193, pp. 168–169, 2010.

Last but not least, let us mention that BenchmarX'10 would not be possible without the support of our sponsors. In particular it was partially supported by the Grant Agency of the Czech Republic, projects of GAČR number 201/09/P364 and P202/10/0573.

We believe that BenchmarX will become a traditional annual meeting opportunity for the whole benchmarking community.

Benchmarking Holistic Approaches to XML Tree Pattern Query Processing
(Extended Abstract of Invited Talk)

Jiaheng Lu

School of Information and DEKE, MOE, Renmin University of China
jiahenglu@ruc.edu.cn

Abstract. In this talk I outlined and surveyed some developments in the field of XML tree pattern query processing, especially focussing on holistic approaches. XML tree pattern query (TPQ) processing is a research stream within XML data management that focuses on efficient TPQ answering. With the increasing popularity of XML for data representation, there is a lot of interest in query processing over data that conforms to a tree-structured data model. Queries on XML data are commonly expressed in the form of tree patterns (or twig patterns), which represent a very useful subset of XPath and XQuery. Efficiently finding all tree pattern matches in an XML database is a major concern of XML query processing. In the past few years, many algorithms have been proposed to match such tree patterns. In the talk, I presented an overview of the state of the art in TPQ processing. This overview shall start by providing some background in holistic approaches to process TPQ and then introduce different algorithms and finally present benchmark datasets and experiments.

1 Research Problem

With the rapidly increasing popularity of XML for data representation, there is a lot of interest in query processing over data that conforms to a *tree-structured* data model. Since the data objects in a variety of languages (e.g. XPath [1], XQuery [2]) are typically trees, *tree pattern matching* is the central issue. For example, the following query

"`Q=//book[author=''Chen'']//chapter/title`"

can be represented as a twig (small tree) pattern. Intuitively, it returns the `title` of `chapter` for a `book` that has an author named by "`Chen`".

In practice, XML data may be very large, complex and have deep nested elements. Thus, efficiently finding all twig patterns in an XML database is a major concern of XML query processing. In the past few years, many algorithms ([10],[9]) have been proposed to match such twig patterns. These approaches (i) first develop a labeling scheme to capture the structural information of XML documents, and then (ii) perform tree pattern matching based on labels alone without traversing the original XML documents. For solving the first sub-problem

M. Yoshikawa et al. (Eds.): DASFAA 2010, LNCS 6193, pp. 170–178, 2010.

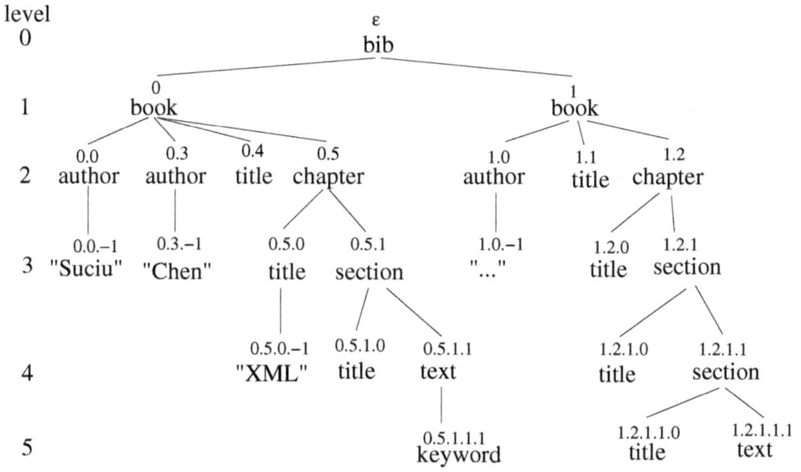

Fig. 1. An XML tree with *extended Dewey* labels

of designing a proper labeling scheme, the previous methods use a *tree-traversal* order(e.g. extended preorder [11]) or textual positions of *start* and *end* tags (e.g. region encoding [3]) or path expressions(e.g. Dewey ID [20]) or prime numbers (e.g. [23]). By applying these labeling schemes, one can determine the relationship (e.g. ancestor-descendant) between two elements in XML documents from their labels alone.

2 XML Tree Pattern Matching Algorithms

In the context of semi-structured and XML databases, tree-based query pattern is a very practical and important class of queries. Lore DBMS [7] and Timber [8] systems have considered various aspects of query processing on such data and queries. XML data and various issues in their storage as well as query processing using relational database systems have recently been considered in [16,25,20,17].

The recent papers (e.g. [15,24,5,4]) are proposed to efficiently process an XML twig pattern. In paper [15], a new holistic algorithm, called OrderedTJ, is proposed to process order-based XML tree query. In paper [24], an algorithm called TwigStackListNot is proposed to handle queries with negation function. Chen et al [5] proposed different data streaming schemes to boost the holism of XML tree pattern processing. They showed that larger optimal class can be achieved by refined data streaming schemes. In addition, Twig^{2}Stack [4] is proposed for answering generalized XML tree pattern queries. Note the difference between *generalized* XML tree pattern and *extended* XML tree pattern here. Generalized XML tree pattern is defined to include optional axis which models the expression in `LET` and `RETURN` clauses of XQuery statements. But extended XML tree pattern is defined to include some complicated conditions like negative function, wildcard and order restriction.

Besides the holistic algorithms, there are other approaches to match an XML tree pattern, such as ViST ([22,21]) and PRIX ([18]), which transform an XML tree pattern match to sequence match. Their algorithms mainly focus on ordered queries, and it is non-trivial to extend those methods to handle unordered queries and extended queries studied in this article. Note that the paper [16] made comprehensive experiments to compare different XML tree query processing algorithms (including sequence match and holistic match) and concluded that the family of holistic processing methods, which provides performance guarantees, is the most robust approach.

From the aspect of theoretical research about the optimality of XML tree pattern matching, Choi et al. [6] developed theorems to prove that it is impossible to devise a holistic algorithm to guarantee the optimality for queries with any combination of P-C and A-D relationships. Shalem et al. [19] researched the space complexity of processing XML twig queries. Their paper showed that the upper bound of full-fledge queries with parent-child and ancestor-descendant edges are $O(D)$, where D is the document size. In other words, their results also theoretically prove that there exists no algorithm to optimally process an arbitrary query $Q^{/,//,*}$.

Most of these works build on some labeling scheme of XML elements to facilitate the verification of the structural relationship. The most commonly used labels are the *containment* and *prefix* labeling scheme. The *containment* labeling was introduced by Zhang et al. [25] to facilitate the containment queries. The verification of *ancestor-descendant* structural relationship is of the same complexity as that of *parent-child* relationship by using regional labeling. Dewey *ID* is the *first* example of using prefix labeling to represent XML data. It can be used to preserve the path information during query processing. Recent work of Lu at el. [14] utilize the *extended Dewey* encoding which encodes path information including not only the element IDs but also the element names.

3 Benchmarking Holistic Algorithms

In this section, we present an extensive experimental study of five holistic algorithm on real-life and synthetic data sets,including TreeMatch [13], TwigStack [3], TJFast [14], OrderedTJ [15] and TwigStackListNot [24]. We implemented all tested algorithms in JDK 1.4 using the file system as a simple storage engine. We conducted all the experiments on a computer with Intel Pentium IV 1.7GHz CPU and 2G of RAM. To offer a comprehensive evaluation of our new algorithms, we conducted experiments on both synthetic and real XML data. The synthetic dataset is generated randomly. There are totally 7 tags A,B,...,F,G in the dataset and tags are assigned uniformly from them. The real data are DBLP (highly regular) and Treebank (highly irregular), which are included to test the two extremes of the spectrum in terms of the structural complexity. The recursive structure in TreeBank is deep (average depth: 7.8, maximal depth: 36). We can easily find queries on this dataset to demonstrate the sub-optimality for our tested algorithms.

3.1 Query Class $Q^{/,//,*}$

In this section, we show the experimental results for queries class $Q^{/,//,*}$. All queries tested in our evaluation are shown in Figure 2 and 3.

Small size of main memory. In the first experiment, we did not allow the *outputlist* in TreeMatch to buffer any elements in the main memory, meaning that any element added to *outputlist* should be output to the secondary storage. Then the requirement for main memory size is quite small. The purpose of this experiment is to simulate the application where the document is extremely large but the available main memory is relatively small. Table 1 shows the number of total output elements (including intermediate and final results) and the corresponding percentage of useful elements. We made the experiments by using three different sizes of random documents. In particular, D1 has 100K nodes and D2 has 500K nodes and D3 has 1M nodes. From Table 1, we observe that for most of queries, TreeMatch achieves the optimality in the sense that each of the output elements does belong to final results. Figure 4(a) compares the performance of

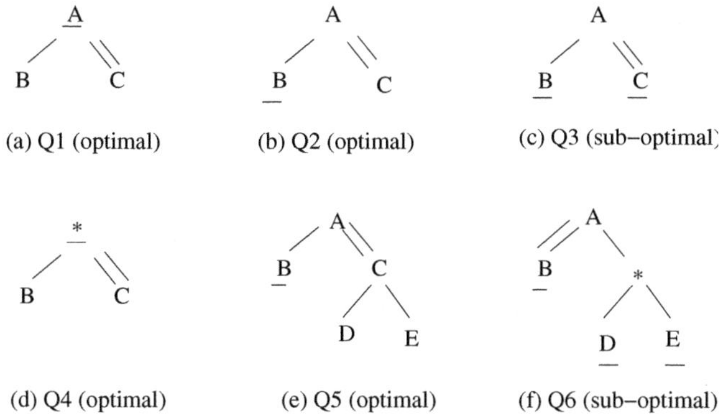

Fig. 2. Queries for random data

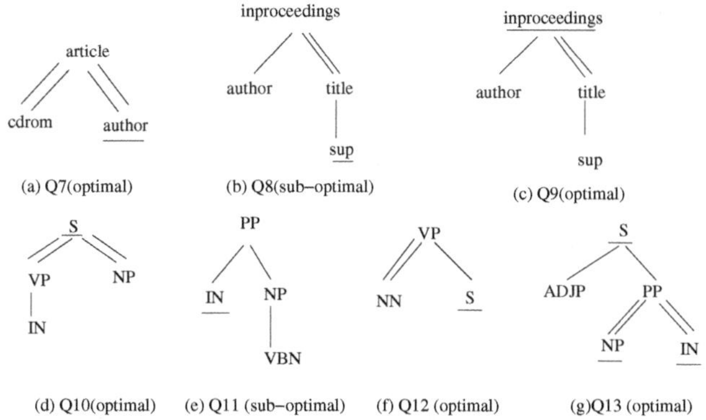

Fig. 3. Queries for DBLP (Q7-Q9) and TreeBank (Q10-Q13) data

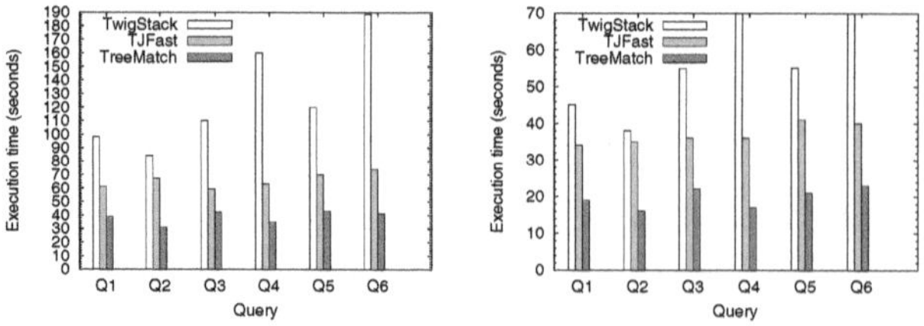

(a) Small memory (b) Large memory

Fig. 4. Execution time of $Q^{/,//,*}$ on random data

TreeMatch with other three existing algorithms. Clearly, TreeMatch is the best for all queries. This advantage is due to the fact that TreeMatch guarantees that (almost) all of output elements belong to final results, which, in general, avoids the I/O cost for outputting useless intermediate results.

Large size of main memory. In the second experiment, we allow the *outputlist* to buffer all elements in the main memory. The purpose of this experiment is to simulate the application where the available main memory is large so that a big portion of documents can fit in the main memory. Table V shows the maximal number of elements buffered in order to avoid outputting any useless intermediate results. An obvious observation is that Q3 and Q6 need to buffer many elements, but all other queries only need to buffer very small number of elements. This also can be explained that all queries except Q3,Q6 belong to the optimal query class. We compared the performance of three algorithms in Figure 4(b) and Figure 5(a). Obviously, TreeMatch is superior to TwigStack and TJFast, reaching 20%−95% improvement in execution time for all queries.

Medium size of main memory. In most real application, the main memory size is not so large that the whole document can fit in memory, neither so limited that only the elements in a single path can load in memory. In order to test whether TreeMatch has the ability to fully exploit the available medium size of main memory, we show the performance of algorithms in terms of the number of output elements with varying the size of main memory in Figure 6. In this

Table 1. Number of output elements (O) and the percentage (P) of useful elements for TreeMatch on random data

	D1		D2		D3	
Query	O	P	O	P	O	P
Q1	1321	100%	6576	100%	13290	100%
Q2	3558	100%	17757	100%	35649	100%
Q3	9575	98.8%	95291	99.9%	156954	94.5%
Q4	6635	100%	33055	100%	65691	100%
Q5	296	100%	1313	100%	2782	100%
Q6	7506	100%	94132	100%	127478	99.9%

Table 2. # of required buffered elements (Random data)

	D_1	D_2	D_3
Q1	5	6	6
Q2	9	10	11
Q3	528	27067	89779
Q4	6	7	8
Q5	7	8	10
Q6	520	26808	89627

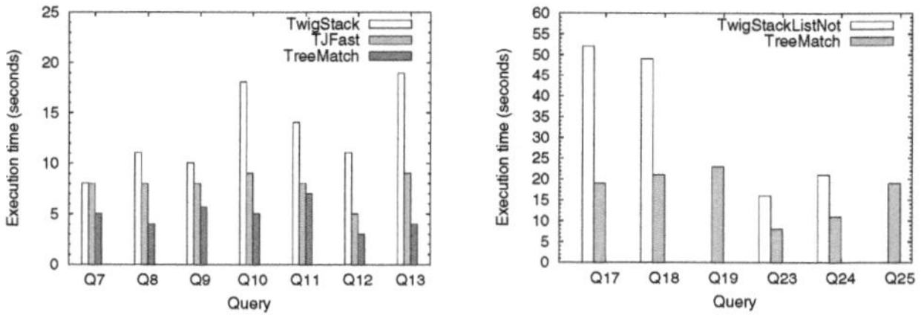

(a) $Q^{/,//,*}$ (b) $Q^{/,//,*,<,\neg}$

Fig. 5. Execution time on DBLP, TreeBank data (large memory)

experiment, we choose $Q1$ and $Q6$, since $Q1$ is an optimal query for TreeMatch, but $Q6$ is sub-optimal. The experimental results show that the number of output elements in TreeMatch is always much less than that in TwigStack and TJFast for all sizes of main memory. In particular, for $Q1$, with the increasing of the size of the available main memory, the number of output elements in TwigStack and TJFast decreases linearly. The reason is that TwigStack and TJFast buffer the intermediate results in the main memory and reduce the output of intermediate results. But the numbers of output elements in TreeMatch remain the same, which always equals the final result size. For query $Q6$, all algorithms are not optimal. But TreeMatch still outputs much less elements than TwigStack and TJFast.

Table 3. # of output elements (O) and the percentage (P) of useful elements for TreeMatch on random data

	D1		D2		D3	
Query	O	P	O	P	O	P
Q14	3596	68.2%	17922	69.8%	35959	68.7%
Q15	2481	100%	12367	100%	24575	100%
Q16	1075	100%	5408	100%	10820	100%
Q17	19792	100%	100008	100%	199727	100%
Q18	3926	100%	20182	100%	39796	100%
Q19	19565	100%	190789	100%	246783	100%

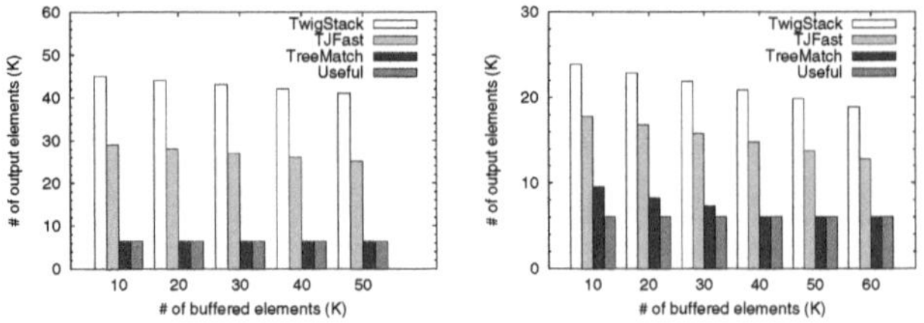

(a) Q1 (b) Q6

Fig. 6. Output data size with varying memory (medium memory)

Table 4. # of required buffered elements (Random data)

	D_1	D_2	D_3
Q14	3926	20182	39796
Q15	9	9	10
Q16	4	5	6
Q17	3	5	6
Q18	6	8	9
Q19	9	11	11

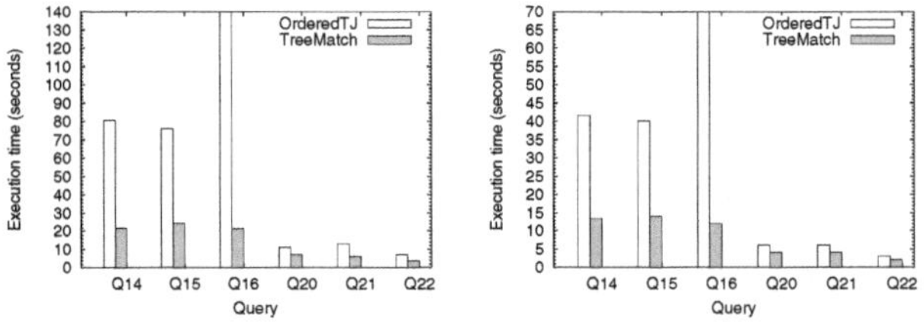

(a) Small memory (b) Large memory

Fig. 7. Execution time of $Q^{/,//,*,<}$ on random data

4 Conclusion

In this paper, we proposed the problem of XML tree pattern matching and surveyed some recent works and algorithms. Our comprehensive benchmarking compared five holistic algorithms and demonstrated their efficiency and scalability. There is no clear winner in all scenarios in our experiments. But TreeMatch[13] has an overall good performance in terms of running time and the ability to process generalized tree patterns. More details and discussion about our experiments can be found in [12].

Acknowledgement

This paper was partially supported by 863 National High-Tech Research Plan of China (No: 2009AA01Z133), National Science Foundation of China (NSFC) (No.

60903056), Key Project in Ministry of Education (No: 109004) and SRFDP Fund for the Doctoral Program (No. 20090004120002) and Program for New Century Excellent Talents in University.

References

1. Berglund, A., Boag, S., Chamberlin, D.: XML path language (XPath) 2.0. W3C Recommendation (January 23, 2007), `http://www.w3.org/TR/xpath20/`
2. Boag, S., Chamberlin, D., Fernandez, M.F.: Xquery 1.0: An XML query language. W3C Working Draft (August 22, 2003)
3. Bruno, N., Srivastava, D., Koudas, N.: Holistic twig joins: optimal XML pattern matching. In: Proc. of SIGMOD Conference, pp. 310–321 (2002)
4. Chen, S., Li, H.-G., Tatemura, J., Hsiung, W.-P., Agrawal, D., Candan, K.S.: Twig2stack: Bottom-up processing of generalized-tree-pattern queries over XML document. In: Proc. of VLDB Conference, pp. 19–30 (2006)
5. Chen, T., Lu, J., Ling, T.W.: On boosting holism in XML twig pattern matching using structural indexing techniques. In: SIGMOD, pp. 455–466 (2005)
6. Choi, B., Mahoui, M., Wood, D.: On the optimality of the holistic twig join algorithms. In: Mařík, V., Štěpánková, O., Retschitzegger, W. (eds.) DEXA 2003. LNCS, vol. 2736, pp. 28–37. Springer, Heidelberg (2003)
7. Goldman, R., Widom, J.: Dataguides: Enabling query formulation and optimization in semistructured databases. In: Proc. of VLDB, pp. 436–445 (1997)
8. Jagadish, H.V., AL-Khalifa, S.: Timber: A native XML database. Technical report, University of Michigan (2002)
9. Jiang, H., et al.: Holistic twig joins on indexed XML documents. In: Proc. of VLDB, pp. 273–284 (2003)
10. Jiang, H., Lu, H., Wang, W.: Efficient processing of XML twig queries with OR-predicates. In: Proc. of SIGMOD Conference, pp. 274–285 (2004)
11. Li, Q., Moon, B.: Indexing and querying XML data for regular path expressions. In: Proc. of VLDB, pp. 361–370 (2001)
12. Lu, J.: Benchmarking holistic approaches to XML tree pattern query processing. Invited talk slides for BenchmarX (2010), `http://datasearch.ruc.edu.cn/paper/keynote03.ppt`
13. Lu, J., Ling, T.W., Bao, Z., Wang, C.: Extended XML tree pattern matching: theories and algorithms. In: IEEE Transacion on Knowledge and Data Engineering (to appear, 2010), `http://datasearch.ruc.edu.cn/paper/TKDE2010.pdf`
14. Lu, J., Ling, T.W., Chan, C., Chen, T.: From region encoding to extended dewey: On efficient processing of XML twig pattern matching. In: VLDB, pp. 193–204 (2005)
15. Lu, J., Ling, T.W., Yu, T., Li, C., Ni, W.: Efficient processing of ordered XML twig pattern matching. In: Andersen, K.V., Debenham, J., Wagner, R. (eds.) DEXA 2005. LNCS, vol. 3588, pp. 300–309. Springer, Heidelberg (2005)
16. Moro, M., Vagena, Z., Tsotras, V.J.: Tree-pattern queries on a lightweight XML processor. In: VLDB, pp. 205–216 (2005)
17. O'Neil, P., O'Neil, E., Pal, S., Cseri, I., Schaller, G., Westbury, N.: ORDPATHs: Insert-friendly XML node labels. In: SIGMOD, pp. 903–908 (2004)
18. Rao, P., Moon, B.: PRIX: Indexing and querying XML using prufer sequences. In: ICDE, pp. 288–300 (2004)

19. Shalem, M., Bar-Yossef, Z.: The space complexity of processing XML twig queries over indexed documents. In: ICDE (2008)
20. Tatarinov, I., Viglas, S., Beyer, K.S., Shanmugasundaram, J., Shekita, E.J., Zhang, C.: Storing and querying ordered XML using a relational database system. In: Proc. of SIGMOD, pp. 204–215 (2002)
21. Wang, H., Meng, X.: On the sequencing of tree structures for XML indexing. In: ICDE, pp. 372–383 (2005)
22. Wang, H., Park, S., Fan, W., Yu, P.S.: ViST: A dynamic index method for querying XML data by tree structures. In: SIGMOD, pp. 110–121 (2003)
23. Wu, X., Lee, M., Hsu, W.: A prime number labeling scheme for dynamic ordered XML trees. In: Proc. of ICDE, pp. 66–78 (2004)
24. Yu, T., Ling, T.W., Lu, J.: Twigstacklistnot: A holistic twig join algorithm for twig query with not-predicates on XML data. In: Li Lee, M., Tan, K.-L., Wuwongse, V. (eds.) DASFAA 2006. LNCS, vol. 3882, pp. 249–263. Springer, Heidelberg (2006)
25. Zhang, C., Naughton, J.F., DeWitt, D.J., Luo, Q., Lohman, G.M.: On supporting containment queries in relational database management systems. In: Proc. of SIGMOD Conference, pp. 425–436 (2001)

Benchmarking the Compression of XML Node Streams*

Radim Bača, Jiří Walder, Martin Pawlas, and Michal Krátký

Department of Computer Science, VŠB–Technical University of Ostrava
17. listopadu 15, Ostrava, Czech Republic
{radim.baca,martin.pawlas,jiri.walder,michal.kratky}@vsb.cz

Abstract. In recent years, many approaches to XML twig pattern query processing have been developed. Holistic approaches are particularly significant in that they provide a theoretical model for optimal processing of some query classes and have very low main memory complexity. Holistic algorithms are supported by a stream abstract data type. This data type is usually implemented using inverted lists or special purpose data structures. In this article, we focus on an efficient implementation of a stream ADT. We utilize previously proposed fast decoding algorithms for some prefix variable-length codes, like Elias-delta, Fibonacci of order 2 and 3 as well as Elias-Fibonacci codes. We compare the efficiency of the access to a stream using various decompression algorithms. These results are compared with the result of data structures where no compression is used. We show that the compression improves the efficiency of XML query processing.

Keywords: stream ADT, XML node streams, variable-length codes, fast decompression algorithms, XML query processing.

1 Introduction

In recent years, many approaches to XML twig pattern query (TPQ) processing have been developed. Indexing techniques for an XML document structure have been studied extensively and works such as [20,16,11,1,5,12,6,7] have outlined basic principles of streaming scheme approaches. Nodes of an XML tree are labeled by a labeling scheme [20,16] and stored in a stream array. Streaming methods usually use the XML node tag as a key for one stream. Labels retrieved for each query node tag are then merged by an XML join algorithm such as structural join [1] or holistic join [5].

XML joins use a stream abstract data type which is usually implemented using inverted lists or special purpose data structures [12,13]. Since XML node labels are often small values, we can use universal variable-length codes for their compression. The main disadvantage of these codes is their inefficient compression/decompression based on bit-by-bit algorithms. In [18], we introduced fast

* Work is partially supported by Grants of GACR No. P202/10/0573 and SGS, Technical University of Ostrava, No. SP/2010138, Czech Republic.

M. Yoshikawa et al. (Eds.): DASFAA 2010, LNCS 6193, pp. 179–190, 2010.

decoding algorithms for some universal codes. In [4], we introduced a compression scheme for a stream ADT. This data structure allows us to store variable-length labels such as Dewey order without any storage overhead. In the article, the result of Fast Fibonacci coding was compared with often used RLE. In this paper, we propose a benchmarking of this scheme; we compare building and accessing of node streams using fast algorithms of more universal codes.

In Section 2, we describe an XML model. Section 3 introduces the stream abstract data type. Since we utilize prefix variable-length codes, Section 4 includes a brief description of these codes. In Section 5, we describe various compression techniques applied to a stream. Section 6 proposes experimental results.

2 XML Model

An XML document can be modeled as a rooted, ordered, labeled tree, where every node of the tree corresponds to an element or an attribute of the document and edges connect elements, or elements and attributes, having a parent-child relationship. We call such representation of an XML document an *XML tree*. We can see an example of the XML tree in Figure 1. We use the term 'node' to define a node of an XML tree which represents an element or an attribute.

The labeling scheme associates every node in the XML tree with a label. These labels allow us to determine structural relationships between nodes. Figures 1(a) and 1(b) show the XML tree labeled by *Containment labeling scheme* [20] and *Dewey order* [16], respectively.

The containment labeling scheme creates labels according to the document order. We can use a simple counter, which is incremented every time we visit a start or end tag of an element. The first and the second number of a node label represent a value of the counter when the start tag and the end tag are visited, respectively. In the case of Dewey order, every number in the label corresponds to one ancestor node.

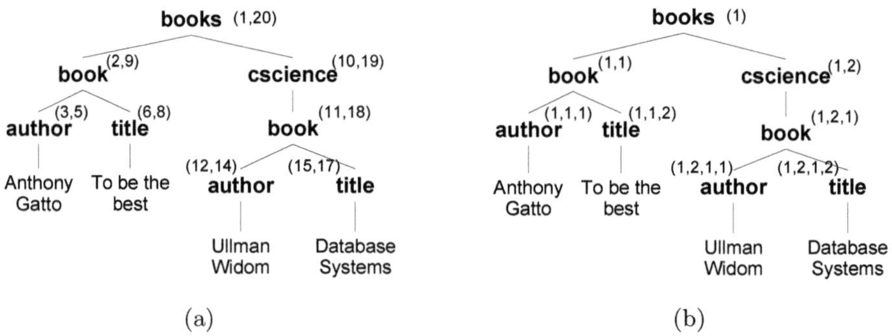

Fig. 1. (a) Containment labeling scheme (b) Dewey order labeling scheme

3 Stream ADT

Holistic approaches [5,7] use an abstract data type (ADT) called a *stream*. A stream is an ordered set of node labels with the same *schema node label.* There are many options for creating schema node labels (also known as *streaming schemes* in holistic works like [5,7]). A cursor pointing to the first node label is assigned to each stream. We distinguish the following operations of a T stream: *head(T)* – returns the node label to the cursor's position, *eof(T)* – returns true iff the cursor is at the end of T, *advance(T)* – moves the cursor to the next node label. Implementation of the stream ADT usually contains additional operations: *openStream(T)* – open the stream T for reading, *closeStream(T)* - close the stream.

The stream ADT is often implemented by an inverted list. In the following section we describe a data structure called *stream array* [4], which implements stream ADT.

3.1 Persistent Stream Array

Persistent stream array is a data structure using a common paged scheme [10], where labels are stored in blocks on the secondary storage and the main memory cache keeps blocks from the secondary storage. In Figure 2, we see an overview of the scheme. The cache utilizes the least recently used (LRU) schema for a selection of cache blocks [10]. Each block includes an array of tuples (node labels) and a pointer to the next block in the stream. Pointers enable a dynamic character of the data structure. We can easily insert or remove tuples from the blocks using the node split or merge. Blocks do not have to be fully utilized; therefore, we also keep the number of tuples stored in each block.

Insert and delete operations. The insert operation is very simple. We first find the position of a new label within the stream and then we test whether there is enough space for the new label or not. We can utilize a common label shift between blocks or block split to create the space for a new label. The delete operation first finds the position of the label which should be deleted and then removes this label from the block. Block merge can be also utilized in this case.

Position searching within the stream during the insert can be quite a time-consuming process since the streams can span many blocks. A more common

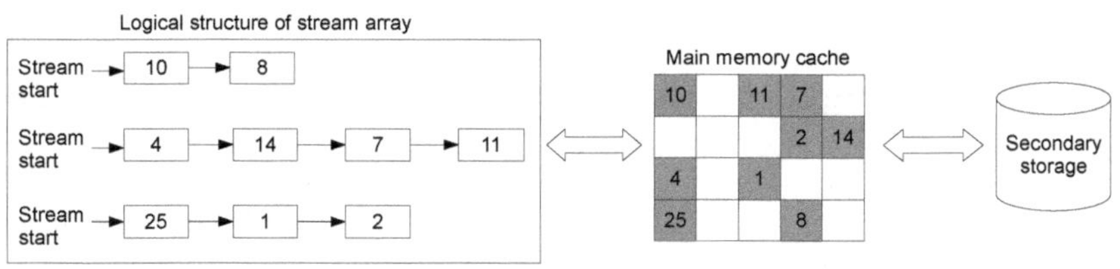

Fig. 2. Overview of the paged data structure

operation in the case of an XML index is the insert operation of many labels which corresponds to an XML tree insert. We address this issue in the next section.

Bulk insert operation. The insert of a whole XML document (or several documents) is a quite common operation when working with XML databases. Loading an XML document into the index can be processed significantly faster then using the insert label-by-label. The situation is simple thanks to the fact that we create labels in the same order in which they are stored in the stream. Therefore, during the bulk insert operation we sequentially read the input XML document, we create labels and we store the labels at the end of each stream. Compared to the insert we do not have to search for the exact position of a new label in the stream. In Section 6, we utilize the bulk insert algorithm to build the indexes.

3.2 Compressed Stream Array

There are two advantages of a stream array compression. The first advantage is that we can decrease the size of the data file and, therefore, decrease the number of disk accesses. Of course, there is extra time spent on the compression and decompression of data. The compression and decompression time should be lower or equal to time saved by having less disk accesses. As a result, the compression algorithm should be fast and should have a good compression ratio. The second advantage is that we can store variable-length tuples. Tuples in a regular stream block are stored in an array with the fixed items' size. The items' size has to be equal to the size of the longest label stored in the stream array and we waste quite a lot of space in this way.

The stream array has a specific feature which enables efficient compression. We never access items in one block randomly during the stream read. Random access to a tuple in the block may occur only during the stream open operation, but the stream open is not processed very often. Therefore, we can keep the block items encoded in the byte array and remember only the actual cursor position in the byte array. The cursor is created during the stream open and it also contains one tuple where we store the encoded label of the current cursor position. Each label is encoded only once during the *advance(T)* operation. The *head(T)* operation only returns the encoded tuple assigned to the cursor. Using this schema we keep data compressed even in the main memory and have to have only one decompressed tuple assigned to each opened stream.

4 Variable-Length Codes and Fast Decoding Algorithms

Since we utilize variable-length universal codes for the compression of XML node streams, we briefly describe variable-length codes and fast decompression algorithms in this section. We chose Elias-delta, Fibonacci of order 2 and 3, and Elias-Fibonacci codes for the compression of streams. This selection is based on benchmarking depicted in [19,17].

4.1 An Overview of Universal Codes

The Elias-delta code is one of the most widely used prefix codes. This code was introduced by Peter Elias [8]. The Elias-delta code $E(n)$ for any positive integer n is coded as follows:

1. Let $B(n)$ be the binary representation of the number n without insignificant 0-bits. Let $B'(n)$ be $B(n)$ without the leading 1-bit.
2. Let $L(n)$ be the length of $B(n)$ as the binary value (meaning the number of bits of $B(n)$).
3. Let $Z(n)$ be a sequence of zeros, the number of zeros is equal to the length of $L(n) - 1$.
4. Elias-delta code is then the concatenation $E(n) = Z(n)L(n)B'(n)$.

The Fibonacci code is based on Fibonacci numbers [14] and it was introduced in [9]. In [2], authors introduced the generalized Fibonacci code. Fibonacci numbers of order m ($m \geq 2$) are defined as follows:

$$F_i^{(m)} = F_{i-1}^{(m)} + F_{i-2}^{(m)} + \ldots + F_{i-m}^{(m)}\,, \text{ for } i \geq 1,$$
$$\text{where } F_{-m+1}^{(m)} = F_{-m+2}^{(m)} = \ldots = F_{-2}^{(m)} = 0,$$
$$\text{and } F_{-1}^{(m)} = F_0^{(m)} = 1.$$

For $m = 2$ we obtain the classical Fibonacci numbers 1, 2, 3, 5, 8, 11, ... etc.

Definition 1. *Fibonacci sum*
Let $S_n^{(m)}$ be the sum of Fibonacci numbers. The sum is defined as follows:

$$S_n^{(m)} = \begin{cases} 0, \; \mathit{for}\; n < -1 \\ \displaystyle\sum_{i=-1}^{n} F_i^{(m)}, \; \mathit{for}\; n \geq -1 \end{cases}$$

Consequently, the coding algorithm for the Fibonacci code $\mathcal{F}^{(m)}(n)$ of order m for any positive integer n is as follows:

1. If $n = 1$, then $\mathcal{F}^{(m)}(n) = 1_m$. `END`.
2. If $n = 2$, then $\mathcal{F}^{(m)}(n) = 01_m$. `END`.
3. Find k such that $S_{k-2}^{(m)} < n \leq S_{k-1}^{(m)}$. Let $Q = n - S_{k-2} - 1$.
4. Compute $F^{(m)}(Q)$.
5. Append 01_m as a suffix to $F^{(m)}(Q)$. If necessary, append leading 0-bits to make $\mathcal{F}^{(m)}(n)$ of length $m + k$.

The Fibonacci code has the property which means that this code starts with a sequence of m adjacent 1-bits; however, this sequence is not presented in another part of the code.

The Elias-Fibonacci code $EF(n)$ for any positive integer n is as follows: $EF(n) = F^{(2)}(L(n))B(n)$ [18]. It means it consists of two parts. The second

Table 1. Examples of codewords for some integers for Elias-delta, Fibonacci of order 2 and 3, and Elias-Fibonacci codes

n	$E(n)$	$\mathcal{F}^{(2)}(n)$	$\mathcal{F}^{(3)}(n)$	$EF(n)$
1	1	11	111	11
2	0100	011	0111	0110
3	0101	0011	00111	0111
4	01100	1011	10111	001100
5	01101	00011	000111	001101
6	01110	10011	100111	001110
7	01111	01011	010111	001111
8	00100000	000011	110111	1011000
9	00100001	100011	0000111	1011001
10	00100010	010011	1000111	1011010
⋮	⋮	⋮	⋮	⋮
1000	0001010111101000	0000010000000011	00000011010111	010011111101000

part is a binary representation of the number n labeled $B(n)$. The first part is the length of $B(n)$, labeled $L(n)$, encoded by the Fibonacci code of order 2. We do not utilize a delimiter in this code; however, we utilize a sequence of two 1-bits between the end of $F^{(2)}(L(n))$ and start of $B(n)$. In other words, if we reach two 1-bits in a code, we read $L(n)$ and we know that we must read $L(n)-1$ bits to complete $B(n)$. Examples of all proposed codes are shown in Table 1.

4.2 Fast Decoding Algorithms

We utilize the fast decoding algorithms introduced in [18]. The basic idea of all fast algorithms is to read an input stream byte by byte instead of bit by bit. This algorithm is based on a finite automaton; a precomputed mapping table is used for each state of the automaton. The precomputed table included in each automaton state allows converting segments of the input stream's bytes directly into decoded numbers for each state. The mapping table also defines the new automaton state for each segment. The algorithm for mapping table building is based on a conventional bit-oriented algorithm. During the building of the mapping table we must consider all states and possibilities when we read the current segment. Authors stated that the fast algorithms are up to 5.2× more efficient than conventional decoding algorithms.

5 Compression of XML Node Streams

In this section, we describe methods utilized for the compression of XML node streams. We must keep in mind that labels are ordered in a block. We use the following methods: 1. Fixed-length tuple, 2. Variable-length tuple, 3. Common prefix compression, 4. Variable-length code compression, 5. Variable-length code compression with the reference item. Obviously, the first two methods are not real compression methods, and we use them for a comparison with other methods. We describe some of these methods in the following sections in more detail. In the following we assume that an integer is stored using 4 Bytes.

5.1 Fixed-Length and Variable-Length Tuple Methods

The variable-length tuple method is usable only in the case of a path-based labeling scheme like Dewey order. In the case of the fixed-length tuple method and Dewey order, we must set a maximal tuple length and all shorter tuples must be filled by a gap value.

Example 1. Let us have these two tuples: $\langle 1, 2\rangle$ and $\langle 1, 2, 3, 7\rangle$. When using the variable-length tuple method they occupy $6 \times 4\,\text{B} + 2\,\text{B}$ for the dimension length of these two tuples. If we use the fixed-length tuple method, the first tuple must be filled, so it looks like $\langle 1, 2, 0, 0\rangle$. Consequently, these two tuples occupy $8 \times 4\,\text{B}$.

5.2 Common Prefix Compression

Common prefix compression is based on the idea of Run Length Encoding (RLE) [15]. Due to ordering of the tuples in a block, the ancestor of a tuple is very similar and therefore we do not have to store each values.

Example 2. Let us have the following tuples: $\langle 1, 2, 3, 7, 9, 7\rangle$, $\langle 1, 2, 3, 7, 5, 6, 7\rangle$, $\langle 1, 2, 3, 7, 7, 0, 0, 7\rangle$. The first tuple cannot be compressed, due to the fact that it has no ancestor. If we compare the second tuple with the first it differs only in the 3 last dimensions, and the third one differs in the last 4 dimensions. Therefore we can store the number of similar dimensions and all differences. The result is as follows: $0 - \langle 1, 2, 3, 7, 9, 7\rangle$, $4 - \langle 5, 6, 7\rangle$, $4 - \langle 7, 0, 0, 7\rangle$. Using this method we obtain $7 \times 4\,\text{B}$ for first, $4 \times 4\,\text{B}$ for second, and $5 \times 4\,\text{B}$ for the third tuple. In total, we obtain $16 \times 4\,\text{B} = 64\,\text{B}$. For fixed-length we need $8 \times 3 \times 4\,\text{B} = 96\,\text{B}$, because all tuples must be extended to the length of 8 dimensions.

5.3 Variable-Length Code Compression

In this case, data is encoded by variable-length codes proposed in Section 4. This kind of compression is based on the behavior of the variable-length codes that the smaller number is coded by a shorter code. This assumption is achieved for both Containment and Dewey order labeling schemes. For the Containment labeling scheme each label includes the range and a small number of the tree depth. We assume that the range represented by a variable-length code will occupy fewer bits than the range represented by binary coding. Similarly, for Dewey order each subtree starts with 1; therefore, the labels are assumed to be small values.

Example 3. Let us have a tuple $\langle 1, 2, 3, 7\rangle$. After encoding the tuple with Fibonacci of order 2, the tuple is stored as a sequence of 11011001101011 bits, which occupy 2 B instead of original 16 B (it means $4 \times 4\,\text{B}$).

5.4 Variable-Length Code Compression with Reference Item

Variable-length codes proposed in Section 4 are appropriate for the compression of small values. However, numbers in the case of the Containment labeling scheme grow rapidly. In this case, the variable-length codes become inefficient and compression does not work appropriately. This issue is less noticeable in the case of Dewey order. Tuples in a stream array are sorted and we can use this feature to compress a tuple with knowledge of its ancestor. The first tuple in the block is stored unchanged. In order to keep all other numbers small, we store the differences between the current tuple and the previous tuple. The first tuple and all differences are than encoded with any of presented codes. Obviously, the difference coding is a well-known technique in the field of data compression [15].

Example 4. Let us have these two tuples: $\langle 1000, 200, 300, 7\rangle$ and $\langle 1005, 220, 100, 7\rangle$. From this example we see that we can subtract first 2 dimensions. After subtraction we get tuples $\langle 1000, 200, 300, 7\rangle$ and $\langle 5, 20, 100, 7\rangle$, which are encoded faster and also occupy less space.

6 Experimental Results

In our experiments[1], we use the XMARK[2] data collection with the factor 2, 240 MB in size; it includes 4,000 k nodes. We generate labels for all nodes by means of two proposed labeling schemes: Containment labeling scheme with the fixed-length of labels and Dewey order labeling scheme with the variable-length. Since labeled path streaming scheme was used [3,7], 512 streams were created. The nodes in streams are ordered. The stream array and all compression algorithms have been implemented in C++[3].

We provide a set of tests where we simulate real work with the stream array and measure the influence of the compression. For each test we randomly select 100 streams and read them until the end. This is processed by holistic join as well structural join approaches. Accessing all labels in one stream is called query processing. As usual, tests are processed with a cold cache (OS cache as well as cache buffer of indices). For all tests we measure index size, query processing time, Disk Access Cost (DAC), and time of index building. The query processing time is the time needed for opening each randomly selected stream and the time needed for decompression of all number codes stored in the stream. DAC is equal to the number of disk accesses during query processing. For the time measurement, we repeat the tests 10 times and calculate the average time. In tables and figures we use the abbreviation 'RI' instead of 'reference item', so 'Fibonacci 2 RI' means 'Fibonacci 2 with the reference item'.

---

[1] The experiments were executed on an Intel® Core 2 Duo 2.4 Ghz, 512 kB L2 cache; 3 GB RAM; Windows 7.

[2] `http://monetdb.cwi.nl/xml/`

[3] Test application: http://db.cs.vsb.cz/download/streamarray.zip

Table 2. Index size, query processing time, DAC, and build time for the Containment labeling scheme

	Index Size [kB]	**Query Processing Time** [s]	**DAC**	**Build Time** [s]
Fixed length	97,708	3.23	3,551	58.22
Common Prefix	85,736	2.37	3,119	52.54
Elias-delta	71,448	2.21	2,611	82.49
Fibonacci 2	73,688	2.18	2,695	97.16
Fibonacci 3	67,860	2.12	2,475	92.29
Elias-Fibonacci	71,000	2.12	2,588	92.36
Elias-delta RI	**36,252**	1.55	**1,356**	**48.30**
Fibonacci 2 RI	37,040	1.56	1,365	61.21
Fibonacci 3 RI	39,472	1.55	1,467	54.98
Elias-Fibonacci RI	38,780	**1.52**	1,437	60.03

6.1 Results for Containment Labeling Scheme

The results for the fixed-length Containment labeling scheme are shown in Table 2 and Figure 3. As we see in Figure 3a the Elias-delta code with the reference item produces the smallest index file; however, the most efficient query processing time was achieved by the Elias-Fibonacci code with the reference item (see Figure 3b). Consequently, Elias-delta code with the reference item achieved the lowest DAC; however, Elias-Fibonacci provides a more efficient decoding time for all numbers larger than 6 due to the fact that these codewords are shorter [18]. The effect of faster decoding for the Elias-Fibonacci code outperforms lower DAC for Elias-delta. All variable-length codes produce very similar results for the index size, query processing time, and DAC and we see that these codes outperform often used RLE; the index size is approximately 2.4× lower. Obviously, the compression with the reference item is more efficient then the compression without reference item. The compression saves approximately 68 % of the index size, 50 % of the query processing time, and 68 % of DAC. The results of the index build time are depicted in Figure 3d. Compression using varible-length codes with the reference item achieved up-to 1.2× more efficient index build time than the fixed-length tuple method. Obviously, the Elias-delta code with the reference item outperforms all other codes.

6.2 Results for Dewey Order Labeling Scheme

The results for variable-length Dewey order are shown in Table 3 and Figure 4. Obviously, all variable-length codes produce very similar results; the compression saves approximately 80% of the index size, 64% of the query processing time, and 80% of DAC. Morevover, the build time is approximately 2.8× more efficient than in the case of the fixed-length tuple method. In this case, value differences are very often zeros which are coded with the shortest codeword. For Elias-delta, the shortest codeword includes only 1 bit while other codes use more bits. Therefore, the Elias-delta code outperforms all other codes. This fact also provides an opportunity to improve compression in the future, when the number of zeros can be reduced by RLE.

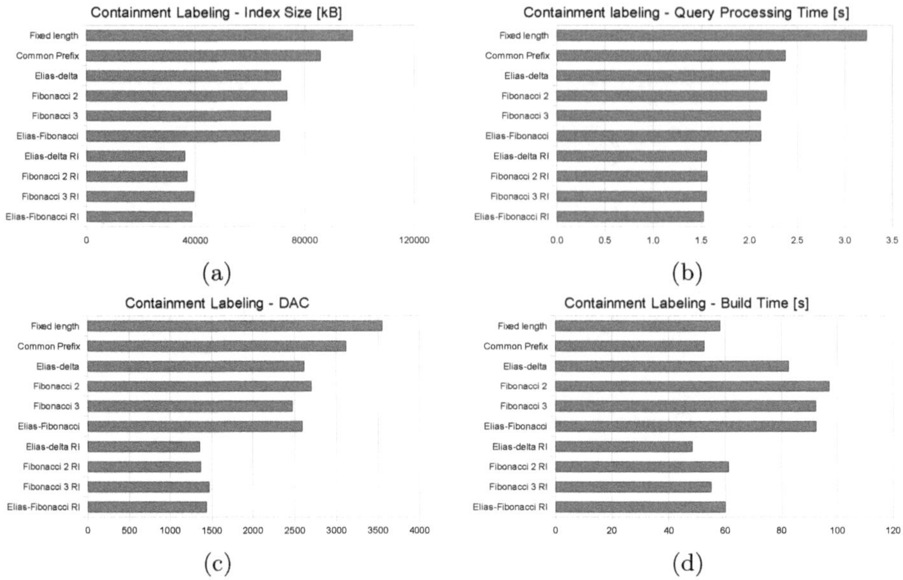

Fig. 3. (a) Index size (b) Query processing time (c) DAC for (d) Build time for the Containment labeling scheme

Table 3. Index size, query processing time, DAC, and build time for the Dewey order labeling scheme

	Index Size [kB]	**Query Processing Time** [s]	**DAC**	**Build Time** [s]
Fixed length	274,620	9.63	9,968	132.98
Variable length	127,156	3.06	4,624	79.81
Common Prefix	77,676	2.35	2,832	55.78
Elias-delta	41,504	1.59	1,516	74.51
Fibonacci 2	41,124	1.58	1,496	86.30
Fibonacci 3	43,232	1.58	1,571	80.00
Elias-Fibonacci	43,192	1.59	1,578	86.24
Elias-delta RI	**28,076**	**1.29**	**1,026**	**46.68**
Fibonacci 2 RI	30,896	1.45	1,126	54.78
Fibonacci 3 RI	35,172	1.51	1,285	48.98
Elias-Fibonacci RI	31,576	1.37	1,157	58.78

Although we utilized conventional bit-by-bit coding algorithms for the variable-length codes, the build time for these methods is more efficient than the build time for methods not using variable-length codes. Consequently, the build time is more influenced by the index size than the coding time.

Dewey order is the more important labeling scheme from the XML data update point of view; therefore, it is important to see that we achieve smaller index sizes than with the Containment labeling scheme. It is because two neighboring labels are similar; they usually differ only in the last positions. The compression using the reference item is more efficient than the compression without the reference item.

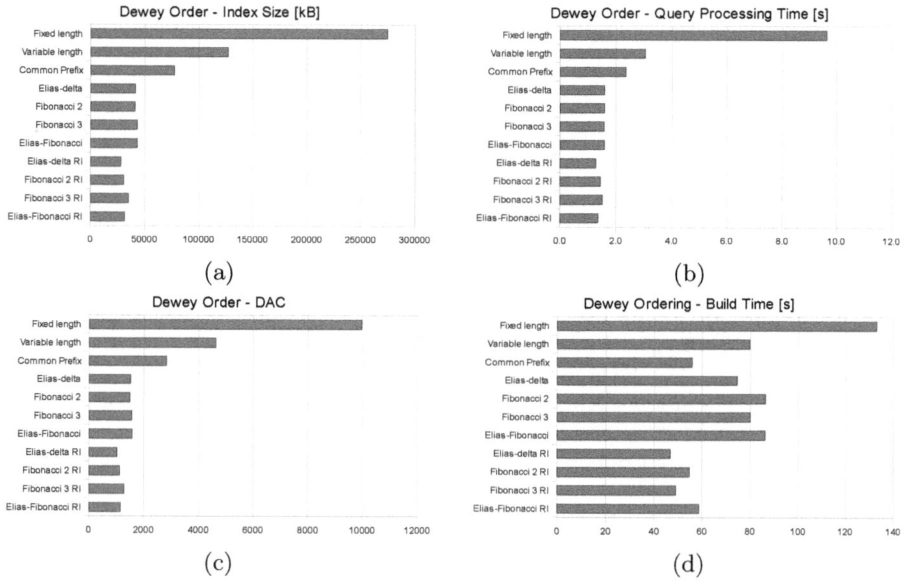

Fig. 4. (a) Index size (b) Query time (c) DAC (d) Build time for the Dewey order labeling scheme

7 Conclusion

In this article, we evaluated various compression methods of XML node steams. This data structure is often used by structural as well as holistic query processing approaches. We tested the two most common labeling schemes: Containment and Dewey order labeling schemes. We performed a series of experiments with various compression techniques. Variable-length codes with the reference item are always more efficient than methods not using the reference item. We propose that Dewey order is more suitable for compression. It is a suitable feature of Dewey order since this labeling scheme is much more appropriate for updates of XML data. Moreover, we see that compression is an interesting way to improve the query processing time; the query processing time was improved up-to 7.5×. In our future research we want to improve the proposed compression methods for XML node streams.

References

1. Al-Khalifa, S., Jagadish, H.V., Koudas, N.: Structural Joins: A Primitive for Efficient XML Query Pattern Matching. In: Proceedings of ICDE 2002, pp. 141–152. IEEE CS, Los Alamitos (2002)
2. Apostolico, A., Fraenkel, A.: Robust Transmission of Unbounded Strings Using Fibonacci Representations. IEEE Transactions on Information Theory 33(2), 238–245 (1987)

3. Bača, R., Krátký, M.: TJDewey – On the Efficient Path Labeling Scheme Holistic Approach. In: Chen, L., Liu, C., Liu, Q., Deng, K. (eds.) Database Systems for Advanced Applications. LNCS, vol. 5667, pp. 6–20. Springer, Heidelberg (2009)
4. Bača, R., Pawlas, M.: Compression of the Stream Array Data Structure. In: Proceedings of the 9th Annual International Workshop on DAtabases, TExts, Specfications and Objects, DATESO 2009. CEUR Workshop Proceedings, vol. 471, pp. 23–31 (2009)
5. Bruno, N., Srivastava, D., Koudas, N.: Holistic Twig Joins: Optimal XML Pattern Matching. In: Proceedings of ACM SIGMOD 2002, pp. 310–321. ACM Press, New York (2002)
6. Chen, S., Li, H.-G., Tatemura, J., Hsiung, W.-P., Agrawal, D., Candan, K.S.: Twig2Stack: Bottom-up Processing of Generalized-tree-pattern Queries Over XML documents. In: Proceedings of VLDB 2006, pp. 283–294 (2006)
7. Chen, Z., Korn, G., Koudas, F., Shanmugasundaram, N., Srivastava, J.: Index Structures for Matching XML Twigs Using Relational Query Processors. In: Proceedings of ICDE 2005, p. 1273. IEEE CS, Los Alamitos (2005)
8. Elias, P.: Universal Codeword Sets and Representations of the Integers. IEEE Transactions on Information Theory 21(2), 194–203 (1975)
9. Fraenkel, A., Klein, S.: Robust Universal Complete Codes as Alternatives to Huffiman Codes. Technical Report Tech. Report CS85-16, Dept. of Appl. Math., The Weizmann Institute of Science, Rehovot (1985)
10. Garcia-Molina, H., Ullman, J., Widom, J.: Database Systems: The Complete Book. Prentice Hall, Englewood Cliffs (2002)
11. Grust, T., van Keulen, M., Teubner, J.: Staircase Join: Teach a Relational DBMS to Watch Its (Axis) Steps. In: Proceedings of VLDB 2003, pp. 524–535 (2003)
12. Jiang, H., Lu, H., Wang, W., Ooi, B.: XR-Tree: Indexing XML Data for Efficient Structural Join. In: Proceedings of ICDE, India, pp. 253–264. IEEE CS, Los Alamitos (2003)
13. Krátký, M., Bača, R., Snášel, V.: Implementation of XPath Axes in the Multidimensional Approach to Indexing XML Data. In: Lindner, W., Mesiti, M., Türker, C., Tzitzikas, Y., Vakali, A.I. (eds.) EDBT 2004. LNCS, vol. 3268, pp. 219–229. Springer, Heidelberg (2004)
14. Leonardo of Pisa (known as Fibonacci). Liber Abaci. 1202
15. Salomon, D.: Data Compression: The Complete Reference, 3rd edn. Springer, New York (2004)
16. Tatarinov, I., et al.: Storing and Querying Ordered XML Using a Relational Database System. In: Proceedings of ACM SIGMOD 2002, pp. 204–215. ACM Press, New York (2002)
17. Walder, J., Krátký, M., Bača, R.: Benchmarking Coding Algorithms for the R-tree Compression. In: Proceedings of the 9th Annual International Workshop on Databases, Texts, Specifications and Objects, DATESO 2009. CEUR Workshop Proceedings, vol. 471, pp. 32–43 (2009)
18. Walder, J., Krátký, M., Bača, R., Platoš, J., Snášel, V.: Fast Decoding Algorithms for Variable-Lengths Codes. Submitted in Information Science (February 2010)
19. Williams, H.E., Zobel, J.: Compressing Integers for Fast File Access. The Computer Journal 42(3), 193–201 (1999)
20. Zhang, C., Naughton, J., DeWitt, D., Luo, Q., Lohman, G.: On Supporting Containment Queries in Relational Database Management Systems. In: Proceedings of ACM SIGMOD 2001, pp. 425–436. ACM Press, New York (2001)

Generation of Synthetic XML for Evaluation of Hybrid XML Systems

David Hall and Lena Strömbäck

Linköpings universitet, S-581 83 Linköping, Sweden

Abstract. Hybrid XML storage offers a large number of alternative shredding choices. In order to automatically determine optimal shredding strategies it is crucial to have an insight into how the structure of a XML data set affects the performance. Since the structure can take many forms and the number of possible mappings is huge it is important to gain insights on the relation between structure and performance for formats that are actually used. By taking real-world data sets and modify the structure in steps you can see how the performance and other measurable properties change. We describe how a data generator can be used to produce a synthetic data set based on an existing data set, by using four different models. We compare the performance on the original data set with the performance on the different synthetic models.

1 Introduction

The world wide web has evolved into a platform where diverse systems and applications exchange data and documents. Many commonly used data formats used by these applications are based on XML and there is an increasing need for efficient data management for the web. The structure of XML documents may vary from a flat, regular, structure to a deep, irregular, structure. The flat, *data-centric*, structure is common for formats exported directly from relational databases, while the *document-centric* structure is common for documents containing text with markup. The large variation of possible structures is one important characteristic of XML.

The flexibility of XML puts new demands on data management systems to capture all properties of the XML data model while achieving high performance. Three main approaches for storage of XML data have been used: native XML databases; shredding XML documents into relations; and hybrid storage that combines native and relational solutions. In principle, data-centric structures are easy to map into relations with both a performance-efficient and easy-to-use relational structure while it is harder to find a good shredding for the more irregular document-centric structure.

Hybrid storage is provided by the major relational database vendors (Oracle, IBM and Microsoft). It allows data to be stored using mapping to relations but also allows storage of sub-trees of XML data using the XML support available in the different RDBMSs. By using the hybrid storage model the user is not limited to either native or relational storage but can choose storage model for different

M. Yoshikawa et al. (Eds.): DASFAA 2010, LNCS 6193, pp. 191–202, 2010.

parts of the data based on for instance query performance, bulk loading speed or document reconstruction speed.

This leaves the user with a large number of possible choices for one schema and the choice between relational and XML storage of different parts of the schema is a trade-off between speed and a representation as close to the original XML schema as possible. The large number of possible mappings makes it practically hard to compare the choices to find metrics to easily determine suitable mapping in terms of speed and ease of use. For this purpose tools such as HShreX[1] can be used to aid the user in the process of mapping. HShreX makes it possible to map XML data to database systems with hybrid storage support and allows us to evaluate different storage alternatives in an efficient manner.

As a new field, storage of XML have seen much improvement over the last decade. There was early a need to compare systems when it comes to their capabilities and performance to allow users to select database system which match their need. In traditional database research benchmarks have been used to find a common ground for testing and comparing existing and proposed systems. Benchmarks are also important since they help developers of database systems to pinpoint limitations in their own systems. The benchmarks typically consist of one or several data sets and sets of queries for that data. Examples of such benchmarks are the Wisconsin benchmark[2] and the Datamation benchmark[3] for relational database systems and OO7[4] for object-oriented database systems. Since the possible ways to represent and structure data in the XML data model is far greater than in relational and object databases the data sets used in these benchmarks must be more diverse or only cover a certain application of XML. A number of benchmarks, such as XMach-1[5], XMark[6] and XOO7[7], have been developed since the advent of XML.

However, most existing benchmarks only allow limited possibilities of varying the XML structure. In this work our aim is to create a data set that as far as possible resembles real data but also allows us to vary different parameters so that we can evaluate connections between the parameters and performance. By varying these parameters we could find thresholds for where different storage strategies are optimal for the given data.

In this paper we evaluate the possibility of recreating a data set using synthetic data to the extent that the synthetic data can be used for testing the behavior of hybrid XML systems when altering XML structural properties such as depth and fan-out. The paper starts with motivating why these structural properties are interesting and why we want to recreate existing data sets. We then give an overview of existing benchmarks and systems for generation of synthetic XML data and why the latter can be used to create data sets useful in testing hybrid XML storage. This is followed by a description of the properties of the original data set that we want to model in the data generator to be able to test for their influence when it comes to measurable characteristics. After this we evaluate the approach by comparing authentic and synthetic data in a hybrid XML system and show that by using a data generator and a template, that specifies an element structure that is similar in number and depth to the original, we can generate a synthetic data set that behaves similar to the original data in terms of performance.

2 Motivation

In order to automatically determine optimal mapping strategies for hybrid XML storage it is crucial to have an insight into how the structure of a certain XML data set affects the performance of the hybrid XML database system. The speed at which queries are processed, bulk loading is performed and documents are reconstructed depends on the structure of the original XML document and the mapping chosen for storing it in the hybrid XML system. We have studied the structure of several real-world XML-based formats, such as UniProt[8], SBML[9], DBLP[10], Open Street Map[11] and House Legislative Documents[12], and have found a large variation of structure between them. Some formats also show variation in structure between different documents adhering to one standard or within one document itself. The large variation of structure in XML can be illustrated by the fact that different measures for describing structures of XML documents have been proposed in the literature[13,14,15,16].

Since the structure of XML can take many forms and the number of possible hybrid mappings based on the different structures is huge it is important to gain more interesting insights on the relation between structure and performance that are relevant for formats that are actually used. This can be done by taking real-world data sets and modify the structure in steps and see how the performance and other measurable properties change. Since we want to be able to modify the existing data set in a number of ways we need a description of the data set that lends itself to easy manipulation. Using the description we should not only be able to produce an artificial version of the data set that for all practical purposes behaves identically to the original but also allows for modification of structure and/or data properties. The identically behaving version is to be used for verifying that the artificial model of the format behaves identical to the original version. If it does not we have not been able to model the format with enough precision.

As an example on how the structure affects performance we can look at the UniProt[8] data set and some of the different storage alternatives for data affected by the XPath query

```
/uniprot/entry[comment/subcellularLocation/location/text()="Cytoplasm"]/accession
```

We could potentially make nine different choices when it comes to use the two alternatives of shredding or store as XML; (1) shred everything and store nothing as XML or store any sub-tree beneath (2) `location`, (3) `subcellularLocation`, (4) `comment`, or (5) `entry` as XML and shred everything above that. In addition to that we also have the previous mentioned choices (1)–(4) with `accession` either shredded or stored as XML, leaving us with a total of nine choices. The purely shredded version will result in high performance for query processing while reconstruction and serialization of data into a XML tree will take longer time than the alternative where the `entry` sub-tree is stored as XML. Figure 1

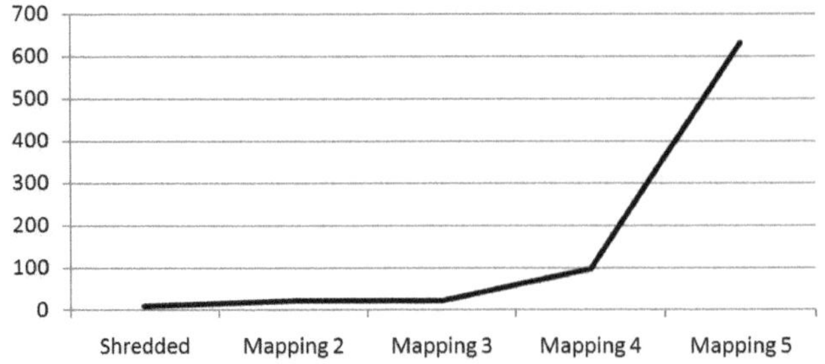

Fig. 1. Run time [ms] for different mappings in UniProt

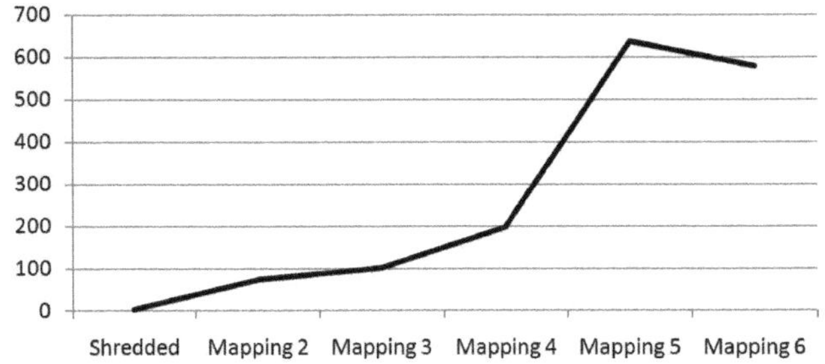

Fig. 2. Run time [ms] for different mappings in PSI-MI

shows the run-times for the different mappings. In fig. 2 we have choosen a similar query and set of mappings for another data set, PSI MI. For this data set, we get a similar performance increase by shredding the XML. However, the increase in performance for shredding one level is not the same as in the first data set due to the difference in structure between the data sets.

To further explore this we need a synthetic data set that is easy to modify. Modifications that could be interesting to perform using the artificial data set are e.g. change of depth or fan-out of the element tree, change of size of data or change of selectivity when used in queries. The description language for the format should thus have parameters for specifying both the overlying structure (as a schema for the XML-based format) but also, a varying number of elements and different instances of data of varying values and size. The number of elements, size and values of data often occur according to some distribution why a way to define such is needed.

3 Current Benchmarks and Data Generators

By using constructed data sets and queries the community has been given tools to test systems and techniques for handling XML data. Benchmarks are thought of as ways to capture data sets and queries typical of one or several applications of XML systems. They are aimed at comparing capabilities and performance of said systems, but not mainly intended for testing different techniques for storage and querying in the development of XML data management systems. A number of benchmarks have been proposed, e.g. [5,6,7]. They use data sets with both data-centric and document-centric properties. Some of them ([5,6]) use synthetically generated data with a scaling factor of the resulting data set as the only parameter that can be adjusted by the user.

Micro benchmarks are data sets (and queries) aimed at testing one particular property. The Michigan benchmark[17] is a micro benchmark made for testing basic operations like selections, joins and aggregation and how it is affected by particular properties of XML structure such as fan-out and depth. The main purpose of the Michigan benchmark is to pinpoint particular properties of XML database systems in order to improve them, not to compare different systems. They also aim at development of efficient ways to store data and process queries when it comes to structures with different fan-out and depth.

Data generators are used to create data sets when real data sets are not available or when you want more flexibility in the data to test with. Several of the benchmarks use some kind of data generator to create their data set which makes it possible to change some input parameters (in the case of benchmarks often a scaling factor of the total database size). There are a number of different features a data generator can have, but in principle all use some format specification and a repetitive, random, iteration. The specification states the structure as well as the data (values). In some of the more advanced data generators[18,19] a number of constraints can be added so that certain wanted properties can be achieved, such as how often a certain element or element value should appear (e.g. if a value should be unique or appear several times to allow joins).

ToXgene[20] was developed as a part of the Toronto XML engine and is used as a data generator in the XBench benchmark. ToXgene uses a template format similar to XML schema but with added elements for specifying distributions (used for e.g. element counts, numerical values and size of text data). Geng and Dobbie describes a method[21] for modifying existing XML data sets to achieve specific selectivity, depth, fan-out and size, meant to be used for producing data sets to be used for XML semantic query optimization.

In our case we want to study the efficiency for any given XML schema and data set when stored in a hybrid XML database system. Therefore, we cannot get satisfying results using a fixed data set from a benchmark. Since benchmarks are aimed at other goals than ours they usually have structure and data that allow a multitude of queries interesting for comparing performance of XML systems. They are not meant for studying how structure affects performance. Micro benchmarks have such a goal, however, but the data set, like the one used in the Michigan benchmark, has structures that differ a great deal from real-world data formats we have studied. In this work we would like to benefit from using a data generator to allow us to base experiments on existing structures and data but allow for easy manipulation to test how different characteristics affects performance.

4 Generating Synthetic Data

Our goal in this work is to generate data similar to real data sets, but where we can vary properties to determine thresholds for storage strategies. As a first step we will investigate if the relation between data size and query times for a selected database holds for generated data sets with a somewhat other structure. We say that the generated artificial data sets behave like the original if it has the same results on performance tests.

The following definitions will be used hereafter in this article:

Definition 1. *Two measures A and B are similar if* $|A - B|$ *is less than 10% of A and B.*

Definition 2. *The selectivity* $Sel(Q, D)$ *of a query Q on a data set D is the number of answers for Q on D.*

We will use ToXgene and try a number of different methods to generate data sets in order to see what parameters influence the performance of the queries. Other goals are to see what is needed to get the same results for a certain query and if ToXgene has enough expressiveness to achieve this. First we only generate the parts of the data set needed to get a result for the query that is similar to the original data. We need to have a selectivity that reflects that of the original document, i.e. we need to have about the same number of rows in the result. For this part we only reconstruct the paths that are needed to represent the data we use in the query.

We continue by testing how we can modify the generated data set to get behavior like the original. We suspect that the size of the document affects speed and thus will add random string data so the amount of data in the XML parts stored in the database is equal to that in the original document. We also want to test if the number of XML elements and its structure affects the performance of queries when taking size into consideration. This will be achieved by specifying different recursive element structures with different depths and widths.

We define four different models of increasing complexity: *Skeleton* – the minimum structure that is needed for a certain query, *Random data* – the previous model with the addition of strings of random data to get the correct size of the data set, *Flat elements* – the skeleton model but with addition of elements with depth 1 to achieve the correct size and right amount of XML elements of the data set, *Recursive elements* – the skeleton model but with addition of elements with varying depth to recreate both data size and element structure of the data set.

4.1 Skeleton Model

Our first model is a rudimentary model that is enough to perform a certain query on the data set.

Definition 3. *A Skeleton data set S given a query Q and a data set D, is a dataset where* $Sel(Q, D)$ *is similar to* $Sel(Q, S)$*. This means the selectivity is similar for the query on the two data sets.*

For our tests we generate a minimal dataset that is a Skeleton model of Q. We illustrate how it works by using the previous mentioned XPath query for the UniProt data set. Thus we need to construct elements for the paths **/uniprot/entry/accession** and **/uniprot/entry/comment/subcellularLocation/location**. Since child elements can occur several times under one element we need to specify occurrence to get a structure similar to the original document. The ToXgene Template Specification Language allows you to set minimum and maximum occurrence of an element. Here we specify that the root element, `uniprot`, should occur once, the `entry` element exactly 1000 times and for `accession` we have specified a distribution to use.

```
<tox-document name="output/up">
      <element name="uniprot" minOccurs="1" maxOccurs="1">
          <complexType>
              ...
              <element name="entry" maxOccurs="1000" minOccurs="1000">
                  <complexType>
                      <element name="accession" tox-distribution="r1" maxOccurs="30">
                       ...
```

By examining a subset consisting of 1000 entries from the original data set we have found that `accession` occurs between one (the most common) and 23 times (for one entry) in an entry with a distribution that can best be approximated as a exponential distribution and with a mean of 1.458 times. We therefore define a distribution like this and refer to it in `accession`.

```
<tox-distribution name="r1" type="exponential" mean="1.45" minInclusive="1" maxInclusive="30"/>
```

Similar distributions are added for `comment`, `subcellularLocation` and `location`. We also need to specify how often the value *cytoplasm* should occur to achieve the right selectivity. The value "Cytoplasm" occurs 49 percent of the instances in the location node, "Secreted" 7 percent, and so on (the rest have been omitted from the listing).

```
<element name="location" tox-distribution="locdist" minOccurs="1" maxOccurs="3">
     <complexType>
         ...
         <tox-alternatives>
            <tox-option odds="49"><tox-expr value="'Cytoplasm'"/></tox-option>
            <tox-option odds="7"><tox-expr value="'Secreted'"/></tox-option>
            ...
        </tox-alternatives>
     </complexType>
</element>
```

We now get a number of `location` elements with the value "Cytoplasm" that is near the number in the original data set. The actual number will differ some due to the random process. We also get a number of `accession` elements for the query described earlier that is near the results for the original data set.

4.2 Random Data

Our second approach is based on the fact that earlier tests have suggested a link between data size and query times. Therefore we fill the document with elements containing random data until the size is the same as in the original data set.

Definition 4. *Path(Q, D) is the set of all sub-paths accessed while executing a query Q on the data set D.*

Definition 5. *A Random dataset R given a query Q and a data set D is a Skeleton dataset such that for all paths in Path(Q, D) the size of data stored in the path is similar in R and D.*

For our example data set and query this means that the `entry` elements are filled with random data. We insert new elements with given distribution whose only role is to create more content that is really never used. One of these payload elements are placed between the `accession` and the comment element, the second in `comment` and the third after `comment`. The resulting synthetic data set is now also similar in total size to that of the original, authentic, data set.

```
<element name="x_payload">
    <simpleType>
        <restriction base="string">
            <tox-string maxLength="36656" minLength="1100"
                  tox-distribution="entryfirstpayload"/>
        </restriction>
    </simpleType>
</element>
```

4.3 Flat Elements

The next step is to add an additional number of elements so we reach the number of elements present in the original data set.

Definition 6. *A Flat dataset F given a query Q and a data set D is a Random data set such that for all paths in Path(Q, D) the number of elements stored in the path is similar in F and D.*

Here we produce a constant number of elements in each `entry`. 77 elements between `accession` and `comment`, and 126 elements after `comment`.

```
<tox-distribution name="firstelemrepeat" minInclusive="126" maxInclusive="126" type="constant"/>
...
<element name="rec_payload_1" maxOccurs="77" tox-distribution="firstelemrepeat">
    <simpleType>
        <restriction base="string">
            <tox-string minLength="5" maxLength="10"/>
        </restriction>
    </simpleType>
</element>
```

4.4 Recursive Elements

By specifying a recursive element with constraints for number and distributions for recursion that reflects the original data set, and adding a small amount of data to each element we now have both a structure and size of the data set that is similar to the original data set.

Definition 7. *A Recursive data set R given a query Q and a data set D is a Flat dataset such that for all paths in $Path(Q, D)$ the path lengths of each sub-tree are similar in R and D.*

```
<element name="rec_payload_1" maxOccurs="77" tox-recursionLevels="reclev1">
    <complexType>
        <element name="name" minOccurs="1" maxOccurs="3">
            <simpleType>
                <restriction base="string">
                    <tox-string minLength="5" maxLength="20"/>
                </restriction>
            </simpleType>
        </element>
        <element name="rec_payload_1" maxOccurs="3"></element>
    </complexType>
</element>
```

5 Evaluation

The goal with the evaluation is to test if our synthetic data sets have a similar performance as the real data.

As a first step we have to verify that we get approximately the same number of answers as we get from the original data set for a given query. This is necessary for comparing response times with the original data set. Table 1 shows that we managed to achieve a number of values that are approximately the number in the original data set. The column for "Cytoplasm" shows the number of `location` elements with that value, the column for "accession" shows the number of `accession` values our example query will produce. Since ToXgene randomly select the number of elements and what value to insert, the number will vary somewhat between runs. The other models for synthetic data sets produce the same number of resulting rows as *skeleton*.

Table 1. Resulting rows for authentic and synthetic data

	Cytoplasm	accession
original	384	271
skeleton	392	237

To test performance for each of the synthetic models and for the original model we have measured the run time for the XPath query mentioned in section 2. For each of the mappings (1)–(5) we have repeated the query 20 times and the number given here is an average. These test have been performed using Microsoft SQL Server 2008 which has support for XML types and using HShreX for generating table definitions and transforming data. The tests have been performed on a system with AMD Athlon 64X2 Dual Core processor 5600+ with 2.90 GHz clock frequency and 4 GiB RAM running the 64-bit version of Windows Vista. No XML indexes have been created.

Table 2. Timings for original and synthetic data

	shredded (1)	location (2)	subcell... (3)	comment (4)	entry (5)
original	8.6 ms	21.1 ms	22.7 ms	96.1 ms	631.1 ms
skeleton	8.2 ms	21.9 ms	22.7 ms	77.3 ms	62.4 ms
random	8.6 ms	23.4 ms	30.4 ms	99.9 ms	112.3 ms
flat elements	8.6 ms	20.3 ms	25.8 ms	103.0 ms	609.2 ms
recursive elements	7.0 ms	24.2 ms	26.5 ms	98.1 ms	633.3 ms

In table 2 the timings for the query using the different mappings (1)–(5) in the original and the different synthetically constructed data sets are shown.

Our tests show that the query processing times for our skeleton model data set is substantially faster than that of the original data set which shows that we have not captured enough properties of the original data set to mimic it. For the random data model the query times for native XML storage increases somewhat but only with a factor less than 2 for `entry` compared to the skeleton model. By using the recursive element model we have achieved a run time for the example query when `entry` is mapped as XML that is within 1 percent of run time for the original data set with same mapping. For the shredded storage alternative the difference between the models is very low.

6 Discussion and Future Work

We have found that a synthetic model of an XML document needs to reflect not only the amount of data but also have structure reminding of that in the original document to get similar performance in a hybrid XML database.

In general it is possible to build the synthetic data with available tools. However, the selectivity of the data set, as exemplified in table 1, can be hard to model. If there are both global and local constraints, for example: 14 `location` elements with the value "cytoplasm" in the entire document but maximum 2 such elements under each `subcellularLocation`, there is a need to calculate how both these constraints boil down to the probability of the value being "cytoplasm". With even more constraints it gets even more complicated to keep track of and model. The difficulty with modeling constraints can be exemplified by the comment element in the *Flat elements* model. Here the number of comment sub-elements were over-shot by 30 percent when striving for getting local constraints right. Thus the resulting run time, as shown in table 2, for the query on mapping 4 in the model is higher than expected. As a solution, [18,19] discusses using global and local count constraints, DTD and XPath expressions to generate XML data. These techniques look promising for accurate and simple modeling of data sets.

Our tests have been performed on unindexed data. If the existing support for XML indexes is used the resulting performance will be different. Therefore it would be interesting to study if the performance similarity holds also when using

XML indexes and if so, use this knowledge to find mappings that are optimal when using XML indexes.

Our final goal is to automatically vary the structure of the data set and test the efficiency of different mappings for each structure variation. This could be achieved by building an environment that analyze existing data sets, then generate synthetic variants of these data sets, iterates over a number of possible parameters and for each of those variants evaluate and compare mappings by running queries over the different mappings.

7 Conclusion

In this paper we studied the problem of finding relevant XML data sets to experimentally study the properties of hybrid XML storage. We first discussed current benchmarks for relational databases, object databases and XML databases, and the special characteristics of XML structure and what demands it poses on benchmarks. We gave a short overview on benchmarks, micro benchmarks and data generators in the XML area. We then described how a data generator can be used to produce a synthetic data set based on an existing data set, by using four different approaches. One approach, *skeleton model*, only contains enough data to answer a certain query. In the next approach, *random data*, we add random string to different elements in the document to get the same size as in the original. The third approach, *flat elements*, is to create the same amount of elements in the document as in the original. The last approach, *recursive elements*, is to create the same amount of elements but with a overall structure that matches that in the original data set.

We compared the performance of an example query on the original data set with the performance on the different models we created. This comparison showed that it is possible to use a data generator, like ToXgene, to create a synthetic data set that behaves like a, rather complex, original data set.

Acknowledgements

We acknowledge the financial support from the Swedish Research Council and the Center for Industrial Information Technology.

References

1. Strömbäck, L., Åsberg, M., Hall, D.: HShreX - A Tool for Design and Evaluation of Hybrid XML Storage. In: Int. Work. on Database and Expert Systems Applications (DEXA), pp. 417–421 (2009)
2. Bitton, D., DeWitt, D.J., Turbyfil, C.: Benchmarking Database Systems: A Systematic Approach. In: Proc. of the 1983 Very Large Database Conf. VLDB (1983)
3. Anon, et al.: A Measure of Transaction Processing Power. In: Stonebraker, M. (ed.) Readings in Database Systems. Morgan Kaufmann, San Francisco (1988)

4. Carey, M.J., DeWitt, D.J., Jeffrey, F.N.: The OO7 Benchmark. In: Proc. of the 1993 ACM SIGMOD International Conference on Management of Data, pp. 12–21 (1993)
5. Böhme, T., Rahm, E.: XMach-1: A Benchmark for XML Data Management. In: Proc. of German database conference BTW 2001, Oldenburg. Springer, Berlin (2001)
6. Schmidt, A.R., Waas, F., Kersten, M.L., Florescu, D., Manolescu, I., Carey, M.J., Busse, R.: The XML Benchmark Project. Technical report, CWI, Amsterdam, The Netherlands (2001)
7. Nambiar, U., Lacroix, Z., Bressan, S., Li Lee, M., Li, Y.: XML Benchmarks Put to the Test. In: IIWAS (2001)
8. The UniProt Consortium The Universal Protein Resource (UniProt). Nucleic Acids Res. 36, D190–D195 (2008)
9. Hucka, M., Finney, A., Sauro, H.M., et al.: The Systems Biology Markup Language (SBML): A Medium for Representation and Exchange of Biochemical Network Models. Bioinformatics 19(4), 524–531 (2003)
10. DBLP XML Records, `http://acm.org/sigmoid/dblp/dp/index.html`
11. Haklay, M., Weber, P.: OpenStreetMap: User-generated Street Maps. IEEE Pervasive Computing 7(4), 12–18 (2008)
12. Legislative Documents in XML at the United States House of Representatives, `http://xml.house.gov/`
13. Nierman, A., Jagadish, H.V.: Evaluating Structural Similarity in XML Documents. In: Proc. of the 5th Int. Work. on the Web and Databases (2002)
14. Freire, J., Haritsa, J., Ramanath, M., Roy, P., Simeon, J.: StatiX: Making XML Count. In: Proc. of ACM SIGMOD Conference, pp. 181–191 (2002)
15. Flesca, S., Manco, G., Masciari, E., Pontieri, L., Pugliese, A.: Fast Detection of XML Structural Similarities. IEEE Trans. Know Data Eng. 7(2), 160–175 (2005)
16. Polyzotis, N., Garofalakis, M.N.: XCLUSTER Synopses for Structured XML Content. In: Proc. of the 22nd Int. Conf. on Data Engineering (2006)
17. Runapongsa, K., Patel, J.M., Jagadish, H.V., Chen, Y., Al-Khalifa, S.: The Michigan benchmark: Towards XML Query Performance Diagnostics. In: Proc. VLDB Conference, vol. 31 (2003)
18. Cohen, S.: Count-Constraints for Generating XML. In: Etzion, O., Kuflik, T., Motro, A. (eds.) NGITS 2006. LNCS, vol. 4032, pp. 153–164. Springer, Heidelberg (2006)
19. Cohen, S.: Generating XML Structure Using Examples and Constraints. In: Proc. of the VLDB Endowment, pp. 490–501 (2008)
20. Barbosa, D., Mendelzon, A., Keenleyside, J., Lyons, K.: ToXgene: A Template-based Data Generator for XML. In: Proc. of the 2002 ACM SIGMOD int. conf. on Management of data (2002)
21. Geng, K., Dobbie, G.: An XML Document Generator for Semantic Query Optimization Experimentation. Int. J. of Web Information Systems 3(1), 26–40 (2007)

Benchmarking Publish/Subscribe-Based Messaging Systems

Kai Sachs[1,*], Stefan Appel[1,*], Samuel Kounev[2], and Alejandro Buchmann[1]

[1] Databases and Distributed System Group, TU Darmstadt, Germany
lastname@dvs.tu-darmstadt.de
[2] Descartes Research Group, Karlsruhe Institute of Technology
skounev@acm.com

Abstract. Publish/subscribe-based messaging systems are used increasingly often as a communication mechanism in data-oriented web applications. Such applications often pose serious performance and scalability challenges. To address these challenges, it is important that systems are tested using benchmarks to evaluate their performance and scalability before they are put into production. In this paper, we present *jms2009-PS*, a new benchmark for publish/subscribe-based messaging systems built on top of the SPECjms2007 standard workload. We introduce the benchmark and discuss its configuration parameters showing how the workload can be customized to evaluate various aspects of publish/subscribe communication. Finally, we present a case study illustrating how the benchmark can be used for performance analysis of messaging servers.

1 Introduction

Publish/subscribe-based messaging systems are used increasingly often as a communication mechanism in data-oriented web applications such as Web 2.0 applications, social networks, online auctions and information dissemination applications to name just a few [1]. Moreover, the publish/subscribe paradigm is part of major technology domains including Enterprise Service Bus, Enterprise Application Integration, Service-Oriented Architecture and Event-Driven Architecture. With the growing adoption of these technologies and applications, the need for benchmarks and performance evaluation tools in the area of publish/subscribe systems increases. While general benchmarks for message-oriented middleware (MOM) exist, no benchmarks specifically targeted at publish/subscribe communication have been proposed. In this paper, we present a new benchmark for publish/subscribe-based messaging systems built on top of the SPECjms2007 standard workload.

SPECjms2007 is the current industry-standard benchmark for MOM servers based on the JMS (Java Message Service) standard interface [2]. It was developed by the Java subcommittee of the Standard Performance Evaluation Corporation (SPEC) with the participation of TU Darmstadt, IBM, Sun, BEA,

* Partly supported by the German Federal Ministry of Education and Research under grant 01IA08006 (ADiWa).

M. Yoshikawa et al. (Eds.): DASFAA 2010, LNCS 6193, pp. 203–214, 2010.

Sybase, Apache, Oracle and JBoss. One of the major benefits of SPECjms2007 is that, in addition to providing a standard workload and metrics for MOM performance, the benchmark provides a flexible and robust framework for in-depth performance evaluation of messaging infrastructures. It allows to create custom workload scenarios and interactions to stress selected aspects of the MOM infrastructure. Examples of such user-defined scenarios can be found in [3] and [4]. While SPECjms2007 includes some limited publish/subscribe communication as part of the workload, the focus of the benchmark is on point-to-point (PtP) communication via queues which dominate the overall system workload [5]. Moreover, the workload does not exercise message filtering through JMS selectors which is an important feature of publish/subscribe messaging that typically causes the most performance and scalability issues.

To address the need for a workload focused on publish/subscribe messaging, we developed the new *jms2009-PS* benchmark which uses the SPECjms2007 workload as basis. A preliminary version of the benchmark was demonstrated at the SIGMETRICS/Performance 2009 Demo Competition [6]. In this paper, we introduce the benchmark and discuss its configuration parameters showing how the workload can be customized to evaluate different aspects of publish/subscribe communication. Overall, jms2009-PS provides more than 80 new configuration parameters allowing the user to customize the workload in terms of the number of topics, the number of subscriptions, the number and type of selectors, and the message delivery modes. After discussing the configuration parameters, we present a case study, in which we demonstrate how to use jms2009-PS for evaluating alternative ways of implementing publish/subscribe communication in terms of their overhead, performance and scalability.

The rest of this paper is structured as follows: We start with some background on message-oriented middleware and the SPECjms2007 benchmark in Section 2. Following this, we present the jms2009-PS benchmark in Section 3. We introduce the various configuration parameters and show how the workload can be customized. Finally, in Section 4, we present our case study and wrap up with some concluding remarks in Section 5.

2 Background

2.1 Message-Oriented Middleware

Message-oriented middleware (MOM) is a specific class of middleware that supports loosely coupled communication among distributed software components by means of asynchronous message-passing as opposed to a request/response metaphor. The loose coupling of communicating parties has several important advantages: i) message producers and consumers do not need to know about each other, ii) they do not need to be active at the same time to exchange information, iii) they are not blocked when sending or receiving messages [7].

The Java Message Service (JMS) [2] is a standard Java-based interface for accessing the facilities of enterprise MOM servers. JMS supports two messaging

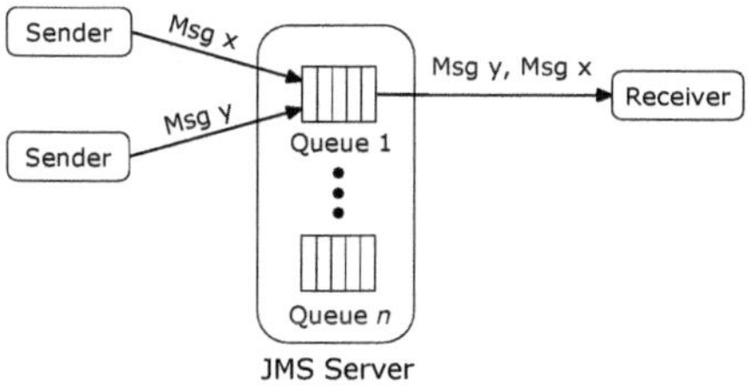

Fig. 1. Point-to-point messaging

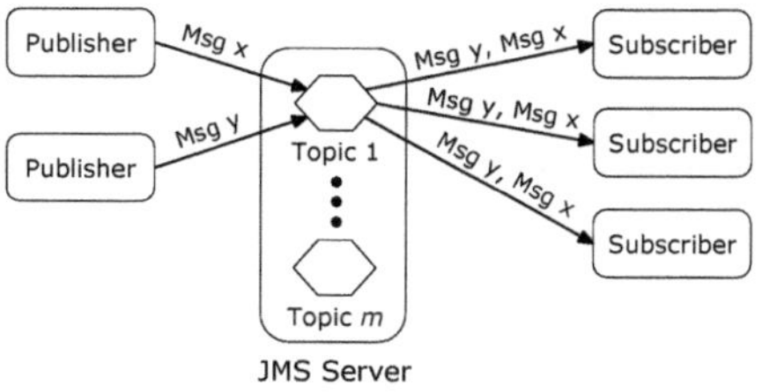

Fig. 2. Pub/sub messaging

models: *point-to-point (PtP)* and *publish/subscribe (pub/sub)*. With PtP messaging each message is sent to a specific *queue* and is retrieved and processed by a single consumer whereas with pub/sub messaging each message is sent to a specific *topic* and it may be delivered to multiple consumers interested in the topic. Consumers are required to register by subscribing to the topic before they can start receiving messages. In the pub/sub domain, message producers are referred to as *publishers* and message consumers as *subscribers*. JMS queues and topics are commonly referred to as *destinations*. The two messaging models are depicted in Figures 1 and 2.

The JMS specification defines several modes of message delivery with different quality-of-service attributes:

Non-Persistent/Persistent: In non-persistent mode, pending messages are kept in main memory buffers while they are waiting to be delivered and are not logged to stable storage. In persistent mode, the JMS provider takes extra care to ensure that no messages are lost in case of a server crash. This is achieved by logging messages to persistent storage such as a database or a file system.

Non-Durable/Durable: JMS supports two types of subscriptions, durable and non-durable. With non-durable subscriptions a subscriber will only receive messages that are published while he is active. In contrast to this, durable subscriptions ensure that a subscriber does not miss any messages during periods of inactivity.

Non-Transactional/Transactional: A JMS messaging session can be transactional or non-transactional. A transaction is a set of messaging operations that are executed as an atomic unit of work.

In addition to the above described delivery modes, JMS allows the specification of *selectors* to enable message filtering. When publishing messages, producers can specify property-value pairs (e.g., *"color=red"*) which are stored in the message headers. When subscribing, consumers can specify a selector to receive only messages with certain property values (e.g., *"color=blue AND size=42"*). Selectors are specified using a subset of the SQL92 conditional expression syntax. For a more detailed introduction to MOM and JMS the reader is referred to [8,2].

2.2 SPECjms2007

The SPECjms2007 benchmark models a supermarket supply chain where RFID technology is used to track the flow of goods. The participants involved are the headquarters (HQ) of the supermarket company, its stores (SM), its distribution centers (DC) and its suppliers (SP). SPECjms2007 defines seven interactions between the participants in the scenario:

1. Order/shipment handling between SM and DC
2. Order/shipment handling between DC and SP
3. Price updates sent from HQ to SMs
4. Inventory management inside SMs
5. Sales statistics sent from SMs to HQ
6. New product announcements sent from HQ to SMs
7. Credit card hot lists sent from HQ to SMs

Interactions 1 and 2 represent a chain of messages while the rest of the interactions include a single message exchange [4]. A single parameter called `BASE` determines the rate at which interactions are executed and is used as a scaling factor. The benchmark is implemented as a Java application comprising multiple JVMs and threads distributed across a set of *client nodes*. For every destination (queue or topic), there is a separate Java class called *Event Handler (EH)* that encapsulates the application logic executed to process messages sent to that destination. Event handlers register as listeners for the queue/topic and receive call backs from the messaging infrastructure as new messages arrive. In addition, for every physical location, a set of threads (referred to as *driver threads*) is launched to drive the benchmark interactions that are logically started at that location.

2.3 Related Work

Over the last decade several proprietary and open-source benchmarks for evaluating MOM platforms have been developed and used in the academia and industry including SonicMQ' Test Harness [9], IBM's Performance Harness for Java Message Service [10], Apache's ActiveMQ JMeter Performance Test [11] and JBoss' Messaging Performance Framework [12]. Using these and other similar benchmarks, numerous performance studies have been conducted and published, see for example [13,14,15,16,17,18,19,20]. While the benchmarks we mentioned have been employed extensively for performance testing and system analyses, unfortunately, they use artificial workloads that do not reflect any real-world application scenario. Furthermore, they typically concentrate on stressing individual MOM features in isolation and do not provide a comprehensive and representative workload for evaluating the overall MOM server performance. For a more detailed discussion of related work we refer the interested reader to [4,21].

Table 1. Configuration parameters supported for each message type

Intr.	Message	Location	T	P	D	Q	TD	ST	Description
1	order	DC	✓	✓	✓	✓	✓	-	Order sent from SM to DC.
	orderConf	SM	✓	✓	✓	✓	✓	-	Order confirmation sent from DC to SM.
	shipDep	DC	✓	✓	✓	✓	✓	-	Shipment registered by RFID readers upon leaving DC.
	statInfo-OrderDC	HQ	✓	✓	✓	✓	✓	-	Sales statistics sent from DC to HQ.
	shipInfo	SM	✓	✓	✓	✓	✓	-	Shipment from DC registered by RFID readers upon arrival at SM.
	shipConf	DC	✓	✓	✓	✓	✓	-	Shipment confirmation sent from SM to DC.
2	callForOffers	HQ	✓	✓	✓	-	✓	✓	Call for offers sent from DC to SPs (XML).
	offer	DC	✓	✓	✓	✓	✓	-	Offer sent from SP to DC (XML).
	pOrder	SP	✓	✓	✓	✓	✓	-	Order sent from DC to SP (XML).
	pOrderConf	DC	✓	✓	✓	✓	✓	-	Order confirmation sent from SP to DC (XML).
	invoice	HQ	✓	✓	✓	✓	✓	-	Order invoice sent from SP to HQ (XML).
	pShipInfo	DC	✓	✓	✓	✓	✓	-	Shipment from SP registered by RFID readers upon arrival at DC.
	pShipConf	SP	✓	✓	✓	✓	✓	-	Shipment confirmation sent from DC to SP (XML).
	statInfo-ShipDC	HQ	✓	✓	✓	✓	✓	-	Purchase statistics sent from DC to HQ.
3	priceUpdate	HQ	✓	✓	✓	-	✓	-	Price update sent from HQ to SMs.
4	inventoryInfo	SM	✓	✓	✓	✓	✓	-	Item movement registered by RFID readers in the warehouse of SM.
5	statInfoSM	HQ	✓	✓	✓	✓	✓	-	Sales statistics sent from SM to HQ.
6	product-Announcement	HQ	✓	✓	✓	-	✓	-	New product announcements sent from HQ to SMs.
7	creditCardHL	HQ	✓	✓	✓	-	✓	-	Credit card hotlist sent from HQ to SMs.

3 jms2009-PS – A Pub/Sub Benchmark

We now present the new *jms2009-PS* benchmark which is specifically targeted at pub/sub systems. We developed jms2009-PS using the SPECjms2007 [4] workload and its scaling strategy as a basis [22]. Overall, we added more than 80 new configuration parameters allowing the user to customize the workload to his needs. All configurations are identical in terms of the number of subscriptions and the message throughput generated for a given scaling factor, however, they differ in six important points:

1. number of topics and queues used
2. number of transactional vs. non-transactional messages
3. number of persistent vs. non-persistent messages
4. total traffic per topic and queue
5. complexity of used selectors (filter statements)
6. number of subscribers per topic

While the benchmark is targeted at pub/sub workloads, it allows to use queue-based PtP messaging in cases where messages are sent to a single consumer. This allows to compare the costs of queue-based vs. topic-based communication for different message delivery modes. In the case of topic-based communication, for each interaction several implementations are supported. In the first implementation, all types of messages are exchanged using one common topic per interaction. Each message consumer (e.g., orders department in DC1) subscribes to this topic using a selector specifying two filters that define the messages he is interested in: message type (e.g., orders) and location ID (e.g., DC 1). The message type and location ID are assigned as properties of each message published as part of the respective interaction. In the second implementation, a separate topic is used for each type of message (e.g., one topic for orders, one for invoices). Consequently, message consumers do not have to specify the message type at subscription time, but only their location ID. It is easy to see that the number of subscribers per topic is lower and the filtering is simpler (only one property to check) in the second implementation compared to the first one. In the first implementation, more traffic is generated per topic, while in the second implementation the traffic per topic is less but the system has to handle more topics in parallel. Therefore, the two implementations stress the system in different ways and allow to evaluate different performance aspects. In addition to these two implementations, the benchmark supports several further implementations which allow to stress additional aspects of topic-based communication. The user can select an implementation by means of the Target Destination (TD) parameter discussed in the next section.

3.1 Configuration Parameters

In this section, we describe in detail the new configuration parameters introduced in jms2009-PS. The parameters can be configured on a per message type basis. Table 1 shows the parameters supported for each message type. In the following, we briefly describe each parameter.

Transactional [*true*|*false*] (T). Specifies whether messages should be sent as part of a transaction.

Persistent [*true*|*false*] (P). Specifies whether messages should be sent in persistent mode.

Durable [*true*|*false*] (D). Specifies whether a durable subscription should be used by message consumers.

Queue [*true*|*false*] (Q). Specifies whether a queue or a topic should be used in cases where there is a single message consumer.

Target Destination (TD). Specifies for each message type the set of topics and respective selectors that should be used to distribute messages to the target consumers. The benchmark supports six different target destination options. Depending on the selected configuration, it automatically takes care of configuring message properties (set by producers) and selectors (set by consumers at subscription time) to guarantee that messages are delivered to the correct consumers. The

Table 2. Target destination options

Setting	Description	Selector
LocationID-MessageType	A separate topic for each combination of location instance and message type is used, e.g., a topic per DC for order messages: `DC1_OrderT` for DC 1, `DC2_OrderT` for DC 2, etc.	– No selectors are needed.
MessageType	A single topic per message type is used, e.g., a topic `DC_OrderT` for order messages of all DCs.	– TargetLocationID= '*locationID*'
Interaction	A single topic per interaction is used, e.g., a topic `Interaction1_T` for all messages involved in Interaction 1.	– TargetLocationID= '*locationID*' – MessageType= '*messageType*'
LocationType	A single topic per location type is used, e.g., a topic `SM_T` for all messages sent to SMs.	– *TargetLocationID*= '*locationID*' – MessageType= '*messageType*'
LocationID	A separate topic for each location instance is used, e.g., a topic `SM1_T` for all messages sent to SM 1.	– MessageType= '*messageType*'
Central	One central topic for all messages is used, e.g., one topic `T` for all messages that are part of the seven interactions.	– LocationType= '*locationType*' – TargetLocationID= '*locationID*' – MessageType= '*messageType*'

target destination options supported by jms2009-PS are shown in Table 2. For each option, the set of topics and the required selectors are described.

Subscription Type [*IN*|*OR*|*SET*] (ST). In Interaction 2, a distribution center (DC) sends a `CallForOffers` to suppliers (SP). Each SP offers a subset of all product families and is only interested in the `CallForOffers` messages targeted at the respective product families. There are multiple ways to implement this communication pattern and jms2009-PS supports the following options:

- **Use a separate topic for each product family**: The SP has to subscribe to all topics corresponding to the product families he is interested in and no selector is needed.
- **Use one topic for all product families**: The SP has to subscribe to this topic using a selector to specify the product families he is interested in. jms2009-PS offers three ways to define the respective subscription:
  - **Using multiple OR operators**: The SP places a single subscription using the following selector: *ProductFamily*="PF1" `OR` *ProductFamily*="PF2" `OR` ... `OR` *ProductFamily*="PF*n*"
  - **Using a single IN operator**: The SP places a single subscription using the following selector: *ProductFamily* `IN` ("PF1","PF2",...,"PF*n*")
  - **Using a set of subscriptions**: The SP subscribes for each product family he is interested in separately:
    ProductFamily="PF1" [· · ·] *ProductFamily*="PF*n*"

4 Case Study

4.1 Introduction

We now present a case study illustrating how jms2009-PS can be used for performance analysis of messaging servers. The environment in which we conducted our case study is depicted in Figure 3. ActiveMQ server was used as a JMS server installed on a machine with two quad-core CPUs and 16 GB of main memory. The server was run in a 64-bit JRockit 1.6 JVM with 8 GB of heap space. A RAID 0 disk array comprised of four disk drives was used for maximum performance. ActiveMQ was configured to use a file-based store for persistent messages with a 3.8 GB message buffer. The jms2009-PS drivers were distributed across three machines. To further increase the network capacity, a separate GBit link was installed between the JMS server and the third driver machine. The latter was configured to always use this link when accessing the server. The drivers were distributed across the machines in such a way that the network traffic was load-balanced between the two networks.

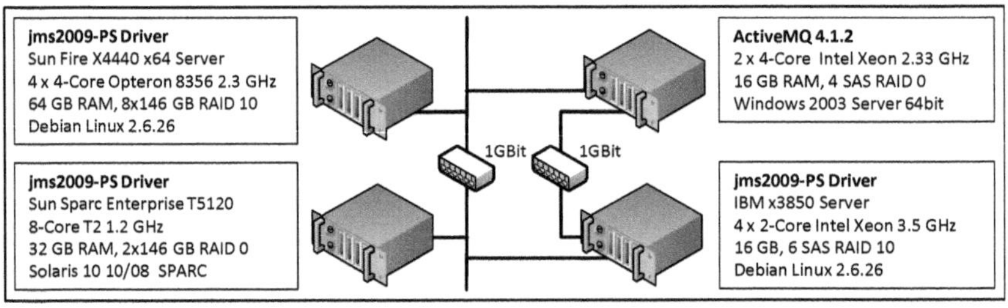

Fig. 3. Experimental Environment

4.2 Test Scenarios

We studied three different scenarios which were identical in terms of the total number of messages sent and received for a given scaling factor (`BASE`). Transactions and persistent message delivery were configured as defined in the SPECjms2007 workload description [4]. The scenarios differ in the number of message destinations and destination types used for communication. Figure 4 illustrates the configurations used in the three scenarios for two of the message types: `order` messages sent from SMs to DCs and `orderConf` messages sent from DCs to SMs (cf. Table 1).

- **Scenario I (SPECjms2007-like Workload):** The workload is configured similar to the SPECjms2007 workload, i.e., it uses mainly queues for communication. Each location instance has its own queue for each message type and therefore there is no need for selectors.
- **Scenario II (Pub/Sub with Multiple Topics):** For each message type, a separate topic is used, i.e., the TD configuration parameter is set to `MessageType` (cf. Table 2).

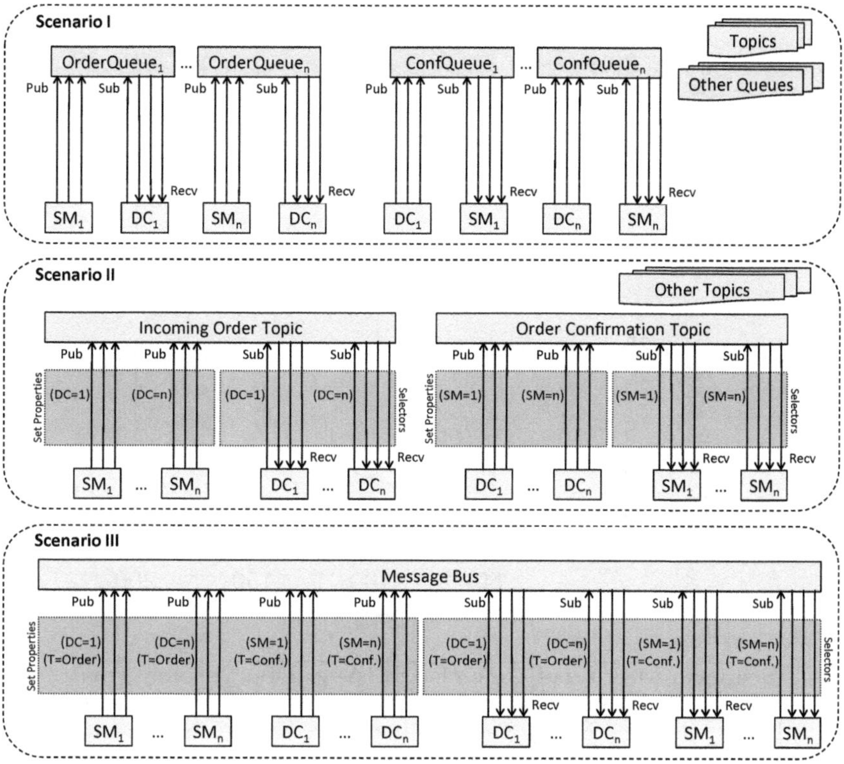

Fig. 4. Considered Scenarios

– **Scenario III (Pub/Sub with Message Bus):** One topic is used for all messages, i.e., the TD configuration parameter is set to `Central` (cf. Table 2).

The three scenarios differ mainly in terms of the flexibility they provide. While Scenario I is easy to implement given that no properties or selectors are necessary, it requires a reconfiguration of the MOM server for each new location or message type since new queues have to be set up. In contrast, Scenarios II and III, which only use topics, provide more flexibility. In Scenario II, a reconfiguration of the MOM server is necessary only when introducing new message types. Scenario III doesn't require reconfiguration at all since a single topic (message bus) is used for communication. In addition, Scenarios II and III support one-to-many communication while the queue-based interactions in Scenario I are limited to one-to-one communication. One-to-many communication based on pub/sub allows to easily add additional message consumers, e.g., to maintain statistics about orders. On the other hand, the use of a limited number of topics in Scenarios II and III degrades the system scalability. As shown in the next section, the jms2009-PS benchmark allows to evaluate the trade-offs that different configurations provide in terms of flexibility, performance and scalability.

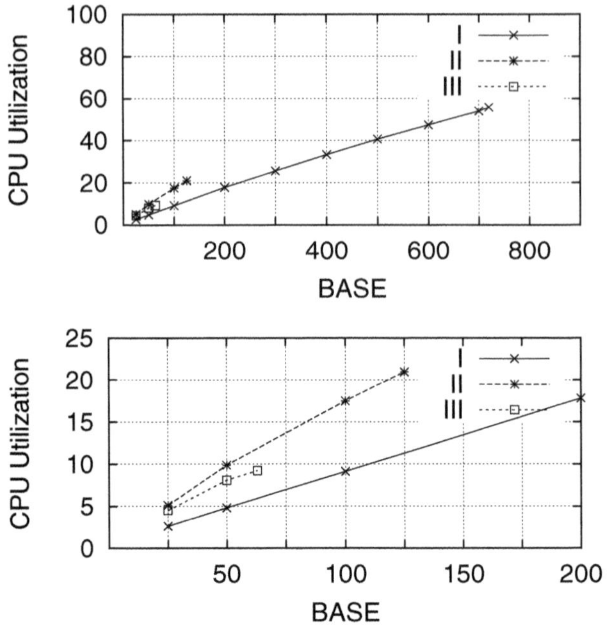

Scenario	Max Load	CPU/BASE	Avg. Dlv. Latency (ms)
I	720	0.077	123
II	125	0.168	1587
III	63	0.147	3235

Fig. 5. Experimental Results

4.3 Experimental Results

Figure 5 presents the experimental results for the three scenarios described above. It shows the CPU utilization for increasing workload intensities (`BASE`), the maximum load that can be sustained by each scenario, the CPU time per unit of the BASE parameter and the average message delivery latency. The results show the scalability and performance of the three configurations as well as their costs in terms of CPU consumption. Scenario I scales up to BASE 720 and exhibits the lowest message delivery latency ($123ms$). The flexibility provided by Scenario II and III comes at the cost of much worse scalability and performance. The maximum load that can be sustained in Scenario II and Scenario III is respectively 6 and 12 times lower than that in Scenario I. Similarly, the average message delivery latency is about 13 times higher for Scenario II compared to Scenario I and about 26 times higher for Scenario III. Thus, the flexibility provided by Scenario II and III comes at a high price. This is due to two reasons: i) the use of selectors leads to roughly two times higher CPU processing time per message as shown in Figure 5, ii) the use of topics for communication leads to synchronization delays. Comparing Scenarios II and III reveals that the selector complexity in this case does not have a significant impact on the CPU processing time per message. What is much more significant is the number of topics used for communication. The single topic in Scenario III clearly leads to a scalability bottleneck and explosion of the message delivery latency. In the third scenario, the throughput was limited by the performance of a single CPU core.

Overall, the results show that topic-based communication using selectors is much more expensive than queue-based communication and, depending on the number of topics used, it limits the scalability of the system. We demonstrated how, by using jms2009-PS, the performance and scalability of different messaging workloads and configuration scenarios can be quantified. The high configurability of the benchmark allows to tailor the workload to the user's requirements by customizing it to resemble a given application scenario. The user can then evaluate alternative ways to implement message communication in terms of their overhead, performance and scalability.

5 Conclusions

We presented a new benchmark for publish/subscribe-based messaging systems built on top of the SPECjms2007 standard workload. We discussed its configuration parameters showing how the workload can be customized to evaluate different aspects of publish/subscribe communication. Overall, jms2009-PS provides more than 80 new configuration parameters allowing the user to customize the workload in terms of the number of topics, the number of subscriptions, the number and type of selectors, and the message delivery modes.

We presented a case study demonstrating how using jms2009-PS, alternative ways to implement publish/subscribe communication in an example application scenario can be evaluated in terms of their overhead, performance and scalability. We defined three different scenarios with different communication patterns. The case study showed that the flexibility provided by topic-based publish-subscribe communication comes at a high price. The use of selectors in our scenario led to roughly two times higher CPU processing time per message. The most critical factor affecting the system performance however was the number of topics used for communication. Having a low number of topics provides maximum flexibility, however, it introduces a scalability bottleneck due to the synchronization delays. Especially, the scenario in which a single topic was used to implement a message bus clearly identifies the limitations of such an approach.

Overall, with jms2009-PS we provide a powerful benchmarking tool. Through its configurability it allows the user to evaluate publish/subscribe platforms for certain communication patterns using a complex real-world workload. Our next steps will be to extend the benchmark workload with new interactions and to prepare a complex case study analysing and comparing different scenarios on alternative platforms.

References

1. Hinze, A., Sachs, K., Buchmann, A.: Event-Based Applications and Enabling Technologies. In: Proceedings of the International Conference on Distributed Event-Based Systems, DEBS 2009 (2009)

2. Sun Microsystems, Inc.: Java Message Service (JMS) Specification - Ver. 1.1 (2002)
3. Happe, J., Friedrich, H., Becker, S., Reussner, R.H.: A pattern-based Performance Completion for Message-oriented Middleware. In: Proc. of the ACM WOSP (2008)
4. Sachs, K., Kounev, S., Bacon, J., Buchmann, A.: Performance evaluation of message-oriented middleware using the SPECjms2007 benchmark. Performance Evaluation 66(8), 410–434 (2009)
5. Sachs, K., Kounev, S., Buchmann, A.: Performance Modeling of Message-Oriented Middleware - A Case Study (2009) (in review)
6. Sachs, K., Kounev, S., Appel, S., Buchmann, A.: A Performance Test Harness For Publish/Subscribe Middleware. In: SIGMETRICS/Performance 2009 Demo Competition, June 2009. ACM, New York (2009)
7. Eugster, P.T., Felber, P.A., Guerraoui, R., Kermarrec, A.M.: The Many Faces of Publish/Subscribe. ACM Computing Surveys 35(2), 114–131 (2003)
8. Hohpe, G., Woolf, B.: Enterprise Integration Patterns: Designing, Building, and Deploying Messaging Solutions. Addison-Wesley, Reading (2003)
9. Sonic Software Corporation: Sonic Test Harness (2005), `http://communities.progress.com/pcom/docs/DOC-29828`
10. IBM Hursley: Performance Harness for Java Message Service (2005), `http://www.alphaworks.ibm.com/tech/perfharness`
11. ActiveMQ: JMeter performance test (2006), `http://incubator.apache.org/activemq/jmeter-performance-tests.html`
12. JBoss: JBoss JMS New Performance Benchmark (2006), `http://wiki.jboss.org/wiki/Wiki.jsp?page=JBossJMSNewPerformanceBenchmark`
13. Crimson Consulting Group: High-Performance JMS Messaging - A Benchmark Comparison of Sun Java System Message Queue and IBM WebSphere MQ (2003), `http://www.sun.com/software/products/message_queue/wp_JMSperformance.pdf`
14. Krissoft Solutions: JMS Performance Comparison (2006), `http://www.fiorano.com/comp-analysis/jms_perf_report.htm`
15. Sonic Software Corporation: Benchmarking E-Business Messaging Providers. White Paper (January 2004)
16. Carter, M.: JMS Performance with WebSphere MQ for Windows V6.0 (2005), `http://www-1.ibm.com/support/docview.wss?rs=171&uid=swg24010028`
17. Fiorano Software Inc.: JMS Performance Comparison - Performance Comparison for Publish Subscribe Messaging (2010), `http://www.fiorano.com/whitepapers/fmq/jms_performance_comparison.php`
18. Rindos, A., Loeb, M., Woolet, S.: A performance comparison of IBM MQseries 5.2 and Microsoft Message Queue 2.0 on Windows 2000. IBM SWG Competitive Technical Assessment, Research Triangle Park, NC (2001)
19. Maheshwari, P., Pang, M.: Benchmarking message-oriented middleware: TIB/RV versus SonicMQ. Concurrency Computat.: Pract. and Exper. 17(12) (2005)
20. Menth, M., Henjes, R., Zepfel, C., Gehrsitz, S.: Throughput performance of popular JMS servers. SIGMETRICS Perform. Eval. Rev. 34(1), 367–368 (2006)
21. Kounev, S., Sachs, K.: Benchmarking and Performance Modeling of Event-Based Systems. IT - Information Technology 51(5), 262–269 (2009)
22. Sachs, K., Kounev, S., Appel, S., Buchmann, A.: Benchmarking of Message-Oriented Middleware. In: Proc. of the DEBS 2009 (2009)

An Experimental Evaluation of Relational RDF Storage and Querying Techniques

Hooran MahmoudiNasab[1] and Sherif Sakr[2]

[1] Macquarie University, Sydney, Australia
Hooran@ics.mq.edu.au
[2] University of New South Wales, Sydney, Australia
ssakr@cse.unsw.edu.au

Abstract. The Resource Description Framework (RDF) is a flexible model for representing information about resources in the web. With the increasing amount of RDF data which is becoming available, efficient and scalable management of RDF data has become a fundamental challenge to achieve the Semantic Web vision. The RDF model has attracted a lot of attention of the database community and many researchers have proposed different solutions to store and query RDF data efficiently. In this paper, we focus on evaluating the state-of-the-art of the approaches which are relying on the relational infrastructure to provide scalable engines to store and query RDF data. Our experimental evaluation is done on top of recently introduced SP^{2}Bench performance benchmark for RDF query engines. The results of our experiments shows that there is still room for optimization in the proposed generic relational RDF storage schemes and thus new techniques for storing and querying RDF data are still required to bring forward the Semantic Web vision.

1 Introduction

The Resource Description Framework (RDF) is a W3C recommendation that has rapidly gained popularity as a mean of expressing and exchanging semantic metadata, i.e., data that specifies semantic information about data. RDF was originally designed for the representation and processing of metadata about remote information sources and defines a model for describing relationships among resources in terms of uniquely identified attributes and values. The basic building block in RDF is a simple tuple model, (subject, predicate, object), to express different types of knowledge in the form of fact statements. The interpretation of each statement is that subject S has property P with value O, where S and P are resource URIs and O is either a URI or a literal value. Thus, any object from one triple can play the role of a subject in another triple which amounts to chaining two labeled edges in a graph-based structure. Thus, RDF allows a form of reification in which any RDF statement itself can be the subject or object of a triple. One of the clear advantage of the RDF data model is its schema-free structure in comparison to the entity-relationship model where the entities, their attributes and relationships to other entities are strictly defined. In RDF,

M. Yoshikawa et al. (Eds.): DASFAA 2010, LNCS 6193, pp. 215–226, 2010.

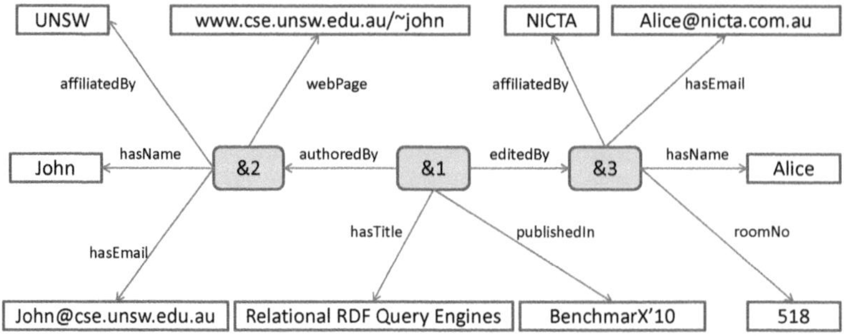

Fig. 1. Sample RDF Graph

```
SELECT  ?Z
WHERE   {?X hasTitle "Relational RDF Query Engines".
         ?X publishedIn "BenchmarX'10".
         ?X authoredBy ?Y.
         ?Y  webPage ?Z.}
```

Fig. 2. Sample SPARQL query

the schema may evolve over the time which fits well with the modern notion of data management, dataspaces, and its *pay-as-you-go* philosophy [11]. Figure 1 illustrates a sample RDF graph.

The SPARQL query language is the official W3C standard for querying and extracting information from RDF graphs [14]. It represents the counterpart to *select-project-join* queries in the relational model. It is based on a powerful graph matching facility which allows binding variables to components in the input RDF graph and supports conjunctions and disjunctions of triple patterns. In addition, operators akin to relational joins, unions, left outer joins, selections, and projections can be combined to build more expressive queries. Figure 2 depicts a sample SPARQL query over the sample RDF graph of Figure 1 to *retrieve the web page information of the author of the paper published in BenchmarX'10 with the title "Relational RDF Query Engines"*.

Efficient and scalable management of RDF data is a fundamental challenge at the core of the Semantic Web. Relational database management systems (RDBMSs) have repeatedly shown that they are very efficient, scalable and successful in hosting types of data which have formerly not been anticipated to be stored inside relational databases such as complex objects [18], spatio-temporal data [3] and XML data [8]. In addition, RDBMSs have shown their ability to handle vast amounts of data very efficiently using powerful indexing mechanisms. Several research efforts have been proposed to provide efficient and scalable RDF querying engines by relying on the relational infrastructure [2,9,10,19]. These relational RDF query engines can be mainly classified to the following categories:

Subject	Predicate	Object
Id1	publishedIn	BenchmarX'10
Id1	hasTitle	Relational RDF Query Engines
Id1	authoredBy	Id2
Id2	hasName	John
Id2	affiliatedBy	UNSW
Id2	hasEmail	John@cse.unsw.edu.au
Id2	webPage	www.cse.unsw.edu.au/~john
Id1	editedBy	Id3
Id3	hasName	Alice
Id3	affiliatedBy	NICTA
Id3	hasEmail	Alice@nicta.com.au
Id3	roomNo	518

```
Select T3.Object
From Triples as T1, Triples as T2,
     Triples as T3, Triples as T4
Where T1.Predicate="publishedIn"
and T1.Object="Book Chapter"
and T2.predicate="hasTitle"
and T2.Object="Relational RDF Query Engines"
and T3.Predicate="webPage"
and T1.subject=T2.subject
and T4.subject=T1.subject
and T4.Predicate="authoredBy"
and T4.Object = T3.Subject
```

Fig. 3. Relational Representation of Triple RDF Stores

- **Vertical (triple) table stores:** where each RDF triple is stored directly in a three-column table (subject, predicate, object).
- **Property (n-ary) table stores:** where multiple RDF properties are modeled as n-ary table columns for the same subject.
- **Horizontal (binary) table stores:** where RDF triples are modeled as one horizontal table or into a set of vertically partitioned binary tables (one table for each RDF property).

Figures 3,4 and 5 illustrate examples of the three alternative relational representations of the sample RDF graph (Figure 1) and their associated SQL queries for evaluating the sample SPARQL query (Figure 2).

Experimental evaluation and comparison of different techniques and algorithms which deals with the same problem is a crucial aspect especially in applied domains of computer science. Previous studies of RDF query engines [15,16] have been presented in the literature. However, they were different in their focus. For example, [15] compares between the native RDF engines (with no database backend) while [16] compares the performances of triple stores and binary tables in the context of a column-oriented RDBMS, *MonetDB*. This paper takes a different focus by providing an extensive experimental study for evaluating the state-of-the-art of the *relational*-based RDF query engines in the context of traditional and most frequently used row-oriented RDBMS (e.g: PostgreSQL, Oracle, SQL Server, ...,etc). The remainder of this paper is organized as follows. Section 2 gives a brief overview over the state-of-the-art of the relational RDF query engines. Section 3 gives on overview of the SP^{2}Bench performance benchmark which we used to perform our experiments. Detailed description of the experimental framework and the experimental results are presented in Section 4. Section 5 concludes the chapter and suggests for possible future research directions on the subject.

Publication

ID	publishedIn	hasTitle	authoredBy	editedBy
Id1	BenchmarX'10	Relational RDF Query Engines	Id2	id3

Person

ID	hasName	affiliatedBy	hasEmail	webPage	roomNo
Id2	John	UNSW	John@cse.unsw.edu.au	www.cse.unsw.edu.au/~john	
Id3	Alice	NICTA	Alice@nicta.com.au		518

```
Select Person.webPage
From Person, Publication
Where Publication.publishedIn = "BenchmarX'10"
and Publication.hasTitle = "Relational RDF Query Engines"
and Publication.authoredBy = Person.ID
```

Fig. 4. Relational Representation of Property Tables RDF Stores

publishedIn

Id1	BenchmarX'10

hasTitle

Id1	Relational RDF Query Engines

hasName

Id2	John
Id3	Alice

affiliatedBy

Id2	UNSW
Id3	NICTA

hasEmail

Id2	John@cse.unsw.edu.au
Id3	Alice@nicta.com.au

roomNo

Id3	518

webPage

Id2	www.cse.unsw.edu.au/~john

authoredBy

Id1	Id2

editedBy

Id1	Id3

```
Select webPage.value
From PublishedIn, hasTitle,
        authoredBy, webPage
Where publishedIn.value = "BenchmarX'10"
and hasTitle.value = "Relational RDF Query Engines"
and publicationType.ID = hasTitle.ID
and publicationType.ID = authoredBy.ID
and authoredBy.value = webPage.ID
```

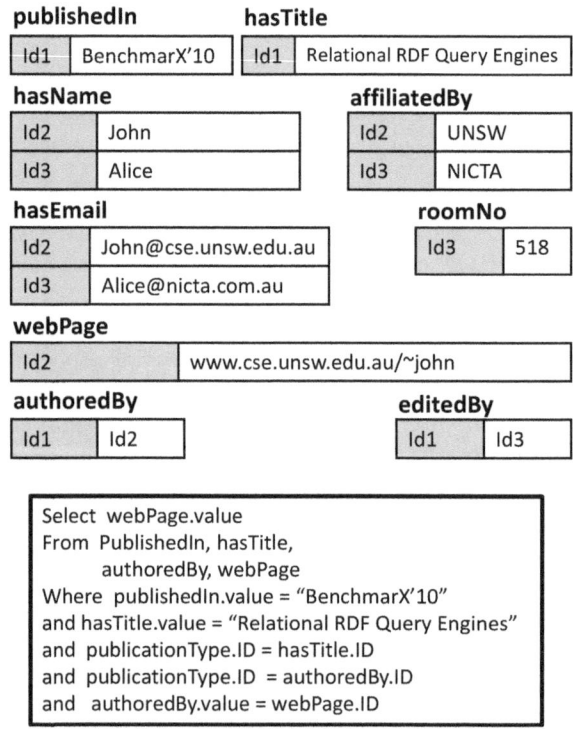

Fig. 5. Relational Representation of Binary Tables RDF Stores

2 Relational RDF Query Engines: State-of-the-Art

2.1 Vertical (Triple) Stores

Harris and Gibbins [9] have described the 3store RDF storage system which is based on a central triple table that holds the hashes for the subject, predicate, object and the RDF graph identifier. A symbols table is used to allow reverse lookups from the hash to the hashed value and to allow SQL operations to be performed on pre-computed values in the data types of the columns without the use of casts. To produce the intermediate results table, the hashes of any SPARQL variables required to be returned in the results set are projected and the hashes from the intermediate results table are joined to the symbols table to provide the textual representation of the results.

Neumann and Weikum [13] have presented the RDF-3X (RDF Triple eXpress) query engine which tries to overcome the criticism that triples stores incurs too many expensive self-joins by creating the exhaustive set of indexes and relying on fast processing of merge joins . The physical design of RDF-3x is workload-independent and eliminates the need for physical-design tuning by building indexes over all 6 permutations of the three dimensions that constitute an RDF triple. Additionally, indexes over count-aggregated variants for all three two-dimensional and all three one-dimensional projections are created. The query processor follows RISC-style design philosophy [4] by using the full set of indexes on the triple tables to rely mostly on merge joins over sorted index lists. The query optimizer relies upon its cost model in finding the lowest-cost execution plan and mostly focuses on join order and the generation of execution plans.

Weiss et al. [19] have presented the Hexastore RDF storage scheme with main focuses on scalability and generality in its data storage, processing and representation. Hexastore does not discriminate against any RDF element and treats subjects, properties and objects equally. Each RDF element type have its special index structures built around it and every possible ordering of the importance or precedence of the three elements in an indexing scheme is materialized. Each index structure in a Hexastore centers around one RDF element and defines a prioritization between the other two elements. Two vectors are associated with each RDF element (e.g. subject), one for each of the other two RDF elements (e.g. property and object). In addition, lists of the third RDF element are appended to the elements in these vectors. In total, six distinct indices are used for indexing the RDF data. A clear disadvantage of this approach is that Hexastore features a worst-case five-fold storage increase in comparison to a conventional triples table.

2.2 Property Table Stores

Jena is a an open-source toolkit for Semantic Web programmers [20]. It uses a denormalized schema in which resource URIs and simple literal values are stored directly in the statement table. In order to distinguish database references from literals and URIs, column values are encoded with a prefix that indicates the type of the value. A separate literals table is only used to store literal values whose length exceeds a threshold, such as blobs. Similarly, a separate resources table is used to store long URIs. By storing values directly in the statement table it is possible to perform many queries without a join. However, a denormalized schema uses more database space because the same value (literal or URI) is stored repeatedly. Jena permit multiple graphs to be stored in a single database instanceand supports the use of multiple statement tables in a single database so that applications can flexibly map graphs to different tables. In this way, graphs that are often accessed together may be stored together while graphs that are never accessed together may be stored separately.

Chong et al. [5] have introduced an Oracle-based property table approach which translates the RDF query to a self-join query on Triple-based RDF table store. The resulting query is executed efficiently by making use of B-tree indexes as well as creating materialized join views for specialized subject-property. Subject-Property Matrix materialized join views are used to minimize the query processing overheads that are inherent in the canonical triples-based representation of RDF. The materialized join views are incrementally maintained based on user demand and query workloads. A special module is provided to analyze the table of RDF triples and estimate the size of various materialized views, based on which a user can define a subset of materialized views. For a group of subjects, the system defines a set of single-valued properties that occur together.

Levandoski and Mokbel [12] have presented another property table approach for storing RDF data without any assumption about the query workload statistics. The approach provides a *tailored* schema for each RDF data set based on two main parameters: 1) *Support threshold* which represents a value to measure the strength of correlation between properties in the RDF data. 2) The *null threshold* which represents the percentage of null storage tolerated for each table in the schema. The approach involves two phases: *clustering* and *partitioning*. The clustering phase scans the RDF data to automatically discover groups of related properties. Based on the support threshold, each set of n properties which are grouped together in the same cluster are good candidates to constitute a single n-ary table and the properties which are not grouped in any cluster are good candidates for storage in binary tables. The partitioning phase goes over the formed clusters and balances the tradeoff between storing as many RDF properties in clusters as possible while keeping null storage to a minimum based on the null threshold.

2.3 Horizontal Stores

Abadi et al. [2] have presented *SW-Store* a new DBMS which is storing RDF data using a fully decomposed storage model (DSM) [6]. In this approach, the triples table is rewritten into n two-column tables where n is the number of unique properties in the data. In each of these tables, the first column contains the subjects that define that property and the second column contains the object values for those subjects while the subjects that do not define a particular

Table 1. SP^2Bench Benchmark Queries

Q1	Return the year of publication of "Journal 1 (1940)".
Q2	Extract all inproceedings with properties: *creator, booktitle, issued, partOf, seeAlso, title, pages, homepage,* and optionally *abstract*, including their values.
Q3abc	Select all articles with property **(a)** pages **(b)** month **(c)** isbn.
Q4	Select all distinct pairs of article author names for authors that have published in the same journal.
Q5	Return the names of all persons that occur as author of at least one inproceeding and at least one article.
Q6	Return, for each year, the set of all publications authored by persons that have not published in years before.
Q7	Return the titles of all papers that have been cited at least once, but not by any paper that has not been cited itself.
Q8	Compute authors that have published with Paul Erdos or with an author that has published with Paul Erdös.
Q9	Return incoming and outgoing properties of persons.
Q10	Return publications and venues in which "Paul Erdös" is involved either as author or as editor.
Q11	Return top 10 electronic edition URLs starting from the 51th publication, in lexicographical order.
Q12abc	**(a)** Return yes if a person is an author of at least one inproceeding and article. **(b)** Return yes if an author has published with "Paul Erdös" or with an author that has published with "Paul Erdös". **(c)** Return yes if person "John Q. Public" exists.

property are simply omitted from the table for that property. Each table is sorted by subject, so that particular subjects can be located quickly, and that fast merge joins can be used to reconstruct information about multiple properties for subsets of subjects. For a multi-valued attribute, each distinct value is listed in a successive row in the table for that property. The implementation of SW-Store relies on a column-oriented DBMS, C-store [17], to store tables as collections of columns rather than as collections of rows.

3 SP^2Bench Performance Benchmark

In [15] Schmidt et al. have presented the **SP**ARQL **P**erformance **Bench**mark (SP^2Bench) which is based on the DBLP scenario [1]. The DBLP database presents an extensive bibliographic information about the field of Computer Science and, particularly, databases. The benchmark is accompanied with a data generator which supports the creation of arbitrarily large DBLP-like models in RDF format. This data generator mirrors the vital key characteristics and distributions of the original DBLP dataset. The logical RDF schema for the DBLP dataset consists of *Authors* and *Editors* entities which are representation types of *Persons*. A superclass *Document* which is decomposed into several sub-classes: *Proceedings, Inproceedings, Journal, Article, Book, PhDThesis, MasterThesis, Incollection, WWW resources.* The RDF graph representation of these entities reflects their instantiation and the different types of relationship between them.

In addition, the benchmark provides 17 queries defined using the SPARQL query language on top of the structure of the DBLP dataset in a way to cover the most important SPARQL constructs and operator constellations. The defined queries vary in their complexity and result size. Table 1 lists the SP^2Bench

Benchmark Queries. For more details about the benchmark specification, data generation algorithm and SPARQL definition of the benchmark queries, we refer the reader to [15].

4 Experimental Evaluation

4.1 Settings

Our experimental evaluation of the alternative relational RDF storage techniques are conducted using the IBM DB2 DBMS running on a PC with 3.2 GHZ Intel Xeon processors, 4 GB of main memory storage and 250 GB of SCSI secondary storage. We used the SP^2Bench data generator to produce four different testing datasets with number of triples equal to: 500K, 1M, 2M and 4M Triples. In our evaluation, we consider the following four alternative relational storage schemes:

1. **Triple Stores (TS):** where a single relational table is used to store the whole set of RDF triples (subject, predicate, object). We follow the RDF-3X and build indexes over all 6 permutations of the three fields of each RDF triple.
2. **Binary Table Stores (BS):** for each unique predicate in the RDF data, we create a binary table (ID, Value) and two indexes over the permutations of the two fields are built.
3. **Traditional Relational Stores (RS):** In this scheme, we use the Entity Relationship Model of the DBLP dataset and follow the traditional way of designing normalized relational schema where we build a separate table for each entity (with its associated descriptive attributes) and use foreign keys to represent the relationships between the different objects. We build specific partitioned B-tree indexes [7] for each table based on the referenced attributes in the benchmark queries.
4. **Property Table Stores (PS):** where we use the schema of *RS* and decompose each entity with number of attributes ≥ 4 into two subject-property tables. The decomposition is done blindly and based on the order of the attributes without considering the benchmark queries (workload independent).

4.2 Performance Metrics

We measure and compare the performance of the alternative relational RDF storage techniques using the following metrics:

- **Loading Time:** represents the period of time for shredding the RDF dataset into the relational tables of the storage scheme.
- **Storage Cost:** depicts the size of the storage disk space which is consumed by the relational storage schemes for storing the RDF dataset.
- **Query Performance:** represents the execution times for the different SQL-translation of the SPARQL queries of SP^2Bench over the alternative relational storage schemes.

Table 2. A comparison between the alternative relational RDF storage techniques in terms of their loading times

	Loading Time (in Seconds)			
Dataset	Triple Stores	Binary Tables	Traditional Relational	Property Tables
500K	282	306	212	252
1M	577	586	402	521
2M	1242	1393	931	1176
4M	2881	2936	1845	2406

Table 3. A comparison between the alternative relational RDF storage techniques in terms of their storage cost

	Storage Cost (in KB)			
Dataset	Triple Stores	Binary Tables	Traditional Relational	Property Tables
500K	24721	32120	8175	10225
1M	48142	64214	17820	21200
2M	96251	128634	36125	43450
4M	192842	257412	73500	86200

All reported numbers of the query performance metric are the average of five executions with the highest and the lowest values removed. The rational behind this is that the first reading of each query is always expensively inconsistent with the other readings. This is because the relational database uses buffer pools as a caching mechanism. The initial period when the database spends its time loading pages into the buffer pools is known as the warm up period. During this period the response time of the database declines with respect to the normal response time.

For all metrics: the lower the metric value, the better the approach.

4.3 Experimental Results

Table 2 summarizes the loading times for shredding the different datasets into the alternative relational representations. The RS scheme is the fastest due to the less required number of insert tuple operations. Similarly, the TS requires less loading time than BS since the number of inserted tuples and updated tables are smaller for each triple.

Table 3 summarizes the storage cost for the alternative relational representations. The RS scheme represents the cheapest approach because of the normalized design and the absence of any data redundancy. Due to the limited percentage of the sparsity in the DBLP dataset, the PS does not introduce any additional cost in the storage space except a little overhead due to the redundancy of the object identification attributes in the decomposed property tables. The BS scheme represents the most expensive approach due to the redundancy of the ID attributes for each binary table. It should be also noted that the storage cost of TS and BS are affected by the additional sizes of their associated indexes.

Table 4. A comparison between the alternative relational RDF storage techniques in terms of their query performance (in milliseconds)

	1M				2M				4M			
	TS	BS	RS	PS	TS	BS	RS	PS	TS	BS	RS	PS
Q1	1031	1292	606	701	1982	2208	1008	1262	3651	3807	1988	2108
Q2	1672	1511	776	1109	2982	3012	1606	1987	5402	5601	2308	3783
Q3a	982	1106	61	116	1683	1873	102	198	3022	3342	191	354
Q3b	754	883	46	76	1343	1408	87	132	2063	2203	176	218
Q3c	1106	1224	97	118	1918	2109	209	275	3602	3874	448	684
Q4	21402	21292	11876	14116	38951	37642	20192	25019	66354	64119	39964	48116
Q5	1452	1292	798	932	2754	2598	1504	1786	5011	4806	3116	35612
Q6	2042	1998	1889	2109	3981	3966	3786	4407	7011	6986	6685	8209
Q7	592	30445	412	773	1102	58556	776	1546	2004	116432	1393	2665
Q8	9013	8651	1683	1918	15932	13006	3409	3902	27611	24412	8012	8609
Q9	2502	15311	654	887	4894	26113	1309	1461	9311	37511	2204	2671
Q10	383	596	284	387	714	1117	554	708	1306	2013	1109	1507
Q11	762	514	306	398	1209	961	614	765	2111	1704	1079	1461

Table 4 summarizes the query performance for the SP^{2}Bench benchmark queries over the alternative relational representations using the different sizes of the dataset. Remarks about the results of this experiment are given as follows:

- There is no clear winner between the triple store (TS) and the binary table (BS) encoding schemes. Triple store (TS) with its simple storage and the huge number of tuples in the encoding relation is still very competitive to the binary tables encoding scheme because of the full set of B-tree physical indexes over the permutations of the three encoding fields $(subject, predicate, object)$.
- The query performance of the (BS) encoding scheme is affected badly by the increase of the number of the predicates in the input query. It is also affected by the *subject-object* or *object-object* type of joins where no index information is available for utilization. Such problem could be solved by building materialized views over the columns of the most frequently referenced pairs of attributes.
- Although their generality, there is still a clear gap between the query performance of the (TS) and (BS) encoding schemes in comparison with the tailored relational encoding scheme (RS) of the RDF data. However, designing a tailored relational schema requires a detailed information about the structure of the represented objects in the RDF dataset. Such information is not always available and designing a tailored relational schema limits the schema-free advantage of the RDF data because any new object with a variant schema will require applying a change in the schema of the underlying relational structure. Hence, we believe that there is still required efforts to improve the performance of these generic relational RDF storages and reduce the query performance gap with the tailored relational encoding schemes.

– The property tables encoding schemes (PS) are trying to fill the gap between the generic encoding schemes (TS and BS) and the tailored encoding schemes (RS). The results of our experiments show that the (PS) encoding scheme can achieve a comparable query performance to the (RS) encoding scheme. However, designing the schema of the property tables requires either explicit or implicit information about the characteristics of the objects in the RDF dataset. Such explicit information can not be always available and the process of inferring such implicit information introduces an additional cost of a pre-processing phase. Such challenges call for new techniques for flexible designs for the property tables encoding schemes.

5 Concluding Remarks

A naive relational way to store a set of RDF statements is using a relational database with a single table including columns for subject, property, and object. While simple, this schema quickly hits scalability limitations. Therefore, several approaches have been proposed to deal with this limitation by using extensive set of indexes or by using selectivity estimation information to optimize the join ordering [13,19]. Another approach to reduce the self-join problem is to create separate tables (property tables) for subjects that tend to have common properties defined [5,12]. In [2] Abadi et al. have explored the trade-off between triple-based stores and binary tables-based stores of RDF data. The main advantages of binary tables are:

– **Improved bandwidth utilization:** In a column store, only those attributes that are accessed by a query need to be read off disk. In a row-store, surrounding attributes also need to be read since an attribute is generally smaller than the smallest granularity in which data can be accessed.
– **Improved data compression:** Storing data from the same attribute domain together increases locality, improves data compression ratio and reduce the bandwidth requirements when transferring compressed data.

On the other side, binary tables do have the following main disadvantages:

– **Increased cost of inserts:** Column-stores perform poorly for insert queries since multiple distinct locations on disk have to be updated for each tuple.
– **Increased tuple reconstruction costs:** In order for column-stores to offer a standards-compliant relational database interface (e.g. ODBC, JDBC, etc.), they must at some point in a query plan stitch values from multiple columns together into a row-store style tuple to be output from the database.

In [2] Abadi et al. reported that the performance of binary tables is superior to clustered property table while [16] reported that even in column-store database, the performance of binary tables is not always better than clustered property table and depends on the characteristics of the data set. Moreover, the experiments of [2] reported that storing RDF data in column-store database is better than that of row-store database while [16] experiments have shown that the gain of performance in column-store database depends on the number of predicates in a data set. Our experiments have shown that no approach is dominant for all queries and none of these approaches can compete with a tailored relational model. Therefore, we believe that there is still required efforts for improving the performance of the proposed generic relational RDF storage schemes and thus new techniques for storing and querying RDF data need to be developed to support the achievement of the Semantic Web design goals.

References

1. DBLP Computer Science Biliography, http://www.informatik.uni-trier.de/~ley/db/
2. Abadi, D., Marcus, A., Madden, S., Hollenbach, K.: SW-Store: a vertically partitioned DBMS for Semantic Web data management. VLDB J. 18(2) (2009)
3. Botea, V., Mallett, D., Nascimento, M., Sander, J.: PIST: An Efficient and Practical Indexing Technique for Historical Spatio-Temporal Point Data. GeoInformatica 12(2) (2008)
4. Chaudhuri, S., Weikum, G.: Rethinking Database System Architecture: Towards a Self-Tuning RISC-Style Database System. In: VLDB (2000)
5. Inseok Chong, E., Das, S., Eadon, G., Srinivasan, J.: An Efficient SQL-based RDF Querying Scheme. In: VLDB (2005)
6. Copeland, G., Khoshafian, S.: A Decomposition Storage Model. In: SIGMOD (1985)
7. Graefe, G.: Sorting and Indexing with Partitioned B-Trees. In: CIDR (2003)
8. Grust, T., Sakr, S., Teubner, J.: XQuery on SQL Hosts. In: VLDB (2004)
9. Harris, S., Gibbins, N.: 3store: Efficient Bulk RDF Storage. In: PSSS (2003)
10. Harth, A., Decker, S.: Optimized Index Structures for Querying RDF from the Web. In: LA-WEB (2005)
11. Jeffery, S., Franklin, M., Halevy, A.: Pay-as-you-go user feedback for dataspace systems. In: SIGMOD (2008)
12. Levandoski, J., Mokbel, M.: RDF Data-Centric Storage. In: ICWS (2009)
13. Neumann, T., Weikum, G.: RDF-3X: a RISC-style engine for RDF. PVLDB 1(1) (2008)
14. Prud'hommeaux, E., Seaborne, A.: SPARQL Query Language for RDF, W3C Recommendation (January 2008), http://www.w3.org/TR/rdf-sparql-query/
15. Schmidt, M., Hornung, T., Lausen, G., Pinkel, C.: SP^{2}Bench: A SPARQL Performance Benchmark. In: ICDE (2009)
16. Sidirourgos, L., Goncalves, R., Kersten, M., Nes, N., Manegold, S.: Column-store support for RDF data management: not all swans are white. PVLDB 1(2) (2008)
17. Stonebraker, M., Abadi, D., Batkin, A., Chen, X., Cherniack, M., Ferreira, M., Lau, E., Lin, A., Madden, S., O'Neil, E., O'Neil, P., Rasin, A., Tran, N., Zdonik, S.: C-Store: A Column-oriented DBMS. In: VLDB (2005)
18. Türker, C., Gertz, M.: Semantic integrity support in SQL: 1999 and commercial (object-)relational database management systems. VLDB J. 10(4) (2001)
19. Weiss, C., Karras, P., Bernstein, A.: Hexastore: sextuple indexing for semantic web data management. PVLDB 1(1) (2008)
20. Wilkinson, K., Sayers, C., Kuno, H., Reynolds, D.: Efficient RDF Storage and Retrieval in Jena2. In: SWDB (2003)

Analyzer: A Framework for File Analysis*

Martin Svoboda, Jakub Stárka, Jan Sochna, Jiří Schejbal, and Irena Mlýnková

Department of Software Engineering, Charles University in Prague, Czech Republic
analyzer.contact@gmail.com

Abstract. This paper aims to introduce *Analyzer* – a complete framework for performing statistical analyses of real-world documents. Exploitation of results of these analyses is a classical way how data processing can be optimized in many areas. Although this intent is legitimate, ad hoc and dedicated analyses soon become obsolete, they are usually built on insufficiently extensive collections and are difficult to repeat. *Analyzer* represents an easily extensible framework, which helps the user with gathering documents, managing analyses and browsing computed reports. This paper particularly attempts to discuss proposed analyses model, standard application usage and features, and also basic aspects of *Analyzer* architecture and implementation.

1 Introduction

Exploitation of results of statistical analyses of real-world data is a classical optimization strategy in various areas of data processing. It is based on the idea to focus primarily on efficient implementation of constructs that are used in real-world data most often. However, working with real-world data is not simple, since they can often change, are not precise, or even involve a number of errors. Firstly, we need to gather a reasonably large and representative set of real-world data. There exists a huge number of crawlers, however we usually require data having a particular format or structure, so a wide range of filters must be supported. Secondly, since the data are usually human-written, they contain a number of errors. In this case we can either discard the incorrect data, and, hence, loose a significant portion of them, or provide a kind of *corrector*. In the next step we want to make the analyses themselves. In this case we have to cope with the fact that the data can change and hence the analytical phase must be repeatable and extensible. And, finally, having obtained the results of the statistics, we need to be able to visualize and analyze the huge amount of information efficiently and mutually compare the results.

In this paper we describe a proposal background, architecture outline, implementation aspects and usage scenarios of a general framework called *Analyzer* that aims to cope with all the previously named requirements. In other words it provides all essential functionality for an easy management of files to be analyzed,

* Supported by the Czech Science Foundation (GAČR), grant no. 201/09/P364, and the Ministry of Education of the Czech Republic, grant no. MSM0021620838.

M. Yoshikawa et al. (Eds.): DASFAA 2010, LNCS 6193, pp. 227–238, 2010.

configuration and execution of selected analyses and an advanced graphical user interface for browsing generated reports.

The fundamental feature of *Analyzer* is extensibility. This not only means the ability to implement own and more suitable kernel components responsible, e.g., for storing computed analytical data, but primarily the open concept of plugins. *Analyzer* provides a general environment, whereas all analytical computations themselves are defined solely within the implementation of plugins. The user is therefore expected to first install *Analyzer* itself and then create his/her own plugins designed to correspond to the determined research intents. Although our initial motivations were related to XML [8] data, *Analyzer* usage is not limited only to this area.

Simplified functionality overview of *Analyzer* can be started by already mentioned file management. Its usage is based on projects, where each project represents an isolated analytical work. New files can be automatically downloaded into projects via provided crawlers or can be manually imported from locally reachable locations. Using the mechanism of following previously recognized links between documents, new documents can also be automatically sought out. The user has a complete control over the analytical computations through the composition of selected and configured methods from available plugins. All computations are executed in parallel by multiple threads. Despite this fact, the performance was not the primary goal and more crucial emphasis was put on document model complexity and implied analytical possibilities the user can utilize. Finally, documents can be grouped into collections, which form the basis for presentation of computed statistical reports.

The current plugins support essential processing of general files and basic analysis of XML documents, schemas and queries. In particular, we focus on structural characteristics of XML data files, their schemata written in DTD [8] or XML Schema [24,12] and XQuery [9] and XPath [7] querying languages.

The paper is structured as follows: Section 2 discusses existing related works. Section 3 focuses on the proposed model of documents, their description and mutual linking, as well as the model of grouping documents into collections and collections into clusters. In Section 4 we describe *Analyzer* architecture and functionality of key components. Section 5 provides basic overview of plugins and their collaboration with *Analyzer*. Section 6 introduces basic experimental results and, finally, Section 7 provides conclusions.

2 Related Work

Currently there exist several papers that describe the results of analysis of real-world XML data. Firstly, there occurred several analyses of the structure of DTDs [23,14,16] which analyzed mainly the complexity of content models and usage of various constructs. With the arrival of XML Schema [24,12], as the extension of DTD, a natural question arised: Which of the extra features of XML Schema not allowed in DTD are used in practice? Papers [11,19] are trying to answer it using statistical analysis of real-world XML schemas. Finally, there exist also papers that analyze the structure of XML documents. Paper [20] analyzes the structure of XML documents regardless eventually existing schema. On the other hand, paper [22] focuses on the question which of the constructs that appear in XML schemas are really exploited in XML documents.

Naturally, there also exist multiple approaches that exploit the results of the analyses. For instance, the finding that the depth of XML documents is on average less than 10 [20] is widely exploited in techniques which represent XML documents as a set of points in multidimensional space and store them in corresponding data structures, e.g. R-trees, UB-trees, or BUB-trees [17]. On the other hand, the authors of [11] define several classes of commonly used regular expressions and exploit their finding in later papers on inference of identifiable classes of languages [10]. Or, in paper [21] the authors exploit the results of paper [22] for tuning weights of a similarity metric.

However, though the amount of existing works is significant and the findings are important, all the papers have the same common disadvantage. Soon each analysis becomes obsolete and it should be repeated. However, the respective crawlers, data analyzers and their settings are not available any more or they have limited functionality and cannot be extended with new features easily.

3 Analyses Proposal

Let us suppose the following standard life cycle of each analysis from the point of view of the way it can be performed in *Analyzer*:

1. Creation of a new project and its configuration,
2. Selection and configuration of required analyses,
3. Insertion of documents to be analyzed,
4. Computation of analytical results over documents,
5. Selection and configuration of collections,
6. Document classification and assignment into collections, and
7. Computation of reports over collections.

Projects encapsulate inserted documents, configuration of analyses and computed data, and represent a single research intent. Each project has its own repository for saving computed data, at least one storage for storing data contents of inserted documents and at least one crawler for downloading new documents. If these three components or their content remain reachable, projects themselves can be easily ported from one computer or location to another.

Document Insertion. The subject of analyses are *documents*. Documents can be inserted into the project in three different ways. Two of them are explicit in a way that the user directly describes particular files and initiates the process of insertion (import or download), the third one represents automatic seeking of linked documents previously not inserted using first two mechanisms.

The *import* functionality enables the user to select a sub-tree of locally reachable files (e.g. on hard or optical drives). These files can be optionally hard copied to the project home folder or can be left at the original location. Consider that the user has previously downloaded the entire sub-tree of some web site and all files are stored on the drive. In this case the user can specify the original base URL address and *Analyzer* attempts to map relative paths of these files to this base address.

The second way is a *download* using one of the supported crawlers. Depending on particular crawler behavior, the user is able to either request a set of particular addresses to be downloaded or select a set of addresses the unlimited download should be initiated from. In the first mode the crawler downloads exactly the selected files, the second mode can be characterized like flooding crawling.

Document Model. Each document is characterized by a pair of physical and logical *resources*. The first one is the URL address from which the file was really imported, downloaded or sought from, the second one represents an address *Analyzer* "thinks" the original file should be located at. However, the heuristic guessing is not currently completely implemented and is a subject of our future work. *Analyzer* itself is able to maintain multiple versions of the same document. This more precisely means that all individual import or download *sessions* are grouped into *chains*. Each chain is described by a relative *age* and it is not possible to have more than one document of the same logical resource in it, thus two same documents of the same relative age in a project.

As we have already discussed, since each document is described by a relative age and a pair of logical and physical resource, the document entity is only an abstraction of a file – data *content* of a given file is treated independently. Once a new document is inserted into the project, the corresponding original file is bounded with this document. In order to support file corrections, one type of plugin methods can perform content modifications. Whenever a new version of content is generated, the previously valid one is thrown away, unless the previous one is the original one. Plugins always work with the current content version.

During first analytical steps of document processing, document *types* are recognized. Because this detection is realized by plugins, the typing concept is not limited and programmers are allowed to work with their own typing namespace. We have proposed to harness standardized MIME types [18]. The most important fact about types is that each document is described by a set of recognized types, not only one type. The idea behind types is simple: plugins recognize types, plugins analyze only documents of selected known types and finally projects can be restricted to processing of selected types only.

Analyzer also supports detection and processing of *links* between documents. A link is a reference from a source document to a target document. It can be a reference defined in an XML type document and pointed to its schema file. Another example can be a link from an HTML type document to an image included in the given page. It does not matter whether links represent aggregation, composition or only association. *Analyzer* is able to delay analytical processing of a given document until all required and accessible referenced documents are present in the project.

Collections Model. Let us suppose that some methods published by plugins are dedicated to computation of analytical data over documents. These data are called *results*, thus a result is a small piece of information computed by a given plugin over a given document. It is expected that results are not the goal of analyses, they are created in order to be aggregated over multiple documents later in a form of reports and then presented.

Collections are introduced in order to allow grouping of documents. Formally we can define a collection as a set of documents. Once again collections are defined by plugins in a way that plugins are responsible for classification of individual documents. Despite this fact, the user is also able to filter documents using general criteria like, e.g., resources or relative age restrictions. Since each project can have a higher number of collections and some collections can be related (e.g. they classify documents into multiple categories using a shared set of criteria), *Analyzer* enables also grouping of collections into *clusters*.

When the classification of all documents is done and the user does not want to add new documents, computed results can be aggregated as previously outlined. This is done separately in each collection and thus generated *reports* are always derived only from documents that are members of a given collection.

Analyses Course. In a project life cycle, the recommended sequence of steps a user should perform may not be followed. However only advanced users should do this, because not well considered actions may lead to computed data recision. Although *Analyzer* automatically detects these situations and invokes the minimal set of required recalculations, extra work and time is needed.

During a new project creation the user (besides other configuration) can optionally select types the project should be dedicated for. This selection is defined by a set of regular expression patterns over types (in default typing namespace over MIME types).

The next step is a selection of *analyses* to be used in a given project. *Analyzer* lists all *plugins* that are currently accessible, but the user can only select those which seem to be consistent. Some plugins can be configured, in the other case the plugin can be selected only once. As it will be explained later, plugins offer their functionality through methods. An integral part of analyses selection and configuration is also definition of fixed order of all analytical methods, this means the order in which *Analyzer* executes these methods over documents.

Now the user can import or download required documents. Even during this insertion the computation of results over documents can be processed. If a project involves types filtering, the given document is removed from a project if it does not match any of the provided patterns.

The next step is a creation of new clusters and thus sets of collections. Once a new collection is created, *Analyzer* automatically starts the classification of all existing documents satisfying other filtering criteria defined during the cluster creation and shared by all collections of the given cluster.

The final step is the closure of clusters which invokes aggregation of the results into reports. *Analyzer* ensures that all reports that can be generated are computed without any user endeavor. Reports are stored permanently and the user can browse them any time later.

4 Implementation

Analyzer is implemented in *Java 6* language [1] as a desktop application with robust GUI. It is built on the top of *NetBeans 6.8* platform [2] and capable of the cross platform usage. Its simplified architecture is depicted in Figure 1.

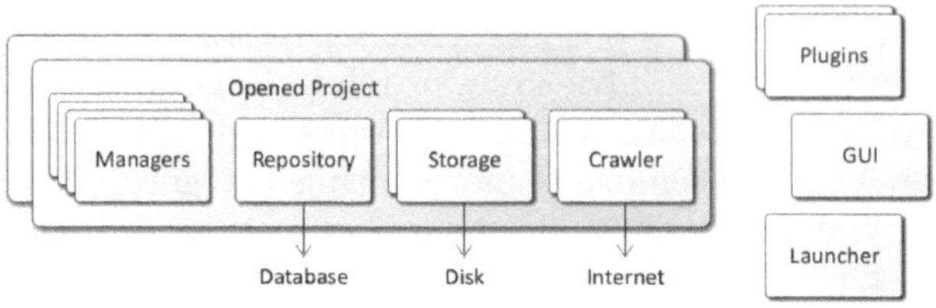

Fig. 1. A simplified architecture of *Analyzer*

From the runtime point of view *Analyzer* architecture can be divided into two layers. First of them represents components of opened application shared by all opened projects, the second layer represents components exclusively used and created separately in each opened project.

Project Components. Components at the project level involve particularly repositories, storages and crawlers. They are exclusively owned by each project, but this does not mean that, e.g., a real relational database server behind a repository cannot be used by multiple projects. It is allowed and the given component only has to ensure the required isolation between projects (which can be done easily in the given example using different databases).

Each project must have a single *repository.* It serves for storing all computed data and even the majority of metadata like, e.g., analyses configuration or created collections. Although *Analyzer* design does not require it, all three provided repositories are based on standard relational databases (MySQL server database through *MySQL Connector 5.1.7* [3], embedded *Apache Derby 10.5.1.1* database [4] and embedded *H2 Database 1.1.117* [5]).

Storages are used for storing document contents. The only stable implementation is based on a native file system, but experiments were taken with native storages for XML files.

Analyzer is able to work with two orthogonal categories of *crawlers.* First differentiation is based on explicit and flooding behaviors. In order to limit the crawling explosion, the user can specify maximum allowed depth. The second division is based on the way how new download requests are created, processed and finished from the point of view of whether these actions are synchronous or asynchronous. *Analyzer* currently contains one simple embedded downloader and is able to work with the *Egothor* crawler [15].

Principal design feature of all these three components is extensibility. Although a typical user would probably not need it, new components can be implemented and added relatively easily.

The project layer also contains the set of *managers*, which are responsible for creating, editing and processing of all entities such as documents, collections or reports. As all computed data and data on entities are stored permanently in a repository, in order to increase efficiency these managers are able to cache loaded data and even release them, if they are no longer required. Some managers are also able to postpone and aggregate update operations, but the consistency of computed data is still guaranteed.

Shared Components. In a running *Analyzer* a user is able to concurrently open more projects than only just one. Passing over other auxiliary components, the most important one is a *launcher*, which is responsible for executing tasks over all such projects.

Tasks represent fragments of analytical or other computations, which have been scheduled. For example each download of a selected resource, computation over a given document or aggregation of reports over collections is internally encapsulated and processed in a form of tasks. Once *Analyzer* decides that some work should be done, a new task is created, scheduled and thus prepared for execution. Clearly this model is a compromise, since it increases computational demands, but gives the user nearly full control over processing with a small granularity.

The user is able to attach or detach the project from the launcher and therefore say whether tasks from a given project should be executed now or not. As a consequence the user can pause started computations and resume them later. Scheduled tasks are performed in parallel by worker threads from a prepared pool. If a given task could not be successfully finished (for whether reasons), *Analyzer* attempts to execute it repeatedly with a defined number of attempts. In order to enhance performance, *Analyzer* also makes an effort to, e.g., run tasks over one document successively to minimize required disk reading operations.

GUI Browser. The GUI of *Analyzer* is based on the possibilities of the NetBeans platform. It brings the complete and robust environment for creating and managing projects and performing analyses from their configuration to browsing of computed reports. An example of screenshot image can be found in Figure 2.

The browser itself contains adjustable windows through which the user is able to monitor the progress of computations and browse all existing entities in opened projects. These data are provided mainly in a form of interactive *trees* or *listings* and the user is able to easily navigate between them according to the analyses model and entities relations.

More complicated actions like creation of new components or analyses configuration are implemented as *wizards*.

Analyzer *Download.* The current distribution of *Analyzer* and all implemented plugins can be downloaded from `http://urtax.ms.mff.cuni.cz/anaxml/`. This site includes also other related information and complete documentation including manual for creating new plugins.

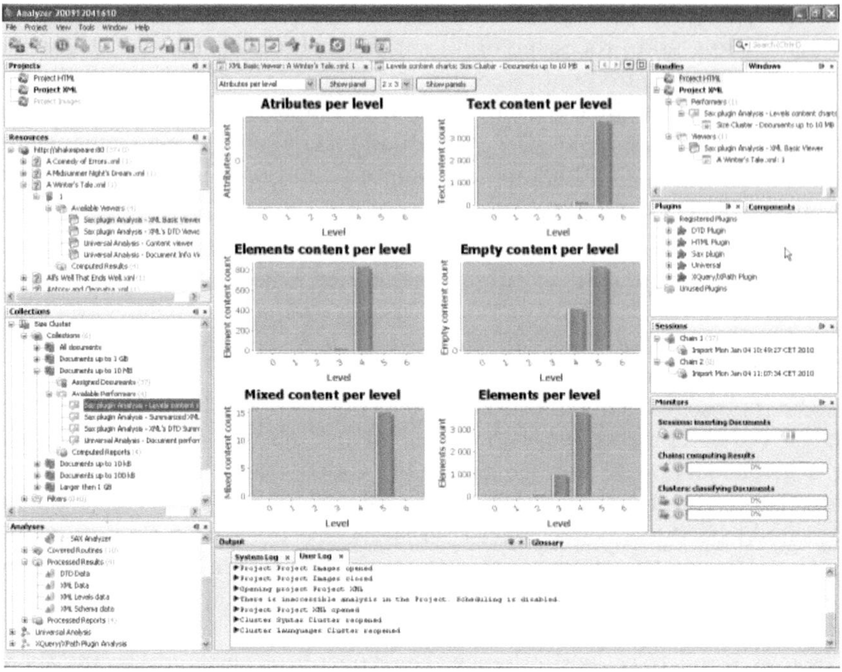

Fig. 2. A screenshot of *Analyzer*

5 Plugins

Analyzer itself provides a general environment for performing analyses over documents and collections of documents, but the intrinsical analytical logic is not a part of it. All analytical computations and mechanisms are implemented in plugins. The current distribution of *Analyzer* includes a few basic plugins for processing general files and XML related files, but the user is the one who is expected to create and use own plugins.

Each *plugin* is in fact a Java class that satisfies particular structural conditions. It is expected, that each plugin is determined for analyzing files of specific types. When *Analyzer* starts, it attempts to load all accessible plugins, therefore their usage is simple and without any complicated integration. Briefly, the plugin publishes the functionality and *Analyzer* makes it usable.

Analyses Computation. Disregarding the ability of a plugin to be configured (and thus, e.g., adjusted to particular analytical intents), each plugin specifies a set of types that can be processed by it. This restriction is defined by regular expression patterns. The plugin functionality is provided through implemented *methods*. They are of predefined eight different types. Although these methods are not java methods but classes, we can omit this fact for simplicity. Each of these methods and even the plugin itself contains also meta-data, which enable *Analyzer* to inspect the provided capabilities.

First four method types serve for analyzing documents. They produce results, which form the basis for reports generation:

- The *detector* recognizes types of a given document,
- The *tracer* looks for links starting in a given document,
- The *corrector* attempts to repair content of a given document, and
- The *analyzer* primarily produces results.

After the user selects and configures all required analyses (therefore plugins the user wants to use), the selection of particular available detectors, tracers, correctors and analyzers must be managed. This comprises not only selection, but also ordering of these methods.

Continuing with description of types of methods, a *collector* is a method that is responsible for classifying documents, thus saying, whether the given document should be part of a related collection or not. Once the user closes a cluster, *Analyzer* invokes *provider* methods over all its collections in order to aggregate results into reports. This step is complicated, because *Analyzer* has to process all documents in given collections in order to compute really all reports.

Finally, *viewer* and *performer* methods are used for presenting computed results over documents and computed reports over collections respectively.

Execution of Methods. The execution of tasks representing methods is similar to execution of other tasks, *Analyzer* only wraps the code written by the plugin programmer, invokes the own computation and handles potentially raised errors or other forms of incorrect processing.

All methods share the way how they access the functionality of *Analyzer* and how they acquire data about documents or other entities they are processing or generating. These requests are processed by *mediators*, objects with well known interface and contract. Each method type has own specialized mediator, which allows only the relevant operations.

Because requests initiated by a plugin programmer may be formally correct, but may violate selected rules for behavior of methods, *Analyzer* attempts to detect and prevent these situations by disallowing the successful ending of execution of such methods. The mediator in fact only pretends processing of all requests, internally simulates required actions and the real execution is postponed until the very end of a given task execution.

Implemented Plugins. The implementation of *Analyzer* comes with a few created plugins, which are ready for use. If we omit sample plugins demonstrating only framework possibilities, there are three main groups of plugins: a universal plugin for basic analyses of documents regardless their types, a plugin for XML documents and their schema analyses and finally a plugin for XQuery and XPath analyses.

The universal plugin is, among others, capable of detecting document types using the mechanism of combined file suffix processing and content guessing based on *MIME Magic* [18].

The XML plugin is able to analyze elements and attributes count, distribution of content at different levels or usage of DTD/XML Schema. XML Schema file analysis contains usage of constructs like `simpleContent`, `complexType`, `restriction` or `group`. DTD file analysis focuses on elements and attributes definitions, usage of `ANY`, `EMPTY`, allowed or required constructs.

The XQuery and XPath plugin is capable of, e.g., analysis of FLWOR constructs occurrence, path expressions, constructors etc.

6 Experiments

This section provides a short presentation of the computing possibilities of *Analyzer*. Apparently, the key impact on computation speed represent repositories and, thus, the main effect brings primarily the number of analyzed documents. Therefore we configured 2 simple analyses with 4 methods for generating results. The documents were inserted into a project using a soft import without copying. A single cluster with 6 collections was created.

Table 1. Results of experiments with computation speed

Set name	Document count and size	Repository database	Document import	Result computation	Collection filling	Report computation
A	1,000 x 100 kB	Derby	7 s	60 s	14 s	12 s
		H2 DB	2 s	12 s	6 s	1 s
		MySQL	3 s	19 s	9 s	< 1 s
B	10,000 x 10 kB	Derby	45 s	13 min	5 min	11 min
		H2 DB	10 s	100 s	90 s	60 s
		MySQL	15 s	135 s	70 s	10 s
C	100,000 x 1 kB	H2 DB	1 min	150 min	150 min	16 h
		MySQL	3 min	22 min	14 min	1 min

Table 1 shows the speed of the performed experiments over 3 different sets of documents. All tests were executed using a PC with Intel Core 2 Quad Q9550 2.83 Ghz processor, 4 GB RAM and *Gentoo Linux 10.1* [6] OS. The analyzed documents were stored on a local hard disk and also all three repositories stored their internal data locally on the same disk. The MySQL Community Server 5.0.84 was installed locally and used through JDBC connector 3.0. Both Collection filling and Report computation phases are based only on repository querying (documents are never read). As we can see, there is a significant difference between H2 and MySQL. It can be explained by the inability to work with defined indexes during selection queries.

Last but not least we will demonstrate the purpose and required output of *Analyzer*. Due to space limitations we made only a basic set of analyses over a simple collection. A more comprehensive analysis of a set of real-world XML documents is the very next step of our future work. Figure 3 depicts the output of computed XML statistics over the set A generated by the *XMark* generator [13]. From the additional information we select the following ones: maximum depth = 12; average depth = 9.4; minimum depth = 5; average element count per a document = 1,455; average attribute count per a document = 333.

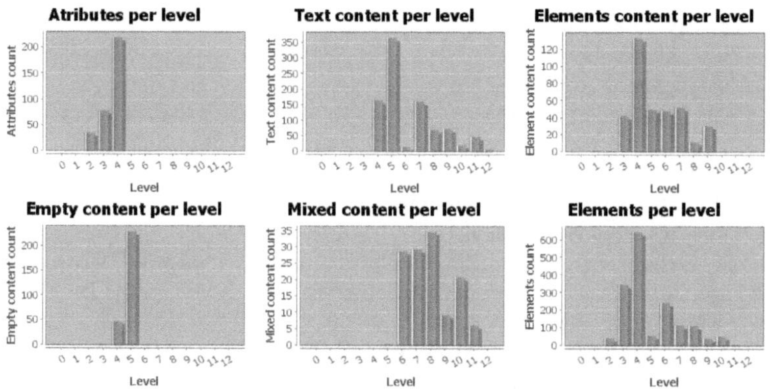

Fig. 3. Elements content statistics

7 Conclusion

Despite our original motivations related to XML technologies, we finally implemented an application that is completely capable of performing analyses over documents of whatever types. *Analyzer* represents a framework, that gives a user an environment for gathering documents, configuring analyses, managing and scheduling computations, permanent storage for files and computed data, and a browser for presenting generated reports. The key advantages of *Analyzer* are as follows:

- Multiple versions of the same document are supported,
- Documents can be described by multiple types concurrently,
- Automatic attempts to download referenced documents are performed,
- Projects can be forced to process only documents of selected types,
- All analytical logic is implemented separately in plugins,
- Executing scheduled tasks in multi-threaded environment is exploited,
- Started computations can be interrupted and resumed later, and
- Computed data are permanently stored and available for browsing.

Our future plans will primarily be targeted to improvements of existing plugins related to XML file analyses. We particularly want to extend the set of metrics that are computed over XML files and their schemas. One partial intent is, e.g., based on pattern matching against documents content and implied documents classification. We also plan to perform experiments over vast document sets and especially over sets of real-world data automatically gathered by the supported flooding crawler. Since these data are often not well-formed or valid, we also want to create more sophisticated corrector that would decrease the set of XML documents that we are not able to analyze.

References

1. `http://java.sun.com/javase/6/`
2. `http://platform.netbeans.org/`
3. `http://dev.mysql.com/downloads/connector/j/`

4. http://db.apache.org/derby/
5. http://www.h2database.com/
6. http://www.gentoo.org/
7. XML Path Language (XPath) 1.0. W3C (1999), http://www.w3.org/TR/xpath
8. Extensible Markup Language (XML) 1.0, 4th edn. W3C (2006), http://www.w3.org/XML/
9. XQuery 1.0: An XML Query Language. W3C (2007), http://www.w3.org/TR/xquery/
10. Bex, G.J., Gelade, W., Neven, F., Vansummeren, S.: Learning Deterministic Regular Expressions for the Inference of Schemas from XML Data. In: WWW 2008, pp. 825–834. ACM, New York (2008)
11. Bex, G.J., Neven, F., Van den Bussche, J.: DTDs versus XML Schema: a Practical Study. In: WebDB 2004, pp. 79–84. ACM, New York (2004)
12. Biron, P.V., Malhotra, A.: XML Schema Part 2: Datatypes, 2nd edn. W3C (2004), http://www.w3.org/TR/xmlschema-2/
13. Busse, R., Carey, M., Florescu, D., Kersten, M., Manolescu, I., Schmidt, A., Waas, F.: XMark Generator 0.96, http://www.xml-benchmark.org/
14. Choi, B.: What are Real DTDs Like? In: WebDB 2002, Madison, Wisconsin, USA, pp. 43–48. ACM, New York (2002)
15. Galamboš, L.: Egothor 1.0, Java Search Engine (2006), http://www.egothor.org/
16. Klettke, M., Schneider, L., Heuer, A.: Metrics for XML Document Collections. In: XMLDM 2002 Workshops, Prague, Czech Republic, pp. 162–176 (2002)
17. Krátký, M., Pokorný, J., Snášel, V.: Indexing XML Data with UB-Trees. In: Manolopoulos, Y., Návrat, P. (eds.) ADBIS 2002. LNCS, vol. 2435, pp. 155–164. Springer, Heidelberg (2002)
18. McArdle, S.: MIME Utils 2.0, Mime Type Detection Utility for Java (2009), http://www.medsea.eu/mime-util/
19. McDowell, A., Schmidt, C., Yue, K.: Analysis and Metrics of XML Schema. In: SERP 2004, Las Vegas, Nevada, USA, pp. 538–544. CSREA Press (2004)
20. Mignet, L., Barbosa, D., Veltri, P.: The XML Web: a First Study. In: WWW 2003, pp. 500–510. ACM, New York (2003)
21. Mlýnková, I., Pokorný, J.: Similarity of XML Schema Fragments Based on XML Data Statistics. In: Innovations 2007, pp. 243–247. IEEE Press, Los Alamitos (2007)
22. Mlýnková, I., Toman, K., Pokorný, J.: Statistical Analysis of Real XML Data Collections. In: COMAD 2006, New Delhi, India, pp. 20–31. Tata McGraw-Hill Publishing Company Limited, New York (2006)
23. Sahuguet, A.: Everything You Ever Wanted to Know About DTDs, But Were Afraid to Ask. In: Suciu, D., Vossen, G. (eds.) WebDB 2000. LNCS, vol. 1997, pp. 171–183. Springer, Heidelberg (2001)
24. Thompson, H.S., Beech, D., Maloney, M., Mendelsohn, N.: XML Schema Part 1: Structures, 2nd edn. W3C (2004), http://www.w3.org/TR/xmlschema-1/

SNSMW 2010
Workshop Organizers' Message

Yoshinori Hijikata and Guandong Xu

Osaka University, Victoria University

The First International Workshop on Social Networks and Social Media Mining on the Web (SNSMW 2010) was held in Tsukuba, Japan on 4 April, 2010, in conjunction with the DASFAA 2010 conference. The aim of the workshop is to provide an opportunity to present papers on social networks and social media mining. The web has evolved since its birth. Currently, the role of the web is not only the media for information transmission but the media for people's collaboration. Social aspects are not negligible for web computing. The topics of interest include computational models for social media, trust and privacy, social-network analysis/mining, community detection and evolution, Blog search and retrieval, human interface and interaction techniques for social media, and so on.

The workshop has attracted 22 submissions. All submissions were peer reviewed by program committee members. The program committee selected 14 papers for inclusion in the proceedings (Acceptance ratio is 63.6%). The accepted papers covered important research topics and novel applications on web computing. About 50 people participated in the workshop as audiences and deeply discussed in the above topics.

The workshop would not be successful without the help of many organizations and individuals. First, we would like to thank program committee co-chairs of SNSMW 2010. Prof. Lin Li prepared the CFP and a submission system for the workshop. Prof. Munehiko Sasajima managed all the review process for the workshop. Next, we would like to thank the program committee members for evaluating the assigned papers in a timely and professional manner. Also, the workshop committee members and local arrangement committee members of DASFAA 2010 gave us a lot of help for preparing the workshop. Finally, we would like to thank all the authors and participants of the workshop. The authors submitted very innovative and challenging impressive papers. The audiences gave precious comments and discussed the research direction in this area. We believe that they are the main factors for our succession.

M. Yoshikawa et al. (Eds.): DASFAA 2010, LNCS 6193, p. 239, 2010.

Task-Oriented User Modeling Method and Its Application to Service Navigation on the Web

Munehiko Sasajima, Yoshinobu Kitamura, and Riichiro Mizoguchi

I.S.I.R, Osaka University. 8-1 Mihogaoka, Ibaraki-shi, Osaka, 567-0047, Japan
{msasa,kita,miz}@ei.sanken.osaka-u.ac.jp

Abstract. Value of information accumulated on the Web should be enhanced if it is provided to the user who just faces to a problematic situation which can be solved by the information. The authors have been investigating a task-oriented menu, which enables users to search for mobile internet services not by category but by situation of the users. Construction of the task-oriented menu is based on a user modeling method which supports descriptions of user activities, such as task execution and defeating obstacles encountered during the task, which in turn represents users' situations and/or needs for certain information. We have built task models of the mobile users which covered about 97% of the assumed situations of mobile internet services. Then we reorganized "contexts" in the model and designed a menu hierarchy from the view point of the task. We have linked the designed menu to the set of actual mobile internet service sites included in the i-mode service operated by NTT docomo, consists of 5016 services. Among them, 4817 services are properly connected to the menu. This paper introduces a framework for real scale task-oriented menu system for mobile service navigation with its relations to the SNS applications as knowledge resources.

Keywords: User modeling, Mobile internet services, Knowledge-based Systems, Task Ontology.

1 Introduction

Today, various kinds of information are accumulated on the web including SNS. Wikipedia provides generic knowledge about things with hierarchical structure, while Twitter provides real-time information via short messages, for example. Subscribing such services, people are executing many kinds of tasks in daily life.

Providing appropriate information for users in a specific situation should enhance value of information, because value of information is proportional to the necessity of the information for the user. Short messages on Twitter, a late breaking SNS, give latest and dynamic information to users, thus suitable for users who need the latest information to solve certain problem. Messages on Twitter about current train situation support users who seek for the fastest train route to the destination just now, while the service does not work well for users who want to understand whole subway networks of the train-services in Tokyo, for example.

To realize situation-oriented information services, the authors have been investigating a framework to navigate users to the information resources along with the user's

M. Yoshikawa et al. (Eds.): DASFAA 2010, LNCS 6193, pp. 240–251, 2010.

situation. For the purpose, we have modeled daily activity of the users who subscribe Japanese mobile internet service as the first step.

Here we explain characteristics about the Japanese mobile internet services. While they provide many mobile internet services via mobile handsets in Japan, such as online shopping, mobile banking, and news services, current methods for mobile service navigation have proven insufficient to guide users efficiently to the mobile internet services they need. To solve this problem, the authors have been investigating a task-oriented menu which enables users to search for services by "what they want to do" in certain problem-solving situations, instead of by "name of category" [1]. On this first prototype system, Naganuma proved that the task-oriented menu system has ability to navigating novice users to the mobile services they want faster than conventional domain oriented menu system. The first prototype system mentioned in [1], however, was a limited one. In terms of task and domain knowledge, the first prototype assumed only limited situations, thus limited services were built in the menu system.

To extend the first prototype menu system to the real scale one, we need to investigate two issues. The first one is how to enhance scalability. The second one is how to develop a menu system with real scale on the basis of the investigation about the scalability. The authors discussed these two issues and developed a new menu system with real scale for navigating users to the mobile services they want, which is linked to a real scale of mobile services consisting of about 9,000 services. We have described about the user modeling issues in [3].

This paper describes design and development process of the new menu system, with the system's possibility to work with SNS services.

2 Task-Oriented Menu for Mobile Service Navigation

Fig. 1 shows the process of service selection using a task-oriented menu on the first prototype system [1]. First, the most abstract task candidates are shown on the mobile phone (Fig. 1 left). A user selects one of them (e.g. "Go to a department store") to solve current problem (e.g., "need to buy clothes"). Then, tasks and/or subtasks associated with each task are unfolded and displayed under the task nodes (Fig. 1 center). Finally, services associated with the task selected by the user are shown, and each of them leads to access to the actual service (Fig. 1 right).

As shown in this example, the task-oriented menu is easy to use for novice users of mobile internet services. By just selecting what he/she wants to do in the real world from the menu, he/she will be led to a service for solving the current problem. Knowledge about the hierarchy of the domain-oriented menu labeled like "hobbies", "local info", "life" and so on, is not necessary.

Although such a generic task hierarchy looks like the hierarchical structure of the category-based menus of today, there are fundamental differences. In certain cases, it is possible to label a concept with a noun instead of a verb or action. It is acceptable to label a mobile internet service that sells tickets as "Ticketing" or "Buy a ticket", for example. In the same manner, abstract tasks can be labeled with nouns. Although it seems that any concept can be labeled by both verbs and nouns, it is a hasty generalization. Such a generalization may lead to the misunderstanding that we just followed the process used by the designer of the category-based menu in classifying the mobile internet services, thus introducing an abstract hierarchy of the tasks.

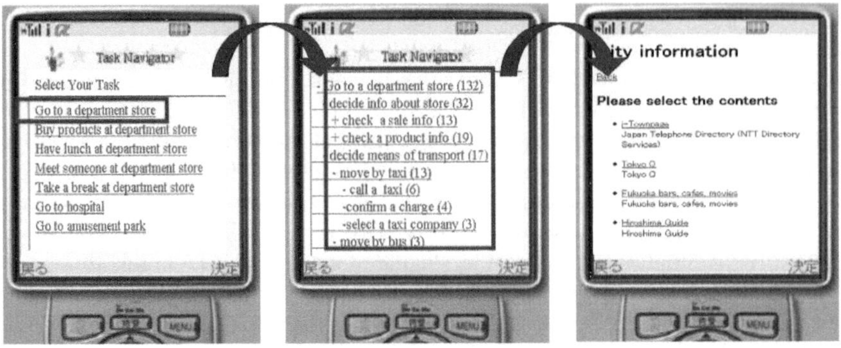

Fig. 1. Task oriented menu (The first prototype by Naganuma[1])

An important point is that the difference between "Ticketing" and "Buy a ticket" is just the expression of the label. The concepts are the same task. We focus on the concept and essential characteristics of the mobile user's task. Comparing them at the conceptual level, a category-based classification of objects is totally different from a task-based one in terms of its structure.

In the case of category-based classifications today, generally speaking, the boundary or definition of each category becomes vague or implicit. Classification of an object or a concept heavily depends on the intention of the designer who developed the menu. The categories "Hobbies" and "Shopping" are both located at the top level of the Japanese i-mode menu, for example. A mobile internet service that sells cars is classified in the former if the designer considers driving a car as a hobby. On the other hand, the service is classified in the shopping category if the designer focuses on the commercial aspect of the service rather than its object.

On the other hand, in classification of actions from the viewpoint of tasks, the boundary or definition of each category becomes more explicit. Since the criteria for the classification, such as pre-conditions, processes, and effects of the action, appear in both the label of the category and the classified concepts, it is easy to find the location of a new concept in a hierarchy which is classified based on task. For the same reason, it is easy to add a new concept to the task-based classification. A service that sells cars is classified in a sub-category of the task "Buy", whether driving a car is a hobby or not.

For the reasons described so far, task-based categories are more suitable for the classification of mobile services. On this point, Naganuma [1] conducted a user test involving nine adult subjects to confirm the effectiveness of a task-oriented menu system and evaluate the process used to find services for problem-solving purposes in terms of process functionality. Subjects were divided into three groups according to their experience of mobile internet services: 1) subjects using mobile internet services every day, 2) subjects using mobile internet services a few days a week, and 3) subjects with no experience in using mobile internet services.

Subjects were asked to retrieve appropriate services to given problems by using the task-oriented menu system, a keyword-type full-text search system newly developed for the experiment, and a major commercial directory-type menu system.

Analyzing the results by the user types, only the task-oriented menu system allowed non-expert users to find the appropriate services with the same success rate as experienced users. The results show that the task-oriented menu system is effective for mobile internet service navigation.

3 Issues on Building Real-Scale Task Oriented Menu

For realization of task-oriented menu system in real scale, we have to tackle two issues: (1) Scalability of the system and (2) Building a task-oriented menu system with real scale. For the first issue, the authors have identified four kinds of scalabilities to be satisfied [2][3]: (a) Coverage for domains of mobile services (b) Granularity of user modeling (c) Coverage for mobile services in real world (d) Coverage for mobile users' situations in which they rely on mobile services. For the item (a) and (b), we have already proposed a new ontology-based modeling method which is named OOPS (abbreviation of "Ontology-based Obstacle, Prevention and Solution).

Fig. 2 represents a process of building an OOPS model. The dotted rectangle labeled (1) corresponds to the basic model of users' activities. It is described by instantiating generic models or ontologies. Description of the OOPS model starts from the task at the level of large granularity.

Next, ways to achieve the task are linked, and each of the ways consists of a sequence of sub-tasks. Our "way" is similar to the "method" of CommonKADS [4] and "how to bundle" of the Business Process Handbook [5]. Following this process, the task of large granularity is decomposed into sub-tasks via ways. Area (1) in Fig. 2 represents that a task "Move to a theme park" is achieved by three ways. Among them, the way "Move by driving my own car" consists of three sub-tasks, "Go to the parking space", "Drive from home", and "Park the car at the parking lot".

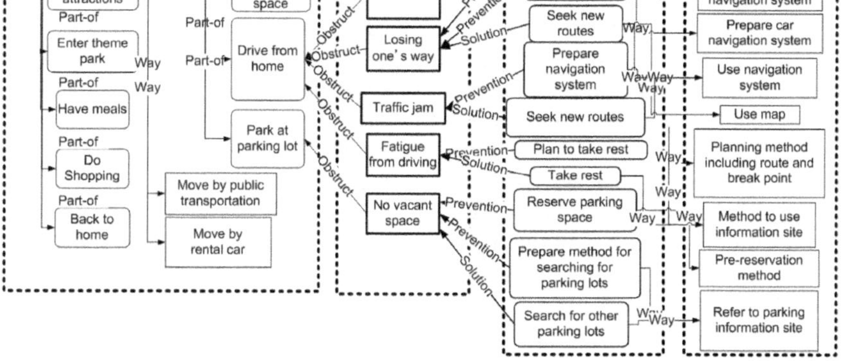

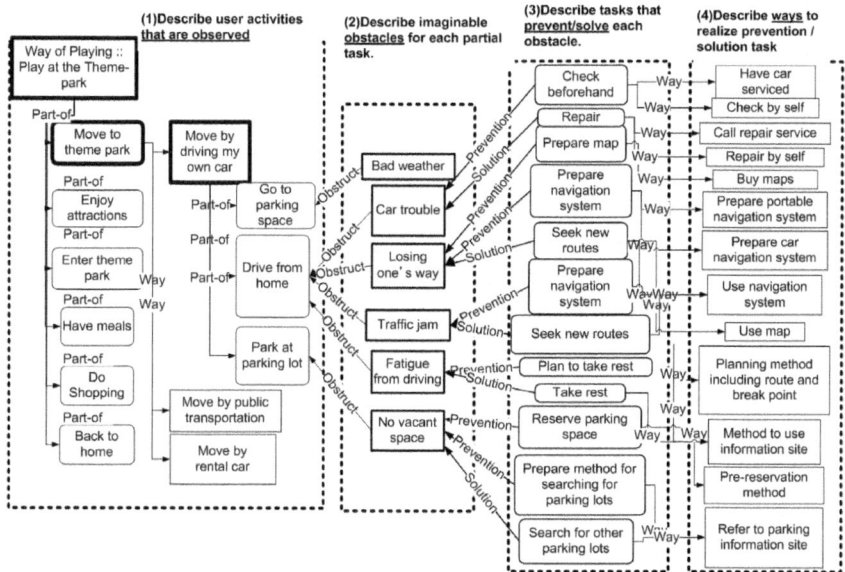

Fig. 2. The process of building OOPS models

We have designed and developed an ontology which covers users' daily tasks and necessary domain knowledge. Modeling method based on the ontology solves complicated domain modeling (i.e., (a)) and gives guidelines for granularity of the task modeling (i.e., (b)). The modeling method supports descriptions of users' activities and related knowledge, such as how to solve problems that the users encounter and how to prevent or solve them on the spot. By experiments in [3], OOPS modeling method showed performance that promotes generation of idea for modeling users' daily activities. Further details are described in [3].

4 Prototyping Real-Scale Task-Oriented Menu

In this research, we concentrated on the issue (2) as well as scalability issues of (c) and (d). For testing the coverage of mobile services and mobile users' situations (item (c) and (d)), a new menu system with real scale is definitely needed.

4.1 Analysis of User Activities

To make such a system, analysis of the user activities in a wide range of domains is required. For such analysis, we have applied the OOPS modeling method to "Tourism" domain which covers a broader spectrum of actions from traveling around and consuming money to staying at a hotel. We have evaluated the coverage of the OOPS model by comparing situations assumed and represented in the model which we developed on tourism setting with those situations assumed to be supported by current mobile services.

We have tested coverage of the model by a full set of mobile services which are available at the official sites of NTT docomo in 2004. Among about 5,000 officially authorized service sites, excluding entertainment services sites (Games, ring-tone downloading, etc), there are 2,732 sites that consist of 9,162 specific services inside. We analyzed a situation for each of the 9,162 services. Among them, our OOPS user model covered about 98% of the typical situations assumed by the mobile service sites, and just 199 services (2.17% of the 9, 162 official services) were not covered by the situations represented by our OOPS model.

4.2 Development of New Prototype System

Based on the OOPS user model, we developed a menu system with real scale. Fig.3 depicts our environment for developing the task-oriented menu, which is based on an environment by NTT docomo for building i-appli (applications for i-mode mobile handsets). On the left part of the figure, the menu we designed is displayed hierarchically.

Fig.4 depicts the first two levels of the menu. The OOPS model on tourism domain consists of 5 tasks. At first, we built a menu hierarchy where the 5 tasks are at the top level("Move", "Have meal", "Have fun", "Buy" and "Stay overnights"). Those at the second level (17 items) have how users achieve the tasks, those at the third level (97 items) have subtasks which consist of methods, those at the fourth level (112 items) have obstacles which can occur when users do subtasks and those at the fifth level (445 tasks) have tasks which can prevent or solve obstacles such as "Go to somewhere", "Have meal", "Draw cash", "Buy things", and so on. As a whole, the menu consists of 5 levels at the deepest level.

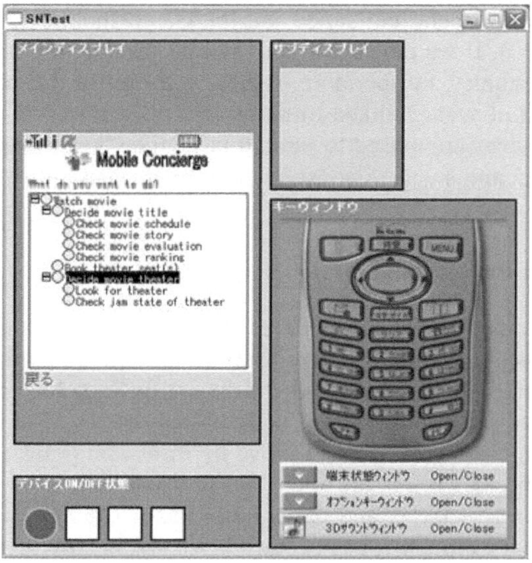

Fig. 3. Environment for developing task-oriented menu

Menu top
- Move
    - On foot
    - By public transportation
  - By taxi
    - By car
    - By rent-a-car
- Have meal
    - At a restaurant
    - Take out
    - Cook by self
- Have fun
    - By sight seeing
    - By playing at a theme park
    - By watching sports/play/etc.
- Buy
    - In a town
    - By internet shopping
    - By auction
- Stay over nights
    - Stay at a hotel
    - Stay at friends

Fig. 4. First two levels of the menu

The menu hierarchy enables users to search the mobile internet services they need if they select task, method, subtask, obstacle, and prevention/solution task in order. Then we implemented the menu system and assigned all of the officially authorized service sites. Fig.5 shows statistics about mobile services. As a result, 96% of 5,016 mobile internet services were allocated to the real-scale menu properly (Fig.5 (a)).

Although the entire menu contained 445 tasks, no mobile service is allocated to 100 tasks (Fig.5, (b)). If we develop a new mobile service for such tasks, it will be a new business opportunity. Furthermore, issues on usability still remain. For example, 11 % of task menu items are linked to more than 50 services. A cause of this is that today's mobile services are biased to limited tasks like "know weather forecast", "get movie information", and so on. Also we plan to do other usability tests without limitations of task and domain.

4.3 Separation of Prevention and Solution Tasks

The authors have considered that there are two situations when users need mobile services. The one is the situations where users want to prevent problems they encountered, and the other is the situations where they want to solve problems. We should have clearly divided the two situations and applied the result to the menu hierarchy. For example, when users who want to move by train cannot take it because the seats are not available and they select the node "No seat available", we can find the prevention task "Make a reservation" and the solution task "Change transportation". When the problem "no seat available"; has occurred already, however, users would be upset because they cannot make a reservation for the seats after they have been fully booked. This means the menu hierarchy should show the node "Make a reservation" before the problem occurs.

Therefore we have developed the menu system where users can select "before problems" or "after problems" at the first step, following which they can find services which suit their situation. For the example mentioned above, when users select the node "Seat not available" they can find the prevention task "Make a reservation" if they choose "before problems" and the solution task "Change transportation" if they choose "after problems" at the first step.

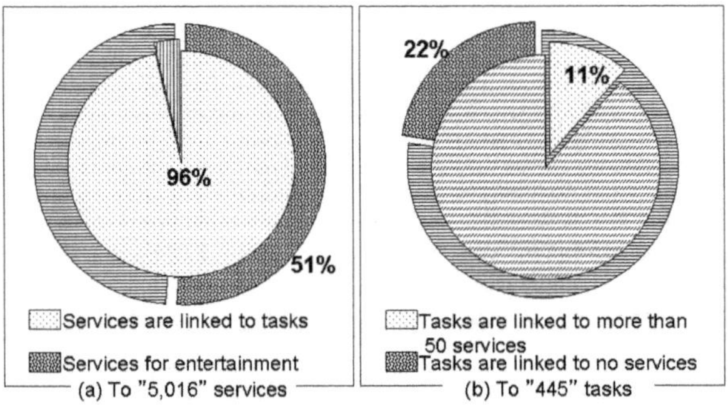

Fig. 5. Statistics about service contents

4.4 Process of Mobile Service Navigation

Fig.6 shows screen shots of the developed system. When a user selects one of them (e.g. "Move") to achieve the current goal (e.g., "go to a shop"), methods which can achieve the task are unfolded. By selecting an item among the menu, tasks and subtasks associated with each task are unfolded and displayed under the task nodes.

Finally, at the deepest level of the menu, each of the menu items is linked with a URL of an internet service like "City map service".

Suppose a scenario that a user wants to go to a shop by public transportation system. Fig.6 depicts a sample process of service selection using screen shots of the menu system of the latest version. First, the most abstract task candidates are shown on the mobile phone (Fig.6, Upper-left). Since the user wants to go to the shop by public transportation system, he/she selects one of them (e.g. "Move") to achieve the current goal (go to a shop). Then, five methods which can achieve the task "Move" are unfolded (Fig.6 Upper-right). By selecting the second item among the menu (e.g., "By public transportation"), tasks and/or subtasks associated with each task are unfolded and displayed under the task nodes (Fig.6, Lower-left). Selecting tasks further, plausible obstacles for the subtasks and their solution tasks are unfolded (Fig.6 Lower-right). The user might lose his/her way to a ticket station, for example. In that case, selecting such a troublesome situation among the menu items, solutions for the trouble are unfolded (e.g., "Find a ticket information" and "Seek for a route map" in Fig.6). Finally, services associated with the task selected by the user are shown, and each of them leads to access to the actual service.

4.5 Design Review by Experts

Our new prototype menu system is now under the design review by experts of mobile services. Compared to the original menu system prototyped by Naganuma [1], they positively point out followings.

(1) Granularity of the menu has become uniform. Since original menu was an ad hoc one, granularities of some menu items were coarse and others were fine. As a result, understandability of the menu has become better.

(2) Since the new menu system is composed of finer grained menu items, users who have definite purpose (e.g., go to a department store to buy cloths) will be guided more easily to the target information services.

(3) Those services which are not utilized before are "revealed" and are able to access now. Some television companies, for example, provide information about recipes introduced within their TV programs. Since their sites have been in the "TV" category before, some users should miss the recipes because they cannot imagine TV companies provide such recipes. New menu system guides to the recipes by "Have meal (task) > Cook by self (method) > Look for recipes (sub-task)". Then links for recipes are listed including those provided by the TV companies.

5 Social Network Services as a Knowledge Resource

Since valuable knowledge are generated and accumulated on variety of SNS services such as Wikipedia, Twitter, Blog, and so on, appropriate selection of the knowledge source should be done according to the "context" of the users. Suppose that a user plans to do a long business trip on next Monday. He/she has to survey an appropriate route, select and reserve a train, buy tickets, and do the trip. When the user wants to select the route, he/she should refer to the encyclopedia-like knowledge resource from which we can get a quick overview of things. Wikipedia would play the role. On the other hand, if he/she needs dynamic information on the way to the destination, such as train situation of local trains near the destination, Twitter, on which people always tweet the latest information might play the role.

Our service navigation framework based on OOPS model has potential to indicate the knowledge resource suitable for the users' context. Task model of "Reservation of the seat of the train", for example, is a prevention task to avoid occurrence of the obstacle "The train is full and cannot sit down". Since such preventive tasks are always carried out before the execution of the main task, i.e., goes to the business trip, we can set a heuristic rule reasonably: "For the users seeking information to do preventive task, "static" information services like Wikipedia should be preferred." On the other hand, solution tasks which are carried out when certain problems occur on the spot, dynamic information is should be preferred more to solve the problem on the spot. To solve a problem "Train services are temporally not available", for example, real-time tweets about train situation on Twitter should be helpful for users. Referring to such preferences about the information resources, our task-oriented service navigation system will be able to recommend suitable social network services to users who seek for solution.

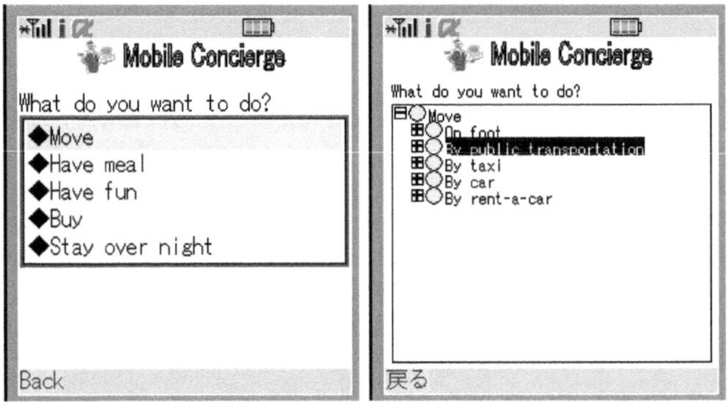

(Left)Top menu: "Move" task is selected by user. (Right) Five methods for "Move" are unfolded and "By public transportation" method is selected.

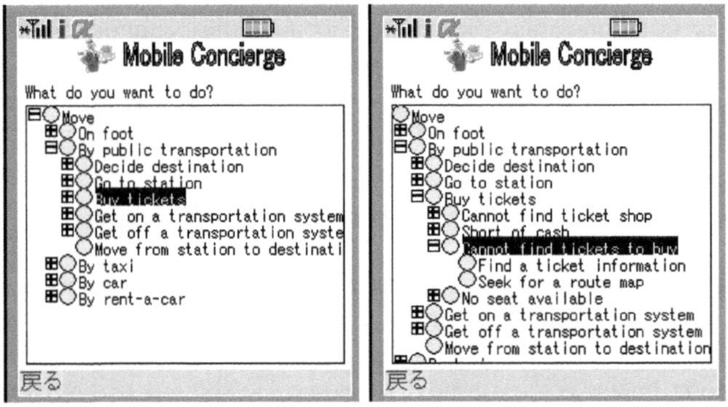

(Left)Subtasks of "move by public transportation" are unfolded. (Right) Plausible obstacles for the subtasks and their solution tasks are unfolded.

Fig. 6. Sample screen shots

6 Related Work

Boreum et al. investigated which factors of mobile internet services are important for users [6]. They interviewed people from three countries, Japan, Korea, and Finland, which have mature mobile internet service markets. According to their analysis, both the "logical order of the menu" and "meaningful classification of the contents" are considered to be important by many subjects from the three countries. The results validate our approach for improving the menu system and classification of the contents by user tasks, which should contribute to user satisfaction.

To satisfy users' needs, many researchers today focus on better composition of existing mobile internet services. Our modeling method, which focuses on better analysis of users' needs, is able to strengthen the research explained in the following. Hierarchical Task Network planning (a general explanation is given in [7], and applications for web services are described in [8]) supports how to divide and conquer a web user's "problem", which resembles our task decomposition process in OOPS modeling. In the process of composing web services, Motahari-Nexhad [9] proposes how to identify mismatches of the interfaces and protocols between two services to be composed. Domingue [10] describes how to cope with heterogeneous interaction patterns with the framework of IRS-III, and Ashri [11] discusses the interaction protocols in their experience of IRS-II. In such an organization process, alignment of the ontologies behind the services is necessary. Omelayenko [12] proposes a method for mapping meta-ontologies among web services, and Ehrig [13] describes a machine-learning method for an initial stage of ontology alignment. Tsz-Chiu Au [14] points out that it is unrealistic to assume that the information provided by the web services is static in many cases. They propose another framework to deal with volatile information, taking a ticket reservation service problem as an example.

These studies, however, do not consider the contents of the mobile internet services. In contrast, our approach starts from analyzing users' activities, including problematic situations which require mobile internet services. We then design the menu system for user navigation based upon the user model. Most research on web services implicitly assumes that web browsing is done on desktop computers; thus, the time and cost involved in searching and evaluating the answers are not of much concern. On the other hand, in the case of our mobile internet service problem, users need prompt answers. Thus, we pay attention to navigating users directly from the obstacles which they face to the proper service which is the source of the answer. We leave evaluation of the answers to the users themselves.

Masuoka proposed a Task Computing framework and built a ubiquitous environment which provides more than 100 web services [15]. The web services are described by OWL-S, and the environment changes dynamically. The ubiquitous environment is unique because it deals with dynamic changes such as sudden appearance/ disappearance of clients/services, like the real world.

MIT's Process Handbook Project [5] deals with knowledge models about businesses. It focuses on modeling business activities and has a taxonomy of basic business activities. However, the method for building the model is implicit, and confusion of task concepts with way concepts occurs with some models. One of the models, "buy in a store", consists of a task concept "buy" and a way concept "in a store", for example. Such confusion lowers the generality of the model, and does not meet our requirements.

In the field of the human–computer interactions, although there are many studies about web interfaces, there are not so many studies specific to mobile phones. James [16] compares the efficiency of two text input methods used on mobile phone: multitap and prediction. Kamvar [17] analyzed search patterns of a search engine specifically designed for mobile internet services on a large scale. The search patterns resembled those of desktop search engines. The results show that mobile internet services are still not organized well for mobile users. The users rely on search engines, as they do on desktop computers, since they cannot reach the necessary services. As mentioned in section 1, basically task-oriented menu system navigates users along with their necessity of the services, thus not so much depends on search technologies.

7 Conclusion and Future Work

This paper introduced our research on the task-oriented menu system with real-scale mobile internet services in it, as well as its possibility to work with SNS. Now the system is under the design review by experts and we plan to do field test by general users of mobile phones in longer term.

Furthermore, we plan to improve user interface for the task-oriented menu system. First, it is unrealistic to replace everything with a task-oriented style; rather, integration of a search engine and/or domain-oriented classification will be necessary for some tasks. For example, the task "buy" deals with millions of items which require conventional search technologies.

Secondly, we are designing "shortcut" menus for some frequently accessible services. The menu hierarchy has some subtasks which frequently appear under different tasks. Such subtasks are possible to be carried out as not only subtasks associated with each task but also independent tasks. For example, if users who want to draw cash to buy train tickets intend to search services about ATM information, in the current menu system, they must select "Move", "By public transportation", "Buy tickets", "Short of cash", "Draw cash" and "Search ATM" step by step. Although the task oriented menu system can support users to search for the ATM services to solve problems, the shortcut menu should be a good help for users because the services for drawing cash are necessary in many other situations. Therefore, we have been trying to define the problems which happen frequently and build the shortcut menu for such services.

Lastly, we plan to utilize SNS as resource of knowledge and solution for users. Each SNS services has both strong point and weak point, appropriate recommendation along with user's context should be helpful.

References

1. Naganuma, T., Kurakake, S.: Task Knowledge Based Retrieval for Services Relevant to Mobile User's Activity. In: Gil, Y., Motta, E., Benjamins, V.R., Musen, M.A. (eds.) ISWC 2005. LNCS, vol. 3729, pp. 959–973. Springer, Heidelberg (2005)
2. Sasajima, M., Kitamura, Y., Naganuma, T., Kurakake, S., Mizoguchi, R.: Task Ontology-Based Framework for Modeling Users' Activities for Mobile Service Navigation. In: Sure, Y., Domingue, J. (eds.) ESWC 2006. LNCS, vol. 4011, pp. 71–72. Springer, Heidelberg (2006)

3. Sasajima, M., Kitamura, Y., Naganuma, T., Fujii, K., Kurakake, S., Mizoguchi, R.: Obstacles Reveal the Needs of Mobile Internet Services -OOPS: Ontology-Based Obstacle, Prevention, and Solution Modeling Framework. J. of Web Engineering 7(2), 133–157 (2008)
4. Schreiber, G., Akkermans, H., Anjewierden, A., de Hoog, R., Shadbolt, N., de Velde, W.V., Wielinga, B.: Knowledge Engineering and Management - The CommonKADS Methodology. MIT Press, Cambridge (2000)
5. Malone, T.W., Crowston, K., Herman, G.A.: Organizing Business Knowledge - The MIT Process Hand Book. MIT Press, Cambridge (2003)
6. Choi, B., Lee, I., Kim, J., Jeon, Y.: A Qualitative Cross-National Study of Cultural Influences on Mobile Data Service Design. In: Proc. of the SIGCHI conference on Human factors in computing systems, CHI 2005, pp. 661–670 (2005)
7. Kambhampati, S.: Refinement Planning as a Unifying Framework for Plan Synthesis. AI Magazine, 67–97 (summer 1997)
8. Kuter, U., Sirin, E., Nau, D., Parsia, B., Hendler, J.: Information gathering during planning for web service composition. J. of Web Semantics 3(2-3), 183–205 (2005)
9. Motahari-Nexhad, H.R., Martens, A., Curbera, F., Casati, F.: Semi-Automated Adaptation of Service Interactions. In: Proc. of WWW 2007, pp. 993–1002 (2007)
10. Domingue, J., Galizia, S., Cabral, L.: Choreography in IRS-III- Coping with Heterogeneous Interaction Patterns in Web Services. In: Gil, Y., Motta, E., Benjamins, V.R., Musen, M.A. (eds.) ISWC 2005. LNCS, vol. 3729, pp. 171–185. Springer, Heidelberg (2005)
11. Ashri, R., Denker, G., Marvin, D., Surridge, M., Payne, T.: Semantic Web Service Interaction Protocols: An Ontological Approach. In: McIlraith, S.A., Plexousakis, D., van Harmelen, F. (eds.) ISWC 2004. LNCS, vol. 3298, pp. 304–319. Springer, Heidelberg (2004)
12. Omelayenko, B.: RDFT: A Mapping Meta-Ontology for Web Service Integration. In: Omelayenko, B., Klein, M. (eds.) Knowledge Transformation for the Semantic Web, pp. 137–153. IOS Press, Amsterdam (2003)
13. Ehrig, M., Staab, S., Sure, Y.: Bootstrapping Ontology Alignment Methods with APFEL. In: Gil, Y., Motta, E., Benjamins, V.R., Musen, M.A. (eds.) ISWC 2005. LNCS, vol. 3729, pp. 186–200. Springer, Heidelberg (2005)
14. Au, T., Kuter, U., Nau, D.: Web Service Composition with Volatile information. In: Gil, Y., Motta, E., Benjamins, V.R., Musen, M.A. (eds.) ISWC 2005. LNCS, vol. 3729, pp. 52–66. Springer, Heidelberg (2005)
15. Masuoka, R., Parsia, B., Labrou, Y.: Task Computing - The Semantic Web Meets Pervasive Computing. In: Fensel, D., Sycara, K., Mylopoulos, J. (eds.) ISWC 2003. LNCS, vol. 2870, pp. 866–881. Springer, Heidelberg (2003)
16. James, C.L., Reischel, K.M.: Text Input for Mobile Devices: Comparing Model Prediction to Actual Performance. In: Proc. of CHI 2001, pp. 365–371 (2001)
17. Kamvar, M., Baluja, S.: A Large Scale Study of Wireless Search Behavior: Google Mobile Search. In: Proc. of CHI 2006, pp. 701–709 (2006)

Tag Disambiguation through Flickr and Wikipedia

Anastasia Stampouli[1], Eirini Giannakidou[1,2], and Athena Vakali[1]

[1] Aristotle University of Thessaloniki, Department of Informatics, 54124 Thessaloniki, Greece
{astampou,eirgiann,avakali}@csd.auth.gr
[2] Centre of Research & Technology - Hellas
Informatics and Telematics Institute
6th km Harilaou - Thermi, 57001, Thessaloniki, Greece
igiannak@iti.gr

Abstract. Given the popularity of social tagging systems and the limitations these systems have, due to lack of any structure, a common issue that arises involves the low retrieval quality in such systems due to ambiguities of certain terms. In this paper, an approach for improving the retrieval in these systems, in case of ambiguous terms, is presented that attempts to perform tag disambiguation and, at the same time, provide users with relevant content. The idea is based on a mashup that combines data and functionality of two major web 2.0 sites, namely Flickr and Wikipedia and aims at enhancing content retrieval for web users. A case study with the ambiguous notion "Apple" illustrates the value of the proposed approach.

Keywords: term disambiguation, flickr, Wikipedia, DBpedia project, mashup.

1 Introduction

With the development of social tagging systems a great amount of information was created in a relatively short time interval. This led a lot of researchers to think of various ways in which they could exploit this kind of information for various aims. However, an issue that emerges regarding this information that comes from many users is that it can be interpreted in many different ways because of its clearly subjective character. This subjective character is based on the fact that in most systems of such type users select the labels (i.e. tags) that they use, in order to characterize/describe digital objects, without any control over the procedure of choice through some concrete vocabulary.

An important issue that arises in such systems that the users have the possibility of selecting freely the tags that they use is the disambiguation of certain notions. The meaning of the tags may be obvious for the author but not for all the other users. Thus, because of the ambiguous character of tag information, a need was identified for combination of information from various sources of data, so that the information that is provided in the users has a more valid character and better quality results are produced in the various user queries. A solution towards that direction was the creation of mashups (i.e. concurrent use of information from multiple social data sources for users' benefit). The applications that are based in mashups do not receive static

M. Yoshikawa et al. (Eds.): DASFAA 2010, LNCS 6193, pp. 252–263, 2010.

information but high quality processed elements that render the user information more useful. There are certain examples of tags that are used as a basis for the development of mashups which support in an efficient way the interconnection between the sources of information and operations concerning the management of their content [1].

The idea of creating customized applications (i.e. mashups) to use interlinked web 2.0 content and improve retrieval quality in social sites is often seen in various approaches [2]. Beyond this, there are also approaches that aim at resolving tag ambiguities and achieving better retrieval rates, by analyzing the tag space or using external resources [3, 4, 5].

In this paper, a mashup idea is presented that attempts to perform tag disambiguation and, at the same time, provide users with relevant content. The mashup combines data and functionality of two major web 2.0 sites, namely Flickr and Wikipedia and aims at enhancing content retrieval for web users. The rest of the paper is organized as follows. In the next section, a description of the "mashup" term is given, along with some indicative examples of successful and, currently, well adopted by users mashups that use either Flickr or Wikipedia. The proposed mashup framework is presented, in detail, in Section 3. Experimental results with real datasets follow and illustrate the value of the approach. Finally, the paper concludes with some conclusions and some ideas for future research.

2 Mashups

Mashups have recently gained special attention as concerns to the creativity that is included in their development and their functionality with regard to the users. Substantially, a mashup is a combination of data that are found in the World Wide Web via some processing. If we consider that the web is constituted by levels (the *physical* one that is referred to the equipment, the *logical* one that is referred to the communication protocols, the *data* level that is referred to the content and the *social* one that is referred to users and applications), then, the mashups are classified between the data level and the social one [6]. In this way, mashups achieve to change the way that the users are related to the content of web sites.

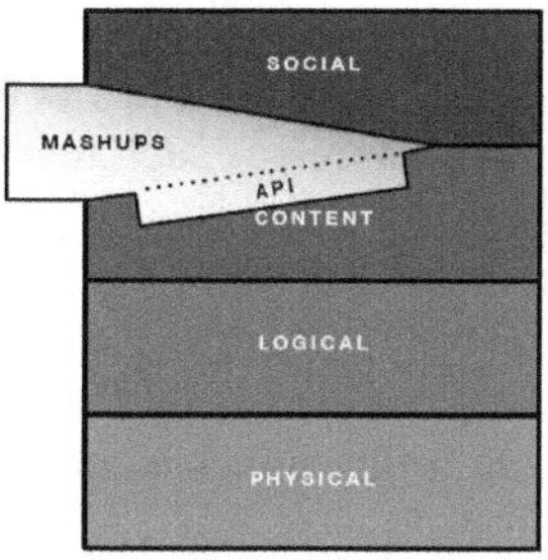

Fig. 1. Mashups in the web levels hierarchy ([6])

In web development the term mashup is defined as a web application which combines data that originate from more from than one source in one functionally completed tool. The term mashup implies easy and quick incorporation which is realized mainly with access to APIs and to sources of data aiming at the production of more relevant results. The mashup developers use in a dynamic way data from a source and incorporate them in another application. This intra-application communication sparks interoperability concerns. Most developers of web 2.0 sites address these concerns by offering compatible technologies (e.g. APIs), web services and other tools that allow the users to create mashups [6].

A lot of users experiment with mashups using sources of information such as Microsoft, Google, eBay, Amazon, Flickr, Facebook and APIs of Yahoo [6]. As the majority of web users, in the past few years, have begun exploiting the services of the web in a way that approaches more their daily activities, a lot of mashups have been deployed towards this direction. Below we will report some of the basic mashups that have been created in the past few years, so that we can have a better view in reference to this phenomenon which is considered to be one of the technology trends that will shape the future web. Mainly, we focused on mashups that use Wikipedia, DBpedia and Flickr which are related immediately to our work.

Wikipedia Mashups. An example of such a mashup is Wikipedia Vision[1] that is a mashup in which for each wikipedia edit a box is displayed in a world map with the title of the article, the summary of the edit and other information such as geographical location of the Wikipedia user and the time the edit happened. The social resources utilized in this mashup are Wikipedia and Google Maps.

Flickr Mashups. It is observed that there are a lot of mashups that have been structured based on Flickr API. It should be placed emphasis on Flickr Wrappr[2] which is a mashup that combines data from DBpedia and Flickr that are two sources of information used in the development of the mashup, presented in this paper. Flickr Wrappr combines geographic information and assigns them in tags from Flickr and Wikipedia aiming at the favoring of pictures from Flickr which have high correlation with the notion that is relevant to the search of the user. Other examples of mashups that are based on Flickr are Flickr Mania[3], Flickr Fight[4], Feelimage[5], Semapedia[6], InSuggest[7], Flicktionary[8], etc.

DBpedia mashups. The basic idea in these mashups is to exploit the structured data offered by the DBpedia project. An example of such mashups is DBpedia Mobile that locates in the map locations that exist in DBpedia and gives the user the possibility of exploring relative information that exists for these places [7].

---

[1] Wikipedia Vision: http://www.lkozma.net/wpv/
[2] Flickr Wrappr: http://www4.wiwiss.fu-berlin.de/flickrwrappr/
[3] Flickr Mania: http://www.flickrmania.com/
[4] Flickr Fight: http://flickrfight.net/
[5] Feelimage: http://www.feelimage.net
[6] Semapedia: http://en.semapedia.org/
[7] InSuggest: http://www.insuggest.com/
[8] Flicktionary: http://imagine-it.org/flickr/flicktionary.htm

3 Framework Description

In this work we present a mashup that connects DBpedia with Flickr, in an effort to combine information that provides DBpedia with the information that is provided by the tags that are assigned to the photos of Flickr. This convergence aims at improving the retrieval quality and, thus, returning more relevant results to various user queries in Flickr site.

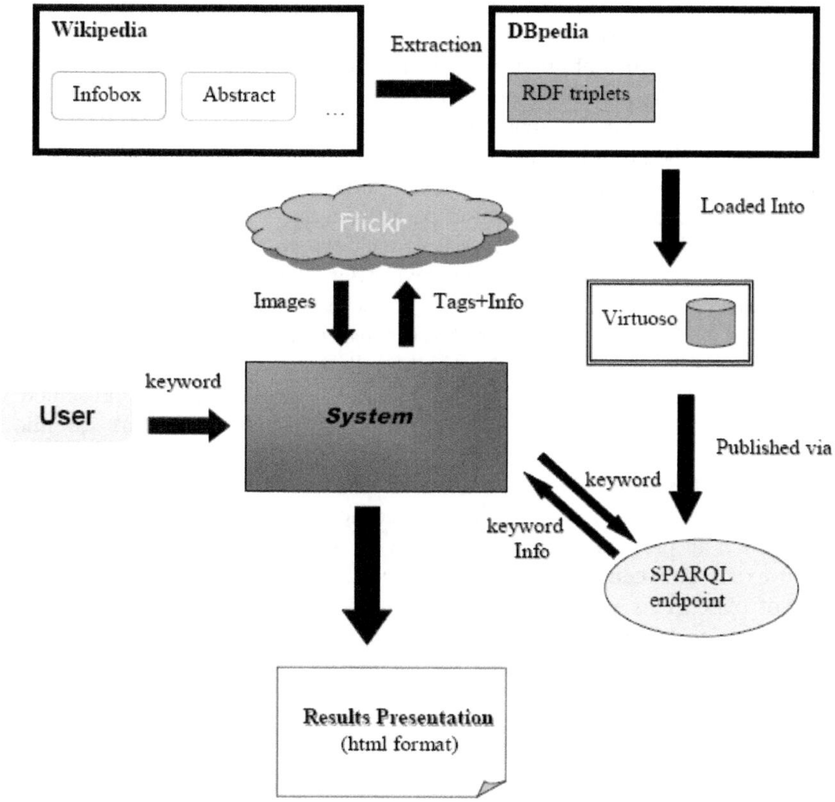

Fig. 2. Proposed framework overview

As it is widely known, Flickr constitutes one of the largest world sources of published photographs. It gives the opportunity to the users to characterize their photos with tags. Aiming at the facilitation of the user, there are not strictly determined rules for the potentially used tags. That is to say, there are no restrictions with regard to the name, the level of detail, as well as the relativity of tags. As a consequence, disambiguation may arise in cases, such as when certain photos are characterized with tags that are referred to general terms. To ensure better retrieval, users often use multiple related tags to describe a resource, which results in tag redundancy.

To the same extend with Flickr, as popularity is concerned, Wikipedia constitutes an enormous collection of semi-structured content from which the project of DBpedia.org extracts structured information. Here we will focus on a special functionality offered by Wikipedia, the so-called *term disambiguation*. With the term disambiguation in Wikipedia we refer to the activity of resolution of conflicts that result from the titles of articles in Wikipedia. These conflicts occur when a term is connected with more than one subjects, therefore this term is likely to appear in the title of more than one articles. In such cases, there must be a way that redirects the user in the page of a certain article that corresponds to the correct sense of the notion. What is reported above is widely known in Wikipedia as disambiguation. For example the term Texas appears to more than 20 different entities in Wikipedia such as university, musical album etc. The term disambiguation in Wikipedia enables the user to select the exact sense of Texas he/she is looking information for.

The system we present here materializes the interconnection of DBpedia and Flickr, in an effort to tackle the disambiguation issue that worsens the retrieval in Flickr. In Figure 2, the developed system is described graphically, along with the tools that were used in the proposed implementation. When the user performs a query at Flickr, a SPARQL query is executed via the DBpedia public SPARQL endpoint to the DBpedia data source. The DBpedia data source is hosted and published using OpenLink Virtuoso RDF Store. The SPARQL query returns the various senses of the user query terms. Then, an individual query is posed in Flickr for each different sense and the user gets Flickr photos grouped by the various senses. A more detailed description follows.

First of all, we will describe the way the Wikipedia data is represented in the DBpedia project. Each notion in DBpedia is found at a link of the form *http://dbpedia.org/page/Resource* where Resource is the name of the corresponding notion. In this particular page certain basic information that refers to the specific notion is included, in RDF triplets. More specifically, there is a column named "property" in which all predicates are recorded. With the term predicate we define the relation that exists between the basic notion and the values that are found in the right column of page. This way, the information that the DBpedia project extracts from Wikipedia for each notion exists in structured form. Therefore, the user is given the possibility of having access in these data via queries expressed in SPARQL.

As mentioned above, there is a term disambiguation page in Wikipedia for each basic notion, where there are links that redirect the users to pages describing each one of the ambiguous senses of the specified notion. The predicate (i.e. property) that is used to refer to the various senses of a notion, in the DBpedia project, is named `dbpprop:disambiguates`. In this property a list of disambiguations is included, that is substantially links that lead to the various senses of the particular senses.

Below, we quote a SPARQL query that returns the various senses of the notion `Paris`.

```
PREFIX rdfs: <http://www.w3.org/2000/01/rdf-schema#>
      SELECT DISTINCT ?label ?disambiguates  WHERE {
          dbpedia:Paris dbpprop:disambiguates ?disambiguates .
          ?disambiguates rdfs:label ?label.
          FILTER(lang(?label) = "en").
```

The results of the above SPARQL query include all the various ambiguous senses of the notion in question. More specifically, for each of these senses a list of related words that describe each particular sense is returned. Then, a preprocessing occurs that removes special characters from the returned words, such as parentheses and commas. Finally, each list contains labels that are supposed to characterize a photograph wrt a particular significance of the initial concept-notion. Such lists of words constitute tag lists that are given as input to the `flick.photos.search` Flick API function.

The user may define the number of the pictures that he/she wants to be returned for each of the disambiguations. The results are stored in an xml file that includes information for all the photographs that are returned from the search in Flickr and fulfill certain criteria that are defined by the user and concern the certain sense of the initial word (notion). Moreover, these photographs are stored in jpeg format at a certain user-defined path, and they are also presented in thumbnail format at html pages, grouped by each sense. In that way the user has the complete monitoring of the returned results.

4 Experimentation

To study the retrieval quality of our proposed approach, we tested with various ambiguous notions, such as paris, jaguar, apple, bush and many others. The results were satisfying, as the script returned photos grouped by sense. Here, we demonstrate a case study, where user wants to discover the possible disambiguation of the word Apple. The DBpedia page for the particular notion is *http://dbpedia.org/resource/Apple*. In Figure 3, the various senses extracted from Wikipedia and related to Apple notion appear[9].

dbpprop:disambiguates	▪ dbpedia:Apple_%28automobile%29
	▪ dbpedia:Apple_Corps
	▪ dbpedia:Apple_River
	▪ dbpedia:Apple_%28band%29
	▪ dbpedia:Apple_Inc.
	▪ dbpedia:Apples%2C_Vaud
	▪ dbpedia:Apple_%28album%29
	▪ dbpedia:Apple_Cup
	▪ dbpedia:Apple_Daily
	▪ dbpedia:Apple_Records
	▪ dbpedia:Apple_Store_%28online%29
	▪ dbpedia:Apple_Valley
	▪ dbpedia:Apple_Bank
	▪ dbpedia:Apple_Store_%28retail%29
	▪ dbpedia:Apple_Brook
	▪ dbpedia:Apple_Inc.%5D%5D_since_1976'

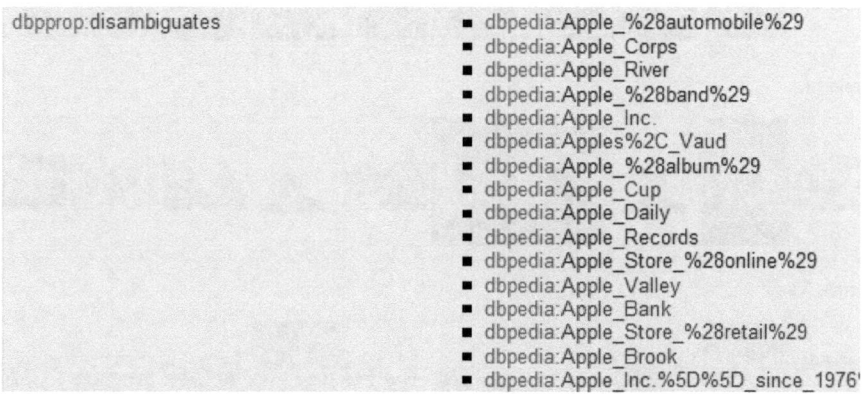

Fig. 3. Values of DBpedia `dbprop:disambiguates` property for the word Apple

---

[9] Some of them it is likely not to have the property `rdfs:label` therefore they will not be presented in the results in the html page.

After the processing of the `dbprop:disambiguates` property values (as described in the previous section), we perform one query to Flickr for each different sense of the word Apple. In Figure 4, the Flickr results for these queries are given, that is to say the photographs that were returned as relevant for each different sense.

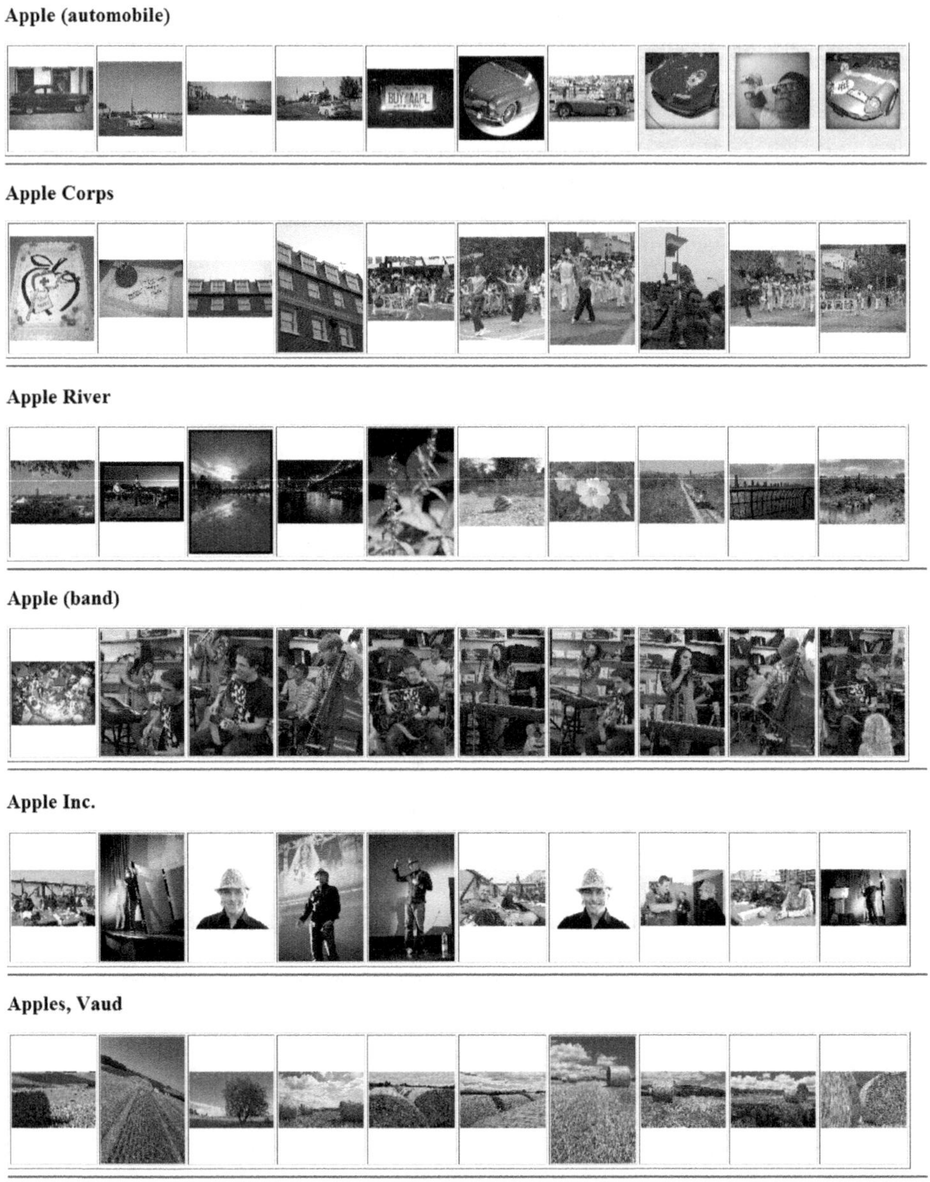

Fig. 4. Flickr photos related to "Apple" grouped by sense meaning, after DBpedia information exploitment (no further processing)

Fig. 4. *(continued)*

These results were returned when the search for the relevant photographs in the site of Flickr is conducted with criterion each photograph to be characterized with the total of the tags that corresponds in each sense. It is observed that for certain senses the photographs that are returned from Flickr are highly relevant with the subject, such as Apple (automobile), Apple (band), Apples, Vaud etc. However for certain senses the photographs that are returned are not highly relevant with the real meaning of the particular sense. Some cases of this kind of search are Apple Daily, Apple Cup and Apple Inc. For example, in the case of "Apple Daily" which is a newspaper that is published in Hong-Kong, the search that was conducted in Flickr for photographs that would be characterized with both tags (Apple and Daily) did not return any relevant results. This happened because these two tags are possible to be assigned in photographs that depict other relevant things. As an example for the above case might be a photograph that depict the fruit apple and it has been also assigned with the tag "daily" while it could depict a daily moment from the life of person.

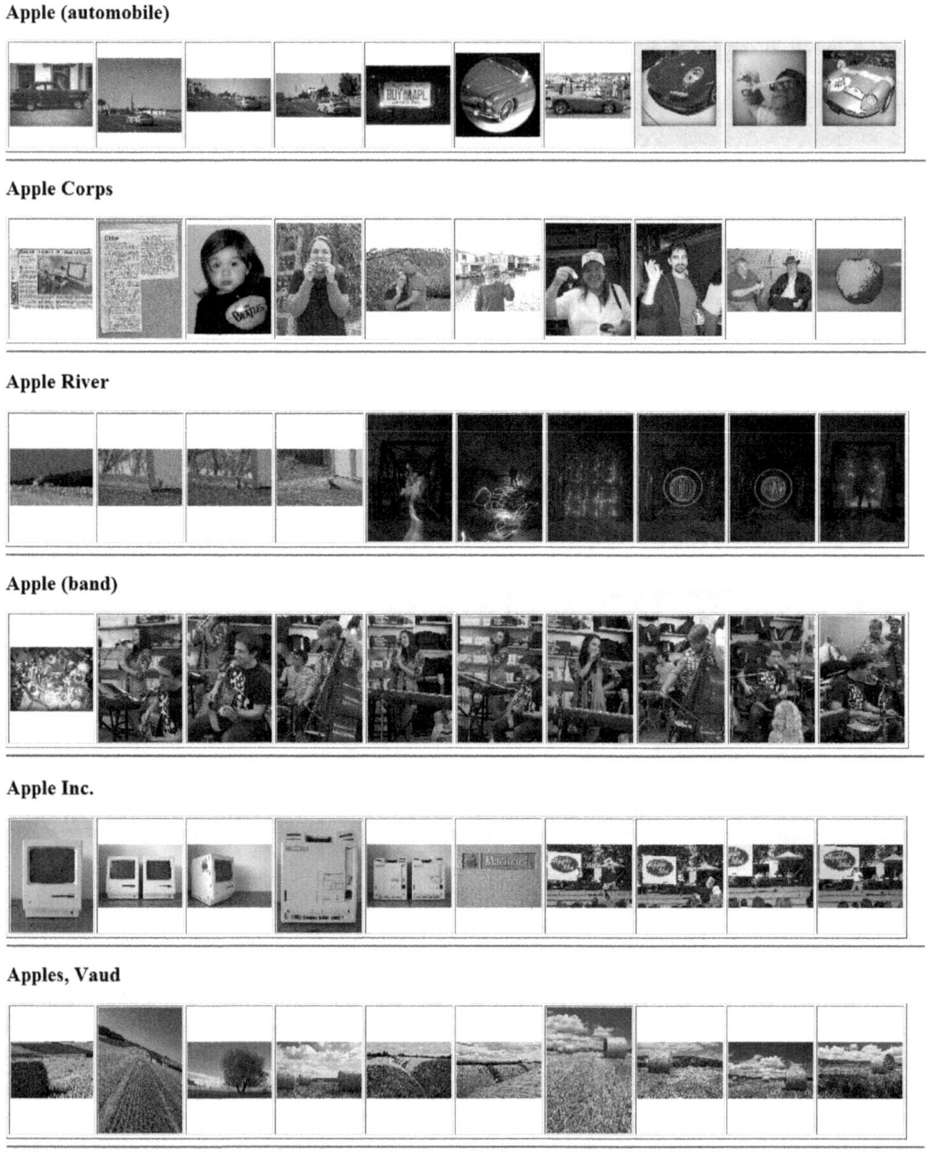

Fig. 5. Flickr photos related to "Apple" grouped by sense meaning, after DBpedia information exploitment (**with** further processing)

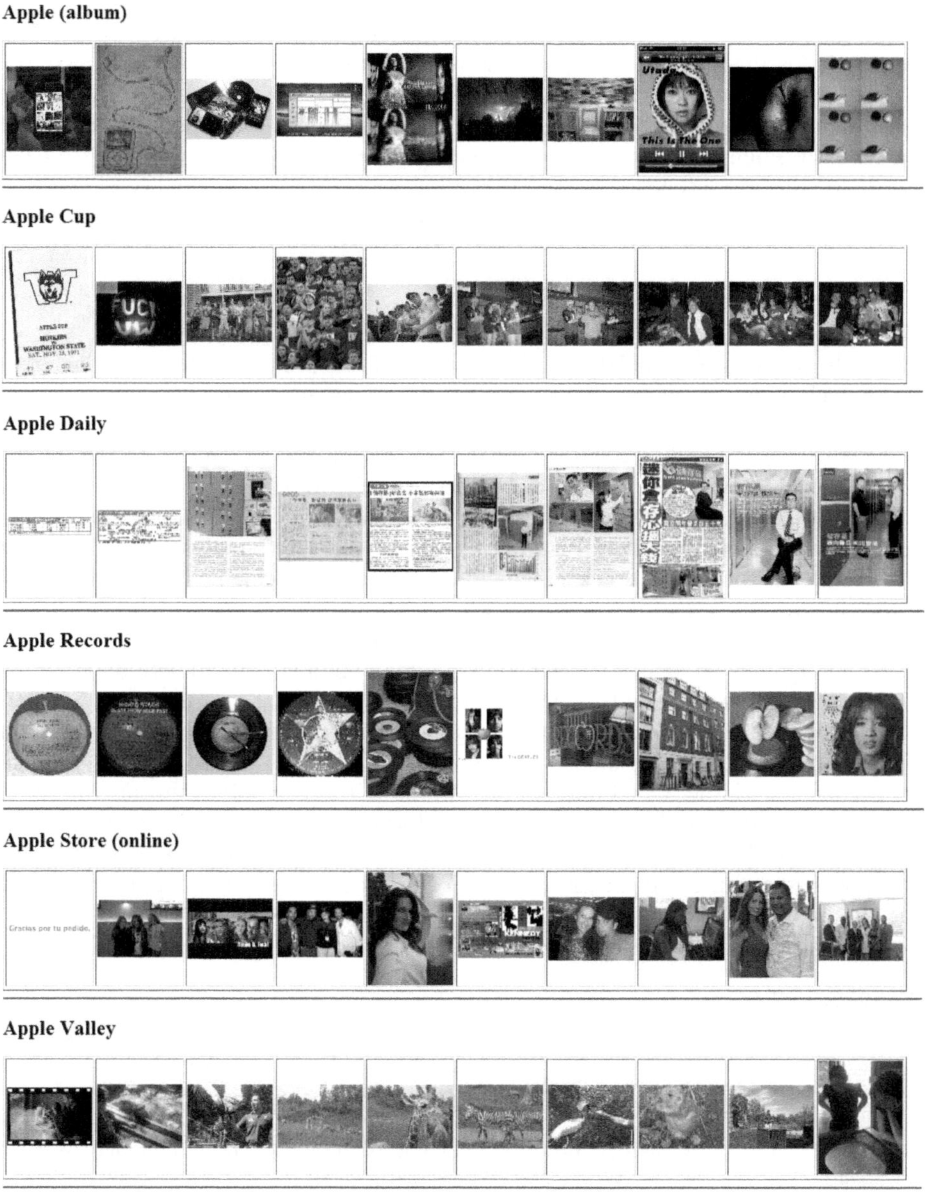

Fig. 5. *(continued)*

After the preprocessing that we applied that concerns the removal of special characters and the joint use of words that describe one sense as a single tag in the Flickr query, we get the results that appear in Figure 5. The difference in the retrieval between the two cases is observed especially in senses that the words that describe them are separated from each other with a void. For example, in the case of "Apple Cup" sense, in the first case where the search was conducted with two tags (`Apple' and 'Cup') the results do not approach at all the real meaning of the concept Apple Cup. Apple Cup is the annual football's game between the two biggest universities in the United States. In the second case is observed that after the code modification that result in a search with only one tag (`Apple Cup') the results correspond completely in the actual meaning of "Apple Cup" according to DBpedia. The described case study illustrates that the proposed framework achieves high retrieval quality in terms of grouping together really relevant Flickr photos, in case of ambiguous terms.

5 Conclusions

Given the popularity of social tagging systems and the limitations these systems have, due to lack of any structure, we presented in this paper an approach for improving the retrieval in these systems, in case of ambiguous terms. The developed system may also contribute in familiarizing the user with various senses of a given notion, as they are described in Wikipedia, and may be used in order to inform users for a particular sense of the word. It can also be used as a presentation tool that describes each sense of an ambiguous term with optical means via the relevant photographs from Flickr. Furthermore it could be used as a recommendation system which will be embedded in a site such as Flickr, and it would help users in the choice of relevant tags by proposing tags relative with the various senses of a certain word.

As ambiguities are bound to happen very often in non-structured text, the proposed approach may, also, be used in the text processing domain, to resolve ambiguities of particular terms. For as long as natural language terms are used, without any formal or other representation that embeds structural linkage between terms, term disambiguation remains an issue. Our future work towards this aim involves testing with other sources, apart from DBpedia, for gaining information about various senses of ambiguous terms. Furthermore, we plan to extend the current framework to an approach that renders structure and semantics to data from social sites, stepping, thus, towards the direction of Web 3.0.

References

1. Hagemann, S., Vossen, G.: ActiveTags: Making Tags More Useful Anywhere on the Web. In: Proc. of the Twentieth Australasian Database Conference (ADC 2009), New Zealand (2009)
2. Bizer, C., et al.: DBpedia - A crystallization point for the Web of Data. Journal of Web Semantics: Sci. Serv. Agents World Wide Web (2009), doi:10.1016/j.websem.2009.07.002
3. Au Yeung, C.M., Gibbins, N., Shadbolt, N.: Understanding the Semantics of Ambiguous Tags in Folksonomies. In: Proc. of the International Workshop on Emergent Semantics and Ontology Evolution (ESOE 2007) at ISWC/ASWC, South Korea (2007)
4. Giannakidou, E., Koutsonikola, V., Vakali, A., Kompatsiaris, I.: Co-clustering Tags and Social Data Sources. In: Proc. of the 9th International Conference on Web-Age Information Management (WAIM 2008), China, pp. 317–324. IEEE Computer Society, Los Alamitos (2008)

5. Giannakidou, E., Kompatsiaris, I., Vakali, A.: SEMSOC: SEMantic, SOcial and Content-based Clustering in Multimedia Collaborative Tagging Systems. In: Proc. of the 2nd IEEE International Conference on Semantic Computing (ICSC 2008), CA, USA, pp. 128–135. IEEE Computer Society, Los Alamitos (2008)
6. Palfrey, J., Gasser, U.: Mashups Interoperability and eInnovation. Berkman Publication Series (2007)
7. Becker, C., Bizer, C.: DBpedia Mobile: A Location-Enabled Linked Data Browser. In: Proc. of the Linked Data on the Web (LDOW 2008), China, (2008)

Measuring Attention Intensity to Web Pages Based on Specificity of Social Tags

Takayuki Yumoto[1] and Kazutoshi Sumiya[2]

[1] Graduate School of Engineering, University of Hyogo
2167 Shosha, Himeji, Hyogo 671-2280, Japan
yumoto@eng.u-hyogo.ac.jp

[2] School of Human Science and Environment, University of Hyogo
1–1–12 Shinzaike-honcho, Himeji, Hyogo 670-0092, Japan
sumiya@shse.u-hyogo.ac.jp

Abstract. Social bookmarks are used to find Web pages drawing much attention. However, tendency of pages to collect bookmarks is different by their topic. Therefore, the number of bookmarks can be used to know attention intensity to pages but it cannot be used as the metric of the intensity itself. We define the relative quantity of social bookmarks (RQS) for measuring the attention intensity to a Web page. The RQS is calculated using the number of social bookmarks of related pages. Related pages are found using similarity based on specificity of social tags. We define two types of specificity, local specificity, which is the specificity for a user, and global, which is the specificity common in a social bookmark service.

1 Introduction

Recently, social bookmarks are not only used to save private bookmarks on the Web but also for users to be notified of popular or interesting Web pages, therefore, the number of social bookmarks is an important metric. This number, however, depends on not only the quality of Web pages but also users' interests in the social bookmark service. Suppose that there are two pages A and B. The topic of page A is popular and the topic of page B is not popular. In this case, page A tends to gather more social bookmarks than page B. However, if pages A and B have the same number of social bookmarks, the attention intensity to page A is smaller than that of page B. To eliminate this bias of users' interests, we need to compare the number of social bookmarks with those of related pages. We define the relative quantity of social bookmarks (RQS) to measure the attention intensity to Web pages. The RQS is calculated using the numbers of social bookmarks of related pages.

Related pages are found using social tags. In social tags, however, there are synonymity and ambiguity problems. An example of a synonymity problem is that some users use the tag "Programming" (capitalized) and other users use "programming" (not capitalized) to bookmark the same page. An example of an ambiguity problems is that tag "apple" can mean "Apple Computer" or a

M. Yoshikawa et al. (Eds.): DASFAA 2010, LNCS 6193, pp. 264–273, 2010.

fruit. This problem also contains a granularity problem of tags. Suppose that some users use the tag "programming" to bookmark pages about a specific programming language, but others use that tag only to bookmark pages whose topic is common in several programming languages. To bookmark pages about a specific programming language such as perl, these other users would use the tag "perl". In this case, the granularity of concept of "programming" for these users is different.

We focus on the fact that synonymity and ambiguity problems do not occur in tags of one user. To find related pages, we use pages bookmarked with the same tags with which the users bookmark the target page. We also focus on the granularity of the concept of tags, and we propose a method for finding related pages using the specificity of tags. We define two types of specificity, global, which is specificity for a social bookmark service, and local, which is specificity for a user.

The rest of this paper is organized as follows. In Section 2, we describe related work. In Section 3, we explain the specificity of social tags. In Section 4, we define relative quantity of social bookmarks to measure the attention intensity to Web pages. In Section 5, we explain our experiments for specificity and for the RQS. In Section 6, we give the concluding remarks and discuss future work.

2 Related Work

Social bookmarks are often modeled as $(user, page, tags)$ or $(user, page, tags, time)$. There have been many studies on social bookmarks for various purposes. Most research defines some kind of relationship between the one of the elements of the model using the other elements. For example, Krestel and Chen extracted a user graph of social bookmarking data to find spammers[1]. This is an example of the relationship between users. On the other hand, Niwa et al. proposed a Web page recommending system, in which they use tag clustering[2]. This is an example of the relationship between tags. Sugiyama et al. proposed a method for finding related pages using the similarity between pages[3]. To measure the attention intensity to Web pages, we need to obtain pages related to the target page and also define similarity between pages. In general, similarities using social bookmarks can be defined as follows:

$$Sim(o_1, o_2) = Sim(S_1, S_2), \tag{1}$$

where o_i is an element in the social bookmark model and S_i is the other elements. In Sugiyama et al.'s and our research, o_i is a page and S_i is user-tag pairs. These similarities are also based on the similarity measure for sets such as cosine similarity and the Jaccard coefficient. These are generalized as:

$$Sim(S_1, S_2) = \frac{|S_1 \cap S_2|}{Univ(S_1, S_2)} \tag{2}$$

If we change the function $Univ(S_1, S_2)$ in formula (2), this function becomes various similarity measure listed in Table 1. In formula (2), all the elements

Table 1. Universe Function of Similarity between Sets

	$Univ(S_1, S_2)$
Cosine	$\sqrt{\|S_1\|\|S_2\|}$
Jaccard	$\|S_1 \cup S_2\|$
Dice	$(\|S_1\| + \|S_2\|)/2$
Simpson	$\min(\|S_1\|, \|S_2\|)$

$s \in S_1 \cap S_2$ are evenly treated. When we weight s by weighting function f, we can describe formula (2) as follows:

$$Sim(S_1, S_2) = \frac{\sum_{s \in S_1 \cap S_2} f(s)}{Univ(S_1, S_2)} \tag{3}$$

Formula (2) equals formula (3) where $f(s) = 1$. In many studies, this weighting function is defined in various forms. For example, Sugiyama et al. defined it based on corresponding ratios of tags and we define it based on the specificity of tags.

Liang et al. proposed recommendation system based on each user's personal usage of tags and the common usage of tags by many users[4]. Their idea is partly similar to ours but the approaches are different. Though they focused on the tags frequently used by each user, we focused on the tags specifying the bookmarked pages in detail.

Chi et al. focused on the specificity of social tags and reported that this specificity decreases through observing the transition of entropy of social tags[5]. We focus on the concept of this specificity to define similarity between pages.

3 Specificity of Social Tags

3.1 Overview of Specificity

Specificity means the ability of a tag to differenciate the page from a set of pages. For example, if the contents of pages bookmarked using a tag vary, the specificity of the tag is low. On the other hand, if the pages bookmarked using the tag describe narrow topic, the specificity of the tag is high. To calculate the specificity, we analyze the pages that the same user bookmarked using the same tag. We used another method that does not depend on content analysis. Furthermore, we propose two types of specificity, local, which is the specificity for a user, and global, which is the specificity common in a social bookmark service.

3.2 Local Specificity

When the user bookmarks fewer pages using the tag against the number of pages the user bookmarks, the local specificity becomes higher. We define the local specificity of tag t for user u, $sp_l(u, t)$ as follows:

$$sp_l(u,t) = 1 - \frac{|Pages(u,t)|}{|Pages_U(u)|}, \tag{4}$$

where $Pages(u,t)$ is a set of pages that are bookmarked by the user u using the tag t and $Pages_U(u)$ is a set of the pages that are bookmarked by the user u. When user u bookmarks using the tag set T, we define the specificity as follows:

$$sp_l(u,T) = \min_{t' \in T}(sp_l(u,t')) \tag{5}$$

In both cases, the range of local specificity is $[0,1]$.

3.3 Global Specificity

Considering the number of the users who use the tag and the frequency of the tags, we define the global specificity of tag t as follows:

$$sp_g(t) = \min\left(1, \frac{|Users(t)|}{|Pages_T(t)|}\right), \tag{6}$$

where $Users(t)$ is a set of users who use tag t and $Page_T(t)$ is a set of pages bookmarked using tag t. The range of $sp_g(t)$ is $[0,1]$. When the number of pages bookmarked using tag t is large against the number of users who use tag t, the global specificity becomes high. When the number of pages bookmarked using tag t is larger than the number of users who use tag t, we regard the global specificity is high enough and set the value as 1. This specificity is weak at polysemy and synonymity. However, it is used to reduce the effect of the biased usage of user tags.

3.4 Combination of Two Specificities

We discuss the relationship between local and global specificity. If the tendency of local specificity matches that of global specificity, tag's usages are the same. Next, we consider the case when the tendency of local specificity does not match that of the global specificity. Suppose that local specificity is high and the global specificity is low. A user uses general tags for bookmarking a few pages. Therefore, this user seems to be familiar with the topic and the specificity of the tag is high. When the local specificity is low and the global specificity is high, the user uses the tag in his/her own way. In this case, the tag may specify the contents in detail but it does not always specify them. In short, when local and global specificities are high, the specificity of the tag should be high. Otherwise, it should be low. Then, the combined specificity of the tag for the user is defined as follows:

$$sp(u,t) = sp_l(u,t) \times sp_g(t) \tag{7}$$

4 Measuring Attention Intensity to Web Page

4.1 Relative Quantity of Social Bookmarks

Tendency of pages to collect bookmarks is different by their topic. because the number of users who are interested in each topic is different. We need to

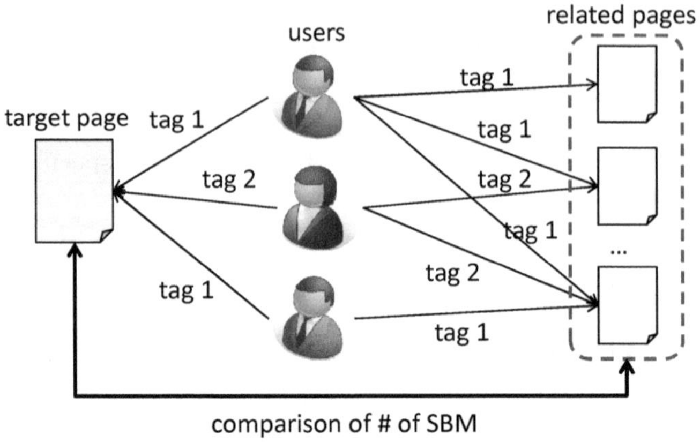

Fig. 1. Schematic of Relative Quantity of Social Bookmarks

normalize the number of social bookmarks of the target page using those of related pages. We define the RQS as the normalized number of social bookmarks. We define RQS of page p, $RQS(p)$ as follows:

$$RQS(p) = BM(p)/\left(\frac{1}{m}\sum_{i=1}^{m} BM(p_i)\right) \tag{8}$$

where $BM(p)$ is the number of social bookmarks of page p, and p_i is a related page of page p. We use the RQS as an estimated value of the attention intensity to the Web page. We show a schematic of this in Figure 1. Related pages are selected from the pages bookmarked with the same tags used by the user to bookmark the target page. RQS is calculated by comparing the numbers of the social bookmarks of the target page and the ones of the related pages.

4.2 Discovering Related Pages

Related pages are found using their similarity to the target page. Similarity is defined using specificity and is based on the Jaccard coefficient.

$$Sim(p_1, p_2) = \frac{\sum_{(u,t)\in UT(p_1)\cap UT(p_2)} sp(u,t)}{|UT(p_1) \cup UT(p_2)|} \tag{9}$$

where $UT(p_i)$ is a set of pairs of users who bookmark page p_i and tags which they use for bookmarking that page. However, if $|UT(p_1) \cap UT(p_2)|$ is large, calculation of $Sim(p_1, p_2)$ requires a large amount of time. Regarding this, there have been studies focused on users who bookmark pages earlier than others. Noll et al. called them discoverers and introduced the concept of discoverers into the HITS algorithm[6] to find experts and spammers among social bookmark users[7]. We use discoverers for approximation and define them as follows:

$$\{u_i | (u_i, p_i, t_i, \tau_i), \tau_i \leq \tau_{i+1}, i = 1, \cdots, n\} \tag{10}$$

where (u_i, p_i, t_i, τ_i) means that user u_i bookmarked page p_i with tags t_i at time τ_i and n is a parameter. We approximate the similarity function (9) using only discoverers to calculate the numerator. We define the approximate similarity function as follows:

$$Sim_n(p_1, p_2) = \frac{\sum_{(d,t) \in UT(p_1,n) \cap UT(p_2)} sp(d,t)}{|UT(p_1) \cup UT(p_2)|} \tag{11}$$

where $UT(p_1, n)$ is a set of user-tag pairs whose users are discoverers and d denotes a discoverer. $|UT(p_1, n)| \leq |UT(p_1)|$ and $sp(d, t) \geq 0$ are always satisfied. Hence, the following formula is also satisfied.

$$Sim_n(p_1, p_2) \leq Sim(p_1, p_2) \tag{12}$$

We use $Sim_n(p_1, p_2)$ instead of $Sim(p_1, p_2)$.

The candidate pages related to the target pages are obtained using those bookmarked by users who bookmarked the target page with the same tags. When we want to obtain the related page candidates of pages bookmarked by many users, however, it requires a large amount of time to obtain the candidates. To avoid this problem, we consider only pages that are bookmarked by the discoverers as the candidates. We developed an algorithm for collecting the candidates of the related pages. If the discoverer d bookmarks page p with the tag t, we collect pages $Pages(d, t)$ bookmarked by d with t. Then, we calculate $sp(d, t)$ of each discoverer d with tag t. We show the pseudo-code as follows:

```
for all (d, t) ∈ UT(p, n) do
  if sp_l(d, t), sp_g(t) is undefined then
    calculate sp_l(d, t) and sp_g(t).
  end if
  for all p' ∈ Pages(d, t) do
    if sim[p'] is undefined then
      sim[p'] ← sp_l(d, t) × sp_g(t)
    else
      sim[p'] ← sim[p'] + sp_l(d, t) × sp_g(t)
    end if
  end for
end for
for all p' in sim do
  sim[p'] ← sim[p'] / |UT(p) ∪ UT(p')|)
end for
```

sim[p'] is an array to reserve the similarity between the pages p and p'.

5 Evaluation

5.1 Evaluation on Specificity

We used Livedoor clip data[1] in December 2008 for the experiments. We found the URLs listed in Table 2 from pages bookmarked by discoverers. The discoverers are defined by formula (10) with $n = 10$. We list the URLs, the number of social bookmarks, and the number of the related page candidates in Table 2. We selected ten pages whose similarity with the target pages were highest from our algorithm using each $sp(d,t)$ function. Pages we could not visit are removed from the experimental targets in advance. All of the related page candidates were sorted in ascending order of their URLs and were presented to the three volunteers who did not know which function each page derived from. The volunteers rated them using the following standard.

- 3: almost the same topic as the target page
- 2: deeply related topic with the target page
- 1: related topic with the target page
- 0: unrelated topic with the target page

We evaluate the similarity ranking using the average of discount cumulated gain(DCG)[8], which is defined as follows:

$$DCG[i] = \begin{cases} G[i], \text{if } i = 1 \\ DCG[i-1] + G[i]/\log i, \text{otherwise} \end{cases} \tag{13}$$

where i is the rank in the similarity ranking and $G[i]$ is the average score rated by the volunteers.

The results are listed in Table 3. The scores in bold are the highest scores for each target page. If $sp(d,t) = 1$, then the similarity function equals the Jaccard coefficient of user-tag pairs. We regard this as the baseline. From the results, the average DCG when only global specificity is used ($sp(d,t) = sp_g(t)$) is highest, and the average DCG when local and global specificity are used ($sp(d,t) = sp_l(d,t) \times sp_g(t)$) is second highest. On the other hand, the average DCG of the case when only local specificity is used ($sp(d,t) = sp_l(d,t)$) is lower than that of the baseline. We also counted the number of URLs whose DCG was higher than the baseline. The number increased the most when only global specificity is used or global and local specificities are used. The number was 8 out of 10. The number when only local specificity was used was 5 out of 10. We discuss the reason local specificity does not contribute to a high DCG. In URL2, the DCG score of local specificity is very low. Therefore, we analyzed the URL2. Most of the tags used to bookmark URL2 were related to movies such as "Movie" but some users used tags related to April Fool. They bookmarked URL2 on April 1. In April 1, this page might have contained contents related to April Fool. On the other hand, we found that most of the related pages of URL2 derived from local specificity contained joke or parody related to April Fool and

[1] `http://clip.livedoor.com/`

Table 2. Pages used for Experiments

ID	URL	#SBM	candidates
URL1	`http://codezine.jp/`	47	56
URL2	`http://eiga.com/`	12	28
URL3	`http://javascriptist.net/`	188	292
URL4	`http://lifehacking.jp/2008/03/life-instructions/`	45	265
URL5	`http://otoko-cooking.com/index.html`	77	32
URL6	`http://staff.aist.go.jp/toru-nakata/sotsuron.html`	299	45
URL7	`http://www.asahi.com/`	84	54
URL8	`http://www.hereticanthem.com/webdesign/295/`	144	562
URL9	`http://www.iknow.co.jp/`	112	18
URL10	`http://www.uta-net.com/`	22	11

Table 3. Experimental Results for Specificity

$sp(d,t)$	$sp_l(d,t) \times sp_g(t)$	$sp_l(d,t)$	$sp_g(t)$	1
URL1	**5.74**	4.84	**5.74**	5.01
URL2	**6.64**	0.05	**6.64**	0.79
URL3	5.74	**6.21**	6.03	5.95
URL4	6.45	5.97	**6.50**	5.55
URL5	7.78	7.78	7.78	**8.59**
URL6	**4.31**	2.28	**4.31**	3.59
URL7	8.51	**9.01**	7.93	8.45
URL8	**6.69**	2.91	**6.69**	6.66
URL9	**6.66**	6.57	6.58	4.08
URL10	6.99	**7.05**	6.99	6.45
AVG.	6.47	4.97	**6.54**	5.18
# of improved	**8**	5	**8**	-

were published in April 1. Thus, certain users who have different tendencies in tagging can easily affect local specificity. To solve this problem, we need to consider the meaning of the tag.

In addition, the DCG scores were the same in 6 out of 10 tasks between when only global specificity was used when global and local specificities are used. This is because the narrow range distribution of the value of $sp_l(d,t)$ and $sp_l(d,t)$ does not have much effect on the value of $sp(d,t) = sp_l(d,t) \times sp_g(t)$. Hence, we need to analyze the differences in the usage of tags between users and the design of the local specificity function.

5.2 Evaluation of Relative Quantity of Web Pages

To evaluate the RQS as a measure of the attention intensity to Web pages, we use the attention degree of Web pages, which we define as **the attention intensity a user feels when he/she knows the number of social bookmarks**

Table 4. Experimental Results for RQS

ID	#SBM	RQS	User
URL1	47	2.749	0
URL2	12	0.381	-1
URL3	188	20.889	1
URL4	45	1.282	0
URL5	77	4.583	1
URL6	299	25.556	1
URL7	84	3.000	0.667
URL8	144	4.816	1
URL9	112	2.363	0.667
URL10	22	1.424	0
Spearman	0.877	0.922	-

of the target page and its related pages. If the RQS has a strong correlation with the attention degree, the RQS is useful as a measure of the attention intensity to Web pages. The values of the attention degree are obtained from volunteers ratings. Considering the title and the number of social bookmarks of the target pages and those of its related pages when $sp(d,t) = sp_l(d,t) \times sp_g(t)$, the volunteers rated the pages using the following standards:

- 1: Attention degree is high
- 0: Attention degree is medium
- -1: Attention degree is low

If all pages of a blog site have the same title, we use the title of each blog entry instead of the page title. Three volunteers rated each page listed in Table 2 and we used the average of these scores as the attention degree.

If the RQS is useful for measuring the attention intensity to Web page, the Spearman rank correlation coefficient between it and the attention degree should be high. Therefore, we evaluated the RQS using the Spearman rank correlation coefficient between attention degree. To evaluate the RQS, we compared it with the number of social bookmarks. We used Spearman rank correlation coefficient between it and the attention degree as the baseline. The results are shown in Table 4. In Table4, #SBM means the number of social bookmarks and User means the attention degree obtained from user evaluation. Spearman means the Spearman rank correlation coefficient against the attention degree. We found that RQS has a stronger correlation with attention degree than the number of social bookmarks. Therefore, the RQS is more useful than the number of social bookmarks for estimating the attention degree.

6 Conclusions

We proposed a similarity measure based on the specificity of social tags and a method for obtaining related pages using the measure. We defined local and global specificity and evaluated their effectiveness and the effectiveness of their combination. From the evaluation, we found that global specificity improves the similarity measure but local specificity sometimes makes it worse. One of the reasons seems that certain users who have different tendencies in tagging can easily affect the local specificity. We also define the RQS to measure the attention intensity to the Web pages using related pages. We compared the Spearman rank coefficient between the RQS and attention degree and the one between the number of social bookmarks and attention degree. We found that the Spearman rank coefficient between the RQS and attention degree is higher. For future work, we need to improve local specificity.

Acknowledgment

This work was supported in part by the National Institute of Information and Communications Technology.

References

1. Krestel, R., Chen, L.: Using co-occurence of tags and resources to identify spammers. In: ECML/PKDD Discovery Challenge (RSDC 2008), Workshop at ECML/PKDD 2008 (2008)
2. Niwa, S., Doi, T., Honiden, S.: Web page recommender system based on folksonomy mining. In: ITNG 2006: Third International Conference on Information Technology New Generations, pp. 388–393 (2006)
3. Sugiyama, N., Seki, Y., Aono, M.: A method for finding related pages by users' tagging behavior from social bookmarks (in Japanese). Journal of the DBSJ 7(1), 239–244 (2008)
4. Liang, H., Xu, Y., Li, Y., Nayak, R.: Collaborative filtering recommender systems based on popular tags. In: ADCS 2009: Proceedings of the Fourteenth Australasian Document Computing Symposium (2009)
5. Chi, E.H., Mytkowicz, T.: Understanding the efficiency of social tagging systems using information theory. In: HT 2008: Proceedings of the nineteenth ACM conference on Hypertext and hypermedia, pp. 81–88. ACM, New York (2008)
6. Kleinberg, J.M.: Authoritative sources in a hyperlinked environment. J. ACM 46(5), 604–632 (1999)
7. Noll, M.G., Au Yeung, C.M., Gibbins, N., Meinel, C., Shadbolt, N.: Telling experts from spammers: expertise ranking in folksonomies. In: SIGIR 2009: Proceedings of the 32nd international ACM SIGIR conference on Research and development in information retrieval, pp. 612–619. ACM, New York (2009)
8. Järvelin, K., Kekäläinen, J.: Ir evaluation methods for retrieving highly relevant documents. In: SIGIR 2000: Proceedings of the 23rd annual international ACM SIGIR conference on Research and development in information retrieval, pp. 41–48. ACM, New York (2000)

SQL as a Mashup Tool: Design and Implementation of a Web Service Integration Approach Based on the Concept of Extensible Relational Database Management Systems

Yoshihiko Ichikawa[1], Yuuki Matsui[2], and Minoru Tanaka[2]

[1] Media and Information Technology Center, Yamaguchi University, Minami Kogushi 1-1-1, Ube, Yamaguchi, Japan
ichikay@yamaguchi-u.ac.jp

[2] Graduate School of Science and Engineering, Yamaguchi University, Japan

Abstract. Recently Web services based on the HTTP and XML technology have become widely used, and application programs or mashups integrating such services have also proliferated. In order to support the integration process, we have developed a tool to convert user-defined function specifications written in XML to the corresponding user-defined functions loadable to PostgreSQL, an extensible relational database management system. With this conversion layer provided by the tool, multiple Web services and relational databases can be integrated in SQL, and therefore, integrated applications or mashups can be built quickly without being bothered by variety of Web service interfaces defining the calling sequences and result data types. Moreover, even if one of the Web service providers that a particular mashup depends on changes its service specification, the application does not need to be modified accordingly, when the corresponding function's calling interface remains intact by changing the specification of the function body. This property which we refer to as Web service independence is quite important since Web service interfaces may change without any previous notices, and so some management methodology is needed for mashups.

Keywords: Web Service, Mashup, Extensible Relational Database Management System.

1 Introduction

After proliferation of the World Wide Web and the technologies to support services on the Web, HTTP-based services such as Yahoo! Search Web Services and Flikr [1], Amazon Web Services [2] and Twitter API [3] have become freely available, and hybrid applications integrating these services, called mashups due to its similarity to music and video mashups, have become popular. These services are referred to as Web services and each of them "*is a software system designed to support interoperable machine-to-machine interaction over a network. It has an interface described in a machine-processable format (specifically*

M. Yoshikawa et al. (Eds.): DASFAA 2010, LNCS 6193, pp. 274–284, 2010.

WSDL). Other systems interact with the Web service in a manner prescribed by its description using SOAP-messages, typically conveyed using HTTP with an XML serialization in conjunction with other Web-related standards" according to the definition of W3C [4].[1] While W3C definition is based on the rigid RPC-like protocols such as WSDL and SOAP, we include REST style services in Web services here.[2] Moreover, HTML based services like search engines, bulletin boards, news sites, weather reports may also be included, since they also provide quite valuable information and a simple gateway script defining a wrapper, an intermediate process working between clients and servers to adapt data formats, may make them look like Web services in a narrow sense.

The success of Web services has lead to mashups, i.e., Web pages or services built from other existing Web services. Typical mashups include a news reader which collects news update data from multiple news sources, a meta-search engine making use of more than one search engine service, and a mapping mashup that lays out information retrieved from an index server on top of a map image retrieved from a map service. A programmer trying to develop mashups must understand the interfaces of the services, and integrate the returned results. Although data returned from these services are often formatted in the standardized language XML, they usually defined in different schemas or DTDs, and hence integration process can be done only in an ad hoc manner. To lessen the burden of the application programmers, utilization of declarative programming languages is attractive. YQL [5], for instance, allows a data source to be defined from multiple data sources using JavaScript, and support filtering, projection and sub-querying functionality. Recent database technologies, such as XQuery [6], a query language designed for XML databases, and SQL/XML [7], which is a part of the SQL2003 standard and defines an abstract data type for XML data in SQL, have been proposed for storing and integrating XML databases, Web-services and/or relational databases.

New declarative languages and data types provide us with new exploration opportunities, but application programmers still take care of variety of Web service interfaces and schemas of returned data. Instead of adhering to XML data and its flexibility, we propose another approach in which Web services are encapsulated in user-defined functions of extensible relational database management systems (DBMSs). Recently, major free or commercial relational DBMS products support extensibility to some extent, and when database administrators need procedures or functions which are not supported by default, they can write their own definitions and make them available in SQL statements. Note that the discussion in this paper is based on PostgreSQL [8], an extensible relational DBMS. The proposed approach, however, may apply to other DBMS. The following is a simply query making use of Yahoo! Search Service:

```
SELECT *
FROM getcontents_yahoo(
  $${{'numberperpage','50'},{'startnumber','1'},{'reqnumber','100'}} $$,
```

[1] We will shortly describe WSDL and SOAP below.

[2] We will briefly explain SOAP and REST in Section 2.

```
'Web Service','any')
```

`getcontents_yahoo` is a user-defined function encapsulating the process of interacting with the service and converting the returned result into a relation. The first argument gives optional parameters[3] , followed by the search keyword and the search type. The function's return type is

```
SET OF (rank integer, title text, summary text, url text).
```

Since the result is just a relation, it can be arbitrarily filtered, projected and joined with other relations including stored relations, views and those from Web services as far as SQL permits. Our approach hides the details of Web services, and provides application programmers with declarative simplicity and flexibility of SQL. This approach is attractive especially when we want to build data-intensive mashups like news mashups and search mashups, since the main part of the data returned from each underlying Web service has some iterative structure, and thus can be easily translated into a table format. We call our system as SQL/MT short for SQL as a mashup tool. In contract to YQL which does not support arbitrary combination of data sources in its basic syntax, our approach can make use of the expressive power of SQL directly.

While the burden of application programmers with respect to Web service utilization is eased in this approach, most part of it now has been moved to those who define the user-defined functions. We call the latter library programmers to discriminate them from application programmers. In order to further lessen the burden of library programmers, we provide them with a translator that maps a specification in XML of a user-defined function encapsulating Web service utilization into the corresponding definition of the function directly loadable to PostgreSQL. We call the specification language Pg/WAFL, short for PosgreSQL Web service accessing function markup Language. A sample description in Pg/WAFL is shown in Appendix A. The approach taken by Ohshima et al. [9,10] is similar to ours in the sense that their system, EaRDB, also makes use of user-defined functions to access outer information sources, while they do not propose any mechanism to support development of user-defined functions.[4]

Our approach also provides another benefit. A particular Web service interface may change without any previous notices, and thus the programs depending on the service may have to be modified accordingly. When a wrapper is used for accessing the service, the wrapper may absorb the effect of modification of the Web service by modifying the wrapper definition. In our approach, the user-defined functions for accessing Web services work as wrappers, and hence, even if one of the Web service providers that a particular mashup depends on changes its service specification, the application does not need to be modified, as long as the header part of the corresponding function can remain intact, while the

[3] $$ is used to introduce literals in PostgreSQL as well as '. In this case, a two-dimensional array literal whose first row is 'numberperpage' and '50', second row is 'startnumber' and '1', and third row is 'reqnumber' and '100' is given.

[4] To be precise, the term "stored procedure" should be used, since the target of [9] is Transact-SQL supported by Microsoft SQL Server and Sybase.

function body is changed accordingly. So DBMSs with user-defined functions for accessing Web services support this property, which we refer to as Web service independence, as well as logical and physical data independence [11], one of the most important concepts that database management systems support.

The rest of this paper is organized as follows. In Sections 2 and 3, we will describe target Web services first and then explain Pg/WAFL and its translator implementation. Section 4 shows some applications we have developed with our proposed technique. The last section concludes and addresses some future work.

2 Target Web Services

While all the Web services make use of HTTP for sending a request and receiving its result, some formally or informally defined protocols are usually put on top of HTTP. These protocols specifically define how to format the request and how the result is formatted. For instance, information regarding the updated content of a particular on-line news site may be accessed by simply accessing the Web page specified by the service and parsing the returned data formatted in a particular feed format (or simply feed), where typical feed formats include RSS1.0 family, RSS 2.0 family, and ATOM, all of which are extended from XML. In this case, the request is simply implied by the URL of the Web page itself, and the result format is the feed. Serialization of returned data is typically done with XML, but other methods such as PHP serialization (a character representation of PHP data)and JSON (the JavaScript correspondent) are also used.

Similar, but more general-purpose service style is called REST (Representational State Transfer). A typical Web service adopting REST accepts service parameters usually as HTTP GET parameters, and returns the result, which is serialized typically in XML or JSON, as part of the HTTP response. Although there is no W3C recommendation for REST, there have been a lot of REST-based Web services, and is easy to comprehend and use. So in this paper, we mainly treat REST style Web services as the target.

More abstract and standardized Web service specifications are given and implemented with WSDL (Web service description language) and SOAP (Simple Object Access Protocol), respectively. Since WSDL is used to formally specify a particular Web service, automatic generation of user-defined functions for the Web service might be possible. And probably, WADL (Web application description language) designed for formally describing REST-style Web services might be used as the starting point of automatic generation. This paper, however, does not cover the issue, and we only name it as one of the future work.

3 Pg/WAFL and Its Translator

A user-defined function description in Pg/WAFL comprises three parts as shown in Appendix A. The first part specifies the header part of the user-defined function, i.e., the function name, the list of arguments and the return type, specified by the `FuncName` element, `FuncArg` and `RetType`, respectively. We use two kinds of arguments. First, ordinary parameters (we call them "positional parameters" since they are given in a particular position in the argument list) are used to pass mandatory arguments. In the example, "query" and "format" are positional parameters, and specify the second and the third arguments of the corresponding functions, respectively. The first argument of the function, on the other hand, is used to pass parameters of the second kind, that we call them "keyword parameters" as every actual parameter value is preceded by a keyword giving the parameter name. "reqnumber", "numberpage" etc. are keyword parameters. The keyword parameters are passed to functions as the first argument using an array of keyword-value pairs. The following is a sample query we explained above:

```
SELECT *
FROM getcontents_yahoo(
  $${{'numberperpage','50'},{'startnumber','1'},{'reqnumber','100'}} $$,
  'Web Service','any')
```

The array passed as the first argument specifies the "numberparpage", "startnumber", and "requnumber" keyword parameters, and the second argument "Web service" and the third one "any" are parameter values for "query" and "format", respectively. We use keyword parameters due to two reasons. First, many of Web service parameters are optional. So giving optional parameter some positions on a particular function argument list might lead to a lot of null values when the function is actually used. Second, this is an implementation-dependent issue though, PostgreSQL's user-defined functions can have up to eight parameters. Although raising this threshold is possible, that would result in reducing the server performance.[5] The `required` attribute specifies optionality of arguments.

The `RetType` element specifies the return type. In the example, the result is table, i.e., a set of tuples, and has four columns, i.e., "rank" of type integer, "title" of type text, "summary" of type text and "url" of type text. Note that "rank" is of type "rank" in the Pg/WAFL specification. This indicates that each tuple in the table has its ranking information as the value of the "rank" column.

How to call web services with the given parameters is described in the `Request` part. `baseurl` gives the base url of the corresponding Web service, and the `param` elements and `param_paging` element gives the parameters passed to the Web service. Since we support only REST style parameters, the actual url with its base url *baseurl* and parameter values v_i for p_1, v_2 for p_2 $\cdots$ and v_n for p_n is "$baseurl?p_1 = v_1\&p_2 = v_2\& \cdots \&p_n = v_n$." The `required` attribute specifies optionality of parameters, again. The value of a particular parameter is defined by the `source` attribute, and the default value is given in the content of the corresponding `param` element. Note that we only support query parameters for now, while path and matrix parameters may be used to access some Web services.

`param_paging` is used for paging parameters. When we want to retrieve, say, one hundred, items from, say, a Web search engine service, we can not necessarily

[5] Note that PostgreSQL supports type hierarchies and overloading. Therefore, which function is actually called is determined at runtime according to the combination of the argument types. So at worst, the function searching algorithm may exponential with respect to the number of function arguments.

accomplish the task by sending only one request. A typical Web service has some maximum number of items that can be requested by a single request. So, when we want more items than the limit, we have to make multiple requests to achieve our task. This is called "paging" . In this example, "start" and "result" Web service parameters are used to specify the start position and the page size of a particular page request, and the "start", "reqnumber" and "numperpage" function arguments define the initial item position, the total number of items, and the page size, respectively. In the generated function body, these paging parameters control iterative access to the Web service.

The last part, "Returning", specifies how to translate data returned by a Web service to a relation. We can split the translation process into two sub-processes. The first sub-process maps returned XML data to another XML data representing the result relation, while the second one further maps the relation described in XML to the actual relation stored in PostgreSQL. Since the second sub-process is trivial from the context, we require library programmers to write only the first sub-process. Any method of XML data transformation may be applied to the first sub-prosess, as it is just a XML-to-XML translation process. We now support only XSLT[12] as the specification language, but other languages such as XQuery and even DSSSL[6] might be used here. Note that the stylesheet in this sample defines only three columns, while the return type defines four columns. This is because the "rank" column of a particular tuple in the table is automatically filled by the system according to the position of the tuple in the result. Note also that the current implementation of SQL/MT does not support verification. Hence, even if the `Returning` element contains an incorrect code fragment, it is executed as is. This is another issue yet to be explored.

We use plPHP[7] as the description language of generated user-defined functions. As the name indicates, the plPHP module allows the programmers to write user-defined functions of PostgreSQL in PHP. We choose plPHP, since PHP itself supports DOM and XSLT libraries for XML data manipulation. This choice, however, is not inherent in our approach. Other procedural languages supported by PostgreSQL such as Perl, Tcl and Python might be used, as long as XML data manipulation is supported at runtime.

The SQL command automatically generated from the sample include about 120 lines. Although the difference between the command and the the Pg/WAFL description may not seem so much for expert programmers, SQL/MT provides us with a few favorable (probably future) properties. First of all, the Pg/WAFL description might be used for other types of DBMSs than PostgreSQL if we write an appropriate Pg/WAFL translator, and therefore it allows us to have the chance to support good portability. Second, if the similar descriptions were provided by Web service providers themselves, application programmers would be able to build mashups in SQL without resorting to library programmers. Lastly, as we mentioned in the introduction, even if a Web service specification

---

[6] This is a Lisp-like predecessor of XSLT. DSSSL is not an XML-based language, but might be used by CDATA elements.

[7] See `http://sourceforge.net/projects/plphp/` for more detail.

is modified, applications depending on the service may remain intact, if only modifying the Pg/WAFL description can absorb the effect of modification.

4 Sample Applications

To show effectiveness of SQL/MT, we have implemented several applications. We explain two application in this section. The first one is a so-called meta-search engine, which sends a request to more than one search engine, and combines the results to generate an aggregated result. For each query term, it sends a query request to Yahoo! Web Search service, and also sends another query request to Yahoo! Image Search service. The two results are simply joined by SQL's standard functionality:

```
SELECT
 ysearch.rank, ysearch.title, ysearch.summary, ysearch.url,
 yimg.title, yimg.summary, yimg.url
FROM
 getcont_yahoo($${{'reqnumber','100'}}$$, :QUERY, 'any') AS ysearch
  LEFT JOIN
 getcont_yahooimage($${{'reqnumber','100'}}$$, :QUERY, 'any') AS yimg
ON url_compare(ysearch.url,yimg.url)>=1
ORDER BY ysearch.rank ASC;
```

where ":QUERY" is replaced with an actual query keyword at runtime, `getcont_yahoo` and `getcont_yahooimage` are functions for two Yahoo!'s services, respectively, and `url_compare` is a user-defined function to evaluate the similarity between given two URLs. In this sample, `url_compare` returns a value greater than or equal to 1, when at least the site names of the URLS given as actual parameters are equal to each other. Without using SQL/MT, application programmers would have to write code for sorting data, merging data and generating result explicitly, which are coded in the above SQL statement implicitly in "LEFT JOIN".

Figure 1 shows our second sample, New Analyzer, which illustrates how remote Web applications, local non-DBMS services and local databases are integrated. This is a tool for collecting word occurrence frequencies in news pages and storing them in a database table, periodically. Words in news pages are extracted with a morphological analyzer, Chasen[13]. The overall architecture is shown in Figure 1 (b). NewsAnalyzer is accompanied by a data viewer to browse the stored data as a tagcloud. A partial screenshot of the viewer is shown in Figure 1 (a). The frequency of a word is represented by the size and the color of the font: larger and more redish fonts indicate higher frequencies. Frequently used words in the screenshot include "application", "sales activity", "development", "management", "corporation", "function" and "business". Note that since we do not eliminate common words, they do not necessarily indicate interesting words. With the slide bar, users can choose the date of interest. Every step of the collection process is written in SQL. Since the interface to the morphological analyzer is also written as a function returning a table representing the analysis

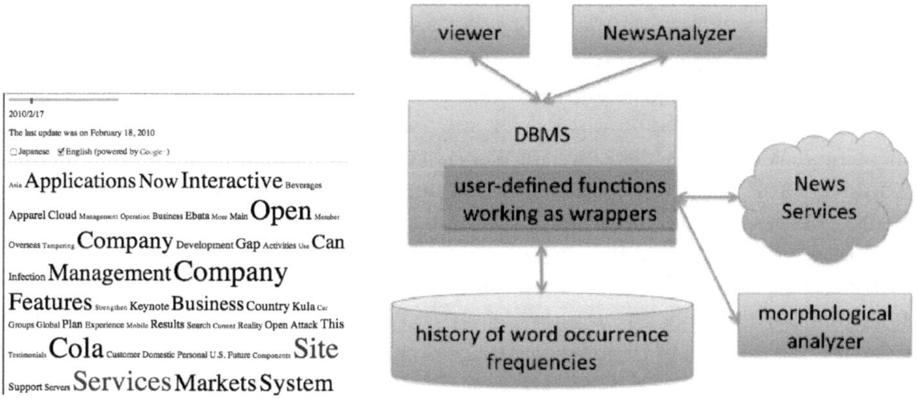

(a) a partial screenshot of the viewer (b) the overall architecture

Fig. 1. A sample application: *News Analyzer*. (NB: The viewer support both Japanese and English, though all of the collected articles are written in Japanese. Japanese-English translation is perfomed by utilizing Google AJAX Language API.)

result, the final source code of the collection tool comprises about a dozen of lines for calling SQL statements.[8]

5 Conclusion

We explained a novel approach to building mashups of Web services using the extensibility of recent relational database management systems, and introduced its implemenation, SQL/MT short for SQL as a mashup tool. In our approach, details of Web services are encapsulated in the corresponding user-defined functions which are used to extend the functionality of DBMSs. This particularly ease the burden of application programmers, but there remains the burden of those who write user-defined functions. So we have developed a tool converting the specification of a particular user-defined function accessing a Web-service into the corresponding loadable user-defined function definition. We refer to the language for describing the input as Pg/WAFL, which is an extension of XML. By using this approach, we can improve construction efficiency, portability and maintainability of mashups. Moreover, if Web service providers provide their service descriptions in Pg/WAFL, application programmers would be able to build mashups in SQL by simply writing some SQL statements. Our approach also introduces another concept into database management systems, Web-service independence akin to physical/local data independence: even if a Web service specification is modified, applications depending on the service may remain intact, when changing the Pg/WAFL description can absorb the effect of modification.

[8] If you really adhere to SQL itself, you might use a procedural extension of SQL such as Pl/PgSQL to execute all the steps on the server side.

While we have shown two applications to illustrate effectiveness of our approach, there are some issues to be explored in the future. First, some quantitative comparison of our approach to the previously known approaches should be needed to clarify the pros and cons of our approach. Second, formal descriptions of Web services in WSDL and WADL may be utilized in forming Pg/WAFL specifications. When this were accomplished completely, applications programmers would be able to access some Web services instantly with no additional cost. Third, we need some verification mechanism to check validity of Pg/WAFL descriptions. Otherwise, reliability of applications is difficult to ensure. Lastly, we also have to study the effect of external resources to the transactional properties, especially atomicity[9] and isolation[10][11], which may be easily broken when external resources are utilized.

References

1. Yahoo! Inc.: Yahoo! Search Services, `http://developer.yahoo.com/search/`
2. Amazon.com: Amazon Web Services, `http://aws.amazon.com/`
3. Twitter: Twitter API Documentation, `http://apiwiki.twitter.com/Twitter-API-Documentation`
4. W3C: Web Services Glossary (February 2004), `http://www.w3.org/TR/ws-gloss/`
5. Yahoo! Inc.: Yahoo! Query Language, `http://developer.yahoo.com/yql/`
6. W3C: W3C XML Query (XQuery), `http://www.w3.org/XML/Query/`
7. Eisenberg, A., Kulkarni, K., Melton, J., Michels, J.E., Zemke, F.: Sql:2003 has been published. SIGMOD RECORD 33(1), 119–126 (2004)
8. PostgreSQL Global Development Group: PostgreSQL: The world's most advanced open source databases, `http://www.postgresql.org/`
9. Ohshima, H., Oyama, S., Tanak, K.: Eardb: A platform for processing web aggregate queries. DBSJ Letters 6(2), 49–52 (2007) (in Japanese)
10. Ohshima, H., Oyama, S., Tanak, K.: Cloud as virtual databases: Bridging private databases and web services. In: Yoshikawa, M., et al. (eds.) DASFAA 2010. LNCS, vol. 6193, pp. 274–284. Springer, Heidelberg (2010)
11. Date, C.J.: Introduction to Database Systems, 7th edn. Addison-Wesley, Reading (2001)
12. W3C Consortium: XSL Transformations (XSLT) Version 2.0. W3C Consortium (January 2007)
13. Computational Linguistics Laboratory, Graduate School of Information Science, Nara Institute of Science and Technology: Chasen (2007), `http://chasen-legacy.sourceforge.jp/`

[9] Atomicity is a property that database updates submitted from a transaction should be performed in an all-or-nothing manner.

[10] Isolation is a property that correctness of a transaction should not be affected by other concurrently executed transactions. More specifically, when a transaction does not modify an database item, the value of the item should be the same whenever it is read in the transaction, even if other transactions may modify the item.

A A Sample Description in Pg/WAFL

```
<?xml version="1.0" encoding="UTF-8"?>
<FuncSpec>
 <!-- Part I: function header -->
 <FuncName>getcont_yahoo</FuncName>
 <FuncArgs>
   <FuncArg argname='reqnumber' argtype='keyword'
            required="true">integer</FuncArg>
   <FuncArg argname='numberperpage' argtype='keyword'
            required="false">integer</FuncArg>
   <FuncArg argname='query' argtype='positional'>text</FuncArg>
   <FuncArg argname='format' argtype='positional'>text</FuncArg>
   <FuncArg argname='appid' argtype='keyword'>text</FuncArg>
   <FuncArg argname='startnumber' argtype='keyword'
            required="false">integer</FuncArg>
 </FuncArgs>
 <RetType srf='Yes'>
   <RowType name='contents_yahoo'>
     <SrfElement name='rank' type='rank' />
     <SrfElement name='title' type='text' />
     <SrfElement name='summary' type='text' />
     <SrfElement name='url' type='text'/>
   </RowType>
 </RetType>
 <!-- Part II: Web service binding -->
 <Request type='xml'>
  <url>
    <baseurl>http://search.yahooapis.jp/WebSearchService/V1/webSearch</baseurl>
    <param_paging start='start' size='results'
                  source_start='start' source_total='reqnumber' source_size='numperpage'/>
    <param name="appid" type="xsd:string" source="appid"
          required="false">############</param>
    <param name="query" type="xsd:string" source="query"
          required="true" />
    <param name="format" type="xsd:string" source="format" required="true" />
  <url>
 </Request>
 <!-- Part III: conversion of responce data to table data -->
 <Returning lang='xslt'>
   <xsl:stylesheet version="1.0"
      xmlns:xsl="http://www.w3.org/1999/XSL/Transform"
      xmlns:xsi="http://www.w3.org/2001/XMLSchema-instance"
      xmlns:yahoo="urn:yahoo:jp:srch">
     <xsl:output method="xml" indent="yes"/>
     <xsl:template match="/">
       <table>
        <xsl:apply-templates/>
       </table>
     </xsl:template>
     <xsl:template match="yahoo:Result">
```

```
      <record>
        <title><xsl:value-of select="yahoo:Title"/></title>
        <summary><xsl:value-of select="yahoo:Summary"/></summary>
        <url><xsl:value-of select="yahoo:Url"/></url>
      </record>
     </xsl:template>
   </xsl:stylesheet>
 </Returning>
</FuncSpec>
```

Design of Impression Scales for Assessing Impressions of News Articles

Tadahiko Kumamoto

Department of Information and Network Science,
Faculty of Information and Computer Science,
Chiba Institute of Technology,
2–17–1, Tsudanuma, Narashino, Chiba 275–0016, Japan
kumamoto@net.it-chiba.ac.jp

Abstract. This paper focuses on the impressions that people get from reading articles in newspapers. We have already proposed web application systems that extract and use several types of impressions from news articles. However, the types of impressions extracted and used in these systems were intuitively defined by us on the basis of a basic emotion model, which the well-known psychologist Robert Plutchik proposed to represent human emotions. That is, the characteristics of news articles that result in different impressions have not been taken into consideration in much detail. Therefore, we have tried to design one or more impression scales suitable for assessing impressions generated by news articles. First, we conducted nine experiments in each of which 100 people read ten news articles and indicated their impressions on 42 five-point scales, where 42 impression-related words such as "happy" and "strained" were assigned for the 42 scales. Consequently, we obtained impression-estimation data for the 42 impression-related words. Next, we applied factor and cluster analysis to these impression-estimation data, and analyzed similarities among the impression-related words in terms of their scores. In our results, the words that convey similar impressions are classified into a single group and the words that convey opposite impressions are classified into different groups of words. Finally, we designed six impression scales suitable for assessing impressions generated by news articles on the basis of these results, each of which consisted of two contrasting groups of impression-related words.

1 Introduction

In recent years, in the field of "Affective Computing," that is, computing that relates to, arises from, or deliberately influences emotions [1], many research groups around the world have been trying to model the roles of emotion in interactions between people or between people and computers, and to make computers recognize and express emotions. In particular, there have been numerous studies in which computers explicitly express their computed affective state to users as dialogue participants, or convey the affective state of a user to other users as intermediaries, where the embodied conversational agents are equipped with synthesized emotional facial expressions in order to play their roles [2,3].

M. Yoshikawa et al. (Eds.): DASFAA 2010, LNCS 6193, pp. 285–295, 2010.

However, there are few studies that extract and use the impressions that people feel upon seeing or listening to information that someone has presented. Although for works of art such as music and painting several impression-based music and image retrieval methods [4,5,6] have been proposed as a means to identify pieces of music and paintings that convey similar impressions with those that users have entered, there have been very few proposed impression-based methods for texts such as news articles, novels, and poems. According to the Daijirin[1], the term "emotion" is defined as a "movement of mind; becoming happy or suffering sadness, affections, sentiments, moods," while the term "impression" is defined as a "feeling that people get by seeing or listening to something." That is, "emotion" means the affective state of people, or a change in this state, and represents a psychological aspect of mind at a deep level. In contrast, an "impression" is the mental picture that people have at a perceived level, and represents a perceptive aspect of mind at a surface level.

We previously focused on impressions generated by news articles, and proposed an impression mining method for extracting several types of impressions from news articles [7] and web application systems that effectively use the extracted impressions [8,9,10,11]. However, the impressions that were extracted and used in these systems were intuitively determined on the basis of the basic emotion model[2] [12], which well-known psychologist Robert Plutchik proposed to represent human emotions, while we considered the intended use of the systems. This means that the characteristics of news articles with regard to impressions have not been taken into consideration in much detail.

Therefore, in this study, we tried to design one or more scales suitable for assessing impressions of news articles. First, we conducted nine experiments with a total of 900 participants, and collected impression-estimation data that represent the relationship between news articles and the impressions that they generate. In each experiment, 100 participants read ten news articles, and rated each of them on 42 scales, where 42 impression-related words such as "happy" and "strained" were assigned for the scales, and each scale was used to assess, on a five-point scale from 1 (strongly) to 5 (not at all), how much each of the news articles generates the target impressions in the participants. Next, we applied factor and cluster analysis [13] to the impression-estimation data, and analyzed similarities among the impression-related words in terms of their scores. In our results, the words that conveyed similar impressions were classified into a single group and the words that conveyed opposite impressions were classified into different groups. Finally, we designed and proposed six impression scales suitable for assessing impressions of news articles on the basis of these results, each of which consisted of two contrasting groups of impression-related words.

---

[1] The Daijirin is one of the most famous Japanese dictionaries, which can be accessed in the form of an online version at `http://dictionary.goo.ne.jp/`.

[2] According to Plutchik, basic emotions are defined as those that form the basis of all the emotions that people have, and all other emotions are explained by mixing the basic emotions.

The rest of this paper is organized as follows. In Section 2, some related work about emotions, reputations, and impressions is introduced. In Section 3, we describe nine online experiments that we conducted to collect the impression-estimation data that represented the relationship between news articles and the impressions they generate. In Section 4, we analyze the impression-estimation data, and design six impression scales suitable for assessing impressions of news articles. Finally, in Section 5, we present our conclusions.

2 Related Work

Studies for inferring the emotions of people are most prevalent in the field of "Affective Computing." The goal of these studies has been to enable smoother communication with robots and avatars and smoother communication between people using e-mail. For instance, a commercial system that extracts vocal features from users' utterances and determines their emotions from six types of emotion, namely, "anger," "joy," "sadness," "normal," "laughter," and "excitement," has been released to the public [14]. There is also a system that recognizes users' emotionally charged or offensive utterances like "wow" and "oh my god" and locates their emotions in the emotion space designated by three axes: "acceptance — refusal," "relaxation — impatience," and "pleasant — unpleasant" [15]. A system has been proposed to measure users' facial expressions with a three-dimensional measuring instrument, which matches the facial expressions with the five typical facial expressions that represent "joy," "anger," "surprise," "fear," and "disgust" [16]. A system that infers users' emotions using the positive feelings [17] associated with the words appearing in their utterances has been proposed [18], while the degree of positive feelings associated with a word was determined by workers on the basis of their experiences. There is a difference between these studies and ours in that our focus is on the impressions that are generated in people due to text through which information is transmitted, rather than the associated emotion or affective state.

Methods of extracting writers' reputations and evaluation from movie reviews, book reviews, and production evaluation questionnaires have also been studied. For example, Turney proposed a method of classifying various genres of reviews into "recommended" or "not recommended" [19]. The primary characteristics of his method are the following: one is that the class into which a text is classified is determined on the basis of the co-occurrence relationship between each of the words extracted from the text and predefined reference words, namely, "excellent" and "poor," and the other is that the relationship is determined on the basis of the number of hits obtained using the AltaVista Advanced Search engine[3]. This method was designed only for a specific scale: "recommended — not recommended."

We have already proposed not only an impression mining method that extracts several types of impressions from news articles [7] but also web application systems

[3] The URL at that time was `http://www.altavista.com/sites/search/adv`, but it is not available now.

that effectively use the extracted impressions [8,9,10,11]. The News Reader with Emotional Expressions or wEE [8] automatically generates news-program-like animations with synthesized emotional speech and background music. A distinctive aspect of the wEE is that it automatically determines appropriate background music and an appropriate tone of voice for the animated newscaster in the animation generation according to impressions of news articles to be read by the newscaster. The Web OpinionPoll [9] collects web pages that are related to users' questions through web retrieval when users ask questions in the form of "What do people think about ···?" and plots impressions of the collected web pages on two impression planes: one is a plane spanned by two impression scales "anticipation — surprise" and "acceptance — disgust," and the other is a plane spanned by another two impression scales "joy — sadness" and "fear — anger." My Portal Viewer Plus [10] and Fair News Reader [11] manage users' preferences for impressions of news articles on four impression scales, and recommend news articles that users might want to read, not only from the viewpoint of topics, but also from impressions, where the four impression scales are "happy — unhappy," "acceptance — rejection," "relaxation - strain," and "fear — anger." These impression scales were all intuitively designed on the basis of a basic emotion model, although impression-related words constituting each impression scale were determined depending on the intended use of the application systems.

3 Collection of Impression-Estimation Data

We conducted online impression-estimation experiments with a total of 900 participants, and collected the impression-estimation data that represented the relationship between news articles and their impressions.

First, 900 participants were divided equally into nine groups, and ninety different news articles that had been selected from the society or local-news pages of Mainichi newspapers published in 2002 were also equally divided into nine groups. This means that a total of 100 participants, 50 male and 50 female, read ten different news articles. Each participant was asked to read the ten news articles presented in a random order and rate each of them on 42 scales corresponding to the 42 impression-related words listed in Table 1. That is, each participant was asked to assess, on a scale of 1 to 5, how much she/he felt the impressions represented by the corresponding impression-related word upon reading a target news article, with 1, 2, 3, 4, and 5 being "strongly," "comparatively strongly," "comparatively weakly," "weakly," and "not at all," respectively.

Only the first paragraphs of the original news articles were presented to the participants in order to reduce their workload. In addition, personal information such as individual names, organization names[4], and regional names[5] were

[4] Names of public institutions were not replaced except for the parts denoting regional names, but names of sections in the public institutions were replaced with symbols. The parts denoting the types of organization such as "University" and "Corporation" were not replaced.

[5] The parts denoting the types of region such as "Prefecture" and "City" were not replaced.

Table 1. Forty-two impression-related words presented to participants in a random order

Common, Strained, Untroubled, Fear, Anger, Grief-stricken, Idyllic, Surprising, Sophisticated, Unsophisticated, Interesting, Pitiful, Pathetic, Deplorable, Favorable, Brutal, Cool, Arrogant, Modest, Naive, Daring, Bright, Dark, Favorite, Fortunate, Unfortunate, Happy, Refreshing, Unpleasant, Glad, Sad, Peaceful, Optimistic, Uncomfortable, Pessimistic, Sick, Unexpected, Lamentable, Uninteresting, Awful, Least favorite, Serious

replaced with diamond, circle, and square symbols and hidden so that people could not identify anything specific from the news articles. The ten news articles presented to each group were selected in a balanced manner in terms of the impressions that they generated. That is, several hundred news articles published in 2002 in the society or local-news pages of the Mainichi newspaper were extracted from a database, and were then classified into seven impression classes: "joy," "anger," "sadness," "delight," "surprise," "fear," and "others." Then, one or two news articles were selected from each impression class so as to obtain a total of ten news articles.

The forty-two impression-related words were selected from a Japanese thesaurus [20] using the following method.

(1) Impression-related words that can represent impressions of news articles were exhaustively extracted from the thesaurus, and 532 impression-related words were obtained.
(2) Context-dependent words such as "large" and "low" and document-structure-dependent words such as "felicitous" and "simple" were excluded from the 532 impression-related words.
(3) Synonymous and semi-synonymous words were grouped together, and consequently 42 groups were formed. One impression-related word was finally selected from each of the groups as determined by the number of hits obtained by entering a character string concatenated with the impression-related word and the term "article" into the Google search engine [21].

By performing the experiments mentioned in this section, 9,000 impression-estimation data were obtained for each of the 42 impression-related words.

4 Design of Impression Scales

In this section we analyze the impression-estimation data obtained in the preceding section, and determine similarities among the 42 impression-related words. We design one or more scales suitable for assessing impressions of news articles on the basis of these results.

4.1 Analysis of Basic Statistics

Averages and standard deviations of the 9,000 data were computed for each of the 42 impression-related words. The results are arranged in ascending order of standard deviation and shown in Table 2.

Table 2 shows that the standard deviations are between 0.84 and 1.50, and that they vary substantially among the impression-related words. Since small standard deviations mean that the corresponding impressions were rarely observed among the 9,000 data, we decided to exclude the words "modest" and "sophisticated," whose standard deviations were less than 1.0, and their antonyms "arrogant" and "unsophisticated" from the list of 42 impression-related words.

Table 2. Averages (Ave) and standard deviations (SD) of all data for each impression-related word

Impression-related word	Ave	SD	Impression-related word	Ave	SD
Modest	4.58	0.84	Strained	4.10	1.26
Sophisticated	4.54	0.93	Idyllic	4.16	1.26
Untroubled	4.37	1.07	Sick	4.13	1.29
Naive	4.36	1.08	Pessimistic	4.06	1.30
Uninteresting	4.34	1.09	Bright	4.12	1.30
Optimistic	4.35	1.09	Fear	4.02	1.34
Unsophisticated	4.40	1.11	Surprising	3.83	1.35
Interesting	4.32	1.11	Grief-stricken	3.91	1.39
Glad	4.34	1.12	Pathetic	3.93	1.39
Unexpected	4.24	1.12	Least favorite	3.98	1.41
Fortunate	4.32	1.12	Brutal	3.99	1.41
Daring	4.32	1.13	Uncomfortable	3.83	1.42
Favorite	4.31	1.14	Dark	3.84	1.42
Refreshing	4.31	1.15	Sad	3.79	1.46
Common	4.21	1.16	Anger	3.84	1.47
Happy	4.26	1.18	Pitiful	3.83	1.47
Cool	4.22	1.19	Unfortunate	3.79	1.47
Arrogant	4.27	1.22	Serious	3.69	1.49
Favorable	4.17	1.24	Lamentable	3.74	1.50
Deplorable	4.17	1.25	Awful	3.75	1.50
Peaceful	4.18	1.25	Unpleasant	3.76	1.50

4.2 Factor Analysis

As described in the preceding subsection, four impression-related words were excluded from the list of 42 impression-related words. Therefore, we applied factor analysis to the data for the remaining 38 impression-related words while changing the number of factors from three to seven in the factor analysis, where the Varimax method was adopted and used for rotation of factors so as to create an orthogonal space. The highest accumulated contribution ratio of 64.4% was obtained when the number of factors was four. Therefore, we adopted this result. The result is shown in Table 3.

Table 3. Results of factor analysis for all data for 38 impression-related words

Factor	Impression-related word	Factor loadings			
		First-order factor	Second-order factor	Third-order factor	Fourth-order factor
First-order factor	Sad	0.86	-0.09	-0.04	-0.06
	Unfortunate	0.86	-0.09	-0.02	-0.08
	Lamentable	0.82	-0.13	0.02	0.03
	Dark	0.81	-0.08	0.10	0.00
	Serious	0.81	-0.12	-0.02	0.08
	Brutal	0.81	-0.05	0.01	0.01
	Pitiful	0.81	-0.07	-0.07	-0.11
	Grief-stricken	0.80	-0.04	0.07	0.10
	Pathetic	0.80	-0.04	0.10	-0.02
	Awful	0.79	-0.15	0.17	0.10
	Fear	0.79	-0.03	0.03	0.16
	Uncomfortable	0.78	-0.08	0.03	0.15
	Anger	0.78	-0.13	0.10	0.13
	Pessimistic	0.77	0.01	0.11	0.07
	Unpleasant	0.75	-0.16	0.21	0.13
	Deplorable	0.73	0.02	0.21	0.08
	Sick	0.72	-0.01	0.14	0.20
	Strained	0.71	0.05	0.05	0.19
	Least favorite	0.70	-0.05	0.30	0.14
Second-order factor	Happy	-0.11	0.87	-0.01	0.07
	Bright	-0.17	0.86	-0.01	0.03
	Fortunate	-0.06	0.86	0.03	0.04
	Favorite	-0.04	0.86	-0.01	0.09
	Idyllic	-0.15	0.85	0.09	-0.05
	Glad	-0.05	0.85	-0.01	0.09
	Favorable	-0.11	0.85	-0.02	0.05
	Refreshing	-0.07	0.85	0.04	0.01
	Peaceful	-0.15	0.79	0.16	-0.05
	Untroubled	0.00	0.78	0.13	0.03
	Interesting	-0.05	0.74	0.03	0.25
	Naive	0.00	0.72	0.25	-0.03
	Optimistic	0.02	0.70	0.24	0.10
Third-order factor	Uninteresting	0.17	0.23	0.67	0.07
	Common	0.17	0.33	0.55	-0.04
Fourth-order factor	Surprising	0.52	0.19	-0.05	0.53
	Unexpected	0.30	0.38	0.12	0.51
—	Cool	0.49	0.07	0.49	0.18
	Daring	0.39	0.30	0.21	0.42

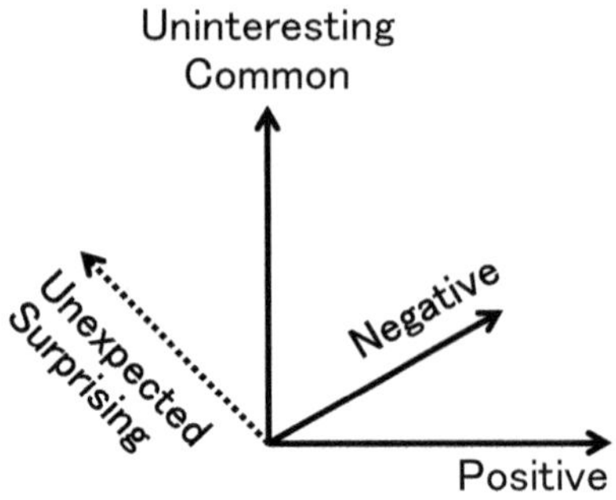

Fig. 1. Four-dimensional orthogonal space representing relationships among impression-related words

We can see from Table 3 that negative words such as "sad" and "dark," positive words such as "happy" and "bright," impression-related words "uninteresting" and "common," and impression-related words "surprising" and "unexpected" were grouped into the first-order factor, the second-order factor, the third-order factor, and the fourth-order factor, respectively. Therefore, we created a four-dimensional orthogonal space spanned by these four factor axes. This space is illustrated in Figure 1.

4.3 Cluster Analysis

Since the two factor axes "positive" and "negative" in the space created in the preceding subsection exhibit a limited resolution, we do not consider that they are suitable for assessing impressions of news articles.

Therefore, we decided to analyze the data[6] from another viewpoint, and applied cluster analysis to the data, where we adopted Ward's method as a clustering method and used the squared Euclidean distance as a measure of similarity. Consequently, the impression-related words were grouped according to score patterns of the participants for the data.

The results are illustrated in Figure 2. From Figure 2, we find that the cluster size is the most appropriate when the number of clusters is ten. That is, the word "optimistic" is added to the word group consisting of "peaceful," "idyllic," "naive," and "untroubled" when the number is nine, and the words "unexpected" and "surprising" are separated from each other when the number is 11. We consider that this addition and separation are inappropriate. Note that, in the figure, this case is denoted by a dashed line. For readers' reference, impression-related words constituting each cluster are enumerated below.

[6] Two impression-related words "cool" and "daring" were excluded from the 38 impression-related words before applying cluster analysis to the data. This is why these two impression-related words were not grouped into any factors, as shown in Table 3.

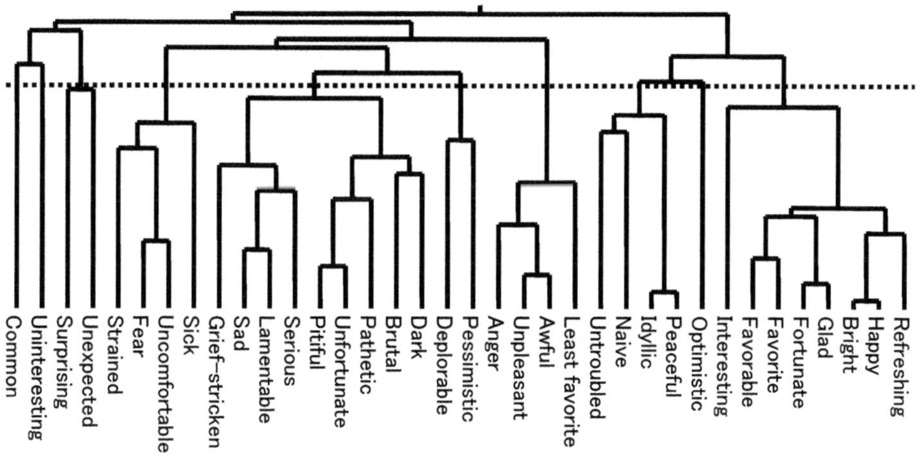

Fig. 2. Results of cluster analysis for all data for 36 impression-related words

- Happy, Bright, Glad, Fortunate, Favorite, Favorable, Refreshing, Interesting
- Peaceful, Idyllic, Naive, Untroubled
- Optimistic
- Sad, Dark, Brutal, Pathetic, Unfortunate, Pitiful, Serious, Lamentable, Grief-stricken
- Anger, Least favorite, Awful, Unpleasant
- Strained, Fear, Sick, Uncomfortable
- Pessimistic, Deplorable
- Uninteresting
- Common
- Surprising, Unexpected

4.4 Design of Impression Scales

Although there is some degree of similarity between the results of cluster analysis and the results of factor analysis, there are differences in at least the following two points. The first is that, in the clustering analysis, the positive words constituting the second-order factor and the negative words constituting the first-order factor were classified into three and four clusters, respectively. The second is that the impression-related words "uninteresting" and "common" constituting the third-order factor were separated into two clusters.

Upon taking these findings into consideration, impression scales are designed by the following procedures. First, since the number of negative clusters is larger than that of positive clusters and is four, we consider separating all the impression-related words in the three positive clusters into four groups. In this separation, it is essential that the four negative clusters correspond with the four newly generated positive groups and that each positive group has an antonymous relationship with the corresponding negative cluster. Consequently, four impression scales are generated. Next, the impression-related words "uninteresting" and "common" constituting the third-order factor are separated, and then pair off with their antonyms and "interesting" and "surprising/unexpected," respectively. Consequently, two impression scales are generated. We summarize these, and propose the following six impression scales as measures for assessing impressions of news articles. Note that each impression-related word group can be represented by one or two words within it.

- Happy, Bright, Refreshing
  versus Sad, Dark, Brutal, Pathetic, Unfortunate, Pitiful, Serious, Lamentable, Grief-stricken
- Glad, Fortunate, Favorite, Favorable
  versus Anger, Least favorite, Awful, Unpleasant
- Interesting
  versus Uninteresting
- Optimistic
  versus Pessimistic, Deplorable
- Peaceful, Idyllic, Naive, Untroubled
  versus Strained, Fear, Sick, Uncomfortable
- Surprising, Unexpected
  versus Common

5 Conclusion

We have proposed six impression scales as those suitable for assessing the impressions generated by news articles. First, we conducted nine experiments with a total of 900 participants, and collected impression-estimation data in order to analyze similarities among 42 impression-related words. In each experiment, 100 participants read ten news articles in a random order, and rated each of them on 42 scales. These 42 scales correspond to the 42 impression-related words that were extracted from a Japanese thesaurus as words suitable at some level for assessing the impressions generated by news articles. Each scale was used to assess, on a scale of 1 (strongly) to 5 (not at all), the strength of impressions that were generated in the participants by the news articles. There were no overlaps in the participants and news articles in all of the experiments. As a result of these experiments, we obtained 9,000 impression-estimation data for each of the 42 impression-related words. Next, we applied factor and cluster analysis to the collected data, and analyzed similarities among the impression-related words. On the basis of the results of this analysis, we designed six impression scales.

Our future work will be as follows. The validity and usability of the proposed impression scales will be tested through more impression-estimation experiments. We are also planning to analyze the characteristics of news articles in terms of impressions in more detail using the proposed impression scales.

References

1. Picard, R.W.: Affective Computing. MIT Press, Cambridge (1997)
2. Massaro, D.W.: Perceiving Talking Faces: From Speech Perception to a Behavioral Principle. MIT Press, USA (1998)

3. Bartneck, C.: How Convincing Is Mr. Data's Smile: Affective Expressions of Machines. User Modeling and User-Adapted Interaction 11, 279–295 (2001)
4. Kumamoto, T., Ohta, K.: A Query by Musical Impression System using N-gram Based Features. In: Proc. of IEEE Conference on Cybernetics and Intelligent Systems, pp. 992–997 (2004)
5. Kumamoto, T.: Design and Evaluation of a Music Retrieval Scheme that Adapts to the User's Impressions. In: Ardissono, L., Brna, P., Mitrović, A. (eds.) UM 2005. LNCS (LNAI), vol. 3538, pp. 287–296. Springer, Heidelberg (2005)
6. Kurita, T., Kato, T., Fukuda, I., Sakakura, A.: Sense Retrieval on an Image Database of Full Color Paintings. Trans. Information Processing Society of Japan 33(11), 1373–1383 (1992)
7. Kumamoto, T., Tanaka, K.: Proposal of Impression Mining from News Articles. In: Khosla, R., Howlett, R.J., Jain, L.C. (eds.) KES 2005. LNCS (LNAI), vol. 3681, pp. 901–910. Springer, Heidelberg (2005)
8. Kumamoto, T., Nadamoto, A., Tanaka, K.: Automatic Generation of Computer Animation Conveying Impressions of News Articles. In: Lovrek, I., Howlett, R.J., Jain, L.C. (eds.) KES 2008, Part I. LNCS (LNAI), vol. 5177, pp. 588–597. Springer, Heidelberg (2008)
9. Kumamoto, T., Tanaka, K.: Web OpinionPoll: Extensive Collection and Impression-based Visualization of People's Opinions. In: Advances in Communication Systems and Electrical Engineering, ch.17. Lecture Notes in Electrical Engineering, vol. 4, pp. 229–243. Springer, US (2008)
10. Kawai, Y., Kumamoto, T., Tanaka, T.: User Preference Modeling Based on Interest and Impressions for News Portal Site Systems. In: Bressan, S., Küng, J., Wagner, R. (eds.) DEXA 2006. LNCS, vol. 4080, pp. 549–559. Springer, Heidelberg (2006)
11. Kawai, Y., Kumamoto, T., Tanaka, T.: Fair News Reader: Recommending News Articles with Different Sentiments Based on User Preference. In: Apolloni, B., Howlett, R.J., Jain, L. (eds.) KES 2007, Part I. LNCS (LNAI), vol. 4692, pp. 612–622. Springer, Heidelberg (2007)
12. Plutchik, R.: The Emotions: Facts, Theories, and a New Model. Random House, New York (1962)
13. Kan, T.: Multivariate Statistical Analysis, Gendai-Sugakusha, Kyoto, Japan (2000)
14. SGI Japan Ltd., `http://www.sgi.co.jp/newsroom/press_releases/2004/sep/st.html`
15. Fukui, M., Shibazaki, Y., Sasaki, K., Takebayashi, Y.: Multimodal Personal Information Provider Using Natural Language and Emotion Understanding from Speech and Keyboard Input. IPSJ SIG Notes, HI64-8, 43–48 (1986)
16. Kuraishi, H., Shibata, Y.: Feeling Communication System by Facial Expression Analysis/Synthesis Using Individual Models. IPSJ SIG Notes, DPS74-14, 79–84 (1996)
17. Mera, K., Ichimura, T., Aizawa, T., Yamashita, T.: Invoking Emotions in a Dialog System Based on Word-Impressions. Trans. Japanese Society for Artificial Intelligence 17(3), 186–195 (2002)
18. Ren, F.M., Mitsuyoshi, K., Kuroiwa, S., Lin, S.G.: Researches on the Emotion Measurement System. In: Proc. IEEE International Conference on System, Man and Cybernetics, pp. 1666–1672 (2003)
19. Turney, P.D.: Thumbs Up or Thumbs Down? Semantic Orientation Applied to Unsupervised Classification of Reviews. In: Proc. of the Conference on Association for Computational Linguistics, Philadelphia, USA, pp. 417–424 (2002)
20. Ohno, S., Hamanishi, M.: Ruigo-Kokugo-Jiten. Kadokawa Shoten Publishing Co., Ltd., Tokyo (1986)
21. `http://www.google.co.jp/`

An Evaluation Framework for Analytical Methods of Integrating Electronic Word-of-Mouth Information: Position Paper

Kazunori Fujimoto

Kinki University, Osaka, 5778502, Japan
kfujimoto@kindai.ac.jp
http://ccpc01.cc.kindai.ac.jp/english/

Abstract. This paper presents an evaluation framework for analytical methods of integrating eWOM Information. This framework involves a communication model that assumes a set of human subjective probabilities called an *belief source* and includes two translation processes: (1) encoding the belief source into a representation to communicate with a computer; these encoded messages are called *eWOM messages*, and (2) in the computer, decoding the eWOM messages to estimate the probabilities in the belief source. The efficiency of reducing the difficulty of describing the belief source and the accuracy of reconstructing the belief source are quantitated using this model. The evaluation processes are illustrated with an analytical method of integrating eWOM messages for probabilistic classification problems.

Keywords: electronic word-of-mouth, opinion analysis, belief representation, probabilistic reasoning, subjective probability.

1 Introduction

The World Wide Web enables people to electronically exchange such individual information as opinions, experiences, recommendations, and so on. As a result, an immense quantity of not only objective information but also subjective information is stored on the Web. Studies of subjective information on the Web are considered a crucial issue in social psychology [2,1] and computer science [11,8]. This paper uses the term "electronic word-of-mouth (eWOM) information," which is often used in the area of social psychology [6,9,7] rather than of computer science, to refer to subjective information that is provided electronically for the general public.

Probabilistic reasoning [10], which is a useful framework for handling uncertainty, has been applied to various fields [12]. This framework may help provide intelligent systems that summarize and explain eWOM information to people. However, a number of subjective probabilities must be given to a computer to ensure a workable framework. The application domain for reasoning is restricted because of the difficulty of acquiring subjective probabilities.

M. Yoshikawa et al. (Eds.): DASFAA 2010, LNCS 6193, pp. 296–307, 2010.

In human word-of-mouth communication, subjective information is usually communicated after being translated into a natural language with which people are familiar. They reconstruct the belief contained in the information held by the sender with the pieces obtained from the described information. A communication framework can be established from humans to computers based on this fact. This paper focuses on the communicating subjective probabilities from humans to computers. A human communicates subjective probabilities to a computer after translating them into a familiar representation that is available to describe beliefs for computers. The computer estimates the subjective probabilities using the described information provided by humans.

This paper presents an evaluation framework for analytical methods of integrating eWOM information. Section 2 describes the basic idea of the framework that involves a communication model. This model assumes a set of human subjective probabilities called an *belief source* and includes two translation processes: (1) encoding the belief source into a representation to communicate with a computer; these encoded messages are called *eWOM messages*, and (2) in the computer, decoding the eWOM messages to estimate the probabilities in the belief source. The efficiency of reducing the difficulty of describing the belief source and the accuracy of reconstructing the belief source are quantitated using this model. These two measures allow evaluation of the analytical methods for integrating eWOM information. Section 3 develops an analytical method to integrate the eWOM information that does not directly use subjective probabilities but uses logical conditions with verbal expressions of uncertainty. Section 4 illustrates the evaluation processes for the analytical method with a probabilistic classification problem [4]. For comparison, the uncertainty calculation based on the certainty factors [14] and a simple method that uses subjective probabilities directly are also introduced in the illustration. Section 5 discusses the significance of the proposed framework and describes future work.

2 Communicating Subjective Probabilities

2.1 Basic Idea

Fig. 1 shows the model for the communicating subjective probabilities. The belief source is communicated to a computer in the form of eWOM messages translated using the belief source encoding. In the computer, the belief source is decoded using the belief source decoding from the eWOM messages. As a result, the information of the belief source is stored in the computer memory. In these processes, the belief source encoding does not describe the belief source completely and the belief source decoding must estimate the belief source using the incomplete information obtained from the eWOM messages. Thus, there is a deficiency of information at the time of both translations, so the exact probabilistic values in the belief source can not be obtained. The utility of the communication can be evaluated from the efficiency of reducing the difficulty in describing the belief source and the accuracy in reconstructing the probabilities in the belief source.

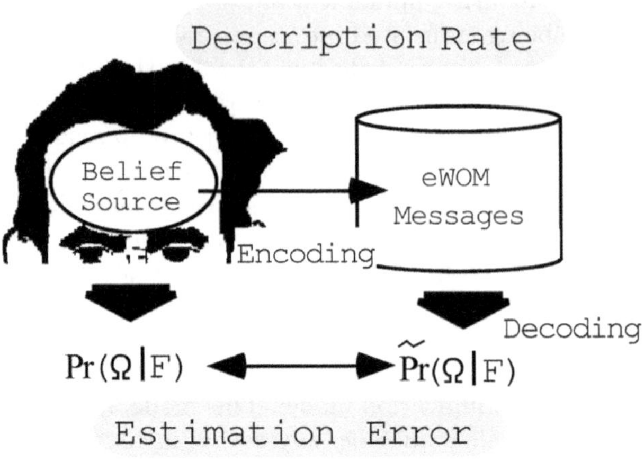

Fig. 1. Communication Model

2.2 Two Evaluation Measures

In this subsection, the efficiency and accuracy are quantitated as Description Rate for belief source encodings and Estimation Error for belief source decodings, respectively. The notations used in this quantization are explained below.

- Ω denotes a discrete random variable which range is $\{e_1,\ldots,e_N\}$. For an example of digital equipment evaluation, Ω may be introduced as evaluation results for the equipment, where e_1 and e_2 means the equipment is good for a professional use and is good for a novice use, respectively.
- F denotes a discrete random variable which range is all subsets, except the null set, of $\Upsilon = \{f_1,\ldots,f_R\}$. For the example, F may be introduced as the set of observed features of the equipment, where f_1 and f_2 means the equipment has a lot of switches and has a lot of interfaces, respectively. M and $\boldsymbol{f}$ denotes the number of all subsets of Υ and a subset of Υ, respectively.
- $\tilde{\Pr}(\Omega|F)$ denotes the estimated value for the $\Pr(\Omega|F)$. The estimation for the belief source means the estimation for all $\Pr(\Omega|F)$s in the belief source, which is the complete probabilistic data that allow the calculation of any $\Pr(\Omega|F)$.

Description Rate. Description Rate for belief source encoding represents the efficiency of reducing the difficulty in describing the belief source. The idea for quantitating Description Rate is described below.

When a human directly describes a value for a probability, the human must choose an appropriate value for the probability from all possible choices. For example, consider two translations, E_0 and E_1. Translation E_0 describes the probabilistic values with two decimal places. There are 101 possible choices for describing the probability value. (The reason for this is that there are 101 possible values from 0.00 to 1.00 at intervals of 0.01.) On the other hand, E_1 describes whether or not a feature f contributes to gain the possibility of the result e. There are only two possible choices for E_1, i.e., a feature f contributes to gain the possibility the result e or not. Translation E_1 has fewer choices than E_0. This reduction in the number of possible choices can be considered as reducing the difficulty in the description because the number of possible choices determines the degree of ease for humans to describe.

With this notion, Description Rate for the belief source encodings is quantitated using the number of possible choices for describing the domain.

Definition 1. *Description Rate R for belief source encoding E of belief source $\mathcal{S}$ is defined as*

$$R(\mathcal{S}, E) = \frac{log_2 \mathcal{N}(\mathcal{S}, E)}{log_2 \mathcal{N}(\mathcal{S}, E_0)}, \tag{1}$$

where $\mathcal{N}$ denotes a function that gives the number of possible choices for the description using the encoding, and E_0 denotes an encoding that directly describes the belief source.

Estimation Error. Estimation Error for belief source decoding represents the accuracy of the estimated probabilities. The error mean square of the estimated posterior probabilities is used for quantitating Estimation Error.

Definition 2. *Estimation Error E for belief source decoding D of eWOM messages $\mathcal{K}$ is defined as*

$$E(\mathcal{K}, D) = \frac{1}{N \times M} \sum_{(\Omega, F)} \{\tilde{\Pr}(\Omega|F) - \Pr(\Omega|F)\}^2, \tag{2}$$

where N and M denotes the size of the range of Ω and the number of all subsets of Υ, and $\tilde{\Pr}(\Omega|F)$ denotes the estimated value for $\Pr(\Omega|F)$ in the belief source using eWOM messages $\mathcal{K}$ and decoding D.

3 Communication Based on Logical Statements

This section describes belief source encoding that encodes the belief source into the eWOM messages involving logical conditions with some verbal expressions of uncertainty. This encoding is called *ELV* (Encoding in Logical conditions with Verbal expressions). Belief source decoding corresponding to the *ELV* is also described. This decoding is called *DLV* (Decoding of Logical conditions with Verbal expressions). These *ELV* and *DLV* are described and formalized in the next following subsections.

3.1 Encoding in Logical Conditions with Verbal Expressions

The *ELV* procedure is shown below.

For each e_i for Ω,

1. extract the set of features, f, that satisfies $\Pr(\Omega = e_i|F = f) > \Pr(\Omega = e_i)$ from the belief source (This set is denoted by $Spt(e_i)$.),
2. calculate the value for $\Pr(\Omega = e_i|F = Spt(e_i))$ using the belief source (This value is denoted by μ_i.),
3. obtain the verbal expression v_i for each μ_i by using a mapping table from probability values to verbal expressions. (An example of the table is shown in Appendix [A].)
4. make logical statements with verbal expressions such as $e_i \leftarrow f_1 \wedge \cdots \wedge f_{r_i} : v_i$, where $f_1, \ldots, f_{r_i}$ are all features in $Spt(e_i)$ and v_i is the verbal expression for μ_i.

Using this *ELV*, the belief source is translated into a set of logical statements each which has a verbal expressions of uncertainty.

3.2 Decoding of Logical Conditions with Verbal Expressions

The purpose of *DLV* is to reconstruct all $\Pr(\Omega|F)$s in the belief source using the eWOM messages and the *ELV* encoding rules. The sets of features $Spt(e_i)$s with verbal expressions v_is are extracted from the eWOM messages and are exploited for the reconstruction.

Any $\Pr(\Omega = e_i|F = \boldsymbol{f})$ in the belief source can be calculated[1] using the equation

$$\Pr(\Omega = e_i|F = \boldsymbol{f}) = \left\{1 + \frac{N-1}{\prod_{f \in \boldsymbol{f}} L(f|e_i)}\right\}^{-1}, \tag{3}$$

where N is the size of the range of Ω and $L(f|e_i)$ is the likelihood rate $\Pr(F = f|\Omega = e_i)/\Pr(F = f|\Omega = \neg e_i)$. Thus, the problem of reconstructing the belief source results in the problem of estimating all $L(f|e_i)$ parameters.

In this subsection, constraints for $L(f|e_i)$s is derived by using the *ELV* encoding rules and the probabilistic axioms. Some assumptions are then introduced based on the properties of the belief source in order to construct the $L(f|e_i)$ parameters estimation. The estimation for $L(f|e_i)$s is formalized by using the constraints and the assumptions.

Parameter Constraints. Based on the statements in the *ELV*, some constraints can be obtained for the $L(f|e_i)$ parameters. The condition $f \in Spt(e_i)$ implicates $\Pr(\Omega = e_i) < \Pr(\Omega = e_i|F = f)$, so that

$$L(f|e_i) > 1 \tag{4}$$

[1] For simplicity, it is assumed that the prior probability of any e_i is the same value and any feature f depends only on whether ot not e_i is determined.

for all $f \in Spt(e_i)$, and for all e_i that are obtained. The value μ_i for e_i implicates $\Pr(\Omega = e_i | F = Spt(e_i)) = \mu_i$, which value is decoded from the verbal expression in the statement, so that

$$\prod_{f \in Spt(e_i)} L(f|e_i) = \frac{\mu_i}{1-\mu_i}(N-1) \tag{5}$$

for all e_i that are obtained.

Based on the probabilistic axiom "the sum of the probabilities for all e_i becomes 1,"

$$\sum_{e_i} \frac{1}{1+(N-1)/L(f|e_i)} = 1 \tag{6}$$

for all f that are obtained.

Each constraint is not derived from the others, so that the number of the independent equations is $R+N$, even though the number of parameters is $R \times N$. The solution for the parameters is indeterminate because the number of parameters is larger than the number of equations.

Assumptions. Three assumptions, described below, are introduced in order to construct the $L(f|e_i)$ parameter estimation.

1. When a feature, f, where $L(f|e_i) \leq 1$ is observed, the posterior probability of e_i takes a smaller value because the observation works negatively on the probability. In this case, the exact estimation of the posterior probability is less important because Estimation Error will be smaller even if the estimated value is fixed to a small value. With this notion, the $L(f|e_i)$, which is less than or equal to 1, is assumed to take a constant small value, ε_i.
2. For $L(f|e_i)$ that is greater than 1, $L(f|e_i) = W(f)K(e_i)$ is assumed, where $W(f)$ and $K(e_i)$ take positive real numbers, $W(f)$ denotes the degree of effectiveness of observing f, and $K(e_i)$ denotes the degree of ease in recognizing e_i in the domain.
3. When all features in Υ are observed, the posterior probability $\Pr(\Omega = e_i|F = \Upsilon)$ takes the same value as the prior probability $\Pr(e_i)$ because the Υ contains all features of all e_is, so that all feature observations become meaningless. Using eq. (3) this assumption is formalized below.

$$\prod_{f \in \Upsilon} L(f|e_i) = 1 \tag{7}$$

   for all e_i.

As these assumptions are not always true, the DLV involves an estimation error, which is measured by Estimation Error in the framework.

Approximate Solution for DLV. The estimation for $\Pr(\Omega = e_i|F = \boldsymbol{f})$ is derived in four steps:

1. equations that calculate $W(f)$s is defined as the approximate equation obtained from eqs. (4) and (6),
2. equations that calculate $K(e_i)$s is derived from eq. (5) with the set of $W(f)$s,

3. equations that calculate ε_is is derived from eq. (7) with $W(f)$s and $K(e_i)$s, and
4. express using $W(f)K(e_i)$s and ε_is instead of $L(f|e_i)$s in eq. (3).

These steps are formalized below.

Equation (6) means that the sum of $\Pr(\Omega = e_i|F = f)$s for all e_is becomes 1. $\Pr(\Omega = e_i|F = f)$ takes a small value that is near 0 if $f \notin Spt(e_i)$ because $L(f|e_i)$ takes ε_i. So the volume of $\Pr(\Omega = e_i|F = f)$ can be determined by the number of e_i which satisfies $f \in Spt(e_i)$. With this notion, the $W(f)$ is defined as

$$W(f) = \frac{1}{Inv(f)}, \tag{8}$$

where $Inv(f)$ denotes the number of e_i including the f in $Spt(e_i)$.

By substituting $L(f|e_i) = K(e_i)/Inv(f)$ into eq. (5),

$$K(e_i) = \left\{ \frac{(N-1)\mu_i}{1-\mu_i} \prod_{f \in Spt(e_i)} Inv(f) \right\}^{\frac{1}{r_i}}, \tag{9}$$

where r_i, the number of features in $Spt(e_i)$ is obtained.

By substituting eqs. (8) and (9) into eq. (7),

$$\varepsilon_i = \left\{ \frac{1-\mu_i}{(N-1)\mu_i} \right\}^{\frac{1}{R-r_i}}, \tag{10}$$

where R is the number of features in Υ are obtained.

Using $W(f)K(e_i)$s and ε_is instead of $L(f|e_i)$s, the estimation is written

$$\tilde{\Pr}(\Omega = e_i|F = \boldsymbol{f}) = \left\{ 1 + \frac{N-1}{\varepsilon_i^{\beta} K(e_i)^{\alpha} \prod_{f \in \{\boldsymbol{f} \cap Spt(e_i)\}} W(f)} \right\}^{-1}, \tag{11}$$

where α is the number of features in both $\boldsymbol{f}$ and $Spt(e_i)$, and β is the number of features in $\boldsymbol{f}$ but not in $Spt(e_i)$.

Using eq. (11), the estimated value for any $\Pr(\Omega|F)$ in the belief source can be calculated using the eWOM messages translated by the *ELV*.

4 Examples

In this section, the *ELV-DLV* is demonstrated using a probabilistic classification problem. The efficiency of the *ELV* and the accuracy of the *DLV* are evaluated using Description Rate and Estimation Error.

4.1 Belief Source and eWOM Messages

Table 1 shows the belief source used in the example. Discrete random variables Ω and F, each which range is $\{e_1, \ldots, e_4\}$ and $\{f_1, \ldots, f_6\}$, is introduced as evaluation results for the equipment and a set of observed features of the equipment, respectively. All the posterior probabilities in the belief source can be calculated using the equation

Table 1. Belief Source: $\Pr(F = f_j | \Omega = e_i)$

	f_1	f_2	f_3	f_4	f_5	f_6
e_1	0.9	0.1	0.1	0.1	0.9	0.1
e_2	0.1	0.9	0.1	0.1	0.1	0.9
e_3	0.1	0.1	0.9	0.1	0.1	0.9
e_4	0.1	0.1	0.1	0.9	0.9	0.1

(a) e_1 is very likely because it has f_1 and f_5.
(b) e_2 is very likely because it has f_2 and f_6.
(c) e_3 is very likely because it has f_3 and f_6.
(d) e_4 is very likely because it has f_4 and f_5.

Fig. 2. eWOM Messages

$$\Pr(\Omega = e_i | F = \boldsymbol{f}) = \frac{\prod_{f \in \boldsymbol{f}} P(f|e_i)}{\sum_{k=1}^{4} \prod_{f \in \boldsymbol{f}} P(f|e_k)}, \tag{12}$$

which is derived from Bayes' theorem.

Fig. 2 shows eWOM messages, which is formed into a regular expression, used in the example. In the framework, some clues as to shapes of the belief source are extracted from the eWOM messages. For example, *DLV* extracts the list of features, each which increases the value of posterior probabilities of e_i compared to the prior probabilities, from the body part of each message, e.g., $\{f_1, f_5\}$ are extracted as the list for e_1 from message (a). The verbal expressions are also extracted to obtain the value for $\Pr(\Omega = e_i | F = Spt(e_i))$, e.g., the expression "very likely" is extracted and is interpreted as a probabilistic value 0.9 by using Table 2. These pieces of clues are used in *DLV* to reconstruct the belief source.

4.2 Evaluation

Fig. 3 shows the Description Rate for the *ELV* and the Estimation Error for the *DLV*. In this figure, the horizontal and vertical lines represent Description Rate and Estimation Error, respectively. For comparison, the Description Rate for the belief source encoding that directly describes the belief source (this is denoted by E_0 and describes the probabilistic values with a decimal place) and the Estimation Error for the uncertainty calculation based on the certainty factors (this is denoted by *CF*) are shown together. (Appendix [B] shows how the possible choices for the description are calculated, Appendix [C] shows important parameter values calculated by *DLV*, and Appendix [D] shows the uncertainty calculation.)

This figure shows that the Description Rate for E_0 and *ELV* is 1.0 and 0.46, respectively. This means that the *ELV* reduces the difficulty of the description by nearly one second. The uncertainty calculation uses the same eWOM messages

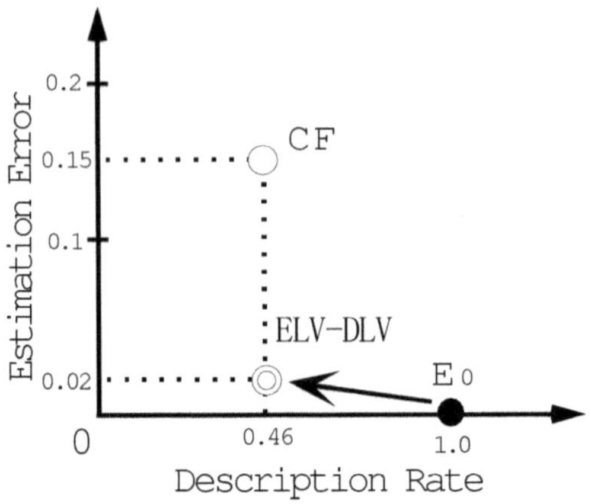

Fig. 3. Description Rate and Estimation Error

as the *DLV* uses, so that the Description Rate for these are the same as shown in the figure. The Estimation Error for the *DLV* and the uncertainty calculation is 0.02 and 0.15, respectively. The *DLV* can estimate the probabilities in the belief source more accurately than the uncertainty calculation.

As described above, each method is mapped on a two-dimensional plane formed by Description Rate and Estimation Error. A method can be evaluated using the distance between its point and the origin. (The smaller the distance, the better calculus.)

5 Discussion and Future Work

This paper presented two evaluation measures for analytical methods to integrate eWOM information: Description Rate and Estimation Error. Even though many uncertainty calculi can reduce the difficulty of describing the belief source [13,15], especially the number of probabilistic values for the calculation, the efficiency of reducing the difficulty and the calculation accuracy have not been studied. In [5], only the qualitative relationships between the certainty factors and the probabilities were studied. The proposed framework enables the efficiency and the accuracy to be measured by using Description Rate and Estimation Error. These measures provide one of the most fundamental evaluation frameworks for analytical methods.

Description Rate represents the efficiency of reducing the difficulty of describing the belief source. Analytical methods with smaller Description Rates simplify the description of eWOM messages because there are fewer possible choices for describing them. From a different viewpoint, the Description Rate represents the degree of the complexity of the message understanding because it measures the number of possible choices for understanding as well. In both cases, analytical methods that allow simple eWOM messages are evaluated better with respect to Description Rate.

Estimation Error represents, on the other hand, the accuracy in reconstructing the belief source. Different from Description Rate, analytical methods that allow simple messages are not always evaluated better with respect to Estimation Error. Detailed information is necessary to correctly estimate the belief source and to derive new variable information, as shown by the evaluation illustrated in Section 4. The belief source encoding, E_0, which directly describes the belief source, has a smaller Estimation Error and a larger Description Rate. In addition, the belief source encodings, *ELV-DLV* and *CF*, which have the same Description Rate, do not always have the same Estimation Error. Although the example is quite simple, it explains well the basic idea of the evaluation framework.

Showing that humans have subjective information in the shape of subjective probabilities is not easy. However, once subjective probabilities are obtained, many powerful tools in probabilistic reasoning can be applied. With such probabilistic tools, the proposed framework can be used to develop a promising approach for integrating eWOM messages and deriving new knowledge from them.

This paper describes a case where eWOM messages were only provided by a single person. The idea has to be extended for a multiple person case where eWOM messages are provided by the general public. In the extension, additional random variables are introduced to discriminate between each person. This extended model will be reported in the near future.

References

1. Chen, Y., Xie, J.: Online consumer review: Word-of-mouth as a new element of marketing communication mix. Management Science 54(3), 477–491 (2008)
2. Chiou, J.S., Cheng, C.: Should a company have message boards on its web sites? Journal of Interactive Marketing 17(3), 50–61 (2003)
3. Druzdzel, M.: Qualitative verbal explanations in bayesian belief networks. Artificial Intelligence and Simulation of Behaviour Quarterly 94, 43–54 (1996)
4. Duda, R.O., Hart, P.E.: Pattern Classification and Scene Analysis. John Wiley and Sons, Chichester (1973)
5. Heckerman, D.: Probabilistic interpretations for mycin's certainty factors. In: Proceedings of the First Conference on Uncertainty in Artificial Intelligence (UAI-85), pp. 9–20. Elsevier Science, Amsterdam (1985)
6. Hennig-Thurau, T., Qwinner, K.P., Walsh, G., Gremler, D.D.: Electronic word-of-mouth via consumer-opinion platforms: What motivates consumers to articulate themselves on the internet? Journal of Interactive Marketing 18(1), 38–52 (2004)
7. Lee, J., Lee, J.N.: Understanding the product information inference process in electronic word-of-mouth: An objectivity-subjectivity dichotomy perspective. Information and Management 46(5), 302–311 (2009)
8. Pang, B., Lee, L.: Opinion mining and sentiment analysis. Foundations and Trends in Information Retrieval 2(1-2), 1–135 (2008)
9. Park, D.H., Kim, S.: The effects of consumer knowledge on message processing of electronic word-of-mouth via online consumer reviews. Electronic Commerce Research and Applications 7, 399–410 (2008)
10. Pearl, J.: Probabilistic Reasoning in Intelligent Systems: Networks of Plausible Inference. Morgan Kaufmann, San Francisco (1988)

11. Riloff, E., Wiebe, J., Phillips, W.: Exploiting subjectivity classification to improve information extraction. In: Proceedings of the 20th National Conference on Artificial Intelligence (AAAI 2005), pp. 1106–1111 (2005)
12. Shafer, G., Pearl, J. (eds.): Readings in Uncertainty Reasoning. Morgan Kaufmann, San Francisco (1990)
13. Shafer, G.: A Mathematical Theory of Evidence. Princeton University Press, Princeton (1976)
14. Shortliffe, E.H.: Computer-Based Medical Consultations: MYCIN. Elsevier Publishing Company, Amsterdam (1976)
15. Wellman, M.P.: Fundamental concepts of qualitative probabilistic networks. Artificial Intelligence 44(3), 257–303 (1990)

Appendix

[A] An Example of Mapping Tables

Table 2 shows an example of mapping tables from probability values to verbal expressions. This is made by referring to a sample table in [3].

Table 2. Mapping Table [3]

Probability	Adjective	Adverb
0.0	impossible	never
0.1	very unlikely	very rarely
0.2	unlikely	rarely
0.3	fairly unlikely	fairly rarely
0.4	less likely than not	less often than not
0.5	as likely as not	as often as not
0.6	more likely than not	more often than not
0.7	fairly likely	fairly often
0.8	likely	commonly
0.9	very likely	very commonly
1.0	certain	always

[B] Calculations for the Number of Possible Choices

The Description Rate is calculated using eq. (1). In the calculations, the number of possible choices for the description is determined as follow:

E_0 The number of the possible choices is $11^{4\times6}$ because each relationship between f and e_i has 11 possible values from 0.0 to 1.0 at intervals of 0.1 and the number of the relationships is 4×6.

ELV Without value μ_i, the number of possible choices is $2^{4\times6}$ because each relationship between f and e_i has two possible choices ($\Pr(\Omega = e_i|F = f) > \Pr(\Omega = e_i)$ or not) and the number of the relationships is 4×6. The number of possible choices to describe μ_is is 11^4 so that the number of total possible choices is $2^{4\times6} \times 11^4$.

[C] Parameter Values Calculated by the *DLV*

Using eq. (8), $W(f_1) = W(f_2) = W(f_3) = W(f_4) = 1$ and $W(f_5) = W(f_6) = 0.5$ are obtained. Using eq. (9), $K(e_i) = 7.35$ for all e_i are obtained. Using eq. (10), $\varepsilon_i = 0.44$ for all i are obtained. The posterior probabilities in the belief source are calculated using eq. (11) with these values.

[D] Uncertainty Calculation

The uncertainty calculation for $e_i \leftarrow f_1 \wedge \cdots \wedge f_r$: μ_i used in the evaluation is

$$\begin{aligned} &if \quad \{f_1, \cdots, f_r\} \subseteq \boldsymbol{f} \quad then \quad \tilde{\Pr}(\Omega = e_i | F = \boldsymbol{f}) = \mu_i \\ &\qquad\qquad\qquad\qquad otherwise \quad \tilde{\Pr}(\Omega = e_i | F = \boldsymbol{f}) = 0. \end{aligned}$$

A Framework for Finding Community in Complex Networks

Naoki Okada, Kyohei Tanikawa, Yoshinori Hijikata, and Shogo Nishida

Graduate School of Engineering Science, Osaka University, Japan

Abstract. There is an increasing number of researches of complex networks such as the WWW, social networks and biological networks. One of the hot topics in this area is community detection. Nodes belonging to a community are likely to have common properties. For instance, in the WWW, a community may be a set of pages which belong to a same topic. Community structure is undoubtedly a key characteristic of complex networks. In this paper, we propose a new framework for finding communities in complex networks.This framework uses the idea of intersection graph and uses semantic information such as texts and attributes which appear in networks.

1 Introduction

Many researchers have studyed complex networks such as the WWW, social networks and biological networks and have found the property of a scale free, a small world, a large clustering coefficient, and so on [1]. Recently, the community structure in complex networks gains increased attention from researchers. The community structure means the appearance of densely connected groups of nodes, with only sparser connections between groups. Based on the definition, many methods of community detection have been proposed and the analyses of community structure in various complex networks have been conducted [2].

Against this problem of community detection, the point whether the overlaps between communities can be extracted starts to gather emphasis [6-8]. The overlaps mean that one node belongs to several communities. For example, one person belongs to several communities like a group of college members and a group of business members in social networks. In the WWW, a page can be categorized to several groups like Apple Inc.'s page can be categorized to "computer" and "audio." It is important that a method of community detection can assign a node to not only one community but several communities.

A network is assumed constant in exisiting methods of community detection. That is, all edges between nodes are treated as homogeneous in many cases. However, it is rare the edges are homogeneous in real networks. For example, in the WWW, there are various links such as internal links, advertisement links, and links to other cites. Similarly, there are various human connections such as bussiness, hobby and organization in social networks.

We propose new framework which can solve above two problems. The framework can extract overlaps between communities by using the idea of an intersection

M. Yoshikawa et al. (Eds.): DASFAA 2010, LNCS 6193, pp. 308–315, 2010.

graph. And we address a problem of the edge's inhomogeneity in complex networks by using the similarity of semantic information such as texts and attributes which appear in networks.The attribute information is machine-readable and is given expressly in networks. For example, the information is birthday and hobby in SNS.

The remainder of this paper is organized as follows. We describe related works in Section 2 and our proposed framework in Section 3. We describe our implementation of community detection in social networks and the result of experiment using the implementation in Section 4. The experiment is an example of application to an actual complex network. Finally, we describe some conclusions and future works.

2 Related Work

The problem of community detection in complex networks has been studied in various areas such as social networks, the WWW, and biological networks. One community in social networks shows a set of people related each other such as business, hobby, and organization. At the same time, that in the WWW shows a set of Web pages about certain one topic [4]. When we divide one network into some communities in community detection, there is a problem how we evaluate the division. Addressing the problem, Newman et al. proposed the indicator called modularity and some methods based on the modularity [5].

Some researchers have tried to extract communities in complex networks including the overlaps between communities. Fuzzy clustering is one of the major method [6]. One node can belong to several communities in these methods. Some researchers proposed some methods of community detection using the fuzzy clustering [7,8].

Our proposed framework uses a semantic information appeared in a network. This framework addresses a problem of the edge's inhomogeneity. We examine how change the result of extracting community by using the semantic information in our experiment.

3 Proposed Framework

3.1 Step 1. Enumeration of Dense Subgraphs

Our system enumerates dense subgraphs in the input graph $G = (V, E)$ in Step 1. One of typical dense subgraphs is the maximal clique. A clique is a set of nodes with every pair of nodes in the set connected by an edge and a maximal clique is a clique to which no node in the graph can be added to create a larger clique. There are various types of clique which relaxes a condition such as n-clique, n-clan, k-plex and k-core [9]. For example, n-clique is a group of at least size n within which each node is n or fewer steps from every other node.

We need to select one dense subgraph from these types. The choice criteria are the clustering coefficient and the average number of dense subgraphs which each node belongs to. Because nearby nodes are connected densely in the case of the network where a clustering coefficient is high, many dense subgraphs can be extracted even if the condition is strict. On the other hand, in the case of the network where a cluster coefficient is low, enough number of dense subgraphs can't be extracted if the condition is strict.

3.2 Summary of Our Framework

Our proposed framework can extract the overlaps between communities by using the idea of the intersection graph. Our system weights edges by calculating the similarity of the semantic information and address a problem of the edge's inhomogeneity in network. The input is one graph $G = (V, E)$. V is the set of nodes and E is that of edges. Additionally, semantic information are given to the nodes and edges. We apply the following four steps to this graph. We describe the detail about each step from Section 3.2-3.5.

- **Step 1. Enumeration of dense subgraphs:** Our system enumerates dense subgraphs (generally, it is called clique) from graph $G = (V, E)$.
- **Step 2. Conversion to the intersection graph:** Our system regards each subgraph enumerated in Step 1 as one node and convert them to the intersection graph.
- **Step 3. Calculation of the weight of edges:** Our system calculates the weight of edges by using the degree of overlaps of the sets (dense subgraphs) and the similarity of semantic information between the sets.
- **Step 4. Clustering based on the modularity:** Our system divides the nodes in the intersection graph into clusters by using a clustering method based on the modularity.

3.3 Step 2. Conversion to the Intersection Graph

When there are several sets (dense subgraphs) $S_i(i = 1, \cdots, n)$, our system generates a node v_i for each set S_i. If there are common component for two arbitrary nodes v_i and v_j, our system puts the edge between the two nodes. The undirected graph obtained like this is called the intersection graph [3]. Our system sets each dense subgraph enumerated in Step 1 as one set and make the intersection graph G'=(V',E') from the input graph G=(V,E) in Step 2.

3.4 Step 3. Calculation of the Weight of Edges

Our system calculates the weight of edges in the intersection graph in Step 3. The weight is calculated from two indicators. The first is the degree of overlaps of the two sets which correspond to both endpoints of an edge in the intersection graph. The second is the similarity of the semantic information such as texts and attributes appeared in above two sets.

There are the co-occurrence frequency, the Jaccard coefficient and so on as the degree of overlaps of two arbitrary sets X, Y [10]. We express this degree as $d(X, Y)$ and implement the following Jaccard coefficient in this paper.

$$d(X, Y) = \frac{| X \cap Y |}{| X \cup Y |} \tag{1}$$

The method which uses vector space model as the similarity of the semantic information of two arbitrary sets X, Y can be considered. For example, in case our system calculates the similarity from the texts, our system regards each set as one vector, evaluates $tf \cdot idf$ values for the keyword which is occurred in the texts of the set, and characterizes the vector. Then set x, y as vector of the two sets X, Y and calculate the similarity between the vectors by using the cosine. The texts corresponding to the nodes and the edges between the sets are the page texts and the anchor texts (text around anchor) in the case of the WWW, and those are self-introduction profiles and friend introduction sentences in the case of the SNS. We call this the similarity of the semantic information $sim(X, Y)$.

$$sim(X, Y) = cos\theta = \frac{x \cdot y}{\| x \| \| y \|} \tag{2}$$

We define the weight for the edge between node v_i and v_j in the intersection graph corresponding to the set X, Y by using the degree of overlaps of the sets and the similarity of the semantic information.

$$w(i, j) = w(X, Y) = \frac{d(X, Y)}{1 + \epsilon - sim(X, Y)} \tag{3}$$

Now ϵ is the invariable for the denominator not to be 0.

3.5 Step 4. Clustering Based on the Modularity

Our system divides the intersection graph generated in Step 3 into the community in Step 4. When our system divide one network into several communities in the community detection, there is a problem how we evaluate the division. Addressing the problem, the idea called modularity that is very instinctive despite simple idea is now recognized generally. This is defined by Newman et al [5]. This is based on an idea that a random network does not show the community structure. When the division result P_k (P_k is a divition of the nodes into k groups) is given, the modularity is represented by following module function $Q(P_k)$.

$$Q(P_k) = \sum_{i=1}^{k} (e_{ii} - a_i^2) \tag{4}$$

Briefly speaking, e_{ii} represents the ratio of the edges for the total edges that exists in the community i. And a_i represents the expected value of the ratio of the edges that exist in the community i. If the division become more properly, the rate of the edge in the community become higher value. As a result, the value of the module function Q is increased. This coincides with the definition of the community described in Section 1. The clustering based on the modularity is the clustering method that aims maximizing module function Q.

3.6 Expectation to the Friend Recommendation System

We apply the above clustering framework to SNS network in Section 4. Generally, the SNS user tends to connect actual world's friends. The way to find the friends is that user traces the existing connections on SNS. Another way is to use a friend search function which is equipped in SNS. However it is difficult to find friends in the former case because the user need to see many pages of the people irrelevant to him. It is also difficult in the latter case because he need to see many pages of the people who have same name but not related to him. Now it is thought that people in the same cluster might be friends each other if it assumes that our proposed method can get a proper cluster. Wherein, we can help the user to find his friends effectively by introducing the people unconnected to him in the same cluster.

4 Application to SNS Network

Our study targets a following network. It has various relationships between the nodes and we can use semantic information represented these relationships. Then we select mixi ($http : //mixi.jp/$) that is the most popular SNS in Japan as a network of an implementation example. Users write self-introduction profiles and write friend introduction sentences for their friends in mixi, therefore it is easy to get the semantic information. Additionally, there are various relationships between users such as the connection of university, the working place, the connection of hobby. However, service of friend introduction sentences is unique service in mixi and is not equipped in all SNS.

4.1 Dataset

Examinees are the users of mixi. Then the examinee is put as a center user and the link structure from the center user to two in the radius is extracted. The friend introduction sentences between users in dataset are collected as semantic information. We invited four users as central users.

4.2 Implementation

We select the maximal clique as dense subgraphs in Step 1 and the Jaccard coefficient as the degree of overlaps of the sets in Step 3. We select friend introduction sentences as semantic information in Step 3 and use the vector space model for calculating the weight of edges in the intersection graph. Only the nouns are extracted by the morphological analysis of these friend introduction sentences and our system regards this as the component of each vector in vector space model. Our system evaluates $tf \cdot idf$ value for each noun extracted from all friend introduction sentences in certain maximal clique (corresponding with node in intersection graph) and replace the noun by one vector, then calculate the similarity between the nearby maximal cliques by equation(3). We also set ϵ in equation(3) as 0.1. We use the method of repeatedly finding combination that maximizes increment of the module function in Step 4. In this method, firstly we regard each node as one community. When one community i and another community j are merged, the increment ΔQ of the module function Q is following.

$$\Delta Q = 2(e_{ij} - a_i a_j) \tag{5}$$

Until the figure of the community becomes one, our system finds the combination of the communities maximized Q value and merge these communities. Q value is calculated in each merged step. Finaly, our system outputs the division result of merged step of the highest Q value. We call this method *proposed method* from now on. We also implement the method using only the Jaccard coefficient as weight of edges in Step 3. By comparing *proposed method* with this, we can research the contribution of the similarity of the semantic information. This method equals the method of Evrett et al [3]. We call this method *Evrett method* from now on.

4.3 Result of Experiment

We extracted the communities from the data of examinee 1. We exclude the communities that the examinee do not contain and show the result in Figure 1 and 2. Figure 1 is in the case of proposed method and Figure 2 is in the case of Evrett method. The node of examinee 1 is surrounded by thick circle. In Figure 1, there are five communities(A-E). The diamond nodes show nodes which belong to two or more communities. The white nodes in A and the diamond node belong to the community A. The black nodes in B and the diamond node belong to the community B. In Figure 2, there are two communities. The black nodes show the first community, and all nodes show the second community. We leave out the figures showed the result of examinee 2-4 for convenience of space.

Fig. 1. Result of community detection for examinee 1 (proposed method)

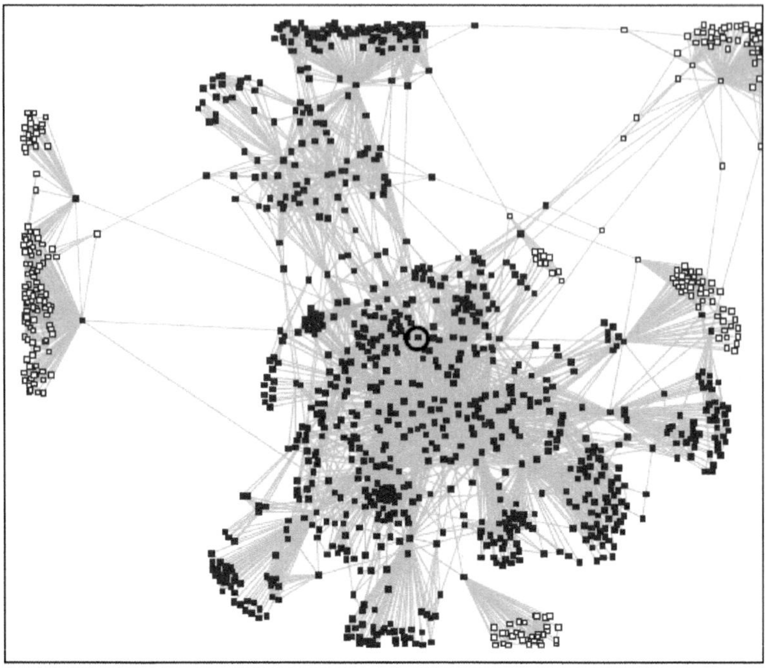

Fig. 2. Result of community detection for examinee 1 (Evrett method)

4.4 Consideration

We can see that the proposed method could extract meaningful five communities for examinee 1. In Figure 1, A showed the connection of club in the examinee's university, B showed the connection of his university, C showed the connection of his friends in hometown, D showed the connection of university in Tokyo, and E showed the connection of university in Okayama. In A and B, the examinee locates in the center of the community, but in C-E, the examinee locates in the surface of the community. For D and E, the three nodes surrounded by dashed circle show the connection of same high school. It is thought that these three nodes and examinee 1 act as intermediary of D and E. Using the term of the field of social network analysis [9], examinee 1 is high centrality in A and B but low centrality in C-E. However he is at the location where the betweenness is high in D and E.

Evrett method for examinee 1 extracted two communities. One is big community and the other is bigger community including it. These two communities are not useful because they mixed communities extracted in proposed method.

Proposed method for examinee 2 extracted five communities (F-J). F and H show the connection of the same high school and the same grade, therefore it is more appropriate to merge them. G shows the connection of the club in high school. I and J show the connection of the same university, therefore it is appropriate to merge them. For both pairs ($F, H$and I, J), the person who have numerous number of friends exist in the one of communities (H and I). He tends to make a big community with his surroundings and it is hard for another community to merge the big community. As a result, it is thought the big community tends not to be merged but to be remained.

Proposed method for examinee 3 and 4 can not get useful result. The feature is similar to the result of Evrett method. The reason is that because the correct communities included a lot of common nodes each other, it is hard to separate them. Additionally, even if the critical words appear, it can not affect to separate because we use all nouns appeared in friend introduction sentences. We try the method using the only critical words or using another definition as dense subgraphs in the future work.

5 Conclusion and Future Work

In this paper, we proposed the new framework for the community detection. This framework can extract the overlaps of communities by using an idea of the intersection graph. We also addressed a problem of the edge's inhomogeneity. We applied this framework to actual social network. We will conduct a detailed analysis for the result of the community detection and apply it to friend recommendation system in the future.

References

1. Newman, M.E.J.: The Structure and function of complex networks. SIAM Review 45, 167–256 (2003)
2. Danon, L., Duch, J., Guilera, A.D., Arenas, A.: Comparing community structure identification. Statistical Mechanics, P09008 (2005)
3. Everett, M.G., Borgatti, S.P.: Analyzing Clique Overlap. Connections 21(1), 49–61 (1998)
4. Flake, G.W., Lawrence, S., Giles, C.L., Coetzee, F.: Self- Organization of the Web and Identification of Communities. IEEE Computer 35(3), 66–71 (2002)
5. Newman, M.E.J., Girvan, M.: Finding and evaluating community structure in networks. Physical Review E 69(2), 026113 (2004)
6. Dunn, J.C.: A fuzzy relative of the ISODATA process and its use in detecting compact well-separated clusters. J. Cybernet. 3, 32–57 (1973)
7. Reichardt, J., Bornholdt, S.: Detecting fuzzy community structures in complex networks with potts model. Physical Review Letters 93(21), 218701 (2004)
8. Reichardt, J., Bornholdt, S.: Statistical mechanics of community detection. Physical Review E 74(1), 016110 (2006)
9. Scott, J.: Social Network Analysis: A Handbook, 2nd edn. Sage Publications, London (2000)
10. Rasmussen, E.: Clustering Algorithms. In: Frakes, W.B., Yates, R.B. (eds.) Information Retrieval: Data Structures and Algorithms. Prentice Hall, Englewood Cliffs (1992)

C&C: An Effective Algorithm for Extracting Web Community Cores*

Xianchao Zhang, Yueting Li, and Wenxin Liang**

School of Software, Dalian University of Technology, China
xczhang@dlut.edu.cn,
liyueting@mail.dlut.edu.cn,
wxliang@dlut.edu.cn

Abstract. Communities is a significant pattern of the Web. A community is a group of pages related to a common topic. Web communities are able to be characterized by dense bipartite subgraphs. Each community almost surely contains at least one core. A core is a complete bipartite graph (CBG). Focusing on the issues of extracting such community cores from the Web, in this paper we propose an effective **C&C** algorithm based on *combination* and *consolidation* to extract all embedded cores in web graphs. Experiments on real and large data collections demonstrate that the proposed algorithm **C&C** is efficient and effective for the community core extraction because: 1) all the largest emerging cores can be identified; 2) identifying all the embedded cores with different sizes only requires one-pass execution of **C&C**; 3) the extraction process needs no user-determined parameters in **C&C**.

Keywords: Web mining; Community core; Bipartite graph.

1 Introduction

Web communities is a significant structure of the Web. A web community is defined as a set of web pages concerning a group of individuals sharing a common interest. These communities play an important role in analyzing the structures of the Web. Therefore, automatically finding those communities would be a great help to modern search engines.

Previous work on the issues of extracting communities using link analysis in web graphs can be roughly divided into two categories. One category is based on the availability of one or more seeds for a possible community whose members are those pages closest to the given seed or seeds. Technologies involved in this category refer to max-flow/min-cut [6,7,10,15], HITS [8,11,4] and so on.

The other category does not require any seeds and aims to extract communities existing in the Web as many as possible. Our work here also belongs to

* This work was partially supported by NSFC under grant No. 60873180, and by the start-up funding (#1600-893313) for newly appointed academic staff of Dalian University of Technology, China.

** Corresponding author.

M. Yoshikawa et al. (Eds.): DASFAA 2010, LNCS 6193, pp. 316–326, 2010.

the second category. Previous work mostly focused on finding dense subgraphs with certain predetermined characteristics, such as [12,9,5,14]. It is worthwhile to note that Kumar et al. [12] proposed a method named Trawling to identify cyber-communities by extracting community cores. However, there are no efficient techniques in common for discovery of abundant objective communities without subjective parameters.

In this paper, we pay attention to the problems of distinguishing all objective cores of communities in a large collection of web pages. We propose a novel algorithm based on *combination* and *consolidation* (**C&C** algorithm for short) using several heuristic methods. In the **C&C** algorithm, a number of unit cores are firstly extracted by the technique of *combination*, and then the cores that belong to larger complete bipartite graphs are automatically combined by the algorithm of *consolidation*. The **C&C** algorithm is much more efficient and effective than the Trawling algorithm because: 1) **C&C** does not need any user-determined parameters; 2) Identifying all the embedded cores with different sizes only requires one-pass execution of **C&C**, while it needs many times of iterative execution of Trawling; 3) **C&C** is capable of extracting all the largest complete bipartite subgraphs emerged in the web graph, which are more valuable than the fixed-size cores extracted by Trawling.

The reminder of the paper proceeds as follows. Section 2 reviews some related techniques and backgrounds. In Section 3, Algorithm **C&C** is introduced. We report our experimental results and discuss performance of proposed algorithms and other related issues in Section 4, followed by conclusion and future work in Section 5.

2 Backgrounds

This section first reviews several related technologies, followed by a profile of Trawling and some characteristics we conclude.

2.1 Link Analysis

Link analysis [17,13] is a major tool in the field of the World Wide Web. One central property of web information retrieval is the relativity among web pages, and linkages imply predicting information to determine the importance of web pages, which is the start of link analysis.

From the view of linkage analysis, Web is a directed graph $G = (V, E)$, where V is a set of nodes representing web pages, and E is the representation of linkages. Given u, v be a pair nodes of a directed graph G, if there exists an edge $e = (u, v)$ delegating a linkage from u to v, then e is an *outlink* of u, and an *inlink* of v. In addition, u is called a *parent* of v, and v is a *child* of u. For each node u, we use $P(u)$ and $T(u)$ to represent the set of its parents and children, respectively. Then, the *outdegree* of u, $O(u) = |T(u)|$, i.e., the number of u's children, and the *indegree* of u, $I(u) = |P(u)|$, i.e., the number of u's parents. Heuristically, communities can be regarded as dense subgraphs of web pages [5].

2.2 Trawling

In [12], Kumar et al. developed a mathematical intuition in which web communities are able to be characterized by dense directed bipartite subgraphs, and a random large enough and dense enough bipartite directed subgraph of the Web almost surely has a core.

A bipartite graph is a graph whose nodes can be partitioned into two disjoined sets, which are symbolized by L and R, and every directed edge $e(u, v)$ in the graph is pointed from a node u in L to a node v in R. Moreover, every node in L is named a *fan* and each node in R is called a *center*. A graph $G = (V, E)$ is a complete bipartite graph (CBG) or a *core* if $\forall u \in L$ of G, $T(u) = R$, and $\forall u \in R$, $P(u) = L$. A largest core is a core that is not a subset of other complete bipartite subgraphs. Furthermore, $C(u)$ denotes the cores including node u, and $C\{X\}$ indicates the cores in which set X is contained. The graph depicted in Fig.1 is a $(3, 4)$ core, i.e. a core with 4 fans in L and 3 centers in R, and it is denoted as $C_{4,3}$.

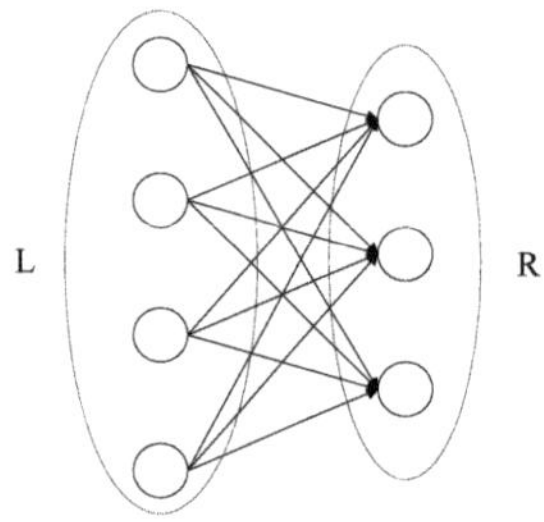

Fig. 1. A $C_{4,3}$ Bipartite Graph

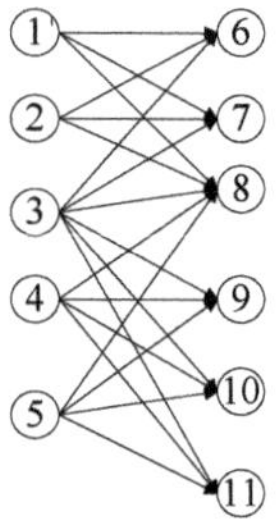

Fig. 2. An example of bipartite graph

Based on the hypothesis that dense bipartite graphs are signatures of web communities, Kumar et al. proposed Trawling, an approach to extract cores from the Web. To identify community cores, Trawling system is divided into four steps. The first step is iterative pruning, which is to prune nodes in L whose *outdegrees* are smaller than j and nodes in R with *indegree* smaller than i when looking for (i, j) cores. In the process of pruning nodes, the associate edges also should be deleted, and therefore this step should be iteratively. After iterative pruning, the second step is inclusion-exclusion pruning, which either eliminate a page from contention, or discover an (i, j) core. Given a node x whose *outdegree* is exactly equal to j, Kumar et al. employed *Criterion 1* to determine whether x belongs to a core. The third step is to generate cores and filter nepotistic ones whose fans come from the same Website. Finally, a priori algorithm of Agrawal and Srikanth [2] is employed to finish off.

Criterion 1. *Let* $c_1, c_2, \ldots, c_n$ *be centers adjacent to* x. *Let* $N(c_i)$ *represent the neighborhoods of* c_i. *Then,* x *is part of a core if and only if the intersection of sets* $N(c_i)$ *has size at least* i.

2.3 Discussion on Trawling

The goal of Trawling is to find non-overlapped cores as many as possible, and it appears that virtually all of these cores correspond to real communities rather than coincidental occurrences of complete bipartite subgraphs.

Example 1. *In Fig.2, when looking for* $(3, 3)$ *cores, the output of Trawling is* $C\{L(1, 2, 3), R(6, 7, 8)\}$. *While, when* $i = 3$, $j = 4$, *the final result of Trawling is* $C\{L(3, 4, 5), R(8, 9, 10, 11)\}$

As shown in *Example 1*, the consequential cores of Trawling are yielding to values of i and j. Under the circumstances that $i > 3$ or $j > 4$, no complete bipartite subgraphs would be identified from Fig.2. While, the unknown and tremendous characteristics of the Web make the initialization of i and j become a big challenge. In addition, some removal strategies of Trawling would destroy the structures of other complete bipartite subgraphs and certain cores would be missing. Let's return to the graph in Fig.2, node 3 belongs to both $C_{3,3}$ and $C_{3,4}$, while the removal of nodes that related to $C_{3,3}$ would destroy the structure of $C_{3,4}$. Besides, one community might has more than one cores, it is unreasonable that those bipartite cores are non-overlapped. For example, both $C_{3,3}$ and $C_{3,4}$ in Fig.2 might be the cores of certain communities.

3 C&C Algorithm

To overcome the drawbacks of Trawling described in Section 2.3, we put over an efficacious algorithm C&C. To extract all the largest cores, C&C could be approximately divided into two phases. The first phase is to extract all unit cores according to Criterion 2, and the second phase is the consolidation of unit cores output by the first one.

3.1 Unit Cores Extraction

The criterion of finding a core proposed by Kumar et al. [12] is just suit to vertices whose *ourdegrees* are exactly equal to j. Heuristically, a new criterion is proposed to estimate whether an arbitrary potential fan qualifies to be a part of a community.

Criterion 2. *Let* c_1,c_2,...,c_n *be* n *centers adjacent to a node* x. *Let* $N(c_i)$ *represents the neighborhoods of* c_i, *i.e., the set of fans that point to* c_i. *Then,* x *is part of a core if and only if one kind of its combinations* $c^j_{N(x)}$ *meets the intersection of its neighborhood sets has size at least* i.

All cores from a node are output if more than one type of combinations satisfy Criterion 2; otherwise, none is output. The cores generated in this step are the units to be consolidated next step. In other words, the values of i and j indicate the basic unit of cores and we initialize them both to be 3 which is the smallest value of Trawling [12]. The goal of this step is to enumerate all existing $C_{3,3}$ of the graph. For convenience of operation, A map *seeds* of elements $< O, V >$ is introduced, where O are integer keys indicating values of *outdegree*, and V are sets containing pages whose *outdegrees* are equal to their corresponding keys in O. In the process of finding $C_{3,3}$, always the first element of *seeds* is fetched until *seeds* is empty. The detailed process of extracting the unit cores based on combinations is illustrated in *Algorithm 1.*

Algorithm 1. Cores extraction

```
Input:  seeds: a map of nodes and their corresponding outdegree
        G: a web graph < V, E >
        i: number of fans
        j: number of centers
Output: all existing C_{3,3}
for r ∈ seeds, compute C^3_{T(r)} do
    for each C^3_{T(r)} of T(r) do
        compute the intersection size of fans pointed to these 3 centers;
        if the intersection size ≥ 3 then
            output these fans and 3 centers;
        end if
    end for
    delete r and iteratively modify seeds and G;
end for
```

Example 2. *Still taking Fig.2 for example, C&C can extract five* $C_{3,3}$ *from it, which are* $C\{L(1,2,3), R(6,7,8)\}$, $C\{L(3,4,5), R(8,9,10)\}$, $C\{L(3,4,5), R(8,9,11)\}$, $C\{L(3,4,5), R(9,10,11)\}$ *and* $C\{L(3,4,5), R(8,10,11)\}$.

As depicted in *Example 2*, this step outputs all existing $C_{3,3}$, while only one $C_{3,3}$ was extracted by Trawling showing in *Example 1.* However, a great number of $C_{3,3}$ have the same fans or centers, therefore, we need next step to consolidate these closely related cores.

3.2 Cores Consolidation

In order to consolidate these closely related cores, a heuristic step is adopted to merge these cores based on *Theorem 1.*

Theorem 1. *Given two complete bipartite graphs* C_1, C_2, *if fans or centers of* C_1 *are exactly the same as those of* C_2, *then a graph whose fans are the union of* $C_1^{'}s$ *fans and* $C_2^{'}s$ *fans and centers are the union of* $C_1^{'}s$ *centers and* $C_2^{'}s$ *centers still be a complete bipartite graph.*

Proof 1. C_1 *and* C_2 *are both complete bipartite graphs,* L_1, L_2 *are two sets of fans of* C_1 *and* C_2 *respectively, and* R_1, R_2 *are two sets of centers of* C_1 *and*

C_2. $\forall u \in L_1$, $T(u) = R_1$ and $\forall u \in L_2$, $T(u) = R_2$. Besides, $\forall u \in L_1$ (or R_1), u also $\in L_2$ (or R_2), hence $\forall u \in L_1$ and L_2 (or R_1 and R_2), $T(u) = R_1 \cup R_2$ (or $P(u) = L_1 \cup L_2$). According to the definition of complete bipartite graph in Section 2.1, Theorem 1 is proved.

According to *Theorem 1*, combine cores that have the same fans or centers could obtain plenty of non-fixed-size bipartite complete graphs. A map *Cores* of elements $< T, I >$ is introduced, where T is a set containing fans of cores, and I is a set including corresponding centers of cores. Then cores stored in the map *Cores* are united according to the keys or values of them. *Algorithm 2* illustrates the process of consolidating bipartite cores generated by *Algorithm 1*.

Algorithm 2. Cores consolidation

Input: *Cores*: a map of cores output by Algorithm 1
T: a set of fans
I: a set of centers
Output: merged cores

set Cores to $\emptyset$;
for each core output by algorithm 1 **do**
  set T to $\emptyset$;
  set I to $\emptyset$;
  read fans of core to set T;
  read centers of core to set I;
  if T has exist in Cores **then**
    insert $\langle T, I \cup Cores[T] \rangle$ into Cores;
  end if
  if I has exist in Cores **then**
    insert $\langle T \cup Cores[I], I \rangle$ into Cores;
  else
    insert$\langle T, I \rangle$ into Cores;
  end if
end for

Example 3. *After consolidation, the cores enumerating in Example 2 are merged into $C\{L(1,2,3), R(6,7,8)\}$, $C\{L(3,4,5), R(8,9,10,11)\}$.*

This step consolidates all the unit cores $C_{3,3}$ output by *Algorithm 1* into largest bipartite graphs. As described in *Example 3*, two largest cores embedding in Fig.2 are totally discovered.

4 Experiments

This section gives a presentation of our experiments, followed by some experimental results and analysis on real, large web collections. We apply our method on uk-2007-05 data collection [3], which includes 105,896,555 nodes and 3,738,733,648 links. All of our experiments are performed on a single PC with an Intel 2.67GHz Pentium processor and 2GB memory.

4.1 Dataset

For such a huge data collection, some pre-processing steps are necessary to prune meaningless linkages and pages that surely cannot be any parts of bipartite cores. Then, the web graph is translated into advisable data structures.

Data Preprocess. Since most linkages among pages come from the same website are just for navigation instead of adoration that such linkages were pruned from the page collection. Then we removed the possible duplicates or mirrors according to *mirror_similarity* given in *Definition 1.* It is efficient for that the similarity of two pages just rests on the ratio of their common children. The empirical threshold we chosen to determine whether two pages are mirrors is 0.85. The code is available online [16].

Definition 1. *Let x, y be two pages of a graph, the mirror_similarity of x and y is calculated by next equation 1.*

$$mirror\_similarity(x, y) = \frac{0.5*(|x \cap T(y)| + |y \cap T(x)|) + (T(x) \cap T(y))}{min\{|T(x)|, |T(y)|\}} . \quad (1)$$

Drawn lessons from [12], we pruned both popular and unpopular pages. The popular pages, such as www.yahoo.com are pages that are highly referred; the unpopular pages are those that are seldom referred. The pages that have more than 50 parents were removed from the data sets in our experiments. We consider a page is unpopular if its parents less than 2 [14], and hence the pages that have less than 2 parents were also removed.

As a result of pre-process, the rest nodes, less than 4,000,000, are capable of fitting into 2G memory so that both Trawling and **C&C** were carried out without accessing hard disk.

Data Structure. An unique integer was allocated as ID for each *URL*, which indexes two adjacency lists *outLinks* and *inLinks*. The entry of *outLinks* and *inLinks* is corresponding to each URL by storing its ID. For *outLinks*, each entry holds IDs which its URL points to. As expected, IDs of its parents are saved in every entry of *inLinks*. The reasons using adjacency lists are because: 1) parents or children of a node can be immediately obtained just through an integer index of arrays; 2) the number of parents or children of a node can be easily acquired just by the size of list, and if a node is deleted, the size of a list will dynamically change.

To heighten the efficiency of subsequent operations to find $C_{3,3}$, iteratively pruning was employed the here. We iteratively pruned the all the nodes and corresponding edges in *outLinks* whose *outdegree* less than 3, meanwhile, pruned nodes and corresponding edges in *inLinks* whose *indegree* less than 3.

4.2 Results

At the beginning, for the convenience of comparing the consequential cores, a tiny synthetic data collection including 20 nodes was used. Then, both C&C and Trawling were executed on processed uk-2007-05 data collection.

Fig.3 shows the link relationship of the synthetic data set with 20 nodes. The results of **C&C** versus Trawling on the synthetic data set are summarized in Table 1: 1) All the embedded cores can be extracted by only one-pass execution of **C&C**; 2) **C&C** is capable of identifying the largest and non-fixed-size complete cores, which is more valuable than only discovering the fixed-size cores; 3) the extraction process in **C&C** needs no user-determined parameters.

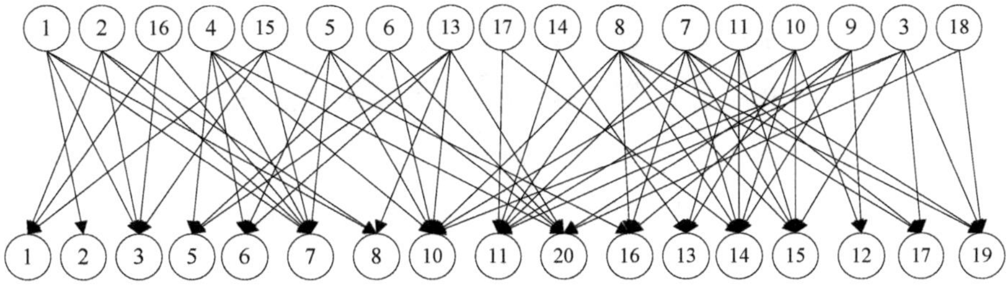

Fig. 3. Synthetic data set

Table 1. C&C vs. Trawling on synthetic data set

	C&C	Trawling
Parameters	No	Yes
Execution	1	2
Results	C{L(2,15,16), R(1,3,7)}	$i = 3, j = 3$
	C{L(4,6,13), R(5,10,20)}	C{L(2,15,16), R(1,3,7)}
	C{L(4,5,13), R(6,10,20)}	C{L(4,6,13), R(5,10,20)}
	C{L(7,8,10), R(11,14,15)}	$i = 3, j = 4$
	C{L(3,7,8), R(11,15,17,19)}	C{L(3,7,8), R(11,15,17,19)}

Algorithm 1 found 59,877 unit $C_{3,3}$ from uk-2007-05 data. After employed Algorithm 2, there were 3204 cores left. Fig.4 presents the distribution of core sizes output by **C&C** algorithm and number of corresponding cores output by Trawling. From Fig.4, we can see that the number of most kinds of cores identified by **C&C** algorithm are greater than Trawling, which better achieve the goal of Trawling to find cores embedded in web graphs as many as possible. It is also forgivable that Trawling extracts more cores than **C&C** under some circumstances, as **C&C** merely output the largest $C_{i,j}$ while Trawling also takes the super cores of a $C_{i,j}$ as $C_{i,j}$.

In addition, Finding all these $C_{3,3}$, $C_{3,4}$, $C_{3,5}$, $C_{4,3}$ and so on just take one time running of **C&C**, while Trawling would be executed more than 20 times according to various values of i or j. Since **C&C** leaves out a time-consuming procedure, the iterative pruning, the total running time of **C&C** reduces to less than 20 minutes. In contrast, one round execution of Trawling costs more than 100 minutes. Fig.5 depicts the distribution of cores versus the number of their

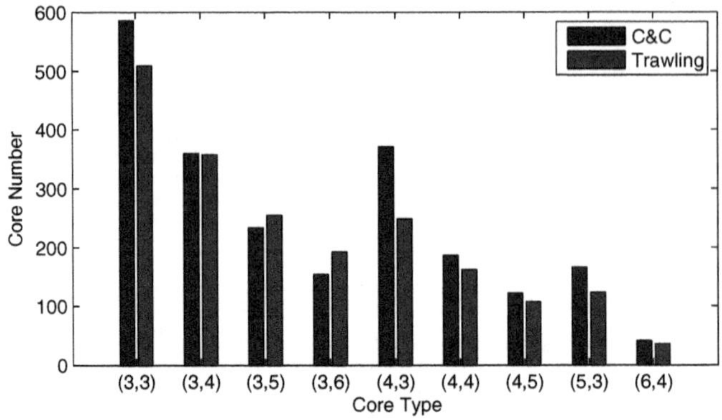

Fig. 4. C&C vs. Trawling on distribution of consequential cores

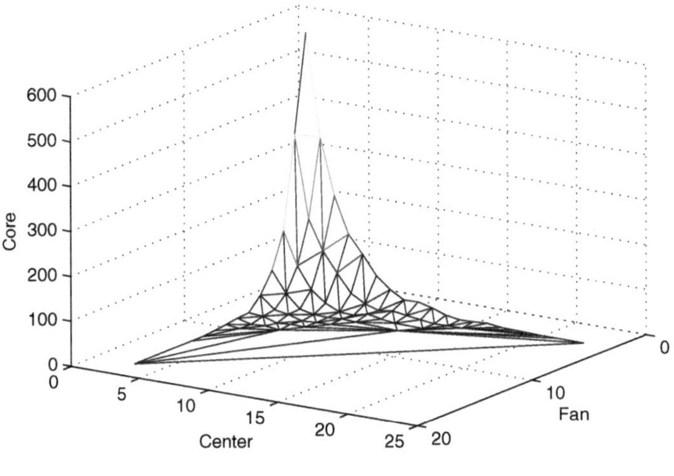

Fig. 5. Distribution of cores vs. Fans and Centers

fans and centers, which shows that the distributions of cores versus fans and centers obey power-law [1]. This phenomenon indicates that the distributions of cores are concordant with the distributions of links.

Furthermore, relying on manual inspection, we randomly chose 100 cores in five times to analysis whether they correspond to real communities, which demonstrated that almost all these cores had community patterns. To reflect the community pattern of identified cores, we present *Example 4* to show a core whose members are all related to e-shop identified by **C&C**.

Example 4. Core of e-shop output by C&C
Fans:
http://www.ldb.co.uk/index.htm
http://www.ldb.co.uk/urc/urchome.shtml
http://www.lichfieldwebdesign.co.uk/watercolourlandscapes/
http://www.vitaminshop.org.uk/
Centers:
http://www.cathedralchemdry.co.uk/
http://www.conveyorbeltsuk.co.uk/
http://www.dragsys.co.uk/
http://www.emuoils.co.uk/
http://www.iso9000uk.co.uk/
http://www.jointgenie.co.uk/ http://www.sugarsurgeons.co.uk/
http://www.suttoncoldfieldymca.org.uk/

Example 5 shows an $e-shop$ $C_{3,3}$ found by Trawling, which is a subgraph of the core depicted in *Example 4*. Comparison of *Example 4* and *Example 5* shows that **C&C** is capable of finding more complete and abundant community cores.

Example 5. Core of e-shop output by Trawling
Fans:
http://www.ldb.co.uk/urc/urchome.shtml
http://www.lichfieldwebdesign.co.uk/watercolourlandscapes/
http://www.vitaminshop.org.uk/
Centers:
http://www.dragsys.co.uk/
http://www.iso9000uk.co.uk/
http://www.suttoncoldfieldymca.org.uk/

5 Conclusion and Future Work

Communities are very important structures for people to obtain valuable information from the Web. Therefore, to effectively discover meaningful communities related to specific topics from a large number of webpages in the Web becomes a challenge job. In this paper, we proposed a novel **C&C** algorithm based on combination and consolidation techniques. The **C&C** algorithm overcomes the drawbacks of the typical CBG-based algorithm Trawling in the following aspects: 1) **C&C** is more efficient because all the embedded cores can be extracted by only one-pass execution; 2) **C&C** is capable of extracting all the largest complete cores, which are more valuable than the fixed-size cores extracted by Trawling; 3) the extraction process in **C&C** needs no user-determined parameters. We conducted experiments using both synthetic and real data sets to evaluate the effectiveness of **C&C** comparing with the Trawling algorithm. The experimental results indicate that our method is superior to the original Trawling algorithm.

As one part of our future work, the page's context should be considered when finding bipartite cores. In addition, an efficient algorithm to divide massive data collection into independent memory-suitable sub-collections is desirable. Besides, investigation on chasing down the relationships among the extracted cores and the corresponding communities and organizing them into hierarchical structures is another part of our future work. In addition, automatically assigning themes to each community level is also a worthwhile research.

References

1. Adamic, L.A., Huberman, B.A.: Pawer-Law Distribution of the World Wide Web. Science 287, 2115 (2000)
2. Agrawal, R., Srikanth, R.: Fast algorithms for mining association rules. In: proceedings of 20th International Conference on Very Large Data Bases, pp. 487–499. Morgan Kaufmann, San Fransisco (1994)
3. Boldi, P., Vigna, S.: The Web Graph Framework: Compression Techniques. In: Proceedings of the Thirteenth International World Wide Web Conference, pp. 595–601. ACM, New York (2004)
4. Borodin, A., Gareth, O., Jeffrey, S., Tsaparas, P.: Finding authorities and hubs from link structures on the World Wide Web. In: Proceedings of the 10th international conference on World Wide Web, pp. 415–429. ACM, New York (2001)
5. Dourisboure, Y., Geraci, F., Pellegrini, M.: Extraction and classification of dense communities in the web. In: 16th international conference on World Wide Web, pp. 461–470. ACM, New York (2007)
6. Flake, G.W., Lawrence, S., Giles, C.L.: Efficient identification of Web communities. In: Proceedings of the sixth ACM SIGKDD international conference on Knowledge discovery and data mining, pp. 150–160. ACM, New York (2000)
7. Flake, G.W., Lawrence, S., Giles, C.L., Coetzee, F.M.: Self-Organization and Identification of Web Communities. Computer 35, 66–71 (2002)
8. Gibson, D., Kleinberg, J.M., Raghavan, P.: Inferring Web communities from link topology. In: Proceedings of the ninth ACM conference on Hypertext and hypermedia: links, objects, time and space, pp. 225–234. ACM, New York (1998)
9. Gibson, D., Kumar, R., Tomkins, A.: Discovering large dense subgraphs in massive graphs. In: 31st international conference on Very large data bases, pp. 721–732. ACM, New York (2005)
10. Hao, J.X., Orlin, J.B.: A faster algorithm for finding the minimum cut in a graph. In: Proceedings of the third annual ACM-SIAM symposium on Discrete algorithms, pp. 165–174. SIAM, Philadelphia (1992)
11. Kleinberg, J.M.: Authoritative sources in a hyperlinked environment. Journal of the ACM 46, 604–632 (1999)
12. Kumar, R., Raghavan, P., Rajagopalan, S., Tomkins, A.: Trawling the Web for emerging cyber-communities. Computer Networks 31, 11–16 (1999)
13. Park, H.W., Thelwall, M.: Hyperlink Analyses of the World Wide Web: A Review. Journal of Computer Mediated Communication 8(4) (2003)
14. Reddy, P.K., Kitsuregawa, M.: An Approach to Find Related Communities Based on Bipartite Graphs. Institute of Electronics, Information and Communication Engineers 101, 7–14 (2001)
15. Stoer, M., Wagner, F.: A simple min-cut algorithm. Journal of the ACM 44, 585–591 (1997)
16. WISDOM Lab.: `http://wisdom.dlut.edu.cn/`
17. Zhang, Y.C., Yu, J.X., Hou, J.Y.: Web communities: analysis and construction. Springer, Berlin (2006)

Extracting Local Web Communities Using Lexical Similarity*

Xianchao Zhang, Wen Xu, and Wenxin Liang**

School of Software, Dalian University of Technology, China
xczhang@dlut.edu.cn,
wendyxuwen@mail.dlut.edu.cn,
wxliang@dlut.edu.cn

Abstract. The World Wide Web contains rich textual contents that are interconnected via complex hyperlinks. Most studies on web community extraction only focus on graph structures. Consequently, web communities are discovered purely in terms of explicit link information without considering textual properties of web pages. This paper proposes an improved algorithm based on Flake's method using the maximum flow algorithm. The improved algorithm considers the differences between edges in terms of importance, and assigns a well-designed capacity to each edge via the lexical similarity of web pages. Given a specific query, it also lends itself to a new and efficient ranking scheme for members in the extracted community. The experimental results indicate that our approach efficiently handles a variety of data sets across a novel optimization strategy of similarity computation.

Keywords: Community Extraction, Maximum Flow Algorithm, Lexical Similarity.

1 Introduction

The World Wide Web holds numerous communities, each providing resources on a specific topic, such as movies, associations and companies. Generally the web is reckoned as a directed graph, regarding web pages as nodes and hyperlinks as edges. A web community is a dense subgraph of a given web graph whose members are, in some sense, more similar to each other than to other non-community members.

The problem of detecting such communities within networks has been well studied. Early approaches such as spectral partitioning [12], the Kernighan-Lin algorithm [10], hierarchical clustering [13], and G-N algorithm [8] work well for specific types of problems (particularly graph bisection), but generally perform poorly in real networks. Recently, most works focus on graph partitioning approaches. In this case, discovering web community is identical to finding a proper

* This work was partially supported by NSFC under grant No. 60873180, and by the start-up funding (#1600-893313) for newly appointed academic staff of Dalian University of Technology, China.

** Corresponding author.

M. Yoshikawa et al. (Eds.): DASFAA 2010, LNCS 6193, pp. 327–337, 2010.

cut that separates a subgraph from the web graph. For example, Anderson and Lang [1] explore the problem of incubating seed sets into communities through random walks. Flake et al. [5, 6] firstly extract the community structure by recasting the problem into a maximum flow framework. Flake's community algorithm is fast in practice because its runtime is often determined by the size of the community it finds (not the whole graph). Moreover, it yields communities that have strong theoretical guarantees on their local and global properties.

In Flake's community identification algorithm, Flake heuristically assigns all edge capacities with a constant value but fails to take the semantic information of pages into account. Therefore, the extracted community often contains many noisy pages (which are irrelevant to the topic of the community) and the precision of the community decreases accordingly. Noriko Imafuji et al. assign edge capacities using hub and authority scores obtained from HITS calculation [9]. Yasuhito Asano et al. build a site-oriented framework to displace Flake's page-oriented framework [3]. Because these improvements only focus on the link structures of the web graph, we utilize the lexical similarity between web pages to represent differentiated importance of each edge, taking both link and text information into account. To compute the content-based similarity, we quantify each page using TF-IDF (Term Frequency-Inverse Document Frequency) vector, a popular metric for measuring the relevance of entities in documents, which also has effective performance when applied to web mining applications such as ranking of web pages [4, 16] and classification of hyper-linked document objects [2].

In summary, our main contributions in this paper are as follows:

Firstly, we examine the performance of Flake's method based upon the maximum flow algorithm and summarize possible drawbacks and problems caused by simply assigning a constant value to edge capacities.

Secondly, we apply TF-IDF to max-flow/min-cut algorithm by devising a new edge capacity assignment based on the semantic similarity (lexical similarity in specific), thus utilizing both link information and content information during community extraction.

Thirdly, we propose a new ranking strategy which not only considers text similarity but also strengthens the difference between candidate seeds. Besides, taking user's query into account, our strategy can be implemented as dynamic on-line algorithm.

Finally, by conducting experiments on randomly selected 20 topics, we show that our improved maximum flow algorithm outperforms the Flake's by greatly decreasing the number of noisy pages and extracting more topic-related pages with high efficiency and accuracy.

The rest of the paper is organized as follows. Section 2 states related work on Flake's maximum flow algorithm. In Section 3, the delicate assignment of edge capacities is addressed, followed by the heuristic approach for optimizing the computing and the explanation of our improved algorithm. Experimental results and analysis are conducted in Section 4. The conclusion and future work are summarized in Section 5.

2 Related Work

As stated in the previous section, our objective is to find a dense web subgraph given a specific topic. The method using the maximum flow algorithm for extracting web communities is first proposed by Flake [5, 6]. In this section, we begin with a subsection describing $s - t$ maximum flow algorithm. Next, we describe Flake's community algorithm followed with analysis and discussion about its performance in the context of quality and quantity.

2.1 Maximum Flow Algorithm

Let $G = \{V, E\}$ be a directed graph where V and E are a set of nodes and edges respectively. Denote (u, v) be a directed edge from the node u to v and each edge $(u, v) \in E$ has an assigned capacity $c(u, v) \in \mathbb{Z}^+$. Suppose s, t be the fixed nodes in V. The flow from s to t of G is a non-negative integer function f which satisfies the following conditions: $0 \leq f(u, v) \leq c(u, v)$ *for all* $(u, v) \in E$ and $\sum_{(u_i,v)\in E} f(u_i, v) = \sum_{(v,u_j)\in E} f(v, u_j)$ *for all* $v \in V - \{s, t\}$. The latter condition implies the total flow out of s equals to the total flow into t. The value of total flow is called a graph flow of G. The maximum flow algorithm finds the maximum flow of the graph.

Let $S \subseteq V$, $T = V/S$, and $s \in S$, $t \in T$. The set of edges $\{(u, v) \in E | u \in S, v \in T\}$ is called a $s - t$ cut on a graph G. A minimum cut is a cut whose capacity which minimizes the total capacities of the cut edges. The famous max flow - min cut theorem [7] proves that a maximum graph flow equals to the value of a minimum cut.

2.2 Community Extraction Based on the Maximum Flow Algorithm

According to the graph theory, Flake et al. define a community on the web as a set of sites that have more links (in either direction) to members of the community than to non-members [5, 6] (Fig. 1).

They have proved a theorem that after the s-t maximum flow algorithm performed on the web graph, all the nodes accessible from s through unsaturated edges satisfy the definition of a web community. Because it is not practical to apply s-t maximum flow algorithm on the whole web graph due to the web size,

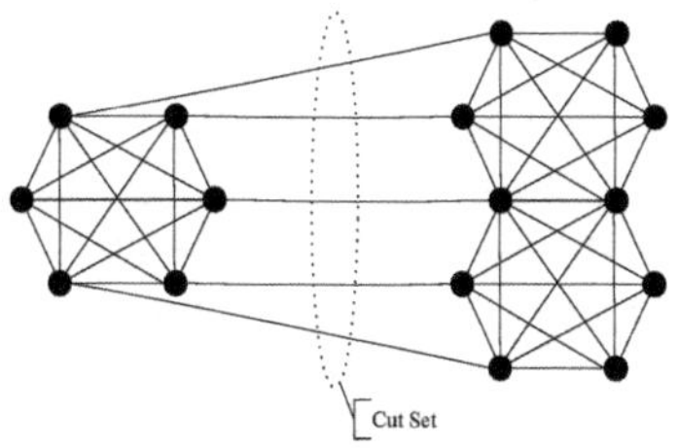

Fig. 1. A simple example of Flake's community (a node set in the left)

Flake devises a procedure to obtain the web community that approximately satisfies the definition proposed previously. The process of Flake's algorithm is summarized as follows:

First step: crawl a graph. Suppose S is a set of seed nodes. Crawl in depth 2 from the nodes in S to gain a subgraph of the web graph $G = (V, E)$ which is also called a vicinity graph.

Second step: assign edge capacities. Suppose any edge $e \in E$ is dual directed with the edge capacity $c(e) = |S|$. Add a virtual source node s to V with the edges connecting to all the nodes in S with the edge capacity $= \infty$. Add a virtual sink node t to V with the edges connected from all the nodes in $V - S \bigcup s \bigcup t$ with the edge capacity $= 1$.

Third step: perform s-t maximum flow algorithm for G. All the nodes accessible from s through unsaturated edges become the new member pages of a web graph.

Forth step: add some new nodes in the community to S, repeat the procedure until the desired community can be obtained.

Fig. 2 shows a simple procedure starting with three seeds in S and a vicinity graph of depth 2.

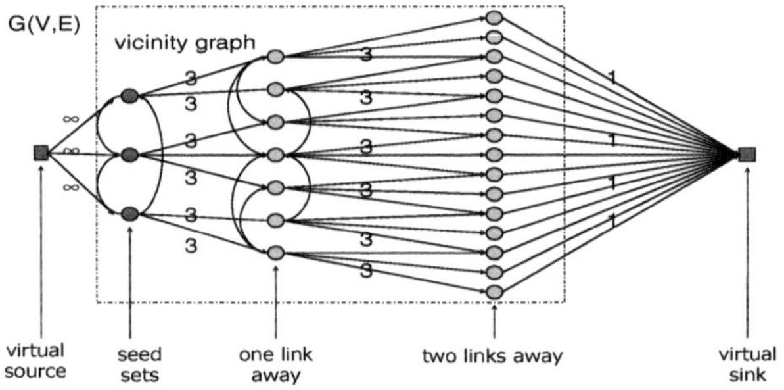

Fig. 2. An example of applying maximum flow for obtaining an appropriate web community. For simplifying, suppose all the edges are going the same direction.

Flake's maximum flow algorithm is a E-M process that iteratively applies estimation (the "E" step) and maximization (the "M" step). It solves the topic drifting problem in community extraction effectively. However, there still exist problems to be tackled with.

During the "E" step in which a subset of the community is found, it heuristically assigns the capacity of each edge with a constant $|S|$, which equals to the seed numbers in the procedure. On the one hand, graph structures containing many noisy pages are often extracted, thus no community of appropriate size is obtained; on the other hand, some valuable links are reckoned as cut edges, causing the extracted community too small.

Another problem lies in the "M" step in which some newly discovered sites are relabeled as seeds. Flake's method just rank the candidates via link numbers.

However, this strategy can not distinguish the candidates effectively since some sites with many links turns out not so relevant with the seeds or the communities topic in content.

The relationship between assignment of edge capacities and community quality and quantity has been intensely studied [9]. By increasing the edge capacities, we can easily enlarge the desired community size. However, along with the simple increment of edge capacity, the phenomenon of topic drifting occurs and more noisy pages are added in. The main reason for this is that the methods treat all the edges in the web graph the same and deny the differences between edges.

3 Method

In order to solve the problems mentioned in the former section, we propose a new assignment of edge capacities combining links and contents, which reflects the diverse influence that each edge devotes to the community.

3.1 Assignment of Edge Capacities Using the Lexical Similarity

The flow produced between two web pages can be viewed as the exchange of authority between each other [11]. Intuitively, more similar contents the two pages have, more authority they exchange. Therefore, edge capacities in the web graph are supposed to be set according to the content similarity between two web pages.

To compute the content-based similarity, we quantify each page using TF-IDF (Term Frequency-Inverse Document Frequency) vector, a popular metric for measuring the relevance of entities in documents. To construct the TF-IDF vector of each page's features, we perform the following pre-processing: (1) For page content and title, we first eliminate stop words and then further conflate remaining words using the standard Porter Stemmer. Term space dimension are reduced even further by using document frequency threshold to de-emphasize the impact of rare terms unlikely to influence global performance. (2) For meta data and anchor text, we perform analogous preprocessing except that the features shun stemming.

We employ the extended Jaccard coefficient to compute the similarity between various string data objects, since this metric has been shown to produce superior results for many clustering approaches [14]. The extended Jaccard coefficient for page u and v with respect to a feature g (such as meta description) is defined as

$$\sigma_g(u, v) = \frac{u^g \cdot v^g}{|u^g|^2 + |v^g|^2 - u^g \cdot v^g} \tag{1}$$

where u^g, v^g is the TF-IDF vector representative of feature g on page u, v. Using this measure, we can compute the similarity between each pair of pages with respect to various features. Finally, we compute the similarity between page

u and v by combining all similarity values associated with each page in the form of a weighted linear sum:

$$S(u,v) = \sum_{g_k \in \Omega} \sigma_{g_k}(u,v) \cdot \phi_k \tag{2}$$

where ϕ_k is a suitable weight for each $g_k \in \Omega$. The similarity value $S(u,v)$ generated from TF-IDF vector lies in the range that $0 \leq S(u,v) \leq 1$. It's not appropriate to be used in the assignment of edge capacity, because in the maximum-flow algorithm, the edge capacities are supposed to be a positive integer. Therefore, we have to add a constant adapter into the equation of edge capacity:

$$c(u,v) = f_q \cdot S(u,v) \tag{3}$$

where f_q is the upper limiting value of edge capacities in Flake's method using maximum flow algorithm, at which the edge capacities are set, all edges become unsaturated and all nodes in the vicinity graph turn out to be community members. The computing of f_q is at hand and described in detail by Noriko Imafuji [9]. We call this method the **MT** (**Max-flow+TF-IDF**) assignment.

3.2 Optimization of Similarity Computing

Inspired by the concept of co-citation in IR field, we propose an optimal method to compute the lexical similarity between pages using the seeds, thus to improve the efficiency of algorithm. The resulting method is named as **MTS** (**Max-flow + TF-IDF + Seed**) assignment.

Namely, we regard the lexical similarity of a page p to the good seeds as a probability that p belongs to the community. In other words, if two pages are both more similar to good seeds, the edge between them would have greater influence for the desired community and the edge capacity should be set larger accordingly.

More precisely, let $\omega^g = \{\omega_1^g, \omega_2^g, \ldots, \omega_{|\omega|}^g\}$ be the TF-IDF vector representative of seeds with respect to content feature g. Then the similarity between page u, v with respect to the feature g can be described as follows:

$$\sigma_g(u,v) = \sigma_g(u,w) \cdot \sigma_g(v,w) \tag{4}$$

Note that sometimes we may not confident about our seeds, or it might be expensive to provide many. In this case, we can construct manually a TF-IDF vector representing keywords and terms for the desired community to alternate the TF-IDF vector of seeds.

3.3 Improved Algorithm Based on the Maximum Flow

The algorithm based on the maximum flow to extract community which assigns edge capacities using the lexical similarity requires a good seed set and generates a community cohesive to a specific topic. It iterates until the members in the community converge or generally remain the same. The whole process is described in algorithm 1.

When choosing new seeds in the "M" step, we propose a new ranking strategy for each node in the extracted community which is different from Flake's method [5]. Let $v_{Ci}^{(in)}$ be the number of nodes which link to v_{c_i} , $v_{Ci}^{(out)}$ be the number of nodes to which v_{c_i} links. Assume $R_c(v_{c_i})$ to be the rank value of the node v_{c_i} in the community C, and the equation for it is as follows:

$$R_c(v_{c_i}) = S(v_{c_i}, w) \times (v_{Ci}^{(in)} + v_{Ci}^{(out)}) \tag{5}$$

Algorithm 1. Improved Maximum Flow Algorithm

Input: seed set $S = \{v_{s1}, v_{s2}, \cdots, v_{sl}\}$
Output: a web community $C = \{v_{c1}, v_{c2}, \cdots, v_{cm}\}$

```
repeat
starting from each seed v_{s_l} ∈ S, crawl pages in depth of 2 for a web subgraph G(V, E);
compute the similarity between each node and the seeds according to the equation (1) (2) or (4) (2);
add source s and sink t to V;
for ∀v_{s_i} ∈ S do
    add edge (s, v_{s_i}) into E;
    c(s, v_{s_i}) = ∞
end for
for ∀(u, v) ∈ E do
    set c(u, v) using MT or MTS;
    if(u, v) ∉ E then
    add edge (v, u) into E;
    c(v, u) = c(u, v)
end for
for ∀v ∈ v and v ∉ S⋃{s, t} do
    add edge (v, t) into E;
    c(v, t) = 1;
end for
execute s − t maximum flow algorithm;
return C = {v | v ∈ C, v is connected to seed nodes };
compute the value for ∀c(v_{s_i}) ∈ C using equation (5) described later;
rank the nodes list according to the value;
add the top 10 nodes into S;
until the nodes in C remain steady
```

Flake ranks the nodes only according to their link numbers (including in-links and out-links), however, it's not sufficient since certain top nodes are probably have the same number of links. We take the lexical similarity between nodes and seeds into account, thus combining both link and content information to strengthen the difference between nodes. For nodes with the same number of links, we tend to rank higher the one which is more similar to seed nodes in the content.

4 Experiments

In this section, using the original capacity, **MT** capacity, **MTS** capacity, we perform experiments to evaluate the algorithms.

4.1 Data Collecting and Pruning

Data Sets. In order to assure that the experimental data sets will not affect the reliability of our research outcome, 20 well-known and specific web pages relevant to distinct topics are selected randomly as seed pages, including 10 Chinese web pages and 10 English ones. Pages that have more than 200 (empirical value) in-links or out-links are avoided since they will result in a huge vicinity graph causing the topics drift easily. We collect about 3.8 G raw pages in Sep. 2009 using a famous focused crawler NUTCH. The queries equal to the seed nodes and the constructing of vicinity graph begins from crawling from the seeds. The outgoing links come from parsing the HTML pages of crawler, while the incoming links are provided by the Google search engine.

Data Pruning. 1) Remove the pages whose numbers of incoming links or outgoing links exceed 500 (empirical value), because these pages are probably the well-known pages such as Yahoo, Sina and so on which can be found easily without any mining strategy. 2) Cut pages whose URLs include %, ?, bbs, cgi-bin, diary, news, since most of these pages are irrelevant to user's query. 3) Merge mirrors.

4.2 Experimental Results and Discussion

Let $C1$ be the community obtained by the Flake's maximum flow algorithm with a constant edge capacity, $C2$ and $C3$ be the community obtained by our improved algorithm with **MT** capacity and **MTS** capacity respectively. In our experiments, we choose the shortest augmenting path algorithm which adopts the breadth-first search to solve the $s-t$ problem, since it's appropriate to be used in identifying web communities with time complexity limited to $O(VE^2)$.

Table 1 shows the general size of $C1$, $C2$ and $C3$ for each seed node. The left three columns in table 1 represent topic ID, seed url, and topics which are based on keywords or page titles. $|V|$, $|C1|$, $|C2|$, $|C3|$ indicate the numbers of nodes in the vicinity graph, the number of nodes in the web community obtained by using the original constant capacity, **MT** capacity, **MTS** capacity respectively. It demonstrates that the communities $C2$ and $C3$ obtained by the improved algorithm excel in quantity than Flake's $C1$. For No. 2, 9 and 20, no matter what values are assigned for edge capacities, we cannot obtain ideal communities of appropriate size.

We browse the highest 15 pages in the obtained communities and check whether the pages have the same topics with the seeds or not. The experimental results are shown in fig. 3. The average numbers of relevant pages in $C1$, $C2$ and $C3$ are 5.95 (ranges from 2 to 10), 10.7 (ranges from 8 to 15) and 12.1

(ranges from 10 to 15) respectively. As shown in fig. 3 (a), $C2$ and $C3$ obviously outperform $C1$. For example, in 18 among 20 topics, $C2$ is better than $C1$, and only in 2 cases, $C2$ is inferior to $C1$.

Table 1. Seed nodes, topics, size of the vicinity graph and the extracted community

No.	Seed URLs	Topics	$\|V\|$	$\|C1\|$	$\|C2\|$	$\|C3\|$
1	http://www.scientificamerican.com/	science	2089	26	38	42
2	http://www.aaai.org/home.html	artificial intelligence	1380	8	25	28
3	http://www.ca.gov/	state of California	6175	36	46	49
4	http://www.epa.gov.cn/	environmental agency	4603	60	89	72
5	http://succulent-plant.com/	succulent-plant	471	21	28	29
6	http://www.ncac.org/	censorship	1123	18	30	35
7	http://www.olmpic.org/	olympic	620	17	29	31
8	http://www.rockclimbing.com/	rock climbing	2154	24	33	38
9	http://www.jaguarcars.com	jaguar	1289	4	26	27
10	http://www.gulfwarvets.com	gulf war	2013	17	22	26
11	http://www.jcrb.com/	legal system,prosecution	3890	66	79	84
12	http://junshi.xilu.com/	China's military	2248	31	35	44
13	http://www.fec.com.cn/	financial securities	5540	28	41	47
14	http://www.yishu.com/	art appreciation	982	21	29	38
15	http://www.shufa.org/	calligraphy	3161	58	60	64
16	http://www.5ijk.net/	health care	3452	13	18	21
17	http://www.chinacars.com/	automobile	7240	14	72	85
18	http://www.edu.cn/	education	5012	18	26	24
19	http://www.zhb.gov.cn/	environmental protection	1409	19	33	32
20	http://www.lknet.ac.cn	landscape garden	345	2	20	18

We also browse all the other member pages in the obtained communities using three capacities and calculate the precision of extracted $C1$, $C2$ and $C3$ as shown in fig. 4. The precision of community C is defined as follows: precision (C) = number of relevant pages in C / total pages in C. Compared **MTS** capacity

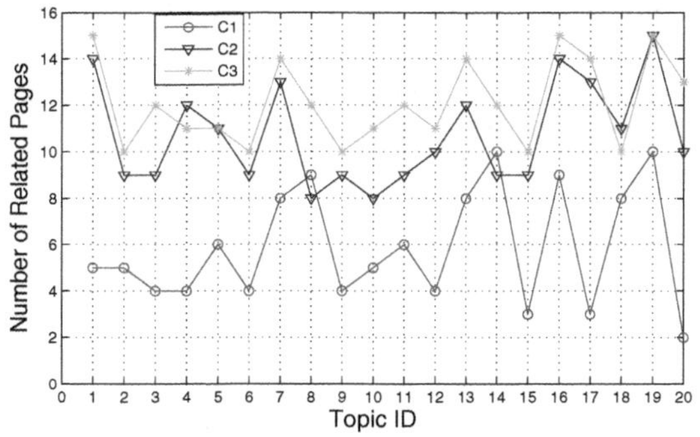

Fig. 3. The number of related pages ranked top 15 in the community

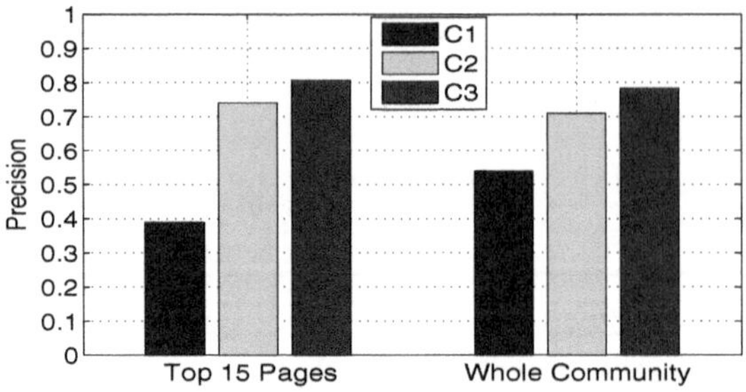

Fig. 4. The precision of top 15 pages and the whole community

to **MT** capacity, there is a slight increase in precision due to the use of seeds. For $C2$ and $C3$, the precision of the top 15 pages is generally in accordance with that of the whole community. For $C1$, the precision of top 15 pages is rather lower than that of the whole community. On the contrary, our algorithm provides better precision for top 15 pages (0.74 for $C2$, 0.8066 for $C3$) than that of the whole community (0.7091 for $C2$, 0.7833 for $C3$). Because web users usually browse top few pages when using a search engine, our algorithm using the lexical similarity therefore is better for user recommendation.

5 Conclusions and Future Work

We have analyzed features and problems of the Flake's maximum flow algorithm and explored benefits of page contents in the extraction of web communities from a given graph. Based on the original maximum flow algorithm, we devise new methods to assign edge capacities according to different importance. By introducing the lexical similarity, we exploit fully both content and link information of the web. We also propose a new ranking strategy combining text with links, thus strengthening the difference between pages. Our preliminary experiment conducted on randomly selected 20 seeds has shown that the community obtained by the improved algorithm has much better precision than the original algorithm, thus proving that using our content-combined method is better than purely link-based methods. In the future, we will investigate further how the setting of seeds and community keyword vector influence the performance of communities and provide the alternatives. Another promising direction is to use WordNet to disambiguate word senses [15] in the computing process of lexical similarity.

References

1. Andeson, R., Lang, K.J.: Community from seed sets. In: 15th International Conference on WWW, New York, USA, pp. 223–232 (2006)
2. Angelova, R., Weikum, G.: Graph-based Text classification: learn from your neighbors. In: 29th ACM Conference on Research and Development in Information Retrieval, Seattle, Washington, pp. 485–492 (2006)

3. Asano, Y., Nishizeki, T., Toyoda, M., Kitsuregaw, A.M.: Mining Communities on the Web Using a Max-Flow and a Site-Oriented Framework. IEICE Trans. on Information and Systems (2006)
4. DeRose, P., Shen, W., Chen, F.: Building Structured Web Community Portals: A Top-down, Compositional, and Incremental Approach. In: 33rd International Conference on VLDB, Vienna, Austria, pp. 399–410 (2007)
5. Flake, G.W., Lawrence, S., Giles, C.L.: Efficient Identification of Web Communities. In: sixth ACM International Conference on KDD, pp. 150–160. ACM Press, Boston (2000)
6. Flake, G.W., Lawrence, S., Giles, C.L., Coetzee, F.M.: Self-Organization and Identification of Web Communities. Computer (2002)
7. Ford, L.R., Fulkson, D.R.: Maximal Flow through A Network. Canadian Journal of Mathematics 8, 399–404 (1956)
8. Girven, M., Newman, M.E.J.: Community Structure in Social and Biological Networks. Proc. Nati. Acad. 99, 7821–7826 (2002)
9. Imafuji, N., Kitsuregawa, M.: Finding Web Communities by Maximum Flow Algorithm Using Well Desinged Edge Capacities. IEICE Trans. on Information and Systems (2004)
10. Kernighan, B.W., Lin, S.: Tech. J. 49, 291 (1970)
11. Lee, H.C., Borodin, A., Goldsmith, L.: Extracting and Ranking Viral Communities Using Seed and Content Similarity. In: 19th ACM Conference on Hypertext, Pittsburgh, PA, pp. 139–148 (2008)
12. Pothen, A., Simon, H., Liou, K.P.: Matrix Anal. Appl. 11, 430 (1990)
13. Scott, J.: Social Network Analysis: A Handbook, 2nd edn. Sage, London (2000)
14. Strehl, A.: Relationship-based Clustering and Cluster Ensembles for High-Dimensional Data Mining. Phd thesis, Univ. of Texas at Austin (2002)
15. Voorhees, E.M.: Using WordNet to disambiguate word senses for text retrieval. In: 16th ACM Conference on Research and Development in Information Retrieval, New York, USA, pp. 171–180 (1993)
16. Xu, G., Ma, W.Y.: Building Implicit Links From Content For Forum Search. In: 29th ACM Conference on Research and Development in IR, Seattle, Washington, pp. 300–307 (2006)

An Improved Algorithm for Extracting Research Communities from Bibliographic Data

Yushi Nakamura[1], Toshihiko Horiike[1],
Yoshimasa Taira[1], and Hiroshi Sakamoto[12]

[1] Kyushu Institute of Technology
680-4 Kawazu, Iizuka-shi, Fukuoka, 820-8502, Japan
[2] PRESTO JST
Kawaguchi Center Building 4-1-8, Honcho, Kawaguchi-shi, Saitama 332-0012, Japan
{y_nakamura,t_horiike,taira,hiroshi}@donald.ai.kyutech.ac.jp

Abstract. In this paper we improve the performance of the community extraction algorithm in [1] from bibliographic data, which was originally proposed for web community discovery by [2]. A web community is considered to be a set of web pages holding a common topic, in other words, it is a dense subgraph induced in web graph. Such subgraphs obtained by the max-flow algorithm are called *max-flow communities*, and this algorithm was improved to obtain research communities from bibliographic data by the strategy for selection of community nodes in [1]. We propose an improvement of this algorithm by carefully selecting initial seed node, and show the performance of this algorithm by experiments for the list of many keywords frequently appearing in data.

1 Introduction

We develop an algorithm for extracting research communities from bibliographic data, which is based on the maximum flow algorithm to find dense subgraphs as web communities [2]. We consider a web community to be a set of web pages holding a common topic, which is represented by a connected subgraph in web graph. We apply this idea to research community extraction.

For given bibliographic data, the list of frequent keywords are obtained. For such keywords, we design our algorithm to compute suitable research communities related to the keywords. The relevance of keyword to obtain community depends on initial seed. In [1], initial seeds are randomly chosen from candidates. We thus propose a careful strategy for the selection of initial seeds, and show the performance of our improvement.

Study of extracting web communities has attracted many researchers since its wide application to web technology, like trend discovery and information recommendation, and many algorithms were presented. The algorithms in [2,3,4] aim to find dense subgraphs using local information of web graph. On the other hand, algorithms in [5,6,7] try to extract communities by using global information, like HITS [8].

M. Yoshikawa et al. (Eds.): DASFAA 2010, LNCS 6193, pp. 338–345, 2010.

Related to such pioneering studies, the problem handled in this paper is to extract research communities from bibliographic data, and we focus on the former research strategy, i.e. extracting dense subgraphs using local information. This problem motivate us to extract interesting research communities as follows.

In [7], a community is defined as a subgraph which contains at least one *clique*. Here, indegree/outdegree of nodes are closely related to extracted communities, and consequently, a small degree node is hardly selected as a member of a community. This method is basically equal to [8].

Such a method based on hub-authority is effective for extracting a global relation in a graph. However, not all important communities are extracted by this method. For instance, consider to find communities from network constructed by the relation of researchers, which is represented by a bibliographic data. An important community is constructed by several outstanding papers and other related studies. It is difficult to extract such communities by global information only since there is very few study which impacts on the whole research field or many different research fields. In order to extract such *compact* relations, we adopt the strategy of *maximum flow community*.

In [2,3], a community is defined to be a set of web pages that link to more web pages in the community than to pages outside of the community. Generally the problem of finding such subsets is computationally hard. However by exploiting various properties of web, identifying web communities becomes identical to solving the tractable max-flow problem [9]. Flake et al. introduced an efficient method of extracting communities using such max-flow algorithm. So we call a community extracted by the max-flow algorithm a *max-flow community*.

Efficiency of max-flow communities depends on the ranking of community nodes. In [1] we proposed a modification for the ranking by careful evaluation according to connectivity to seed nodes. In original strategy, ranking is decided by only the number of sum of indegree and outdegree of an extracted node. Such communities are very sensitive to the number of edges, and there is a possibility that irrelevant nodes are associated to a community due to their many edges. We thus considered that ranking of community nodes should be evaluated by also the relation to seed nodes, which are some cores of a community, i.e. some nodes deeply related to seeds should be ranked as higher positions. By this modification, we obtained good communities related to [2] for several keywords.

However, in this method, the selection of initial seed is critical. By experiment for CiteSeer bibliographic data, we can confirm that many communities are not suitable, i.e. they are often too large. So it is hard for us to understand the main topic of such a research community. To improve the inconvenience, we propose a new strategy for the selection of initial seeds. This strategy is based on the special characteristic of research network. Generally such a network is *acyclic*, i.e. the flow going from a node cannot came in the same node. Thus, if an initial seed has no indegree edge, the resulting community maybe decided by the seed only. To avoid such situation, our improved algorithm takes account of the indegree edges of seeds as well, and we show the efficiency by experiments.

The remainder of this paper is divided into four additional sections. In Section 2 we give the definition of web community in [2] and a summary of the algorithm for extracting research community in [1]. In Section 3 we propose an idea of selection of seed nodes, and present experimental results in CiteSeer bibliographic data. Finally we discuss a future work on this study.

2 Research Community by Max-Flow Algorithm

The definition of web community is given bellow.

Definition 1. (G.W. Flake et al. [2]) A community of undirected graph $G = (V, E)$ is a subset $C \subseteq V$ such that for all nodes $v \in C$, v has at least as many edges connecting to nodes in C as it does to nodes in $(V - C)$.

It is easy to expand this definition to directed graph like WWW. In web graph, each node is corresponding to a web page, and an edge (u, v) is a link from u to v with a unit capacity $c(u, v) = 1$. Initially we assume a set S of seed nodes and a set $C = \emptyset$ of community nodes.

Here we summarize the original algorithm by [2]. For any nodes s, t, we can compute $s-t$ maximum flow such that s, t are separated by a minimum *cut set* of saturated edges[1]. All such saturated edges are removed, and all nodes reachable from a node in S are added to C. Next we compute the ranking of nodes in C with respect to their indegree/outdegree numbers. Upper ranked nodes are moved to S, and we continue the above process until C is steady. Then obtained connected subgraphs are called max-flow communities. A virtual source s and a virtual sink t are assumed such that $c(s, v) = 1$ and $c(v, t) = \infty$ for any $v \in V$. In [2], by this assumption, we can extract such web communities without a *priori* knowledge about web graph.

Next we summarize the modified algorithm in [1] for research community based on the above max-flow community. In this modification, a new ranking method for the node set C was proposed. When we obtain a set C of community nodes, for the next iteration, we must compute the ranking of all members in C according to a criterion.

In [2] the ranking is computed by the value $indegree(v) + outdegree(v)$, which is independent of the number of seed nodes directly associated with v, while the relation between S and C is important information for our communities. On the other hand, in [1], the ranking is computed by the number of edges associated with S, i.e. $indegree(v, S) + outdegree(v, S)$.

In Fig. 1, the modified ranking method is illustrated. The seed nodes are denoted by the black nodes, and the community nodes are labeled by integers 1, 2, 3, and 4. Since node 1 is maximum in the measure $indegree(v) + outdegree(v)$, this node is ranked in the top by the original method. On the other hand, in our ranking method by $indegree(v, S) + outdegree(v, S)$, node 3 is ranked in the top, and

[1] For max-flow algorithm, see [9].

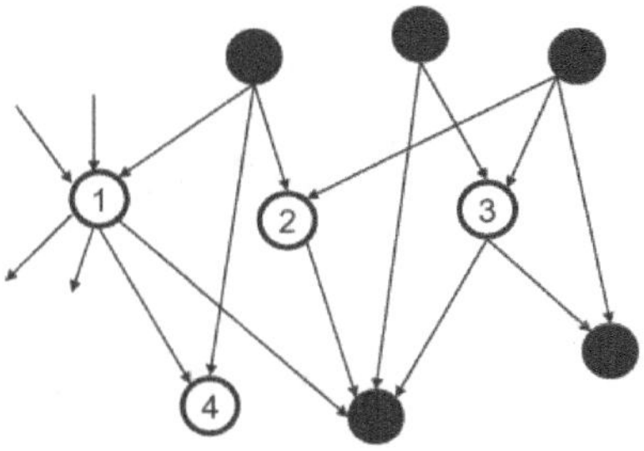

Fig. 1. Seed nodes and ranking of community nodes

the community nodes are sorted as $3, 2, 1, 4$. Using this ranking measure, we describe the max-flow community algorithm below.

Research Community Extraction Algorithm

Input: The set of seed nodes, S, and a web graph $G(V, E)$ whose nodes are reachable from a seed node within 2 edges.

Output: Web community C.

Preprocess: For $(u, v) \in E$, set the capacity $c(u, v) = |S|$, for the virtual source s and sink t, and $v \in V$, set $c(s, v) = 1$ and $c(v, t) = \infty$, and let $C = \emptyset$.

(1) Execute the max-flow algorithm on G.

(2) Compute all $v \in V$ which are reachable from an $s \in S$ by only unsaturated edges, and add all of them to C.

(3) Decide the ranking for $c \in C$ by $indegree(c, S) + outdegree(c, S)$, and move the higher ranked nodes from C to S.

(4) Continue (1)-(3) until C become to be steady, and output C.

In Fig. 2, we show flow of extracting communities from web graph. The highest node is the virtual source and the lowest is the virtual sink. Any seed node is associated by the source, and the sink is associated by any node. By the step (1) of the algorithm, a maximum flow is obtained. At this time, the saturated edges, which are illustrated by bold broken lines in Fig. 2, denote the cut edges. Intuitively, an extracted web community is consisting of nodes which are reachable from the source without cut edges. In the next section we examine the efficiency of our improvement.

3 Proposed Method and Experimental Results

In this section we explain our improvement for selection of initial seed node in the algorithm, and show experimental results of the improved algorithm compared to the previous one [1].

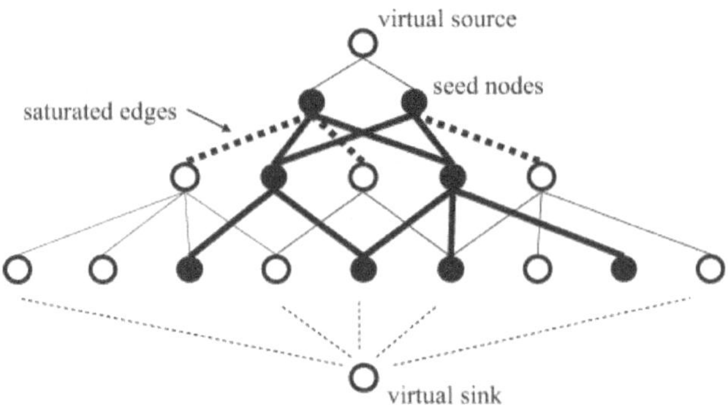

Fig. 2. The flow of community extraction

In the previous algorithm, initial seed node is randomly chosen from candidates which are consisting of all nodes having at least k outdegree edges for a threshold k. On the other hand, in the proposed algorithm, candidates for initial seed nodes must satisfy at least k indegree and outdegree edges.

In this experiment, we set $k = 3$ and we use CiteSeer bibliographic data [12], which includes over 700,000 entries for research documents. The following example is a typical record in this data.

```
<record>
  <id>7348</id>
  <title>Parallel Sorting by Overpartitioning</title>
  <description>In this paper we propose... </description>
  <ref>14421,40374,91922,40140,372786,4945,8848</ref>
</record>
```

In this data, any paper has its unique ID defined inside `<id>` tag. In the above example, paper `7348` is referring other studies indicated by 7 integers inside `<ref>` tag. Thus, we can regard a collection of such records as a directed graph. For such a bibliographic graph, we examine the efficiency of the proposed algorithm compared to the previous algorithm in [1].

We first preprocess the bibliographic data to obtain keywords. From the frequency list of all keywords, we get 20 keywords related to computer science field. For each keyword, the algorithm computes an initial seed node from candidates, where each candidate must contain an occurrence of the keyword in its title or abstract.

In Table 1, we show the experimental result. In this table, all keywords are sorted according to the frequency. For each keyword, the efficiency of the proposed algorithm is compared with the previous algorithm in [1]. Each integer indicated by "size" denotes the number of nodes in the community obtained for the corresponding keyword, and each rational indicated by "relevance" denotes the ratio of the nodes in the community which are closely related to the corresponding keyword. We measured this value by reading all records. The character "-" means that the obtained community is too small. In such a case, we regard the extraction as being unsuccessful.

Compared with the result of the previous algorithm, we can confirm that the proposed algorithm outputs compact research community, and the proposed algorithm can produce suitable communities related to given keywords. Therefore, we conclude that compact communities are obtained from bibliographic data by this improved community extraction algorithm.

Table 1. Comparison of two algorithms

keyword	frequency	proposed		previous	
		size	relevance	size	relevance
mining	13550	31	0.710	89	0.191
infinite	13472	6	0.667	2	-
paths	13277	16	0.875	17	0.294
integer	13082	26	0.154	43	0.093
automata	12912	23	0.174	34	0.147
robots	12534	3	0.667	8	0.750
clusters	12224	10	0.300	2	-
grammar	11914	26	0.654	60	0.433
formula	11732	1	-	15	0.533
game	11396	2	-	4	1
graphics	11152	9	1	16	0.563
www	11116	17	0.059	135	0.237
logics	10774	9	0.778	33	0.606
boolean	10519	68	0.338	19	0.105
string	10204	7	0.857	21	0.762
xml	9798	46	0.065	89	0.090
category	9755	9	0.444	1	-
encoding	9567	14	0.286	13	0.231
indexing	9249	36	0.361	56	0.018
heuristics	8657	7	0.429	18	0.833

4 Conclusion

We propose an improvement for the selection of initial seed node on the community extraction. Our method is based on the previous community extraction algorithm in [1] using careful evaluation of the relation between seed nodes and community nodes. The effectiveness of our improvement is shown by experiments for finding research communities from CiteSeer bibliography data. More compact and close communities are obtained by the proposed algorithm compared to the privies one. We thus conclude that our algorithm is effective for extracting relatively compact research communities closely related to keywords. Next we must try to show the precision and recall of our extracted communities using benchmark data.

As future work we would develop a hybrid algorithm for community extraction. In [13], comparison of two types of algorithms based on complete bipartite graphs and max-flow network was presented, and it was reported that more generic communities are obtained by the former method and more specific communities are obtained by the latter method. In [14], a method for extracting relation among web communities using HITS was proposed. We thus try to expand our strategy to the above different types of community extraction.

Acknowledgements

This work was supported by JST PRESTO program. The authors would be grateful to the anonymous referees for their careful reading of the draft and uesful comments.

References

1. Horiike, T., Takahashi, Y., Kuboyama, T., Sakamoto, H.: Extracting research communities by improved maximum flow algorithm. In: Velásquez, J.D., Ríos, S.A., Howlett, R.J., Jain, L.C. (eds.) KES 2009, Part II. LNCS, vol. 5712, pp. 472–479. Springer, Heidelberg (2009)
2. Flake, G.W., Lawrence, S., Giles, C.L.: Efficient identification of web communities. In: KDD 2000, pp. 150–160 (2000)
3. Flake, G.W., Lawrence, S., Giles, C.L., Coetzee, F.: Self-organization and identification of web communities. IEEE Computer 35(3), 66–71 (2002)
4. Kumar, R., Raghavan, P., Rajagopalan, S., Tomkins, A.: Trawling the web for emerging cyber-communities. Computer Networks 31(11-16), 1481–1493 (1999)
5. Chakrabarti, S., Dom, B., Raghavan, P., Rajagopalan, S., Gibson, D., Kleinberg, J.M.: Automatic resource compilation by analyzing hyperlink structure and associated text. Computer Networks 30(1-7), 65–74 (1998)
6. Gibson, D., Kleinberg, J.M., Raghavan, P.: Inferring web communities from link topology. In: Hypertext 1998, pp. 225–234 (1998)
7. Kumar, R., Raghavan, P., Rajagopalan, S., Tomkins, A.: Extracting large-scale knowledge bases from the web. In: VLDB 1999, pp. 639–650 (1999)
8. Kleinberg, J.M.: Authoritative sources in a hyperlinked environment. In: SODA 1998, pp. 668–677 (1998)
9. Goldberg, A., Tarjan, R.: A new approach to the maximal flow problem. In: STOC 1986, pp. 136–146 (1986)
10. Ford Jr., L., Fulkerson, D.: Maximal flow through a network. Canadian Journal of Mathematics 8, 399–404 (1956)
11. Edmonds, J., Karp, R.M.: Theoretical improvements in algorithmic efficiency for network flow problems. J. ACM 19(2), 248–264 (1972)
12. CiteSeer.IST: `http://citeseer.ist.psu.edu/`
13. Imafuji, N., Kitsuregawa, M.: Effects of maximum flow algorithm on identifying web community. In: WIDM 2002, pp. 43–48 (2002)

14. Toyoda, M., Kitsuregawa, M.: Creating a web community chart for navigating related communities. In: Hypertex 2001, pp. 103–112 (2001)
15. Imafuji, N., Kitsuregawa, M.: Finding a web community by maximum flow algorithm with hits score based capacity. In: DASFAA 2003, pp. 101–106 (2003)
16. Dean, J., Henzinger, M.R.: Finding related pages in the world wide web. Computer Networks 31(11-16), 1467–1479 (1999)
17. Asano, Y., Nishizeki, T., Toyoda, M., Kitsuregawa, M.: Mining communities on the web using a max-flow and a site-oriented framework. IEICE Transactions 89-D(10), 2606–2615 (2006)

Proposal of Deleting Plots from the Reviews to the Items with Stories

Kaori Ikeda, Yoshinori Hijikata, and Shogo Nishida

Graduate School of Engineering Science, Osaka University, Japan

Abstract. Recently, there are a lot of commercial web sites in which users can write reviews. Many people see the reviews of an item they are interested in. The opinions in reviews are useful when they want to measure whether a certain item is good. However, some reviews about items that contains stories (e.g. novels, movies, and computer games) have spoilers (undesirable descriptions of the story) as well as the opinions of review authors (reviewers). If users see a review involving spoilers, they might feel less interesting when you read or watch the item. We try to make a system that helps users see reviews without seeing plots.

1 Introduction

Recently, many people do online shopping. Before they make a decision on whether they buy an item they are interested in, they often undertake information gathering about the item. They decide whether they buy it or not based on the gathered information. People can exchange information easily in a community website, such as BBS and SNS. There are some websites in which users can write and read reviews of items easily (e.g. Amazon.com [1] and eBay [2]). Many people use these websites when they want to get the information about a certain item. They can get a lot of users' opinions from reviews, which is useful for evaluating a certain item.

However, in the reviews about items that contains stories (e.g. novels, movies, and computer games), there may be spoilers (undesirable descriptions of the stories) in addition to useful opinions. Here is an example.

<example review>
Half-Blood Prince is easily one of the better books in the Harry Potter series, though each is a masterpiece. Several of the chapters are particularly well-written, with great suspense and imagery. After completing this book, I was in a state of total shock and to this moment I wish only to read the seventh book. The end of the book is very sad indeed, yet, I was not crying–I was merely shocked, flabbergasted at the circumstances. before reading this book, if I had to make a list of impossible things that could never happen... Snape killing the Headmaster and fleeing the school with a bunch of Death Eaters, would have

[1] http://www.amazon.com
[2] http://www.ebay.com

M. Yoshikawa et al. (Eds.): DASFAA 2010, LNCS 6193, pp. 346–352, 2010.

been right at the top of the list. But, I'd have been wrong. I had a very strong feeling that Dumbledore would be the one to die in this book. But I never saw the way it happened coming. Disturbing ending leaves you frustrated waiting for the next book.

Users can realize that the item is a good book of this series from this review. The opinion in this review can be useful for those who are making a decision on whether they buy the item.

However readers are forced to know about the crucial plot "Snape killing the Headmaster", which they would not have known before they read the item. After reading this review, they may be less interesting when they read this item. Social Survey Research Information Co. conducted an online inquiry survey of spoilers in reviews, and reported that the answerers said "I was disappointed at knowing the ending of the story from a review.", "I was shocked because I saw the criminal person's name while reading the reviews of the mystery novel.", and so on. Furthermore, more than half of respondents insist they do not want to see spoilers.

We try to detect and hide plots from reviews. We assign scores that indicate the likelihood of "plots" to each phrase by machine learning to detect the plots.

In this paper, we present a system that helps users see reviews without seeing plots. Here, plots mean the description of items' stories. Our system treats English reviews.

In Section 2, we refer to related works. We explain our approach in Section 3. We present a method for detecting plots and a method for presenting users reviews with plots hidden in Section 4. We give some conclusions and future works in Section 5.

2 Related Work

The most relevant region of research to ours is opinion mining, and the most representative theme in this region is opinion classification. Dave et al. [1] and Wilson et al. [6] conducted opinion classification. Dave et al. [1] presented a polarity classification method at sentence-level using Naive Bayes. Wilson et al. [6] proposed a system that classifies each phrase as positive or negative, considering a priori polarity and contextual polarity of words in the phrase. These researches both treated product reviews.

There are some researches that presented integrated systems for opinion analysis. Morinaga et al. [3] proposed a framework for gathering and analyzing reputations for a certain product. In their system, an extracted statement is attached a numerical value expressing a degree of confidence that the statement is indeed an opinion, as well as the label indicating the statement is positive or negative. The system also presents a map that shows the relationships between items and characteristic words contained in the statements of opinions. Hu et al. [2] presented a method for extracting opinions from reviews and summarizing them with regard to each product feature. They treated reviews about digital cameras, cellular phones, and mp3 players.

In addition, there are researches that classified sentences as subjective or objective. These researches could be useful for opinion acquisition. Pang et al. [4] classified sentences as either subjective or objective using Naive Bayes. Furthermore, the subjective sentences were classified as positive or negative. They treated movie reviews. Yu et al. [7] separated opinions from facts at either document-level or sentence-level. Riloff et al. [5] presented a bootstrapping process to allow classifiers to learn from unlabeled texts. The process finds common patterns in which subjective sentences have, using original training data (known subjective vocabulary). It classifies sentences as subjective or objective using the patterns as well as the original training data. These classified sentences were used as a training set to learn extraction patterns associated with subjectivity. Yu et al. [7] and Riloff et al. [5] both treated newspaper articles.

Our research aims at detecting plots from reviews about items that contain stories (e.g. novel, movie). We classify each phrase in reviews as a plot or not in order to detect plots. Our research is similar to the researches detecting opinions from reviews and classifying them as positive or negative. However, we focus not on opinions but on plots. As far as we know, no research works on detecting plots. Opinions are comparatively easy to classify using dictionaries of expressions for evaluation. On the other hand, no effective tool exists for detecting plots. It seems that detecting plots from reviews is rather difficult than polarity classification.

3 Approach

In order to develop the system described above, we have to consider how to detect plots from a review. It is difficult to detect plots perfectly from a review. This is because the understanding of the meaning of sentences is needed to detect plots and computers are weak at understanding them even when we introduce deep natural language processing techniques.

In addition, whether a certain plot should be eliminated or not depends on the reader. Some users think it is OK to see some plots unless they read the core of the story, other users may think they do not want to see a subtle depiction about the story because they want to be moved while reading or seeing the item. If we show users the reviews in which same plots are eliminated, it seems impossible to satisfy all of them.

We checked 100 reviews in Amazon.com to find any clues to judge whether a phrase is a plot or not. We noticed that there are specific words that are likely to appear in plots, and words that seldom appear in plots. For example, words "kill" and "island" seldom appear in sentences except for plots. On the other hand, words "think" and "be moved" are frequently used for representing reviewers' opinions. We think we can detect plots using this feature, without introducing deep natural language processing techniques.

In our research, we assign scores that indicate the likelihood of "plots" to each phrase by machine learning. We try to detect plots based on the scores and provide an interface on which users can adjust a rate at which plots are hidden. We present users a slider to adjust the rate in this interface. We think that users can see reviews with plots hidden as they like. In Section 4, we explain these methods in detail.

4 Detecting Plots

We assign scores that indicate the likelihood of "plots" to each phrase, and detect plots based on the scores. We use Naive Bayes method to get the scores. Plots and opinions usually appear in different sentences, however, sometimes plots and opinions both appear in one sentence. Thus we treat phrase as a unit. We explain how to detect and hide plots in detail as below.

4.1 Assigning Scores to Phrases

We assign scores that indicate the likelihood of belonging to the "plot" category to phrases by Naive Bayes method. The manually labeled data are used to train Naive Bayes classifier. Naive Bayes Classifier calculates the probability that indicates how much each word is likely to appear in plots. A probability of appearance of a certain word ω in plots $P(plot|\omega)$ is calculated as

$$P(plot|\omega) = \frac{\text{a number of appearance of } \omega \text{ in plots}}{\text{a number of appearance of } \omega} \tag{1}$$

Each sentence in the reviews is separated into phrases and each phrase is checked whether it is regarded as a plot or not. To check whether a certain phrase is regarded as a plot, the probability that indicates how much the phrase is likely to belong to the "plot" category is calculated based on words appearing in the phrase. (See (2).)

$$P(plot|phrase) = \prod_{i=1}^{n} \frac{P(w_i|plot)P(plot)}{P(w_i)} \tag{2}$$

In (2), w_i is the i-th word that appears in the phrase. n is the number of the words the phrase has. The probability $P(other|phrase)$ can be calculated as $1-P(plot|phrase)$. Consequently, if $P(plot|phrase) > 0.5$, the phrase is classified in the "plot" category, and vice versa.

We consider generalizing character names and author names respectively. Here, a character name means a name that a character who appears in an item has, and an author name means a creator's name of the item. We found that phrases that contain character names are comparably plots and the phrases that contain author names are likely not to be plots. However, character names and author names are of huge variety, so same words seldom appear in reviews. Little important scores are given to these words by Naive Bayes method because it highly depends on how many times each word appears in reviews. If we generalize those words and train the classifier, we can utilize the existence of character names and author names in plots. We make a list of personal names in advance for generalizing character names. We compare the list to words that appear in a content summary in an item description page provided by e-commerce site (e.g. Amazon.com and eBay), in order to treat words that appear in both of them as character names. We extract author names from each item description page for generalizing author names. It seems easy because each author name appears in a uniform manner in the item description page.

We introduce some options for scoring. We try to use bigram and trigram in addition to monogram, so as to take into account the order of words. We also consider using simple syntactic information. In reviews, sentences whose subject is "I" frequently express reviewers' opinions, hence they are likely not to be plots. On the other hand, the sentences whose subject is a character name are likely to be plots, because reviewers tend to choose the character name for subject in order to describe character's action or feeling. It is useful to use syntactic information to judge a phrase as a plot or not.

We also try to use scores that indicate the likelihood of opinions. Here, opinions mean reviewers' impressions or requests. We found that opinions are likely to exist apart from plots in reviews. Hence it seems that phrases whose probability of belonging to "opinion" are high are likely not to be plots. We want to utilize this for detecting plots by reducing the probability of opinions from the probability of plots.

4.2 Interface

Each phrase is assigned the probability of belonging to the "plot" category by Naive Bayes classifier. The phrases whose probabilities are higher than a threshold are hidden. We plan to provide an interface to show users reviews with plots hidden, shown in Figure 2. The interface has a slider to enable users to adjust the threshold. In this way, users can see reviews with plots hidden as they like.

Figure 1 shows a raw review before hiding plots. Figure 2 shows a review with some plots hidden. In Figure 2, the threshold of the bottom review is lower than that of the top review, hence more plots are hidden than the top review.

The Big Chill--on acid, August [redacted]

By [redacted]

Leopold Bloom King ("Leo" to friends) is the narrator of Pat Conroy's first novel in 14 years. The story opens on Bloomsday, 1969, in Charleston, South Carolina. Most families don't commemorate this celebration of the work of James Joyce, but then again, most parents don't name their sons after fictional Joycean characters. At the tender age of 18, painfully shy Leo has had enough drama to last a lifetime. Trouble began early with his radiant older brother's suicide. Leo found the body. This led to years of therapy and adventures within the mental health care system. Finally released from institutions, Leo is immediately convicted of a crime he didn't commit, but for which he won't defend himself. All of this has occurred before the events of the novel, and are exposited in the first 50 pages or so.

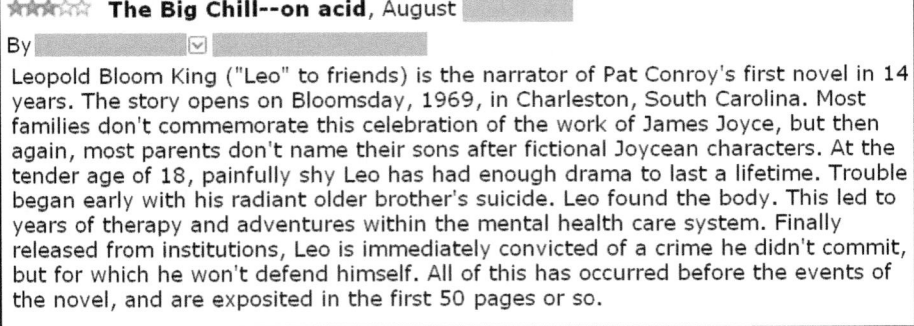

Fig. 1. A raw review before hiding plots

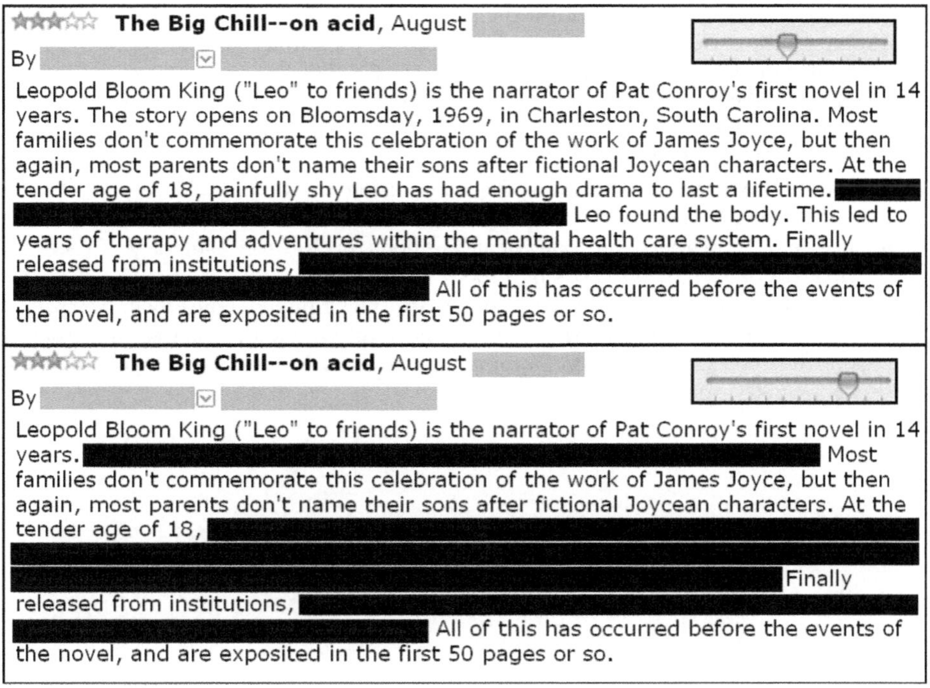

Fig. 2. A review with some plots hidden

5 Conclusion

In our research, we try to hide plots in reviews. We propose a system that helps users see reviews without seeing plots. In order to detect plots, we assign scores that indicate the likelihood of "plots" to each phrase by Naive Bayes. The phrases whose score is higher than a threshold are hidden. Users can see reviews with plots hidden as they like by adjusting the threshold using a slider. We create the supervised data to train Naive Bayes and implement the system in the future.

References

1. Dave, K., Lawrence, S., Pennock, D.: Mining the Peanut Gallery: Opinion Extraction and Semantic Classification of Product Reviews. In: Proceedings of the Twelfth International World Wide Web Conference (WWW 2003), pp. 519–528 (2003)
2. Hu, M., Liu, B.: Mining and Summarizing Customer Reviews. In: Proceedings of International Conference on Knowledge Discovery in Databases (KDD'04), pp. 168–177 (2004)
3. Morinaga, S., Yamanishi, K., Tateishi, K., Fukushima, T.: Mining Product Reputations on the Web. In: Proceedings of International Conference on Knowledge Discovery in Databases (KDD'02), pp. 341–349 (2002)

4. Pang, B., Lee, L.: A Sentimental Education: Sentiment Analysis Using Subjectivity Summarization Based on Minimum Cuts. In: Proceedings of the Association for Computational Linguistics (ACL'04), pp. 271–278 (2004)
5. Riloff, E., Wiebe, J.: Learning Extraction Patterns for Subjective Expressions. In: Proceedings of the 2003 Conference on Emprical Methods in Natural Language Processing (EMNLP 2003), pp. 25–32 (2003)
6. Wilson, T., Wiebe, J., Hoffmann, P.: Recognizing Contextual Polarity in Phrase-Level Sentiment Analysis. In: Proceedings of Human Language Technology Conference and Conference on Empirical Methods in Natural Language Processing (HLT/EMNLP 2005), pp. 347–354 (2005)
7. Yu, H., Hatzivassiloglou, V.: Towards Answering Opinion Questions: Separating Facts from opinions and Identifying the Polarity of Opinion Sentences. In: Proceedings of the 2003 Conference on Emprical Methods in Natural Language Processing (EMNLP 2003), pp. 129–136 (2003)

Basic Study on a Recommendation Method Considering Region-Restrictedness of Spots

Kenta Oku and Fumio Hattori

College of Information Science and Engineering, Ritsumeikan University,
1-1-1 Nojihigashi, Kusatsu-city, Shiga, Japan
oku@fc.ritsumei.ac.jp, fhattori@is.ritsumei.ac.jp

Abstract. We propose a recommendation method that considers region-restrictedness. In this study, we define a spot as an establishment such as a restaurant, amusement facility, or tourist attraction in the real world. A spot with high region-restrictedness indicates that the spot is located in a restricted area but not in a user's home area. We define the region-restrictedness score to extract region-restricted phrases from text data about spots (such as promotional descriptions about spots). Then, spots including these phrases are recommended to the user. In this paper, we present our proposed method and discuss it on the basis of basic experimental results.

Keywords: Recommendation, Region-restrictedness, Local search.

1 Introduction

In recent years, many users have begun using local search services to search for spots matching queries in a specific area. Google Maps[1] and Yahoo! Maps[2] are examples of such local search services. When users search for an area using an address or a place name along with keywords such as "bar" or "lunch," close spots matching the keywords are shown on the map.

However, simply providing information about the close spots does not always satisfy the users. For example, suppose Ken, who lives in Osaka, Japan, goes on a trip to Matsusaka, Mie prefecture, Japan. At night, he searches for restaurants close to Matsusaka station and the foods available at these restaurants using a local search service. Although he can obtain information about many restaurants close to the station, some of the restaurants listed are also available in Osaka; for example, Ken can eat a "teriyaki burger" at "McDonald's" or a "hamburg steak" at "Gusto" (a chain of family restaurants in Japan). Because Ken has been eagerly awaiting this trip, he might not feel like going to these restaurants knowing that they are also available in Osaka. A better solution would be to provide Ken with information about restaurants and food available in Matsusaka but not in Osaka (e.g. "Matsusaka beef" (a well-known food available in Matsusaka)).

In case of "Matsusaka beef," a well-known specialty, Ken can retrieve information using keyword queries because he can easily associate "Matsusaka" with "Matsusaka beef." However, when he goes on a trip to an unknown place,

M. Yoshikawa et al. (Eds.): DASFAA 2010, LNCS 6193, pp. 353–364, 2010.

he would not know the names of special food. In order to find such foods, it is necessary to automatically extract keywords related to the foods available in a restricted area and show them to users.

In this paper, we propose a recommendation method for region-restricted spots. We define a region-restricted spot as a spot that is located in a restricted destination area but not in a user's home area. Here, the destination area implies an area that the user is visiting when on a trip. The user's home area implies an area where the user lives.

The remainder of this paper is organized as follows. In Section 2, we present related works and services and describe the difference between our proposed method and such existing methods. In Section 3, we explain the recommendation method for region-restricted spots. Section 4 presents basic experimental analyses of the validity of our method when applied to real areas in Japan. Finally, Section 5 presents the conclusions of this paper.

2 Related Work

Tezuka et al. [3] have proposed a method for predicting the regionality of Web pages and objects (e.g., "red leaves" or "noodles"). For example, when a user wants to know about places that are famous for red leaves, he/she can input "red leaves" as a search query, and this will display areas related to red leaves. Therefore, the user can find related areas from the names of objects. On the other hand, in this paper, we aim to extract region-restricted phrases based on the input area.

Tarumi et al. [4] proposed the SpaceTag system to provide information to users in a restricted area. The SpaceTag is an object such as text, an image, a sound, or a program that is accessible in a restricted time and an area. A SpaceTag is made by enterprises, public organizations, and general users. Therefore, their opinions and intentions might be included in the SpaceTag. On the other hand, our proposed method automatically extracts region-restricted phrases from a large amount of spot data associated with real-world locations.

Many location- and time-based information delivery systems for tourism have also been proposed [5][6][7]. However, these systems provide information about only those spots that are close to a user's current location. In other words, they do not aim at region-restrictedness.

Many gourmet Web sites provide information about restaurants that serve local specialties. However, such sites might also include the owner's subjective intentions. Moreover, although sufficient information is available about well-known places, little or no information is available about unknown places. On the other hand, if spot data were to be associated with real-world locations, our proposed method can be applied to any place, including unknown ones. Furthermore, because our method automatically extracts region-restricted phrases, unexpected phrases could also be discovered, such as minor phrases that a site owner might not notice.

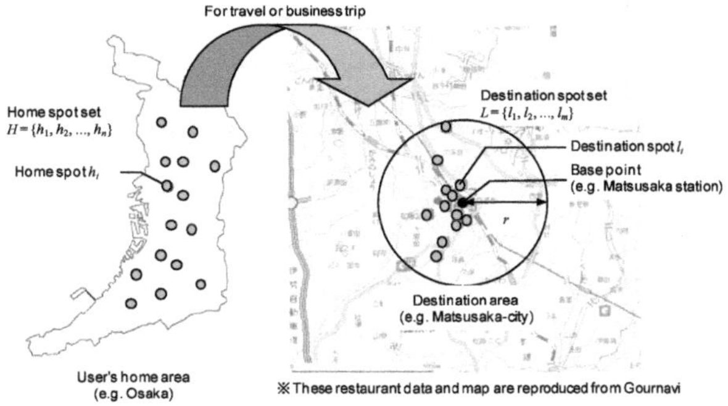

Fig. 1. Home spots and destination spots

3 Recommendation Method Considering Region-Restrictedness

In this section, we explain our proposed recommendation method that considers region-restrictedness.

Our proposed method focuses on the region-restrictedness of spots, and it recommends spots with high region-restrictedness. In this study, we define a spot as an establishment such as a restaurant, amusement facility, or tourist attraction in the real world. A spot with high region-restrictedness indicates a spot that is located in a restricted area but not in a user's home area.

We can acquire spot data such as location and other information from spot information sites such as Gournavi[8]. The proposed method utilizes the following information as spot data:

– Spot name
– Location (latitude/longitude or an address)
– Text data such as promotional descriptions

The proposed method recommends spots based on the following steps:

i Acquire home spots and destination spots.
ii Extract phrases from text data about each destination spot.
iii Calculate region-restrictedness score of each extracted phrase.
iv Recommend spots based on the region-restrictedness score.

In the remainder of this section, we explain each step.

3.1 Acquire Home Spots and Destination Spots

First, we define a home spot and a destination spot (see Figure 1).

We define a home spot h_i as a spot in a user's home area. A home spot set is represented as follows:

$$H = \{h_1, h_2, \ldots, h_n\} \tag{1}$$

Table 1. Extracted patterns of a part of speech

Phrase	Part of speech	Part of speech in Japanese	# of the parts
Prefix	prefix(+noun)	「接頭詞-名詞接続」	0 or 1
	Noun(verbal)	「名詞-サ変接続」	0 and over
Base word	Noun(general) or Noun(proper)	「名詞-一般」または「名詞-固有名詞」	1 and over
Suffix	Noun(verbal)	「名詞-サ変接続」	0 and over
	Noun(suffix)	「名詞-接尾」	0 or 1

Here, n is the total number of home spots. For example, if a user's home area is "Osaka prefecture," the home spot set H includes all spots in "Osaka prefecture" with n being the number of spots.

We define a destination spot l_j as a spot in a user's destination area (e.g., area visited for tourist or business purposes). A destination spot set, which includes spots existing within a radius of r from a base point in the destination area, is represented as follows:

$$L = \{l_1, l_2, \ldots, l_m\} \tag{2}$$

Here, m is the number of spots existing within the range. For example, for the destination "Matsusaka" with the base point as "Matsusaka station," the destination spot set L includes all spots within a radius of r from "Matsusaka station" with m being the number of spots.

3.2 Extract Phrases from Text Data of Each Destination Spot

Our method extracts phrases included in text data about each destination spot $l_j \in L$. We can use a morphological parser such as ChaSen[9] to extract these phrases. Phrases are extracted by the following steps:

i Extract words included in text data about each spot l_j using morphological parser.

ii Let a basic word be a word whose part of speech is "noun (general)" or "noun (proper)" among the extracted words. If "noun (general)" or "noun (proper)" occurs before or after the basic word in a sequence, combine these words into one basic word. This prevents the loss of their features that may occur by splitting them, for example, "Matsusaka beef (松阪牛)" into "Matsusaka (松阪)" and "beef (牛)." On the other hand, exclude a basic word consisting of only "noun (proper.place)." Although the method may extract a name of an area such as "Matsusaka" as a region-restricted phrase, in this case, "Matsusaka" is obvious to the user.

iii Combine the basic word and a prefix and suffix dependent on it into one phrase. In other words, extract a noun phrase consisting of patterns of a part of speech shown in Table 1.

iv In the case of a noun phrase that can be combined by "particle (pronominal)," combine these words into one phrase. In this manner, the method can extract more restricted phrase such as "well-established restaurant in Matsusaka-city (松阪市の老舗料亭)" or "store with Sukiya architecture in a purely Japanese style (純和風数寄屋造りの店構え)."

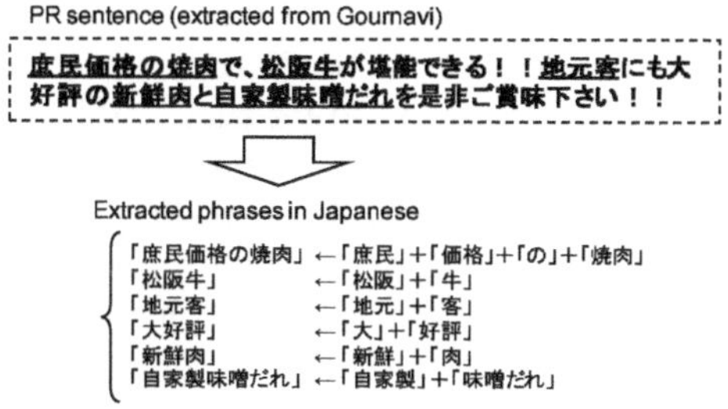
PR sentence (extracted from Gournavi)
庶民価格の焼肉で、松阪牛が堪能できる！！地元客にも大
好評の新鮮肉と自家製味噌だれを是非ご賞味下さい！！
Extracted phrases in Japanese
「庶民価格の焼肉」←「庶民」+「価格」+「の」+「焼肉」
「松阪牛」←「松阪」+「牛」
「地元客」←「地元」+「客」
「大好評」←「大」+「好評」
「新鮮肉」←「新鮮」+「肉」
「自家製味噌だれ」←「自家製」+「味噌だれ」

Fig. 2. Example of the extraction of phrases from text data about a sample spot

In Figure 2, we show an example of the extraction of phrases from text about a spot. For example, a phrase "grilled meat with unpretentious price (庶民価格の焼肉)" was extracted by combining "unpretentious (庶民)," "price (価格)," "with (の)," and "grilled meat (焼肉)."

We represent an extracted phrase set for a spot l_j as follows:

$$W_j = \{w_{j1}, w_{j2}, \ldots\} \tag{3}$$

3.3 Calculate Region-Restrictedness Score of Extracted Phrase

Our method examines how each extracted phrase $w_{jk} \in W$ is restricted to the destination area. In order to find it, we apply Inverse Document Frequency (IDF), which is widely used in the field of document retrieval. Generally, the IDF is represented as follows:

$$\text{idf} = \log \frac{d}{d_e} \tag{4}$$

Here, d is the total number of documents and d_e, the number of documents including a word w_e. That is, a lower weight is assigned to a general word that commonly occurs in many documents and a higher weight is assigned to a feature word that occurs in specified documents.

Based on this notion, we define the restrictedness ν_{jk}. The restrictedness denotes how each extracted phrase w_{jk} in text about a destination spot is restricted against a user's home spot set. In equation (4), when we regard the text data of spots as documents, the restrictedness is represented as follows:

$$\nu_{jk} = \log \frac{n+1}{n_{jk}+1} \tag{5}$$

Here, n is the number of spots included in a home spot set H (refer to 3.1) and n_{jk}, the number of spots whose text includes a phrase w_{jk} among the H. By using this restrictedness, our method can extract a restricted phrase that occurs only in the destination spots but not in the user's home spots.

However, by considering only the restrictedness, a unique catch copy about a spot, such as "with salad Vikings of coupon" or "vegetables for alcoholic drinks," may also be extracted. Most phrases used for such catch copy are unique. Therefore, the restrictedness of these phrases is higher. Therefore, it is not necessary that some content has regionality for a destination area.

Therefore, we consider the regional weight γ_{jk} in addition to the restrictedness ν_{jk}. The regional weight γ_{jk} indicates how a phrase w_{jk} is related to the destination area. That is, a higher weight is given to a phrase that is strongly related to the destination area, such as "Matsusaka beef" in "Matsusaka," and a lower weight is given to a phase that is weakly related to one such as "with salad Vikings of coupon."

In order to take the regional weight, we use WebPMI[10], which indicates the similarity between words based on their co-occurrence frequencies on the Web. The WebPMI between words p and q is represented as follows:

$$\mathrm{WebPMI}(p,q) = \begin{cases} 0 & \text{if } H(p \cap q) \leq c \\ \log \frac{\frac{H(p\cap q)}{N}}{\frac{H(p)}{N}\frac{H(q)}{N}} & \text{otherwise} \end{cases} \tag{6}$$

Here, $H(p), H(q)$, and $H(p \cap q)$ denote the number of Web search results obtained using the queries "p," "q," and "$p + q$," respectively. N is the number of documents a search engine indexes. c is a threshold for avoiding noise caused by words with low frequency.

By calculating the WebPMI(w_{jk}, local) between a phrase w_{jk} and the name of a destination area local, the method obtains γ_{jk}, which is the regional weight of the phrase w_{jk} for an area. γ_{jk} is defined as follows:

$$\gamma_{jk} = \mathrm{WebPMI}(w_{jk}, \mathrm{local}) \tag{7}$$

Here, we utilize reverse geocoding [1] to detect the name of a destination area. Let local be the name of a city, such as "Matsusaka city," that has been acquired by reverse geocoding from the latitude and longitude of the base point.

Finally, we obtain the region-restrictedness score s_{jk} of a phrase w_{jk} based on the above two measures, namely, the restrictedness ν_{jk} and the regional weight γ_{jk}. The score is calculated as follows:

$$s_{jk} = \nu^{\star}_{jk} \times \gamma^{\star}_{jk} \tag{8}$$

Here, $\nu^{\star}_{jk}$ and $\gamma^{\star}_{jk}$ are normalized ν_{jk} and γ_{jk} as $[0, 1]$ in spot l_j, and they are respectively calculated as follows.

$$\nu^{\star}_{jk} = \frac{\nu_{jk} - \min_k \nu_{jk}}{\max_k \nu_{jk} - \min_k \nu_{jk}} \qquad \gamma^{\star}_{jk} = \frac{\gamma_{jk} - \min_k \gamma_{jk}}{\max_k \gamma_{jk} - \min_k \gamma_{jk}} \tag{9}$$

3.4 Recommend Spots Based on Region-Restrictedness Score

For the threshold δ, we regard phrases that satisfy $s_{jk} \geq \delta$ as region-restricted phrases. Our recommendation method provides users with spots with these phrases.

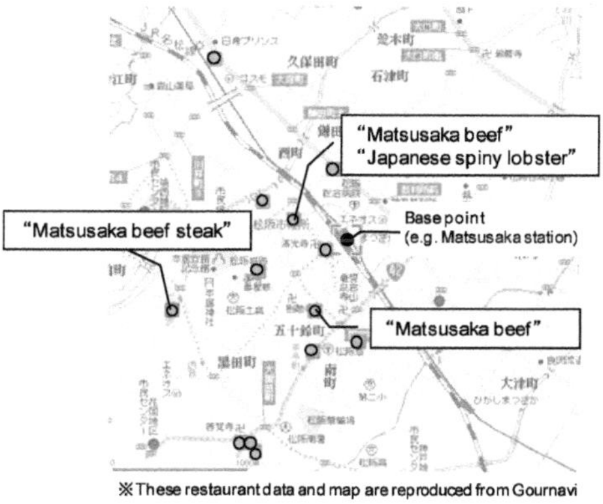

Fig. 3. Example of spot recommendation using region-restrictedness phrases

Table 2. Example of restaurant data used in this experiment

Data type		Content in Japanese
Restaurant name	–	相生亭
Location	Latitude	34.574997
	Longitude	136.534744
Text data	PR sentence (long)	心あたたまる日本の味覚を『相生亭』にて心ゆくまでお楽しみください。
	PR sentence (short)	【松阪肉会席】極上の松阪肉を、こだわりの素材と相生の味わいでバリエーションも豊かな…

Figure 3 shows an example of spot recommendation using region-restricted phrases. For a base point as the user's current or input location, the method shows the surrounding spots with the region-restricted phrases on the map. As shown in Figure 3, our method might extract multiple phrases for one spot or the same phrase for multiple spots. A user can choose spots that he/she wants to use by referring to such phrases.

4 Basic Experiments

We carried out basic experiments in order to analyze the tendency of extraction of phrases based on the region-restricted score described above. First, we explain the data sets used in the experiments in Section 4.1. In Section 4.2, we show the results of qualitative analysis to evaluate the relevance of the region-restricted score and discuss the results. In Sections 4.3 and 4.4, we discuss the results of extracted phrases depending on the destination spot areas and home areas, respectively.

4.1 Data Set

Although our proposed method can be applied to a restaurant, amusement facility, or tourist attraction, in these experiments, we applied it to restaurants as a genre of spots.

We acquired restaurant data from Gournavi [8], a Japanese restaurant guide. We obtained the following restaurant data using the Gournavi API [8] provided by Gournavi:

Table 3. Prefectures used as home areas in this experiment

Prefecture	# of restaurant data
Osaka	5,956
Tokyo	5,660
Aichi	3,041

Table 4. Base points used as destination areas in this experiment

Base point	Latitude	Longitude	City name	# of spots
Nara Park	34.685454	135.843411	Nara-city	30
Matsusaka station	34.576917	136.535790	Matsusaka-city	10
Ohmihachiman station	35.122875	136.102753	Ohmihachiman-city	30

- Restaurant name
- Location (as latitude/longitude)
- Text data (short and long versions of promotional descriptions)

Table 2 shows an example of the data.

In these experiments, we set the prefectures listed in Table 3 as home areas. Let a home spot set of each prefecture be all restaurant data acquired by the Gournavi API for each prefecture.

We also set the base points listed in Table 4 as destination areas. Let a destination spot set of each base point be all restaurant data existing within a radius of $3,000$ m from each base point. However, in cases where the number of restaurants exceeded 30, the closest 30 restaurants from the base point were chosen.

4.2 Qualitative Analysis of Region-Restrictedness Score

We carried out a qualitative analysis of the tendency of phrase extraction based on the region-restrictedness score in order to evaluate the relevance of the score.

In this analysis, let the home area be "Osaka" and the base point in the destination area be "Nara Park." Phrases were extracted from text data about each restaurant data in the destination spot set according to the steps described in Section 3.2. The number of extracted phrases was 483 (except for repeated phrases).

The region-restrictedness score was calculated for each extracted phrase. Then, we constructed a phrase ranking based on the score. Here, let $c = 5$ in Equation (6). The number of phrases that satisfies $H(p \cap q) \leq c$ was 47. We then ranked 436 phrases and excluded these 47 phrases. Figure 4 shows a part of the ranking results. In order to evaluate the relevance of the ranking, we showed the following:

(a) Top 30: 1st to 30th
(b) Worst 30: 407th to 436th (the lowest)

In the next section, we discuss each result.

(a) Top 30

Rank	Phrase in English	Phrase in Japanese	Score	Category
1	Right in the middle of Nature in Mt. Kasuga	春日山の大自然ただ中		C
2	The middle of famous temples	名立たる社寺の中心		C
3	Hirokuni Akiyoshi *(a chef's name at a hotel in Nara)*	秋吉博国		B
4	Inn of ancient city	古都の宿		B
5	Garden bonito	庭の鰹		A
6	Kasuga Grand Shrine *(a Shinto shrine in Nara Park)*	春日大社		C
7	Nara Park *(a public park located in the city of Nara)*	奈良公園		C
8	Specially made bonito	特製の鰹		A
9	Yamato chicken *(a traditional chicken in Nara)*	大和肉鶏		A
10	Dining bar open	ダイニングバーオープン		B
11	French terrace	フレンチテラス		B
12	Woody	木質調		B
13	Yoshino Kudzu *(a traditional specialty in Nara)*	吉野本葛		A
14	Todai-ji *(a Buddhist temple complex located in Nara Park)*	東大寺		C
15	Town of Nara	奈良の町		B
16	In Higashimuki shopping street *(a shopping street in Nara)*	ひがしむき商店街内		C
17	Kintetsu Nara station	近鉄奈良駅		C
18	Fastidious bonito	こだわりのかつお		A
19	Kudara *(a restaurant name)*	百楽		D
20	Primeval forest in Kasuga Okuyama *(one of the world heritages in Nara)*	春日奥山原始林		C
21	Front of Kintetsu Nara station	近鉄奈良駅前		C
22	Vicinity of Sarusawa pond *(a pond in Nara Park)*	猿沢池のほとり		C
23	Terrace style	テラススタイル		B
24	Yamato vegetables *(traditional vegetables in Nara)*	大和野菜		A
25	Yamato beef *(a traditional beef in Nara)*	大和牛		A
26	Sister restaurant to beer hall Fujin *(a restaurant name)*	ビアホール風神の姉妹店		D
27	Japanese-style restaurant inn	料理旅館		D
28	Banzai *(a restaurant name)*	萬菜		D
29	Kimono fabric	呉服		B
30	Japanese-style restaurant Miyama *(a restaurant name)*	和風レストラン三山		D

(b) Worst 30

Rank	Phrase in English	Phrase in Japanese	Score
407	Reserved	貸切	0.1021
408	Mind	心	0.1008
409	Popular	人気	0.0991
410	Drink	ドリンク	0.0978
411	Woman	女性	0.0969
412	Lunch at restaurant	お店のランチ	0.0928
413	This restaurant	当店	0.0920
414	Taste	味	0.0876
415	Summer	夏	0.0870
416	Wine	ワイン	0.0856
417	Ingredient	素材の食材	0.0770
418	Alcoholic drink	お酒	0.0767
419	Maximum	最大	0.0766
420	Banquet	ご宴会	0.0751
421	Other wine	他のワイン	0.0746
422	Atmosphere	雰囲気	0.0744
423	Farewell and welcome party	歓送迎会	0.0727
424	Walking	徒歩	0.0681
425	Pace of a month	月のペース	0.0615
426	Customer	お客様	0.0589
427	Space	空間	0.0581
428	Menu	メニュー	0.0575
429	Location by walking	徒歩の立地	0.0526
430	Dinner party	宴会	0.0475
431	Economical	お得	0.0400
432	Private separate room	個室	0.0372
433	Inside of this restaurant	店内	0.0316
434	Restaurant	お店	0.0227
435	As much as one likes	放題	0.0178
436	Course	コース	0.0000

Fig. 4. Ranking results of phrases based on region-restrictedness scores (home: Osaka, destination: Nara Park)

Discussion of Top 30 Phrases. As shown in Figure 4 (a), we found that many phrases that were strongly related to Nara but not to Osaka, such as "Yamato chicken (大和肉鶏)" (9th), "Yoshino Kudzu (吉野本葛)" (13th), "right in the middle of Nature in Mt. Kasuga (春日山の大自然ただ中)" (1st), and "Todaiji (東大寺)" (14th) were extracted. We focused on the contents of extracted phrases, and found that the phrases could be broadly categorized as follows.

A. Phrases related to foods or ingredients
B. Phrases characterizing a restaurant in terms of its ambience or facilities
C. Phrases including a name of a landmark around a restaurant
D. Phrases related to a restaurant name

Each alphabet in Figure 4 (a) indicates one of the above categories. We now discuss each category.

A. Phrases related to foods or ingredients

Phrases related to foods or ingredients, such as "Yamato chicken (大和肉鶏)" (9th), "Yoshino Kudzu" (吉野本葛) (13th), and "Yamato beef (大和牛)" (25th), that were peculiar to Nara were assigned higher ranks.

However, although "tea gruel (茶粥)" and "kakinoha sushi (柿の葉寿司)" are also specialties peculiar to Nara, these phrases could not be extracted in this experiment because they were not included in the promotional sentences used as text data about restaurants. On the other hand, some restaurant data include these phrases in their details pages or menu pages. Therefore, we would like to consider these pages as text data about spot data in future work.

B. Phrases characterizing a restaurant in terms of its ambience or facilities

"Inn of ancient city (古都の宿)" (4th) and "woody (木質調)" (12th) were phrases that characterized the restaurant's ambience, and they were assigned higher ranks. "French terrace (フレンチテラス)" (11th) and "terrace style (テラスス

(a) Destination: Matsusaka station

Rank	Phrase in English	Phrase in Japanese	Score
1	Matsusaka merchant *(a traditional merchant in Matsusaka)*	松阪商人	1.0000
2	Gojoban Yashiki *(a historic residence in the city of Matsusaka)*	御城番屋敷	0.9828
3	Matsusaka beef *(a specialty in Matsusaka)* etc.	松阪牛等	0.9547
4	Matsusaka meat *(a specialty in Matsusaka)*	松阪肉	0.9298
5	Old-established restaurant in Matsusaka-city	松阪市の老舗料亭	0.8169
6	Old-established restaurant times	老舗時代	0.8039
7	Beef Kaiseki *(a traditional multi-course Japanese dinner)*	牛肉懐石	0.7866
8	Look of a store with Sukiya structure in a purely Japanese style	純和風数寄屋造りの店構え	0.7812
9	Yachiyo *(a restaurant name)*	八千代	0.7802
10	Matsusaka beef steak *(a specialty in Matsusaka)*	松阪牛ステーキ	0.7348

(b) Destination: Ohmihachiman

Rank	Phrase in English	Phrase in Japanese	Score
1	Hachiman Konnyaku *(a specialty in Ohmihachiman)*	八幡蒟蒻	0.9226
2	Natural bittern *(a bittern from Ohmihachiman)*	天然苦汁	0.8948
3	Kansai sushi	関西寿し	0.8690
4	Chojifu *(a specialty in Ohmihachiman)*	丁字麩	0.8393
5	JR Ohmihachiman station	JR近江八幡駅	0.8126
6	Dashimaki with Akaji Tamago *(Japanese style omelet with eel)*	赤地玉子のだし巻き	0.8080
7	Prelude to autumn	秋の序曲	0.7869
8	Funazushi *(a sushi with a crucian carp)*	鮒寿し	0.7659
9	Dengoroh *(a restaurant name)*	伝五郎	0.7604
10	Front of Ohmihachiman station	近江八幡駅前	0.7185

Fig. 5. Ranking results of phrases depending on destination areas (home: Osaka)

タイル)" (23th) were phrases that characterized the restaurant's facilities and "Hirokuni Akiyoshi (秋吉博国)" (3rd) was the name of a chef; these phrases were also assigned higher ranks.

Using such phrases, a user can choose restaurants by also referring to the ambience or facilities peculiar to the destination area.

However, "French terrace" and "terrace style" are not region-restricted phrases for Nara alone. These phrases were extracted because there were a few samples in Osaka that included these phrases in the promotional sentences. In the future, we intend to examine whether it is better to consider spots available not in a home area or only in a destination area.

C. Phrases including a name of a landmark around a restaurant
"Right in the middle of Nature in Mt. Kasuga (春日山の大自然ただ中)" (1st), "the middle of famous temples (名立たる社寺の中心)" (2nd), "Todaiji (東大寺)" (14th), and "primeval forest in Kasuga Okuyama (春日奥山原始林)" (20th) were assigned higher ranks as phrases including a name of a landmark around a restaurant. Because most landmarks indicate the regionality, it is also effective to provide such landmarks in addition to the phrases characterizing a restaurant.

D. Phrases related to a restaurant name
"Kudara (百楽)" (19th) and "Banzai (萬菜)" are the names of restaurants. First, because most restaurant names are peculiar, these phrases can be extracted easily. However, the names do not always characterize their contents. Therefore, it is not effective to show these phrases to users. Therefore, it is necessary to exclude these phrases related to a restaurant name from the ranking.

Discussion of Worst 30 Phrases. Figure 4 (b) shows the worst 30 phrases.

(a) Home: Tokyo

Rank	Phrase in English	Score
1	Right in the middle of Nature in Mt. Kasuga	1.0000
2	The middle of famous temples	0.9807
3	Hirokuni Akiyoshi *(a chef's name at a hotel in Nara)*	0.9756
4	Inn of ancient city	0.9687
5	Garden bonito	0.9644
6	Kasuga Grand Shrine *(a Shinto shrine in Nara Park)*	0.9157
7	Nara Park *(a public park located in the city of Nara)*	0.9149
8	Specially made bonito	0.9079
9	Yamato chicken *(a traditional chicken in Nara)*	0.9032
10	Dining bar open	0.8980
11	French terrace	0.8970
12	Woody	0.8920
13	Yoshino Kudzu *(a traditional specialty in Nara)*	0.8850
14	Todai-ji *(a Buddhist temple complex located in Nara Park)*	0.8787
15	Town of Nara	0.8725
16	Yamato vegetables *(traditional vegetables in Nara)*	0.8663
17	In Higashimuki shopping street *(a shopping street in Nara)*	0.8592
18	Kintetsu Nara station	0.8467
19	Fastidious bonito	0.8370
20	Kudara *(a restaurant name)*	0.8194

(b) Home: Aichi

Rank	Phrase in English	Score
1	Right in the middle of Nature in Mt. Kasuga	1.0000
2	The middle of famous temples	0.9804
3	Hirokuni Akiyoshi *(a chef's name at a hotel in Nara)*	0.9767
4	Inn of ancient city	0.9690
5	Garden bonito	0.9626
6	Kasuga Grand Shrine *(a Shinto shrine in Nara Park)*	0.9167
7	Nara Park *(a public park located in the city of Nara)*	0.9159
8	Specially made bonito	0.9094
9	Yamato chicken *(a traditional chicken in Nara)*	0.9024
10	Dining bar open	0.8996
11	French terrace	0.8963
12	Woody	0.8938
13	Yoshino Kudzu *(a traditional specialty in Nara)*	0.8834
14	Todai-ji *(a Buddhist temple complex located in Nara Park)*	0.8799
15	Town of Nara	0.8694
16	Yamato vegetables *(traditional vegetables in Nara)*	0.8675
17	In Higashimuki shopping street *(a shopping street in Nara)*	0.8610
18	Kintetsu Nara station	0.8472
19	Fastidious bonito	0.8440
20	Kudara *(a restaurant name)*	0.8192

Fig. 6. Ranking results of phrases depending on home areas (destination: Nara Park)

We found that general phrases such as "course (コース)" and "restaurant (店)" were assigned lower ranks. As a result, we confirmed that the general phrases could be assigned lower ranks using the region-restrictedness score.

4.3 Discussion of Phrases Depending on Destination Areas

We compared the ranking results of extracted phrases for the home area "Osaka" and destination areas as the base points listed in Table 4. Figure 5 shows the top 10 phrases when the base points were "Matsusaka station (松阪駅)" and "Ohmihachiman station (近江八幡駅)." 165 and 265 phrases were extracted for these respective base points.

As shown in Figure 5, phrases restricted to each area could be extracted, such as "Matsusaka beef (松阪牛)" at "Matsusaka station" and "Hachiman Konnyaku (八幡蒟蒻)" at "Ohmihachiman station." In particular, foods based on "Matsusaka beef" such as "Matsusaka beef steak (松阪牛ステーキ)" (10th) were extracted in various phrases at "Matsusaka station" and various foods such as "Hachiman Konnyaku (八幡蒟蒻)" (1st), "natural bittern (天然苦汁)" (2nd), and "Chojifu (丁字麩)" (4th) were extracted at "Hachiman station"; in addition, various landmarks such as "Kasuga Taisya (春日大社)" and "Todaiji (東大寺)" were extracted at "Nara Park." Therefore, the characteristics tend to depend on the destination areas. In the future, we intend to carry out further detailed analyses using various areas.

4.4 Discussion of Phrases Depending on Home Areas

We compared the ranking results of extracted phrases for the destination area "Nara Park" and home areas as the prefectures listed in Table 3. Figure 6 shows the top 20 phrases when the home areas were "Tokyo" and "Aichi."

As shown in Figure 6, there was not much difference among the three prefectures in this experiment. In only one case, we found that "Yamato vegetable" was ranked 16th in "Tokyo" and "Aichi," whereas it was ranked 24th in "Osaka." Actually, according to data obtained from Gournavi, there were three restaurants serving this food in Osaka but none in Tokyo and Aichi. This implies that users have some opportunities to eat this food in Osaka but none in Tokyo and Aichi. This is why its rank was lower in the case of Osaka than in Tokyo and

Aichi. This implies that the ranking results tend to change depending on the home areas.

Although there was not much difference in this experiment, we intend to examine the effect of the home area in greater detail in future work.

5 Conclusion

We proposed a recommendation method that considers region-restrictedness. In this study, we define a spot as an establishment such as a restaurant, amusement facility, or tourist attraction in the real world. A spot with high region-restrictedness indicates a spot that is located in a restricted area but not in a user's home area. Then, our proposed method recommends spots with high region-restrictedness. We define the region-restrictedness score to extract region-restricted phrases for the destination area from text data about spots.

We carried out a qualitative analysis of the region-restrictedness score. From the ranking results based on the score, we found that many phrases related to destination areas could be extracted with higher ranks. Moreover, we found that the extracted phrases could be broadly categorized into four categories, and we discussed each category separately.

Although we have presented a basic analysis of the recommendation method, we intend to examine this method further with the aim of developing a practical recommendation system that considers region-restrictedness.

References

1. Google maps, `http://maps.google.com/`
2. Yahoo! maps, `http://maps.yahoo.com/`
3. Tezuka, T., Kondo, H., Tanaka, K.: Estimation of relevant regions for web content by gaussian mixture models for object level local search. Information Processing Society of Japan: Database 1(1), 13–25 (2008) (in Japanese)
4. Tarumi, H., Morishita, K., Kambayashi, Y.: Public applications of spacetag and their impacts, digital cities: Technologies, experiences and future perspectives. In: Ishida, T., Isbister, K. (eds.) Digital Cities 1999. LNCS, vol. 1765, pp. 350–363. Springer, Heidelberg (2000)
5. Abowd, G.D., Atkeson, C.G., Hong, J., Long, S., Kooper, R., Pinkerton, M.: Cyberguide: A mobile context-aware tour guide. Wireless Networks 3(5), 421–433 (1997)
6. Sumi, Y., Etani, T., Fels, S., Simonet, N., Kobayashi, K., Mase, K.: C-map: Building a context-aware mobile assistant for exhibition tours. In: Community Computing and Support Systems, Social Interaction in Networked Communities, pp. 137–154. Springer, London (1998)
7. Cheverst, K., Davies, N., Mitchell, K., Friday, A.: Experiences of developing and deploying a context-aware tourist guide: the guide project. In: Proceedings of the 6th Annual international Conference on Mobile Computing and Networking (MobiCom 2000), pp. 20–31. ACM, New York (2000)
8. Gournavi, `http://www.gnavi.co.jp/en/`
9. Chasen (in Japanese), `http://chasen.naist.jp/hiki/ChaSen/`
10. Bollegala, D., Matsuo, Y., Ishizuka, M.: Measuring semantic similarity between words using web search engines. In: WWW 2007 (2007)

A Hybrid Recommendation Method with Double SVD Reduction

Yusuke Ariyoshi[1] and Junzo Kamahara[2]

[1] Faculty of Economics Management and Information Science, Onomichi University
1600 Hisayamada-cho, Onomichi, Hiroshima, 722-8506 Japan
y-ariyoshi@onomichi-u.ac.jp
[2] Graduate School of Maritime Sciences, Kobe University
5-1-1 Fukaeminami, Higashinada-ku, Kobe, Hyogo 658-0022 Japan
kamahara@maritime.kobe-u.ac.jp

Abstract. An issue related to recommendation is the requirement of considerable memory for calculating the recommendation score. We propose a hybrid information recommendation method using singular value decomposition (SVD) to reduce data size for calculation. This method combines two steps. First, the method reduces the number of documents on the basis of the users' rating pattern by applying SVD based on collaborative filtering (CF). Second, it reduces the number of terms on the basis of the term frequency pattern of the reduced documents by applying SVD based on content-based filtering (CBF). The experimental results show that the proposed method has almost the same mean absolute error (MAE) as the SVD-based CBF. Originally, our data set has 9924 terms. The SVD-based CBF reduces the number of terms to 45 and the proposed method to 15 while preserving the same MAE. This means that the proposed method is effective for calculating recommendation.

Keywords: Recommender System, Content-Based Filtering, Collaborative Filtering, Singular Value Decomposition.

1 Introduction

A recommendation system recommends an item by predicting a user's ratings for the item that the user does not evaluate. There are two methods of rating prediction. One is content-based filtering (CBF), which predicts the rating on the basis of the content of items, such as word appearance frequency. The other is collaborative filtering (CF), which predicts the rating on the basis of other users' ratings of an item.

There are actively researches of method which improve prediction[1, 2]. Singular value decomposition (SVD) is one of the approaches used to improve predicts. There is an improvement method that uses SVD for both CBF and CF[3, 4].

Advantages of SVD are (1) an increase in accuracy and (2) low memory requirement. However, in some cases, the size of memory required is not reduced. Data used for recommending an item are represented as large sparse matrices. Since the matrices

M. Yoshikawa et al. (Eds.): DASFAA 2010, LNCS 6193, pp. 365–373, 2010.

are often dense after SVD, size of the memory required for storing them can greater than that required for the original matrix. Originally, SVD was used with latent semantic indexing (LSI) for information retrieval. In the case of LSI, a sparse 5,526 × 1,033 matrix generated from MEDLINE requires 0.4 Mbytes of memory to store the original matrix, and 2.6 Mbytes to store the corresponding matrices after SVD [5].

In this paper, we propose a new recommendation method that requires a small memory. SVD-based CBF predicts ratings on the basis of a term's appearance-frequency data. Theoretically, if unnecessary information is removed from the term's appearance-frequency data, the size of the memory required can be reduced.

The proposed method combines two reduction steps. First, the method reduces the number of documents used on the basis of the users' rating pattern by applying SVD-based CF to eliminate irrelevant information for prediction. Second, it reduces the number of terms used on the basis of the term's appearance-frequency pattern in these reduced number of documents by applying SVD-based CBF.

The next section describes the conventional recommendation methods. Section 3 discusses the proposed method. Section 4 presents the experimental results, and section 5 discusses the conclusions.

2 Existing Methods

In this section, we present LSI and the existing methods of content-based filtering and collaborative filtering using SVD. We also describe Soboroff's hybrid recommendation method, which uses SVD.

2.1 Latent Semantic Indexing (LSI)

LSI is an information retrieval technique based on the vector space model. In LSI, the term weight of a document (e.g., term frequency) represents the document vector and the entire set of retrieved documents represents the document-term matrix F.

The document-term matrix F is a $d \times t$ matrix since the entire document set has d documents and t unique terms. Each element of matrix F refers to a term weight of the corresponding term in the corresponding document. Each row of the document-term matrix is equivalent to the document vector that represents the term weights in the corresponding document. In the same way, each column of the document-term matrix is equivalent to the term vector that represents the term weights for the corresponding term in the documents.

LSI can reduce the document-term matrix using SVD. The SVD of the document-term matrix F is

$$F = D \times R \times T^t . \tag{1}$$

The superscript t of a matrix indicates that the matrix is a transposed matrix.

The rank of matrix F can be described as $rank(F) = r$. D is a $d \times r$ orthogonal matrix, and T is a $d \times r$ orthogonal matrix. R is an $r \times r$ diagonal matrix in which all elements on the main diagonal have some value and all other elements are equal to zero.

When we compare matrix D with matrix F, we observe that both matrices have d rows; however, the number of columns in matrix D is reduced from t to r. Matrix D, which exists in an r-dimensional space is reflected in matrix F, which exists in a t-dimensional space for each d document. This means that SVD reduces the number of document dimensions from t to r.

The term vector of matrix D (R and T) on the left is significant as it implies that the distribution is high. Let us build a matrix D_k (R_k and T_k) using the k ($<r$) term vectors extracted from the left side of matrix D (R and T). Then, D_k becomes a $d \times k$ orthogonal matrix and represents each document in a k-dimensional space. This means that the number of term dimensions is reduced to k. Further, the reduced k terms might be sufficient to retrieve d documents from similarity on the basis of the term frequency pattern.

Reducing the number of terms in LSI means that the synonyms can be intuitively summarized as one term. Therefore, a search keyword can retrieve the documents that contain the corresponding synonyms.

2.2 Content-Based Filtering with SVD (SVD-CBF)

Content-based filtering with SVD (SVD-CBF) is a type of CBF that applies LSI during information retrieval. In the case of CBF, the interests of each user are represented using a term vector called "user profile." In the user profile, terms that appear frequently in a document valued by the user have significant weight, and the terms that appear frequently in a document not valued by the user have less weight. Further, the entire set of user profiles is represented as the profile matrix P. P is a $u \times t$ matrix since the number of users is u.

In CBF, filtering is carried out by matching a user profile with a document vector. CBF calculates the $u \times d$ matrix G_{CBF}, which represents the predicted ratings between users' interests and documents by using the profile matrix P and the document-term matrix F;

$$G_{CBF} = P \times F^{t}. \tag{2}$$

SVD-CBF filters the content using matrix D_k instead of matrix F. Furthermore, the profile matrix is reduced by product of matrix T_k and matrix R_k^{-1}.

$$P_{SVD-CBF} = P \times T_k \times R_k^{-1}. \tag{3}$$

SVD-CBF calculates the matrix $G_{SVD\text{-}CBF}$ that represents the predicted ratings by using the reduced profile matrix $P_{SVD\text{-}CBF}$ and matrix D_k;

$$G_{SVD-CBF} = P_{SVD-CBF} \times D_k. \tag{4}$$

Therefore, the recommendations on a certain keyword would include documents that contain the corresponding synonyms.

2.3 Soboroff's Hybrid Method

All of the known recommendation methods have strengths and weaknesses, and many researchers have chosen to combine methods in different ways [6]. Soboroff's method is one of the hybrid method which combines CBF and CF with SVD [7].

In Soboroff's hybrid method, SVD is applied to the profile matrix P. The rank of matrix P can be described as rank(P) = v. The equation of SVD for matrix P is

$$P = J \times V \times L^t . \tag{5}$$

Let J be a $u \times v$ orthogonal matrix and L be a $t \times v$ orthogonal matrix. V is a $v \times v$ diagonal matrix.

On comparing matrix J with matrix P, we observe that both matrices have u rows; however, the number of columns in matrix J is reduced from t to v. Originally, in matrix P, each user is represented in a t-dimensional space; however, in matrix J, the user is represented in a v-dimensional space. The number of term dimensions is reduced from t to v.

The term vector of matrix J (V and L) on the left is significant as implies a high distribution. Let us build a matrix J_n (V_n and L_n) by extracting n ($<v$) column term vectors from the left side of matrix J (V and L). Then, J_n becomes a $u \times n$ orthogonal matrix and represents each user in an n-dimensional space. This means that the number of term dimensions is reduced to n. The reduced n terms may be sufficient to make a recommendation for u users from the similarity on the basis of the term weight pattern in the user profile.

Soboroff's hybrid method filters content using matrix J_n instead of matrix P. Furthermore, the document-term matrix is reduced by the product of matrix L_n and matrix V_n^{-1}.

$$F_n = F \times L_n \times V_n^{-1} . \tag{6}$$

Soboroff's hybrid method calculates the matrix $G_{Soboroff}$, which represents the predicted ratings by using the reduced profile matrix J_n and the matrix F_n.

$$G_{Soboroff} = J_w \times F_n . \tag{7}$$

2.4 Collaborative Filtering with SVD (SVD-CF)

The technique using SVD used for improving the accuracy of the recommendation in a manner similar to that of SVD-CBF is collaborative filtering with SVD (SVD-CF).

Collaborative filtering represents the relationship between users and documents as a user-document matrix G. Since u is the number of users and d is the number of documents, the user-document matrix G is a $u \times d$ matrix. The elements of the user-document matrix are values of the corresponding user's rating for the corresponding document. However, some elements do not have any value because the user did not rate the document.

SVD-CF also reduces the user-document matrix G by using SVD like LSI. The rank of matrix G can be described as $rank(G) = s$. The equation of SVD for matrix G is

$$G = U \times S \times E^t . \tag{8}$$

Let U be a $u \times s$ orthogonal matrix and E be a $d \times s$ orthogonal matrix. S is an $s \times s$ diagonal matrix.

On comparing matrix U with matrix G, we observe that both matrices have u rows; however, the number of columns in matrix U is decreased from d to s. Originally, although in matrix G, each u user is represented in a d-dimensional space, in matrix U, the user is represented in an s-dimensional space. The number of document dimensions decreases from d to s.

The left side of matrix U (S and E) is significant as it implies a high distribution. Let us build a matrix U_j (S_j and E_j) by extracting j ($<s$) column document vectors from the left side of matrix U (S and E). Then, matrix U_j becomes a $u \times j$ orthogonal matrix and represents each user in a j-dimensional space. This means that the number of document dimensions is reduced to j. The reduced j documents might be sufficient to make a recommendation for u users from the similarity on the basis of the rating pattern.

In order to predict the value of the user ratings, the user-document matrix G' is recomposed by using the reduced matrix Uj, Sj, and Ej. Although there are elements that do not have the value of an unevaluated document in matrix G, the corresponding elements have a predicted value in matrix G'.

$$G' = U_j \times S_j \times E_j^t . \tag{9}$$

3 Proposed Hybrid Method Using SVD

The recommendation system filters information by predicting the value of the user's evaluation. The CBF predicts evaluation value based on the term frequency information. However, there are effective or non-effective values of term frequency for predicting values.

Further, when we compare Uj with G of SVD-CF in equation (8) and (9), G represents characteristics of u users by evaluation values of d documents. Though, documents which have a similar evaluation pattern in G are reduced to one document in Uj. Uj represents u users' characteristics by evaluation values of j reduced documents. These j documents have different evaluation patterns. Therefore, it is important to distinguish these j documents in order to estimate evaluation. On the other hand, distinguishing documents, which are separate in G, but become one document in Uj, is not important to estimate evaluation.

Hence, the proposed method has the following steps. In the first step, the document set that should be recommended will be reduced on the basis of the similarity of user evaluations. In the next step, terms in document set will be reduced on the basis of the similarity of term frequencies by applying SVD-CBF. In the last step, we will predict the values of the user ratings for the original document set by using SVD-CBF in the reduced term set. These predicted values will be used for making the recommendation.

3.1 Reducing the Number of Documents

As described above, in the SVD-CDF, the number of dimensions (i.e., the number of documents) will be reduced from d to s by processing SVD for matrix G, which represents the values of the user ratings for the documents.

Let us transform equation (8) as follows:

$$G \times E \times S^{-1} = U \ . \tag{10}$$

We can consider the matrix $E \times S^{-1}$ as the projection that reduces the number of columns (documents) from d to s because the number of columns in matrix G is d and the number of columns in matrix U is s. Furthermore, in the matrix $E_j \times S_j^{-1}$, the number of columns (documents) is decreased from d to j.

Then, the number of documents in the term-document matrix F will be reduced by using matrix $E_j \times S_j^{-1}$. For this reduction, the number of rows (documents) in matrix F is reduced from d to j by multiplying $(E_j \times S_j^{-1})^t$ with the $d \times t$ matrix F as follows:

$$S_j^{-1} \times E_j \times F = F_j \, . \tag{11}$$

Matrix F_j, which has j documents, is reduced from matrix F, which has d documents, on the basis of the similarity of user ratings.

3.2 Reducing the Number of Terms and Predicting User Ratings

Next, we apply the method of SVD-CBF to matrix F_j in order to reduce the number of terms.

We can represent the following equation of SVD after replacing matrix F by matrix F_j in the same way as that in SVD-CBF for the term-document matrix (see equation (1)).

$$F_j = D' \times R' \times T'^t \ . \tag{12}$$

We multiply matrix T' and R'^{-1} on the both sides of equation (12), starting from the right:

$$F_j \times T' \times R'^{-1} = D' \, . \tag{13}$$

The rank of matrix F_j can be described as $rank(F_j) = w$. The matrix $T' \times R'^{-1}$ is a projection that can reduce the number of columns (terms) from t to w because the number of columns in matrix F_j is t and the number of columns in matrix D' is w. Furthermore, declaring matrix D_m (T_m and R_m), which is built by extracting the m column vectors of matrix D' (T' and R'), can reduce the number of columns from t to m.

Then, we would reduce the number of terms in the original term-document matrix F by using the matrix $T_m \times R_m^{-1}$. Firstly, multiplying the $d \times t$ matrix F with $T_m \times R_m^{-1}$ on the left reduces the number of columns (terms) from t to m.

Table 1. Histogram of Ratings

Ratings	1	2	3	4	5
# of Documents	6815	2308	1774	1461	1250

Table 2. MAE and Number of Terms

	SVD-CBF	Soboroff's Hybrid Method	Proposed Method
MAE	0.818	0.869	0.813
# of Dimensions	45	22	15

$$F \times T_m \times R_m^{-1} = F_m . \tag{14}$$

Matrix F_m is a $d \times m$ matrix.

Matrix F_m, which has m documents, is reduced from matrix F, which has d documents, on the basis of the similarity of term frequencies (and the similarity of user ratings).

The profile matrix is also reduced by multiplying it with the matrix $T_m \times R_m^{-1}$.

$$P_m = P \times T_m \times R_m^{-1} . \tag{15}$$

Finally, we can calculate the matrix $G_{proposed}$, which represents the predicted ratings by using the reduced profile matrix P_m and matrix F_m.

$$G_{proposed} = P_m \times F_m . \tag{16}$$

4 Experimental Evaluation

To evaluate the ability of reduction and the accuracy of the proposed method, we compare the proposed method with SVD-CBF and Soboroff's hybrid method.

4.1 Experimental Data

In the experiment, we use a data set of a technical document recommendation service. This data set has the term frequency data of each document and the user ratings data. In this data set, there are 86 users. These users have provided 13,608 ratings for 3,560 documents. Further, there are 9,924 terms in this data set. User ratings are recorded as integer numbers in the range of 1 to 5. Table 1 is a histogram of the ratings.

4.2 Results

To compare each method and to decide the value for each parameter, a 10-fold cross-validation is carried out. The accuracy of prediction is measured in terms of MAE (mean absolute error). We perform the 10-fold cross-validation while changing the number of dimensions after reduction, and determine the number of dimensions that gives the best value of MAE.

Table 2 shows the MAE and the number of dimensions after reduction by each method. Figure 1 shows each user's MAE. In the figure, users are sorted according to the value of the MAE. The MAE of the proposed method and that of SVD-CBF are almost the same. The performance of Soboroff's hybrid method is slightly worse in the case of this data set. Further, the number of dimensions in the case of SVD-CBF is 45, that in the case of Soboroff's hybrid method is 22, and that in the case of the proposed method is 15. That is, the number of dimensions in the proposed method is one-third the number in SVD-CBF with almost the same prediction accuracy. The number of dimensions in Soboroff's hybrid method falls in between these two values.

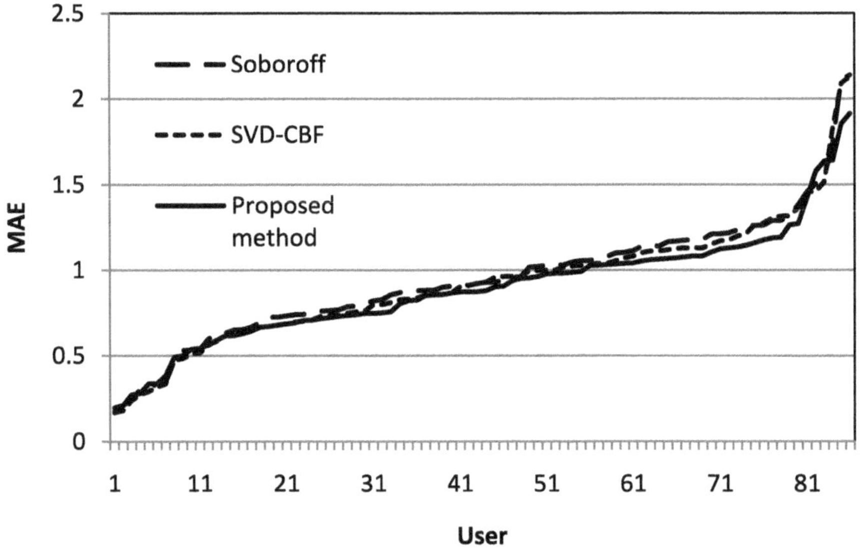

Fig. 1. MAE of Each User

5 Conclusions

In this paper, we proposed a hybrid information recommendation method by using SVD to reduce the data size for calculations. This method combined two reduction steps. First, the method reduced the number of documents used on the basis of the users' rating pattern by applying SVD based on CF. Second, it reduced the number of terms used on the basis of the term frequency pattern of these reduced documents by applying SVD based on CBF.

The evaluation experiment was performed with a data set of a technical document recommendation service. The experimental results showed that the proposed method had almost the same MAE as that of the SVD-CBF. Originally, our data set had 9924 terms. The SVD-CBF reduced the number of terms to 45. The proposed method reduced the number of terms to 15 while preserving almost the same MAE. This implied that the proposed method is effective for calculating recommendations about memory size.

For example, there are two documents whose evaluation patterns were same, but term frequency patterns were different. Information of term frequency to distinguish these two documents is left in SVD-CBF. However, it does not have to distinguish these two documents in order to predict evaluations. Therefore, two these documents would reduced into one document in Uj. Thus, the proposed method can reduce the number of documents than SVD-CBF more.

The test set, which was used in the experimental evaluation, was small. Therefore, we would like to perform experiments with a larger test set. The proposed method uses SVD which is basic dimensions reduction technique. We also plan to compare the proposed method with other dimension reduction technique (pLSI[8], etc.).

Acknowledgements

We would like to express our sincere gratitude to the entire research team and Prof. Shinji Shimojo, Associate Professor Yuichi Teranishi of Osaka University, in particular. In addition, the basic idea of the proposed method was conceived at the NEC Internet system laboratories. We would also like to thank everyone at the laboratories who contributed to the discussion of this research.

References

1. Herlocker, J., Konstan, J., Terveen, L., Riedl, J.: Evaluating Collaborative Filtering Recommender Systems. ACM Trans. on Information Systems 22(1), 5–53 (2004)
2. Kamishima, T.: Algorithms for Recommender Systems. Journal of JSAI 22(6), 826–837 (2007)
3. Foltz, P.W., Dumais, S.T.: Personalized Information Delivery: An Analysis on Information Filtering Methods. Comm. of the ACM 35(12), 51–60 (1992)
4. Sarwar, B.M., et al.: Application of Dimensionality Reduction in Recommender System—A Case Study. In: Proc. KDD Workshop on Web Mining for e-Commerce: Challenges and Opportunities (WebKDD). ACM Press, New York (2000)
5. Berry, M.W., Drmac, Z., Jessup, E.R.: Matrices, vector spaces, and information retrieval. SIAM Review 41(6), 391–407 (1999)
6. Burke, R.: Hybrid recommender systems; Survey and experiments. User-modeling and user-adapted interactions 12(4), 331–370 (2002)
7. Soboroff, I.M., Nicholas, C.K.: Related, but not Relevant: Content-Based Collaborative Filtering in TREC-8. Information Retrieval 5(2-3), 189–208 (2002)
8. Hofmann, T.: Probabilistic latent semantic indexing. In: Proc. of SIGIR 1999, pp. 50–57 (1999)

Monitoring Geo-social Activities through Micro-blogging Sites

Tatsuya Fujisaka, Ryong Lee, and Kazutoshi Sumiya

School of Human Science and Environment, University of Hyogo
1-1-12 Shinzaike-honcho, Himeji, Hyogo 670-0092, Japan
nc06h211@stshse.u-hyogo.ac.jp,
{leeryong,sumiya}@shse.u-hyogo.ac.jp

Abstract. Micro-blogging sites are not only a place for sharing instant update sharing, but also an unexplored land where we can monitor and analyze our society from a great deal of everyone's buzz. Interestingly, recent smartphones are enabling us to easily write some micro-blogs outdoors and publish them with additional tags about automatically identified location and time. In the respect of the great number of participating users and their global distribution, we can regard such micro-blogging sites as an unprecedented sensor network in which each person is a kind of sensor to aware the real world events and reporting their observations and opinions voluntarily. In this paper, we first introduce our efforts to develop a geo-social activity monitoring system based on the micro-blogging sites by aggregating and analyzing such a novel dataset. We also present our preliminary work to find meaning geo-social activities with their influence regions through extracting characteristic moving patterns of mobile micro-bloggers.

Keywords: Micro-blog, Human Sensor Network, Geographic Social Activity.

1 Introduction

Micro-blogs represented by Twitter [19] are recently attracting a great deal of attentions all over the world. From a report by Sysomos Inc. in June 2009 [5], Twitter has experienced an explosive growth over the past two years; it has over 11.5 million users and reached the position as the number one micro-blogging tool. The reason the site has been used popularly can be summarized in two respects. At first, micro-bloggers are able to send their most up-to-dates instantly to acquaintances or simply to the public. Especially, one of the most significant characteristics is on the limited size of writable texts. However, the restriction does not seem so critical problem, since our update reporting would be enough represented even in such short length. Second, on behalf of the wide availability of smartphones where we can easily write and browse micro-blogs anytime and anyplace, it becomes much and much easier to input a short length of texts for sending to other people or remaining some notes about favorable events.

Furthermore, some micro-blogging applications available in smartphones such as iPhone can attach a geographic location with the equipped positioning sensor by

M. Yoshikawa et al. (Eds.): DASFAA 2010, LNCS 6193, pp. 374–384, 2010.

cell-stations or GPS. This functionality is also greatly expanding the usages of the micro-blogging sites in an innovative way we have not experienced yet. The most crucial difference is that such micro-blogs written with mobile devices capable of geo-tagging about current place on the earth are exploding over the micro-blogging sites. If we consider the diversity of the micro-bloggers who are participating at globally different places and writing messages often about social events occurring at nearby places where they are now, the geo-tagged micro-blogs are very useful and rapid social media to monitor and analyze geographically social activities.

One interesting fact we should focus on is that human beings are voluntarily writing their experiences, thoughts, opinions, feelings, etc. Sometimes, people are even uploading photos or videos to the micro-blogging sites [18]. In this paper, we model such human beings as sensors which are usually used to monitor some kinds of environmental statues such as wild fire [1,14,17]. Surely, humankinds have developed various kinds of sensing abilities such as 'see', 'hear', 'taste', etc. to protect themselves from a lot of dangers in the nature. We can further arrange such sensing experiences together and intellectually make a decision about what we will do next, etc. Of course, micro-bloggers are a group of such evolved humankinds, while lots of their messages look like useless babblings [8] or can include little information to the public. In the respect of generic wireless sensor network model, each person makes a short length of report and sends it to some specific people or simply broadcast to the public, whenever he or she wants to share some experiences or for other personal memories. Completely uncontrolled, each person can move to any place or take a photograph to share. Furthermore, the total number of human sensors through the micro-blogging sites is rapidly explosively growing all over the world. We cannot simply regard such buzzing as a noise, since, in some important social events, the sites showed its usefulness and effectiveness such as Iran's demonstration [16] and India's terror [12] cases.

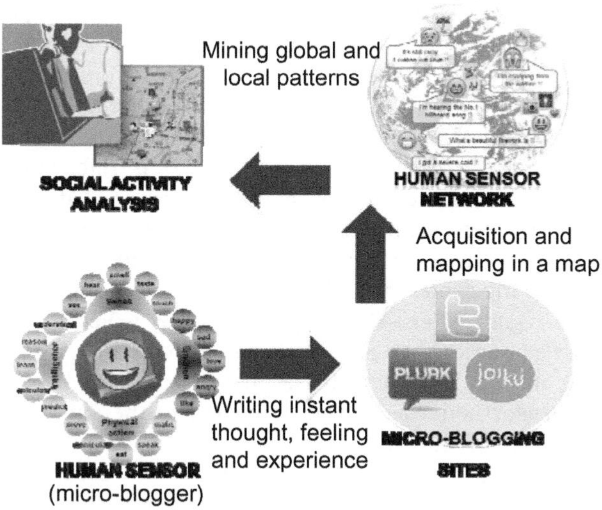

Fig. 1. Human Sensor Network based on Mass Micro-blog Data

Based on the concept of human sensor network over the micro-blogging sites, we will build a framework to aggregate such uncontrollable and unexpectedly occurring micro-blogs and develop a geographic social activity analysis system. In this paper, we especially endeavor to estimate influence regions of social events based on micro-blogging sites. In particular, we focus on the movement patterns of mass micro-bloggers who make instant updates with geo-tagged and time-stamped data.

In order to achieve our goal, we have developed a micro-blogging monitoring system to obtain mass geo-tagged and time-stamped micro-blog data at first. Then, we performed a clustering to examine the spatial distribution of the data. Finally, we find out clusters which heavily were occurring users' movement and perform estimation of influence region.

The remainder of this paper is constructed as follows. Section 2 describes our initial motivation and reviews related work. Section 3 explains our system for gathering mass micro-blog data. Section 4 presents full details of methods to estimate influence region of spatio-temporal regional events. Section 5 illustrates the experiment conducted with a real dataset collected from the Twitter. Section 6 will discuss some research issues derived from our experiences. Section 7 concludes this paper with future work.

2 Human Sensor Network over Micro-blogging Sites

2.1 Human Beings as Sensors

With the great advance of mobile web accessing infrastructures, people can easily use web access anytime and anywhere, and share a variety of information about the real world in real-time. Particularly, micro-blogging sites such as Twitter, Plurk, Jaiku, Pownce, etc. are surprisingly accelerating the speed of personal up-to-date sharing and distribution expanding their geographic coverage over all around the world instantly. Nonetheless, some people considered that micro-blogs have too much personal information and nonsense messages are often found. In fact, Grove [8] negatively reported that the public's pointless 40.5% babbles over the Twitter. However, we can regard them in a completely different view as a human sensor network. Conventionally, a sensor network [1,14,17] is referring to a monitoring framework with a lot of elementary sensing nodes embedded in an environment, where each node can periodically sense surrounding situations such as sudden uprising temperatures to detect a wildfire in a forest and report periodically to an administrative monitoring center through usually wireless communication technology.

Likewise, if we regard **Micro-Blogging Services as a Sensor Network** with the thought of Humans as Sensors, we are able to see them as a huge-scale human sensor network spreading all over the world. In the first place, each micro-blog user can be seen as a unique sensor node. However, compared to the simple electronic sensor nodes usually used in conventional sensor network, we human being are sure to have much intelligent and sophisticated sensing capabilities. In general, we human being can see, listen, feel, taste, smell, etc. In addition, our ability to recognize surrounding natural or social environments is generally superior to the other devices. Of course, there can be differences among the Human Sensor Nodes in their own abilities, features, and even views to the world. With this novel view, the Twitter's function would take on a major significance to obtain sensing reports from all over the world. Furthermore, there are really lots of human nodes whose quantity has been explosively increasing; some nodes are reporting their daily life experiences, more surprisingly, with no payment for their efforts with less privacy concerns. Thus, in order to sense a globe for various purposes, we consider that it is very important to establish such kinds of huge systems easily based on these open-minded human sensors. In this paper, we especially make an effort to analyze the regional events based on the noble concept as this human sensor.

2.2 Related Work

Micro-blogging is still in the state of evolution, simultaneously becoming many academic and practical issues. Java et al. [7], Zhao et al. [22] and Krishnamurthy et al. [10] examined the use of Twitter in relation to its impact on lifestyles and topical discussions. Iwaki et al. [6] considered the discovery of useful topics from micro-blogs. Both studies paid attention to the contents of messages and the link structure of follows among users. These researches mainly analyzed the trends in remarks and the discovery of tastes based on the context of the messages and link structures. Our study differently focuses on the location and time when users actually write micro-blogs, in order to detect unusually crowded places from movement patterns.

For a research analyzing the social movements of people, Wang et al. [21] analyzed a dataset which were extracted from GPS-equipped taxis and found places which were passengers were often picked up passengers or dropped -off them to analyze the movement of human flows. In their research, they needed a large budget and the support of taxi companies to collect datasets. However, we developed a system that is easily able to extract datasets for any region everywhere. As a result, we can analyze movement histories in various regions with almost zero cost.

Moriya et al. [11] developed a system that estimates situation of a region from textual messages, in relation to geographic information provided by blogs, and displayed the results on a digital map. This research is similar to our work in terms of social analysis being the point used to consider tendencies, but in our research we try to analyze movement patterns.

As a research analyzing the social movements of people, Otsuka et al. [13] and Mohan et al. [15] discovered a relationship between the real world and network and analyzed how behavior on the web reflects in real world. Our study detects unusually crowded places based on micro-blogs where people's movements are directly reflected in the data.

3 Acquiring Mass Higher-Resolution Buzzes

In this section, we will explain a method for gathering mass human sensing data from micro-blog sites. For the purpose, we developed a system that can obtain sensing data for a region designated for analysis. Fig.2 presents the outline of system. This system can receive various requests from analysts who want to obtain data on a large region, such as at a nation-wide level, or for a narrow region such as for a city.

Among many micro-blogging sites, we utilized the most popular site, Twitter to acquire our experimental data.

Users first need to specify the region for examination. The system then locates the geographic region, accesses the micro-blog site and obtains data through the Twitter's API [20]. We explain our preliminary experiments to reveal where most twitter users are publishing their messages in Japan. Given the limitations of Twitter's Open API, a naïve approach to examining such spatial distribution of human activities through Twitter would be to split the entire region of interest into grid with a lot of small cells(in Twitter, the minimum size should be 1-km.), and to place a virtual radar station in every cell. For a circular area with a 100 km radius, we would need $\lceil 100^2 \pi \rceil$ cells to cover the area.

Instead of such a naïve approach, we applied quad-tree based space splitting, where a space is recursively split into four rectangular sub areas of the same size, until each area is larger than the minimum radius permitted in the query specification and the number of results will be under 1,500 (This is the maximally acquirable answers in Twitter.). For practical processing and a simple discussion, we assume the basic shape in this study is a rectangular region.

However, each rectangle should be examined with a circular query. Thus, we made a circum-circle for every cell to cover the rectangular bound as show in Fig.2 (a).This method can help us to utilize general planar-based space indexing algorithms when asking for on-line APIs which usually only support a circular query. The resulting number of required queries to aggregate the whole twitter-blogs occurred in the specified region can be greatly improved, since usual occurrence pattern is not uniform, instead, resulting in a high density in urban areas and a low density in other places.

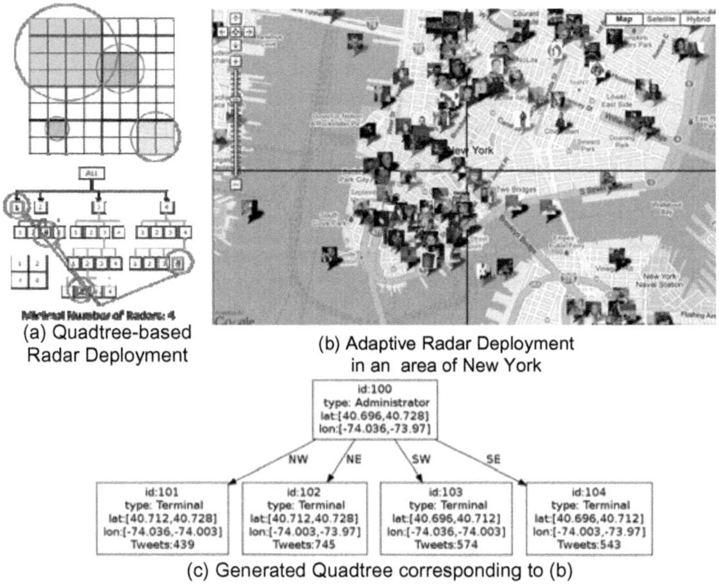

(c) Generated Quadtree corresponding to (b)

Fig. 2. Outline of Micro-blog Monitoring System

As shown in Fig.2 (a), 8*8 cells can be managed only by 4 monitoring queries which have adaptively computed radius and well-positioned centers. For example, we investigated in an area of New York by adaptively deploying on queries, and eventually 4 queries were formed to completely cover the whole target region. Of course, the constructed quadtree depicted in Fig.2 (c), can be periodically re-generated to follow the most up-to-date status. Consequently, in the timely drawn trees in Fig.2 (c), a root node and 4 leaf nodes were made: each of them have a node id, links to children, deployed location, a coverage by a radius, and actually acquired tweets (message acquired from twitters). As another example, we illustrate an experimental result of collecting tweets in Asia as shown in Fig.3.

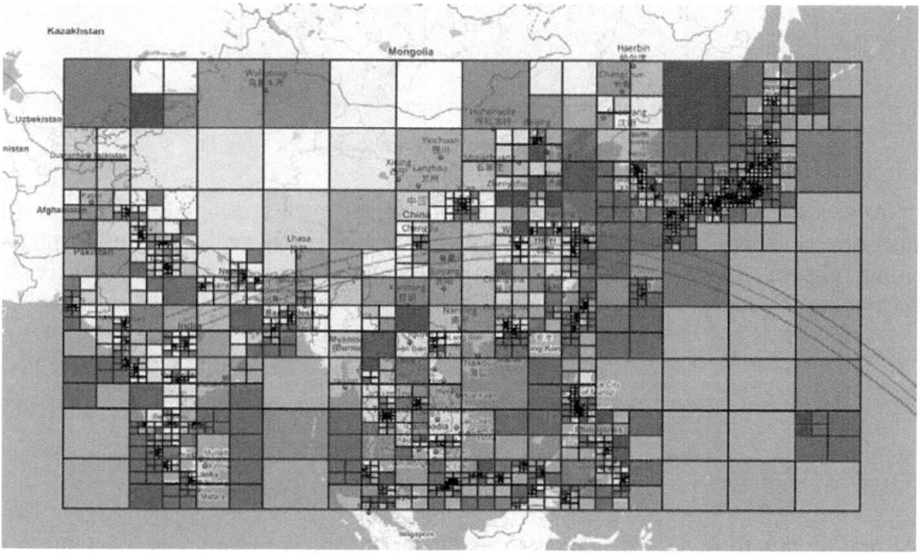

Fig. 3. Geographic Distribution of Tweets in Asia (July, 2009)

4 Analyzing Influence Regions of Social Events

In this section, we explain a method to estimate influence regions of social events based on movement pattern models [2, 3, 4]. At first, we have to find out unusually crowed places where regional events may happen. In order to detect such places from the mass micro-blog data, we need to decide selection of observed regions before movement analysis based on movement pattern models. For this, we conducted distribution of regions which depend on quantity of the data and we detect the change of each cluster in a periodic time based on the constructed clusters. In this paper, we preliminarily adopt the K-means [9] algorithm as a simple approach based on location. By using the method, we regard each cluster as crowded regions.

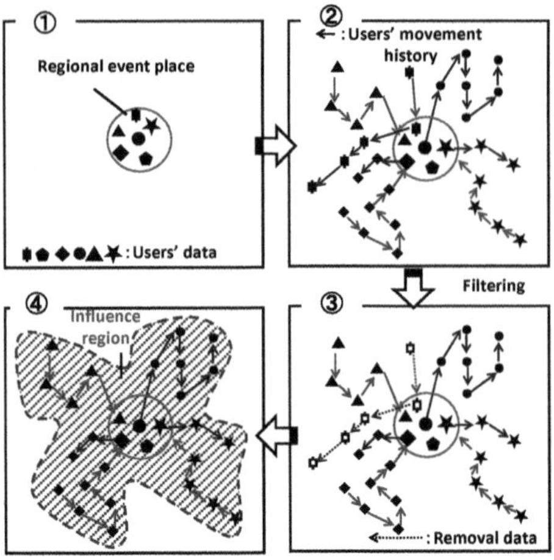

Fig. 4. Outline of method to estimate influence region

At second, we estimate influence region of social events using users' movement histories as shown in Fig.4. As previously noted, we firstly find out unusual places using "*Crowd Activity*" as follow. In other word, we discover the places where the movement of people is intense.

$$Activity_i = \frac{\sum_{j}^{\#user_i} moving\ distance(user_j)}{radius_i\,(km) \times \#users_i} \tag{1}$$

$$\begin{cases} radius_i : the\ radius\ of\ i-th\ cluster \\ \#users_i : the\ number\ of\ found\ users\ in\ i-th\ cluster \end{cases}$$

At first, in this formula, we calculate movement distance of users which belong to in a cluster. After we add up users' movement distance, we calculate the average of clusters by considering the size of the cluster. Therefore, we can discover unusual places which were occurring movement patterns such as aggregation and dispersion using a measure of "*Crowd Activity*". Next, we analyze users' movement histories of the crowd region which calculated high *Crowd Activity* score. In other words, we analyze only movement histories of users who are in the crowd region by finding out an unusual place with *Crowd Activity* beforehand. Next, we analyze whether the movement of the users is related to a regional event and filter it as show in the right lower side of Fig.4 if a user don't relate. Finally, we decide to estimate effective region based on movement distance from a crowd region to the place which were occurring a regional event. In order to estimate influence region closely, we have to consider a probability that the movement happens from a crowd region to an unusual place. For instance, a lot of people in a region may move the unusual place; on the one hand, a few of people in a region may go the place. However, we mainly want to know which regional people were entering / leaving into the place. Therefore, we estimate influence region based on moving distance without considering how much probability movements in crowd regions would be.

5 Experiment

At first we obtained the micro-blog data in Japan using our monitoring system and geo-tagged data only extracted. The number of data was 128,901 and the number of user was 4,382. Next, we performed the detection of unusually places based on "Crowd Activity". Table1 presents 10 clusters which have high Crowd Activity scores.

Table 1. The top 10 results of high Crowd Activity score

rank	latitude	longitude	address	radius (km)	#user	#moving user	moving distance (km)	avg. distance (km)	Activity
1	35.644	139.741	Mita, Minatoku, Tokyo	2.6	83	19	3291.6	173.2	65.4
2	35.673	139.7329	Akasaka, Minatoku, Tokyo	2.1	99	23	2875.1	125.0	58.3
3	35.655	139.8043	Edogawa, Koutouku, Tokyo	2.7	41	13	1500.2	115.4	42.2
4	35.671	139.7113	Jinguumae, Shibuyaku, Tokyo	2.1	76	13	1167.9	89.8	41.9
5	35.694	139.8176	Etoubashi, Sumidaku, Tokyo	4.6	52	19	3593.1	189.1	41.0
6	35.506	139.5703	Kamoi, Midoriku, Kanagawa	8.3	35	12	3630.8	302.6	36.5
7	35.735	139.6925	Kanamecho, Toyoshima, Tokyo	2.7	19	4	397.6	99.4	36.4
8	35.66	139.6241	Hachimanyama, Setagaya, Tokyo	3.8	45	10	1397.5	139.8	36.4
9	35.62	139.7715	Hegashiyashio, Shinagawa, Tokyo	3.7	59	19	2443.9	128.6	34.8
10	35.672	139.6833	Motoyoyogicho, Shibuya, Tokyo	1.9	49	11	716.6	65.1	34.7

From the result, we performed analysis of a cluster (id=40) which located around Odaiba where many events seemed to be performed particularly. In fact, there are a famous tourist spot where the Fuji broadcasting center, amusement parks, and a number of shopping malls. In fig.5 (a), the circle is the cluster which was formed in the periphery of Odaiba. Yellow icons represent micro-blog data in the cluster and there were 2,411 data. Next, we examined the user number of people in the cluster and the number of users who really left movement histories.

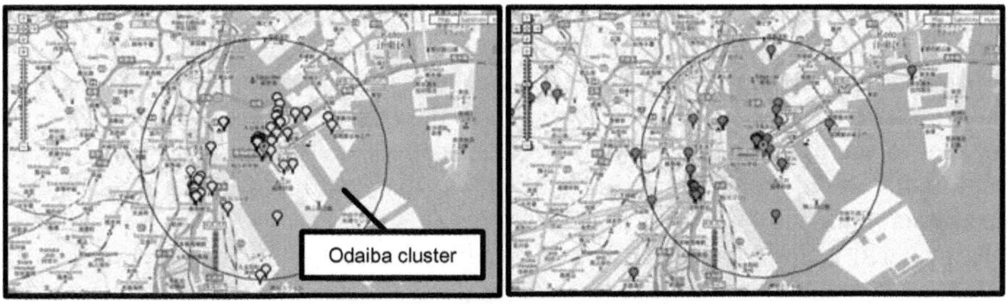

(a) The periphery of Odaiba

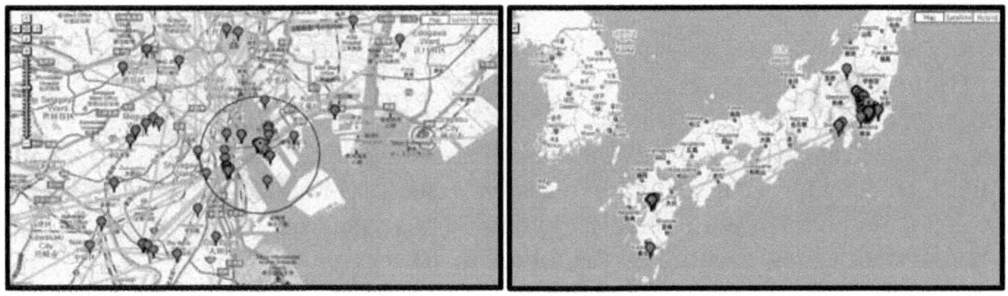

(b) Kantou area (c) Japan area

Fig. 5. Movement histories analysis (Aug. 5-11th, 2009)

As the result, they were obtained from 19 moving users among 59 found users. In the figure, we depicted movement histories by using red icons and red lines on the map as shown in Fig.5.

We can easily understand that there were many people coming to Odaiba from the Kanto area. Also, users came to there from not only kantou area but also far-off places such as Niigata, Fukuoka or Kagoshima. The result shows that a lot of people from various parts of the country congregated in this region during this period. In fact, various events took placed in Odaiba in this time.

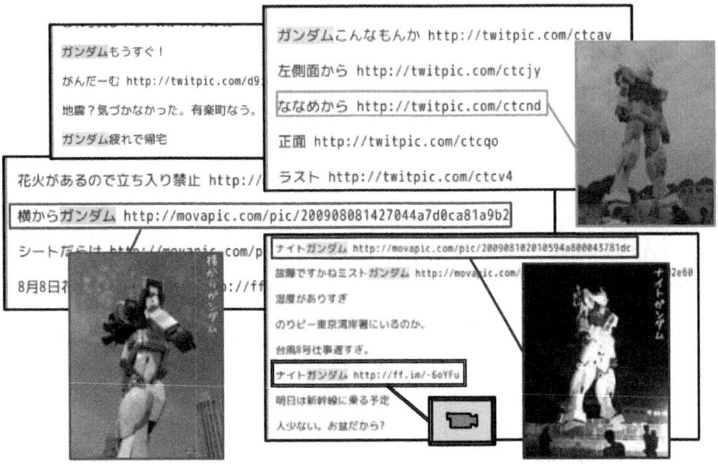

Fig. 6. Miro-bloging messages with photo or video

In addition, it attracted attention, since huge Gundam was built there this summer. Gungam is a very popular high animated cartoon among some Japanese people, and a lot of goods is sold. In fact, size of life of the Gundam was exhibited in Odaiba during this summer and we discovered that people in the considerably remote region visited this spot to see the Gundam. In other words, we revealed that this was a nationwide event to affect wide regional people. In fact, we analyzed messages in the cluster and can extract "gundam" word. In Fig.6, we present some real messages with photos or videos related to the topic word among the found messages. Therefore, we consider that by analyzing micro-blog textual messages, we can not only discover explicit social events or the real interesting patterns, but also know crowd's thoughts and emotions.

6 Discussion

In our pioneering work, we utilized mass micro-blogs for demographic survey. This unprecedented approach, actually, requires a lot of practical implementation and research from collecting the huge-scale data to analyzing useful social patterns. This on-going work is now focused on the following issues:

-Real-time Buzz Monitoring: In order to fully access the flowing data stream of upcoming twitter's data around the word, our quadtree-based acquisition framework needs to work much dynamically for tracing most up-to-dates with a well-scheduled monitoring plan.

-Geo-Social Pattern Analysis: While our initial efforts to find characteristic moving patterns was able to extract a little predicted pattern, there are much great possibilities to extract unexpected and useful social patterns. For this, we primarily observed much objective clue, that is, moving histories of crowd.

7 Conclusion

In this paper, we first presented a noble concept to model human beings as a unique intelligent sensor for the purpose of dealing with micro-blogging sites as a valuable resource of geo-social patterns analysis. In this fundamental model, we can easily imagine the numerous numbers of applications utilizing such seemingly noisy babbles, but actually invaluable reports through everyone's voice and life style. The bound of availability would be unlimited. We believe that we can find much useful social patterns from the micro-blogging sites in the respects of the huge quantity and their global distribution. In this paper, we showed a nation-wide pattern occurred in Japan with the simple clustering and movement tracing. In the future work, we will examine much deeper and unknown social patterns targeting for other countries or continents, eventually realizing a real-time global geo-social event monitoring system.

Acknowledgment

This research was supported in part by a Grant-in-Aid for Scientific Research (B)(2) 20300039 from the Ministry of Education, Culture, Sports, Science, and Technology of Japan.

References

1. Kansal, A., Nath, S., Liu, J., Zhao, F.: SenseWeb: An Infrastructure for Shared Sensing. IEEE MultiMedia 14, 4 (2007)
2. Fujisaka, T., Lee, R., Sumiya, K.: Exploring Urban Characteristics Using the Movement History of Mass Mobile Microbloggers. In: The Eleventh Workshop on Mobile Computing Systems and Applications (HotMobile 2010) (February 2010) (to appear)
3. Fujisaka, T., Lee, R., Sumiya, K.: Discovery of User Behavior Patterns from Geo-tagged Micro-blogs. In: 4th International Conference on Ubiquitous Information Management and Communication (ICUIMC 2010) (January 2010) (to appear)
4. Fujisaka, T., Lee, R., Sumiya, K.: Detection of Unusually Crowded Places through Micro-Blogging Sites. In: The 6th International Symposium on Web and Mobile Information Services (WAMIS 2010) (April 2010) (to appear)
5. Inside Twitter: An In-depth Look Inside the Twitter World. Sysomos (June 10, 2009) (Retrieved on 2009-06-23)

6. Iwaki, Y., Jatowt, A., Tanaka, K.: Supporting finding read-valuable articles in microblogs. DEIM Forum 2009 A6-6 (2009)
7. Java, A., Song, X., Finin, T., Tseng, B.: Why we twitter: understanding microblogging usage and communities. In: Proceedings of the 9th WebKDD and 1st SNAKDD 2007 workshop on Web mining and social network analysis, San Jose, California, pp. 56–65 (2007)
8. Grove, J.V.: Twitter Analysis: 40% of Tweets Are Pointless Babble (from a survey by Pear Analytics)
9. K-means algorithm, http://docs.scipy.org/doc/scipy/reference/cluster.vq.html
10. Krishnamurthy, B., Gill, P., Arlitt, M.: A few chirps about twitter. In: WOSP 2008: Proceedings of the first workshop on Online social networks, Seattle, WA, USA, pp. 19–24 (2008)
11. Moriya, K., Sasaki, S., Kiyoki, Y.: A Dynamic Creation Method of Environmental Situation Maps Using Text Data of Regional Information. DEIM Forum 2009 B1-6 (2009)
12. Mumbai terror, http://japan.cnet.com/news/media/story/0,2000056023,20384390,00htm
13. Otsuka, S., Takaku, M., Kitsuregawa, M., Miyazaki, N.: A Study for Analysis of User Behavior in The Free Magazine Site for Women. DEIM Forum 2009 B8-4 (2009)
14. Pottie, G.J., Kaiser, W.J.: Wireless integrated network sensors. Commun. ACM 43(5), 51–58 (2000)
15. Mohan, P., Padmanabhan, V.N., Ramjee, R.: Nericell: rich monitoring of road and traffic conditions using mobile smartphones. In: Proceedings of the 6th ACM conference on Embedded network sensor systems, Raleigh, NC, USA, pp. 323–336 (2008)
16. Protests in Iran reported through Twitter, http://zen.seesaa.net/article/121677479.html, http://shinyai.cocolognifty.com/shinyai/2009/06/twitterfriendfe.html
17. Haenselmann, T.: An FDLíed Textbook on Sensor Networks, http://pi4.informatik.uni-mannheim.de/~haensel/sn_book/
18. Twitpic, http://twitpic.com/
19. Twitter, http://twitter.com/
20. Twitter Open API, http://apiwiki.twitter.com/Twitter-Search-API-Method%3A-search
21. Wang, H., Zou, H., Yue, Y., Li, Q.: Visualizing hot spot analysis result based on mashup. In: Proceedings of the 2009 International Workshop on Location Based Social Networks (2009)
22. Zhao, D., Rosson, M.B.: How and why people Twitter: the role that micro-blogging plays in informal communication at work. In: Proceedings of the ACM 2009 international conference on Supporting group work, Sanibel Island, Florida, USA, pp. 243–252 (2009)

UDM2010
Workshop Organizers' Message

Katsumi Tanaka, Yutaka Kidawara, and Ki-Joune Li

Kyoto University, Japan
National Institute of Information and Communications Technology, Japan
Pusan National University, Korea

Ubiquitous computing technologies provide a pervasive base for a real world environment such that we can acquire and deliver information at every place. Advances in the technologies of displays, electronic papers, digital architecture, sensors, RFID tags and storage devices etc. may bring a new real world environment for data access. The Second International Workshop on Ubiquitous Data Management (UDM2010) held in Tsukuba, Japan on 4 April 2010, in conjunction with the DASFAA 2010 conference. The UDM2010 aims to focus more on new emerging issues of data management (acquisition, storage, retrieval, and delivery) involved with respect to pervasive, ubiquitous and sensor computing.

The UDM2010 was prepared and helped by a lot of people. First, we would like to thank the program committee members for evaluating the assigned papers in a timely and professional manner. Especially, we would like to express our sincere appreciation to the great work by the following persons: Program Co-Chairs: Dr.Koji Zettsu (NICT: National Institute of Information and Communications Technology, Japan), Dr.Hannu Jaakkola (Tampere University of Technology, Finland), Publicity Chair: Dr. Mitsuru Minakuchi (Kyoto Sangyo University, Japan), Publication Co-chairs: Dr.Kyoungsook Kim (NICT, Japan), Dr.Sungwoo Tak (Pusan University, Korea), and Local Arrangement Co-Chair: Dr. Takafumi Nakanishi (NICT, Japan), Dr.Hisashi Miyamori (Kyoto Sangyo University, Japan), Mr. Yuhei Akahoshi(NICT, Japan). The success of the conference is due to the hard work of these committee chairs and other volunteers.

We also thank Ms. Junko Masuda for their hard and diligent work for the workshop secretariat.

Finally, we thank you for your contributions to UDM2010: for attending sessions, presenting papers, being session chairs, and performing all the other functions that are needed.

M. Yoshikawa et al. (Eds.): DASFAA 2010, LNCS 6193, p. 385, 2010.

Distributed SLCA-Based XML Keyword Search by Map-Reduce

Chenjing Zhang[1,2], Qiang Ma[2], Xiaoling Wang[3], and Aoying Zhou[2,3]

[1] College of Information Technology, Shanghai Ocean University, China
cjzhang@shou.edu.cn
[2] School of Computer Science and Technology, Fudan University, China
{cjzhang,maqiang}@fudan.edu.cn
[3] Shanghai Key Laboratory of Trustworthy Computing,
Software Engineering Institute, East China Normal University
{xlwang,ayzhou}@sei.ecnu.edu.cn

Abstract. Large scales of XML information comes continually from new Web applications, and SLCA (Smallest Lowest Common Ancestor)-based XML keyword search is one of the most important information retrieval approaches. Previous approaches focus on building index for XML documents. However in information dissemination scenario, it is impossible to build index in advance for continuous XML document streams. This paper addresses SLCA-based keyword search for continuous XML documents by Map-Reduce mechanism. We use parallel algorithms to process plenty of XML documents in Hadoop environment. A distributed SLCA computation method is designed, where each net node computes SLCA independently and just a little information needs be transmitted. A real Hadoop environment is built and we demonstrate the efficiency of our algorithms analytically and experimentally.

Keywords: SLCA, keyword search, XML, distributed system.

1 Introduction

XML is widely-used format for exchanging and storing information. Plenty of XML data are produced continually and what users are interested in are some parts of one XML document in many applications, for example publish/subscribe system. It's widely used in news, stock tickers, sports tickers, entertainment delivery and so on. Many attentions focus on meaningful information filtering and extracting. [6,4] filter XML data based on XPath queries. All of them demand users to write XML path queries. However, many users aren't familiar with XML data schema and XPath query language. Most users tend to use keywords to describe requirements.

SLCA-based keyword search is an important approach to extract information in XML documents. A lot of work focus on the efficiency of XML keyword search algorithms, such as [10,12,11]. They all store XML tree nodes in DB and index them. They can't process continuous XML data streams, because it is impossible to build index in advance for data produced continually.

M. Yoshikawa et al. (Eds.): DASFAA 2010, LNCS 6193, pp. 386–397, 2010.

Distributed system is a better choice for processing large scales of data. XML data placement in distributed environment attracts many attentions, such as [3,9,14]. Most of them give XML data placement strategy aiming at path queries.

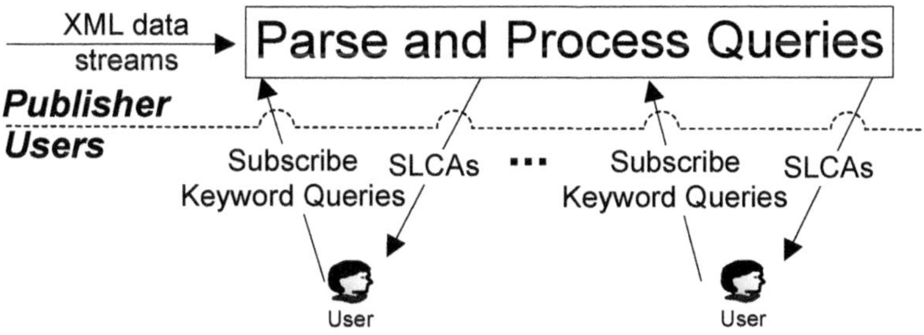

Fig. 1. Keyword Search in XML Dissemination. Users commit keywords to subscribe what they want. Publisher parses continuous XML data and returns SLCAs matching the keywords.

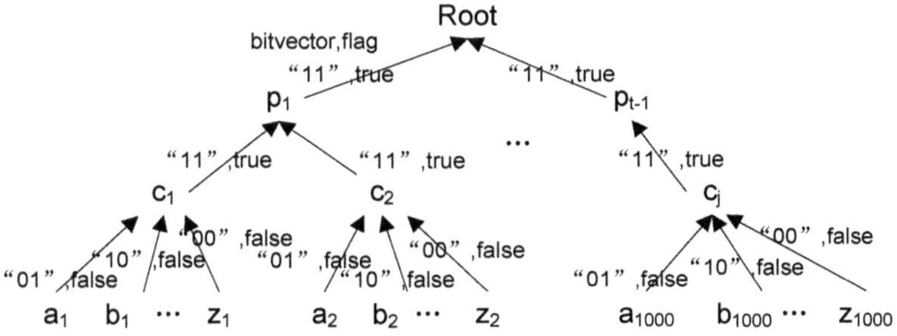

Fig. 2. An XML Tree. The label of arrows are transmitted information, *bitvector* and *flag*. *Bitvector* ="*01*" means the first keyword appears. *Flag* ="*false*" means there aren't SLCAs in the current subtree.

This paper presents an approach to filter XML data using distributed SLCA-based keyword search. It not only finds documents which contain users' keywords, but also locates meaningful contents. The application scenario is abstracted in Fig. 1. Main contributions of our work are described briefly as follows:

- The paper introduces SLCA-based keyword search into XML filtering application.
- The paper computes SLCAs in distributed environment. A series of algorithms for distributed SLCA computation are also given.
- We experimentally demonstrate the performance of our solution for distributed SLCA computation.

The rest of paper is organized as follows. Section 2 gives problem definition of our approach. Then is the system implementation in Section 3. The detail algorithms are shown in subsection 3.2, which include partition strategy, SLCA computation

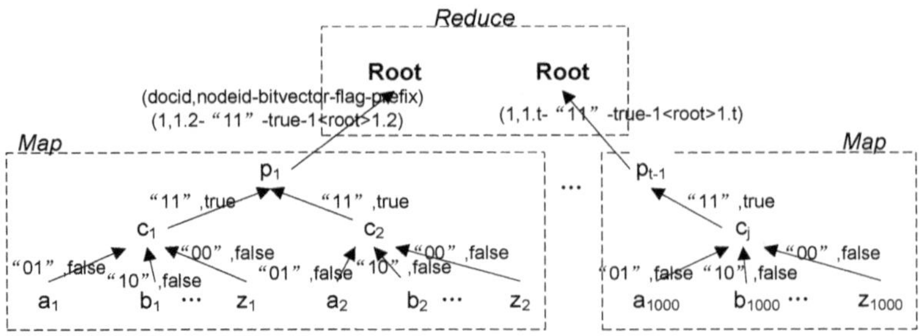

Fig. 3. Separated XML Tree. Data in one dotted box means one processing unit of *Map* or *Reduce* task. "*(docid,nodeid-bitvector-flag-prefix)*" is the information from *Map* task to *Reduce* task. "*(1,1.2-11-true-1<root>1.2)*" is an instance of it.

on local data and combination algorithm. Following are experiments in Section 4, which show features and performance of our algorithms. Section 5 is related work. Conclusions and future work are given in Section 6.

2 Problem Definition

SLCAs for given keywords are nodes in an XML tree which satisfy two conditions: (1) all keywords appear in subtree rooted by the nodes, and (2) no descendant of the nodes satisfies condition (1). Previous approaches build centralized index for XML data and ids for different keywords need be joined to compute SLCAs. Intermediate results including improper SLCAs will be involved. However, building centralized index for large scales of XML data is time consuming and it's impossible to build centralized index for continuous XML data. Therefore, XML filtering method without index is needed in information dissemination.

Our goal is to compute SLCAs in distributed environment. All documents in dataset are distributed to different net nodes. SLCA computation algorithm runs on each net node to obtain SLCAs of local data. The information from each net node is combined finally to compute rest SLCAs.

The best case is that one document can be placed wholly on one net node. We run SLCA computation algorithm on each net node. Thus the results are obtained directly.

However, one document needs be split and be placed on different net nodes when we take size and parallelism into account. We give the placement strategy of data to improve parallelism and to keep lower communication cost. The whole work includes three steps.

- Step1: Documents in dataset are distributed to net nodes. Fig.2 shows an document tree wholly placed on one net node. If one document needs be split, we detach child subtrees from the whole document tree, as is shown in Fig. 3. Upper common ancestor nodes (node *root* in Fig.3) are duplicated in each subtrees. Each subtree is treated as an XML record and is distributed to different net nodes. Fig. 3 gives a partition of the XML tree in Fig. 2.

- Step2: Each *Map* task processes local data to obtain SLCAs (may be empty). If a document is split, each part transmits some information (*docid, nodeid-bitvector-flag-prefix*) to *Reduce* task.
- Step3: Finally, non-processed nodes (duplicated ancestors) of separated documents in *Map* task will be processed in *Reduce* task to get the rest of SLCAs.

3 Distributed SLCA-Based XML Keyword Search

In the section, we give the system architecture and system implementation.

3.1 System Architecture

Fig. 4 shows the architecture to compute SLCAs in distributed environment. We use Hadoop [2] as the main platform and adopt MapReduce [5] program paradigm to carry out the distributed system.

Processing logic of *Map* and *Reduce* are shown in two functions:

Map: $(K1, V1) \rightarrow list(K2, V2)$

Reduce: $(K2, list(V2)) \rightarrow (K2, V3)$

Map function processes a pair of (K1,V1) to get a list of intermediate key-value pairs (K2,V2). *Reduce* function merges intermediate results sharing same K2 and output result V3.

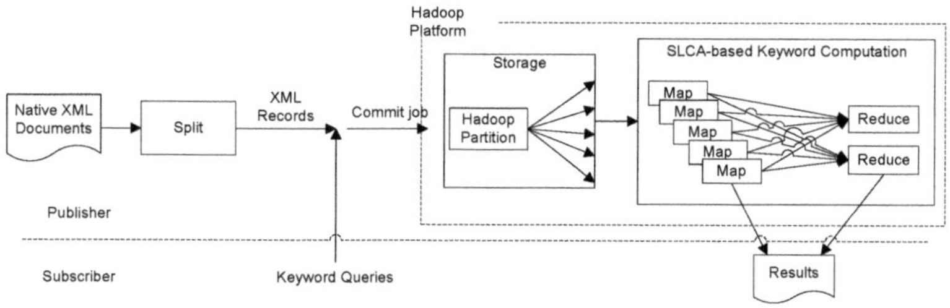

Fig. 4. System Architecture

There are three key steps in the system.

— The XML dataset is pre-split before committed to Hadoop. Each big native XML document will be split into small XML records in function *Split*(shown in Fig. 4) and original document id will be saved in each record. Small native document is treated as an XML record. Then all XML records, keyword searches are committed to Hadoop platform. Hadoop divides the XML records to several processing nodes transparently.

— *Map* tasks process local XML records and obtain SLCAs. Some information of each part of split documents need be transmitted to Reduce task.

— *Reduce* tasks use information from *Map* tasks to compute rest SLCAs of split documents.

3.2 Algorithms

According to the description in subsection 3.1, detail algorithms are presented in the following subsections.

Document Partition. If an XML document is bigger than a certain threshold, which equals to default max input data size(64M) in Hadoop, the document needs be split. Splitting XML document in our system is shown in algorithm 1. If the size of subtree rooted by node n isn't bigger than the threshold, algorithm 1 translates the content of subTree(n) to a line and add it into *recordSet* in lines 2-5(*prefix* is added also.). Otherwise, it detaches each child from node n as an independent XML segment and recursively call algorithm 1 on them(lines 6-15). We use Pres label [11] to labeling XML elements.

Algorithm 1. Split()

```
    Input: n is the root node of current XML tree; prefix is the information of
           upper nodes; recordSet stores split XML records.
    Output: recordSet stores split XML records.
 1  parent_id = get last Pres_id from prefix;
 2  if size of subTree(n) ≤ threshold then
 3      translate content of subTree(n) to a line;
 4      recordSet.addALine(prefix + sep_char1 + subTree(n)); /* here, "+" is
        string concatenation operation.*/
 5  end
 6  else
 7      n_content = all contents of node n;
 8      prefix = prefix + sep_char2 + n_content;
 9      List eleList = n.elements();
10      for each node c_node in eleList do
11          childPres_id = construct current child's Pres_id from parent_id;
12          prefix = prefix + sep_char2 + childPres_id;
13          Split(c_node, prefix, recordSet);   /*recursive call*/
14      end
15  end
16  return recordSet;
```

The efficiency of algorithm 1 is $O(n)$, in which n is the number of words in XML tree. If the efficiency of XML Parsing is $O(n)$, the whole efficiency is $O(n)$.

After splitting raw XML data, XML records set and keyword queries are committed to Hadoop. The XML records will be distributed to several net nodes transparently. The detailed algorithm on each net node to process local data is described in the following subsections.

SLCA computation by Map. In the subsection, how to obtain SLCAs from current input data are described in algorithm 2.

Algorithm 2. myMap()

Input: *key* is the position of current XML segment in whole file; *value* is content of current segment.
Output: *collector* store pairs of (*docid*, *current_id- bitvector - flag - prefix*).

1 *prefix* = split *value* by *sep_char1* and return the first part;
2 split *prefix* by *sep_char2*;
3 *docid* = the first part of *prefix*;
4 *current_id* = the last part of *prefix*;
5 *root* = get root by way of using *SAXReader* to parse the second part of *value*;
6 (*bitvector*, *flag*) = GetSLCA(*root*);
7 *collector*.add(*docid*, *current_id- bitvector - flag - prefix*);/*here, "-" is another char to separate strings. */
8 return *collector*;

Algorithm 3. Reduce()

Input: *key* is docid of current document; *values* includes the information from different net machines.
Output: *restSLCAs* stores the rest of SLCAs of current document.

restSLCAs = ∅;
levelList = ∅;
while *values.hasNext()* **do**
    curnodeinfo = *values*.Next();
    level = *curnodeinfo*.getLevel();
    if *level exists in levelList* **then**
        insert *curnodeinfo* into *levelList* ascending by *nodeid* in *curnodeinfo*;
    end
    else
        insert new *sublist* to *levelList* descending by level number;
        add *curnodeinfo* to the the new *sublist*;
    end
end
restSLCAs = GetRestSLCA(*levelList*);
return *restSLCAs*;

The input *value* is the content of the current XML segment. Lines 1-5 get document id *docid*, current XML segment id *current_id* and root node *root*. Then line6 calls function GetSLCA() to compute SLCA and gets returns (*bitvector*, *flag*). The current segment will transmit key-value pairs to the next step in line7. *Docid* in line7 is the output key. Records sharing same *docid* will be hashed into the same *Reduce* task.

According to semantics of SLCA, whether a node is SLCA or not depends on whether there exist SLCAs in all its descendants. GetSLCA() traverses XML tree bottom-up. Each tree node incorporates information from its children into itself. It uses the information to test whether itself is SLCA node or not. Then it returns the information to its parent. As is shown in Fig.2. Transmitted information is "*bitvector,flag*" and "'*11*',*true*" is an instance of it. "*Bitvector*" shows

Algorithm 4. GetRestSLCA()

Input: ArrayList *levelList* contains sorted information from *Map* task.
Output: restSLCAs stores the rest of SLCA of current document.

```
restSLCAs = ∅;
for each level >1 in levelList do
    levelNum = current level number;
    curList = current nodeinfo list in levelList;
    archor = null;
    d_bitvector = 0;
    d_flag = false;
    for each nodeinfo in curList do
        if archor is null then
            archor = current nodeinfo;
            d_bitvector = archor.getBitvector();
            d_falg = archor.getFlag();
        end
        else
            if archor and current nodeinfo(cur_nodeinfo for short) has same
            parent then
                d_bitvector = combine their bitvector by bit OR operator;
                d_flag = combine their flag by Boolean OR operator;
            end
            else
                SLCAid = processParent(archor, d_bitvector, d_flag, levelList);
                if SLCAid != null then
                    restSLCAs.add(SLCAid);
                end
                archor = cur_nodeinfo;
                d_bitvector = archor.getBitvector();
                d_flag = archor.getFlag();
            end
        end
    end
    if archor != null then
        SLCAid = processParent(archor, d_bitvector, d_flag, levelList);
        if SLCAid != null then
            restSLCAs.add(SLCAid);
        end
    end
end
return restSLCAs;
```

which keywords appear in the current subtree. "*Flag*" means whether there exist SLCAs in the current subtree.

Let n be the number of words in an XML tree. Let n_1 be the number of words in all subtrees and n_2 the number of words in duplicated ancestors. The sum of n_1 and n_2 is n. The efficiency of algorithm 2 is $O(n_1)$.

Combining Distributed Information by Reduce. Algorithm 3 sorts information from each net node descending by node level number ascending by node id. Then they are processed to compute rest SLCAs bottom-up in algorithm 4.

In the algorithm 3, information sharing same document id is in *values* and is denoted as *curnodeinfo*. *Curnodeinfos* are sorted and are inserted into an array *levelList*(lines 3-13). Line14 calls algorithm 4 to process information in *levelList*. Rest SLCAs in *restSLCAs* are returned in line15.

Algorithm 4 computes SLCAs on the sorted array *levelList*. It gives the priority to lower level nodes. Here, child node has lower level than the parent. In current level, *nodeinfos* sharing common parent will be considered as a group. And *archor* represents the first one in the group(line10 and line24). All their *bitvectors* and *flags* will be combined together (lines 15-18). Their parent's information is constructed and then is inserted into *levelList* (in line20). If the parent is SLCA, id of it will be added to *restSLCAs*(lines 20-23). Lines 24-26 prepare for the next group. All groups in current level are processed in lines 8-29 except the last group. Rest work of the last group, dealing with *parent* of it, will be done in lines 30-35. After all the groups in current level are processed, the upper level will be processed until all *nodeinfos* are processed. (In all algorithms, prefix "*p*" of variables means "parent". Prefix "*d*" means "descendants". For example, "*d_bicvector*" means bitvector of descendants.)

Algorithm 5. ProcessParent()

```
Input: archor gives node information; d_bitvector and d_flag give information
       of descendants; levelList stores rest nodes information sorted by level
       and nodeid.
Output: nodeid equals id of parent node if it is SLCA else null.
nodeid = null;
get p_id,p_content and p_prefix from archor;
if d_flag then
    insert (p_id - d_bitvector - d_flag - p_prefix) into levelList according to
    certain orders;
end
else
    (p_bitvector, p_flag) = keyInNode(p_content);
    p_bitvector = p_bitvector | d_bitvector;
    if p_bitvector shows all keywords occur then
        p_flag = true;
    end
    insert (p_id - p_bitvector - p_flag - p_prefix) into levelList according to
    certain orders;
    if p_flag and !d_flag then
        nodeid = p_id;
    end
end
return nodeid;
```

Algorithm 5 is called by algorithm 4 in line20 and line31. It constructs some information of *archor*'s *parent* in line2. If there exist SLCAs in descendants, the parent transmit *d_flag* and *d_bicvector* to next step directly(lines 3-5). Otherwise, lines 7-12 compute *p_bicvector* and *p_flag* and insert information of the *parent* into *levelList*. If the *parent* is SLCA, id of it will be saved in *nodeid*(lines 13-15). Finally, *nodeid* will be returned in line17.

KeyInNode(p) computes bitvector and flag of a node p. Bitvector and flag of p are set to be "0" and "false" at the beginning. If one keyword appears in p's label, corresponding bit of p's bitvector will become "1". If all keywords appear in it, p's flag becomes "true".

Let t be the number of partitioned document parts. n_2 has the same meaning with n_2 in subsection 3.2. The efficiency of algorithm 5 and KeyInNode() are *O(1)*. The efficiency of algorithm 4 is $O(n_2)$ because algorithm 4 processes all words in duplicated nodes(the number equals n_2 according to assumption). The efficiency of algorithm 3 is the sum of efficiencies of insert-sort and algorithm 4. Then it is $O(t^2 + n_2)$. So the efficient of whole system is $O(n + t^2)$.

4 Experiments

In this section, we evaluate our distributed SLCA computation algorithms. There are three groups of experiments. The first group is to show the impact of keyword number and keyword frequency to distributed SLCA computing algorithms, which is traditional experiment for SLCA computation in centralized environment. The second group is to verify the scalability for query number in our system, which is important in XML data dissemination. The last group is about the scalability for data size, which is needed with the increasing of XML information.

Experiments run in Linux, whose version is ubuntu0.8.4. Version of computing platform Hadoop is 0.19.3. The size of system(# nodes in system) varies from 1 to 6. All the machines are dual-core desktop with 1GB memory. We test our approach on real dataset DBLP [1]. Size of datasets in experiments are 135MB, 208MB, 515MB, 823MB and 1.06GB(The biggest size of DBLP dataset is about 623M. We copy some parts of it to get the bigger dataset.). In information dissemination scenario, most of data streams are small XML segments. So most of them needn't be split and needn't *Reduce*. About one thousandth of XML records will be combined in *Reduce* function in the second and the third experiments. However, in the first experiment all XML records will be combined in *Reduce* step. The queries are denoted as *kN-L-H*, which is the same as [10]. *kN* is the number of keywords in the queries. *L* and *H* are frequencies of the lowest frequency and the highest frequency of keywords separately. In each query, only one keyword has the frequency *L* and other keywords have the frequency *H*. We randomly generate a group of queries and execute them 3 times. Query number of each group varies from 10 to 3000. The average time of each query is recorded.

4.1 Impact of Query Features

The first experiment shows the influence of query features, which include keyword number and keyword frequency. The size of dataset is 135M in Fig. 5(a)and 208M in Fig. 5(b). Keyword frequency pairs, *L-H*, have several options. Keyword number varies from 2 to 4. We record the time from committing job to end of whole work. It includes time of XML parsing, encoding and query processing.

In Fig. 5(a) and (b), query time increases slightly with the increasing of keyword number. In Fig. 5(c),(d),(e) and (f), the trend is unobvious. According to the design of algorithms, the whole XML tree will be scanned once no matter what the keyword number is. Along with the increasing of keyword number, a little check work is added. So it slightly affects the whole processing time. (The processing time of kN=3 is bigger than it of kN=4 — Fig. 5(c) and Fig. 5(d) occur experimental fluctuation when *L-H* are *100-1000* and *1000-10000.*)

Fixing the keyword number, all sub figures in Fig. 5 show our approach isn't sensitive to keyword frequency. If one keyword appears in one XML node, we just update a bit of *bitvector*. So keyword frequency won't impact the algorithms significantly. We also find performance of 6-nodes has no much improvement than 3-nodes. The reason is that small dataset can't make full use of system capacity.

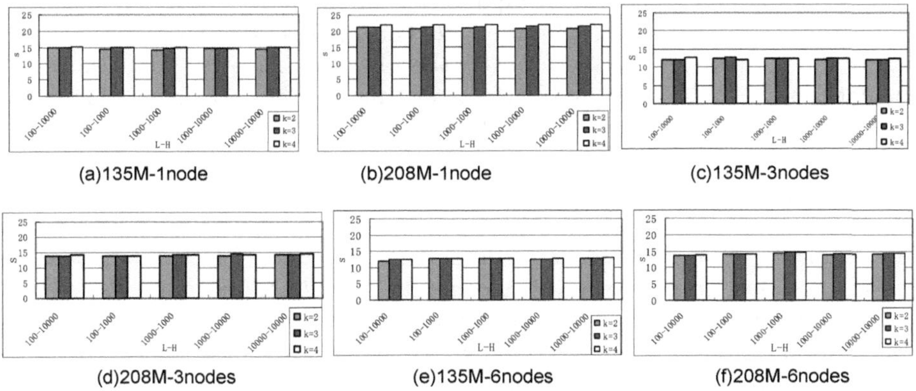

Fig. 5. Impact of Query Features. k is keyword number, which varies from 2 to 4. *L-H* is lowest frequency and highest frequency of keywords. Query number of a group is 10.

4.2 Scalability for Query Number

The second experiment shows the scalability for query number. Let query class be 2-100-10000. System size is 6.

In Fig. 6, the query number varies from 100 to 3000. Whole running time of a group of queries increases linearly with the increasing of query number when data size is fixed. Fig. 6 shows average running time of each query. Fixing data size, the average time of each query descends slightly when the query number ascends. It shows that parsing XML data takes up much time in whole work when query number is small. With the increasing of query number, the whole time depends on query number mostly.

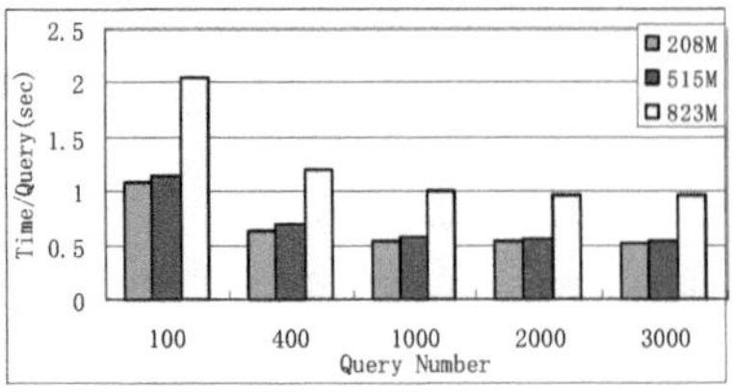

Fig. 6. Average query time varies with query No.

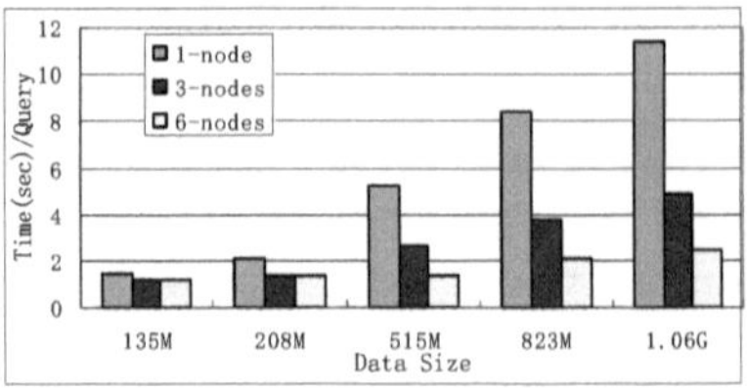

Fig. 7. Average query time varies with datasize

4.3 Scalability for Data Size

Fig. 7 shows the scalability of data size. The query number is 100. Fig. 7 gives average time of each query.

When the system size increases, the whole time of 100 queries and the average time of each query both change slightly. Especially when the system size is 6, processing times for the document size of 135M, 208M and 515M are the same almost. *Hadoop* running report shows the capacity of task is 12 when system size is 6. Map task number of 135M, 208M, 515M, 823M and 1.06G are 3, 4, 9, 14 and 20 separately(The default input size is no more than 64M. The map task number is related with it.). All data splits can be processed parallel when data size is 135M, 208M or 515M. However, the task number of 832M is 14, not all the data splits can be processed at the same time. So the cost time still increases slightly when data size is 823M and 1.06G.

5 Related Work

SLCA-based keyword search is an important approach for XML information extracting. Most of previous SLCA computing [10,11,12] obtain a list of node id for each keyword firstly. Then the id lists are joined to get potential SLCAs. The improper results are deleted finally. [7] gives a stack-based algorithm to get information from a mix of XML and HTML documents and rank the results.

There are also some work to study the semantics for XML keyword search. Meaningful LCA in [8] is a similar semantics to SLCA semantics. [8] presents a novel technology, schema-free XQuery, which enables users to retrieve XML data without knowledge of document schema. [13] gives another XML keyword search semantics, ELCA, which includes more useful LCA nodes.

XML data placement is a key factor in distributed XML processing. [3,9] give different placement strategy to improve parallelism. All of them are designed especially for path queries.

6 Conclusions and Future Work

In this paper, we present parallel algorithms for distributed SLCA computing. XML documents are split into several parts to be processed parallel. In our algorithms, SLCAs are computed bottom-up in one scan of document tree. Each node just communicates with its parent. No intermediate results and no auxiliary complicated data structure. Each net node processes local data parallel and transmits just a little information to the next step. We use Hadoop as the platform and implement distributed SLCA algorithms in MapReduce paradigm. A series of experiments are conducted to verify the efficiency of our approach.

Acknowledgments. This work is supported by NSFC grants (No. 60773075 and No. 60925008), National Hi-Tech 863 program under grant 2009AA01Z149, 973 program (No. 2010CB328106), Shanghai Education Project (No. 10ZZ33) and Shanghai Leading Academic Discipline Project (No. B412).

References

1. DBLP XML records, `http://dblp.uni-trier.de/xml/`
2. Apache. Hadoop, `http://hadoop.apache.org/core/`
3. Bremer, J.-M., Gertz, M.: On distributing XML repositories. In: WebDB, pp. 73–78 (2003)
4. Bruno, N., Gravano, L., Koudas, N., Srivastava, D.: Navigation- vs. index-based XML multi-query processing. In: ICDE, pp. 139–150 (2003)
5. Dean, J., Ghemawat, S.: Mapreduce: Simplified data processing on large clusters. In: OSDI, pp. 137–150 (2004)
6. Gong, X., Yan, Y., Qian, W., Zhou, A.: Bloom filter-based XML packets filtering for millions of path queries. In: ICDE, pp. 890–901 (2005)
7. Guo, L., Shao, F., Botev, C., Shanmugasundaram, J.: Xrank: Ranked keyword search over XML documents. In: SIGMOD Conference, pp. 16–27 (2003)
8. Li, Y., Yu, C., Jagadish, H.V.: Schema-free xquery. In: VLDB, pp. 72–83 (2004)
9. Machdi, I., Amagasa, T., Kitagawa, H.: Gmx: an xml data partitioning scheme for holistic twig joins. In: iiWAS, pp. 137–146 (2008)
10. Sun, C., Chan, C.Y., Goenka, A.K.: Multiway slca-based keyword search in XML data. In: WWW, pp. 1043–1052 (2007)
11. Wang, W., Wang, X., Zhou, A.: Hash-search: An efficient slca-based keyword search algorithm on XML documents. In: DASFAA, pp. 496–510 (2009)
12. Xu, Y., Papakonstantinou, Y.: Efficient keyword search for smallest lcas in XML databases. In: SIGMOD Conference, pp. 537–538 (2005)
13. Xu, Y., Papakonstantinou, Y.: Efficient lca based keyword search in XML data. In: CIKM, pp. 1007–1010 (2007)
14. Yui, M., Miyazaki, J., Uemura, S., Kato, H.: Xbird/d: distributed and parallel xquery processing using remote proxy. In: SAC, pp. 1003–1007 (2008)

FVC: A Feature-Vector-Based Classification for XML Dissemination

Xiaoling Wang[1], Ester Martin[2], Weining Qian[1], and Aoying Zhou[1]

[1] Shanghai Key Laboratory of Trustworthy Computing, Software Engineering Institute, East China Normal University, Shanghai 200062, China
{xlwang,wnqian,ayzhou}@sei.ecnu.edu.cn
[2] School of Computing Science, Simon Fraser University, Burnaby, BC, Canada
ester@cs.sfu.ca

Abstract. With the adoption of XML in a wide range of applications, efficient XML classification has become an important research topic. In current studies, users' interests are expressed by XPath or XQuery queries. However, such a query is hard to formulate, because it requires a good knowledge of the structure and contents of the documents that will arrive and some knowledge of XQuery which few consumers will have. The query may even be impossible to formulate in cases where the distinction of relevant and irrelevant documents requires the consideration of a large number of features. Traditional classification method can't work well for XML dissemination, because the number of training example is often small. Therefore, this paper introduces a data mining approach to XML dissemination that uses a given document collection of the user to automatically learn a classifier modelling his/her information needs. We present a novel XML classifier taking into account the structure as well as the content of XML documents. Our experimental evaluation on several real XML document sets demonstrates the accuracy and efficiency of the proposed XML classification approach.

1 Introduction

Nowadays, Extensible Mark-up Language (XML) becomes pervasive in more and more applications, such as Digital Library, XML subscribe/publish system, and other XML repositories. With the adoption of XML in a wide range of applications, XML classification has become an important application. There are many "news streams" that can be modeled as XML documents arriving at some server that is responsible for managing these documents and disseminating them to a pool of clients. New CS research papers (DBLP), new webpages (GoogleAlert), new movies all are examples of news streams and often use XML as data exchange format. Clients such as computer scientists, businessmen and consumers want to be alerted of relevant news documents without being overwhelmed by "spam" documents. For this purpose, clients subscribe at the server with some specification of their information needs by some kind of keyword-based XML query. Former methods have been proposed to optimize XML dissemination,

M. Yoshikawa et al. (Eds.): DASFAA 2010, LNCS 6193, pp. 398–409, 2010.

improving the efficiency of the simultaneous execution of very large numbers of XML queries by sharing the processing costs for common subqueries [1,2].

Current approaches [3,4] to XML dissemination require the clients to specify their interests as XPath or XQuery queries. Unfortunately, XML queries are hard to formulate for consumers, because they require a good knowledge of the structure and contents of the documents of the news stream. In the case of XML documents, it would also require familiarity with the XQuery language which few clients will have.

On the other hand, in many scenarios a client would have an initial collection of relevant documents obtained from other sources, e.g. a collection of related research papers, a collection of favorite bookmarks or a collection of owned movies. These document collections do implicitly specify the information needs of the client which motivates a data mining approach to XML dissemination based on classifiers that are learned automatically from the given collections of relevant documents:

1. A training collection of "positive" (relevant) XML documents on each client describes the client's (consumer's) interest. Using a sample of other documents as "negative" training documents, a two-class classifier (relevant / irrelevant) is trained on the client.
2. A client subscribes to the server by sending his classifier to the server.
3. The server applies the classifiers of all clients that have subscribed to the incoming XML documents and forwards a document to all clients whose classifier predicts the document as relevant.
4. The client (consumer) receives a potentially relevant XML document, checks the document for actual relevance and records relevance feedback (is / is not relevant).
5. The client maintains and updates the classifier. If too many documents received from the server are judged as irrelevant by the consumer, according to the client relevance feedback, the client re-trains the classifier on the current document collection and sends a new classifier to the server.

The architecture of a data mining-based XML dissemination system is shown in Figure. 1.

Classification methods for XML documents have recently received some attention in the database and data mining communities [6,9]. The information dissemination scenario, however, creates unique challenges for XML classification that have not yet been addressed in the literature. Compared to the classical scenario of text and XML classification, training datasets are small, i.e. contain only a few hundreds or dozens of documents. This makes classifier construction much more difficult. For example, SVM approach needs more training examples in order to achieve high precision.

To deal with small training sets, we introduce a novel classification method that represents both the structure and the contents of XML documents in a natural way. Our method integrates the XRules approach [9], that takes into account the XML structure only, and the Bag of Words text classification approach [6], that exploits only the contents of XML documents.

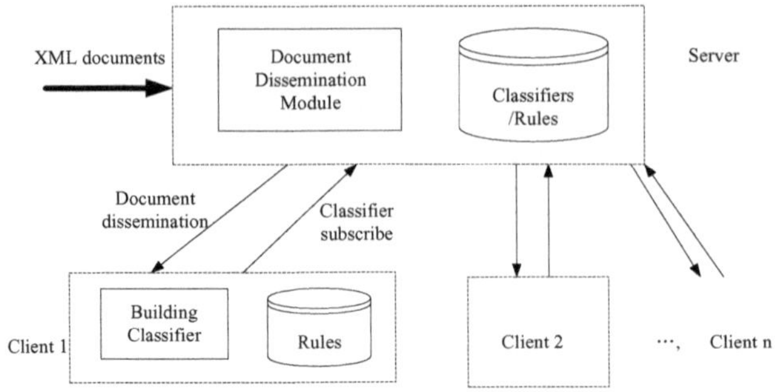

Fig. 1. System Architecture

The main contributions of this paper are as follows:

- We introduce a data mining approach to XML dissemination and a corresponding client-server system architecture is given.
- We present novel XML classification methods taking into account both the structure and contents of XML documents.
- Our experimental evaluation on real XML document sets demonstrates the precision of the proposed methods.

The rest of this paper is organized as follows. Related work is discussed in Section 2. Section 3 introduces the novel XML classification methods for XML documents. The results of our experimental evaluation are presented in Section 4, followed by the conclusion in Section 5.

2 Related Work

There are two kinds of approaches for XML document classification.

Schema-Driven Approach. Mining frequent sub-trees is one main problem in XML classification. Former work [8,7,9] are rules-based approach for frequent sub-tree mining. These methods focus on embedded and ordered trees, and it is based on the property of frequent patterns: a super-pattern is less frequent or as frequent as a sub-pattern. There are two steps of this algorithm: 1) enumerate candidate sub-trees of size k and 2) count the frequency of these sub-trees. The sub-tree of size k +1 is generated from the sub-trees of size k that have frequency larger than the threshold. XRules [9] extend TreeMiner to find all frequent trees, and it is cost-sensitive and uses Bayesian rule based class decision making.

Data-Driven Approach. Another kind of approaches [6,5] for XML classification is based on text classification. They extract two kinds of features from XML data: the first part is content parts - term, the second part is specific structure part - twig, such as leftchild/parent/rightchild. The shortcomings of these approaches are: 1) The separation of structure mining and content mining may result in incorrect rules. 2) SVM [6] for XML text classification is the most used method, however, an SVM classifier needs more training data, in the scenario of XML dissemination, each client has no more examples to train the classifier.

3 XML Classification Methods

As discussed in Section 1, the scenario of information dissemination creates unique challenges for XML classification. In particular, clients typically have only a small number of training documents, but traditional text/XML classification methods require larger training sets to achieve high classification accuracy. Addressing the special characteristics of XML dissemination, this section firstly give the preliminaries of this problem, and then presents our classification methods that take into account both the structure and content of XML documents in an integrated fashion.

3.1 Preliminaries

We first introduce XML document trees and then revisit the XRules method [9], which is the state-of-the-art rule-based XML classifier.

An XML document can be modelled as a labelled, ordered and rooted tree $T = (V, E, root(T))$, where V is a set of nodes, $E \subset V \times V$ is a set of edges, and $root(T) \in V$ is the root node of T. A node $n_i \in V$ represents an element, an attribute, or a value.

All of the classification methods introduced in the following sections work on XML document trees.

Obtaining Training Examples. Firstly, we discuss how to obtain positive training examples and negative training examples at the client side. It is reasonable to assume that a client would have an initial collection of relevant documents obtained from other sources, e.g. a collection of related research papers or email files. This collection is regarded as the positive training examples.

There are two approaches to generate negative training examples. Initially, if we have no irrelevant document in our local storage, we can draw some samples from the entire population of documents, such as DBLP or IEEE digital library. Another approach to obtain negative training examples is by feedback information. Since any XML classifier produces some false positives, some of the documents that the server sends to a client will actually be judged as irrelevant by the user. Such documents can be collected and used as user-specific negative examples.

Note that the positive training examples are more important than the negative examples, because clients are only interested in accurately predicting positive documents. This unique property will be exploited in our algorithms to enhance the precision of classifiers.

XRules Revisited. Secondly, we revisit the XRules [9] method, which is a representative method designed for XML document classification. It employs the concept of structural rules and frequent sub-tree mining. Each rule, i.e., sub-tree, is of the form $T \rightarrow c, (\pi, \delta)$, in which T is a tree structure, c is the class label, π is the support of the rule, and δ is the strength of the rule.

To train the classifier, XRules first mines all frequent structural rules with respect to a specific class c whose support and strength is larger than the predefined parameters π_c^{min} and δ_c^{min}. Then all such rules are ordered according to a precedence relation. Thus the classifier is obtained. In the testing phase, two steps are performed, rule retrieval and class prediction. The former step retrieves all rules that match an example, while the latter one determines the class label by combining all evidence provided by those matched rules.

We argue that XRules is not sufficient for XML document classification. The main reason is that XRules does not consider the content of XML documents. Only structural information is used to generate the rules. Therefore, XRules is useless for XML documents that conform to a given schema. In the following sections, two methods considering both structure and content are introduced for XML classification.

3.2 XRules+: Extending XRules to Handle Content

The first method is a naive approach to extend XRules [9] by adding content leaf nodes into XML structure trees without additional preprocessing. We call this method XRules+.

XRules+ first transforms an XML document into a tree by using the following steps.

1. For each element, create a vertex, whose label is the element name;
2. For elements v_1 and v_2 with parent-child relationships, create a directed edge $e(v_1, v_1)$;
3. For each attribute, create a vertex, whose label is the attribute name;
4. For each attribute value, create a vertex, whose label is the value;
5. For each attribute a and its value a_v pair, create a directed edge $e(a, a_v)$;
6. For each attribute a and the element v containing it, create a directed edge $e(v, a)$;
7. For each term t, create a vertex, whose label is the term;
8. For term t and the element v containing it, create a directed edge $e(v, t)$;
9. For element v and the element v' that v refers to, create a directed edge $e(v, v')$.

If the content of one element $E1$ includes more than one term, each term can be treated as a node, and then element $E1$ has more than one child node. Thus, the inner nodes are structure nodes and the leaf nodes are content nodes. The XRules approach can be applied to mining frequent sub-trees from extended XML trees. Figure 2 depicts an example, where the circles denote the structure nodes and the rectangles denote the content nodes.

Thus, an XML document is transformed to a directed tree automatically. Then, XRules is applied to train the classifier. And the testing phase remains unchanged.

XRules+ is equivalent to considering all possible combinations of a term and a structural pattern. However, for most XML documents, the number of terms

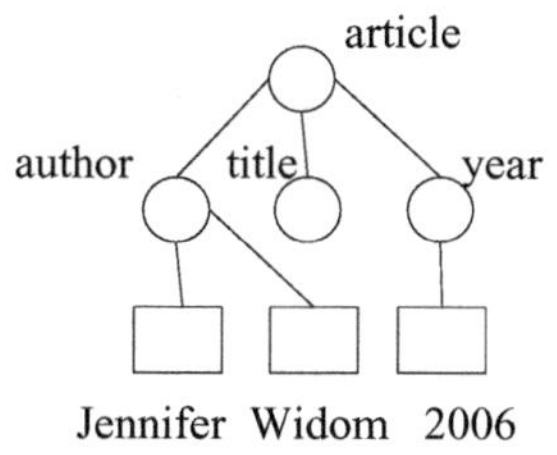

Fig. 2. Extending XML Tree by XRules+

in the content is much larger than the number of structure nodes (elements), so that there are many nodes in extended XML trees. Therefore, too many patterns may be generated, and only few of them will be frequent. Suppose the number of terms in the content of an element Ei is n, which will correspond to n leaf nodes of Ei. Considering ordered trees, there are $C_n^0 + C_n^1 + ... + C_n^n = 2^n$ possible embedded subtrees rooted at Ei. With increasing numbers of nodes in XML trees, the number of candidate sub-trees becomes larger, and the efficiency of XRules+ will suffer significantly.

We do some experiments to verify this argument. The training examples are articles from dblp xml files, we extract the title and author information for each article. The number of training examples are 800 per class and the number of testing examples are 200 per class. The two-class problem are tested using XRules method and XRules+ method. The result are shown in Table 1. It verifies that if one XML document contains value nodes, the candidate subtrees will increase quickly, so the performance will be affected.

Table 1. Num. of Rules in XRules and XRules+

MINSUPPORT	**#rules**		**Execution Time(s)**	
	XRule	XRule+	XRule	XRule+
10%	19	53	0.5	0.8
5%	23	172	2	3
1%	41	3381	48	84

We conduct another group of experiments to test the performance of XRules and XRules+. After changing the training example where the number of nodes in XML tree exceeds 30, the depth of each XML tree is about 8 and the training data set contains 10 documents, XRules can't find frequent sub-trees in 5 hours. So, XRules and XRules+ is limited for many large XML documents.

3.3 FVC: A Feature-Vector-Based Classification Approach

Aiming at the shortcomings of XRules+, in this subsection, we present FVC, an extension of XRules using feature vectors to handle the content of XML documents. Instead of creating one leaf node for every term in an element as in XRules+, we determine the set of all relevant terms in the elements and represent the whole content of a specific element by one corresponding term frequency vector, also called feature vector.

An FVC rule has the form

$(T, V) \rightarrow c, (\pi, \delta)$,

in which T is a structural pattern, V is a feature vector, c is a class label, π is the support of the structural rule T, and δ is the strength of the rule T.

Note that a feature vector in general represents the content of more than one element, namely the content of all leaf nodes of the structural pattern of the FVC rule.

A document is *matched* by the body of the rule, if the following two conditions are satisfied.

1. The document contains the structural pattern T.
2. The distance from V to the feature vector of the matching pattern T is calculated. The Nearest-Neighbour method is used to assign the class label to the tested document.

When a training example matches T, and the class label is the same as c, it is *covered* by the rule. The number of training examples that are covered by a rule is the support of the rule. Similarly, the strength of the rule can be determined.

The mining of FVC rules proceeds in the following steps:

1. **Generation of structural patterns.** For each class, all frequent structural patterns within this class are generated, whose support and strength are above the predefined thresholds π and δ.
2. **Determination of feature vector dimensions.** For each combination of a training XML document and a frequent structural pattern, one feature vector representing the union of all leaf nodes of that structural pattern is constructed. All terms appearing in the corpus of XML documents are considered. Their term-frequencies and inverse-document-frequencies (TF*IDF) are calculated using the standard information-retrieval techniques. The terms with top ranked TF*IDF weights are selected as features[1]. Each preserved term is used as one dimension in the content (feature) vectors.
3. **FVC rule generation.** For each structural pattern, each instance it covers, i.e. the document fragment satisfying that structure, is extracted. Its content is then converted into a feature vector. Each vector, attached with its structural pattern, becomes an *FVC rule.*

The pseudo-code of FVC is presented in Algorithm 1 and Algorithm 2.

In the test (dissemination) phase, all FVC rules with matching structural patterns are retrieved. Among these rules, the feature vector that is nearest to the feature vector of the test document is determined. The class label of the corresponding FVC rule is used to predict the class of the test document.

[1] In our experiments, 3000 terms were used to generate the vectors.

Algorithm 1. `FVCTrain`

Input: training data set $Train$;
Output: rule set rs
Procedure FVCTrain($Train$)

Use XRules to get frequent patterns $PatternSet$ for input documents $Train$;
Get the first 3000 terms by TF*IDF from $Train$;
/* determine the vector dimensions of each pattern in $PatternSet$ */
for all pattern p in $PatternSet$ **do**
    Generate feature vectors v for each p;
    Add (p, v) into rs;
end for
return rs ;

Algorithm 2. `FVC`

Input: testing document d and rule set rs;
Output: Class label L
Procedure FVCTest(d)

for all pattern $p : (T, V) \rightarrow c, (\pi, \delta)$ in the rule set rs **do**
    Parse document d to obtain the pattern set ps where the pattern in d matches T in rs;
    Extract the content and obtain the feature vector v in d;
end for
Obtain the class label L by NN approach;
Assign L to document d;
return L;

4 Experiments

In this section, we report the results of our experimental evaluation using several real life XML datasets. All the experiments were conducted on a Pentium IV 3.2 G CPU platform with 512MB of RAM.

4.1 Experimental Setting

We define two classification tasks in order to evaluate methods presented in this paper.

Classification tasks
The real data comes from two commonly used XML benchmarks called DBLP [10] and SIGMODRecord [11]. Based on these two XML document collections, we design two classification tasks:

1. Task1: SIGMOD-KDD classifier. We extract some documents from DBLP and build dataset I. For a given document, even for an expert, it is not easy to judge whether it comes from the SIGMOD proceedings or the KDD

proceedings, because both conferences have papers focusing on data mining or data management. But there are some hints, for example, some data mining people often publish papers in SIGMOD proceedings. We want to verify that structural classification method can find such patterns.
2. Task2: DB-AI classifier. We extract documents from DBLP according to the ACM categories and build dataset II for task 2. Intuitively, DB and AI are two relatively distinct topics, so that text mining is a good method for classification. Integrated methods considering both structure and content are expected to increase the precision. We want to test this point by our experiments.

Data sets

We extract some XML documents from the DBLP and SIGMODRecord benchmarks, giving a detailed introduction of each dataset below.

- Dataset I comes from DBLP [10], which collects more than 200000 published papers in computer science area. The size of DBLP is about 226MB, the depth of the XML document tree is about 4 to 5. The root of this collection is "dblp", and the second level nodes include "inproceedings", "article" or others. We extract sub-trees of "article" and "inproceedings" from "dblp" tree. Thus, we obtained 533,077 small XML documents, and each document is one paper published in journal or conference proceedings. Based on these documents, we build three datasets I(1), I(2) and I(3).
  1. Dataset I(1): We extract 1000 articles from SIGMOD conference proceedings and 1000 articles from KDD conference proceedings to create a two-class problem: SIGMOD articles are considered as positive and KDD articles as negative examples. We remove other information from these articles/papers and used only the author and title elements in Dataset I(1). This information is common for any published paper in common digital libraries, such as citeseer or ACM/IEEE digital library.
  2. Dataset I(2): In order to test the performance of compared methods for small training document sets, we extracted a subset of 200 articles/papers from each class in Dataset I(1) and obtain Dataset I(2).
  3. Dataset I(3): In order to test the role of content for classification methods, for articles/papers in Dataset I(2), we added the "abstract" element into each document. Thus, we obtain Dataset I(3).
- Dataset II also comes from DBLP [10]. We extract articles for two ACM categories, "DB" and "AI". For these articles, we add abstract information into each XML document. By changing the number of positive and negative examples, we obtain Dataset II(1), II(2) and II(3). We want to test the influence of the negative examples for the classification methods.
  - Dataset II(1): The number of training documents is 160, including 80 "DB" articles and 80 "AI" articles. The testing documents are 20 "DB" articles and 20 "AI" articles. So, we use 160(80+,80-)/40(20+,20-) to denote Dataset II(1).
  - Dataset II(2): The number of training documents is 180, including 120 "DB" articles and 60 "AI" articles. The testing documents are 20 "DB"

articles and 20 "AI" articles. So, we use 180(120+,60-)/40(20+,20-) to denote Dataset II(2).

- Dataset II(3): The number of training documents is 150, including 120 "DB" articles and 30 "AI" articles. The testing documents are 20 "DB" articles and 20 "AI" articles. So, we use 150(120+,30-)/40(20+,20-) to denote Dataset II(3).

Classification Methods

Five methods for XML classification are compared.

1. XRules. This method [9] considers only the structure of XML documents. The XRules implementation was downloaded from the website of its author.
2. FVC. This method is presented in Section 3.3. It considers both structure and content in an integrated approach, extending structural patterns by feature vectors.
3. NN. This method is to implement traditional nearest neighbor based text classification method, which only considers the content (TF*IDF) of a document.

Experiments were conducted concerning the accuracy and the efficiency of the compared methods. The evaluation measures include precision, runtime and number of rules.

4.2 Performance of Classification Methods

In order to make the results more robust to random effects in the training and test documents, all experiments were repeated 5 times, and the results were averaged. In all experiments, we chose 3000 terms as features in FVC method.

Classification precision is the most important factor for XML document dissemination. Firstly, we study the precision of various methods. The precisions of XRules, FVC and NN method over Dataset I are shown in Figure 3 and over Dataset II are shown in Figure 4, always with respect to different minsupport values π.

Figure 3(a) shows that when the number of training examples is large, each method can obtain relatively good precision. However, with decreasing number of training examples, FVC performs better than XRules and NN as shown in Figure 3(b) and Figure 3(c).

From these experimental results, we draw the following conclusions.

- **Influence of the size of training dataset.** Dataset I(1) and I(2) are designed to show the influence on precision when changing the size of training examples. In dataset I(1), the number of training documents is 800 per class. We use 200 documents as testing documents for each class. In dataset I(2), we use 200 examples as training documents for each class.

  XRules performs good enough for dataset I(1) when the size of training documents is large enough. However, the small size of training documents reduces the precision of XRules method. This verifies that XRules is not

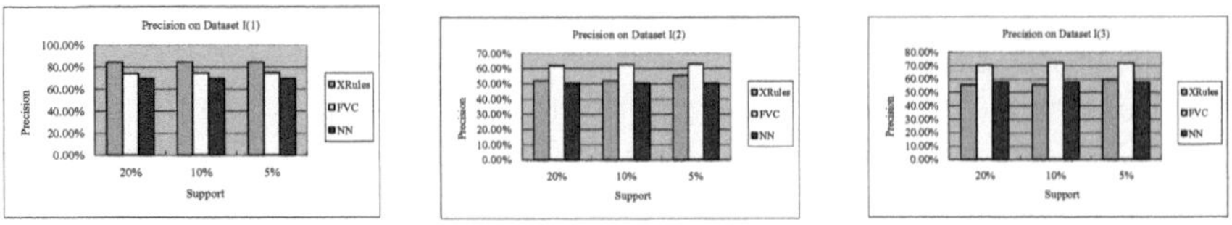

(a) I(1) (b) I(2) (c) I(3)

Fig. 3. Precision on Dataset I

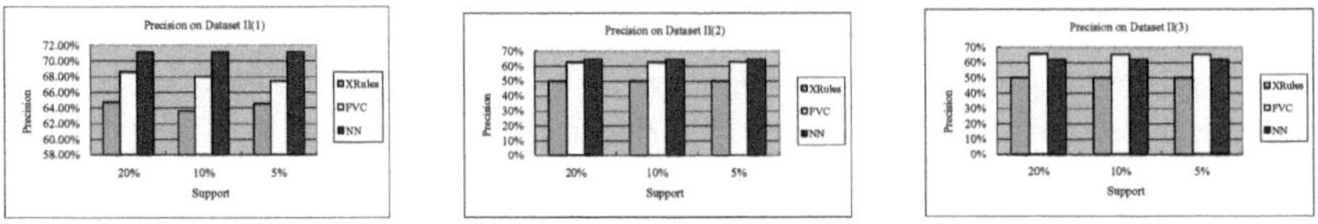

(a) II(1) (b) II(2) (c) II(3)

Fig. 4. Precision on Dataset II

feasible to get good rules for personal users, because there are not enough training documents available in this application context.

FVC performs better than XRules and NN methods, with decreasing number of training documents.

- **Influence of the amount of content.** Dataset I(2) and I(3) are to show the influence when adding more content into XML documents. I(3) adds some "abstract" information for each article into I(2). Figure 3(b) and Figure 3(c) shows that the precision of the NN method is improved because NN is pure text classification, and it does not consider structural information. Adding "abstract" content increases the precision of NN from 50% to 60%.

  We also find that, when comparing the results on I(2) and I(3), XRules does actually improve (from 52% to 56% / from 55.5% to 59%). However from analysis, the precision of XRules method shouldn't improve, because it only consider structure information and there is no more influence when adding content. The reason is that I(3) add another element tag "abstract" and related abstract content. So there is little difference from the structure part between I(2) and I(3). Thus, XRules can obtain more rules from I(3) than I(2). This is the major factor to affect the difference of precision for XRules on I(2) and I(3).

  For FVC, the precision is increasing because they consider both structure and content for the classification task.

- **Influence of the negative examples.** In order to test the influence of negative examples, we changed the number of negative examples in dataset II. II(1) has 80 positive-example/80 negative-examples, II(2) has 120 positive-example/60 negative-examples, and II(3) has 120 positive-example/30 negative-examples.

  Figure 4 shows, with the decreasing number of negative examples, the precision of almost all methods fall. Among these methods, XRules is the most sensitive and after the number of negative examples drops below 60, its precision is only 50%.

5 Conclusion

With the adoption of XML in a wide range of applications, efficient XML dissemination has become an important research topic. To deal with small training sets, we introduced a novel classification method, FVC, that represents both the structure and the contents of XML documents in a natural way. Our experimental evaluation on real XML document sets demonstrated the accuracy of the proposed XML classification approach. As the further work, we want to further exploiting how to optimize a large number of classifiers at the dissemination server. We also want to design the new strategy to improve the performance of proposed method.

Acknowledgments. We would like to thank Weiyan Wang for the discussion and system implementation. This work is supported by NSFC grants (No. 60773075 and No. 60925008), National Hi-Tech 863 program under grant (No. 2009AA01Z149), 973 program (No. 2010CB328106), Shanghai Education Project (No. 10ZZ33) and Shanghai Leading Academic Discipline Project (No. B412).

References

1. Diao, Y., Rizvi, S., Franklin., M.J.: Towards an Internet-Scale XML Dissemination Service. In: Proc. of the 30th VLDB, pp. 612–623 (2004)
2. Gong, X., Yan, Y., Qian, W., Zhou, A.: Bloom Filter-based XML Packets Filtering for Millions of Path Queries. In: ICDE 2005 (2005)
3. Li, G., Hou, S., Jacobsen, H.A.: Routing of XML and XPath queries in data dissemination networks. In: Proc. of ICDCS (2008)
4. Kwon, J., Rao, P., Moon, B., Lee, S.: Fast XML document filtering by sequencing twig patterns. ACM Transactions on Internet Technology 9(4) (2009)
5. Theobald, A., Weikum, G.: The index-based XXL search engine for querying XML data with relevance ranking. In: Jensen, C.S., Jeffery, K., Pokorný, J., Šaltenis, S., Bertino, E., Böhm, K., Jarke, M. (eds.) EDBT 2002. LNCS, vol. 2287, pp. 477–495. Springer, Heidelberg (2002)
6. Theobald, M., Schenkel, R., Weikum, G.: Exploiting structure, annotation, and ontological knowledge for automatic classification of XML data. In: WebDB, pp. 1–6 (2003)
7. Zaki, M.: Efficiently mining trees in a forest. In: 8th ACM SIGKDD Int'l Conference on Knowledge Discovery and Data Mining (2002)
8. Zaki, M.: Efficiently mining frequent embedded unordered trees. Fundamenta Informaticae 66(1-2), 33–52 (2005)
9. Zaki, M.J., Aggarwal, C.C.: XRules: an effective structural classifier for XML data. In: KDD, pp. 316–325 (2003)
10. Ley, M.: DBLP database web site (2000), `http://www.informatik.uni-trier.de/ley/db/index.html`
11. `http://www.acm.org/sigmod/record/xml`

An Object-Field Perspective Data Model for Moving Geographic Phenomena

K.-S. Kim and Y. Kiyoki

[1] Knowledge Creating Communication Research Center
National Institute of Information and Communications Technology
3-5 Hikaridai, Seika-cho, Soraku-gun, Kyoto 619-0289 Japan
ksookim@nict.go.jp
[2] Faculty of Environmental Information, Keio University
5322 Endo, Fujisawa-shi, Kanagawa 252-8520, Japan
kiyoki@sfc.keio.ac.jp

Abstract. We propose a new data model to represent dynamic and continuous geographic phenomena over spatiotemporal domain in moving-object databases. Existing data models of moving objects have shortcomings with respect to the representation of moving geographic phenomena involving continuous fields, such as temperature, elevation, and the degree of pollution. Moreover, in the case of a spatiotemporal model for continuous fields, it is difficult to deal with continuous movements through time. In this paper, we define a data type called moving field to represent both object-based and field-based views of geographic phenomena in spatiotemporal domains. The main feature of our model is that it integrates the spatial field model with the slice representation of moving objects. By introducing moving fields, we provide a new computational environment for analyzing various moving phenomena with numerical as well as geographic processing.

1 Introduction

As the effects of severe weather such as hurricanes, floods, droughts, and global warming have become more apparent, geographic phenomena have been rapidly gaining interest in various fields of the world. With advances in sensor technologies and communication networks, many researchers and organizations have started to monitor and analyze geographic phenomena by using earth observation data. In sensing systems, issues such as how to capture, track, and transfer the data concerning specific phenomena have been dealt with. Further, database systems have been developed for storing and processing various types of spatiotemporal data about geographic phenomena.

Spatial databases have long been an essential part of geographic information system (GIS) applications in order to study geographic phenomena using computers. However, traditional spatial databases are insufficient for analyzing dynamic phenomena over a spatiotemporal space because they assume the static aspects of the phenomena. Generally, geographic phenomena have dynamic

M. Yoshikawa et al. (Eds.): DASFAA 2010, LNCS 6193, pp. 410–421, 2010.

properties that change over time. For example, a hurricane moves from one position to another until it disappears, and its wind speed and temperature vary depending on the location and time. For dealing with the dynamic changes in spatiotemporal data, many data models have been developed to express the real-world spatiotemporal processes [1]. In particular, moving-object databases have focused on data models and operations to manipulate the locations and extent of spatial objects such as vehicles and hurricanes that continuously move or change their shape over time. They have excluded the continuous spatiotemporal field data such as temperature, pressure, and the degree of air pollution; however, these field-based data are important in the analysis of the characteristics and progress of spatiotemporally continuous phenomena.

In this paper, we propose a new data type called *moving field*, e.g., pressure of hurricanes, density of air pollution area, and temperature of forest fires, with an object-based and field-based model in a moving-object database. The moving-field data type represents the range of values for some measured attribute associated with the moving domain of objects in space-time. We try to integrate the spatial field data representation with moving-object database models. The moving object model allows the estimation of the location information at any time during the lifetime of an object, and the spatial field data model contains methods to evaluate the value at any location within the domain. This study contributes to the development of data structures for handling not only the movements but also changes in attribute values corresponding to the locations of a moving object.

The rest of this paper is organized as follows: in section 2, we review data models for moving objects and field-based perspectives, and in section 3, we clarify the motivation for this study and define the problem, on which we focused, involved in the use of earth observation data. In section 4, we define the conceptual model of moving fields, and in section 5, we describe the data structures at the implementation level. In section 6, we have presented the concluding remarks and future research issues.

2 Related Work

Moving objects have been widely studied in the field of research for the past decade. A moving-object database supports data models to estimate the geometric information of objects at any time using sampling location data. In the moving-object data models, there are two categories: one is for anticipating the future movements as they have been introduced in [2,3], and the other is for manipulating past movements of moving objects, i.e., trajectory data. In particular, the data model proposed by [4,5] has been a basis for the analysis of the historical movements of trajectory data. In this paper, we refer to the trajectory model to handle the historical changes of moving phenomena over time.

In general, a moving data type is constructed as a mapping function from time to a data type: *moving-type* : *time* $\rightarrow$ *data-type*. Hence, a moving object with time-varying locations can be modeled as function $mobject : time \rightarrow spatial\text{-}object$. In [4,5], three types of moving objects–moving point, moving line, and moving region–are defined using the concept of spatial object types such as point, line, and region. For example, a moving point (*mpoint*) and a moving region (*mregion*) are defined as the mapping functions $mpoint : time \rightarrow point$ and $mregion : time \rightarrow region$, respectively. In particular, data structures on the basis of the slice representation have been presented for implementing moving regions in [6]. However, existing moving object models have some issues related to the representation of moving geographic phenomena containing continuous spatial fields because they have mainly concentrated on the continuous geometric changes of an object, such as locations and shapes.

The GIS communities have investigated object-based models with a discrete perspective and field-based models with a continuous perspective for the spatial data modeling [7]. While a spatial object represents a discrete and independent entity with a set of attributes, including geographical locations such as a country, a river, and a mountain, a spatial field is a set of attribute values that are determined for each location in a spatial domain, such as elevation, temperature, and air pollution density. Although people prefer to use an object-oriented approach to handle geographic data, a certain geographic phenomenon in the real world needs a field-based representation according to an application task. In [8], Tryfona mentioned that many cases of geographic phenomena are expressed by a combination of spatial fields, e.g., a storm can be represented by a combination of temperature, precipitation, and wind speed. However, most spatial applications need both models of space and time. In [9], Galton introduced *object-field* as a hybrid model type to convert between objects and fields at the conceptual level. In a similar work [10], an object field is presented to link fields and objects for spatial phenomena like weather or wildfire. In particular, the work discusses an example of implementation methods of object fields using the relationships between locations and objects. In [11], a query language is presented to handle continuous field data for geographic phenomena, as well as discrete objects. As we referred to these works, we realized that field data play important roles in describing the state of geographic phenomena at a place. However, they have overhead cost to handle continuous field data with movements of a time-varying spatial object. Therefore, we investigate a new model with object-field perspectives to represent moving geographic phenomena in this study.

3 Problem Definition

This section addresses the problem of dealing with history information of moving geographic phenomena in current moving-object databases. For supporting our work, we consider a client/server application to archive geo-observation data of specific phenomena through geo-sensor networks similar to the application discussed in [12]. Figure 1 shows the application in the case of a hurricane. There are two types of geo-sensors and they monitor two different field data related to a hurricane: pressure and wind speed. When a hurricane happens, the sensors

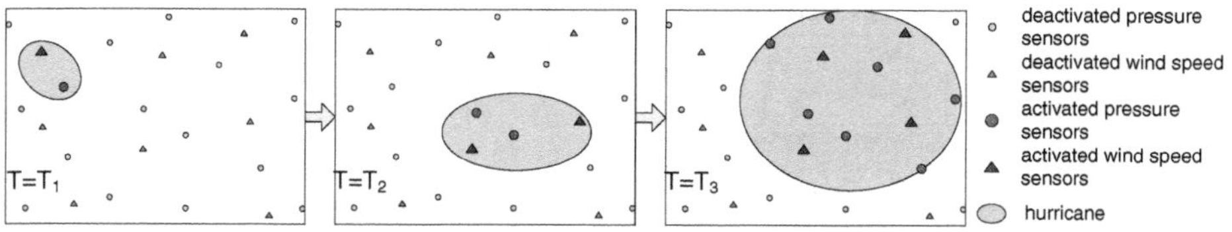

Fig. 1. Example of moving geographic phenomena over a geosensor network

that become activated send the observed field data to a central data server until the hurricane disappears periodically. The server stores these observation data related to each hurricane and processes queries such as the following examples about the hurricane that continuously changes over time.

Q1: In the period *2006* to *2008*, did any hurricane pass through the same area as hurricane "Katrina."
Q2: Show the pressure within *100km* from the eye of hurricane "Katrina".
Q3: Show the hurricane "Katrina" area where wind speed was over *90KTS* from *2005/08/24* to *2005/08/30*.

In the application, a hurricane has object-based and field-based properties in a spatiotemporal domain. That is, it is described by a discrete object that exists at a certain place and time with stable attributes such as its name; it is also perceived as a continuous field of the range of wind speed values of sensors contained within the hurricane area where the sustained speed of the winds reaches 74 mph. Among the above queries, while a query like *Q1* can be answered with a current moving-object database system, others have a few difficulties in being solved. First, most moving-object databases consider the movement of point-based objects such as people, vehicles, and ships, but moving geographic phenomena mainly occupy a certain region and their region changes and evolves continuously over time. Second, they contain continuous spatial fields such as pressure and wind speed of their effect areas. As already mentioned, a spatial field represents values of a certain attribute everywhere in the domain space. However, it is usually impossible to measure continuous locations and values of a moving phenomenon everywhere and every time. Therefore, we need a data model to be able to reconstruct a moving phenomenon from the sampling data at some locations and times and to process the above queries by estimating the field value corresponding to any query point/area and any query time instance/interval.

In this study, we investigate the connection of object- and field-based models of geographical phenomena, such as *object-fields* introduced in [9,10], for modeling and analyzing moving phenomena. However, these works have focused on the static aspects of the phenomena and have not considered the effect of time. Figure 2 shows an example of the representation of object-fields using relationships between locations and objects given in [10]. If we apply this representation for moving phenomena, we should link new field data and new locations whenever the phenomena change their locations or shapes, and field values. This may

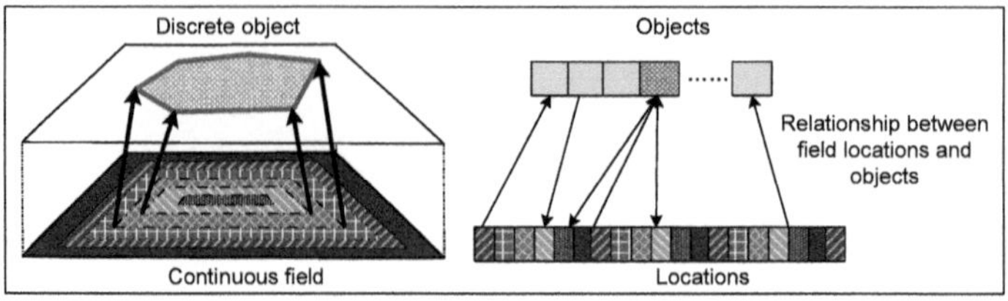

Fig. 2. Representation of object-fields while establishing relationships between field locations and objects

result in a considerable overhead on the system performance due to frequent updating of the relationships. Therefore, we take account of a hybrid data model of moving objects that contain continuous spatial fields.

4 Conceptual Modeling of Moving Fields

4.1 Moving Fields

In order to define a moving field, we first review the concepts of spatial fields and dynamic fields for continuous geographic phenomena [13]. In the field-based models, every location within a spatiotemporal domain is associated with an attribute value or a set of attribute values. A field can be a mathematical mapping function of a given location domain to values. Therefore, a spatial field is denoted as a function sf from a spatial domain of locations S to a value range V, i.e., $sf : S \to V$. It represents the spatial variation of an attribute value assigned to the locations. Let T be a set of time instants or periods, S be the set of spatial locations, and V be the set of possible values of the field. In the same manner, a dynamic field can be derived as a mapping function df from a spatiotemporal domain $S \times T$ into a valid value range V, $df : S \times T \to V$ like that shown in [3]. It can alternatively take the form $df : T \to (S \to V)$ like defined in [12]. Although two mapping functions have different forms, the dynamic field represents the changes in spatial fields across regions of space and periods of time.

Moving fields are motivated from the definition shown in [12] of dynamic fields that consist of the data of active sensors that detect salient events over geo-sensor networks. Compared to in-network monitoring methods of dynamic fields proposed by [12], we focus the development of a data model for processing and analyzing historical data of the continuous changes in the dynamic fields with respect to the continuous movement of phenomena over time. In [14], the efforts of combining continuous and discrete changes in objects and fields in a spatiotemporal domain are presented; the work emphasizes the need of data structures to represent multiple aspects of the phenomena. The moving field suggests a hybrid data model of spatiotemporal object- and field-based representations of moving phenomena, especially spatially and temporally continuous changes. We assume in the following that moving fields are scalar fields. In order to extend our previous work [15], we define a moving field as follows:

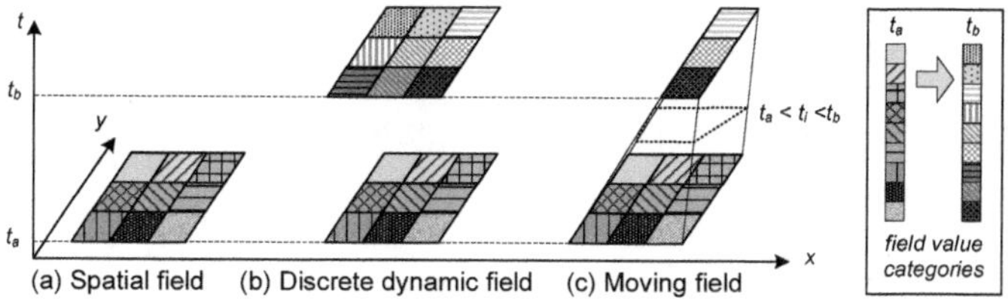

Fig. 3. Field models for incorporating time

Definition 1. Moving fields
A moving field is defined as a continuous mapping function `mf` *from time-varying spatial locations in a moving phenomenon to time-varying scalar values of a field-based attribute over time, i.e.,* `mf:S(t)` $\rightarrow$ `V(t)` *such that* $\forall$ **t** $\in$ *T, where T is the life-time of the phenomenon.* `S(t), V(t)` *is a subset of locations, values at time instance* `t` *of spatial domain* `S` *and field value range* `V`*, respectively. The field values include the real numbers, integers, and Boolean values.*

Figure 3 shows the incorporation of the temporal dimension into the field-based models. Compared to a dynamic field with discrete changes, a moving field is a continuous component that fills a part of space-time. In other words, we can estimate a spatial field bounded by a certain spatial domain at any time between two snapshots of a dynamic field. Intuitively, a moving field is an attribute of a moving phenomenon, but its values vary depending on the location of the phenomenon in a spatiotemporal space. Finally, we are concerned with the historical changes of the moving phenomena. In a moving-object database, a trajectory of a moving object is expressed as a sequence of locations (lc_1, t_1), (lc_2, t_2), ..., (lc_n, t_n) during its life time. That is, the historical change of a moving phenomenon can be described by an indexed sequence of snapshots that are domain-restricted spatial fields at one moment in time. For this, we define the term "history" to represent the historical changes of moving phenomena over time as follows:

Definition 2. Histories
The history of a moving phenomenon represents a region's history as a sequence of the forms (r_1, t_1, v_1), (r_2, t_2, v_2), ..., (r_n, t_n, v_n), *where* r_i *is the region of the spatial domain,* t_i *is the time instance, and* v_i *is the range of a field value of the i-th capturing of the moving phenomenon.*

Figure 4 shows the difference between (a) the trajectory of a moving object with the linear temporal interpolation described as a polyline in a 3D(two spatial and one temporal dimension) space and (b) the history of a point-based moving phenomenon described as a polyline in a 3.5D (space-time with field values) space, including a field dimension.

4.2 Field Operations

Next, we design operations to manipulate moving fields. Since we regard a moving field as a hybrid type of a moving object and a dynamic field, we consider

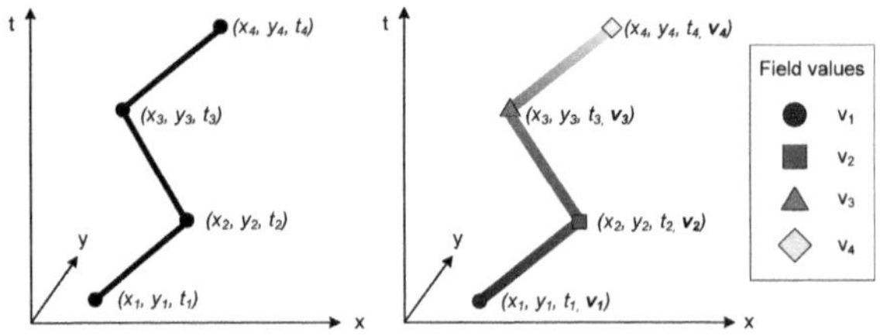

(a) Trajectory (b) History

Fig. 4. History with a moving field of a point-based moving phenomenon in space-time

Table 1. Operation types of moving fields

Types	Operations	Types	Operations
Overlay	`join, merge`	Projection	`domain, range, history`
Interaction	`evaluate, evaluateInverse`	Aggregation	`avg, min, max, sum, count, density, surface`
Numeration	`+, -, *, /, %`	Statistics	`correlation, variance`
Selection	`clipping, slice, section`	Predicates	`<, >, =,` $\neq$`, linear, increases, decreases`

both object-based and field-based operators for the moving fields. In [5], new operations for moving data types are defined, such as *deftime*, *trajectory*, *atinstant*, *speed*, and *turn*, as well as basic spatial operators such as *contains*, *area*, and *distance*. Hence, the moving field can be applied to these operations. For instance, the *atinstant* operation returns a spatial field at a given time instant, and the *defttime* returns the time period when the moving field exists. Moreover, the operations related to continuous field data are brought to our attention, such as operation *overlay* that produces the new field f from more than one field f_1, f_2, ..., f_n. In [8], four types of operations on spatial fields are described: attribute computation, spatial computation, reclassification, and overlay, and particular operations for continuous fields in [11] are defined with three categories: intensity, spatial, and aggregate functions. On the basis of the previous reports, we classify categories of field operations as listed in Table 1. We omit some basic operations of spatiotemporal data types, such as temporal predicates (before, meet, during), spatial predicates (contains, touches, overlaps), spatial operations (distance, buffer, convexhull), and set operations (union, intersection, difference) in this paper. However, these operations should be primitive for moving fields.

Figure 5 shows an example of the overlay operation between two moving fields A and B. We presuppose that the overlay operation and predicates can only operate on the same spatiotemporal location. Therefore, only area C is compatible to perform the operation shown in figure 5(b). We can express a few examples of queries about moving fields using the operations introduced in Section 3. For example, we can assume a relation for hurricanes containing one moving point and two moving fields as follows:

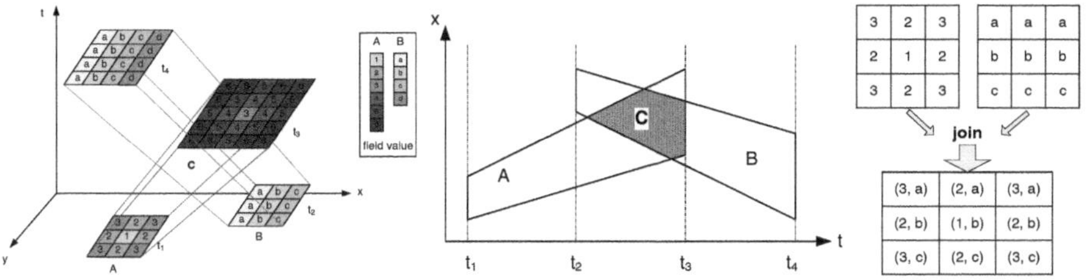

(a) Moving fields in a spatiotemporal space (b) Compatible area (c) Result field

Fig. 5. Join operation between two moving fields

```
hurricanes(id:integer, name:string, eye:mpoint, pressure:mfield,
   windspeed:mfield)
```

Using the relation, we represent each query as followings:

Q1: In the period *2006* to *2008*, find hurricanes passing through the same area as hurricane "Katrina."
`LET` q = SELECT trajectory(eye) FROM hurricanes WHERE name = 'Katrina';
`SELECT` name `FROM` hurricanes
`WHERE` Intersects(q, trajectory(slice(eye, '2006/01/01', '2008/12/31'))) = true;

Q2: Show the pressure within *100km* from the eye of hurricane "Katrina".
`SELECT` clipping(pressure, buffer(eye, 1000))
`FROM` hurricanes `WHERE` name = 'Katrina';

Q3: Show the hurricane "Katrina" area where wind speed was over *90KTS* from *2005/08/24* to *2005/08/30*.
`SELECT` evaluateInverse(slice(windspeed, '2008/08/24', '2008/08/30'),">=90")
`FROM` hurricanes `WHERE` name = 'Katrina';

5 Representing Moving Fields

This section explains how to realize moving fields at the implementation level. Within the spatial database systems, there are two data models for representing spatial data: vector-based models and raster-based models. While the vector data model is expressed by points, lines, and polygons, the raster data model consists of grid cells or tessellations with each containing a value to describe an attribute for the entire spatial domain [16]. In this study, we attempt to integrate the representation spatial field into the data structure for moving objects because moving fields are proposed for describing time-varying attributes of the moving phenomena to be treated like individual objects such as the pressure of hurricanes, density of air pollution area, and temperature of forest fires.

We divide moving objects into three subclasses: moving value, moving geometry, and moving field class types. The class MoValue for representing time-varying values is the base class of moving boolean, moving integer, moving real, and moving string instances. The class MoGeometry represents various types of time-varying vector geometries like moving points, moving lines, and moving

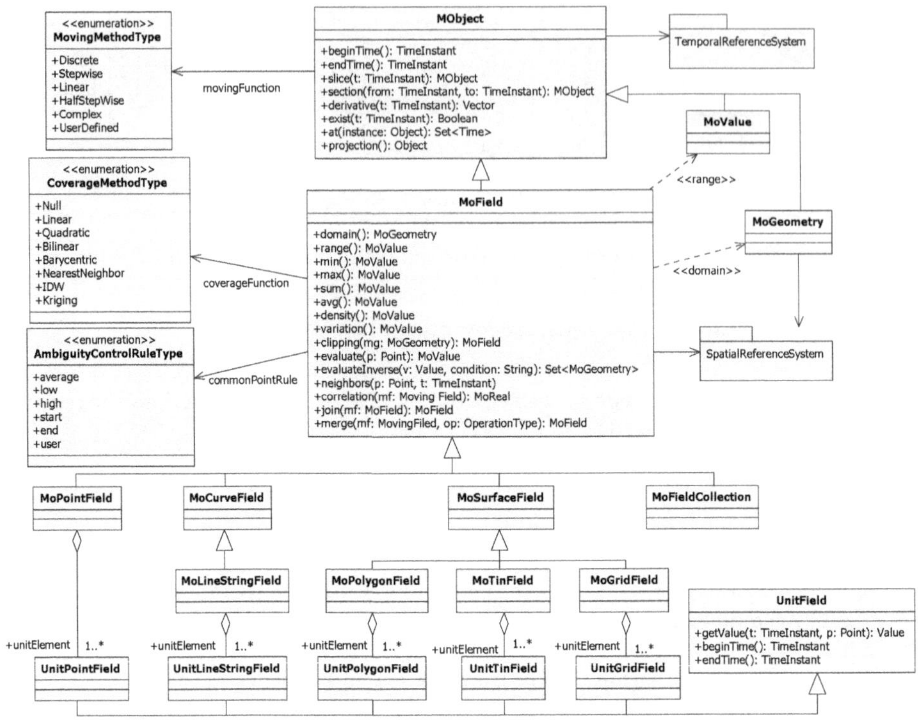

Fig. 6. Class diagram of moving fields

polygons. They have already been defined and implemented through the work of [4,5]. Therefore, we concentrated on the development of the data structures for moving fields for describing time-varying field attributes of the moving phenomena in this study. For the representation of fields, there are six different spatial data models available: cell grids, polygons, TINs (triangulated irregular networks), contour lines, point grids, and irregular points. Although each structure has its own strengths and weaknesses, we exclude the comparison among these models and attempt to exploit some of models in this paper. Figure 6 shows the moving field class (called by MoField), which is specified as the class MoPointField, MoCurveField, MoSurfaceField, and MoFieldCollection, depending on the type of domain geometry of moving phenomena. The class MoPointField is a moving type of a spatial field consisting of irregular points, and MoLineStringField as the subclass of MoCurveField is a moving field type of contour lines. For example, we can represent epidemics using MoPointField and weather fronts using MoLineStringField. However, usually moving phenomena appear with some bounded regions such as floods, wildfires, and hurricanes. In this study, we are devoted to concretize the representation of surface phenomena with MoSurfaceField. The class MoSurfaceField has three subclass types–MoPolygonField, MoTinField, and MoGridField–corresponding to polygons, TINs, and cell grids,

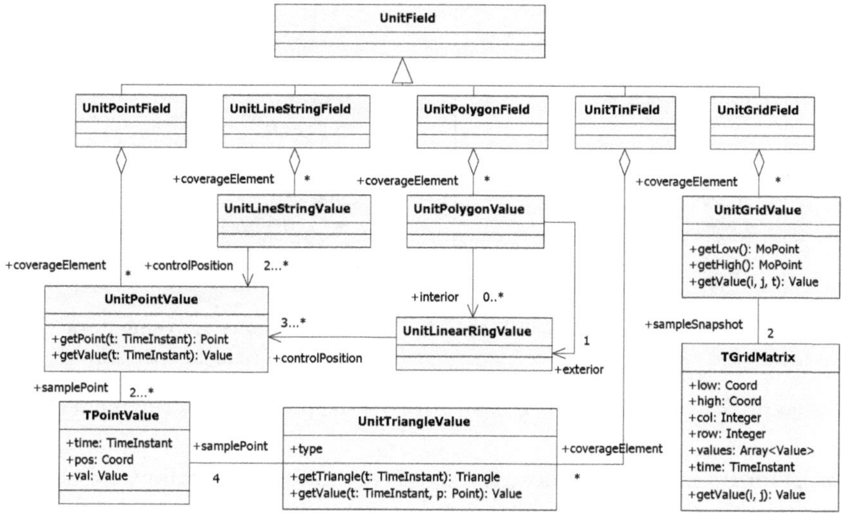

Fig. 7. Unit field-class types for coverage elements of moving fields

respectively. The principal idea of a moving field is that we can estimate the locations and values at any time and any place using a set of explicit samples of the moving phenomenon. For this reason, we need two interpolation functions to reconstruct the moving phenomenon. One is a temporal interpolation function to support the continuous movement, and the other is a spatial interpolation function to evaluate field values with spatial continuity. The former function is denoted by "moving function," and the latter is the "coverage function" on the class diagram of moving field types.

In order to create a moving field type, we take the sliced fragments of moving objects as described by [4]. In the sliced representation, a moving type is composed of unit moving types, and each unit moving type is defined by a pair of a time interval and a unit function that offers the temporal interpolation method, i.e., (*timePeriod*, *unitFunction*). This model allows us to retrieve the locations where an object is located at an arbitrary time instance on the moving object model. Therefore, we also design data structures for moving fields by the aggregation of unit field types of (*timePeriod*, *unitFieldFunction*) except that our *unitFieldFunction* is associated with two interpolation methods as mentioned above. Figure 7 illustrates the primitive unit field types to represent a moving field. The *unitFieldFunction* is realized by the five classes of unit fields: UnitPointField, UnitLineStringField, UnitPolygonField, UnitTinField, and UnitGridField, depending on the interpolation methods. Each unit field respectively consists of coverage elements as instances of UnitPointValue, UnitLineStringValue, UnitPolygonValue, UnitTriangleValue, and UnitGridValue. Finally, values of all units are represented by sampling data at specific time instances. For example, each instance of UnitPointValue and UnitTriangleValue needs two and four sampling points with successive time instances, formed as (c, v, t), where c is a coordinate

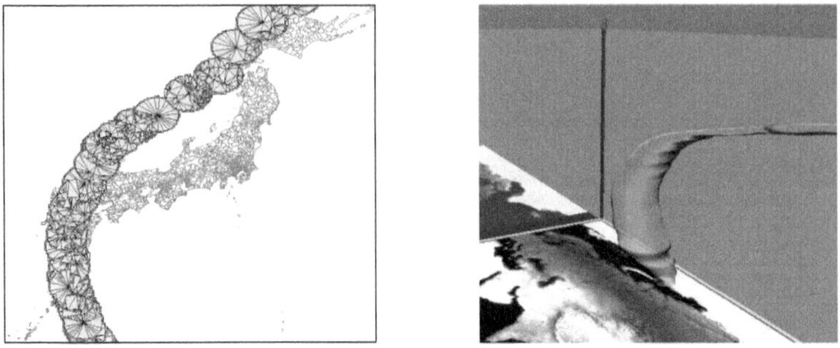

(a) Snapshots of the wind speed field

(b) Continuous movement of the wind speed field in space-time

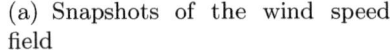

Fig. 8. Example of a moving field within a typhoon area during its lifetime

as (x, y) for its latitude and longitude, v is a value of an attribute of the moving phenomenon, and t is a time instance. In short, a moving field type is composed of instances of a unit moving field type, and an instance of a unit moving field type has explicit sampling data and moving and coverage interpolation methods.

Figure 8 demonstrates a moving field using real geo-observation data such as pressure and wind speed acquired from weather stations and real track data of historical typhoons. In particular, we work with MoTinField because triangular irregular network (TIN) is a popular field model and is based on a set of points and the linear interpolation. In addition, it is congruous to be absorbed in the vector-based moving object model with the linear movement assumption. Figure 8(a) shows snapshots of wind speed sub-TINs around the eye of the typhoon. Next, we created unit TIN fields between two successive sub-TINs. Finally, we can obtain a moving field to show the movement of the hurricane and continuous wind speed field in space-time, as shown by Figure 8(b).

6 Conclusion

Generally, a geographic phenomenon has both object-based and field-based properties in a spatiotemporal domain. In this paper, we have proposed a new data model to represent moving objects containing continuous spatial fields, called moving fields. It represents a spatiotemporal continuous field-based attribute of an object, especially as its value range and domain vary every time depending on the movement of the object. Further, we presented basic data structures on the basis of the representation of spatial fields and moving objects to realize the moving fields at the implementation level and showed an example of a moving field based on the TIN model using the typhoon track and weather station data. By developing the moving field, we can handle region-based moving phenomena not only with geometric processing but also with numerical processing related to correlations. For the future work, we will implement various moving-field types, including raster models such as satellite images and operations in a current database system.

References

1. Pelekis, N., Theodoulidis, B., Kopanakis, I., Theodoridis, Y.: Review of spatio-temporal database models. The Knowledge Engineering Review 19(3), 235–274 (2004)
2. Sistla, A.P., Wolfson, O., Chamberlain, S., Dao, S.: Modeling and querying moving objects. In: Proc. 13th International Conference on Data Engineering, pp. 422–432 (1997)
3. Praing, R., Schneider, M.: A universal abstract model for future movements of moving objects. In: Proc. AGILE International Conference on Geographical Information Systems, pp. 111–120 (2007)
4. Forlizzi, L., Güting, R.H., Nardelli, E., Schneider, M.: A data model and data structures for moving objects databases. In: Proc. 2000 ACM SIGMOD International Conference on Management of Data, pp. 319–330 (2000)
5. Güting, R.H., Böhlen, M.H., Erwig, M., Jensen, C.S., Lorentzos, N.A., Schneider, M., Vazirgiannis, M.: A foundation for representing and querying moving objects. ACM Transactions on Database Systems 25(1), 1–42 (2000)
6. Jin, P., Yue, L., Gong, Y.: A new approach to representing continuously moving regions. In: Proc. 28th Annual International Computer Software and Applications Conference, pp. 70–73 (2004)
7. Couclelis, H.: People manipulate objects (but cultivate fields): Beyond the raster-vector debate in gis. In: Proc. International Conference GIS, pp. 65–77 (1992)
8. Tryfona, N.: Modeling phenomena in spatiotemporal databases: Desiderata and solutions. In: Quirchmayr, G., Bench-Capon, T.J.M., Schweighofer, E. (eds.) DEXA 1998. LNCS, vol. 1460, pp. 155–165. Springer, Heidelberg (1998)
9. Galton, A.: A formal theory of objects and fields. In: Proc. International Conference on Spatial Information Theory, pp. 458–473 (2001)
10. Cova, T.J., Church, R.L., Goodchild, M.F.: Extending geographical representation to include fields of spatial objects. International Journal of Geographical Information Science 16(6), 509–532 (2002)
11. Laurini, R., Paolino, L., Sebillo, M., Tortora, G., Vitiello, G.: A spatial sql extension for continuous field querying. In: Proc. 28th Annual International Computer Software and Applications Conference, pp. 78–81 (2004)
12. Duckham, M., Nittel, S., Worboys, M.: Monitoring dynamic spatial fields using responsive geosensor networks. In: Proc. 13th Annual ACM International Workshop on Geographic Information Systems, pp. 51–60 (2005)
13. Kemp, K.: Environmental Modeling with GIS: A strategy for dealing with spatial continuity. National Center for Geographic Information and Analysis, University of California at Santa Barbara, Technical Report 93-3 (1993)
14. Galton, A.: Fields and objects in space, time, and space-time. Spatial Congnition and Computation 4(1), 39–68 (2004)
15. Kim, K.-S., Zettsu, K., Kidawara, Y., Kiyoki, Y.: A field-based modeling approach for historical disaster data. In: Proc. 2nd International Workshop on Knowledge Cluster Systems, pp. 65–73 (2008)
16. Worboys, M., Duckham, M. (eds.): GIS: A Computing Perspective, 2nd edn. CRC Press, Boca Raton (2004)

GRAMS^3: An Efficient Framework for XML Structural Similarity Search

Peisen Yuan[1,2], Xiaoling Wang[3], Chaofeng Sha[1,2], Ming Gao[1,2], and Aoying Zhou[2,3]

[1] School of Computer Science, Fudan University, Shanghai 200433, P.R. China
[2] Shanghai Key Laboratory of Intelligent Information Processing, Shanghai 200433, P.R. China
[3] Shanghai Key Laboratory of Trustworthy Computing, Software Engineering Institute, East China Normal University, Shanghai 200062, P.R. China
{peiseny,cfsha,mgao}@fudan.edu.cn,
{xlwang,ayzhou}@sei.ecnu.edu.cn

Abstract. Structural similarity search is a fundamental technology for XML data management. However, existing methods do not scale well with large volume of XML document. The *pq*-gram is an efficient way of extracting substructure from the tree-structured data for approximate structural similarity search. In this paper, we propose an effective framework GRAMS^3 for evaluating structural similarity of XML data. First *pq*-grams of XML document are extracted; then we study the characteristics of *pq*-gram of XML and generate doc-gram vector using TGF-IGF model for XML tree; finally we employ locality sensitive hashing for efficiently structural similarity search of XML documents. An empirical study using both synthetic and real datasets demonstrates the framework is efficient.

Keywords: *pq*-Gram, Structural Similarity, Locality Sensitive Hashing, XML Document.

1 Introduction

XML has become a standard for data exchange with the web application development. Efficient management for these tree-structured data is a basic demand. Structural similarity search [1, 2, 3] over XML data is a fundamental technology for XML data management and search processing, which is related to data integration, XML classification and clustering, data cleaning etc. Therefore structural similarity search on XML has become an important research topic in database community recently.

XML is tree-structured data, its complex structure brings challenges for structural similarity comparison. Researchers have proposed tree edit distance technique for structure comparing of tree-structured data. However, its time complexity for ordered tree is $O(n^3)$ with $O(n^2)$ space cost and it's NP-hard for unordered tree [4], where n is the node number of the tree. Thus tree edit distance is time consuming for complex structure XML document comparison.

Recently, approximate similarity has been proposed for tree structural similarity comparison [5,6,7]. Augsten et al. [7] propose *pq*-gram with bag similarity in $O(n\log n)$ time complexity and $O(n)$ space complexity for ordered tree data. Yang et al. [5] present

M. Yoshikawa et al. (Eds.): DASFAA 2010, LNCS 6193, pp. 422–433, 2010.

binary branch tree with L_1 distance for the similarity comparing and Okura et al. [6] propose q-gram for ordered unlabeled tree data with L_1 distance metric.

However, one problem for XML structural similarity comparison is the need of dealing with high-dimensional data. To solve the curse of dimensionality, new algorithms need to be developed for efficiency. In this paper, a scalable and efficient pq-**GR**am-based fr**A**mework for **XML** **S**tructural **S**imilarity **S**earch (**GRAMS**^{3}) is proposed. We employ pq-gram proposed in [7], which is flexible for XML data. Of course, our framework can also be applied to other methods, such as [5]. To measure the characteristics of pq-gram of XML tree, TGF-IGF model is proposed and cosine similarity is adopted as the similarity metric. Furthermore, locality sensitive hashing and random projection techniques are employed for dimension reduction for efficient search. Extensive experiments are conducted to compare with other similarity metrics. The results indicate that our approach is efficient and effective for XML structural similarity search.

The main contributions of this paper are briefly outlined as follows:

- A framework for XML structural similarity search GRAMS^3 is proposed.
- Observations of pq-gram of XML tree for XML structural comparison are proposed.
- Based on the observations, the characteristics of pq-gram of XML tree are introduced, which are measured by the TGF-IGF weight model.
- The locality sensitive hashing and random projection techniques are employed to the solve the problem of curse of dimensionality for efficient search.
- Extensive experiments are conducted to demonstrate the effectiveness and efficiency of our approach.

The rest of paper is organized as follows. Preliminaries are introduced in Section 2. In Section 3, observations and TGF-IGF model are proposed. Architecture and algorithms are presented in Section 4, and experiments evaluation are described in Section 5. We summarize the related work in Section 6 and conclude the paper in Section 7.

2 Preliminaries

2.1 XML Model and pq-Gram

In this paper, the XML document is modeled as a rooted ordered labeled tree. In this model, element nodes and attributes are considered as *structural* nodes, and the text value and attribute value nodes are treated as *text* nodes. Only *structural* nodes are taken into consideration as the structure of XML tree. The *element tag* and the *attribute* name are considered as the node name.

The pq-gram [7] is a flexible way to extract the structural information from tree-structured data. Therefore we employ pq-gram for XML structural similarity search.

According to [7], given a tree T and two integers p and q, an *extended tree* $T^{p,q}$ is built for T firstly. Fig.1 (1) is a tree of an XML document fragment of *dblp* dataset [8], and Fig.1 (2) is the extended tree of T for $p = 2$ and $q = 3$. After building the *extended tree*, pq-grams of tree T can be extracted by algorithm in [7]. The pq-gram is also called tree-gram if not confused in this paper.

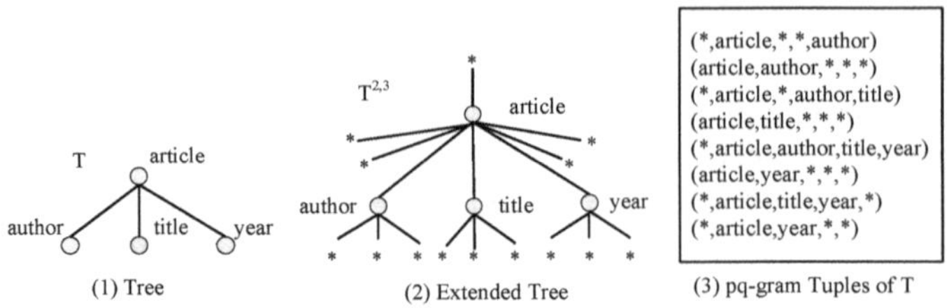

Fig. 1. Example tree and *pq*-gram tuple

2.2 Locality Sensitive Hashing and Random Projection

Locality Sensitive Hashing (LSH) is widely used in nearest neighbor search [9] for high dimension data, similarity search [10] and clustering [11] etc.

LSH is a hash function family $\mathcal{H}$ defined on an object set $\mathcal{O}$, which has a similarity function $sim : \mathcal{O} \times \mathcal{O} \rightarrow [0, 1]$. The scheme of LSH is the hash function family $\mathcal{H}$ with a probability distribution D over the functions such that for two objects $\boldsymbol{o}_1, \boldsymbol{o}_2 \in \mathcal{O}$, a function $h \in \mathcal{H}$ is chosen according to D that satisfies

$$\mathbf{Pr}_{h\in\mathcal{H}}[h(\boldsymbol{o}_1) = h(\boldsymbol{o}_2)] = sim(\boldsymbol{o}_1, \boldsymbol{o}_2). \tag{1}$$

Random Projection (RP) [12] is a method of LSH for dimensionality reduction, which is a powerful tool designed for approximate the cosine distance. Given a collection of objects which is represented by vectors with n dimensions, a random vector $\boldsymbol{r}$ is randomly generated with each component randomly choosing from Gaussian distribution. The hash function family of random projection is defined as :

$$h_{\boldsymbol{r}}(\boldsymbol{u}) = \begin{cases} 1 : \text{if } \boldsymbol{r} \cdot \boldsymbol{u} \geq 0; \\ 0 : \text{otherwise.} \end{cases} \tag{2}$$

The process of random projection multiplies the matrix $\mathbf{M} \in \mathbb{R}^{n \times d}$ by a random matrix $\mathbf{R} \in \mathbb{R}^{d \times k}$ $(k \ll d)$ to generate a compact representation $\mathbf{C} = \mathbf{MR} \in \mathbb{R}^{n \times k}$. Vectors in $\mathbb{R}^{d \times k}$ are normalized with each component randomly choosing from Gaussian distribution.

After projecting each vector into k bits, hamming distance of the bits vector can be evaluated efficiently with much smaller memory and lower computation cost.

3 Observations and TGF-IGF Model

3.1 Observations

Data in the same XML document usually has the same DTD or schema, which leads the XML document to be a *wide-and-shallow* tree with repeated tags in most cases. Therefore, duplicate *pq*-grams are often occurred. However, XML document also includes the optional elements, and they are important for comparing structural similarity. Whereas the characteristic of *pq*-gram of the XML tree is similar with the keywords in the flat document, different *pq*-grams should have distinct weight to differentiate the structure

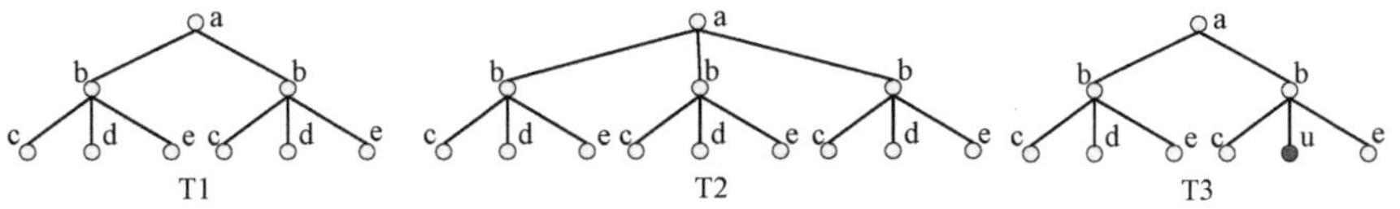

Fig. 2. An Example trees for observations

of XML document. Through the occurrences of some *pq*-grams may be small, they are important to differentiate the structure.

Example 1. In Fig. 2, for p = 2, q = 3, tree T_1 and T_2 contain 20 and 29 *pq*-grams respectively. However, cardinalities of their *pq*-gram sets are 12 and 13 respectively, meaning that their *pq*-gram sets are almost the same with different frequency, though they have different number of entities. This can also be seen from the Example 3. This demonstrates that frequency of *pq*-gram is important to differentiate the XML tree structure. From this example, the first guideline of *pq*-gram for structural similarity comparison is presented as follows.

Guideline 1. *pq*-Gram frequency of XML document tree is important for comparing the structural similarity.

Example 2. From T_1 and T_3 in Fig. 2, for p = 2, q = 3, we get 20 *pq*-grams for each tree, and they share 12 *pq*-grams. However there are 4 *pq*-grams {(a,b,*,c,u), (a,b,c,u,e), (a,b,u,e,*), (b,u,*,*,*)} in tree T_3 with minority frequency due to the node u, but these 4 *pq*-grams are important to differentiate the structure of T_1 and T_3. From this example, the second guideline of *pq*-gram for structural similarity comparison is introduced.

Guideline 2. *pq*-Gram sparsity of XML document tree is also important for differentiating the structural similarity.

After introducing the concept of *pq*-gram , *pq*-gram tuple and doc-gram vector are presented as follows.

Definition 1. *Let g be a pq-gram with the nodes $N(g)$= $\{n_1,..., n_p,n_{p+1},...,n_{p+q}\}$, where n_i is the i-th node in preorder traversal of the pq-gram subtree. The pq-gram tuple $L^*(g)$ = $<l(n_1),..., l(n_p), l(n_{p+1}),..., l(n_{p+q})>$ is called label tuple of pq-gram g, where $l(n_i)$ is the node name of the node n_i.*

Fig.1 (3) is the *2,3*-gram tuples of the tree T. Assume the universe of *pq*-gram label tuples of the corpus composes the alphabet set $\mathbf{G}_{\mathcal{U}}$ and it is sorted lexicographically. Consequently, the structure of XML tree can be represented by a vector with dimension $|\mathbf{G}_{\mathcal{U}}|$, with each entry of the vector is the frequency of the *pq*-grams in the XML document, where $|\mathbf{G}_{\mathcal{U}}|$ is the cardinality of the set $\mathbf{G}_{\mathcal{U}}$.

Definition 2. *Let w_i be the raw frequency of the pq-gram in the XML tree T, $\mathbf{V}(T,p,q)$ = $(w_1,w_2,...,w_{|\mathbf{G}_{\mathcal{U}}|})$ is the pq-gram vector of T.*

Example 3. In the example tree of Fig. 2, *pq*-gram vectors of *2,3*-gram (1, 1, 1, 1, 0, 2, 2, 0, 2, 0, 2, 2, 0, 2, 2, 2, 0),(1, 1, 1, 1, 1, 3, 3, 0, 3, 0, 3, 3, 0, 3, 3, 3, 0) and (1, 1, 1, 1, 0, 2, 1, 1, 1, 1, 1, 2, 1, 2, 1, 2, 1) are respective to T_1, T_2 and T_3.

3.2 TGF-IGF

Based on the above observations, we propose *Tree Gram Frequency* and *Inverse pq-Gram Frequency*(TGF and IGF for short respectively) to implement the above guidelines for XML structural similarity comparison.

Definition 3. *Let $frequency_{i,j}$ be the raw frequency of pq-gram g_i in the XML tree T_j, the normalized Tree Gram Frequency(TGF) $g_{i,j}$ of pq-gram g_i is given by*

$$g_{i,j} = \frac{frequency_{i,j}}{\sum_k frequency_{k,j}} \tag{3}$$

where $\sum_k frequency_{k,j}$ is the sum of all the pq-grams occurrences in the tree T_j.

TGF implements the first guideline, more frequent *pq*-gram has greater weight.

Definition 4. *Let $|T|$ be the total number of trees in the corpus and t_i be the number of trees which pq-gram g_i appears, the Inverse pq-Gram Frequency (IGF) factor of g_i is defined as*

$$igf_i = \log(1 + \frac{|T|}{t_i}), \tag{4}$$

The intuitive of IGF is that minority of *pq*-gram is also important for differentiating XML structure, which materialize the second guideline. The weight of *pq*-gram g_i in XML tree t_j is given by

$$w_{i,j} = g_{i,j} \times igf_i = \frac{frequency_{i,j}}{\sum_k frequency_{k,j}} \times \log(1 + \frac{|T|}{t_i}) \tag{5}$$

Definition 5. *The normalized pq-gram vector of T_j is a vector($w_{1j}, w_{2j}, \ldots, w_{|G_U|j}$), with each dimension w_{ij} representing the normalized weight of the pq-gram defined in Eq.5.*

After introducing the TGF-IGF model, cosine similarity can be adopted to measure the similarity of XML, which is an effective metric in information retrieval [13]. Due to the high dimension of *pq*-gram vector, the locality sensitive hashing technique is used for efficiently evaluating. Then the problem of structural similarity search in high dimensions is reduced into hamming distance evaluation in much lower dimensions.

4 System Architecture and Algorithms

4.1 System Architecture

The architecture of GRAMS^3 is presented in Fig. 3. The preprocessing of GRAMS^3 can be divided into three steps. First, the XML documents are parsed and extracted into *pq*-grams by the *parser module* using the algorithm in [7] . Second, the normalized doc-gram vectors are constructed by the *vector builder* module for each document. Then the *vector sketch* and *inverted list* module generates *random vectors* with Gauss distribution, computes the sketch for each doc-gram vector and builds the sketch inverted

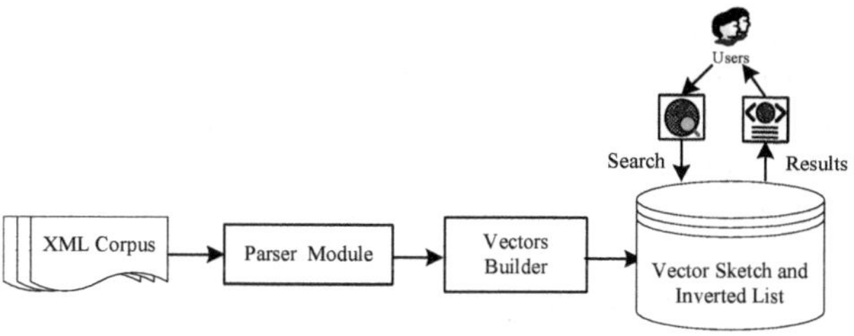

Fig. 3. Architecture of GRAMS^3

index. Given a query $\mathcal{Q}$, the *result* module retrieves the *top-k* results using the sketch inverted list and output to the user at last.

Algorithms are introduced in the following section. Algorithm 1 generates a random matrix from Gaussian distribution firstly. Then for each XML document, the *pq*-grams are extracted and doc-gram vectors are built. Finally sketch inverted list is constructed for the corpus. And the Algorithm 2 is used to deal with search processing.

4.2 Algorithms

Vector Sketch Algorithm. Algorithm 1 first generates a random matrix $\mathbf{R} \in \mathbb{R}^{d \times k}$. Each component of the vector of **R** is i.i.d from $N(0,1)$ and each vector of the matrix **R**

Algorithm 1. Vector Sketch Algorithm

Input: XML corpus, parameters p and q
Output: Vector Sketch Inverted List($VSIL$)

$V = \Phi$; /*normalized vector of document*/
generate a normalized random vector matrix **R**;
foreach $d \in corpus$ **do**
  extract pq-gram with the algorithm from [7];
  compute TGF and IGF for each tree-gram of document d ;
  construct vector $\boldsymbol{v}$ of pq-grams of document d ;
  $\boldsymbol{V} = \boldsymbol{V} \cup \{\boldsymbol{v}\}$;
$\mathbf{S}_V = \Phi$ /*Sketch Bits Stream Vectors*/
foreach $\boldsymbol{v} \in \boldsymbol{V}$ **do**
  foreach $\boldsymbol{v}' \in \boldsymbol{R}$ **do**
    $h = \boldsymbol{v} \cdot \boldsymbol{v}'$;
    if $h \geq 0$ **then**
      $h = 1$;
    else
      $h = 0$;
    $BVector$.append(h);
  $\mathbf{S}_V = \mathbf{S}_V \cup \{BVector\}$;
$VSIL = BuildInvertedList(\mathbf{S}_V)$;
return $VSIL$;

is normalized (line 2). Then each XML document is parsed according to our model and the *pq*-grams are extracted using Algorithm from [7](line 4).

After *pq*-gram extracting, doc-gram vectors of the corpus are built with TGF-IGF model(line 5-7). Consequently the doc-gram matrix $\mathbf{M}^{n\times d}$ is obtained, with each vector of **M** is normalized. Subsequently, the vector sketch inverted list with random projection for the corpus is built. For each doc-gram vector, the algorithm chooses random vectors from **R** to calculate the inner product with hash function defined in Eq. 2, then appends the hash result to the bits vector of the document(line 9-17).

Through random projection, each vector is represented as a bit vector $\{(0,1)^k\}$ and consequently the compact representation of doc-gram matrix $\mathbf{C}^{n\times k} = \mathbf{M}^{n\times d}\,\mathbf{R}^{d\times k}$ is obtained. Finally the inverted list for the sketch vectors is returned (line 18,19).

Search Algorithm. Give a query $\mathcal{Q}$, the function $getSketchVector()$ first retrieves the sketch vector of the query in the sketch inverted list. Then, it evaluates the hamming distance with each bits vector in the sketch inverted list by sequential scanning (line 3-7). Finally, result list of *top-k* structural similarity XML documents are returned after being sorted(line 8,9).

Algorithm 2. Structural Similarity Search

Input: Vector Sketch Inverted List $VSIL$, Query $\mathcal{Q}$
Output: Top-k list
1 $Result = \Phi$;
2 $\boldsymbol{q}'$ = getSketchVector($\mathcal{Q}$);
3 **foreach** $\boldsymbol{v} \in VSIL$ **do**
4 $\quad hammingdist$ = computeHammingDistance($\boldsymbol{q}', \boldsymbol{v}$);
5 $\quad cosinesim$ = cos((1- $hammingdist$)$\times\ \pi$);
6 $\quad sim$ = (1+ $cosinesim$)/2 ;
7 $\quad Result$ = $Result \cup \{sim\}$;
8 sort($Result$);
9 **return** top-*k* list;

Complexity Analysis. Let $|T|$ be the number of the XML trees in the corpus, $|\mathbf{G}_{\mathcal{U}}|$ be the vector length of the corpus. The complexity of Algorithm 1 is analyzed as bellow. To compute the random matrix **R** (line 2), it costs $O(|\mathbf{G}_{\mathcal{U}}| \times k)$. It costs $O(|T|)$ for extracting tree-gram and building normalized doc-gram vector (line 3-7). After generating normalized doc-gram vector, it costs $O(|T| \times |\mathbf{G}_{\mathcal{U}}|)$ for sketch vector evaluation. Thus the time complexity of Algorithm 1 is $O(|T| \times |\mathbf{G}_{\mathcal{U}}|)$. For Algorithm 2, it sequentially scans the sketch vector inverted list, thus it costs $O(|T| \times k)$, and the sorting procedure costs $O(|T| \log |T|)$. Thus the time complexity of Algorithm 2 is $\max\{O(|T| \times k), |T| \log |T|\}$.

5 Experiments

Extensive experiments are conducted to compare the effectiveness and efficiency of the TGF-IGF weighted cosine-based LSH similarity (CosineLSH for short) with different similarity metrics used in [7,5]. First, the search quality is evaluated which is measured by *precision*, *recall*, *F-measure* (denoted as P*R*F for simplicity) [13] and *k-precision*. Second, experiments of the performance of GRAMS^3 are conducted.

For the real data sets, the XML data from [8, 14] are used. As for the synthetic data sets, 30 synthetic XML documents with the size from 100KB to 5MB are generated with XMark [15] with the default DTD.

Due to experiment requirements, the data sets are divided into two parts. The first one includes 596 documents, which is used to test the performance. The second includes 10 different kinds of data[1], which aims at evaluating the *k-precision* against other similarity metrics. For each document in the second group, noises are added randomly with the proportion of 0.01, 0.05, 0.1, 0.15, 0.2, 0.25 of the total structural nodes of the document. Consequently 70 documents are obtained in total including the original ones.

5.1 Experiments Setup

All of the algorithms are implemented in Java SDK1.6 and run on Ubuntu 9.04 with Intel duo core 2.33GHz processor, 2G main memory with 1G being allocated for JVM. The default parameters of p and q are set to 2 and 3 respectively.

5.2 Search Quality

For search quality, experiments are divided into two groups. The first group is used to measure the P*R*F of CosineLSH. The second one is used to measure the *k-precision* of CosineLSH against other similarity metrics.

Group 1. In this group, the P*R*F of CosineLSH against the raw cosine(denoted for RawCosine) are evaluated. Results of RawCosine are used as the baseline. The P*R*F of 15 queries are evaluated with different project numbers and the average results are shown in Fig. 4.

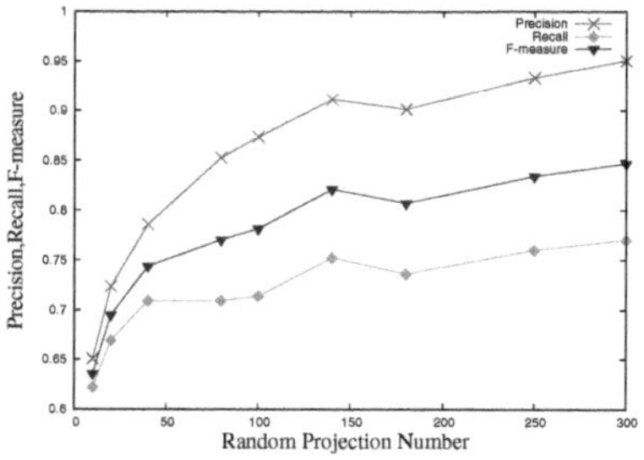

Fig. 4. P*R*F with random projection

[1] These 10 kinds of data are: dblp, customer, mondial, OrdinaryIssue, Proceedings, reed, SigmodRecord, swissprot, Syn, treebank. Syn is the synthetic XML documents.

The x-axis of Fig. 4 represents the number of the random projection, and the y-axis represents the P*R*F. The original dimension of doc-gram vector is 2962. Fig. 4 demonstrates that the P*R*F increase sharply with the random projection number before 50. However, they become smooth after 150. This indicates that there exists a threshold for balancing the P*R*F and the efficiency. For our experiments, the random projection number can be chose from 100 to 150.

Group 2. In this group, the $k\text{-}precision$ for five similarity metrics are evaluated: RawCosine [13], CosineLSH, set-based Jaccard similarity, bag-based [7] and L_1 [5] similarity metrics using the second datasets. The precision metric of $k\text{-}precision$ is defined as $\frac{top_r-k}{k}$, where top_r-k is relevant result in the top-k result list. Files without noise in the second datasets are used for searching with k = 3, 5, 7. The average results of $k\text{-}precision$ are shown from Fig. 5a to Fig. 5d.

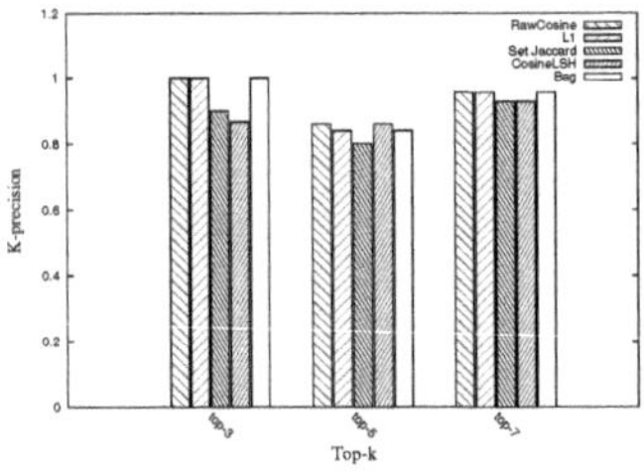

(a) p=1, q=2

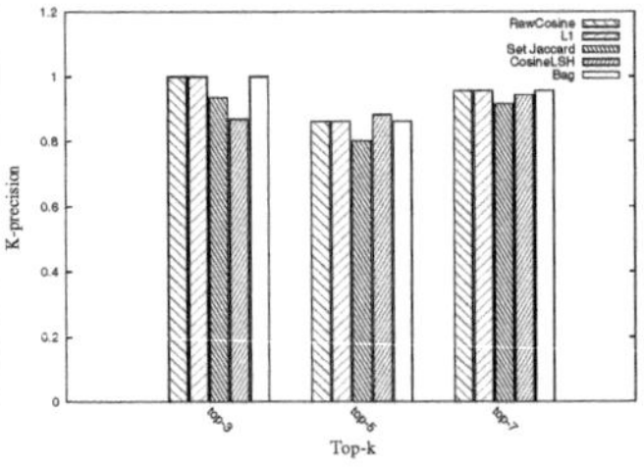

(b) p=1, q=3

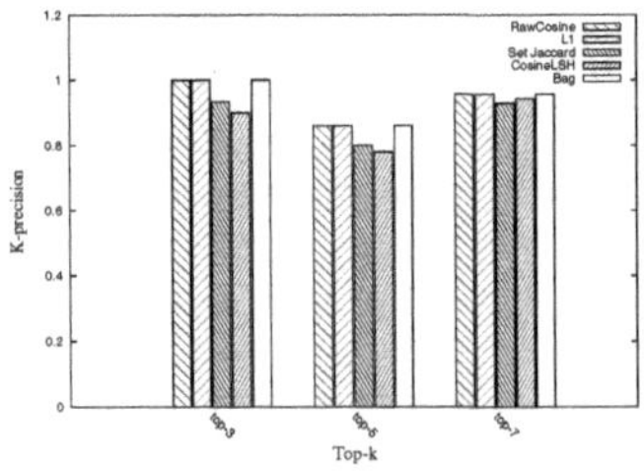

(c) p=2, q=3

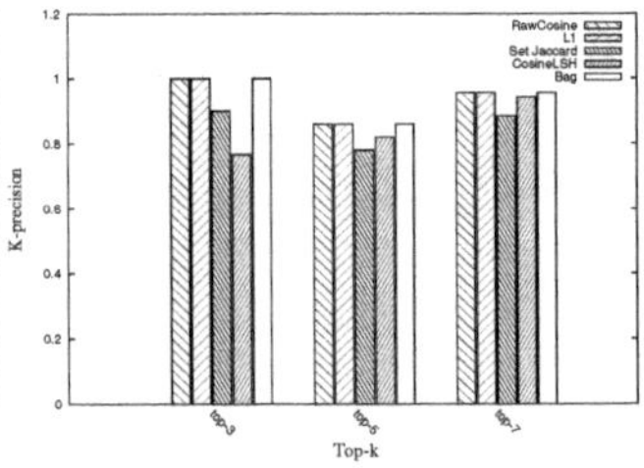

(d) p=3, q=4

Fig. 5. top-k precision for different metrics and p, q

From Fig. 5a to Fig. 5d, two conclusions can be drawn. The first is that RawCosine is better or on par with the other four similarity metrics, which indicates that TGF-IGF model is effective for XML structural similarity search. The second is that CosineLSH is even better than set-based with the increasing of k. These figures also show that the $k\text{-}precision$ of set-based Jaccard similarity is smaller than that of cosine-based, bag-based and L_1 metrics. The reason is that it misses the frequency and sparsity information of the pq-grams.

5.3 Performance

As for the performance, sequential scan is used for similarity evaluation. Each query is run 10 times and the average run time is used as the result. The processing time is shown in Fig. 6 and Fig. 7, and the time unit is millisecond(ms). In Fig. 6, p, q and k are set to 2, 3 and 100 respectively.

Fig. 6 demonstrates that the processing time of CosineLSH is only about 3.3% of RawCosine metric and about 14% of set-based Jaccard similarity, far lower than that of other similarity metrics aslo. This figure also shows that the processing time for Set-based similarity metric is lower than L_1 distance, and the bag metric takes the highest time about 140 ms for each query. For a certain random projection k, Fig. 7 shows that the processing time has little change with different p and q. Fig. 7 also indicates that with the increasing of random projection number, the processing time increases linearly.

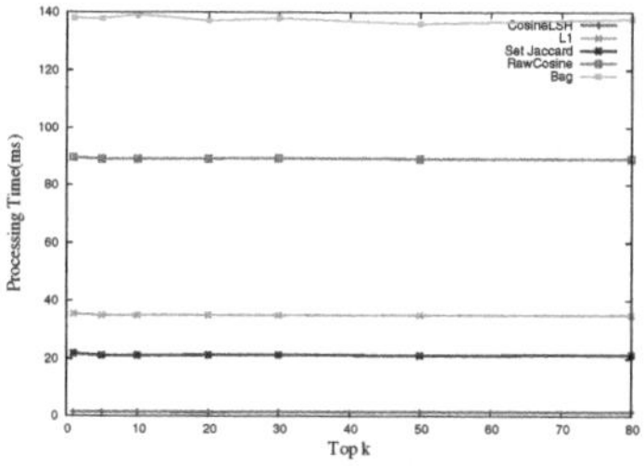

Fig. 6. Time for different metrics

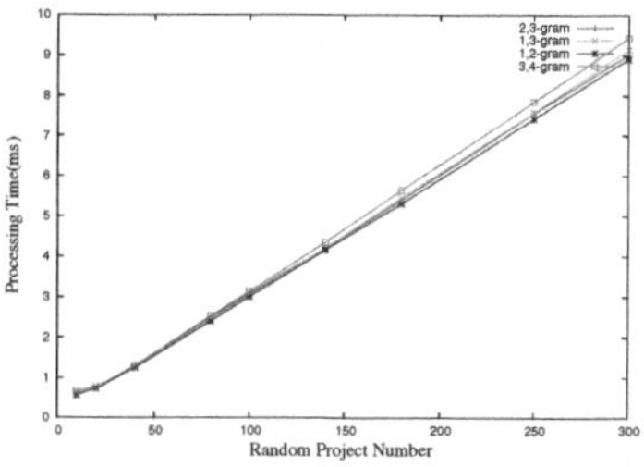

Fig. 7. Time for random projection

In summary, the experimental evaluations of GRAMS^3 show that (1) TGF-IGF with RawCosine similarity has high quality for XML structural similarity search; (2) CosineLSH is efficient and scales well for structural similarity search of XML tree, which can greatly reduce search time comparing with other similarity metrics with minute precision losing.

6 Related Work

Approximate tree structural comparison has been extensively studied and researchers have proposed many approximate methods for XML structural comparison. One key problem of approximate tree structural similarity evaluation is the method of extracting the proper *structural* information.

Nierman et al. [16] propose a simple way of approximate structural similarity computing by extracting node tag and set-based similarity. Due to structural information being ignored, set-based tag similarity has a poor quality for comparing structural similarity. Lian et al. [17] put forward *edge matching* method. They take the edge structure into consideration, which is a more effective way due to the reason that it takes more structural information into account. *Path* similarity method extracts the path set as the structural information of the original XML tree [18]. Path similarity method provides fairly high quality structural information. Recently, tree-gram based methods are proposed to capture the structural similarity for ordered tree [7,5,6], which is becoming an efficient and flexible way for tree data structural similarity evaluation.

Another key problem is the similarity metric. The mostly used similarity metrics for tree similarity are set-based or bag-based [7, 19]. Distance-based dissimilarity as a dual problem of similarity is frequently used for similarity computing, such as L_1 distance [6,5]. However, the above methods either do not take the characteristics of the XML or do not take the efficiency into account for large volume of document similarity retrieving. Thus, we propose an efficient framework for structural similarity search of XML documents.

7 Conclusion

In this paper, an efficient framework GRAMS^3 is proposed for approximate XML structural similarity search with the *pq*-gram and locality sensitive hashing techniques. Two important characteristics of *pq*-gram of XML are identified for structural comparison: frequency and sparsity. To implement these two characteristics, TGF-IGF model is proposed. Based on the TGF-IGF model, cosine similarity and the random projection method are utilized to answer the query efficiently. Experiments show that GRAMS^3 reduces search time greatly with minute precision losing.

Acknowledgments. This work is supported by NSFC grants (No. 60773075, No. 60925008 and No. 60903014), National Hi-Tech 863 program under grant 2009AA01Z149, 973 program (No. 2010CB328106), Shanghai International Cooperation Fund Project (Project No.09530708400) and Shanghai Leading Academic Discipline Project (No. B412).

References

1. Bertino, E., Guerrini, G., Mesiti, M.: A matching algorithm for measuring the structural similarity between an XML document and a DTD and its applications. Information Systems 29(1), 23–46 (2004)
2. Viyanon, W., Madria, S.K., Bhowmick, S.S.: XML Data Integration Based on Content and Structure Similarity Using Keys. In: OTM, pp. 484–493 (2008)
3. Tekli, J., Chbeir, R., Yetongnon, K.: An overview on XML similarity: background, current trends and future directions. Computer Science Review 3(3), 151–173 (2009)
4. Jiang, T., Wang, L., Zhang, K.: Alignment of Trees-An Alternative to Tree Edit. In: CPM, pp. 75–86 (1994)
5. Yang, R., Kalnis, P., Tung, A.K.H.: Similarity evaluation on tree-structured data. In: SIGMOD, pp. 754–765 (2005)
6. Okura, N., Hirata, K., Kuboyama, T., Harao, M.: The q-Gram Distance for Ordered Unlabeled Trees. IEIC Technical Report, 105(273), 25–29 (2005)
7. Augsten, N., Böhlen, M., Gamper, J.: Approximate matching of hierarchical data using pq-grams. In: VLDB, pp. 301–312 (2005)
8. UW XML Repository (2009), `http://www.cs.washington.edu/research/xmldatasets/`

9. Tao, Y., Yi, K., Sheng, C., Kalnis, P.: Quality and efficiency in high dimensional nearest neighbor search. In: SIGMOD, pp. 563–576 (2009)
10. Haghani, P., Michel, S., Aberer, K.: Distributed similarity search in high dimensions using locality sensitive hashing. In: EDBT, pp. 744–755 (2009)
11. Haveliwala, T.H., Gionis, A., Indyk, P.: Scalable techniques for clustering the web. In: WebDB, vol. 129, p. 134 (2000)
12. Goemans, M.X., Williamson, D.P.: Improved approximation algorithms for maximum cut and satisfiability problems using semidefinite programming. JACM 42(6), 1145 (1995)
13. Baeza-Yates, R., Ribeiro-Neto, B.: Modern information retrieval. Addison-Wesley, Reading (1999)
14. Sigmod Record (2009), `http://www.sigmod.org/publications/sigmod-record/xml-edition`
15. Xmark (2009), `http://www.xml-benchmark.org/`
16. Nierman, A., Jagadish, H.V.: Evaluating structural similarity in XML documents. In: WebDB, pp. 61–66 (2002)
17. Lian, W., Cheung, D.W., Mamoulis, N., Yiu, S.M.: An efficient and scalable algorithm for clustering XML documents by structure. In: TKDE, pp. 82–96 (2004)
18. Rafiei, D., Moise, D.L., Sun, D.: Finding Syntactic Similarities Between XML Documents. In: ICDESA, pp. 512–516 (2006)
19. Augsten, N., Böhlen, M., Gamper, J.: The pq-Gram Distance between Ordered Labeled Trees. TODS 35(1), 1–36 (2010)

An Asynchronous Message-Based Knowledge Communication in a Ubiquitous Environment

Petri Rantanen, Pekka Sillberg, Hannu Jaakkola, and Takafumi Nakanishi

[1] Tampere University of Technology (TUT),
Pohjoisranta 11 A, 28100 Pori, Finland
{petri.rantanen,pekka.sillberg,hannu.jaakkola}@tut.fi
[2] National Institute of Information and Communications Technology (NICT),
3-5 Hikaridai, Seika-cho, Soraku-gun, Kyoto, 619-0289, Japan
takafumi@nict.go.jp

Abstract. This paper presents the required operational logic for relaying user requests from traditional Server/Client-based systems to services or additional information sources that require asynchronous communications. The paper describes a simple syntax for user-generated messages that can be used to determine where the messages should be forwarded. The paper also explains how replies to these messages should be processed. In the scope of this paper the Knowledge Grid works as the external source of information, but the same principle could be applied to any information source.

Keywords: IP-based alert message system, Knowledge grid, Message-based System, Asynchronous communication.

1 Introduction

The original context of the topic discussed in this paper is management of disaster related knowledge in connection with serious accidents and catastrophes. In this kind of situation the availability of up-to-date information about the accident is important for the authorities as well as their opportunity to guide people in the accident area to survive in exceptional circumstances. A fast reaction to the situational knowledge is a precondition for successful rescue operations. It provides an opportunity to limit financial losses and human suffering. In the globalized world, major accidents and catastrophes are also becoming global – involving citizens of several countries. As a result, the interest in rescue operations and information distribution is also global. In many cases even the access to public knowledge – available on the Internet – is highly beneficial.

This paper is based on the long-term collaboration between the organizations of the authors – Tampere University of Technology (Finland), and NICT and Keio University (Japan). In addition, the research consortium covers partners from Germany, the Czech Republic, and Indonesia. The purpose of the joint research activity is to develop technologies and processes that improve the availability of knowledge in disasters. The kernel of this joint activity is the GRID

M. Yoshikawa et al. (Eds.): DASFAA 2010, LNCS 6193, pp. 434–444, 2010.

based distributed knowledge management platform. This system has the capacity to mine information items from public sources and authorities repositories, and combine individual information items to create valid knowledge to be utilized in the disaster context. Seamless – place, time, terminal independent, symmetric – access to the sources of knowledge is recognized as vital. This is supported by the Asynchronous Message-based Communication system that is being developed in this joint research activity. The system is based on open protocols and provides two-directional access between the terminals available in the disaster area and the services provided by the connection server. The upward direction may be utilized to transfer data, e.g. photos, data stream or measured data, from the accident area to the authorities, and the downward direction may be utilized to distribute information and guidance to the people in the accident area.

The wider context of the project related to this paper is the openness and interoperability of information systems based on the ideas of the Service Oriented Architecture (SOA) approach. It is based on standardized interfaces and protocols and deep understanding of complex processes crossing organizational borders. The inspiration for the project comes from the fact that every serious accident and catastrophe demands coordinated collaboration between several authorities that may also represent different nations and cultures. The knowledge repositories of authorities – legacy systems – are typically closed, unable to interoperate with each other and with open sources of knowledge. SOA-based interfaces would provide a safe and easily implementable solution to this problem. The Asynchronous Message-based communication protocol further extends access to registered service users using their mobile terminals to communicate with the integrated service architecture.

This paper introduces the results of the joint Finnish-Japanese research activity. The focus of the paper is to describe the integration of the systems designed and developed by the organizations of this paper's authors. The purpose of the integration is to promote the use of the both systems and act as a starting point for developing more features between the systems. Chapter 2 opens the discussion on the motivation to develop asynchronous message-based communication. Chapter 3 describes the IP-based message delivery system developed in the earlier research. Chapter 4 gives an overview of the main components of the extended system, Chapter 5 explains the operational logic of the system, and Chapter 6 includes the summary of the research.

2 Why Asynchronous Message-Based Communication?

The nature of a Knowledge Grid query is that it is unknown beforehand how long it will take. Processing the result may take any amount of time from a few seconds to a very long time. Opening and keeping the request open to the service provider until the result is received is not very efficient and ties up resources for the whole length of the request. There are a few ways to build asynchronous Web services to work around this issue. All listed methods have their own advantages and disadvantages. [10]

One of the approaches is to use one-way notifications between client and service provider. Also a few variations of request/reply operations can be used. The request/reply operations with polling requires the most simple client implementation as it does not need its own Web service but requires the client to implement the polling system to check the service provider periodically for results. It may also require more than one request to retrieve the response if the service provider has not yet completed the query. This approach provides a level of decoupling but leaves the responsibility of retrieving the results to the client.

As the processing time of the Knowledge Grid query may be unknown, it might be better to let the service provider handle the retrieval and sending of results. Both one-way notification and a simple request/reply operation can be used. The client is required to implement its own Web service, supply the endpoint address of this service so the service provider can send the results and supply correlation ID to identify the query. The disadvantages of this type of approach are that it requires quite a large amount of implementation. Also there may be difficulties for the service provider to reach the client when it needs to send the results. On the other hand, if the client is already acting as a Web service for someone else, typically most of the implementation, firewall configurations and so on have already been done. The advantages are a high level of decoupling and the fact that the client can just "fire and forget" the query and let the service provider handle the sending of the results.

One of the possible scenarios for the system could be a traveler or tourist, who uses the message delivery system for receiving travel news, advisories and alerts. When the traveler encounters some event, he or she may want to report that event to other users of the system. Also our traveler may want to know more detailed information on this kind of event. In this case a new Knowledge Grid query may be initiated. The data provided by the Knowledge Grid is background data on the requested subject (and not for example situational awareness data for an emergency), and as such a small delay in response is not critical. The client software may also poll the feeds at some predefined time interval, which means the information will not always be retrieved in real-time in either case.

3 IP-Based Knowledge Delivery System

The system described in this paper is based on the research published in paper [2]. The paper proposes a system architecture that can be used to provide alert messages to mobile and desktop clients using IP-based networks. The system uses a traditional Client/Server architecture and secure server approach [1]. The system offers two alternative messaging channels. The first messaging channel is an SOAP-based [4] synchronous bi-directional communication between the server and the client. The other channel is an Atom feed-based [3] information resource that can be retrieved by any kind of client from proprietary custom software to basic Really Simple Syndication (RSS) readers.

The fundamental idea of the system has been unaltered, but it has received more functionality. The original system concept used RSS-feeds and other information sources provided by trusted parties as resources. Messages from these

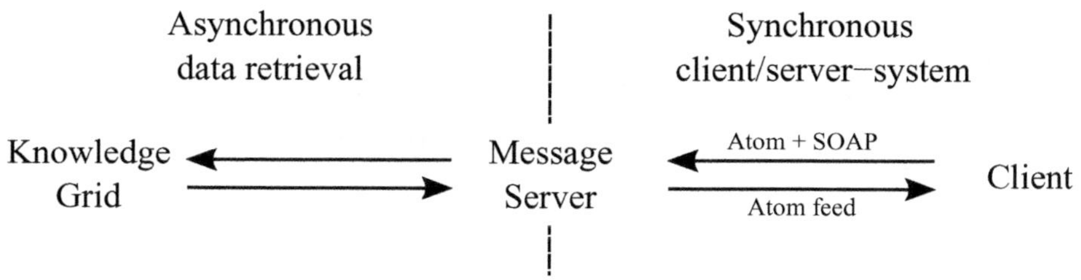

Fig. 1. Communication overview

sources were added to Atom feeds provided by the server or sent directly to clients depending on the use case. The system also offered the possibility for clients to add additional information to existing feeds. In this paper the approach is extended by adding a Knowledge Grid as an additional resource. The server has been added with the ability to process and respond to client generated messages and to relay clients requests to server-known information sources. In this paper, the designed server is called Message Server.

Figure 1 shows the Server/Client-system with the Knowledge Grid working as an additional information resource. The right side of the figure shows the communication between the clients and the Message Server. The feeds are pulled by the clients at some pre-defined time interval using standard HTTP GET commands and SOAP-messages are transferred using HTTP POST. In our use cases, the clients are users, but they could as well be automated sensors or any other kind of devices.

The original system proposal uses Common Alerting Protocol (CAP) [8] encapsulated in SOAP messages. CAP-messages are a standardized way for informing and alerting in emergency situations, but may be cumbersome for more casual messaging. Therefore we added a GeoRSS [5] extended Atom as a new message type. Though GeoRSS has multiple variations [6][7] and is not an official standard, we chose it because it is often used on the Internet and has a standard way of presenting coordinate data [9]. For our experiments, GeoRSS is a good starting point for testing of the system. Adding different kind of message types should be quite easy based on our experience of adding the GeoRSS message type. For more specific cases, a suitable message type should be created and used for better communication and messaging.

The left side shows the asynchronous communication between the Message Server and the Knowledge Grid. The communication is shown in the figure below to give a complete overview of the designed system and is explained in more detail in the following chapter.

4 Asynchronous Communication for a Knowledge-Based System

One of the design goals of accessing Knowledge Grid was to clearly separate the services of the Knowledge Grid and the Message Server. This approach has the

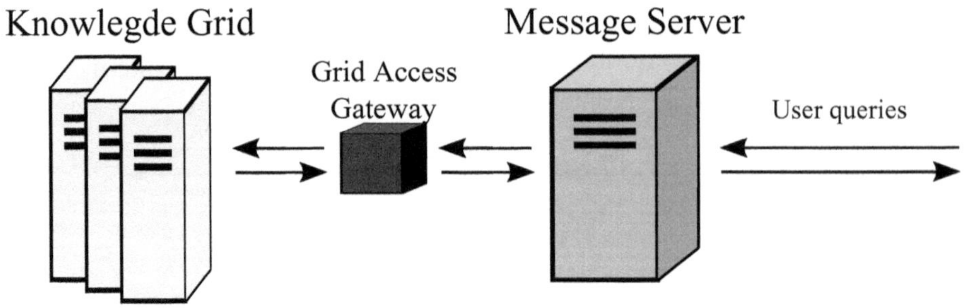

Fig. 2. Asynchronous communication

benefit of requiring both of the systems – Knowledge Grid and Message Server – to implement only the common interface for communication. The systems can be developed independently, and if needed the designed interfaces can be opened to provide additional services to third party clients and servers.

Figure 2 shows an overview of asynchronous communication. The Knowledge Grid and the implemented Grid Access Gateway which is needed to enable communications with the Knowledge Grid and Message Server are shown in the figure. These three components will be explained in more detail in the following section. In our implementation, the Knowledge Grid functioned as the external information source, but the same operational logic could be applied to any source including possible third party systems.

4.1 Knowledge Grid

Recently, a wide variety of knowledge items have been created by using collaborative environments in each community. Unfortunately, this knowledge is mainly utilized only for sharing information resources within each community.

An event affects various aspects of an area, field, or community. For example, in the case of a disaster, a secondary impact and secondary disaster may affect other areas such as the environment, economy, and healthcare. In order to understand the arbitrary concept, it is important to transfer significant knowledge related to accidental or irregular events to actual users from various knowledge bases.

References [11,12,13] have proposed a Knowledge Grid, which provides an infrastructure of acquisition, analysis, and delivery for knowledge sites. In particular, the interconnection method for knowledge bases has been presented by references [12,13]. This method provides the interconnection of heterogeneous knowledge based on the Knowledge Grid and representation of related concepts in heterogeneous fields. It navigates to related contents in these heterogeneous fields depending on the context. Furthermore, these knowledge bases that exist independently can be used more effectively when arranged.

This method represents a lot of different concepts with contents over the heterogeneous fields in a PC client. However, in the case of mobile devices, it is difficult to represent these related contents provided by the method, because a mobile device does not have a screen large enough to represent a lot of various related contents and the mobile user cannot wait for the computation of this method.

In order to solve these issues, it is important to realize asynchronization communications and the resulting delivery by streaming. It is necessary for mobile users to push the halfway result at any time to deliver the results which have been computed by deep analysis during a long processing time. A mobile device can receive the halfway result at any time and it can be presented to the user little by little. In this paper, we have developed asynchronized communication for the interconnection computation of heterogeneous knowledge based on the Knowledge Grid.

4.2 Grid Access Gateway

The Grid Access Gateway works as a common interface between the Message Server and the Knowledge Grid. The Message Server and the Knowledge Grid did not have mutually compatible interfaces, which meant that the design of a middleware between the two systems was necessary. One option would have been to change the interface of either the Knowledge Grid or the Message Server to include compatibility with the other system, but we decided to couple the systems as loosely as possible. This approach allowed the gateway to be developed separately, which also means that the gateway itself would work like any third party system connected to a server.

In its current implementation, the only function of the gateway is to provide simple message translation services. This means converting the messages forwarded by the Message Server to the format understood by the Knowledge Grid and vice versa. The Knowledge Grid messages – or more precisely replies to the forwarded user queries – are converted to the client message format and sent to the Message Server like any other message. In other words, the Grid Access Gateway works like an additional service for the server and like a basic client software.

4.3 Message Server

The original Message Server implementation functioned like a traditional web server and used basic transactions when transferring information to and from the clients. In a strict alert message relay this approach poses no problems, but by itself it does not include internal logic to handle asynchronous data transfers. In the case of an external information source that for some reason cannot send immediate responses to requests this causes a problem. Our solution was not to change the behavior of the Message Server, but to add to it a functionality to recognize and forward to other services user queries that included messages needing additional processing. This way the server could be kept as simple as possible, but still enable enhanced functionality to clients using the server.

If the chosen design is used, there is no need for a separate server interface for the responses of the forwarded queries. The receivers of the relayed requests can work as "clients" to the Message Server and send the responses as a normal message. This message is then processed normally by the server and added to a feed which can be read by other clients or forwarded to clients when needed. Depending on the case, the messages can also be sent directly to clients by the service that processed the request. The latter case will save server resources, but on the other hand it may be easier for the users if they receive all the messages from the same source, and that all the services seem to be offered by the same party.

Relaying the requests also simplifies the addition of new services to the Message Server as it is not necessary to modify the server to understand all the possible different kinds of service responses. The downside of this approach is that the responses that can be added to the servers feeds are limited to the message types recognized by the server. For text-based information relay this should not pose a problem, but for more complex data types – like video or audio – a different approach must be taken. One possible solution could be to provide a link to the data and host the content on another location, which would also reduce the network load on the Message Server. Another option would be to encode the data inside the XML using for example Multipurpose Internet Mail Extensions (MIME).

5 Implementation and Usage Scenarios

In this implementation, encryption is not used by default. Encryption can be enabled if required by the user, but as long as the messages are considered to be casual user-to-user messages, encryption is not necessary. One possible encryption method is for example Transport Layer Security/Secure Socket Layer (TLS/SSL).

Accessing the data in external sources requires the user to type in the query by using special markup recognized by the Message Server. The query can be written to any message type (for example CAP or GeoRSS) and to any element that is allowed by the type to have a clear text description. We chose to use regular expressions to match and extract the query from the message. This gives the possibility to define the query syntax flexibly. The following regular expression is the currently used in our implementation:

Regular expression for matching and extracting the query

```
(\w|\-)+(\?\?)(\w|\s)+(\,(\w|\s)+)*\.
```

The syntax consists of five sections: target, double question marks, method, parameter(s), and end sign. Basically target, method and parameter consist of alphanumeric characters. In addition to this, the target may consist of character "-". The method and the parameter may additionally have whitespace characters. The target is always followed by double question marks. The target method and parameters are separated with a comma, and the end sign is a period. An example of a external query shown below:

Example syntax for invoking external query

```
nict-kcs??article_query,EnvironmentNews,Tokyo,Hurricane.
```

Target in this example is "nict-kcs" and method is "article_query". After the method there is three more parameters: context, place and keyword and values are "EnvironmentNews", "Tokyo" and "Hurricane" respectively. Interpretation of the query would be that user wants NICT's Knowledge Grid to provide some kind of information (articles) about hurricanes around the Tokyo area in the context of environment news.

To reduce the need for memorizing the full syntax, the user does not need to fill in all the parameter(s) and can let the client or Message Server software fill in the missing parameters. For example, if the full method call requires a target, target method and parameters which are context, datetime, place and keyword, the Server software could accept queries with only target, place and keyword. The remainder of the required parameters would be filled in automatically using default values. How and which parameters are requested from the user depends on the service that needs to be invoked and on the client software used.

Based on the given target and the function, the Message Server can relay the request to the actual service provider. The server itself does not process the parameters. This way the server only needs a list of valid targets and their real location, for example the IP address and the function that should be called on the target. Based on the given information the server creates a simple SOAP-encapsulated message targeted to the requested function. The message includes the unprocessed parameters, unique identifier, URI, function and XML namespace information. The identifier can be used by the server to match service responses to specific requests. The servers URI, function and namespace used by the XML are provided to services in order to make returning the results possible. Just like the messages between the server and the clients, the messages between the server and the service providers can be encrypted when required.

5.1 Usage Scenarios

Information retrieval from the Knowledge Grid is divided into two phases, creating the Knowledge Grid query and receiving the results. Figure 3 shows a simplified sequence diagram of creating a Knowledge Grid query. In fact, the Knowledge Grid and the Grid Access Gateway shown in the figure are interchangeable as the user-made query can be directed to basically any other kind of service. These use cases are applying the Knowledge Grid and the Article query as an example. The users query is basically a query for the articles that are related to the context and keywords that the user is interested in, hence the terms "Article query" and "Article feed" which contains the results of the query.

The use case begins when the user creates a *New message*. This new message is then added to the Message Server's own feed database and can then be read by other users. If the message contains the query syntax described in section 5, the Message Server will then generate a corresponding query to the target specified by the user. In this case, this is the *Article query* in the figure. The target of the

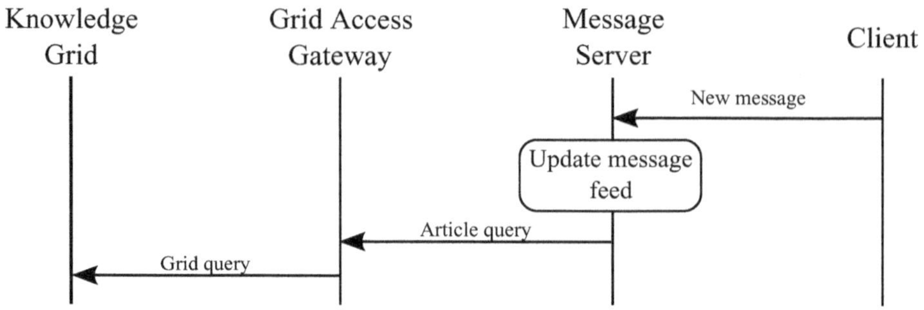

Fig. 3. Creating a new Knowledge Grid query

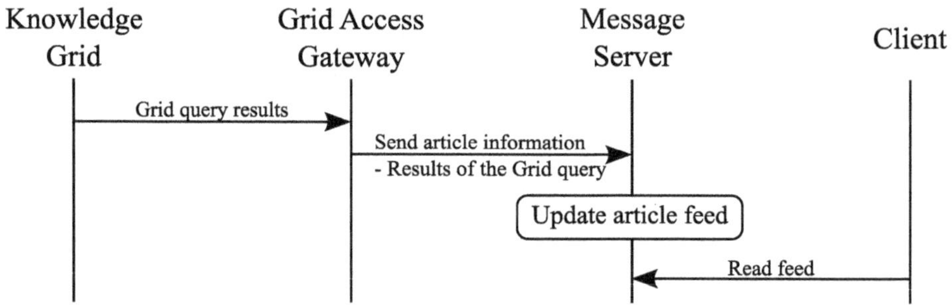

Fig. 4. Receiving the results of the Knowledge Grid query

query, the Knowledge Grid, has a Web service interface to provide the article information. This is the target where the query should be sent by the Message Server. When the Grid Access Gateway receives the query, it will create a *Grid query* which starts processing on the Knowledge Grid.

The second use case – receiving the results of the Knowledge Grid query – is shown in Figure 4. The Grid Access Gateway periodically checks for the status of the grid query and, if the Knowledge Grid has processed the results, they will be returned to the Grid Access Gateway. After this, the Grid Access Gateway will add identification data to the result and send it back to the original caller. The original caller may then process the information received, like in our example, the update article feed. This phase will be repeated until the Knowledge Grid announces to the Grid Access Gateway that there will be no more results.

Users may read the article feed at any point after the initial article query has been made. At first the feed will be empty, but once the Knowledge Grid has processed and returned some results, the feed will be updated and the items in it will increase.

6 Summary

This paper presented a simple operational logic that allows connecting a synchronous Client/Server system with an additional information source or service that requires asynchronous communications. The paper described the required changes on the server side and the use cases involved in forwarding messages from user queries to the Knowledge Grid and returning the replies to the users. In the designed system, the Grid Access Gateway was used to transform message formats between the Message Server and the Knowledge Grid.

In future research, the designed system – including the Message Server, Knowledge Grid and client software – will be further modified to handle a wider range of message types. The research will also concentrate more on general messaging and less on pure alert message delivery. This will include researching the presentation of Knowledge Grid data to an end user who is using a mobile device.

Acknowledgments

This work is partially funded by the Finnish Funding Agency for Technology and Innovation (Tekes) Seamless Services and Mobile Connectivity in Disaster Knowledge Management (SSMC/DDKM) research project and the Academy of Finland UbiKnowS project. In SSCM/DDKM the work is based on the memorandum of understanding – "mobile knowledge management architecture" between Tampere University of Technology (TUT) and the National Institute of Information and Communications Technology (NICT).

References

1. Botterell, A.: An Advanced EAS Relay Network Using the Common Alerting Protocol, White Paper (2003)
2. Sillberg, P., Rantanen, P., Saari, M., Leppäniemi, J., Soini, J., Jaakkola, H.: Towards an IP Based Alert Message Delivery System. In: Information Systems for Crisis Response and Management Conference, Gothenburg, Sweden (2009)
3. The Atom Syndication Format, RFC 4287, `http://www.ietf.org/rfc/rfc4287.txt`
4. SOAP Version 1.2, W3C Recommendation (April 27, 2007), `http://www.w3.org/TR/soap12`
5. GeoRSS Wiki, `http://www.georss.org/`
6. GeoRSS encodings, GeoRSS Wiki, `http://www.georss.org/Encodings`
7. W3C Geospatial Vocabularity, W3C Incubator Group Report October 23 (2007), `http://www.w3.org/2005/Incubator/geo/XGR-geo-20071023/`
8. Common Alerting Protocol v1.1, OASIS Emergency Management TC, `http://www.oasisopen.org/committees/download.php/14759/emergency-CAPv1.1.pdf`
9. World Geodetic System 84 (WGS 84), Implementation manual, version 2.4, World Geodetic System (1998)
10. IBM Developer Works, Asynchronous operations and Web services, Part 2, `http://www.ibm.com/developerworks/webservices/library/ws-asynch2`
11. Zettsu, K., Nakanishi, T., Iwazume, M., Kidawara, Y., Kiyoki, Y.: Knowledge Cluster Systems for Knowledge Sharing. In: Analysis and Delivery among Remote Sites, Information Modelling and Knowledge Bases, vol. 19, pp. 282–289. IOS Press, Amsterdam (2008)

12. Nakanishi, T., Zettsu, K., Kidawara, Y., Kiyoki, Y.: Towards Interconnective Knowledge Sharing and Provision for Disaster Information Systems -Approaching to Sidoarjo Mudflow Disaster in Indonesia. In: Proc. of The 3rd Information and Communication Technology Seminar (ICTS 2007), Surabaya, Indonesia, pp. 332–339 (2007)
13. Nakanishi, T., Zettsu, K., Kidawara, Y., Kiyoki, Y.: Approaching to Interconnection of Heterogeneous Knowledge Bases on a Knowledge Grid. In: Proc. of The International Conference on Semantics, Knowledge and Grid (SKG 2008), Beijing, China, pp. 71–78 (2008)

Providing Scalable Data Services in Ubiquitous Networks

Tanu Malik[1,*], Raghvendra Prasad[2], Sanket Patil[3], Amitabh Chaudhary[4], and Venkat Venkatasubramanian[5]

[1] Cyber Center
[2] Dept. of Computer Science
Purdue University, USA
[3] Dept. of Computer Science
IIIT, Bangalore, India
[4] Dept. of Computer Science and Enggineering
University of Notre Dame, USA
[5] School of Chemical Engineering
Purdue University, USA
tmalik@cs.purdue.edu

Abstract. Topology is a fundamental part of a network that governs connectivity between nodes, the amount of data flow and the efficiency of data flow between nodes. In traditional networks, due to physical limitations, topology remains static for the course of the network operation. Ubiquitous data networks (UDNs), alternatively, are more adaptive and can be configured for changes in their topology. This flexibility in controlling their topology makes them very appealing and an attractive medium for supporting "anywhere, any place" communication. However, it raises the problem of designing a dynamic topology. The dynamic topology design problem is of particular interest to application service providers who need to provide cost-effective data services on a ubiquitous network. In this paper we describe algorithms that decide when and how the topology should be reconfigured in response to a change in the data communication requirements of the network. In particular, we describe and compare a greedy algorithm, which is often used for topology reconfiguration, with a non-greedy algorithm based on metrical task systems. Experiments show the algorithm based on metrical task system has comparable performance to the greedy algorithm at a much lower reconfiguration cost.

1 Introduction

In the vision of pervasive computing, users will exchange information and control their environments from anywhere using various wireline/wireless networks and computing devices [1]. Although such a definition of pervasive computing is very appealing to users, it has been reported that the technological path for building such an anytime, anywhere networking environment is less clear [2]. A primary technical issue is the configuration of the topology between nodes and devices [3], [2]. Traditional computing environments such as the Internet, the native routing infrastructure is fixed and the

* Contact Author.

M. Yoshikawa et al. (Eds.): DASFAA 2010, LNCS 6193, pp. 445–457, 2010.

topology is predominantly static. However in large-scale pervasive computing environments, the topology is mostly deployed and maintained by application service providers (ASPs) who contract with underlying ISPs and buy network bandwidth between nodes to provide value-added network services to end-systems. Thus they can maintain a more dynamic and flexible topology.

We are interested in understanding how and when a topology should be configured in order to support distributed data management services. These services can be in the form of replica or a caching service provided by an ASP in which nodes (both wired and wireless) acquire and disseminate data. In a pervasive computing environment, configuring a topology to support such a distributed data service can be challenging. Firstly, nodes and devices have limited resources [1]. The resource limitation is often due to restricted buffer sizes and storage capacities at nodes, limited bandwidth availability between nodes or limited number of network connections that a node can support. An optimal usage of limited resources requires a topology design that routes the flow of data through most cost-efficient paths. Secondly, the data communication pattern of clients may change drastically over time [1], [3]. This may require a topology that quickly adapts to the change in data requirements.

While the flexibility of reconfiguring a topology as data communication patterns change is essential, reconfiguring a topology every time a communication pattern changes may not be beneficial. Changing network topology is not cost-free: it incurs both management overhead as well as potential disruption of end-to-end flows. Additionally, data in transit may get lost, delayed, or erroneously routed. In the presence of these costs, it might be useful to monitor changes in the communication pattern at for every query request but the topology should only be changed if the long term benefits of making a change justifies the cost of the change.

In this paper, we are most interested in the dynamic topology design problem, *i.e.*, the problem of determining how and when to reconfigure a topology in a resource-constrained pervasive computing environment in which data communication patterns change dynamically. We describe this problem in Section 3. In Sections 3.1 and 3.2 respectively, we describe the operational costs of satisfying a demand pattern in a given topology and the cost of reconfiguring between two topologies. To calculate operational costs on a graph, we describe a linear-programming based solution.

In Section 4, we describe the algorithms that decides when and how to reconfigure. We first describe a greedy algorithm, which is a natural, first-order algorithm that one would choose for deciding when to reconfigure. We then describe a non-greedy algorithm based on metrical task systems [4]. Task systems are general systems that capture the cost of reconfiguration between two states in addition to the cost of satisfying a given demand in a given state. By including the reconfiguration cost the system prevents oscillations into states that are sub-optimal in the long run. The distinguishing part is that task system based algorithms require no statistical modeling or aggregation of the communication requirements from the service provider. This lack of making any assumptions about how the communication requirements may change over time allows the algorithm to provide a minimum level of guarantee of adapting to changes in the communication requirement. Greedy algorithms on the other hand are heuristic and provide no theoretical evidence or a systematic way of understanding when to change a topology. We evaluate the performance of all algorithms in Section 5 and conclude in Section 6.

2 Related Work

The topology design problem has received significant interest in large information systems such as optical networks, data-centric peer-to-peer networks, and more recently complex networks. In these systems the objective is to design an optimal topology under arbitrary optimality requirements of efficiency, cost, balance of load on the servers and robustness to failures. The design of an optimal topology is obtained by deriving these measures from past usage patterns and then using network simulation to obtain an optimal topology. Such simulations, extensively described in [5], [6], are often based on neural networks and genetic algorithms and in which optimal topologies are obtained after executing the software for several hours. The premise is that once an optimal topology is chosen then it will remain static for the duration of the network operation.

In most adaptive networks such as ubiquitous networks [1] and overlay networks [7], communication pattens vary so significantly that it is often difficult to obtain an representative usage pattern to perform a simulation. In the past [6], research proposed to perform simulation repeatedly to obtain an optimal topology and the system reconfigures itself. However, in these systems communication patterns are aggregated over large time scales and the reconfiguration is slow. Recently [8] adaptive networks have focused on auto-configuration [9] in which systems self-monitor the communication requirements and reconfigure the topology when communication patterns change drastically. The dynamic topology problem has been recently studied in the context of overlay networks in which topologies can be designed either in the favor of native networks, which improves performance or the ultimate customers which reduces the operation cost of the whole system [10]. While our problem is similar to theirs, our context and cost metrics are different: We study the dynamic topology problem in the context of ubiquitous environment in which nodes and devices have limited resources and communication requirements change arbitrarily.

Given an optimal topology and a stable communication pattern, the problem of determining how to use the edges of the topology such that the cost of using the topology is minimized is itself an intractable problem. Several versions of the problem have been studied in computer networks under the class of multi-commodity flow problems [11], [10]. In this paper, for simplicity, we have restricted ourselves to single commodity flows [12] which is a suitable model when considering communication requirements over a set of replica nodes. Our primary focus is to understand how to adaptively move between optimal topologies when communication patterns change dynamically.

3 Minimizing the Cost of Data Sharing in a UDN

We consider a ubiquitous computing environment established by an application service provider to provide data sharing services across the network. The provider, strategically, places replicas on the network to disseminate data. Clients (which can be wired or wireless) make connections to one of the replicas and send queries to it. The query results in a variable amount of data being transfered from the replica to the client. Query results are routed according to the topology of the network. The application service provider pays for the usage of the network, i.e., the total amount of data that passes through the network per unit of time. The service provider would like to use those edges of the topology through which the cost of transferring the data is minimized subject to data flow constraints over the network. We now state the problem formally.

Let the topology, T, be represented by a graph $G = (V, E)$ in which V denotes the set of all nodes in the network and E denotes the set of all edges. Let there be P replicas and C clients on the network such that $P \cup C \subseteq V$ and $P \cap C = \emptyset$. Each edge $e \in E$ in the topology T has a cost c_e which is the cost of sending unit data (1 byte) through each pair of nodes. Let b_e denote the maximum amount of bytes that can be sent on any edge. Each client, C_i receives an online sequence of queries $\sigma_{C_i} = (q_1, \ldots, q_n)$. The data requirement of each query, q_i, is assumed equivalent to its result size. We denote the data communication requirements of all clients by $\sigma = (\sigma_{C_i}, \ldots, \sigma_{C_M})$.

A topology T is chosen from a feasible set of topologies. Given $|V|$ nodes, theoretically, there are a total of $2^{|V|(|V|-1)/2}$ possible topologies. However, not all of these topologies are desirable in practice. A topology is usually required to be connected so that every node remains in contact with the rest of the network. In addition a topology may be either symmetric (regular graph) or scale-free [13]. In a symmetric topology nodes have nearly identical degree distributions and share uniform load. In scale-free topologies some of the nodes act as "super nodes" and have a relatively larger load than other nodes. Scale-free topologies have increasingly been shown to be a better design choice for peer-to-peer data networks [6], [5]. To take into account the effect of symmetric and scale-free topologies, we assign a factor, $\rho \in [0, 1]$, for a topology which measures the skew in degree distribution [6]. ρ is defined as:

$$\rho = 1 - \frac{|V|\,(\hat{p} - \bar{p})}{(|V| - 1)(|V| - 2)} \tag{1}$$

in which $\hat{p}$ is the maximum degree in the graph and $\bar{p}$ is the average degree of the graph. Thus ρ is 0 for a scale-free topology such as a star and 1 for a symmetric topology such as a circle. We denote the set of all feasible topologies, which have a given ρ, by 0-1 adjacency matrices $\mathcal{T}_\rho = T_1, T_2, \ldots, T_N$.

Finally, a topology reconfiguration algorithm is the sequence of topologies $T = (T_1, \ldots, T_n), T_i \in \mathcal{T}$ used by the UDN over time in response to the communication requirement, σ, changing over time. The total cost is defined as

$$cost(\sigma, T) = \sum_{i=1}^{n} \sigma(T_i) + \sum_{i=0}^{n-1} d(T_i, T_{i+1}), \tag{2}$$

in which the first term is the sum of costs of satisfying data requirement of all clients σ under the corresponding topology and the second term is the sum of costs of transitioning between topologies in T. In the first term costs under a given topology are calculated under the assumption that data communication pattern remains static. The second term is the cost of reconfiguring a topology. Note, if $T_{i+1} = T_i$ there is no real change in the topology schedule and incurred reconfiguration cost is zero.

The total cost equation is minimized by an algorithm which generates the best topology schedule T. This requires an algorithm to identify when demand characteristics have changed significantly such that the current physical design is no longer optimal and choosing a new topology such that excessive costs are not incurred in moving from the current topology, relative to the benefit. An offline algorithm that knows the entire σ obtains a configuration schedule S with the minimum cost and is optimal. An adaptive algorithm, determines $T = (T_0, ..., T_n)$ without seeing the complete workload $\sigma = (q_1, ..., q_n)$ and works in an online fashion. We first describe the cost estimation functions which can be used by any algorithm and then describe algorithms which decide when and how to configure.

3.1 The Topology Problem under Static Communication Pattern

When the data communication pattern is static, the system will remain in that topology that minimizes the cost of satisfying the pattern. We describe a linear-programming based solution for measuring the cost of satisfying a data communication pattern over a given topology. Given an edge in a topology T, recall that the cost of flowing a unit amount of data through that edge is c_e and the maximum amount of bytes that can be sent on any edge is b_e. If f_e is the amount of bytes that flow through this edge in order to satisfy the communication requirement at a client, then the overall cost to support communication requirement of all clients is the cost of flowing data through all the edges which is defined as

$$\sum_{e \in E} |f_e| \cdot c_e \tag{3}$$

This cost must be minimized to subject to the following constraints:

- The flow in an edge should not exceed its capacity and there is no excess reverse flow in an edge.

$$\forall e = (u, v) \in E : f_{u,v} = -f_{v,u} \textit{ and } |f_e| \leq b_e \tag{4}$$

- The replica nodes do not request data.

$$\forall p \in P, \forall\ u\ \in \textit{neighbors of } p : f_{u,p} \leq 0 \tag{5}$$

- If the communication requirement at each client is static and equals σ_{C_i} then the entire requirement is satisfied:

$$\forall c \in C : \sum_{u \in \textit{ neighbors of } c} f_{u,c} = \sigma_{C_i} \tag{6}$$

- The skew in the flow of data should correspond to the skew in the topology ρ. For this, we also restrict the number of bytes passing through each node $b_u, u \in V$.

$$\rho = max(b_u) - \frac{\sum_u b_u}{|V|}, \tag{7}$$

where $\forall u \in V : b_u = \frac{\sum_{v \in neighbor\ of\ u} |f_{vu}|}{2}$

If the data were routed through using minimum-operation-cost paths, the static topology design problem is the problem of finding a topology T , under the constraints of connectivity and degree-bound, that can minimize the cost in Equation 3 for a communication requirement σ that remains constant over time. We term such a topology, optimal-static topology for σ, and denote it by $T^*(\sigma)$. Similar to most other topological design problems, the static topology design problem can be modeled as a linear programming problem and can be solved efficiently in the worst case.

3.2 The Reconfiguration Cost

Every time the system reconfigures its topology to adapt to changes in communication requirements, a reconfiguration cost is incurred. This cost is the overhead or the impairment to performance incurred by the transition from one topology to another. Various costs could be incurred during a topology reconfiguration, depending on the implementation details of the UDN. For example, establishing and changing links incurs control and management overhead which can be translated to energy costs in a wireless network or costs paid to ISPs in a wired network or a combination of both in wired/wireless setting [8]. Any fraction of data in transit during topology reconfiguration is subject to routing disturbance leading to a rerouting overhead. Depending on the UDN implementation, when topologies change, data in transit may wander through a path with a high operation cost. Finally, rerouting overhead can be magnified at the end-systems.

In this paper, we assume reconfiguration costs as the cost of auto-configuring the entire network. Configuring a network involves first establishing basic IP-level parameters such as IP addresses and addresses of key servers and then automatic distribution of these IP configuration parameters in the entire network [9]. In the wired networking environment, protocols such as Dynamic Host Configuration Protocol (DHCP) [14] and Mobile IP [15] can configure individual hosts. In the pervasive environments, Dynamic Configuration Distribution Protocol (DCDP) is a popular protocol for auto-configuration [2]. In DCDP, auto-configuration is done by recursively splitting the address pool down a spanning tree formed out of the graph topology. Thus the total configuration cost of the network is essentially proportional to the height of the spanning tree. A general approximate measure for the reconfiguration cost is the total number of links that need to be changed during a transition

$$d(T_{old}, T_{new}) = \sum W.(g(T_{old}) + g(T_{new})) \tag{8}$$

in which $g(\cdot)$ is the auto-configuration cost and is proportional to the height of the spanning tree in each topology and W is weight parameter that converts this cost in terms of operation costs.

4 The Topology Reconfiguration Problem with Dynamic Data Requirements

In a real-world, client nodes receive a sequence, σ, of queries, in which the size of the query result differs. Thus the amount of data delivered from the replica to the client changes over time. In such a dynamic scenario no one topology remains optimal and a reconfiguration of topology is needed. In this section, we first describe a greedy algorithm which specifies *when* the topology should be reconfigured by looking at the past workload. We consider several variations of this algorithm by considering different lengths of consideration of the past period. In several environments, request for data is bursty in that arbitrarily large amounts of data are requested over short periods of time. For such environments, it is difficult to ascertain the length of the past period precisely. We describe a more conservative algorithm based on metrical task systems [4]. Algorithms in task systems achieve a minimum level of performance for any workload and provide guarantees on the total cost of satisfying data demands and making transitions.

Greedy Algorithm: Such an algorithm chooses between neighboring topologies greedily. The current topology ranks its neighboring topologies based on past costs of the communication requirement in the other topologies. The algorithm keeps track of the cumulative penalty of remaining in the current topology relative to every other neighboring topology for each incoming data demand. A transition is made once the algorithm observes that the benefit of a new configuration exceeds a threshold. The threshold is defined as the sum of the costs of the most recent transition and next transition that needs to be made. There are various policies of choosing the length of the past interval:

- A reactive policy: The system transitions to another topology every time the cost of satisfying the demand in the current topology is higher than the sum of cost of transitioning and the cost of satisfying the demand in another topology. Thus the system may potentially transition on every input of the demand request.
- A lazy policy: The system is slow in transitioning in that it waits for a delta period before deciding to transition to another topology. Thus the system transitions to another topology when the total cost of satisfying demand in a δ period is lower than the cost of transitioning and satisfying it in the current topology. The reactive and lazy policies are memoryless in that the policy does not take into account the past demand patterns.
- An averaging policy: This policy remembers the demand pattern by considering a demand that is averaged over several δ periods using a weighting scheme. The system switches to that topology which has the lowest cost of executing the averaged demand.

A conservative algorithm: Our conservative policy is based on task systems [4]. We first consider a task system in which there are only two possible toplogies. A conservative algorithm in such a system works similar to the algorithm for the online ski-rental problem. A skier, who doesn't own skis, needs to decide before every skiing trip that she makes whether she should rent skis for the trip or buy them. If she decides to buy skis, she will not have to rent for this or any future trips. Unfortunately, she doesn't know how many ski trips she will make in future, if any. A well known on-line algorithm for this problem is rent skis as long as the total paid in rental costs does not match or exceed the purchase cost, then buy for the next trip. Irrespective of the number of future trips, the cost incurred by this online algorithm is at most twice of the cost incurred by the optimal offline algorithm. If there were only two topologies and the cost function $d(\cdot)$

satisfies symmetry, the reconfiguration problem will be nearly identical to online ski rental. Staying in the current topology corresponds to renting skis and transitioning to another topology corresponds to buying skis. Since the algorithm can start a ski-rental in any of the states, it can be argued that this leads to an conservative policy on two states that costs no more than four times the offline optimal.

When there are more than two topologies the key issue is to decide which topology to compare with the current one. This will establish a correspondence with the online ski rental problem. A well-known algorithm for the N-state task system is by Borodin et. al. [4]. Their algorithm assumes the state space of all topologies to form a metric which allows them to define a *traversal* over N topologies. We show that our reconfiguration function is indeed a metric function and then describe the algorithm.

To form a metric space, the reconfiguration function should satisfy the following properties:

- $d(T_i, T_j) \geq 0, \forall i \neq j, T_i, T_j \in \mathcal{T}$ (positivity),
- $d(T_i, T_i) = 0, \forall i \in \mathcal{T}$ (reflexivity),
- $d(T_i, T_j) + d(T_j, T_k) \geq d(T_i, T_k), \forall\, T_i, T_j, T_k \in \mathcal{T}$ (triangle inequality), and
- $d(T_i, T_j) = d(T_j, T_i), \forall\, T_i, T_j \in \mathcal{T}$ (symmetry).

In our case the reconfiguration function $d(\cdot)$ depends upon the sum of reconfiguration costs in the old (T_i) and the new topology (T_j). Reconfiguration costs are primarily determined by the height of spanning tree over the topologies 3.2 and thus satisfy all the above properties.

When the costs are symmetrical, Borodin et. al. [4] use *components* instead of configurations to perform an online ski rental. In particular their algorithm recursively traverses one component until the query execution cost incurred in that component is approximately that of moving to the other component, moving to the other component and traversing it (recursively), returning to the first component (and completing the

Input: Graph: $G'(V, E)$ with weights corresponding to $d(\cdot)$, Query Sequence: σ
Output: Vertex Sequence to process $\sigma(t)$: $u_0, u_1, \ldots$
Let $B(V, E)$ be the graph G' modified s.t. $\forall (u, v) \in E$ weight $d_B(u, v) \leftarrow d'_G(u, v)$ rounded to next highest power of 2;
Let F be a minimum spanning tree on B;
$\mathcal{T} \leftarrow \mathsf{traversal}(F)$;
$u \leftarrow S_0$;
while *there is a query q to process* **do**
    $c \leftarrow q(u)$;
    Let v be the node after u in $\mathcal{T}$;
    while $c \geq d_B(u, v)$ **do**
        $c \leftarrow c - d_B(u, v)$;
        $u \leftarrow v$;
        $v \leftarrow$ the node after v in $\mathcal{T}$;
    end
    Process q in u;
end

Algorithm 1. A Task System-based Algorithm

Input: Tree: $F(V, E)$
Output: Traversal for F: $\mathcal{T}$
if $E = \{\}$ **then**
| $\mathcal{T} \leftarrow \{\}$;
else if $E = \{(u, v)\}$ **then**
| Return $\mathcal{T}$: Start at u, traverse to v, traverse back to u;
else
| Let (u, v) be a maximum weight edge in E, with weight 2^M;
| On removing (u, v) let the resulting trees be $F_1(V_1, E_1)$ and $F_2(V_2, E_2)$, where $u \in V_1$, and $v \in V_2$;
| Let maximum weight edges in E_1 and E_2 have weights 2^{M_1} and 2^{M_2} respectively;
| $\mathcal{T}_1 \leftarrow \mathsf{traversal}(F_1)$;
| $\mathcal{T}_2 \leftarrow \mathsf{traversal}(F_2)$;
| Return $\mathcal{T}$: Start at u, follow $\mathcal{T}_1$ 2^{M-M_1} times, traverse (u, v), follow $\mathcal{T}_2$ 2^{M-M_2} times, traverse (v, u);
end

Algorithm 2. $\mathsf{traversal}(F)$

cycle) and so on. To determine components, they consider a complete, undirected graph $G'(V, E)$ on $\mathcal{T}$ in which V represents the set of all configurations, E represents the transitions, and the edge weights are the transition costs. By fixing a minimum spanning tree (MST) on G', components are recursively determined by pick the maximum weight edge, say (u, v), in the MST, removing it from the MST. This partitions all the configurations into two smaller components and the MST into two smaller trees. The traversal is defined in Algorithm 2. In [16], the algorithm is shown to have a performance that is atmost $8(N - 1)$ worse than the performance of an offline algorithm (one that has complete knowledge of σ).

5 Experiments

Our current objective is to get a validation of our policies and algorithms through a simulated environment. Thus while our set-up is a representation of a real-world pervasive environment, doing experiments with real data is part of future work. Our setup simulates a replica environment with 10 replicas and a large number of clients i.e., 40 and 90. Thus the total number of nodes, $|V|$, is 50 and 100. To determine the feasible set of topologies that are connected and have a given skew in degree distribution, ρ, we adopt the following procedure: For a given graph, we fix the maximum node degree $\hat{p}$ and the average degree of the graph, $\bar{p}$. This determines the acceptable skew in the degree distribution. We input different values of N, $\hat{p}$, and $\bar{p}$ as parameters to a random graph generator and generate a large number of initial graphs. The generated graphs have no self-loops. In addition, graphs that are disconnected are filtered out as well as graphs that have nodes with less than $\bar{p}$ degree. We assign a cost matrix and an edge capacity matrix with each topology. We choose a set of 100 feasible topologies with a ρ of 0.9. The cost values and the edge capacity values are random values chosen in the range of [100,150] and [50,80] respectively.

The clients receive an on-line query sequence in which each query results in d amount of data from the replica. We are not concerned with the actual syntax of the query but the amount of data it generates on the network. We generate the demand sequence at each client from a normal distribution in which the mean changes as a Markov process. In particular, the change in the value of the mean is done after fixed number of time steps and the change in the value is done using a standard exponential moving average. To model the real world pervasive environment, each client also receives a burst in its demand modeled by a sudden impulse generated randomly for each client. Finally, a sequence of 20,000 events is generated in which data demand at each client is random value in the range [0.1, 100].

We use the GAMS [17] software to solve the static optimal topology problem. GAMS offers an environment to express mathematical constructs of a linear program. It solves the linear program and returns the optimal flow of data, $f_{u,v}$, on a topology. We use the optimal flows returned by GAMS to calculate the operation costs of satisfying a given set of client demands in a given topology. Reconfigurations costs are calculated by the topology structure, the height of the spanning tree varies from 40-200 and by choosing a W parameter that converts reconfiguration cost in terms of operation costs. We choose W as 200. To perform all these simulations, we developed a Python based system that acts as both an event driven simulator and also a simulator for performing experiments on a UDN. The delta period in the greedy algorithm is chosen to be 50. The MST in the conservative algorithm is implemented using Prim's algorithm.

5.1 Cost of Reconfiguration

We compute the total cost of satisfying a query sequence under a topology schedule generated by various policies of the greedy algorithm (Policies `P1-P3`) and the non-greedy algorithm `P4`. We compare the total cost of adaptive policies with a policy, `P5`, that does not change its topology at all but remains in a topology that has the minimum operation cost for the entire demand sequence. We also compare with a static optimal policy `P6` that knows the entire demand sequence in advance. Figure 1(a) and Figure 1(b) shows the total cost and its division into operational cost and the cost of transitioning between topologies.

`P4` improves on the total cost of `P5` by 38%. This is a very encouraging result for pervasive environments where devices are resource-constrained and policies that improve operation costs are needed. However, `P3` further improves cost by 42%. This is because `P3` relies on the predictive modeling of the demand. However, the improvement is low considering that `P4` is general and makes no assumptions regarding workload access patterns. The costs of both `P3` and `P4` are comparable to the cost of `P6`. Both `P1` and `P2` incur high costs. `P1` suffers due to being over-reactive making changes even when they are not required and incurs a very high transition cost. `P2`, by its nature, incurs lower transition costs but high operation costs. On the other hand `P4` incurs much lower transition costs than `P3`. This artifact is due to the conservative nature of `P4`. It evaluates only two alternatives at a time and transitions only if it expects significant performance advantages. On the other hand, `P3` responds quicker to workload changes by evaluating all candidate topologies simultaneously and choosing a topology that benefits the most recent sequence of queries. This optimism of `P3` is tolerable in this workload but can account for significant transition costs in workloads that change even more rapidly.

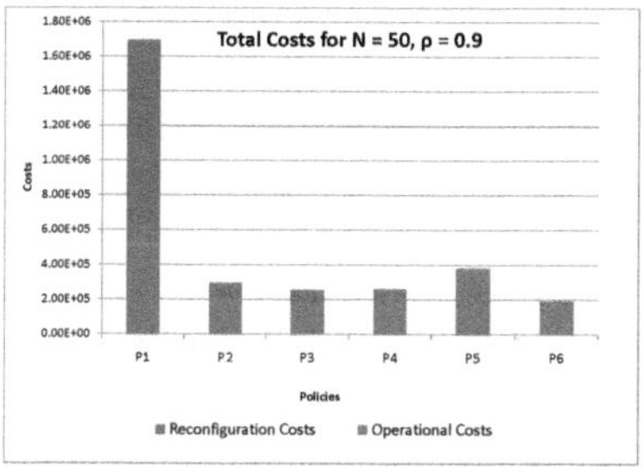

(a) N = 50

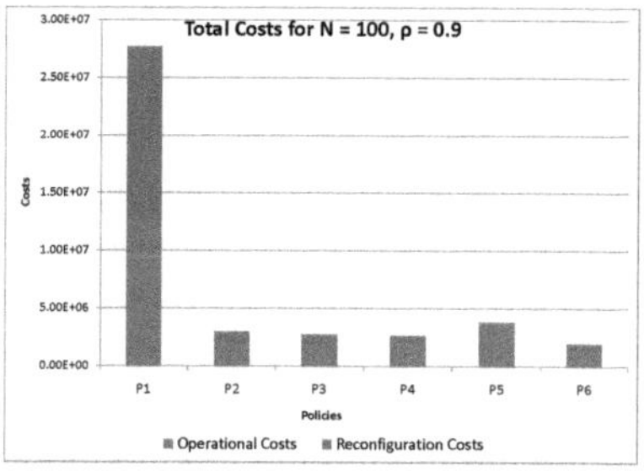

(b) N = 100

Fig. 1. Total operational and reconfiguration costs

5.2 Quality of a Schedule

In this experiment, we compare the quality of a schedule generated over the length of the sequence. We determine the quality of a schedule by comparing the policies with a static optimal policy `P6` that knows the entire demand sequence in advance. For presentation sake (Figure 2(a)), we omit showing the schedule of `P1` as it makes so many transitions over the sequence that it affects the presentation of other policies. We also omit `P5` as it has only one topology in a schedule. We also show the schedule adopted by a policy over 1000 requests as showing over the entire demand sequence suppresses interesting behavior. Results over other demand requests are similar. The experiment is performed over a 50 node topology with W = 2000 and $\rho = 0.9$. Figure shows that `P4` closely follows the static optimal policy, which is an artifact of its conservative nature. `P3` makes lot more transitions than `P4` because it quickly reacts to changes in workload. It does finally settle on the same states as `P4`, however at a much higher transition cost. `P2` does not adapt with the demand sequence and produces a poor schedule.

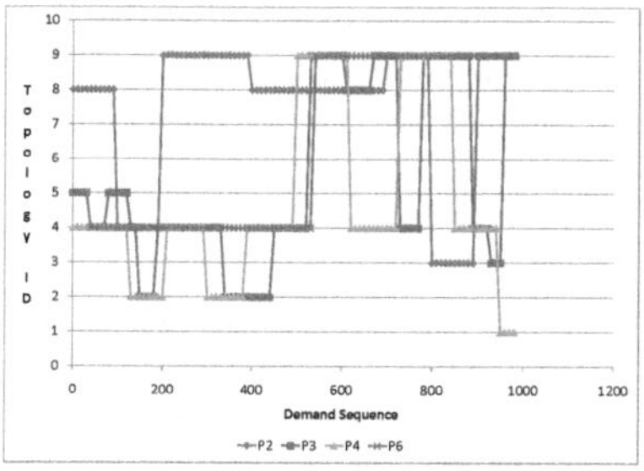

(a) Quality of a Schedule

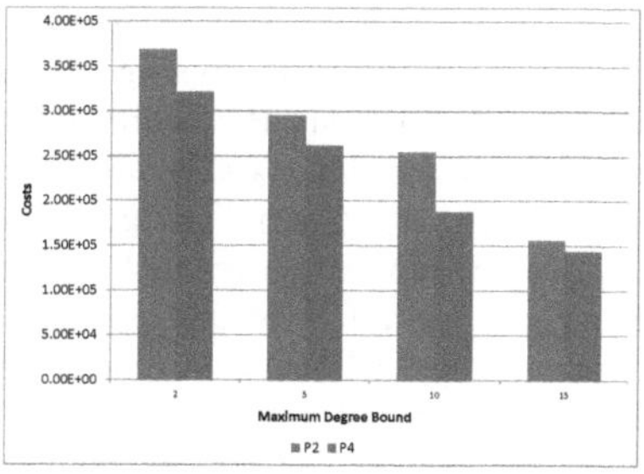

(b) Effect of Degree Bound

Fig. 2. Cost Analysis

5.3 Effect of Degree Bound

We are interested in understanding how dynamic topology reconfiguration policies are affected by the degree bound. We have two observations (Figure 2(b)): First, the cost of the policies decreases when the degree bound increases. With larger degree bound, there are more feasible topologies and thus the system is able to find better topologies with lower operational costs. Larger degree bound may also decrease reconfiguration costs depending upon the protocol implementation as the system may result in a smaller height of the spanning tree. While this suggests that in topology design a larger degree bound should be chosen, increasing the degree bound shows a decrease in the operational and reconfiguration cost. This is an initial result and we plan to work further on the effect of degree bound on reconfiguration costs.

6 Conclusion

We have studied the problem of dynamically reconfiguring the topology of a UDN in response to the changes in the communication requirements. We have considered two costs of using the network: the operational cost of transferring data between nodes and the reconfiguration cost. The objective is to find the optimal reconfiguration policies that can minimize the potential overall cost of using the UDN. Our policies use both greedy and conservative approaches for adapting to the changes in the communication requirements. We tested the performance of our policies on a medium-size ubiquitous data network and observed shown that dynamic overlay topology reconfiguration can significantly reduce the overall cost of providing a data service over a UDN.

References

1. Saha, D., Mukherjee, A.: Pervasive computing: A paradigm for the 21st century. IEEE Computer 36 (2003)
2. Misra, A., Das, S., McAuley, A., Das, S.: Autoconfiguration, registration, and mobility management for pervasive computing. IEEE Personal Communications 8 (2001)
3. Saha, D., Mukherjee, A., Bandyopadhyay, S.: Networking infrastructure for pervasive computing: enabling technologies and systems. Kluwer Academic Publishers, Dordrecht (2003)
4. Borodin, A., El-Yaniv, R.: Online computation and competitive analysis. Cambridge University Press, Cambridge (1998)
5. Patil, S.: Towards General Design Principles for Distributed Indices. Technical report, Indian Institute of Information Technology, Bangalore (2009)
6. Patil, S., Srinivasa, S., Mukherjee, S., Rachakonda, A.R., Venkatasubramanian, V.: Breeding Diameter-Optimal Topologies for Distributed Indexes. Complex Systems 18 (2009)
7. Peterson, L., Shenker, S., Turner, J.: Overcoming the Internet impasse through virtualization. In: Proceedings of the Workshop on Hot Topics in Networks (2004)
8. McAuley, A., Manousakis, K., Telcordia, M.: Self-configuring networks. In: Proceedings of the IEEE Conference on Military Communications (2000)
9. Mcauley, A., Misra, A., Wong, L., Manousakis, K.: Experience with Autoconfiguring a Network with IP addresses. In: Proceedings of the IEEE Conference on Military Communications (2001)
10. Fan, J., Ammar, M.: Dynamic topology configuration in service overlay networks: A study of reconfiguration policies. In: Proceedings of the IEEE Conference of INFOCOM (2006)

11. Awerbuch, B., Leighton, T.: Improved approximation algorithms for the multi-commodity flow problem and local competitive routing in dynamic networks. In: Proceedings of the ACM Symposium on Theory of Computing (1994)
12. Ortega, F., Wolsey, L.: A branch-and-cut algorithm for the single-commodity, uncapacitated, fixed-charge network flow problem. Networks 41 (2003)
13. Barabasi, A.L., Bonabeau, E.: Scale-free networks.. Scientific American 288 (2003)
14. Droms, R.: Automated configuration of TCP/IP with DHCP. IEEE Internet Computing 3 (1999)
15. Perkins, C., Alpert, S., Woolf, B.: Mobile IP; Design Principles and Practices. Addison-Wesley Longman Publishing Company, Amsterdam (1997)
16. Malik, T., Wang, X., Dash, D., Chaudhary, A., Burns, R., Ailamaki, A.: Adaptive physical design for curated archives. In: Proccedings of the Conference on Scientific and Statistical Database Management Systems (2009)
17. Brook, A., Kendrick, D., Meeraus, A.: GAMS, a user's guide. ACM SIGNUM Newsletter 23 (1988)

On-Demand Data Broadcasting for Data Items with Time Constraints on Multiple Broadcast Channels

Ta-Chih Su and Chuan-Ming Liu

Department of Computer Science and Information Engineering
National Taipei University of Technology
Taipei, TAIWAN
{t7598023,cmliu}@ntut.edu.tw

Abstract. Data Broadcasting is an effective approach to provide information to a large group of clients in ubiquitous environments. How to generate the data broadcast schedule to make the average waiting time short for clients is an important issue. In particular, when the data access pattern is dynamic and data have time constraints, such as traffic and stock information, scheduling the broadcast for such data to fulfill the requests becomes challenging. Since the content of the broadcast is dynamic and the request deadlines should be met, such data broadcasting is referred to as on-demand data broadcasting with time constraints. Many related papers discussed this type of data broadcasting with a single broadcast channel. In this paper, we investigate how to schedule the on-demand broadcast for the data with time constraints using multiple broadcast channels and provide two heuristics to schedule the data broadcast. The objective of the proposed heuristics is to minimize the miss rate (i.e., ratio of the requests missing deadlines to all the requests) and latency (i.e., time between issuing and termination of the request). More discussion about the proposed heuristics is given through extensive simulation experiments. The experimental results validate that the proposed heuristics achieve the objectives.

1 Introduction

Advanced technologies in wireless communications, information systems, and hand-held devices make it possible for mobile clients to access different kinds of information services ubiquitously, such as electronic news information, traffic information, stock price information, etc. In such an environment, the bandwidth between server and client is asymmetric [1]. That is, the downlink bandwidth is much greater than the uplink bandwidth. The conventional client-server model hence is a poor match with the wireless mobile environment when the group of mobile clients is large due to the bottleneck of the uplink. Data broadcasting is an attractive solution to this condition and provides an efficient way to disseminate the information to a large pool of clients.

In general, data broadcasting can be classified into two types [3]: *push-based broadcast* and *on-demand broadcast*. In push-based broadcast, the server periodically broadcasts data items on a broadcast channel. Most of the schedule algorithms in this type consider stable data access patterns. In on-demand broadcast, the clients send the requests via an uplink channel. The server then broadcasts the requested data. The on-demand broadcast can be used more widely for dynamic and large-scale data dissemination.

M. Yoshikawa et al. (Eds.): DASFAA 2010, LNCS 6193, pp. 458–469, 2010.

In some information services, data may have temporality, such as traffic information and stock quotes. To ensure the data is timely useful, the clients usually request the data with deadlines and the server then broadcasts the on-demand data. The requested data become invalid when the deadlines are passed. Thus, how to schedule the on-demand broadcast for the data with time constraints becomes an important topic. Many papers discuss this topic and most of them consider a single broadcast channel. For a server, using multiple channels to provide information makes the broadcast cycle shorter than using one channel.

In this paper, we discuss the problem to schedule the on-demand broadcast for data with time constraints in multi-channel environments. We consider each request has its own deadline and has multiple data items associated with it. Such requests will raise an important problem, *data overlap problem*, when multiple channels are used. That is, the requested data items for a request may appear in different channels at the same time and only one channel can be tuned into at a give time instance. More details about the data overlap problem will be given in the next section. The objective of this work is to provide on-demand broadcast schedules that have more requests meet their deadlines and reduce the waiting time for the clients.

After giving the related work and preliminaries in Section 2, we describe the system model in Section 3. The formal definition of the problem in Section 4. Then, we propose two heuristics, MPHH and MPLH, in Section 5. The simulation is presented in Section 6. Section 7 concludes this paper.

2 Related Work

Many papers about data broadcasting have been proposed in the past decade. Part of these papers focused on how to schedule the broadcast in order to achieve a short latency. The *latency* is the time elapsed between issuing and termination of the query and can be used to indicate the Quality of Service(QoS). To reduce the latency, the broadcast schedules considered the data access probabilities and/or dependency. Furthermore, people consider to use multiple broadcast channels to have more deduction on the latency [9,10,11,12,13]. With multiple broadcast channels, the assumption that only one channel can be tuned into at a time instance is usually made. Under such an assumption, the *data overlap* problem happens when the requested data for a query are broadcast at the same time [10]. In this case, only one requested datum can be accessed and the client needs to wait until the next broadcast cycle for the other requested data, thus leading to a longer latency.

The papers related to on-demand data broadcasting considered the urgency and productivity of data to ensure the service quality where each request has a time constraint. For such papers, the *miss rate* is used to be the main measurement to evaluate the service quality. Miss rate is the ratio of requests missing the deadlines to all the requests. In [2], the authors applied the earliest deadline first (EDF) policy to schedule the broadcast. For a request with multiple related data items, all the related data items should be received before the deadline of the request; otherwise, the request is not fully served. To solve this kind of problem, the *slack time* of request is defined to indicate the urgency of request when scheduling the broadcast [3,4,5,6,7,8]. The authors in [4,5,6] observed that the scheduling algorithms which consider data items independently may cause the request to be unserved with only one or two data items missed, thus deteriorating the service quality. Their solutions improve the productivity of data by considering the data dependently.

To the extent of our knowledge, most of the papers about on-demand broadcasting work on a single broadcast channel. The authors in [6] consider multiple channels but do not consider the time constraint of requests. In our work, we consider on-demand data broadcasting using multiple broadcast channels. Each request has its own deadline and multiple related data. The basic idea of our proposed approach is to derive the result by converting the optimal schedule when enough channels are available. This differentiates our work from [6]. When the data overlap problem occurs, it becomes hard to predict when the desired data are broadcast. This will lead to a higher miss rate. In order to minimize the miss rate, our work also focuses on reducing the impact caused by the data overlap problem.

3 System Model

Our system model is shown in Figure 1. The clients send the requests to the server via an uplink channel. Each request contains multiple related data items and has its deadline. Each requested data item has a unique *id*. The server receives the requests and inserts them into a request queue. When the request queue is not empty, the server schedules the data according to the requests in the queue and broadcasts the scheduled data items to serve the requests. To generate the broadcast data items at each time instance, the server will check all of the unserved requests. If the request will miss its deadline, the server removes the request from the request queue.

In order to direct the clients to retrieve the relevant data items, we use an additional channel, *index channel*, to broadcast an index. The rest of the channels are referred to as *data channels*. The index consists of the *id*'s of the data items which will be broadcast on the data channels in the next time slot. For instance, the index i_1 in Figure 1 contains the *id*'s of data items broadcast in time slot 2. After a client sends the request, it immediately tunes into the index channel to retrieve the index. When a client finds the relevant data items from the index, it tunes into one of the relevant data channels to get the data item. Each data item in the data channels also contains an index. The clients hence can retrieve the relevant data items continuously without tuning back into the index channel. If the client retrieves all the related data items before the deadline of the request, we say that the request is served.

4 Problems

We suppose that there are c channels and n data items, $d_1, d_2, \cdots, d_n$, in data set D. Each of data items is of the same size and takes 1 time slot to be broadcast. On the client side, we assume that there are m clients. Each client i, $1 \leq i \leq m$, sends a request Q_i with a deadline dl_i. Request Q_i consists of k data items, $\{d_{i(1)}, d_{i(2)}, \cdots, d_{i(k)}\}$, where $d_{i(j)} \in D$. We denote the number of requests for a data item d_u as N_{d_u}, $1 \leq u \leq n$. U_i indicates the set of unserved data items in the request Q_i at current time. If U_i is not

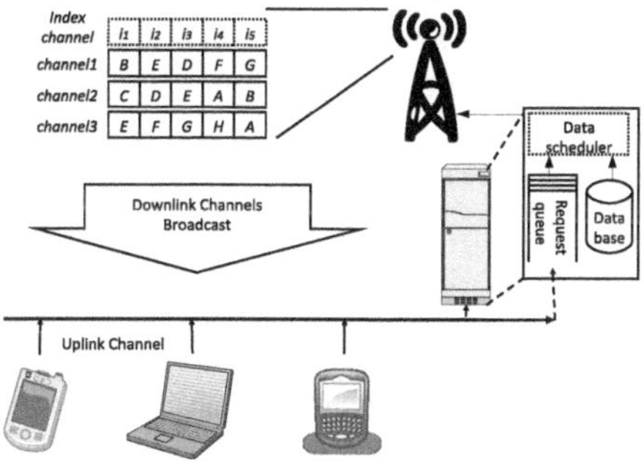

Fig. 1. The architecture of on-demand data broadcasting with 3 broadcast channels; the solid squares presenting the broadcast slots; the dashed squares standing for the indexing channel

empty, the request Q_i is unserved. UR is the set of unserved requests at current time. Let t_c be the current time. The slack time of the request Q_i is defined as $dl_i - t_c - |U_i|$ and denoted by $slack_i$. If $|U_i| > 0$ and $slack_i < 0$, request Q_i will miss its deadline because the remaining time slots are not enough to broadcast the unserved data items in U_i. The miss rate after the data items broadcast at t_c is

$$R_{(t_c - t_0)} = \frac{|miss(Q_{\{t_c - t_0\}})|}{|Q_{\{t_c - t_0\}}|}, \tag{1}$$

where $Q_{\{t_c-t_0\}}$ is the set of the requests received by the server from the time slot t_0 to t_c, $|miss(Q_{\{t_c-t_0\}})|$ is the number of requests missed their deadlines after the data items broadcasted at time slot t_c in the set $Q_{\{t_c-t_0\}}$.

This paper discusses how to generate a broadcast schedule on multiple channels from time t_0 to t_i which has the minimum miss rate as in Equation 1. We refer to such a problem as the *On-demand Broadcasting with Minimum Miss rate (OBMM) Problem* and give a formal definition as below.

Definition 1. *(OBMM Problem)*
Suppose all the notations are defined as above and the set $RD(t_i)$ consists of the unserved data items of all the requests in $Q_{\{t_i-t_0\}}$ at t_i. The On-demand Broadcasting with Minimum Miss rate Problem is to find a mapping $M : RD(t) \rightarrow \{1, 2, \cdots, c\}$, $t \in \{t_0, \cdots, t_i\}$ such that $\sum R_{(t_i-t_0)}$ is minimized.

5 Heuristics

The main idea of our proposed heuristics is to put the broadcast data into c channels as compact as possible. Consider that there are c channels and the number of unserved requests is m where $c < m$. In our proposed approaches, we first assume that there are m channels and the optimal broadcast schedule can be obtained easily. Then, we convert the resulting m-channel broadcast into another broadcast with c channels and keep a low miss rate and latency. The first heuristic, *Most Popular First Heuristic(MPFH)*, first aggregates data items associated with requests efficiently and then selects c data items to be broadcast using current condition. Such a broadcast schedule may not be optimal in terms of miss rate due to the data redundancy in the generated broadcast. As for the second heuristic *Most Popular Last Heuristic(MPLH)*, the idea is to postpone the time to broadcast hot data in order to server more requests in the same time slot.

5.1 Most Popular First Heuristic

With multiple broadcast channels, the data overlap problem is inevitable. In order to reduce the impact caused by the data overlap problem, some data items are repeated broadcast before their deadlines.

There are two phases in our proposed algorithms: Aggregation Phase and Conversion Phase. In aggregation phase, for each request Q_j, $1 \leq j \leq m$, we select data item d_i which has the largest number of requests among all the data associated with Q_j. We refer to d_i as the candidate for serving request Q_j and denote it as ca_j. Each candidate has its own slack time and number of unserved data items. All the candidates are then aggregated into a set CA by union. During the aggregation, if two candidates are the same data item, the new candidate will retain the smaller slack time and the smaller number of unserved data items. For example, there are four candidates, $ca_1 = d_1$, $ca_2 = d_2$, $ca_3 = d_2$, $ca_4 = d_3$ for four requests. After aggregation, the set CA is $\{d_1, d_2, d_3\}$ and the data items in the CA are unique. If the number of of data item in CA is smaller than or equal to c, we just put the data item in the broadcast channels directly. Otherwise, the process moves on to Conversion phase.

In Conversion phase, we select c candidates from CA to broadcast. The selection depends on the slack time. The data item in CA having the smallest slack time will be selected first. If there is a tie, the one with a smaller number of unserved data items will be selected. If exactly one data item can not be selected, we select the one having the most number of requests. After a data item is selected, it is removed from CA. The process repeats until c candidates are selected. Thus, we can have exactly c data items to be broadcast. Besides, if candidate ca_i is selected to be broadcast, ca_i is removed from the associated set of unserved data items, U_i. Notice that only one data item can be removed from each U_i in the process. If candidates ca_i and ca_j are selected to be broadcast in time slot t_c and U_i contains both ca_i and ca_j, we only remove ca_i form U_i. Recall the data overlap problem, ca_i and ca_j are overlapped for Q_i at time t_c. Our process leaves ca_j in the U_i and ca_j will be selected as a candidate for Q_i in the following time slots. The data overlap problem is thus resolved. The MPFH continues selecting data items to be broadcast at each time slot until the set of unserved requests, UR, is empty. The algorithm MPFH shows in Figure 2.

We now use the example in Figure 3 to illustrate how MPFH works. There are two channels and three requests, Q_1, Q_2, and Q_3, in the beginning. As shown in Figure 3(a), Q_1 requests three data items, d_1, d_2, and d_3, with the deadline $dl_1 = 6$; Q_2 requests four data items, d_2, d_3, d_4, and d_5, with the deadline $dl_2 = 9$; Q_3 requests two data items, d_3 and d_4, with the deadline $dl_3 = 3$. The numbers of requests for the data items, N_{d_1}, N_{d_2}, N_{d_3}, N_{d_4}, and N_{d_5}, are 1, 2, 3, 2, and 1, respectively. We first decide the data items to be broadcast at time slot $t = 1$. Data item d_3 will be selected as the candidate in Q_1, Q_2, and Q_3. Then we aggregate these three candidates into set CA.

Input: c channels and m unserved requests.
Output: at most c data items.
(1) find the candidate of each request;
(2) aggregate the candidates into the set CA;
(3) **if** $|CA| < c$ **then** /* $|CA|$ is the number of CA */
    return the data items in CA;
  else
    go to step (4)
(4) **for** n=1 to c **do**
  select the candidate ca_i with minimun $slack_i$
    if more than one candidate be selected **then**
      select the candidate ca_i with the least number of U_i
      if more than one candidate be selected **then**
        select the candidate ca_i with the most number of N_{ca_i}
        remove ca_i from CA
      else
      remove ca_i from CA
    else
      remove ca_i from CA
  return c selected candidates

Fig. 2. The high-level description of Most Popular First Heuristic

There is only one data item d_3 in CA after aggregation. The slack time of data item d_3 is $dl_3 - |U_3| = 1$. Because $|CA| \leq 2$, we can directly broadcast d_3 at time slot $t = 1$. In the meanwhile, the process also receives a new request Q_4 consisting of 2 data items, d_3 and d_6, with deadline $dl_4 = 6$. As show in Figure 3(b), the set of unserved data items for each request at time slot $t = 2$ is $U_1 = \{d_1, d_2\}$, $U_2 = \{d_2, d_4, d_5\}$, $U_3 = \{d_4\}$, and $U_4 = \{d_3, d_6\}$ respectively. N_{d_1}, N_{d_2}, N_{d_3}, N_{d_4}, N_{d_5}, and N_{d_6} now become 1, 2, 1, 2, 1, and 1 respectively. According to the approach, d_2 is selected as the candidate of Q_1 because N_{d_2} is larger than N_{d_1}. In Q_2, because $N_{d_2} = N_{d_4} = N_{d_5}$, we can select any one of d_2, d_4, and d_5 as the candidate. In this case, we select the one has the smallest id. So, d_2 is selected as the candidate of Q_2. Similarly, we select d_4 and d_3 in Q_3 and Q_4, respectively. We then aggregate the candidates, $ca_1(= d_2)$, $ca_2(= d_2)$, $ca_3(= d_4)$, and $ca_4(= d_3)$ into CA. In particular, ca_1 and ca_2 have the same data item. We make a new candidate $ca_{\{1,2\}}$ with slack time $slack_{\{1,2\}} = slack_1$ and the number of unserved data items being $|U_1|$. Hence, after aggregation, CA becomes $\{ca_{\{1,2\}}, ca_3, ca_4\}$.

Since $|CA| = 3 > c = 2$, the process moves to Conversion phase. The candidate with the minimum slack time, $ca_3(= d_4)$, is first selected to be broadcast and then deleted from CA. Then the process continues to select the second data item to be broadcast. CA now becomes $\{ca_{\{1,2\}}, ca_4\}$ and $slack_{\{1,2\}}$ and $slack_4$ are both 3. We then select the one having the least $|U_i|$. Because $|U_1| = |U_4| = 2$, we can select either $ca_{\{1,2\}}$ or ca_4. Again, we select the one with the smaller id. Hence, $ca_{\{1,2\}}$ is selected. So, at time $t = 2$, $ca_3(= d_4)$ and $ca_{\{1,2\}}(= d_2)$ will be broadcast. Figure 3(c) shows the result after d_2 and d_4 are broadcast and the process at time slot $t = 3$. The unserved data items in each request now are $U_1 = \{d_1\}$, $U_2 = \{d_4, d_5\}$, $U_3 = \{\oslash\}$, and $U_4 = \{d_3, d_6\}$, respectively. Because U_3 is empty, we remove Q_3 from the set of

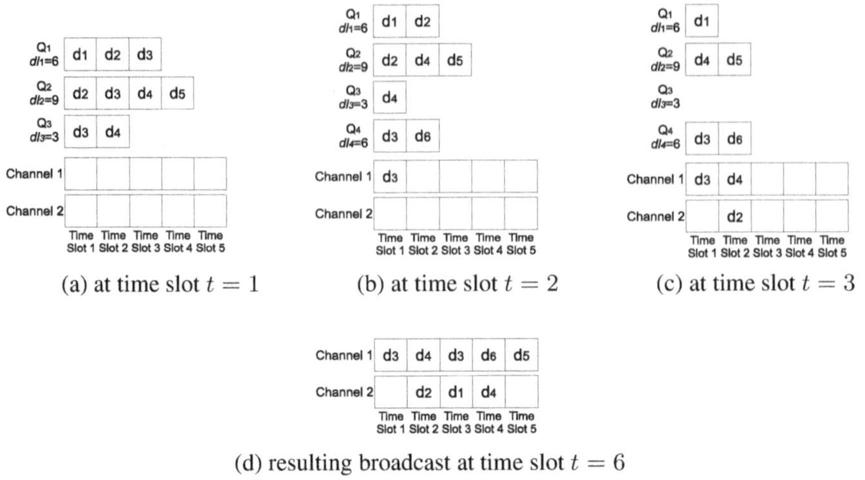

Fig. 3. An example of the execution of MPFH at time slots 1, 2, and 3 and the resulting broadcast

requests. The same process continues until UR is empty. Figure 3(d) shows the result if there are no other requests received.

5.2 Most Popular Last Heuristic

Algorithm MPFH considers the request urgency and service productivity. Consider the example in Figure 4. The broadcast schedule in Figure 4 is generated by MPFH. Data item d_3 is broadcast two times at time slot $t = 1$ and $t = 2$. To server Q_1 and Q_2 before their deadlines, it is sufficient to broadcast data item d_3 at time slot $t = 2$ once. In this case, d_3 is redundant in the broadcast at time slot $t = 1$. By the above observation, we propose the Most Popular Last Heuristic, MPLH, which postpones the time to broadcast popular data in order to server more requests in the same time slot.

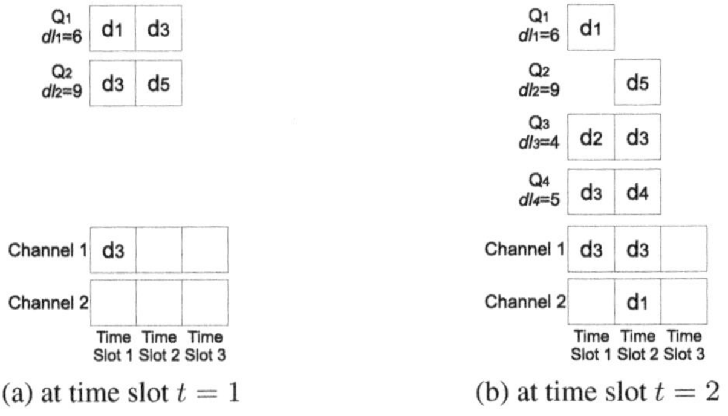

Fig. 4. A broadcast schedule generated by MPFH that can be improved by accumulating more requests for a data item

In order to postpone the time to broadcast popular data, the popular data items will not be selected as candidates in aggregation phase in algorithm MPLH. A popular data item has a higher probability to be requested by the other clients in future, so we accumulate more requests for that data item by postponing the time to broadcast it. Hence, the non-popular data items will be selected as the candidates. The rest of algorithm MPLH is the same as MPFH.

We again use Figure 3 to illustrate how MPLH works. Data items d_1, d_5, and d_4 will be selected as the candidates for Q_1, Q_2, and Q_3, respectively. Then we aggregate these three candidates into set CA and CA now has three data items. Because $|CA| = 3 > c = 2$, the process moves to Conversion phase. With minimal slack time, candidates $ca_3(= d_4)$ and $ca_1(= d_1)$ are selected to be broadcast. In the unserved data items for each request in Figure 5(a), d_4 is removed from Q_2 because $ca_2(= d_5)$ is not selected to be broadcast and no data items in Q_2 are removed before. At time slot $t = 2$, candidates $ca_3(= d_3)$ and $ca_1(= d_2)$ will be broadcast. Figure 5(b) shows the result after d_3 and d_2 are broadcast and the process at time slot $t = 3$. Notice that, candidates $ca_2(= d_5)$ and $ca_4(= d_6)$ are not broadcast at time slot $t = 2$, so we can remove a data item d_i from Q_2 and Q_4 if d_i is broadcast at time slot $t = 2$. We remove d_3 from Q_4. For Q_2, one of d_2 and d_3 can be removed and d_2 is removed in this case. The unserved data items in each request now are $U_1 = \{d_3\}$, $U_2 = \{d_3, d_5\}$, $U_3 = \{\oslash\}$, and $U_4 = \{d_6\}$, respectively. Because U_3 is empty, we remove Q_3 from request queue. The same process continues until UR is empty. Figure 5(c) shows the result if there is no more request received.

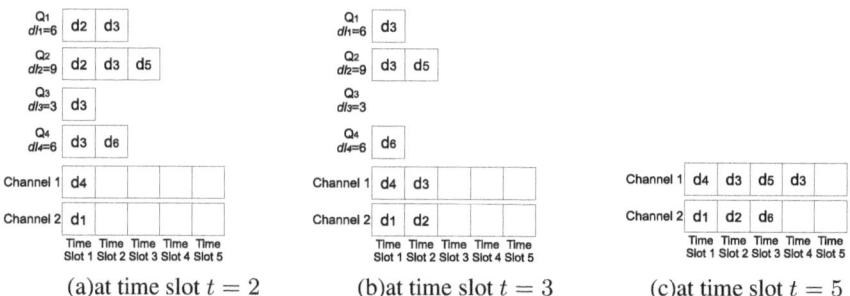

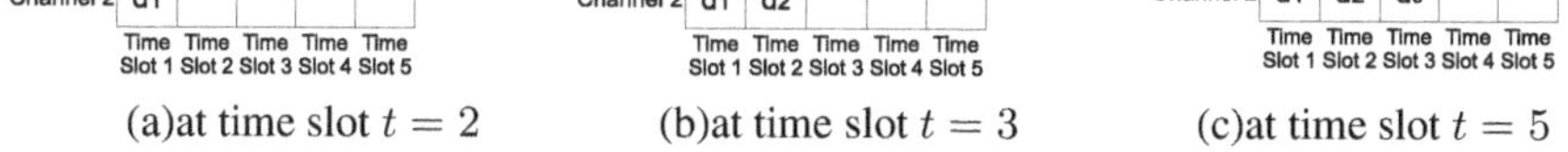

Fig. 5. An example of the execution of MPFH at time slots 2 and 3 and the resulting broadcast at time slot 5 for the case in Figure 3

6 Simulations

This section presents the simulation results and our findings. All the parameters used in our simulation environment are shown in Table 1. In the simulations, we process the requests in batch. When the server broadcasts data items in a time slot, it also collects the new requests. Then, the server processes the new requests and the old unserved requests together. The arrival rate of requests in one time slot is uniformly distributed in the range of [10, 15]. The number of data items associated with each request ranges uniformly from 7 to 14. The deadline of a request is given by: $t_c + (\alpha \times \text{request length})$,

Table 1. Different parameters and values in our simulation

Parameter	Value
Database Size	100, 200, 500, 1000
Size of the data item	Needs one time slot to broadcast
Number of channels	$2 \sim 10$
Arrival rate (# of requests/time slot)	Uniform distribution [10, 15]
Number of data items associated with a request	Uniform distribution [7, 14]
Deadline of a request	$t_c + (\alpha \times \text{request length})$, α =uniform[2,10]
Data items access pattern	Uniform, Zipf=0.8

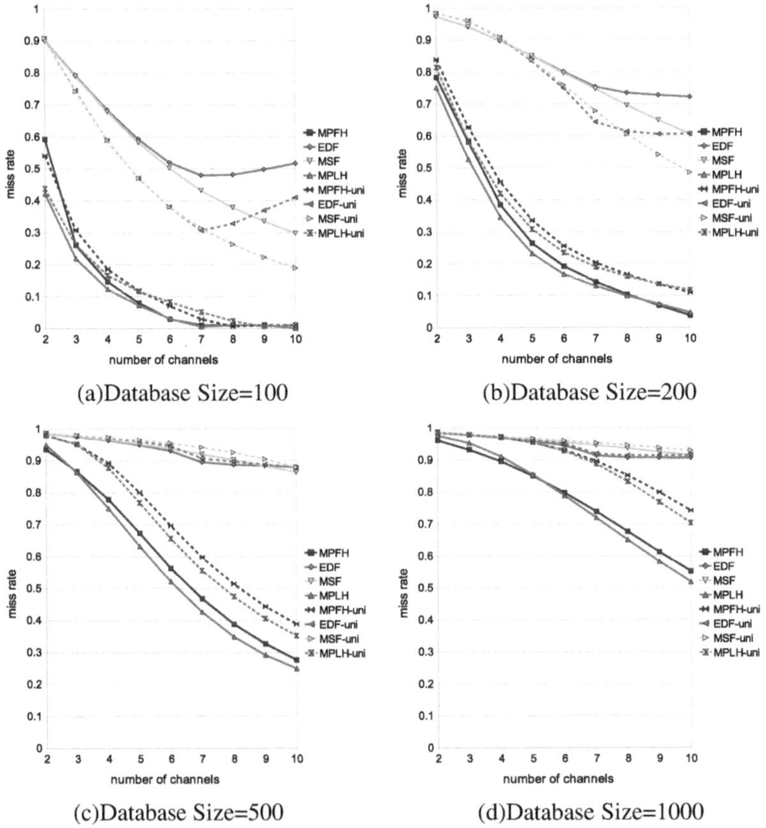

(a)Database Size=100 (b)Database Size=200

(c)Database Size=500 (d)Database Size=1000

Fig. 6. Miss rates for the MPFH, MPLH, EDF, and MSF, when the size of database is (a) 100, (b) 200, (c) 500, and (d) 1000, with different number of channels

where t_c is the current time, *request length* is the number of associated data items of a request, and α is selected uniformly from the range of [2, 10]. The access pattern of data items is uniform distribution or Zipf distribution [14] with parameter $Zipf = 0.8$. In Zipf distribution, data item d_1 is the most frequently accessed data item, while the last data item is the least frequently accessed. We assume that the time spent to process the data items to be broadcast for each time slot is less than one time slot. For each number of channels, we execute 10,000 requests in a round. The reported result is the average of 100 rounds. Two metrics, miss rate and latency, are used to evaluate the performance of our proposed heuristics, MPFH and MPLH. The latency is measured only when the deadline of the request is satisfied.

In the simulation, we compare our proposed algorithms with the other two algorithms, EDF and MSF. Recall that, EDF and MSF are the scheduling algorithms using on a single broadcast channel. In order to use these algorithms on multiple broadcast channels, we modify them to reduce the impact caused by data overlap problem. In EDF and MSF, all the data items associated with the selected requests are placed on the channel having the minimum length.

Figure 6 shows the miss rates using algorithms MPFH, MPLH, EDF, and MSF to process 10,000 requests with different size of database, respectively, on different numbers of channels. Two different access patterns are included. The results using uniform access patterns are presented by MPFH-uni, MPLH-uni, EDF-uni, and MSF-uni, respectively and shown in dashed lines. The results show that our algorithms MPFH and

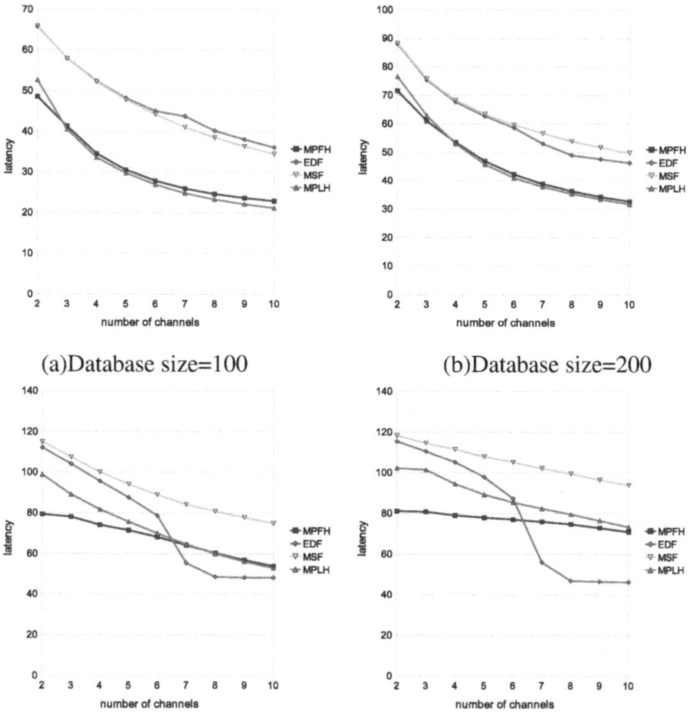

(a)Database size=100 (b)Database size=200

(c)Database Size=500 (d)Database Size=1000

Fig. 7. Latencies for algorithms MPFH, MPLH, EDF, and MSF, when the size of database is (a) 100, (b) 200, (c) 500, and (d) 1000, with different number of channels

MPLH perform better than EDF and MSF in term of miss rate, especially when the size of database is small. The MPFH and MPLH can almost serve all of the requests before their deadlines. When the data access pattern is Zipf distribution, MPFH and MPLH have a lower miss rate than in uniform distribution. Because the similarity of the associated data items between requests is higher in Zipf distribution, our broadcast schedules can serve more requests due to the aggregation of the requests when scheduling the data items.The trend is opposite in EDF and MSF because they don't aggregate the requests.

We now discuss MPLH and MPFH. With a small number of channels, MPLH performs better than MPFH when the database size is small. Recall that, MPLH postpones the time to broadcast hot data in order to server more requests in the same time slot. However, we observe that, as the database size increases, MPFH will do better instead. We conjecture that the similarity between requests is too low, so the effectiveness of postponement disappears. When the number of channels increases, more data items can be broadcast in a time slot. The postponement leads to broadcast fewer redundant data items. Thus, MPLH has a better performance.

Figure 7 presents the results of latencies for algorithms MPFH, MPLH, EDF, and MSF. We only discuss the data access pattern in Zipf distribution because the data access pattern in uniform distribution shows the similar trends. When the size of database is small, the latencies of MPFH and MPLH are almost the same and shorter than the ones of EDF and MSF with a lower miss rate. MPFH performs better than MPLH when the size of database increases. Because the miss rate is high and the similarity between each requests is low, more requests can be served in an earlier stage by the broadcast generated by MPFH without postponement. Thus, MPFH has a shorter latency.

7 Conclusions

In this paper, we discuss how to generate the broadcast schedule for on-demand data broadcast with time constraint on multiple channels. We propose two heuristics, MPFH and MPLH. MPFH aggregates data items associated with requests efficiently. MPLH tries to serve more requests by postponing the popular data items. Both heuristics have good performance in terms of miss rate and latency. The experimental results show that each heuristic has a better performance than other in some specific conditions. MPLH generates a broadcast schedule with lower miss rate when the number of channels and the size of database are both either small or large. When database size is large, the broadcast schedule generated by MPFH has a shorter latency than MPLH, but the miss rate is higher. We conjecture that the ratio of the number of channels and the size of database may affect the performance of our heuristics.

References

1. Acharya, S., Alonso, R., Franklin, M., Zdonik, S.: Broadcast Disks: Data Management for Asymmetric Communication environments. In: Proceedings of the 1995 ACM SIGMOD International Conference on Management of Data, pp. 199–210 (1995)

2. Xuan, P., Sen, S., Gonzalez, O., Fernandez, J., Ramamritham, K.: Broadcast on Demand: Efficient and Timely Dissemination of Data in Mobile Environments. In: Proceedings of the Third IEEE Symposium on Real-Time Technology and Applications, pp. 38–48 (1997)
3. Xu, J., Tang, X., Lee, W.-C.: Time-critical On-demand Data Broadcast: Algorithms, Analysis, and Performance Evaluation. IEEE Transactions on Parallel and Distributed Systems 17(1), 3–14 (2006)
4. Lam, K.-W., Lee, V.C.S., Wu, X.: On-demand Broadcast for Bobile Real-time Multi-item requests. In: Proceedings of the Int'l Conference on Computing & Informatics (2006)
5. Chen, J., Huang, G., Lee, V.C.S.: Scheduling Algorithm for Multi-item Requests with Time Constraints in Mobile Computing Environments. In: Proceedings of the International Conference on Parallel and Distributed Systems, pp. 1–7 (2007)
6. Liu, K., Lee, V.C.S., Leung, K.R.P.H.: Data scheduling for multi-item requests in multi-channel on-demand broadcast environments. In: Proceedings of the 7th ACM International Workshop on Data Engineering for Wireless and Mobile Access (2008)
7. Hu, C.-L.: On-Demand Real-Time Information Dissemination: A General Approach with Fairness, Productivity and Urgency. In: Proceedings of the 21st International Conference on Advanced Information Networking and Applications, pp. 362–369 (2007)
8. Udgata, S.K.: A dynamic, Real-time and On-demand Heuristic Broadcasting Scheme for Multiple Data-item Transactions in Wireless Environment. In: Proceedings of the 4th International Conference on Wireless Communication and Sensor Networks, pp. 40–44 (2008)
9. Lin, K.-F., Liu, C.-M.: Broadcasting Dependent Data with Minimized Access Latency in a Multi-channel Environment. In: Proceedings of the 2006 International Conference on Wireless Communications and Mobile Computing, pp. 809–814 (2006)
10. Fu, S.-Y., Liu, C.-M.: Broadcast Schedules and Query Processing for k Nearest Neighbors Search on Multi-dimensional Index Trees in a Multi-Channel Environment. In: Proceedings of the IEEE International Conference on Systems, Man and Cybernetics (2006)
11. Peng, W.-C., Chen, M.-S.: Dynamic Generation of Data Broadcasting Programs for a Broadcast Disk Array in a Mobile Computing Environment. In: Proceedings of the 9th International Conference on Information and Knowledge Management, pp. 38–45 (2000)
12. Yee, W.G., Navathe, S.B., Omiecinski, E., Jermaine, C.: Efficient Data Allocation over Multiple Channels at Broadcast Servers. IEEE Transactions on Computers 51(10), 1231–1236 (2002)
13. Yi, S.-Y., Nam, S., Jung, S.: Effective Generation of Data Broadcast Schedules with Different Allocation Numbers for Multiple Wireless Channels. IEEE Transactions on Knowledge and Data Engineering 20(5), 668–677 (2008)
14. Zipf, G.K.: Human Behavior and the Principle of Least Effort. Addison-Wesley, Massachusetts (1949)

Author Index

GPSR Compliance

The European Union's (EU) General Product Safety Regulation (GPSR) is a set of rules that requires consumer products to be safe and our obligations to ensure this.

If you have any concerns about our products, you can contact us on ProductSafety@springernature.com

In case Publisher is established outside the EU, the EU authorized representative is:

Springer Nature Customer Service Center GmbH
Europaplatz 3
69115 Heidelberg, Germany

Batch number: 09473985

Printed by Printforce, the Netherlands